About the Author

Gerald R. Horne holds the John J. and Rebecca Moores Chair of History and African American Studies at the University of Houston. His research has addressed issues of racism in a variety of relations involving labor, politics, civil rights, international relations, and war. He has also written extensively about the film industry. Dr. Horne received his Ph.D. in history from Columbia University, his J.D. from the University of California, Berkeley, and his B.A. from Princeton University. His recent books include *Race to Revolution: The U.S. and Cuba during Slavery and Jim Crow*; *The Counter-Revolution of 1776: Slave Resistance and the Origins of the United States of America*; *Black Revolutionary: William Patterson and the Globalization of the African American Freedom Struggle*; and *Negro Comrades of the Crown: African Americans and the British Empire Fight the U.S. Before Emancipation*.

Confronting
BLACK JACOBINS

*The United States, the Haitian Revolution, and
the Origins of the Dominican Republic*

by GERALD HORNE

MR

MONTHLY REVIEW PRESS

New York

Library of Congress Cataloging-in-Publication data available from
the publisher—

ISBN: 978-1-58367-562-5 (paper)
ISBN: 978-1-58367-563-2 (cloth)

Monthly Review Press
146 West 29th Street, Suite 6W
New York, New York 10001

monthlyreview.org

Typeset in Eldorado 10.5/13

5 4 3 2 1

Contents

Introduction

A SPECTER WAS HAUNTING THE SLAVE-HOLDING republic—the specter of an invading army of vengeful Africans.

"Lamentable!" cried George Washington in response to what he described in 1791 as the "unfortunate insurrection of the Negroes in Hispaniola." The president of the fledgling nation was anxious. This is understandable, particularly given the huge population of restive enslaved Africans that inhabited his own nation and the propensity of these bonded workers to unite across borders. Washingon reflected morosely on "a spirit of revolt among the Blacks." "Where it will stop," he said, possibly considering the tenuous state of his own republic, "is difficult to say." The "commencement" of this rebellion, he added sagely, "has been both daring and alarming."[1]

Apparently, the president took seriously the sobering words he had received in August 1791 from the governor of South Carolina, Charles Pinckney, days after the island eruption, who warned nervously about how "nearly similar" Hispaniola was to his state in terms of barely containing an often unruly African majority. He warned: "a day may arrive when" mainlanders too would "be exposed to the same insurrections" as the "flame" of sedition spread northward.[2] It is also possible that the president was simply listening to his colleague, Tench Coxe, a powerful Pennsylvanian who served as a delegate to the Continental Congress. Coxe knew the island well and thought that even if Paris were to prevail over the island's revolutionaries, the French would be inclined to dispatch a "large detachment of republican blacks from St. Domingo to Louisiana." Upon arrival, he surmised, they would precipitate "the sudden emancipation of the blacks there," which would have disastrous consequences for slave-based mainland fortunes—including that of the president and his family.[3]

The U.S. president remonstrated with Pinckney, as he chose to "lament" Carolina's "decision" on "importing slaves after March 1793" in light of the "direful effects of Slavery, which at this moment are presented"—a veiled reference to island turbulence too delicate to mention openly. An early indication of the historic ripples spreading from the Caribbean was his assertion that this uprising of the enslaved should "have operated to produce a total prohibition of the importation of slaves."[4] The eminent historian Rayford Logan may have had the latter in mind when he declared that "at no time in American history have foreign affairs influenced domestic issues more than in the 1790s."[5]

In 1798 Washington's successor was told that "we are vulnerable in the Southern States to an alarming degree." With just a "few ships of war," it was said, the French could "in a few days convoy an army of ten thousand blacks and people of colour in vessels seized from our own citizens. They might land on the defenceless parts of South Carolina or Virginia. Under such circumstances, the slaves would instantly join them & greatly increase their force." This was quite "possible and whatever is possible the enemy will have the enterprise to attempt."[6]

As things turned out, there was no phantom that was haunting the slave-holding republic. The Haitian Revolution by its very nature proved to be a formidable threat to the entire slave system. When what has been described as the "most profitable stretch of real estate on the planet" was upended,[7] a devastating blow was landed simultaneously in favor of all those compelled to toil and sweat for a living.

THIS IS A BOOK CONCERNED with relations between the United States and Hispaniola, more specifically, the reaction of Washington's republic to the revolutionary process in the nation that became Haiti and the splitting of the island in 1844, which led to the formation of the Dominican Republic. As well, this book concludes with the failed attempt by the United States to annex both in the 1870s. This book considers how the island impacted the mainland—and vice versa—and, thus, has a particular emphasis on how the population that came to be called African-American responded. This book is not primarily concerned with internal trends on the island nor with the response there to U.S. policy, which will be the subject of a subsequent volume. This book also considers how leading powers—France, Britain, and Spain most notably—sought to take advantage of a slave-holding republic confronted with militant abolitionism.

What came to be called the Haitian Revolution, 1791–1804, was one of those rare transformative social, political, and economic detonations made all the more remarkable in that it took place in not only the richest and most productive colony of the French Empire but of any empire. But it also implicated the slave-holding republic in that Paris spent heavily in backing North American rebels opposing their seemingly eternal enemy across the channel, which contributed to a crisis in Paris that sparked a transforming revolt in 1789, and this correspondingly contributed mightily to the radicalization of the island. Revolutionary violence in both France and Hispaniola seemed to some U.S. citizens to flow together in a common river of blood that signaled a new departure that could reach the mainland.

This was ironic indeed since North American—then U.S.—residents were heavily implicated in the dramatic increase of the slave trade to the island, which in the 1780s surpassed the British trade, creating a demographic imbalance favorable to a slave revolt.[8]

In the following pages, I will detail a contradictory skein of events: the recently born United States, birthed not least because of its desire to maintain slavery in the face of abolitionist pressure from London,[9] was then confronted by a threatening slave revolt not far from its shores, which created enormous leverage for Britain to wield against its former colony. There was some sympathy for Paris at this time, especially due to the anti-monarchical trends unleashed there in 1789. At the same time, the United States was coming into sharp conflict with France—the island's former colonial master—which created initial pressure to boost the rebellious Africans to gain leverage against Paris, though this was inimical to the interests of the all-powerful slaving forces in Dixie. This laid the basis for an early dual policy toward the island, initially boosting—then in a continuously malignant pattern— undermining the revolutionaries. This also heightened sectional tensions, as the nation hurtled toward civil war. Mercantile interests in New England were increasingly in favor of trade relations with the island—even during the reign of the man respectfully known as "General Toussaint"—while Dixie quaked in its boots at the prospect of armed Africans surging to power on the island.

The United States had not been friendly to "free Negros" and "mulattos," who both fomented and resisted the Haitian Revolution, and was faced with a dilemma when they began arriving on the mainland: should those fleeing revolution be embraced as class comrades or potential subversives who would ally with the enslaved, as some had done on the island? Should the massacre of these *gens de couleur* on the island in the 1840s, as the D.R. was coming into being, be seen as of no consequence to Washington—or a fire bell in the night signaling what would next befall those defined as "white," even in the United States itself?

Simultaneously, there were some Haitians who were eager to welcome Africans fleeing the mainland—but others were uneasy about accepting those defined as "mulatto" in the United States who could then exert weight and influence on the often fragile color equation on the island. The United States had a similar problem:

it encouraged the formation of the D.R., not least as a blow against Haiti, but it was also apprehensive about treating a nation with so many of the darker skinned with equality—which placed Washington at a disadvantage in its jousting with European competitors, particularly London.

In neighboring Cuba, on the other hand, one group of U.S. nationals brought enchained Africans by the boatload, creating the possibility of creating a Haitian twin with incalculable detriment for the mainland—while another group fretted nervously about the same prospect.[10] Inevitably, this created strains that hardly halted the march to civil war. It was in 1799 that a Philadelphia journal opined that "there are two distinct interests" in this new republic: "Southern states that suffer by the curtailment of our trade with Europe" and "Northern states that profit by opening the trade to St. Domingo."[11]

Above all—and this is a central argument of this work—the Haitian Revolution created a general crisis for the system of slavery that could only be resolved with its collapse.[12] The avid 20th century racialist, T. Lothrop Stoddard, found it necessary to study the revolution intensely and emerged with the conclusion that 1791–1804 marked "the first great shock between the ideals of white supremacy and race equality,"[13] a confrontation that compelled a retreat of the racialized slavery that had given rise to the slave-holding republic in the first instance. Indeed, 1791 also marked a fitting rebuff to 1776: the latter seemingly had given a new birth of freedom to slave dealers and the peculiar institution itself—but then the former raised sharply the premium on both. Recently a scholar has suggested that the "elite" of the slave-holding republic "were terrified of the egalitarian implications of Haitian independence, universal and immediate abolition and peasant-based land reform and its attendant stateless egalitarianism."[14] Napoleon Bonaparte suspected that with the Haitian Revolution, "the scepter of the new world would fall sooner or later into the hands of the blacks," a thought that also had occurred in the United States itself.[15] Fanning the flames of concern on the mainland were the bloodcurdling journalistic reports flowing from the island, virtually on a daily basis: in Philadelphia alone between late 1791 and mid-1793 there were hundreds of articles in the local press on events there.[16] Such reports fueled the buoyancy of the slave-holding republic, which simultaneously fueled an antipathy toward emergent Haiti that determined that its subsequent path would be rocky.

Grasping this essential truth of incipient abolitionism early on, London—which had been ousted from its prime slave trading market in North America in any case—prompted by the Haitian Revolution was busily seizing the moral high ground by turning against this global flesh peddling, placing its erstwhile mainland colony on the defensive and, not coincidentally, winning numerous African adherents particularly in the United States itself. Certainly, 1791 gave an immeasurable boost to abolitionism.[17] The influential Londoner James Stephen declaimed portentously in 1807—as Britain was turning decisively against the slave trade—that the "West Indies have probably cost us more money since 1792 than all our military operations on the continent," jeopardizing national security in the face of France's stiff challenge. Redcoats were futilely seeking to suppress Haiti and other slave colonies yearning to be free at an enormous cost of blood and treasure, while a surer path would involve conciliating Africans—which would at once give a cudgel with which to bludgeon its ascending republic enemy. Moreover, he added persuasively, "our opprobrius [*sic*] adherence to this [slave] traffic has added much to the popular prejudice against us."[18]

Such coruscating concerns may have crossed the mind of George Washington when he first contemplated what was to become one of the defining global events in recent centuries. After all, it was during that turbulent time that Edward Stevens, the U.S. consul on the island, argued that the paramount revolutionary leader— Toussaint L'Ouverture—commanded an army of 55,000 men, while the greatest force that his commander-in-chief had led was no larger than 20,000 men.[19] It was Stevens who in 1799, when control of the island remained unclear, reported that a plan had been hatched on the island to "invade both the Southern States of America & the Island of Jamaica," a design that was to be bruited repeatedly in coming years. Toussaint won plaudits from the U.S. consul, when it was reported that he was "determined to prevent this Expedition," a favor he thought would pay dividends.[20]

Adding ballast to this notion of an invasion were the words of Secretary of State Timothy Pickering who advised President John Adams weeks later that not only was Jamaica "in jeopardy in [the] case of an invasion by black troops from St. Domingo" but "our Southern States too . . . are yet in much danger from attempts to excite the blacks to insurrection." This, Pickering maintained, would lead London and his republic to forge an alliance "to guard against the dangers to be apprehended from St. Domingo" in pursuit of "mutual security."[21]

Near that same time, a delegate of London, after conferring with the revolutionaries in Hispaniola, wondered why they were "very inquisitive to know the distance Santo Domingo is from France and also from Jamaica, Cuba, and the other islands"; concerning the latter, they were "very curious to know their strength and in what manner they are governed." Their idea, it was thought, was "to make an attempt on Jamaica," which at minimum would be "alarming."[22] Unsurprisingly, spirited debates over abolition of the slave trade erupted soon after this. One analyst in 1803 pointed out quite properly that "further increase of [the] Negro population in the colony would prove highly dangerous to the white inhabitants," since tumult on the neighboring island had "placed Jamaica in a new and awful position."[23]

As the revolutionaries gained in strength, mainlanders had to worry about these rebels allying with London—or Paris—and landing in Savannah or Charleston with mayhem on their minds. A few years after Stevens spoke, Thomas Jefferson observed that the inflamed Caribbean "appears to have given a considerable impulse to the minds of the slaves in different parts of the United States" itself, contributing to a "great disposition to insurgency" that "manifested itself" in his own Virginia in an "actual insurrection."[24] As early as 1793, as terror raged in Paris, Jefferson warned that two reputed Frenchmen—"a small dark mulatto" and a "quarteron"—were headed to Charleston "with a design to excite an insurrection among the Negroes."[25] This was a Parisian plan he told the governor, "the first branch of which has been carried into execution at St. Domingo."[26]

Five years later in the Palmetto State, there were rumors of a planned invasion of a massive army of Africans from due south.[27] Four years after that there were raging emotions in what is now Washington, D.C., about a revolt of the enslaved spearheaded by island African prisoners deposited there by the French—who were seen as intentionally cavalier about U.S. security.[28] France's Edmond Charles Genêt instructed his nation's consuls in the United States that their enemies were spreading tales about Paris's supposed plans to instigate slave revolts in Dixie; yet the terror then suffusing Paris itself gave weight to the idea that Gallic revolutionaries who did not blanch at the idea of massacring their own compatriots would not flinch at the idea of shedding blood in a nation in which they were now ensnared in a "quasi-war."[29] There was a credible suspicion that Paris would reconcile with island rebels, which—if it had occurred—could have left the United States not as a transcontinental republic but a rump republic pinned along the Atlantic seaboard.[30]

The repetitive articulation of plans to invade Jamaica and Dixie from the island was suggestive of a spreading contagion of unrest in the hemisphere, which reflected, then generated, even more unrest. From 1789–1815 there were dozens of slave rebellions and conspiracies in the Americas. As Paris exploded in 1789, unsettled colonists and frazzled officials began complaining about abolitionist literature and artifacts reaching the Caribbean colonies especially.

But it was in 1795 in Spanish Louisiana—apparently encouraged by the possibility of a French attempt to invade and force retrocession of the former colony—that Africans rose up.[31] This slave conspiracy in Pointe Coupee was blamed by those on the scene on the direct influence of island revolutionaries.[32] There had been an extensive plot in July 1791—days before the ignition in Hispaniola—and in October one conspirator was said to have stated that he and his comrades were simply awaiting word from Hispaniola before deciding to "strike a blow" in concert with islanders. Spanish settlers were accused, in turn, of courting Africans and storing arms for use by the enslaved against French settlers. That this conspiracy was apparently incubating for eighteen months contributed immeasurably to a sense of insecurity, creating conditions for Africans to engage in arbitrage among the major powers, thereby weakening slavery as a whole.[33]

Miles away in St. Lucia, during that very same year, a British general conceded sadly that "the Negroes are completely Masters of the Island."[34] This may have been a booby-prize for the redcoats, since they had only taken this island months before as a result of the dislocation delivered by angry Africans—and now found themselves in a desperate tussle for survival with these alleged allies at their throats.[35]

It was not just St. Lucia and Louisiana that were being contested in this great power struggle involving at least two European powers—and Africans. A similar battle was unwinding in Grenada between Britian and France. London's man announced apprehensively in mid-1796 that the "insurgents" leading the "insurrection" there could be "supplied by canoes from Trinidad and Guadeloupe with arms and ammunition."[36]

British settlers were under siege with repeated complaints as early as December 1791 from Bermuda—within hailing distance of the Carolinas—about "seditious Negroes." One leader expressed "anxiety" about the "disparity in these islands of the whites to the blacks," meaning that "we have not a single soldier or gunman for the guard of the stores and magazines." In fact, "the arms of the Militia are at all times necessarily at the disposal of their black servants."[37] Weeks later another fatigued Bermudian leader confessed that since the commencement of "insurrections, depredations, and murders" in "St. Domingo, a very manifest alteration has taken place in the behaviour of the Negroes here"—which did not bode well, he thought. Before August 1791 a "very dangerous conspiracy" was devised by Africans, but it was "suppressed" with "many of the conspirators executed." But since the "dissemination of opinions respecting the lawfulness of slavery through these islands," buoyed by fear of Hispaniola, he felt a rising sense of power among Africans. Fortifications were "quite insecure" and, thus, "should an insurrection now take place it would be very easy for the Negroes to take possession"—possibly of the entire archipelago. This was "alarming," he asserted with understatement, not least since "Negro slaves greatly exceed the white people in number" and were "hardy and intelligent."[38] "Bermudian Negroes frequent the French islands now," it was noted worriedly, and "more than those from most of the West India islands," it was reported in January 1792.[39] Perhaps reducing the number of Africans by sharply circumscribing the slave trade was a possible remedy—but curbing supply would inexorably suffocate slavery itself, though from London's viewpoint this ban would probably prove more harmful to its rising rival, the slave-holding republic.

But it was not just London that was scrambling to avoid being overtaken by events. In Venezuela in 1795 an enslaved African, Jose Chirino, who had visited Hispaniola returned with militant demands for imposition of "the law of the French."[40] A few years later another revolt shook the northern coast of South America, as a militia leader, Francisco Xavier Pirela, was said to be in touch with crews of ships from Hispaniola.[41] Then the "Revolt of the Tailors" in Bahia, Brazil, raised the provocative issue of racial equality as well as independence.[42] Even the rebellion in Mexico in 1810 was said to have featured the now ubiquitous hand of Haiti.[43]

However, it was London, as a leading global force and frequent antagonist of the ascending power on the west bank of the Atlantic, whose maneuvers would prove most threatening to the slave-holding republic and the human bondage on which it was based, which were now under duress by trends uncorked by revolutionary Hispaniola.

Part of the bill of indictment filed by republicans against London before 1776 and during the resultant war was Britain's frequent deployment of armed Africans on the mainland, a practice seen as deeply dangerous. But the British Empire, seeking to tame the prize that was India while under bombardment in the Caribbean and beginning to eye Hong Kong and China, felt it had little choice in raising armed manpower. Moreover, deploying armed Africans close to a rival's shores—a rival which had reason to fear an armed invasion of Africans, in any case—was a prospect too tantalizing to ignore. Naming this regiment the "Carolina or Black Corps" was not just descriptive but a broad hint at their origins as formerly enslaved Africans, who had fled the mainland and had an incentive to wreak havoc on their former homeland. In the telling year of 1791, it was reported that "many of them had made themselves obnoxious to their former owners" and now had been "taught the use of arms." It was also said that they were "better able to bear fatigue" in the climates in which they had been deployed, notably St. Lucia and Grenada—or an unmentioned Dixie.[44]

The recently born United States had come onto the global stage trumpeting the assertion that its model of development—conspicuously based on enslaving Africans—was a great leap forward for humankind and surely worthy of export. Now, however, with a conflagration raging in Hispaniola and its London sparring partner busily adjusting to same, it was faced with the wrenching prospect of a reconfiguration of its project, just as the ink on its vaunted Constitution and Bill of Rights was drying. A nimble United States was able to delay the most severe of adjustments—until 1865—but this proved to be a torturous path speckled with blood.

West Point = to train soldiers to fight Blacks

A contemporary historian has estimated that "over 100,000 whites and 60,000 blacks lost their lives" during the "thirteen year struggle" encapsulated as the Haitian Revolution, 1791–1804.[45] That more defined as "white" perished, though their numbers were considerably smaller than their counterparts—there were less than 500,000 Africans on the island then—with many survivors fleeing to the mainland imbued with hair-raising tales of woe, was bound to concentrate devilishly the collective mind of the slave-holding republic. The revolution posed starkly an existential question: retreat stolidly from slavery or risk losing everything—including one's life, as in Hispaniola.[46]

This was a "Caribbean genocide" claims another contemporary scholar, a precursor of more familiar 20th century catastrophes, with "neither women nor children" spared.[47] T. Lothrop Stoddard, one of the leading theoreticians of white supremacy in the 20th century, argued that the revolution meant the "complete extermination of the white race" in the western end of the island, where the revolutionaries were strongest.[48]

That so many of these survivors and their relatives wound up playing pivotal roles in maintaining the harshest machinery of slavery on the mainland may not have been accidental.[49] This lengthy list includes Judah P. Benjamin—a loyal leader of the Confederate States of America—whose father-in-law fled the island in horror and proceeded to regale many an audience with the alleged perfidy of incited Africans.[50] Louis Tousard, who served in the revolt against British rule in North America, also owned a plantation on the rebellious island, an enterprise which was marred by frequent unrest in the 1780s. He was involved in seeking to suppress the revolt in 1791—before fleeing to the mainland, where, tellingly, he was intimately involved in establishing the U.S. Military Academy at West Point, New York, which was to be both the sturdy sword and shield, if plans by vengeful Africans to invade the mainland and ignite vengeance of the enslaved were to come to pass.[51]

Then there was Pierre Soule, born in France in 1801 and educated in Bordeaux—a city that generated a veritable tidal wave of opposition to island revolutionaries. Soule had resided in Haiti but left due to an inability to find work: labor was admittedly easier to find for one of his kind in a slave-holding republic than in an abolitionist state. So it was on to Baltimore, then New Orleans by the fall of 1825, and then to the U.S. Senate. Soule would eventually return to Europe as his adopted homeland's chief diplomat in the slave-holding monarchy that was Spain. His tangled ancestry was topped by that of a fellow Pelican State statesman—and historian—Charles Gayarre, whose roots are said to extend back to the conflicted days of the early confrontations in Spain with "invading hordes of Mohammedan Moors," giving him further reason to resist the blandishments of the abolition of African slavery.[52] These newly minted "white Americans" were hardly in the mood to retreat in face of African demands—particularly those backed by Haiti (and London).

On the other hand, as the slave trade and colonizing of the mainland were accelerating hand-in-glove in the late 17th century, Frenchmen—particularly Protestants in conflict with a heavily Catholic Paris—participated with gusto. The Huguenot, John Guerard became one of Charleston's leading slave dealers, as those of his religious faith took to slaving like whales to water.[53] Ultimately, in the antebellum era, French, according to an observer, was spoken on the streets of Beaufort, Savannah, and Charleston "as frequently as English"; it was "the language of trade and diplomacy and citizens in the port cities, particularly the cotton and rice agents, used French as a business language." The tellingly named Beaufort "had a larger concentration of slaves than any other district in the South."[54] As the enslaving republic evolved, those of French ancestry came to play a prominent role.[55] As French refugees poured into the mainland, scurrying from slave revolt in the Caribbean, they augmented an extant pro-slavery tendency.

Their arrival was part of a republican calculation. Tench Coxe, a close colleague of Washington, who had been posted to the island, in 1802 informed Aaron Burr— who, like others, was familiar with the fragility of his new nation—that the "evils of Negro insurrection are so very great, that I hope our legislature will deem a liberal naturalization law" a necessity, since "foreigners with property, professions, and occupations will be a good counterbalance for the blacks."[56]

Burr's mistress, Leonora Sansay, wrote prolifically about Hispaniola and was implicated in Burr's plot to dismember the nation he had served as vice president. As one scholar put it, "perhaps being an eyewitness to the successful overthrow of what she saw as the tyrannical French government in Saint Domingo by the oppressed underdogs lent Sansay special insight into the possibility of effectively severing national ties in another place where many inhabitants were downtrodden and oppressed."[57] Each and every regime in the Americas was unsteady to a degree and the emergent Haiti showed that some of these regimes were susceptible to being toppled.

In sum, the unsteady republic faced a daunting demographic challenge—not only because of the manic energy of slave dealers, who kept depositing ever more Africans on the mainland, but also because of the still potent threat from indigenes. Now with an independent Negro republic looming on the horizon the slave-holding republic perforce was compelled to entice more racial comrades and, thus, fleeing French appeared like manna from heaven.

These arriving "white Americans" not only had little difficulty adjusting to the anti-African bias that characterized the slave-holding republic, they often reveled in

US as refuge for fleeing Frenchmen
The US

it. Their continuing ties to France bolstered illiberal attitudes there too in that the hexagonal revolution was not universally admired, particularly outside of Paris;[58] that 1789 led to 1791 was not viewed as coincidence. This complicated the ability of France to follow through on articulated plans to invade Dixie and stir up the enslaved. Since most of the Europeans massacred in Hispaniola were of French origin, this too stoked antipathy toward the island while encouraging amity toward those who offered their compatriots refuge.

In 1819 the French legation in Washington sought to aid the Euro-American Duncan McIntosh, then residing on the island but not necessarily in the good graces of the regime, since he reputedly aided 3000 French nationals in fleeing. His heroic story was spread throughout Europe and that he was then living in misery— though once he had been wealthy—amidst often unfriendly Africans plucked the heartstrings in his favor. Correspondingly, the Africans he had circumvented were portrayed as "tigers, excited by blood," "monsters," "barbarous," and a "frenetic race" of "wild Africans." Such intensely personal stories bonded "white Americans" and French conservatives, just as these tales pilloried the common African foe.[59] Surely, when U.S. writers—decades after Haiti's founding—referred to the revolutionaries' particular venom toward "merchants," a class lionized on the mainland, this created a combustible brew of race and class antagonisms targeting islanders and those who identified with them, e.g. U.S. Negroes.[60] Predictably, perhaps the planet's reigning racist theorist, Arthur Gobineau of France, who specialized in pillorying Haiti, found an appreciative audience in the slave-holding republic.[61]

Just as surely, the European refugees fleeing in fear from the island and recoiling at the violence inflicted upon so many of them, served to bolster a preexisting conservatism within the republic, buttressing slavery at a time when abolitionism was rising.

Contradictorily, there were other French nationals who had a sense of revulsion upon encountering the pestiferous racism that pockmarked the slave-holding republic.[62]

The fire-breathing Edmund Ruffin of Dixie did not see the *gens de couleur* abandoning the island, at times with human property under their control, as comrades. Indeed, he said, "it was not the slaves of St. Domingo but the wealthy and educated class of free mulattoes that commenced the insurrection"—and who was to say they would not seek to do the same on the mainland?[63] The point is that there was a regnant worry in slave societies that the lighter-skinned and the "free Negroes" (who often overlapped) would ally with the darker skinned enslaved against the ruling elite—and Haiti was cited as Exhibit A.[64] Often in Latin America concessions were made to the lighter-skinned to win their allegiance to slavery, whereas the slave-holding republic—buoyed with hard-line refugees from Hispaniola—begged to differ, as the tendency was to marginalize them too.

As slavery was ossifying on the mainland, forces seeking to disassemble this ogre were gaining strength too. One of the first scholarly explorations of the epochal Virginia slave revolt led by Nat Turner in 1831 declared that Haitian fingerprints were everywhere to be found. Given the frequent commerce between the island and the mainland that preceded 1776 and continued thereafter, said William Sidney Drewry of Johns Hopkins, mainland Africans "had traveled to and from many of the [island] seaports and had ample means of communication with cooks and other servants of the vessels plying between the United States and the West Indies"; moreover, some of the "refugees from St. Domingo settled in Southampton, having brought their Negroes with them" and "recollections of St. Domingo were still vivid in 1831." It is "probable" that the "reports of this catastrophe"—i.e. Negroes who "murdered their masters"—were freely available. Like others before and since, he observed further that the conspirators led by Denmark Vesey in Charleston in 1822 "were detected in active communication with St. Domingo."[65] Fear of another Hispaniola-style revolt caused William Penceel, a slaveholder of color, to expose the plot.[66] Dixie may have known of the ominous words of Pompee Valentine Vastey, a Haitian leader, who in 1816 spoke of a global liberation struggle in which "five hundred million men, black, yellow, and brown" would reclaim their rights[67]—a formula that assuredly included mainland Africans. Enslaving republicans may not have seen it as mere coincidence that organized resistance among U.S. Negroes beginning in the 1790s was said to be sparked by the island insurrection or that their bonded counterparts in Louisiana decades later were known to bellow revolutionary songs originating in Hispaniola.[68]

The problem for the slave-holding republic was that the presence in ever growing numbers on mainland shores of enslaved Africans provided a target for subversion too tempting for adversaries to ignore. The evidence gushing from Dixie leads to the suspicion that enslaved mainland Africans found inspiration—if not aid—for their inclinations in Haiti. Months after the triumph of the revolution and the accession of Louisiana to the federal union, mostly French-surnamed residents of Pointe Coupee—already on edge as a result of the pandemonium of 1795—noted that "the revolution of St. Domingo and other places has become common amongs[t] our Blacks" and, thus, a "Sp[i]rit of Revolt and Mutiny has Crept in Amongst Them," as manifested in the fact that a "few days" previously "we happily discovered a Plan for our Destruction."[69] In Louisiana in 1800 there were complaints that Africans were "completely uncontrollable," possessing the gumption of "not hesitating to strike" masters, while runaways were on the upswing.[70]

Shortly after this nerve-wracking episode, the Mayor of New Orleans wailed about a "scheme to produce an insurrection among the Negroes." He noted that they threatened a "Massacre of the Whites" and planned to either "make themselves masters of the city" or, if that failed, "to destroy it by pillage and fire." The conspiracy was aided by a "white man," who "gave them to understand that he had been formerly engaged in a similar plan in St. Domingo." This man, known as "Le Grand," had been a "soldier in the French Army" before deserting and making his way to the island, where he witnessed the "general massacre of the whites," and then departed for Baltimore, Kentucky—then New Orleans. The Mayor thought that "we shall ever be in danger," from "our contiguity to the West India islands," given "the great number of Slaves and free people of color as well as bad disposed whites now among us" who have "encrimsoned [*sic*] the plains of St. Domingo." The militia was unreliable since it was "mingled with those very Negroes and free people of color" who could well be deemed "political enemies." In New Orleans then there were "twelve thousand souls" comprising the latter, while "not above four thousand whites." Inauspiciously, "the numbers of the former are daily increasing in a much greater proportion than those of the latter," a trend exacerbated by the continued busyness of slave dealers: "our country," he moaned, "is and will continue to be overrun with the wretches of St. Domingo, Martinique & Jamaica instead of the harmless African."[71]

The insecurity of New Orleans—and the mainland as a whole—had been anticipated by Robert Livingston when he was negotiating the historic Louisiana Purchase. While in Paris in 1803 he acknowledged that even taking the strategic port at the mouth of the Mississippi River "would not render us secure." This was not only because the presence of Spain "on the other side" of this artery was threatening, but also because France "might . . . have sent their black troops" to this unsettled town and "upon any dispute" with the republic would have "found a great occasion of slaughter in our southern states" launched from there. With Haitian independence, this foreboding did not disintegrate but metastasized: for now local Africans could not only engage in arbitrage with Spain and France but also unite with fellow avowed abolitionists in Port-au-Prince against the interests of Livingston's slave-holding republic.[72]

Thus, in 1811 in Martinique there was a ramifying plot to set fire to the central urban node and then massacre settlers as they rushed to extinguish the flames. One leader proclaimed that the intent was to "found a second Haitian empire." But the mainland had to be particularly concerned with the confession of one of the key plotters, who had roots in Haiti, that "every month Bonaparte sends a number of emissaries from France who go to New England" and related sites in order to "cause chaos" in places that he "wants to see destroyed." At that point in the Caribbean there was fear of an Atlantic-wide rebellion that did not necessarily exclude the United States itself.[73]

That New Orleans in that very same year was faced with probably the most ambitious slave conspiracy ever to beset the republic, gave sustenance to these claims. In some ways, this 1811 plot was a continuation of what had culminated in Haiti in 1804, notably since this port city had become the locale for numerous slaveholders fleeing the flames of Hispaniola, often with human chattel in tow. The reported leader, Charles Deslondes, and many of his lieutenants had resided in Hispaniola and, likewise, the judges that handed down harsh sentences to the accused—including peremptory executions—also had strong ties to the island.[74]

The Louisiana Purchase had been engineered less than a decade earlier and, given that the loss of the island played a great part in Bonaparte's calculation to relinquish his claim to this vast territory, there was good reason to be fearful about reverberations from Hispaniola. A little more than a decade earlier than the abortive plot in Louisiana, Timothy Dwight, President of Yale University at the turn of the 19th century, was among the many who equated the island revolt with what had just shaken Virginia, a slave conspiracy which took the name of its putative leader: Gabriel.[75] Testifying against him, an African known as "Ben" said that the leader had amassed thousands of combatants and that "two Frenchmen had actually joined."[76] By the time the forbidding news reached the Mississippi Territory, slaveholders were informed that "fifty thousand were to have rose [sic] in arms" and it was likely that the design had its origins in "foreign influence and was intended to exist throughout the United States" in order to "reiterate the horrid scenes of Rapine and Murders, which have been practiced in the French Islands." The recommendation? Keep this news away from the eager ears of the enslaved at all costs.[77]

It is possible that it became easier—and less immediately terrifying—for malevolently guilty slaveholders to point the bloody finger of accusation at Haiti when seeking to understand domestic revolts, rather than blame the murderous scheming of those who often served them food.[78] Painting Haiti in drastically distorting colors at once allowed slaveholders to rationalize the continuation of a brutal enslavement while comforting them in the falsehood that it was the Caribbean "vampire" that was singularly responsible for seditious discontent.[79]

Yet, as frightening as slave revolts were, similarly terrifying was the prospect of Haiti leading to what Jefferson termed an "American Algiers." Anticipating the problem of arbitrage by Africans, which was becoming the most potent tool in their kit, Jefferson worried that London "may play them [island Africans] off on us when they please. Against this," he warned accurately, "there is no remedy."[80]

As early as 1799, this leading slaveholder was expressing his torment to another of his class, James Madison. Both men well knew that in North Africa at that precise moment Africans were harassing U.S. shipping—even enslaving Euro-Americans—and demanding tribute or massive ransoms in return. After fellow U.S. leader Albert Gallatin had warned President Jefferson about "dangers from Saint Domingo,"[81] the Virginian narrowed and expanded his concern by reminding him of the "danger" of "pirates" from there, which was "not peculiar to S. Carolina but threatens all the Southern States."[82]

Typically, Jefferson proved to be prescient. Days after the formal proclamation of the Caribbean republic, his most perfervid nightmare had been realized. The mayor of New Orleans espied "twelve Negroes said to have been brigands" from a Haitian vessel "on shore and in the French language made use of many insulting and menacing expressions to the inhabitants"; supposedly, "they spoke of eating human flesh"—which may have been a reflection of the mayor's own nightmares— "and in general demonstrated great Savageness of Character, boasting of what they had . . . done in the horrors of St. Domingo"—the latter words were quickly becoming a catchphrase summarizing the knife's edge on which slavery rested.[83]

By 1818, Haitian soldiers and sailors were said to be active near the then inflamed and uncertain Georgia-Florida border.[84] It was well-known that Africans had decamped en masse to the Okefenokee Swamp of southern Georgia to the point where James Jackson, the noted duelist and statesman, scoffed in the early years of the 19th century that if his republic "even indirectly recognized the Negro insurrectionists of Haiti, we should logically recognize the independence" of local maroons—which was out of the question but indicative of an African threat that could not be easily subdued.[85]

It was also well known that Toussaint's regime was notorious for seizing slave ships—the lifeblood of the slave-holding republic—and pressing the Africans into his military. Since this meant that slave dealers were, in a sense, adding to an African army, this provided a disincentive for the slave trade.[86]

 "Brigands" or "pirates" were terms used to describe Africans who were prone to seize vessels transporting them from the Upper South to the slave marts that were Savannah and New Orleans—and sail happily to Haiti. The most celebrated case of this genre occurred in 1826 when the infamous slave dealer, Austin Woolfolk, was transporting enslaved Africans from Baltimore to Georgia. The captives subdued the captain and crew, tossed them overboard unceremoniously, and sought to steer the boat to Haiti; unfortunately, they in turn were captured and taken to an uncertain fate in New York.[87] At the same time, Aux Cayes, Haiti, was said to harbor pirates that preyed on the southeastern quadrant of the mainland, which raises the possibility of islanders intercepting this vessel and aiding its escape.[88]

What were described as "pirates" could also be seen as Haitian envoys who realized that an abolitionist republic would have difficulty in surviving in a neighborhood infested with slavery and ventured into nearby territories to make sure the status quo did not persist. "Slavery could not easily be maintained," said one antebellum U.S. leader, Abel Upshur, "in a country surrounded by other countries whose Governments did not recognize that institution."[89] Haiti could agree—and there was the rub—thus reinforcing the irrepressible conflict. For as Christmas was about to be celebrated in Cap-Haïtien in 1825, France's delegate reported to Paris a typical event: a ship had run aground on Haitian soil with scores of enslaved Africans aboard—fresh from the "Ivory Coast"—presumably destined for Cuba, then experiencing a customary spate of imports of human cargo.[90]

In some ways, Haiti was the antipode to the United States, abolitionism confronting enslavement. As the latter gained strength, it was almost inexorable that the former would weaken.

It would have been suicidal, therefore, for Haiti to not respond powerfully to what was becoming a normalized outrage, slave ships and slavery itself in the vicinity. It was in 1822 that a fretful observer declared that a recent slave plot in Martinique was driven by "some persons" from "St. Domingo," who brought with them the "country songs that are now in the mouth of every Negro in the Island."[91] Repercussions were felt quickly in Trinidad, where "some rascals" were "introduced" with a "view to entice the Negroes to desert"—already there was a "large encampment of runaways."[92] Mainlanders reeling from the Haiti-inflected Vesey plot would have been further disconcerted if they had known that the authorities due south had uncovered a "plan upon a very extensive scale" and that they had "little doubt" that "the people of St. Domingo were the instigators & organizers of this diabolical plot." A vessel "loaded with munitions of war and having upwards of 100 men on board" was found and a "very serious attempt [had] been made" by the same Haitians "upon the island of Porto Rico."[93]

As for the Puerto Rican authorities, they condemned these "adventurers and ruffians," who had been recently in Venezuela assisting Simon Bolivar, before sailing to the United States, obtaining in the land of the Second Amendment an "enormous quantity of arms and ammunition." Plans were made in San Juan to "exterminate them" if they dared land there. But what would have infuriated mainlanders if they had been made aware of the vastness of this plot was the notion that it was "hatched and reared" in the United States itself, though the "principal agent" was the "President of Hayti, Boyer, a dangerous and enterprising man who espies at the subversion of all the neighboring islands for the better security of his independence, including the whole archipelago of the Antilles, the very soul of his object being the equality of Colour throughout and the modeling of these Governments similar to that of Saint Domingo."[94] In 1841 San Juan leaders continued to charge Haiti with dispatching subversive literature to Puerto Rico.[95]

The foregoing suggests why so many mainland republicans agreed with Edwin Holland of South Carolina, who in the wake of the Vesey revolt of 1822 said that the Africans who thickly populated his state were "truly the Jacobins of the country," those most disposed to emulate France 1789—or Hispaniola 1791—and overthrow North America 1776.[96]

Scorned as Jacobins, enslaved en masse, hunted down, and slaughtered like wild boar, mainland Africans had little choice but to contemplate emigration—an idea that also had occurred to mainland leaders. By 1821, the U.S. consul in Aux Cayes was complaining about a proliferation of "deserters" from his nation's vessels, "men of colour," a trend which was "extremely vexatious to commerce" since they were not easy to replace.[97] This too was nothing new, particularly the idea that Haiti would be reluctant to cooperate with the United States in returning African refugees. Thousands of black seamen voyaged from the mainland and the island between 1790 and 1830—750 in 1797 alone.[98] If it was any consolation, it was not only the mainland that was being drained of Africans. In 1826 London's emissary in Port-au-Prince noticed that a "very large proportion of the population of the city consists of refugee slaves from the British colonies."[99]

In Haiti seafarers could desert with impunity, which exhilarated U.S. Negroes and enraged their bosses. Days after the triumph of the revolution in 1804, the paramount leader, Jean-Jacques Dessalines, took note of the great number of Africans who were maltreated in the United States and offered to help them—materially— migrate to the island.[100] By 1824, Haiti's President Jean Boyer was dispatching "fifty thousand weight of coffee" to New York for Africans there to sell in order to "facilitate the emigration" to the island.[101] By early 1829, *Freedom's Journal*, the leading U.S. Negro periodical, asserted that "seven or eight thousand people of color from the United States" were now "settled" on the island and that they had "emigrated within eight or nine years."[102] Many of these new residents wound up on the northern coast of the island in what was to become the Dominican Republic and—as shall be seen—a site desperately desired by the United States for strategic and military reasons.

Many of these emigrants not only had agricultural and other skills useful to building the Black Republic, but many also had a burning desire to extirpate

1860's Spain & DR [handwritten annotation]

slavery, making them a continuing threat to the slave-holding republic. There was an anti-slavery society on the island that was in close touch with William Lloyd Garrison.[103] By the 1840s an emigrant was reporting from Porto Plata confidently that "Haiti will soon become a powerful" part of the "Anti-Slavery Society of the United States" with "auxiliaries throughout this country."[104]

In the 1820s Haiti had taken the sprawling—and larger—eastern portion of Hispaniola and then proceeded to denude the mainland of thousands of its hardest working Negro denizens by settling them there. Haiti was implicated in ever more elaborate slave plots—not to mention aboveboard abolitionism, with the likes of Garrison, who was viewed as Public Enemy Number 1 in Dixie—while continuing to cultivate a *de facto* alliance with Washington's adversary in London. In the 1830s and 1840s, Haiti inked far-reaching accords with Paris seeking to restrain the slave trade, which was then captained by U.S. nationals.[105]

But in 1844 the slave-holding republic struck back forcefully by allying with the founders of what became the Dominican Republic, assisting this new nation to independence. The fire-eating Edmund Ruffin confided to his diary that when his comrade, John C. Calhoun, was Secretary of State in 1844, "he used the secret service fund to supply arms" to Haiti's foes in the east with the ultimate aim being "the conquest of Hayti," a plan that overmatched Port-au-Prince's own capacious ambitions and which did not exclude the possibility of reenslavement, rolling back the revolution dramatically.[106] Intriguingly, a self-described "Colored American" concurred, declaring that the slave-holding republic was seeking the "entire overthrow" of the Haitian regime.[107] Paris too, still smarting over the loss of what had been their richest colony, also eagerly backed the secession of eastern Hispaniola.[108]

The same held true for Madrid, whose enmity toward Haiti knew few bounds. By the time the U.S. Civil War erupted, France had moved into Mexico, just as Spain reclaimed the D.R., but even before that Madrid noted knowingly that "the [very] name Spain" commanded "fear and respect" in Port-au-Prince.[109]

With options narrowed, Haiti had little choice but to tighten its ties with London—which only enraged Washington further.[110] The slave-holding republic was disturbed in particular when London helped to foil Washington's attempt to ally further with the D.R. by reminding Dominicans that "nine tenths of their population were rendered liable of arrest and imprisonment . . . should they land in Charleston" because of deep-seated racist biases.[111]

This blocking opened the door to Spain and France making inroads on the island to the detriment of the presumed security of the United States. Simultaneously, Haiti was said to have bought well-armed and equipped vessels from London that could be easily turned against the slave ships festooned with the Stars-and-Stripes then making a beeline to Cuba.[112] The frustrated agent of the slave-holding republic stationed in Haiti told Secretary of State Daniel Webster that a confident Haiti felt that the "political agitation of the slavery question" on the mainland was "favoring their belief that abolitionists of the north will never permit the use of any forcible means against them,"[113] if they were to be so bold as to detain U.S. slavers. Washington was not without weapons, however. By 1857 there were reports about the ill-famed U.S. filibuster—William Walker, in this case, who at one point had taken charge in Nicaragua and had sought to reestablish slavery—was on his way to the island.[114]

Haiti's alienation of the slave-holding bloc on the mainland was no tiny matter. The Mississippi Valley centered on New Orleans and this citadel of still irked and revanchist refugees from the island—besides being a prime slave trading emporium—also happened to contain more millionaires per capita than any other part of the nation, which guaranteed maximum influence in Washington.[115] Arguably, this concentration of wealth was also partly due to the reparations Haiti was made to pay to former island slaveholders, some of whom had decamped to Louisiana.

Hence, understandably, Haiti hailed the raid led by John Brown in Virginia in late 1859, which portended slavery's collapse, a process arguably set in motion in 1791. Correspondingly, Haiti reacted badly when Brown and his comrades were executed. Thus, in 1860 Washington was angered when a "mob" reportedly "assaulted" an arriving U.S. vessel and crew. "Since the affair of Harper's Ferry," said the mainland emissary in Aux Cayes, "feelings of animosity, already existing against American citizens" had "increased" and the "natives seek every opportunity to pour out their bitter cup of hatred." This was hardly irrelevant since the "commerce of the United States" was "so extensive" on the island and "so much American property . . . [was] at stake." The remedy—U.S. vessels of war dispatched forthwith—would only inflame passions more and denude the federal union of armament that would be desperately needed within months.[116]

But it was Dixie that was crying foul in the wake of John Brown's martyrdom. John Tyler, Jr., son of a former president, was among those who charged that the bearded freedom fighter was actually driven—if not sponsored—by Haiti. Brown had studied the revolution in preparation for the raid and it was true that flags flew at half mast in Port-au-Prince when he was executed (as well, three days of mourning were proclaimed and a central boulevard in this capital was named after him). Bridging the sectional divide, Edward Everett of New England agreed that Brown was seeking a replay of 1791.[117] The so-called "Texas Terror" of 1861, an uproar spearheaded by enslaved Africans, was too seen as a harbinger of 1791, a not too distant memory in the minds of many.[118]

This linkage of domestic unrest with foreign motivation was due in part to the fearsomeness of the Haitian reaction to slavery. The message had seeped into the press by early 1861 that Haitian friends not unlike the martyred John Brown would launch an insurrection of the enslaved to "take advantage of [the] first outbreak of war." It was alleged that Haitian troops, according to their ally, James Redpath, would land in the thousands "in the neighborhood of Mississippi" and "march in a body . . . directly for the Gulf, through the portion of the South most thickly populated with slaves to join them, pillage, plunder, murder, and burn"; then "pass through Texas," acting similarly.[119]

This awesome scenario notwithstanding, when civil war arrived on the mainland, Washington finally found out who its true friends were. Spain moved to reclaim the D.R., France muscled into Mexico, and Britain edged towards recognition of the belligerency of the so-called Confederate States of America, a major matter given the proximity of Bermuda and the Bahamas. In contrast, as Haiti's delegate in Washington noted subsequently, it was his republic "alone" that "closed her ports" to "Confederate cruisers" and "allowed U.S. war vessels to refit in her ports and to establish depots for coal and provisions there."[120] Reciprocally, the now abolitionist mainland republic finally chose to recognize diplomatically its southern neighbor, concluding a decades long cold war that had blown hot intermittently[121]—but, alas, the travails inflicted upon Haiti by its more powerful neighbor had simply entered a new stage.

For resolute racists thought that but for external forces like Haiti, slavery on the mainland might have continued. A leading member of a leading South Carolina family was "tempted to assert that every race of men are permanently intolerant of the domination of another race; but we meet with one exception. The Negroes are the only race who have not shown a marked and enduring impatience of the rule of another. In all serious and combined efforts of the blacks to throw off the domination of another people," he advised in the 1860s, "the inspiration and impulse came from abroad, " Hispaniola not least—a lesson that some thought was magnified in the 20th century.[122]

Thus, by early 1862, an all too familiar nightmare made a reappearance off the coast of Hispaniola. "African slaves have been introduced from Cuba into the island of St. Domingo by the Spanish Government" was the controversial allegation communicated to London.[123] This was near Samaná,[124] where many U.S. Negroes had chosen exile, raising the ungainly spectacle that they had fled a republic where this monstrosity was now under siege only to arrive in a land where it seemed to be arriving. Then worse news arrived when a French-American entrepreneur, Antonio Pelletier, was detained near the same site by the Haitian authorities and charged with seeking to collar Haitians and take them to Cuba for enslavement. A diplomatic row ensued that lingered for decades, which complicated unduly the ability of the now dual abolitionist republics to forge accord.[125]

The instability brought to the hemisphere by the mainland civil war was unsettling, not least to Spain, which had been denuded systematically of its holdings in the Americas in recent decades; this anxiety merged with anti-African sentiment to produce heightened concern about Haiti. It was in July 1862 that Madrid's envoy in Haiti worried that the impending arrival of U.S. Negroes to Hispaniola would unduly bolster Black Jacobins and could mean the rise of a "Garibaldi" who by uniting Africans could threaten Spain's tenuous control of its possessions, including Cuba and Puerto Rico and what remained of its control in the Dominican Republic.[126]

This angst about Haiti may have been better directed at the enslaving republic, which already had dominion of California and was lusting for other vast territories once controlled by Madrid. This is suggestive of the point that anger was often displaced to Haiti because, after all, this was the nation that had diverted radically from pre-existing norms—and, it was thought, could do it again. Even in 1863 when the fate of the United States hung in the balance, London discovered that "Americans" were "suspected of having supplied the insurgents" in the D.R. with "arms and ammunition" and had been "unusually busy of late" with "secret expeditions into the country." Although this was presumably aimed at destabilizing Spanish rule, this weaponry could easily have been turned against Haiti. Moreover, it was curious that these "arms and ammunition" were not husbanded for use against slaveholders.[127]

These curiosities remained after the Civil War's conclusion when the newly empowered federal union moved to annex one of the few territories in the vicinity that had not been claimed by competing powers. It was President U.S. Grant who pushed for the annexation of Hispaniola, a measure that was said to envision only the D.R.—where the mass of newly freed U.S. Negroes could be deported—but as the beribboned general conceded later, "if St. Domingo had come we should have had Hayti" too.[128]

Thus, the fiery process of abolition that commenced in 1791 ended ironically in 1871 when Hispaniola barely eluded the grasp of its mainland neighbor who—in a real sense—had driven the process of African enslavement that mandated revolution in the first place.

A MAJOR THEME OF THIS BOOK—as the preceding pages suggest—is the impact of Haiti on mainland Africans, enslaved and free. Daniel Payne, born in Charleston in 1811, was not atypical. The pervasive Huguenot influence there, "aroused" in him a "great desire to learn the French language." "Having heard of Hayti and the

Haytiens, I desired to become a soldier and go to Hayti," he noted militantly, in order to combat their mutual foes.[129] He was walking in the footsteps of the heralded David Walker who—when Payne was still a strapping teenager—sought to bolster black pride, then under attack on the mainland, by pointing to the heroic example of Haiti. "Read the history," he advised, "particularly of Hayti."[130]

As the 19th century proceeded, the desire of numerous U.S. nationals to become a "soldier" in Haiti had not dissipated.[131] Frederick Douglass, who stained his otherwise stellar record by joining with President Grant in the ill-fated effort to annex Hispaniola, compensated for this when he remarked just before passing away— words that echoed the heartfelt sentiments of many Africans slave and free—that it was the Haitian Revolution that was the "original pioneer emancipator of the nineteenth century," whose bold intervention plunged the slave system into a death spiral from which it could not emerge, posing a mortal "threat to all slave-holders throughout the world and the slave-holding world has had its questioning eye upon her ever since." Indeed, "her very name," he concluded correctly, "was pronounced with a shudder."[132]

His 20th century counterpart in eminence, W. E. B. Du Bois—who not so coincidentally had deep roots in Hispaniola—observed in his first book that it was the "wild revolt of despised slaves, the rise of a noble black leader, and the birth of a new nation of Negro freemen," which "frightened the pro-slavery advocates and armed the anti-slavery agitation."[133] What Du Bois could have added was that a central aspect of Haiti's importance was its sovereignty, which meant that—unlike U.S. Negroes behind the bars of the mainland—they could post diplomats worldwide and thereby gather intelligence for the formulation of an estimate of the global correlation of forces, an assessment of which was strategically important for the demise of slavery, then Jim Crow. Thus, in 1874 as the Reconstruction that Du Bois wrote about so effectively was writhing in distress, Haiti's envoy in London was at once assessing the internal scene in London while paying careful attention to German, Russian, and Spanish politics, all of which was necessary for determining Haiti's fate[134]—and was also useful in determining the destiny of the people about to be termed "African-American." Similarly, that same year Haiti appointed a consul in Gibraltar,[135] occupied by Britain and claimed by Spain, which allowed adroit arbitrage between the two for the benefit of Haitians—and potentially African Americans. Being sovereign, Haiti was simply in an advantageous position to leverage its weight not only in favor of its citizenry, but also Africans globally, who were mostly colonized or otherwise bludgeoned. Thus, in 1895, Haiti was presented with a far-reaching proposition that involved "Australian islands, Japan, China, Siam, India, etc."[136]

It was a humdrum matter when Haiti engaged Japanese personnel for infrastructure development[137] at a time when this Asian nation was en route to making special appeals to African-Americans in order to outflank Washington.[138] Washington was quick to forward its laws respecting the barring of Chinese immigration to the United States, though apparently—and for good reason—Haiti did not move in a similar direction.[139] Perhaps understandably, in the prelude to abolition in Brazil in 1888, it was feared that antislavery advocates had in store another Haitian Revolution.[140] Surely, Haiti paid careful attention to U.S. Negroes. For example, in the late 1840s, the Haitian legislature honored the great tragedian Ira Aldridge—who like so many African-American artists had been compelled to make his mark abroad—for his contribution to the arts: he was named Adjutant to the President.[141]

It was left to the less celebrated but no less perceptive William Wells Brown to sum up a developing consensus among U.S. Negroes when he exclaimed in 1854 that "no historian has yet done . . . justice" to the Haitian Revolution.[142] To the extent that these stirring remarks remain true, it may be because this revolution was so profound, so important, so stunning, that it may require an entire school of historians to take its true measure.

In the following pages, I will seek to add to this necessary and perpetual conversation, while keeping in mind that—quite appropriately—in 1804 the Yaqui River in Hispaniola changed course and began to flow into the Bay of Manzanilla, where formerly it emptied into the Bay of Monte Christi.[143] History too changed course in 1804—though this alteration was so far-reaching that we still seek to chart its serpentine flow.

I

Confronting the Rise of Black Jacobins
1791–1793

GEORGE WASHINGTON WAS ELATED.
"I am happy," he rhapsodized in September 1791, weeks after a transforming Caribbean eruption, about "how well disposed the United States are to render every aid in their power to our good friends and Allies [the French] to quell 'the alarming insurrection of the Negroes in Hispaniola'" Signaling the urgent importance of this fraught matter to his own slave-holding republic, President Washington added, "I have not delayed a moment since the receipt of your communications."[1] Quickly, the president advanced French planters on the island a sizeable amount that was to come to $726,000 within months, a sum drawn against the formidable debt incurred by the United States during the anti-London revolt. This is a telling indicator of how the fiscal crisis in Paris, leading to revolt in France and the island alike, was driven in part by the rebellion led by Washington.[2]

The president's alacrity was comprehensible in that on 22 August 1791 at least 1500 Africans acted in concert on the island, an assemblage that dwarfed comparable revolts in South Carolina in 1739 and Jamaica in 1760. It was a grim situation that could be readily envisioned on the mainland. This thought had occurred to Governor Charles Pinckney of South Carolina who, just after the revolt was launched, remarked that it represented a "flame which will extend to all the neighboring islands and may eventually prove not a very pleasing or agreeable example to the Southern states."[3]

Capable of teasing out the abolitionist implications of the revolt, South Carolina—where the African majority had proven to be difficult to control in a manner not unlike Hispaniola—was the first state to take legislative steps to abolish the slave trade when in 1792 it sought to bar the importation of this troublesome property. Neighboring Georgia and North Carolina quickly followed in 1793 and 1794 respectively. It was no secret that the fires of Hispaniola aided immeasurably in assisting enslaving republicans in seeing the light. During a contemporaneous congressional debate concerning taxation imposed on imported Africans, Willis Alston of North Carolina reminded the House that Negroes from the Caribbean were one hundred times more dangerous than slaves imported directly from Africa.[4] The implications for the continent were unpropitious.

The exigency of Washington's response was also driven by the immediacy of the desperation experienced by island settlers. Within hours of the August 1791 turbulence, dire letters were sent northward to the slave-holding republic requesting munitions, troops, and food. The United States was closer to the island than France, a factor that had shaped the island for some time and was to continue.[5] This closeness, in the real and figurative senses, also serves to explain why when frantic messages were sent in the immediate aftermath of August 1791 to Jamaica, Cuba, and the United States for military aid, it was the latter republic that responded with eagerness.[6]

Of course, this reflected enlightened self-interest on the part of the chief executive. Not only were the properties—and lives—of his compatriots in jeopardy on the island,[7] raising searching questions about a similar conflict detonating on the mainland, but also Jefferson already had raised an alarm about the possibility of an "American Algiers" arising nearby. As early as 1580, the notorious Sir Francis Drake himself had found and freed Turks, North African Moors, and even a few Frenchmen and Germans among the Spanish galley slaves toiling ignominiously in Santo Domingo and Cartagena.[8] Who was to say if the future held the prospect of finding Euro-Americans among these island mudsills, but this time with revenge-seeking Africans wielding the whip-hand? In the midst of the "quasi-war" between the United States and France, a few years after Washington's elation, a U.S. Navy man exclaimed, "Look out! United States of America! Or you will share the fate of the Swedes at Tripoli—the Danes at Tunis—and of many other Nations at Algiers."[9]

Jefferson was fixated on this idea, reminding Albert Gallatin in mid-1801 to "expect pirates from St. Domingo." This may have been doubtful but, nevertheless, the possibility was "not peculiar to Charleston but threatens all the Southern states."[10]

Even if this chilling dystopia were ruled out, there were continuing repercussions that proved hard to ignore. The alliance of the North American rebels with Paris effectively had meant an alliance with France's richest—nearby—colony. Just weeks after the hinge moment that was August 1791, complaints were pouring forth from the mainland about the rise in prices of sugar, coffee, and similar articles, too often sourced from the fortress of slavery that was Hispaniola. Elizabeth Drinker, the prim Philadelphia Quaker, after making note of the inflation in the prices of these commodities in her diary, then added "cloudy this evening."[11] Given the circumstances, this appears more like a historical prediction than a weather report.

As President Washington was told subsequently, there was yet another and more frightening deficit that had appeared on the mainland concomitant with the upheaval on the island: Charleston merchants—who shared uneasily a land with often rambunctious Africans—were "deeply impressed with the deplorable condition in which many of the inhabitants of St. Domingo, now residing in this City with their families, have been reduced, from Affluence to Want of the necessaries of life."[12] Was the stark reality of these families a presentiment, perhaps, of what these now affluent merchants might themselves face within decades? And how would they react—not least in their now quotidian maltreatment of Africans—to this potential likelihood?

WHAT HAD ATTRACTED MERCHANTS TO Hispaniola was the wealth there. Gold, silver, copper, mahogany, and iron ore were among the bounty. "Haiti," according to indigenes, was the "mother of nations," but their numbers, estimated to be in the millions on the island before contact with Europeans, had dwindled tremendously by 1791. The soak of bloodletting served to create the harsh conditions that greeted enslaved Africans who were dragged there by the tens of thousands as the numbers of indigenes were dwindling.[13]

By the late 17th century, the island had been split effectively between French colonizers (on the west) and Spanish (on the east)—though what was to mark Hispaniola to this day is that Madrid seized the lion's share, perhaps two-thirds of the territory. Both "Catholic" powers proved to be instrumental in seeking to oust their mutual adversary—"Protestant" London—from its mainland colonies, with Hispaniola being critical to this powerful new reality. As evidenced by the fact that English and Spanish remain the dominant languages of the hemisphere, France wielded less influence in the Americas, which serves to explain why so much Parisian capital flowed into the island. But from the viewpoint of the nascent United States, France's relationship with New Orleans—emerging in the early 18th century was critical.

Certainly the tie between the western portion of the island and the mouth of the Mississippi was close from an early stage. The 1724 Code Noir in Louisiana was borrowed with only slight modification from the island's 1685 slave code,[14] both of which were—in a sense—more "liberal" than their counterparts under the Union

Jack.[15] The 1724 code, for example, forbade masters from breaking up families by selling spouses or children below the age of puberty to different masters. The British retained this regime after 1763, when they formally asserted their claim to Illinois.[16] This did not endear them to settlers on the verge of rebellion—as evidenced by their junking of this blatant restriction on "free trade" upon asserting control over what was to become a powerful midwestern state.

As early as 1763, mainland slaveholders were expressing trepidation about the importation of Africans from the island because of their supposed sinister reputation for revolting, particularly their demonstrated skill in dispensing poisons. This was a reaction to the so-called Mackandal Conspiracy of 1755, when the Africans on the island contemplated poisoning the entire settler population, which was followed in succeeding years by yet another wave of poisonings.[17]

Given the violent ructions that rocked the mainland periodically, it was—in a sense—comprehensible why settlers found it necessary to assume a stance of hawkish vigilance. The Natchez Massacre of 1729 featured a ferocious revolt, against settlers principally led by indigenes—though Africans were involved. The seizing of hundreds of the leading indigenous rebels and their sale into slavery in Hispaniola was guaranteed to bring the two oppressed groups closer together.[18]

In response to such far-reaching plots, French settlers were fleeing to Charleston and other mainland sites too but often continued to hold interests in the Caribbean. This meant that their reaction—or overreaction—to slave conspiracies there could redound to the detriment of enslaved mainland Africans, a trend that was to continue for decades to come.[19] Suggestive of why there was flux in jurisdictions administered by Paris was a comprehensive legal code drafted in France in 1777 that brazenly mandated that "in the end, the race of Negroes will be extinguished in the kingdom,"[20]—this was akin to an invitation to Africans to rebel in response.

Ironically, the man given credit for arriving at the mouth of the Chicago River in 1779 and founding a leading metropolis was thought to be a man of color—with a Gallic name: Jean Baptiste Point Du Sable.[21] It was also not without irony that as this town was being founded, the famed Marquis de Lafayette—still celebrated on the mainland—was happily telling Benjamin Franklin that Senegal had been "taken by our troops" in West Africa. It was "previously in the enemy's hands" and this, he noted, was "preventing the Nigro [*sic*] trade," which had been benefiting "the Southern Gentlemen of America." Thus, he concluded with effervescence, "I believe our conquest will be pleasing to them."[22] What neither correspondent was able to envision was that their energetic enchaining of Africans, who were then dumped in Hispaniola, was to create a demographic nightmare for slavery.

Nonetheless, the developing difference between French and British slavery was then parlayed into a developing abolitionist movement in Paris, which then influenced both the island and the mainland.[23] Nevertheless, it did seem that as Frenchmen came into closer contact with the rougher mainland settlers[24] a coarsening took place, driving them closer to the latter's often harsher modes. This, however, was unsustainable on the island in light of the demographic imbalance. Yet the anti-monarchism of the mainland and the resultant close contact with Paris that led to the founding of the new republic doubtlessly influenced the July 1789 emergence of revolution.

But there were contradictory trends—contrary to and constitutive of the rise of revolution. It was necessary to regulate slavery for the simple reason there were so many enslaved Africans being driven into the Mississippi River basin, not least given the inferno of slave plots that the Caribbean was becoming. This too was connected to Hispaniola insofar as African slavery in Missouri dates at least from 1719 when a Frenchman known as Renault purchased 500 Africans in Hispaniola and brought them to the mainland to work in mines. Yet, again, the ascendancy of the Stars and Stripes marked a qualitative—and quantitative—transformation of slavery, with numerous consequences, often dimly understood. By 1803, as the loss of Hispaniola was influencing Paris to abandon what became known as the Louisiana Purchase, there were almost 3000 enslaved Africans in Missouri—but by 1860 there were 114,931 of this debased group and 3572 free Africans.[25]

There was also a gravitational pull that drove Hispaniola and erstwhile British settlers into a warm embrace: Paris was far away.[26] Though London was driving Paris out of North America during the Seven Years' War of 1756–1763, which—inter alia—would have removed the rear base from which Africans and other antagonists of British settlers could harass Massachusetts and New York from Quebec,[27] these same British settlers continued to trade profitably with the French.[28]

Both Paris and the settlers under British rule on the mainland had grievances with London, which drove the former two closer together. The Sugar Act of 1764, London's handiwork, was an attempt to curb trade between the thirteen colonies and Hispaniola—a bill that contributed to the urgency of mainland revolt, insofar as it was intended to disrupt the mutually profitable relationship between island and mainland.[29] Thus, the influential Carolinian Ralph Izard, born in 1742, eventually owned 594 Africans. He moved to France in 1777 because of his inability to abide British rule and his family lived there until 1783 when the Union Jack was lowered. Izard expired conspicuously enough in 1804, as the emergence of Haiti marked a new stage in the devolution of African slavery.[30]

This mutually beneficial commerce between Hispaniola and the mainland decidedly included trafficking in Africans. By 1784 Paris made official what was evident when—as relations between London and its former mainland colonists reached a new nadir—it formally opened its ports to foreign commerce, putatively violating the leading practices of colonialism, a policy that benefited the infant United States. Predictably, island planters were then incentivized to emulate their mainland counterparts by leaning toward independence themselves, a spark that was to explode shortly thereafter.[31]

By 1785 Charles Pettigrew was journeying regularly from the mainland to the island for slave purchases—though he found "it not a good place to sell Negroes," perhaps because the market had been flooded by his countrymen. Since "they were too suspicious of their morals when brought from the continent," the devious slave dealer sought to "propose to replace in New Negroes if I can," the presumably surly Africans with those who had been acculturated, perhaps from the mainland. The well-connected Pettigrew was in a position to execute his far-reaching plan: "I am to preach in town during my stay at the request of the Governor," he confided to "my dear Polly," writing from the island. The popular flesh peddler was "invited to dine out among [the elite] almost every day"; and "living is high," he also noted, as "I am favored & I have take[n] a private lodging upon a hill above the town."[32]

By 1787, the island was dominating the lucrative business of sugar production, generating a whopping 131 million pounds in that single year, a good deal of it ending up on the delicate palates of Euro-Americans.[33] One observer pointed out that the "number of foreign ships, principally American, which in 1788 assisted in furnishing Saint Domingo with provisions, was considerable." If this had not been the case, said Francis Alexander Stanislaus, the island "would have been in absolute want of many articles of the first necessity."[34] By 1789 an estimated 20% of the vessels arriving in Philadelphia from foreign harbors originated in Saint-Domingue; seven years later, at the height of the revolution, the figure had jumped to more than a third.[35]

A telling vignette also occurred in 1789—days after the storming of the Bastille in Paris—when pirates, infamously disquieting, murdered a captain and cook, who were heading from Port-au-Prince to South America, and they then sailed to the mainland before being jailed in Virginia. This gave U.S. nationals a possible foretaste of what could be expected from an independent Haiti.[36]

Maritime traffic between the island and the mainland was sufficiently intense to attract pirates of various stripes. Just before August 1791, recalled Henry Adams, "such a swarm of Yankee skippers frequented the ports of Saint-Domingue that the trade of the United States with this colony became second only to that with England."[37] Besides the wealth brought by slaves and sugar, there was another reason for mainlanders to keep a close eye on Hispaniola. Early in the 20th century, one

U.S. strategist acknowledged what had been true for some time. "Next to Mexico," said William A. MacCorkle, a former U.S. governor, "this island republic"—Haiti, that is—"is fraught with the greatest importance to the United States in our relation to the Southern and Central American republics, the Gulf of Mexico and the Caribbean Sea." Why? "It is directly on and commands the two great passages of the Atlantic Ocean into the Caribbean Sea from the eastern coast of the United States to and from . . . Panama. . . . It thus practically controls the great bulk of the commerce of the United States to the East and the Pacific Ocean. This island has within its shores more natural wealth than has any other territory of similar size in the world." This island, he continued, "is more capable of supporting life in all its phases, more able to create wealth and diffuse happiness to its people, than any other land of its size on the face of the earth. Its harbours are incomparable and will float the navies of the world. Its atmosphere is salubrious and its climate healthy." Hispaniola sat astride "the two great twin seas, the Gulf of Mexico and the Caribbean Sea," and both were seen as being "more important than the Mediterranean in their effect upon the commerce of the world." Hence, a "fundamental principle of the United States," he stressed in words that were perhaps even truer for the federal union in 1791, is that "we should control the Gulf of Mexico and the Caribbean Sea. This control should be absolute and exclusive."[38]

It was the 20th century Trinidadian intellectual, C. L. R. James, who referred to Môle St. Nicholas, a landmark on the island, as the "Gibraltar of the Caribbean Sea."[39] As early as 1810, an analyst concluded that Samaná, on the northern coast of the island, was a "bay" with "incalculable advantages" on a landmass that was "key to the Mexican gulph [sic]."[40]

This is a compelling picture that suggests why so many mainlanders were to be found on the island in 1791. A great uncle of the late 19th century writer, Samuel G. Perkins was born in Boston in 1767 and by 1785 was toiling in Hispaniola with the mainland firm Perkins, Burling & Co. He stayed until 1794—abandoning the island as flames leapt ever higher.[41] The connection between the island and the enslaving republic had become so close that even as Africans were plotting disruption in 1791, Nathan Cutting, a Massachusetts merchant who had moved to Hispaniola to speculate in the slave trade, suggested that his new homeland would join the United States.[42]

But this luscious status quo grounded in flesh peddling was to be disrupted by August 1791—and before that in July 1789.[43] By mid-1790 Pierce Butler of Carolina was thanking one Founding Father, George Mason, for informative news about France, as he hoped—with a hint of wish fulfillment—that the "French Nation will accomplish their object & secure to themselves & their posterity the equal operation of Laws"[44]—though, like many others in his state, he may have been disappointed by the emerging results. For the French Revolution too sent shock waves coursing to the mainland. Coincident with the latter, debates over slavery commenced, and this along with the debates about rights in the hexagonal nation led directly to a fierce melee on the island.

Thus, the roseate dreams of the merchants of odiousness were too to be dismantled. Fleeing alongside the Perkins scion were others of French surname; some were royalists upset with regime change in Paris and the seismic results on the island, others nested with the Huguenots, who since the late 18th century had flocked to the mainland and had become prominent in the slave trade. Their helter-skelter retreat to the mainland was tangible evidence of a new world birthing at the same time that the newly born mainland republic was moving in an opposing direction. The undulating waves from Hispaniola reached its neighbors, particularly Martinique, where African activism compelled Emmanuel Parius Pons and his brother to abandon their large plantation and scurry to New Orleans, bringing along a large number of enslaved Africans, who carried along startling scenes of presumed superiors bolting for their lives. There in St. James Parish they all settled in the so-called "Maison Blanche" plantation, which was by most measures the most significant plantation Louisiana ever had.[45]

Given the arrival of the likes of Pons, this Caribbean turmoil was not all bad news for the slave-holding republic for such planters had well-developed slave trading networks that arrived with their presence. Thus, between 1790 and 1800, the population of European descent in a key region of the Carolinas—near Andrew Jackson's hometown, the Waxhaws—declined while the population of enslaved Africans nearly doubled; more than half of all households of the former now owned one or more of the latter.[46]

The size and suddenness of this influx of Africans into New Orleans was virtually without precedent on the mainland, with an estimated 9000 arriving there between 1763 and 1796 and an additional estimated 8000 before 1808; most had come from Jamaica and Charleston though many could be traced back to the destabilization of slavery in Hispaniola. That most were male—by a three-to-one ratio by one estimate—did not bode well for the future stability of mainland slavery.[47] Surely, the arrival of island planters, Africans in tow in the thousands, helped to buoy the overall market in Africans.[48]

On the one hand, the United States was wading more deeply into the choppy waters of mass enslavement as Hispaniola was emitting a loudly different signal. This did not augur well for slavery's future given the ability of the island Africans to maneuver diplomatically among the major powers—especially London—to the disadvantage of the enslaving republic. On the other hand, doubling down on slavery by attracting Frenchmen with capital from the Caribbean, in a sense, mirrored the growth of the European population on the mainland before 1776 when settlers fled African unrest in Jamaica and Antigua in the 1730s.

Thus, ultimately the U.S. claim to Alabama was strengthened when the Chapron family of Hispaniola fled in horror to yet another citadel of French culture, the region stretching from Mobile. That the matriarch and male heirs of this clan had barely eluded what the patriarch described as "the torch & the daggers of assassins & Plunderers"[49] insured that their allegiance to a slave-holding republic would not be easy to dislodge. A similar allegiance probably lodged in the breast of Mederic-Louis-Elie Moreau de Saint-Mery, who was about to be arrested on the island and narrowly escaped the guillotine before this relative of Empress Josephine landed in Philadelphia.[50]

The southern neighbor of the then capital of the republic was also deluged with panicked and terrified settlers abandoning the island. As African control of the island was accelerating, a large band of bedraggled refugees decamped to Baltimore from Hispaniola, bearing frightful memories; this party included 1000 described as "white" and 500 denoted as "mulatto." Looking back from 1929, an observer pointed out that this group formed a "rather large percentage of Baltimore's citizenry, just as though 150,000 were to come in upon us" and "never did our quiet homes hear more fearful stories" than during dramatically chilling fireside chats with these refugees.

The volcanic outburst of human passions and hatreds from which they had just fled was said to have been ignited by "Robespierrean words of freedom." Readers of the local press learned that what was at play was not merely the already dreadful "conflict of class against class, but also the much more embittered one of race against race." "They massacred nearly every white person who fell into their power," said one still shocked speaker. "Within two months after the revolt first began, upward of 2000 white persons of all ages had been massacred"; in sum, "1200 Christian families" were instantaneously "reduced from wealth to the necessity of depending altogether on charity," an awful sight to some. At once, this spectacle would deepen allegiances to the slave-holding republic that offered refuge, while causing others to reconsider if the price of slavery was too steep to pay.[51]

It was the latter idea that increasingly was taking hold in London and once implanted there it could only deepen the widening chasm with its former mainland colonies.[52] For ever more frantic accounts of the insurrection on the island were making their way to redoubts of slavery and the slave trade raising ever more searching questions about the ultimate viability of the worst of human bondage.[53]

It did appear that virtually with the moment of the August 1791 devastation of the island, abolitionist voices became ever more insistent. Charges of the "immorality" of slavery and the understandable desire to prevent one's throat from being slit seemed to merge effortlessly in the surging flow of abolition.[54] Inspired explicitly by the Hispaniola rebellion, Percival Stockdale informed Granville Sharp, the veteran abolitionist, that "it appears, even from Liverpool evidence, that if mankind, in general, were to die, in proportion to the mortality of the Slaves during their transportation to the Colonies, the human race would be extinct in ten years."[55]

This hastening velocity of abolitionism was conspicuously the case in London,[56] which soon was to crown itself as the cop-on-the-beat seeking to suppress a slave trade now captained by its former charge in the enslaving republic. Even on the mainland—Newport in this case—by 1792 there was a stern warning about the "doctrine of *retribution*" being visited upon the flesh peddlers who thickly populated Rhode Island; this was "the only reason of hope" it was further stressed.[57]

Jamaica, where great fortunes (for the British) and great revolts (by Africans) were part of the landscape, paid close attention to the Hispaniola revolt from the beginning, a fact facilitated by proximity. It was a "most dreadful calamity" unfolding, it was reported there as early as 1 September 1791, with a "great number of white people . . . butchered."[58] It did not take long for Jamaica to be even more influenced by what was to become Haiti.

Such was the race between two contradictory trends that greeted and, at times, confounded the slave-holding republic: increasing investments in human chattel at home and abroad and, along with it, opening the floodgates to admit more "whites" to overawe growingly restless indigenes and Africans or bowing to the logic of 1791. Would, instead, the growing number of enslaved Africans (and their indigenous comrades) overawe those defined as "white" before reinforcements from Europe would arrive?

As early as 1790, as the waves of change from Paris crossed the channel, grave note was taken in London of debates in France about abolishing the slave trade.[59] Alert investors in the slave-holding republic should have taken heed when testifying before the House of Commons in London in 1790 and 1791 on the increasingly conspicuous matter of abolition was George Baillie, who had resided twenty-five years in South Carolina and Georgia, first as a merchant, afterwards as a planter. William Beverley, born in Virginia and resident there for the first sixteen years of his life, also testified, as did John Clapham, who had spent two decades in Maryland, and Robert Crew, a native of Virginia.[60] Abolitionist tracts reflecting this London debate were also appearing on the mainland with increased frequency.[61]

William Wilberforce, soon to be hailed as the doyen of abolitionism, was instrumental in the April 1791 debate in Parliament on the slave trade. At the same time, Whitehall, in the person of Lord Grenville, worried that the impassioned words coming from London would have the "effect of increasing . . . discontent or dissatisfaction which may at present prevail among the slaves." Thus, he said—underlining the intimate tie between African uproars and reform—planters should seek "mild and gentle treatment of these People," so as to "reconcile them as much as possible to their situation."[62]

Meanwhile in Louisiana, soon to be part of the enslaving federal union, as early as 1792, Africans were seeking to emulate their counterparts on the island.[63] This was not the end of imported trends, thanks to this Caribbean disturbance. As well, tensions accelerated between major political factions, i.e. the Federalists and the Democratic-Republicans. This was particularly unsettling since the conflict infused the entire realm of foreign policy and, thereby, national survival in that the "quasi-war" with France was part of this equation, as well as the seemingly perpetual row with Britain.[64] Certainly, as the slave-holding republic came to recognize that ousting France from North America was sufficiently important that it could even mean countenancing—or even aiding—armed Africans in Hispaniola, slave traders and slaveholders could conclude more easily that leading republicans did not have their best interests at heart.

To make things worse, also arriving in port cities proven to be frail—Norfolk, for example—were a sizeable number of refugees from the island that could be described as "black," but who were not unwilling to back slavery. Still, they too had seen the unraveling of slave society and it was not unreasonable for onlookers to suspect that their allegiance to the status quo was unsteady. Given the primary role played by those regarded as "mulatto" on the mainland in pushing for rights on the island that then led to Africans too revolting, it was understandable why Virginians were nervous about the arrival of these refugees.

Such suspicions were buoyed by the miasmic atmosphere delivered by the radical doctrines of the French Revolution, which did not rule out rights for those with a complement of melanin.[65] How to sideline—or incorporate into the elite—*gens de couleur* and/or "mulattoes" would bedevil the mainland republic until they all were frog-marched into the bottom rung of society, i.e. "blackness" with the arrival of *Plessy v. Ferguson* in 1896.[66]

It was not as if the *gens de couleur* in Guadeloupe and Martinique, for example, during the earliest years of the final decade of the 18th century were gung-ho about general emancipation of the enslaved: *au contraire*. Actually, in mid-May 1791, Julien Raimond, leader of those often described as "mulatto," argued before the

National Assembly in France that granting full political rights to his people would help guarantee the subjugation of the enslaved.[67] But as the mainland republicans saw things, it was Raimond's group who brought down the temple of slavery by making special claims and they balked at igniting a similar process in their backyard. At the same time, the enslaving republic could hardly ignore that in investigating the causes of unrest in Hispaniola, there quickly emerged a focus on the alleged "arrogance" of those seeking to discriminate against those in Raimond's category. By February 1792 already there was serious discussion about granting equality in Paris to "People of Colour and Free Negroes"[68]—a trend that would be resisted on the mainland with ferocity, tearing at the fabric of society in one more step toward civil war.

The problem for the slave-holding republic was that its parlous diplomatic position suggested it could hardly afford to alienate potential allies, even *gens de couleur*. Months before August 1791, the elite Elias Ball of South Carolina was being told that sooner rather than later his nation would be warring with Spain,[69] while even sooner there would be a "quasi-war" with France combined with the seemingly perpetual tensions with Britain. Pierce Butler of the same state unctuously sought to convince Don Diego de Gardoqui of Spain that "we ought to be good neighbours"[70]—but the very utterance betrayed its possible opposite.

Complicating relations between the major powers was the frequent assertiveness of Africans, for as they barged onto the stage, their presence had to be accounted for, which could allow—as was to happen with London—a power to creep toward abolition thereby gaining an advantage over competitors. Still, as African rebelliousness reached the mainland, this also had the potential to unite the major powers on the altar of slave-holding.

Anticipating a larger revolt in 1795, by 1792 Pointe Coupee in Louisiana was afire. Julien Poydras with roots in Nantes—which happened to be a major slave port—was targeted. Though it was alleged he owned a staggering 3700 slaves, another source avers the figure was "only" about 570, still making him one of the largest slaveholders on the mainland; he also had extensive holdings in Bordeaux. This man of French origin was in a territory with close ties to Spain that was about to become a part of the United States, while owning Africans on the verge of seeking to eliminate them all—which could have brought these oppressors together in nervousness.[71] Poydras had departed Hispaniola for Louisiana in 1768 and, thus, was prone to know about the impact of island restiveness on his own riotous "possessions." There was also the possibility, as was happening on the island, that a door could have been opened for a Spanish competitor to destabilize his enterprise by allying with Africans.[72] Poydras was understandably irate when in April 1795 "his" Africans rose as one, spurred on by the victories in Hispaniola. "Sixteen of my best Negroes of the plantation were hung," he griped, "which causes me a loss of thirty thousand piastres in one lump sum."[73]

Louisiana was far from being singular. As soon as the authorities in Missouri recieved word of the 1791 revolt, they anxiously moved to curtail the slave trade with the islands for fear of contagion and opened this hateful commerce with Africa. As well, they moved to assuage the enslaved by guaranteeing them certain rights and immunities. One official acknowledged that "contented subordination" was his goal, which would "prevent" the enslaved "from desiring a liberty which had cost so much blood in Santo Domingo."[74]

The competition among the major powers was made to order for Africans willing to engage in arbitrage, leaning toward one power and against another. Arguably, the increased ability of Africans to engage in arbitrage heightened tensions between and among the "white" powers, as they scrambled hectically to either retreat from—or bolster—slavery, seeking to either take advantage of the debilitated posture of a fellow power or crackdown more mercilessly on invigorated Africans, both of which had a painful downside. This was occurring as a 1792 writer penned an "ode" to the "Insurrection of the Slaves at St. Domingo," urging that the rebels "bathe thy sword in Christian blood!"[75]—suggesting that bolstering enslavement came with a heavy price.

Unfortunately for mainland settlers, their concern had to veer far beyond the import of inflamed poetry. As this ardent ode was being drafted, the thought of such a bloodbath had occurred to Africans in Virginia independently of these passionate words.[76] By May 1792, the governor of Virginia was told by a concerned Smith Snead in Northampton that "people of this county are very much alarmed with the apprehension of the insurrection of the slaves," bringing manifold "dangers," especially since there was "no public ammunition in the county."[77] A neighbor there, Henry Guy, concurred, as he too wrung his hands about the "intended insurrection of our slaves" in a "plot [that] seems to have been general."[78] Then in Portsmouth there was an "intended insurrection" of "our slaves." It was said regretfully, "their conduct has long since warranted the suspicion." A "supply of arms" was requested "speedily" in order to "alleviate the fears" now raging.[79] That same day, Thomas Nelson of Norfolk too was worrying about the "intentions of our slaves" since "we are totally unprepared for such an event, having very few arms in the hands of our militia."[80]

Yet another startled Virginian complained that "the Negroes" were sponsoring "very large night meetings" where they began to "talk of Chewsing [choosing] Delegates & a High Sheriff," as if, like on the island, state power was on their mind.

"In case of invasion," moaned Holt Richardson, "we are totally unprepared."[81] By July 1792, Smith Snead—at least—had not calmed down, warning again of yet another "insurrection," while noting reassuringly that "no white persons"—perhaps presumed sympathizers with the French Revolution—were involved.[82] During that time, the diminutive and bookish James Madison found time to observe incisively that the news from the island "paints the distress of the Island in the most gloomy colours,"[83] a matter of obvious consequence for his commonwealth.

It did not require an oracle to see that if mainland slaveholders could help to squash African rebellion on the island, it could remove any inspiration these rebels supplied to Africans on the mainland. So motivated, it did not take long for U.S. residents on the island to join the fray, taking an active part in the struggle against the enslaved. They were to be found in scouting parties and expeditionary troops dispatched to confront the Africans with lethal force. U.S. seafarers in island ports pitched in, too. In Cap-Français, not only resident U.S. merchants but also such crews were called on to defend against marauding Africans. In a display of class—and "race"—unity, the South Carolina legislature quickly chipped in with a hefty donation of 3000 pounds to the besieged islanders.[84]

What may have influenced the lawmakers was the presence in their state of the likes of Auguste de Grasse, who told President Washington directly of the "great distress" of those like himself who had fled the island one step ahead of angry Africans. He confessed that "after having lost a commodious dwelling & 200 Negroes," he was now drowning in misery.[85] De Grasse's homeland—France—shortly after the igniting of the island revolt had contacted the federal authorities on the mainland, delivering the disturbing news that plantation owners had been killed, plantations immolated, and other Europeans were strangled. An estimated 100,000 armed Africans were said to be on the march, as they enacted a bloody drama of human horrors. French settlers were not simply calling upon altruism for, it was said with some accuracy, this destruction could easily spread. Yet, despite these anguished pleas and the mortal threat articulated to the mainland itself, by 26 January 1792, Paris's man on the mainland was told that the response from the United States was inadequate.[86]

What was not said was that the United States was torn between the felt desire to quell African unrest and the larger desire to weaken France in the hemisphere. Still, the new republic may have thought that Paris was ungrateful for seemingly ample aid was sent, not only by the federal union but by states like South Carolina and Pennsylvania too,[87] who had their own unique foreign policy interests. "Dispensing with their usual procedures," concludes one scholar, "the Assembly" in the Keystone State, "fashioned a bill within a single day which authorized . . .

provisions for the relief of Cap-Français" and provided vessels to transport "any colonists who wished to flee the violence."[88] Another scholar has estimated that the United States supplied island planters with hundreds of thousands of dollars in aid, arms, ammunition, food and the like—after all, it was not preordained that this would always be a French colony and self-interest and buying goodwill among besieged island planters was as good a reason as any to bail out class comrades.[89]

Paris may have not have been wholly aware of the sweeping challenges to North American national security posed by domestic Africans and indigenes, a challenge that had hardly ceased since 1776.[90] But Paris may have known, as early as October 1790, that a number of those from the island described as "mulatto" had gone to the mainland to purchase arms and ammunition in anticipation of taking advantage of the flux brought by July 1789 and visiting the same upon Hispaniola. Some of these men had fought alongside the victorious rebels in their triumph over London a few years earlier. Yet it was dangerous for slave-holding republicans to conspire with Frenchmen sympathetic to revolution since some of the latter also had noticed the odiousness of mainland slavery—and then repaired to Paris to form abolitionist societies.[91]

Such far-sighted attitudes shed light on why some mainland republicans were to find France so distasteful, anti-monarchism aside. One high-level U.S. diplomat, Gouverneur Morris, was horrified upon arriving in a Paris torn by revolution. It was, he thought, "perhaps as wicked a Spot as exists. Incest, Murder, Bestiality, Fraud, Rapine, Oppression, Baseness, Cruelty"—and that was among his milder complaints. How could such a din of iniquity step "forward in the sacred Cause of Liberty"?[92]

Morris was not singular in mainland republican distaste for France and De Grasse was not alone either, though he may have felt that way as he huddled in sufferance in South Carolina. In short, he—and other Parisians and island settlers—may have grasped the ambivalence in the United States about their plight, which may have heightened their already escalating hysteria about what was occurring. At the same time, as Paris itself was enduring a bout of radicalism, often denoted as "terror," their representative in Charleston was plotting as busily as island Africans—invasions of Spanish Florida and Louisiana in his case, and who was to say he would simply stop there?[93] Surely, Paris knew of the fright in Charleston in light of the island frenzy[94] and the spread of this furor to Maryland and Virginia—and what that could portend in terms of destabilizing an infant republic.[95]

Thus, there may not have been much surprise in Paris when General Toussaint, midway during the 1791–1804 epoch, was able to subdue André Rigaud, a leader of both French forces and those of the *gens de couleur*, with ample aid from the mainland. U.S. ships were accused credibly of going so far as to ferry General Toussaint's troops to a strategic point behind Rigaud's lines.[96] Of course, such assistance could easily lead Dixie to conclude that the federal union viewed with insouciance the unique challenges to security within the Slave South, hastening the onset of civil war.

But that was to come years after the commencement of revolt. In the immediate aftermath of August 1791, the great uncle of Samuel Perkins, then on the island, recalled that "the Americans had a guard house assigned to them . . . the guard was commanded by my brother James and I acted as his lieutenant. We drew our forces from the American shipping [community] as well as from the residents . . . the arms and ammunition were kept at our house." The critical "Northern Department" of the island was "commanded by General Galbaud," while "the troops had been fed principally by the American merchants at the Cape"—soon to gain notoriety as the site of a major massacre of settlers. Perkins's great uncle was witness to and partici- pant in bloody warfare aimed at quashing African revolt.

This was not simply a matter of survival but a recognition that if the ramparts were breached on the island, the same could occur on the mainland. This was a gift of prophecy for as things turned out, the Haitian Revolution marked the onset of a general crisis of the entire slave system, unleashing a chain of events that could only eventuate in this system's collapse.

But those Yankees fighting a losing war on the island may not have had the time to reflect upon the world historic meaning of their combat. For, as was reported, "the shock they had received by seeing their companions killed before their eyes, without even a question being asked . . . left them no doubt that equal dispatch would be made with them." "We are Americans," exclaimed this motley mob, as— once again—national identity merged with the imperative to combat the revolt of Africans. Supposedly, one of the Africans who knew enough English to understand their patter, cried out naively: "Stop comrades they are not French; they are from America—a country of liberty." But he was quickly rebuked by another combatant far more attuned to the confluence of class and "race" that had marked colonial slav- ery: "No matter," he said, "they are whites and that is enough; shoot them like dogs."

Some were so dispensed, others were merely jailed. While incarcerated, com- miserating comrades visited and remonstrated with the jailer, who was seen as a "mulatto," for placing them in a confined space with a number of African con- victs. Ever alert to the protocols of racism, they extracted a promise that this affront would cease. [97]

Such protocols were slated for the dustbin of history, though this was not evi- dent in 1791. In July of that fateful year, Sylvanus Bourne, who helped to shape mainland policy toward the island, was informed that a countryman in Aux Cayes was "apprehensive." Already, he was envisioning the "shedding of blood" and, like the great-uncle of Samuel Perkins, this correspondent found that "the Americans who have resided here four to five months are in a military capacity" and are "considered citizens" but are not granted any greater rights.[98] By early 1792, Jacob Mayer of New England found himself in Cap-Français, where, unlike in the period before the onset of the French Revolution, there were "few American vessels" present and "only two from Connecticut." More concerning was that "Negroes and Mulattoes still bear arms against the white people" and, similarly, "everyday you see their fires from the town." Pressure was rising for foreign intervention to save the slave system since "out of the 6000 troops expected from France, 1100 have as yet arrived."[99] Then Mayer's correspondent—Thomas Allen—was told of the "disagreeable intelligence" that "Negroes had arisen in the quarter near Leogane" on the island, "destroying all the plantations adjacent & half of the town."[100]

The contradiction here was that though the enslaving republic was understandably flummoxed by the island revolt, weakening France—which the Africans were perceived as doing—was also a priority. Paris was writhing too and happened to control—or influence—a good deal of North America that the mainland republicans thought should belong to them. The militant self-assertion of the island Africans warped the existing diplomatic chessboard and brought into sharp relief potential alliances and relationships theretofore not foreseen. Months after the turning point that was August 1791, Africans were dickering with the Spanish in Santo Domingo while planters were extending feelers to London and *gens de couleur* were negotiating with the French.[101] The slave-holding republicans had problems with each of these parties and were now forced to reassess. Ousting European powers from the hemisphere was still a top priority, but did that take precedence over the immediate alarm of squashing armed Africans, particularly as the failure to do so would elicit the the most fearful of all outcomes?

Thus, when in October 1791 the colonial satraps on the island requested the urgent assistance of sixty U.S. sailors on shore to participate in an expedition assaulting rambunctious Africans in L'Acul and Haut-du-Cap, far-sighted seafarers may have hesitated, not only due to fear of what the rebels had in store but also due to slyness about the possibility of weakening France's hemispheric position.

As things turned out, only one settler—formerly of Philadelphia—escaped alive from Haut-du-Cap. In fact, the contradiction was so sharp that either way mainland republicans turned, they were bound to be bloodied. Thus, *gens de couleur* were bound to arrive on the mainland, irrespective of who triumphed on the island or irrespective of who sailors ashore leaned toward. And as *gens de couleur* flooded into

Philadelphia, it meant that by the end of 1792 equality for them was now conceivable, a shift in the slave-holding republic with as much consequence as their push for equality on the island. Likewise, when some Philadelphians argued that slavery was a mark of modern democracy while it was monarchy that was inimical to this praxis, it heightened contradictions among abolitionists who thought otherwise.[102]

Greeted uneasily in Philadelphia in September 1791—in many ways the mainland's leading city—was the shocking news from France that lawmakers had given "free Negroes and people of color the same rights and the same weight in government as belong to the white people." Readers of a Jamaican newspaper were told that the latter "almost universally revolved to oppose" this radical measure, guaranteeing enhanced conflict. Similarly shocking was the news item that "vessels with Negroes from Africa are to be sent directly to Bordeaux, where it is supposed the National Assembly will treat them with civility and grant them the rights of citizens"[103]—news designed to arouse racist passions.

The Moline family was among those straggling into Philadelphia in the aftermath of the wrathful ferment, bringing with them from the island enslaved Africans. But influenced by the growing abolitionist fervor—and perhaps now more keenly aware of the wrath that accompanied enslavement—they freed this disturbing chattel upon arriving in the Keystone State.[104]

As suggested by the fact that a periodical in Jamaica was reporting anxiously about how Philadelphians were responding to turmoil in Hispaniola, there was a slave system in the hemisphere, albeit with different masters in different jurisdictions. Yet these slaveholders—at least the perspicacious ones—knew that a challenge to one part of this system could easily materialize in another, making it necessary to pay careful attention to the overall project. This also meant that as slavery was debilitated on the island, it was bound to have similar consequences on the mainland.

Hence, mainland slaveholders interested in perpetuating their hateful system may have noticed—as London did—when as revolt quickened in Paris in late 1790, runaway slaves hastened from Trinidad to Grenada.[105] London's man in Grenada, aware of a growing restiveness regionally, desired that the Carolina Corps—African refugees from Dixie now fighting for Britain—and "volunteer Free Blacks or Mulattoes" be mobilized in response. "Louis La Grenade, a mulatto of the colony, of considerable property," said Edward Matthew, was "well known for many years for his activity against the Runaway Negroes" and should be enlisted.[106] But did not this understandable response feed the regional concern about the growing demands of the "mulatto" that was to singe and sear Hispaniola rather shortly, then leap to the North American mainland to rile Dixie?

French Revolution inspired Black Revolts

There was "discontent among the Negroes of Dominica," it was reported with gross understatement in January 1791. A "serious disturbance" was in the offing, an "insurrection" even, linking the "particularly formidable" indigenous "Charibs [sic]" and "Slaves," necessitating reliance upon the "Black Corps" who were "much better qualified than European Troops for the fatiguing duty of searching out the Fugitives in the interior of the country." Reassuring was the alleged fact that "Our late Guardian Act has been generally productive of a milder treatment" of these rebels—a postulate that reality itself contradicted.[107] What was occurring—even before the sparking of the Haitian Revolution—was that "present unhappy disturbances" in the surrounding "French Colonies" were riling islands that London claimed.[108] In response, the British were "avoiding every interference in their disputes"—but was that wise considering that these islands claimed by Paris were not necessarily reciprocating? For, contemporaneously, Edward Matthew was expressing "much concern that the unhappy disturbances at Martinique are not subsided"[109]—and could spread easily.

Thus, even before August 1791, the Caribbean was in an uproar. A plot in Tortola and an insurrection in Dominica were attributed by London in 1790 to the influence emanating from Paris.[110] Inauspiciously for the major powers, Africans in Dominica had taken advantage of seemingly perpetual London-Paris conflict to seek to upset the entire order. "Depredations" mounted, said one witness, that were "serious," as Africans "robbed and destroyed the property and at length killed some of the English inhabitants." They were "greatly encouraged" by the Marquis Duchilleau of France, who "had actually engaged with them," and "gave them the muskets and bayonets which he took from the English inhabitants," along with "powder and balls" and, amazingly, the "same provisions as [were] allowed to the French soldiers." These Africans had "the audacity to kill and carry away the cattle; and to plunder and set fire to the buildings of the estates," which, inexorably, meant "alarm" at the "daring wickedness of the runaway Negroes."

The accused French officials called "the runaways . . . his friends," as they marauded in "large bodies" with "conk shells blowing and French colours flying." Desperate British planters were reduced to appealing to the French governor in Martinique to little avail, as Africans "retired to the dwelling house on the estate, where they regaled on the stock, provisions, and liquors they found in plenty, their chiefs being served in the silver vessels of the Lieutenant-Governor." Others had "retired among the Carribbees [sic] at Saint Vincent," known to be ferocious fighters with close ties to Africans. All were acquainted with "poisonous herbs that grow in the West Indies" and "by this poison many white people have been killed by poison," with more assuredly facing a similar fate. This was all "occasioned by the revolution in France."[111]

Articulating what was painfully apparent, Major General Adam Williamson admitted that he was "convinced" that the "disturbances at Dominica . . . originated from. . . . the islands of Martinique & Guadeloupe on each side of it, where there were thousands of blacks & people of colour in arms, many of whom crossed over to Dominica." In Jamaica, the colonial prize, the "principal Gentlemen" did not—then—have the "least apprehension of any insurrection or disturbances amongst the slaves," but this may have been an elaborate exercise in calming jangled nerves.[112]

"Disturbances" in Dominica were propelling abolitionist debates in London, complained Lord Grenville, since this uprising brought the "serious alarm" of "contagion" spreading to other islands. More military force was being considered, but London was facing overstretch given its commitments in India and elsewhere. This was a "considerable . . . expense," he carped, both to the "islands and to the mother country"[113]—a cost that would eventuate ultimately in abolition, placing concomitant pressure on the slave-holding republic.

By 1790, it was not just Carolina planters who were agitated about a possible conflict with Spain that too could roil the waters.[114] War with Spain, said Henry Hamilton in Bermuda, could wrack this island and curtail needed supplies—a reality that would be hard to hide from arbitraging Africans,[115] not to mention their nearby comrades in the Carolinas. Soon London was "informed" that "there appeared in the Negroes" of Bermuda a "manifest disposition to revolt."[116] By early 1791, London was frantically searching for "fugitive slaves throughout the Spanish provinces,"[117] as, dismissing solidarity, Madrid's emissaries were providing "protection" to "fugitive slaves."[118]

By June 1791, London was told of the "late turbulent spirit" among the Africans, which was said to be "confined to Dominica"—others were not so sure. There was edgy reassurance that the debate in the House of Commons "relative to the slave trade" had "not caused any alteration in their [Africans'] behavior," as "no revolts were apprehended"—but, again, others were not as certain. Telling was that "during the height of the insurrection at Dominica the Council of Assembly of Montserrat was fearful lest the slaves might become infected, and as their Militia was without firearms, they applied" for more arms—not exactly a vote of confidence.[119]

That is, even before August 1791, there was an unfurling contagion, forcing London to rely more heavily on the dubious remedy of African troops and "mulattoes" in a manner that would strain the redcoats as Hispaniola exploded, instigating even more intense debates in the House of Commons about barring the slave trade—which like falling dominoes would lead to debates about barring slavery itself, which would then put more pressure on a slave-holding republic to contradict its recently concluded founding.

It was also in June 1791 that Edward Matthew noticed that "armaments arrived at Martinique from France," which meant the "inhabitants of St. Domingo would not receive the four battalions of troops" promised, with untoward consequences soon to be evident. Anyway, since the "two battalions formerly sent there [had] created disturbances rather than quieted them," this dispatching was of doubtful utility in any case.[120]

By late July—like a firefighter besieged by determined pyromaniacs—Matthew's gaze had shifted to Barbados. A "coup de main" from an unnamed "neighboring enemy" was not expected, so it should be seen as a "proper place for a military depot." But since similar advice was provided to St. Vincent and Dominica—both then on fire—this consel too was of doubtful utility.[121]

By September 1791, the Earl of Effingham was distraught: he was "very sorry" to hear of "so melancholy an account as I have to given of the situation of our neighbours in St. Domingo." French officials were now there pleading for aid, "cra[ving] assistance on account of a terrible insurrection among the Negroes, who have burnt and destroyed all the plantations for 50 miles in length on both sides of [the] Cape." The untrustworthy "mulattos who were at open violence with the whites have joined them from a sense of common danger and 15,000 of them with 30,000 blacks who remain faithful are crowded in the town of the Cape, almost starving." The benign peer "sent them 500 muskets and 1500 lb. of ball and allowed them to purchase provisions and powder."[122]

Days later, the earl heard that the Hispaniola settlers had "attacked the insurgent Negroes & gained a considerable advantage," though he sensed this was "exaggerated" (and it was). Actually, the "massacres" were "much greater" than imagined, as suggested by the fact that Jamaica was being overrun by distressed Europeans. "My chief care," he said knowingly, "will be to prevent their Negroes from coming to mix with ours" for fear of what the former could impart to the latter about planter vulnerability. For he knew that it was "very possible" that "disturbances might arise here" though he had "endeavoured" strenuously "to avoid such appearance of preparation as might put mischief into people's heads"—which was hardly enough to dissuade the awe-inspiring Maroons of Jamaica, who had almost collapsed the colonial project decades earlier. "What the gossiping of Idle folks may produce I can't tell," he added, but it was not gossip but raging fire, sharp daggers, and hot lead that were more of a concern.[123] Thus, troops were shifted from Barbados to Jamaica, combined with an "augmentation of naval force"[124]—but the shedding of blood and treasure this maneuver portended was hardly the stuff of confidence.

London may have known that by September 1791 enslaved Africans in Jamaica were singing songs about the uprising in Hispaniola and soon slaveholders from

Virginia to Louisiana and from Cuba to Brazil were muttering about an energized insolence now embedded deeply in the hearts of "their" Africans that was inspired by Hispaniola.[125]

By late October of 1791, Stephen Fuller in England was "struck with horror" by what he had heard about Hispaniola. As for London's enslaved in that vicinity, he counseled "keeping them constantly at home, disarming them, preventing caballing, drumming, sounding conch horns, securing the rum & strong liquors, and also ammunition"—but this was easier to articulate from cosseted Southampton than the frontlines of battle. This he sensed since he also stressed that of late "several canoes had arrived at the [east] end of Jamaica with Negroes from Hispaniola"[126]— with unclear intentions.

Fuller may have known that in Spanish Town, Jamaica, a settler had found that the "head Negroes" of "plantations there not only discussed very unreservedly about the rebellion in Hispaniola but declared"—with emphasis—"that the Negroes in the French Country (such is their expression) were Men" and a "similar revolt would soon take place in Jamaica. They went so far as to anticipate the destruction of the whites and to dispute about the distribution of their estates." On the mainland, republicans were busily importing more "whites" so as to overwhelm uproarious Africans and indigenes, but in Jamaica such options did not seem as readily available. Instead, the debate was whether the authorities should "stop the further importation of Negroes from Africa" or increase their number, as some planters suggested. Yet it was known that "no circumstance in life is so pleasing to them [Jamaican Africans] as the addition of new Negroes," so they could better overwhelm the settlers—"which every planter knows to be true."[127]

By 1 November, Matthew had learned from a "gentleman . . . from Spanish St. Domingo" that "there had been an insurrection on several estates at the Cape; that the slaves had killed the proprietors and all the white people on them, to the amount of some hundreds."[128] By 6 November, Major General Williamson, reporting from Jamaica, was seeking to assure a comrade in the now deteriorating Hispaniola by suggesting that "every thing" might be "again quiet." However, he could not help but reveal that the "same spirit of revolt should take place" where he was sited, as "there is no doubt that there are thousands of slaves who would willingly enter into a rebellion if they thought they could succeed," especially since "the greater part of this island is certainly in a very defenceless state."[129]

By mid-November, Fuller demanded that more "small arms" be made available in Jamaica, since it was during the Christian holidays upcoming when "Negroes are most likely to break out, as the white people upon the estates are then all separated." What to do?[130]

By December, Whitehall itself had begun to snap out of bureaucratic inertia, detailing the "commotions" and the "disasters" in Hispaniola, while offering the anodyne advice of "caution" and "circumspection."[131] An official report demanded that the Carolina Corps be augmented in response. Yes, it was said, "an objection may be made to arming of blacks as soldiers," but this understandable concern "has no weight"[132]—though skeptics might well have pondered the viability of a project based on the enslavement of Africans that was then to be policed by Africans.

It was during this tempestuous era that London began frantically "raising Blacks" for the military. The "purchasing of Negroes to be attached to the regiments not exceeding ten percent [of the] company" was recommended. As well, it was recommended to "purchase them from . . . different plantations."[133] The "subject of the Black Troops," said Whitehall, "will have an early consideration; at this moment no plan has been fixed upon." It was also observed that both options—i.e. "embodied as a separate corps or to be attached to the strength of different regiments on duty in Jamaica"—were problematic in their own ways, particularly when discussed—as they were—in the context of Spain providing nearby refuge to "fugitive slaves."[134]

On cue, abolitionist voices became louder and more insistent. By October 1791, one inspired crusader opined that one "cannot look upon a piece of Sugar without conceiving it tainted with spots of human blood." The "iniquity of the Africans Slave Trade," he thundered, "is so glaring that it has met with scarcely any but anonymous defenders," who were mostly grotesquely self-interested, "African merchants and West India planters," sadly, a "numerous body of men."[135] "Resolved" it was declaimed in the House of Commons on 2 April 1792, "that the trade carried on by British Subjects for the purpose of procuring slaves from Africa ought to be gradually abolished."[136]

That is, as of April 1792, motions advocating the abolition of the slave trade were being debated accusingly in the House of Commons with events in Hispaniola fueling the flames. Listeners were told in excruciating detail of "rapes, massacres, of conflagrations, of impaled infants, and acts of parricide"—though this was said in favor of pursuing an untenable status quo, it could just as well be heard as advocating the exact opposite. A "Colonel Tarleton" had just heard from a "respectable officer at Antigua, describing the sickly situation of the King's troops" and wondered whether they were now sufficient to "awe or suppress insurrections amongst the Negroes, throughout the different islands"—a worry that proved to be prophetic.[137] Pro or con, Hispaniola haunted this debate.

There was no unanimity—as of yet—about barring the slave trade. Stephen Fuller, with wide interests in Jamaica, insisted that "the only effectual method to guard us against the evils we have too much to reason to dread, will be by putting an immediate & decisive stop to the impracticable projects of abolishing the African trade." All such inflammatory debates in Parliament did, he huffed, was create a "state of suspense so inviting to the Negroes and so dangerous to the white inhabitants."[138]

But within 48 hours, another Jamaican settler had made an implicit rebuke of Fuller's bold words. This anxious colonist was "diligently preparing for the worst; our Negroes are perfectly acquainted," he said disconsolately, "with everything that has been doing at Hispaniola." Thus, to "ensure the peace of the country it will be absolutely necessary for us to go the expense of at least 100,000 [pounds] in making inlands stations & roads" and also to "double" the "force to be in future stationed here." Why such expenditures and deployments? "I am convinced," he said, "that ideas of Liberty have sunk so deep into the minds of all the Negroes that, wherever the greatest precautions are not taken, they [Africans] will rise."[139]

The tides of history—and Africans—were buoying the latter and foiling Fuller. Initially, Fuller had the better of the argument in London—but a massive British intervention in Hispaniola led to the most stinging and decisive defeats in the empire's checkered history, helping to convince even the most stubborn that only abolition offered a graceful exit.[140]

The vaunted Founding Fathers then administering the slave-holding republic seemed incapable of comprehending the world historic forces that were being unloosed at that time. Thus, the slave-holding republic would then have to contend with an abolitionist London and Haiti, a mighty force that would be difficult to thwart.

2

Confronting Black Jacobins on the March
1793–1797

MAINLAND REPUBLICANS MAY HAVE miscalculated the impact of the French Revolution, which many—including slaveholders—initially embraced, perhaps viewing it as they saw their own revolt, as an uprising that would lead to the further ossifying of slavery.[1]

Pierce Butler of Carolina was among those who seemed to only see the anti-monarchial aspects of July 1789. He seemed unaware that his railing against royals treating commoners like animals could have easily been transposed and reinterpreted by Africans to his own detriment.[2] "France will succeed in their revolution," this Founding Father and one of the richest mainland slaveholders exhorted, insisting that it "would not be in the power of Europe to enslave them." At the same time, Butler was uttering typically pro-slavery sentiments without sensing that due south Africans were fighting a revolution so they would not be enslaved—and this intrepid sentiment could easily reach potential seditionists in the Palmetto State.[3]

Butler was no outlier. An Irish-born officer formerly of the British army, he allegedly wrote the controversial Fugitive Slave Clause of the vaunted Constitution and pushed for adoption of the Electoral College, reducing the influence of the popular vote. He was well-positioned to spread his enthusiasm about Paris.[4] He was ecstatic about the detention of the French monarch, tabbing him enthusiastically as an "Imprudent Man!" Seemingly oblivious to the fact that words that could be applied to a royal could just as easily be applied to a slave-holding republican, he exulted that "one grain of common sense is worth a pound of intrigue" and, thus, "honesty is the best policy."[5]

But it did not take long for slave-holding republicans to rethink their initial enthusiasm when—like a film dissolve—it slowly dawned that enslaved Africans too had imbibed ideas about not being reenslaved, while executing revolution.

It was in August 1793 that Butler heard reports of a planned insurrection of the enslaved in Yorktown, Virginia, planned—it was said—by French radicals and reputedly involving several states, including his own South Carolina. Then the governor of the latter state ordered all free foreign Negroes who had arrived within the past year to depart—quickly—from the state, betraying the nervous apprehension then rising. This was occurring as tumult on the island during the summer of 1793 sent a steady stream of settlers to the shores of Carolina.[6]

"Our Eastern & French friends," sputtered Butler in late 1793, "will do no good to our Blacks. I wish they wou'd mind their own Affairs," he lamented.[7] As 1794 loomed on the horizon, Butler was now in full panic mode, demanding state laws that would bar the importation of Africans not only from the Caribbean but also from northern states, even Virginia. "The Negroes in this State are intolerable," he spluttered, "more . . . insolent than any person who has witnessed it can credit. This is one of the many abuses of the Rights of Man," he concluded with bewilderment.[8]

He had not been paying careful attention for as early as 1791 it was reported from Philadelphia that abolitionists in Paris were seeking to outlaw the slave trade. Adopting Butler's own language, it was said that the revolutionary upsurge "has been the means of exciting . . . more attention to the Rights of Men than has ever occurred at any other period."[9] That Philadelphia was at once the capital city and the leading destination for French exiles fleeing revolution on the island made this message all the more stunning.[10]

By the time Butler realized that a truer revolution was occurring in France, as opposed to the mainland republic, external intervention to reverse the course of events would have been futile. Butler was not unique. William Short, who had served as Jefferson's private secretary in France, was among the numerous republicans who initially hailed July 1789—then shrunk in horror as time passed.[11]

For by early 1794, a French national indubitably aware that such a matter would be of concern "to his friend in America," informed the latter of a "laughable scene" as a "deputation from St. Domingo entered the hall" of the distinguished in Paris: the delegation "consisted of a white man, a mulatto, and a Negro" and even the darkest of them all was greeted warmly by the "President." With outraged emphasis it was added, *"there was no end to the kisses that were given and received amidst the repeated applause of the Convention and the Tribunes. The next day they voted,"* he observed with startled stress, *"emancipation of the slaves."* An African woman, who observed the proceedings, was so stunned that she fainted—as might have Butler if he had read these words. At the "Jacobin Club" there was a warm reception for the Africans; this grouping was a "source of power and those who lead it govern France," it was reported dourly.[12]

As Paris moved to abolish slavery in 1794, the Unites States dispatched to France as an envoy Charles Pinckney, who was as enthusiastic about human bondage as his compatriot, Butler.[13] This should not have come as a surprise in Paris in that Gouverneur Morris, who also had served in Paris, was similarly part of a family that owned dozens of enslaved Africans.[14] As Paris was radicalizing and Hispaniola was moving similarly, the slave-holding republic was maneuvering to stem the tide of abolition—a principle which had driven their anti-London revolt in the first instance.[15]

The "government that ran France in the mid-to-late 1790s," says a recent scholar, has been "credited with an amazing, quiet accomplishment" in aligning with "the French movement for racial equality" and aligning further with "black and mixed-race legislators" in ruling bodies. French revolutionaries, says this analyst, "admitted black and mixed-race representatives among their members as equal," at a time when this was unimaginable on the mainland. Perhaps even more explosively—in terms of the long-term viability of the slave-holding republic—these radicals were providing Africans with "one of the world's finest educations at a time when the English speaking world still considered it a crime for black children to learn to read."[16] Soon there would be fewer books that these youth could read (and denounce) with chapters entitled "the government and care of the Negroes and Cattle," as found in a popular tome about Hispaniola published in 1797.[17]

Though Jacobins were beaten back in Paris with the rise of Napoleon Bonaparte, their African counterparts continued to bestride the stage in the hemisphere and on the mainland, and on the island they were to form the core of the justly heralded Black Abolitionists[18]—literate, sophisticated politically, globally minded, and the ultimate gravediggers of the slave system. Once that genie was out of the bottle, there was no going back, victory was assured—to the point that today, the proud ideological descendants of the Founding Fathers somehow claim the legacy of the founders' antagonists (Black Jacobins) and their vision of a society liberated from slavery and its related noxiousness, which these very same founders surely had not intended.

This was a loud message to the immature slave-holding republic, a message that its own model of development based upon relentless brutalization of Africans was reaching the point of expiry just as it was gaining stride. That this message was at odds with the northern merchants' overarching ambition to push France out of the hemisphere, meaning aiding armed Africans on the island, was hardly grasped at the time.

Nevertheless, Butler and his kin may have been heartened when protests emerged in France against the revolutionary idea of opening public office to Africans,[19] just as they were doubtlessly reassured when at the same time measures—ultimately futile—were devised on the island to bar Africans from gaining arms.[20]

As Africans were on the verge of entering the corridors of power in Paris, Thomas Jefferson happened to notice that a U.S. ship had entered Hispaniola. And its captain, the Founding Father noted, "enticed some Negroes on board his vessel" through subterfuge. The captain then "brought them off and sold them in Georgia as slaves," a fact that when known was bound to inflame ire on the island[21] (not to mention infuriating these newly-minted mainland enslaved, making them more susceptible to aiding mischief). The contradiction underlying these contrasting policies of Paris and the mainland effortlessly impelled friction.

The ongoing massacres of settlers on the island too should have alerted mainlanders that the cost for what had become normalized—the brutalization of Africans—had risen. The same year that Jefferson noticed the dragooning of island Africans, Anne-Louis de Tousard—soon to be a former French settler in Hispaniola—noticed that "the news from St. Domingo is bad. They tell me there has been an uprising among the colored people at the Cape. That is terrifying. Great God! What sorrows are in store for me!"[22]

She was prophetic. For what may also have influenced Butler's souring mood—and hers too—was that an estimated 10,000 Europeans fled from Cap-Français on the morning of 22 June 1793, most of them turning—quite stunningly—directly to the coast of the mainland. That U.S. captains were accused—typically—of plundering these dispirited settlers or of turning them over to pirates did not erode the growing trepidation in the slave-holding republic that they could be glimpsing their very own future while scrutinizing these bedraggled refugees.[23]

By 6 July 1793, arriving in Norfolk from the island were some of these unfortunate exiles bearing morose tales of woe: "Twelve thousand are supposed to have been massacred at the Cape," said Thomas Newton; "many were taken out of the water & thrown on board the vessels without cloathes or any substance whatever." The survivors may not have envied the dead, but, most definitely, they were "unhappy & distressed people."[24] According to another contemporaneous source, "between some French sailors and a number of disaffected *Mulattoes*," there was "carnage and destruction of 14 or 15,000 lives."[25] Whatever the number, summer 1793 was a landmark and not just on the island: as was to be the case in coming years, human hurricanes due south touched the mainland directly, as it became ever more difficult to ignore the increasingly steep price to be paid for the enslavement of Africans.[26]

Reporting from Saint Marc on the island in July 1793, a U.S. national, Captain Thomas Powars of Boston, detailed the burning of Cap Francais. He too suffered losses—fortunately not his life—including his ship register and he was also stuck in port, unable to sell his valuable cargo. "The coast is so infested with British Cruizers," he confided, "it is a neer [sic] miracle that I escaped"—an indication of London's muscular intervention that was to end in tears within years. But rhetoric to the contrary notwithstanding, it was London's fear of spillover effects in Jamaica and other colonies, more than "racial" unity, that was the motivating force, since Powars "need not mention" that "the British would [make] a prize of us yet." There were "several Americans here but none of them sell anything," he added glumly. "Mr. Sam G. Perkins & Mr. Samuel Otis of Boston are both with me" and also were running the risk of massacre of hurried departure.[27]

For Powars was scathed when a "quarrel arose between the sailors of the man of war and Molattoes [sic] which ended in the total destruction of the Cape by fire in consequence of which every vessel that was in Port both French and American" suffered losses.[28]

Newton had another interest besides the "distressed" all around: "our place is crowded with Frenchmen," he warned the governor, "and too many Negroes have been brought in with them."[29] Newton was sagacious for, by the next month, another Virginian was warning the governor of an "intended insurrection of Negroes," with the suspicion lingering that this inundation of Africans was a causative factor.[30] That Petersburg rather than Norfolk was the target did not erode this perception,[31] possibly because an official report determined that the intended revolt—said to be inspired by island events—was said to be the seat of power that was Richmond.[32]

In this latter growing town, John Randolph reported hearing Africans plotting outside his home to liquidate all the settlers and take their homes. In York, in July 1793, credible rumors of an African uprising hung heavily in the night air. By the fall, Norfolk and Portsmouth confirmed what had been reported earlier as eighty—mostly African—men were reportedly planning to burn down the two towns and French ships in the port besides. At the same time, a journalist observed that "the St. Domingo Negroes have sown these seeds of revolt and that a magazine has been attempted to be broken open."[33]

As *gens de couleur* and enslaved Africans alike cascaded onto the shores of the mainland, delivering grave misgivings besides, South Carolina in 1793 sought to limit their arrival with some influential personalities going to the extreme length of proposing that even those who could be defined as "white" also be barred. How could the authorities ignore reports that the enslaved there—inspired by Hispaniola—were plotting to revolt?[34]

As further reports began to materialize of massacres of settlers on the island, customarily epitomizing the panic of his class, Jefferson was blunt in his remarks to Madison in July 1793: "I become daily more and more convinced," he groaned, "that all the West India islands will remain in the hands of the people of color and the total expulsion of whites sooner or later [will] take place." Sensing automatically the impact on the mainland, he continued with urgency, "It is high time we should foresee the bloody scenes which our children certainly and possibly ourselves (South of the Potomac) [might] have to wade through, and try to avert them."[35] As matters evolved, the United States moved to open the floodgates widely, allowing the entry of tens of thousands of European migrants, providing them with emoluments in the form of land expropriated from the indigenous that was stocked with enslaved Africans, and this combination helped to forestall Jefferson's nightmare scenario from reaching the mainland.

Still, like a slow motion film, Jefferson was sluggishly acknowledging that, perhaps, the project that had inspired many of his fellow Virginians to revolt against London—the mass enslavement of Africans—could just be unsustainable. But how could the potential catastrophe be averted if Paris was moving toward radicalism, London was on a steady gallop toward abolition—and, most of all, looming on the horizon was an independent and armed African republic whose realization was hard to block when ousting France from the hemisphere was seen by many as a more important strategic goal?

One response was getting rid of mainland Africans by any means necessary—but this was a non-starter for the enslaved were desperately needed to develop the mainland. Perhaps it could mean limiting the inflow of Africans from the continent, but mainlanders had proven themselves to be past masters at smuggling so this was a de facto non-starter. Whether knowing it or not, Jefferson's class was trapped, with a bloody civil war being the only exit from the dilemma they had constructed so meticulously.

Of course, there were other matters that drew the United States into the maelstrom delivered by 1789 and 1791. A preoccupation of future president James Monroe, serving in Paris in 1794, was "supplies rendered the government of St. Domingo" by his regime in the colonists' quixotic attempt to survive. That same year the United States passed a bill providing relief for the disheveled settlers washing up on their shores who "may be found in want of support."[36]

Eventually, "twenty Frenchmen" told Virginia's governor that they had arrived "almost naked," possessing "nothing but a small number of faithful slaves." We "will never forget," they said, "how much we are indebted to the good citizens" of Norfolk, who "assisted" with "money, victuals, and clothes." But this appreciation notwithstanding, they were now informed of the necessity of returning their slaves to the island—not because of abolitionist fervor but the opposite: fear of a slave revolt not unlike what had driven them bereft to the mainland. This was both "inhuman," these oppressors wailed, and "difficult to be executed" since "we get our living by the means of our Negroes and were we deprived of them we should remain helpless and destitute"; in fact, they moaned, "we should become beggars."[37]

Actual beggars were among the tidal wave of Africans who were surging into the mainland and their presence was also of concern to the authorities. Across the border in North Carolina, there was an attempt to bar "settlers from the West Indies, the Bahamas, or any of the French, Dutch, or Spanish plantations" from bringing "Negroes into the state under the penalty of 100 [pounds] for every Negro over fifteen brought in," as an animating fear of Caribbean Africans took hold. Soon a leading politico claimed that "one hundred Negroes from the West Indies" were "more dangerous than 10,000 from Africa."[38]

Yet this attempt to curtail the arrival of Africans of whatever provenance was bound to conflict with the also obtaining notion that this often perturbing property was the key to prosperity and even bruiting such a curtailment measure would exacerbate domestic tension at a time when relations with the major powers—London, Madrid, and particularly Paris—were far from ideal.

The summer of 1793 was a low point for slavery, but things did not improve in 1794. James McHenry was born in Ireland in 1753 and like many of his countrymen took to the revolt against British rule in North America with enthusiasm once he decamped there. He studied under Benjamin Rush, served as George Washington's secretary, and was present at the creation in 1787 of the fabled Constitutional Convention. But his varied peregrinations did not prepare him for what he heard in 1794 about the massacre of settlers in Hispaniola. It was "the most shocking inhumanity of any that hath taken place," he was informed, since "St. Bartholomew's," a reference to a bitter liquidation of Huguenots at the hands of Catholics in France in the 16th century. In short, the shift from religion to "race" on the mainland, thought to have been a rousing success in ushering in the Enlightenment and bridging the chasm among Europeans, was now also seen to have a negative cost. For what had occurred at Fort Dauphin was "so atrocious that it might not be committed to print," as "every American ashore, or in the harbour met the same fate"—cruel slaughter.[39]

Samuel Perkins of Massachusetts had direct experience with the rough treatment of U.S. nationals on the island, a process that conveyed the point manifestly that slavery delivered a harsh levy. He eyed suspiciously the guillotine on the island, deployed so promiscuously in Paris and gaining popularity in Hispaniola. He could hardly believe his ears when he was told that a way to escape the blade of justice was to "salute all the blacks I had occasion to speak to with the title of *Citoyen*, as all were free and equal"—this at a time when such a praxis on the mainland was diametrically opposed. Instead, he was "cautioned . . . not to use the word *slave* on any occasion, as it might cost me my life." Apparently, when he did not follow this counsel fastidiously—he was speaking in a "low tone" with a fellow U.S. national at the time—he "received a blow on the breast that almost leveled" him "with the ground. On looking up to see whence the blow came, I saw before me a Negro fellow of great size, in full uniform, with his sword half drown, glaring upon me with the most infernal countenance I ever beheld. My first impulse was to break out upon this savage with a heavy curse," mainland style, "but as prudence is the better part of valor, a moment's reflection cooled my anger," though, painfully, he "did not get over the pain in my breast during the day."

Later, Perkins met another African who he suspected of slaying his master. "My blood ran cold at the thought of dining with the murderer of my old friend," so he tried to evade an invitation to dine in a land where the world had been turned upside down. Not fooled, "the fellow looked at me with a malignant eye." Then he met a U.S. national whose invitation to dine aboard his vessel he accepted, but the surprises did not end for "there were perhaps twenty persons at a table—[including] some well-dressed mulatto men." But "scarcely were we seated at a table when a black fellow, without hats or shoes, [and wearing] a dirty checked shirt and trousers, which had apparently been worn for six months entered the room and without ceremony took a chair at [the] table" and proceeded to eat "voraciously," managing to help "himself plentifully with wine from the bottle of his neighbor." As if this rough display of new world manners was insufficient, "after eating to his heart's content and cursing the whites in his Negro Creole, he looked around the table with the fierceness of a tiger." After this African took his leave, "someone asked the host why he permitted such a scamp to take a place at his table. 'If I was to refuse,' said the man, 'I should have my throat cut'" since "'the jealousy of these liberated slaves is such that if you hint that they are not fit company for the whites, you may be sure that they will find some occasion, when you least expect it, to put a knife into you.'" The African, whose invitation to dine he had avoided, had murdered his master, then seized his house and property, a fate that befell numerous settlers, including those straggling into mainland ports.[40]

Since this dire destiny was befalling settlers with origins in Western Europe, this provided a basis for them to unite—alongside the slave-holding republic—against the island Africans. However, squabbling between and among these powers often precluded such unity, virtually guaranteeing setbacks. Moreover, the slave-holding republic had stolen a march on them all by becoming preeminent in doling out rights to those defined as "white," as opposed to those who were royals (e.g. London) or members of a favored religion or ethnicity (e.g. Madrid). The aforementioned Thomas Newton encapsulated the difficulty involved in forging "white" or even settler unity for he had another interest besides the distressed all around: "our place is crowded with Frenchmen," he warned the governor, "and too many Negroes have been brought in with them."[41]

What Perkins did not seem to recognize at the time was an unavoidable reality: it was seemingly preordained that the major powers would be forced to relinquish their jealously guarded holdings in the Caribbean and he was only experiencing the rough edges of this difficult reality. Put crudely, there were just not enough "whites"—nor "mulattos"—for the powers to draw upon to monitor and unnerve the growing population of Caribbean and mainland Africans now duly inspired by events in Hispaniola. Thomas Jefferson should have been thankful for the eventuality that those defined as "white" were able to prevail on the mainland.

AS PARIS RADICALIZED AND THE ISLAND burnt brightly in February 1793, French settlers in Hispaniola were reduced to petitioning His Majesty in London for assistance. They were even willing to make the concession that the *gens de couleur* they had been battling would have privileges akin to those in neighboring Jamaica. But why should Protestant London—as the proposal suggested—continue to grant privileges to the Catholic faith or, for that matter, petition Spanish Cuba for the return of the enslaved who had fled there from Hispaniola?[42]

London had its hands full, in any event, seeking to cork the volcano that had erupted in Dominica and—aroused by Hispaniola—seemed to be spreading throughout the Caribbean. This growing blotch of unrest was confirming Jefferson's worst fears and, as he suggested, was of direct import for the mainland. Ultimately this instability was to push London more speedily toward abolition, hastening conflict with the slave-holding republic.

These petitioners to London should also have realized that their plea could easily fall on deaf ears in light of growing suspicion of France in Britain—class origins aside, unbridled protests in Dominica were marked by accusations of French maneuvering against British interests. Dominica was not unique for something similar was occurring in Grenada.

Still, with the galloping chaos that was suffusing the Caribbean, those who held slavery dear had fewer and fewer options, particularly since the slaveholders themselves were disunited and, instead, seemed fearful of each other—fearful of republican France most of all. "I have been particularly circumspect," said London's emissary in St. Vincent in 1793, "in regard to admitting French people into this colony from the total subversion of every species of Government which at present reigns throughout the French Islands especially at Martinico." Those who violated this diktat somehow were "liable to be imprisoned." He observed that "all the principal proprietors of Martinico and Guadeloupe have emigrated and both islands are in the utmost anarchy and confusion." Many had moved to Trinidad, "where I imagine," said James Seton, "they cannot long exist, being destitute of everything." The Lieutenant-General of the French Windward islands had just arrived, "having also been obliged to abandon Martinico to the Fury of the populace."[43] With British and French nationals scattering hither and yon in self-described confusion and chaos, this provided enormous leverage to Africans to manipulate either—or both.

This too was foreseeable. A group of now bombarded planters and merchants on this besieged island of St. Vincent confronted Whitehall as things were collapsing all about. London gained this island via "cession in 1763," they recounted, from Paris and there were still "some original Indians" and "about two thousand descendants of African Negroes who had escaped from an African slave ship wrecked on the coast of Becouya, a small neighboring island, toward the close of the last century." His Majesty wanted to deport these Africans—anywhere—since they had merged with indigenes forming a fierce fighting force. By 1773, London was compelled to drop this proposal and signed a treaty instead. But, it was said, these fighters committed "treason," backing London's "enemies" in a brazen act of "perfidy and Disloyalty." By the 1790s, they were seeking "avowedly to massacre and extirpate every British white inhabitant not sparing even woman or child. That this they unfortunately accomplished," mimicking Hispaniola and slaughtering "faithful Negroes" besides, inflicting "great losses" on London, was seen as understandably regrettable. The conclusion was clear: They must go. Now.[44] This was to be done eventually, though not without the difficulty that was tearing colonialism itself asunder.

The problem was that buoyed by Hispaniola and conglomerating riotousness, this would be neither simple nor easy. That at the same time proposals were being made in Hispaniola to attain internal peace by massacring Africans and *gens de couleur* was indicative of the extremity of events and the rise of Black Jacobinism,[45] which did not necessarily bode well for the mainland.

As ever, a problem in St. Vincent was attracting those defined as "white," a problem made all the more sensitive now that "mulattoes" were perceived as being unwilling to accept secondary status. In the year that demonstrated the importance of having an adequate complement of "whites"—1776—St. Vincent mandated that for every 30 of the enslaved there should be at least one man in this favored group and for every 15 of the enslaved, at least one woman. But passing a law and attracting this group were separate matters altogether, so the authorities then mandated that the 30 should be raised to 50 and the 15 to 25. However, playing with numbers only exposed the gravity of the threat to settler security.[46] The problem was that mainlanders had stolen a march on islanders when they had begun earlier to entice more "whites" to their shores, thus reducing the possibility of this favored group going elsewhere, virtually guaranteeing that Jefferson's fear of the destiny of the Caribbean being determined by Africans was inexorable.

The narrow attitude toward those defined as "mulatto" and *"gens de couleur"* also made this process inevitable. London's misrule seemed to be designed to provide impetus to insurgents, despite the clear deficit in manpower. When he took over a virtually abandoned Martinique in 1794, His Majesty's emissary emulated mainlanders by circumscribing *gens de couleur*.[47] "Restraining the admission of French and Mulattoes and Free Negroes from entering into this island," said Seton in St. Vincent, was a must. Actually, a frightened Seton mandated a "summary method" of barring "foreigners of every description,"[48] not the ideal method to combat Africans on the march.

Yet Seton was wary of the "aliens and foreigners" who continued to "swarm" where he resided, holding "illegal meetings," sponsoring "clubs and affiliations," and engaging in "illegal treasonable correspondence with divers[e] persons in the French islands." He wanted them all to "take the oath of allegiance and fidelity to His Majesty"—or leave—but this was more bluster than realism. Seeking to expel Europeans while depositing more Africans on these unstable shores via the Carolina Corps or the smuggling of the enslaved was a prescription for disaster—and not just for London.[49]

Worse, Seton was ordering his aides to "raise a certain proportion of Negroes for the conveyance of artillery and ordinance stores to the fortifications," which was myopic in its focus on the French threat and shortsighted in its apparent unawareness of the potential of rising Africans nearby.[50] That the Privy Council commanded "only one Negro" for the militia "for each white man sent from the estates," indicated that they well knew that these ebony men were not altogether reliable either.[51] Worse still, Seton glimpsed "several slaves who have no owners or masters in this island," a ready-made recipe for catastrophe.[52] Moreover, Seton's authorization of the "fitting out [of] a considerable number of privateers" to "take to sea" to prey upon the vessels of fellow powers was bound to complicate further relations.[53]

But did Seton have alternatives? In mid-1793 a French frigate arrived, carrying a man who "commanded the Militia in Martinico," accompanied by "about fifty men and seventy coloured men" alongside, "whom he wishes to be taken into the employment of this colony. It was agreed to admit them to "duty as militia"—but what if they were imposters, actually Jacobins in disguise determined to upset the status quo?[54] What was the beleaguered and undermanned Seton to do?

The problem Seton faced was that there was no adequate filter to distinguish between those bent upon sedition and the "influx of distressed royalists" that was washing up on his shores. The "wretched condition of the royalists emigrated to this island is out of my power to describe," he cried, an upsetting sight that fingered tremulously the heartstrings of class. For "not a month ago" these refugees "enjoyed the greatest ease and affluence" but now were faced with "the most abject situation, literally not having escaped with clothes sufficient to cover them and are now supported by voluntary contributions."[55] Like those administrators similarly situated in Norfolk, it was not hard to envision that the harsh hand dealt these royalists awaited eagerly others unwilling to abjure enslavement. The Exchequer was bound to be strained, if only by ancillary spending on behalf of these arrivals, in a way that was bound to call into question the future of London in the region in a manner that would be similarly threatening to the slave-holding republic.

Yet Seton was dumbfounded by what surrounded him in a way that probably occluded his thinking. By mid-1793, he was facing a "truly alarming situation" featuring indigenes and Africans that were "savage in their nature, prone to plunder, and ready for every kind of mischief" and "excited to acts of rebellion by emissaries distributing money amongst them."[56]

Seton preferred benevolent charity and not government expenditure to aid the distressed[57]—but even private interests had a limit on what they could expend. By October 1793, the attention of a harried Privy Council had jerked toward the inconvenient fact that British vessels were landing infrequently in St. Vincent, while "French ships" and "privateers" were "on the coast of the United States," raising the "probability of the United States joining the French in war" against His Majesty—all of which meant a "famine must inevitably ensue."[58]

Thus, by mid-1794, a harried Seton demanded the "names and descriptions of all Free Mulattoes" who had arrived from surrounding islands in order "to prevent any of that class of people from landing upon this island."[59] A reward was offered "for the apprehending of all Negroes or Mulattoes free or slaves lately come from the French islands."[60] Given the proliferating accusation that *gens de couleur* bore heavy responsibility for August 1791 and given the already evident move toward emancipation of the enslaved under the tricolor, this was understandable—but given London's narrowing alternatives (and staffing options) regionally, it was terribly misguided.

Days after Seton's edict, a report from Philadelphia indicated that a large number of French refugees had just arrived after being "expelled by the British from the Islands."[61] Like those in a similar boat from Hispaniola, they were embittered and impoverished and willing to swear allegiance to the slave-holding republic that had rescued them. Actually, since July 1789, more and more settlers from French colonies in the Caribbean had been arriving on the mainland, particularly in pursuit of education,[62] a process that too tended to solidify allegiance to the slave-holding republic. Yet this was too pushing the mainland toward a diplomatic cul-de-sac: sharper conflict with London when relations with Paris required improvement,[63] all of which worked to the advantage of Africans seeking leverage.

But more than the rising numbers of Africans and "colored" on the island, like its neighbors—and the mainland too—what really made Vincentian settlers fearful about the French contagion was what was forced onto the agenda of the island's Chief Justice, Drewry Ottley: he was "very much alarmed" by the debate in London's Parliament on the "question of abolition"—this was "very dangerous" in the message it sent to the enslaved.[64]

But the Chief Justice should have been made to understand that with the move toward emancipation in the hexagon, a domino effect had been initiated leaving few untouched. Moreover, abolition may have been the "least bad" option—certainly preferable to being murdered, an alternate proposition that the status quo seemed to be bringing, as the suffering royalists then making their way to island and mainland ports could well have attested. For by 1795, the Duke of Portland was told that St. Vincent was under siege by "our internal enemy the Charibs [sic]" who were "aided by the French inhabitants here, every one of whom has formerly sworn before me allegiance" and "all of whom" were now engaged in "insurrection," led by "Chatoue, the Charibe chief at the head of a considerable body of insurgents."[65] The "enemy," said Seton, "has been seen in greater numbers than before" and was "reinforced by a party of regular troops from [French] Guadeloupe."[66]

What was to be done? Whitehall instructed to form a "Corps of Rangers to consist of 100 white volunteers and 500 Negroes" while "confining all such French inhabitants as you have good reason [to] suspect."[67] But cabining the French was dueling with the proposal to mobilize as many "whites" as possible, while the "Negroes" may have had reason to believe that the odds were favoring their taking over the island in the longterm, given regional trends instigated by Hispaniola. These "Negroes" may have been heartened more than Seton, when the governor greeted a "corps of Black Rangers" arriving from Martinique.[68] Yet Seton persisted in pressing for the ousting of the French "without delay"—though sending them to Trinidad & Tobago, "as soon as possible,"[69] even closer to Grenada then undergoing a kind of revolt comparable—if not exceeding—St. Vincent, made clear the staggering dimensions of the problem faced.

Governor Seton also foresaw the "most dangerous consequences" if the "prisoners calling themselves Spaniards should remain longer" on the island since it was "impossible to prevent their communicating with Negroes who they will attempt to seduce." They must go too—wasn't Spain also involved in the seat of precariousness that Hispaniola was thought to be? So, send them to "Martinico" since "the safety perhaps the salvation of the colony may depend upon it."[70] But was not this as feckless an idea as sending suspected dissidents to Trinidad, since Martinique too was being rocked?

Again, slavery was providing a menu of unappetizing choices. The year 1795, as one scholar writes, "the year after the worst excesses of the French Revolution," was equally the "darkest hour" for Caribbean planters, "with the Second Maroon War in Jamaica, slave revolts in Guyana and Venezuela, and an extensive slave conspiracy in Point Coupee."[71] The latter revolt suggested the linkage in the hemisphere between the continents and islands, not just because Africans in a sign of the time were heard singing Jacobin songs.[72] When London felt it necessary to dispatch the Carolina Corps from Martinique to St. Lucia in early 1795 to try to dislodge what were termed the "revolted Negroes," it was an indicator implicating the United States, Britain, and France at once in what seemed to be a losing effort to salvage slavery.[73]

It was in 1795 that what was described as the "insurrection of the Black Charaibs [*sic*]" of St. Vincent showed no signs of dissipating. These militants had pioneered in collaborating with the French against the British in a way various anti-London forces in the hemisphere found easy to emulate. With London bogged down in Hispaniola and, as shall be seen shortly, Grenada too, this collaboration became even more effective. By March of that year they had descended upon British settlers "like a torrent of fire," as one account put it, leading to the apocalyptic conclusion that these skilled fighters "will ever be French" —meaning in this context: Jacobin. This engendered a daunting, though repetitive, conclusion: *that the British planters or the Black Charaibs must be removed from off the island of St. Vincent's.* " The Caribs were duly cleansed and dispatched to Central America, but the crisis of slavery was not so easily handled.[74]

Not coincidentally, 1795 also witnessed the continued influx of French settlers— enslaved Africans in tow—into Norfolk. The latter were supposedly "servants," said Thomas Newton skeptically, a dubious claim along with the companion allegation that "they do not entend [*sic*] to remain here." As he saw it, these refugees, once grand, still traveled in style: for every "100 whites" who arrived, "200 blacks may attend them," as these exiles were recreating the same skewed racial ratios that had led to the Hispaniola revolt in the first place. Newton said that the increase in such arrivals left Norfolk in an "exposed situation for we have too many of the blacks from the islands among us." Many of them had witnessed "great slaughter in the W. Indies,"[75] which some may have been eager to recreate in the commonwealth.

Grousing continued apace in Virginia about these various unwelcome guests,[76] as Newton continued to speak of growing "fears of the French Negroes being trouble-some," which originated in the disturbing fact that the "Negroes have the spirit of freedom among them."[77] Class and race solidarity commanded that the welcome mat be placed appropriately for the arrival of woebegone settlers from the islands, but the baggage they brought—that is, their ebony attendants—combined with unease about somehow further alienating a radicalized Paris, was tearing rifts in the fabric of mainland society.

If the problem could just be limited to arriving Africans, who had the oppor-tunity both to witness the massacring of settlers and now to impart this gruesome sight to local Africans, thereby planting a seed of revolt, this dilemma might have been containable. But as a meeting of the Norfolk authorities suggested, there was also worry about the arriving "French people of color," who had proven to be dis-ruptive on the island, and thus there was a need to "act in concert" to block any tricks they might want to pull.[78] The reluctance to embrace *gens de couleur* was not expanding the base that enslavement of Africans demanded.

When French refugees were arriving—by their own admission—"almost naked," it was not easy for even the most unsympathetic mainland settler to turn them away, thus they kept arriving,[79] along with their annoying property, just as the base for enslavement was constricting due not least to the rise of Black Jacobinism.

As in Louisiana, there was concern in Virginia about the evident extension of Jacobinism among the Africans and what that spelt for settlers. Still, this now rising Jacobin sentiment was detected most directly in Grenada, seen as an inspiration for St. Vincent, with both being influenced by Hispaniola—and all intimidating the slave-holding republic. This sentiment was a reflection of the continuing radicaliza-tion in Paris that, for example, led to U.S. vessels being harassed by French priva-teers and taken to Hispaniola to be condemned.[80] This process had been identified as early as 1793 and continued through the pivotal year of 1795 and two years later amounted to hundreds of U.S. vessels being assaulted.[81]

This process made it difficult for slave-holding republicans to ally with France at a time when relations with Britain were normatively complicated and a new threat loomed in the form of island based Black Jacobins.

That was not all. As noted, the Carolina Corps of Africans armed by London, by August 1791, had hundreds within their ranks and were not only sited menacingly in Newfoundland and Canada but also in Grenada.[82] As was true of a good deal of the Caribbean, there were U.S. nationals present in Grenada, which led to the dif-fusion of tales of mayhem inflicted upon settlers. U.S. vessels were steadily arriving in Grenada in 1795 as the insurrection mounted.[83]

One Briton reported in 1795 that this island was "in great danger" and added that "we hold possession of it by a very precarious tenure," which was accurate.[84] By 1795 there were thousands of free Negroes there, many of whom were of French extraction and, consequently, eager to respond to Jacobinism, along with 25,000 enslaved Africans; the revolt that occurred there included, perhaps, a quarter of the latter grouping, armed mainly with cutlasses or pikes and an occasional blunderbuss.[85]

Thus, by 1795, this spice island too was aflame as London rushed troops from Gibraltar—thus, exposing this strategic site to reclamation by Spain. Just as General Toussaint came to symbolize his island, Grenada's uprising was embodied by the man known as General Julien Fedon, who one U.S. national condemned for his "cruelties," though he freely admitted that "we are yet to know how the force of arms will succeed in [al]laying this unquiet spirit of insurrection." This mainlander with roots in Boston well knew that "those Negroes who have tasted the charms of a life of indolence free from control will return with bitter reluctance to their former subjection"—a lesson equally applicable to Carolina and Virginia.[86]

The Cary family of the Bay State was told of the "insurrection in this island." There were "alarming reports about the French fleet" being dangerously close, since the governor of Guadeloupe had just stirred "commotions" in St. Lucia and had "contrived to get his emissaries" to prepare "the coloured free people here ready for a revolt" to "gain" more islands "for the French republic." Like a typical mainlander, this man too was enraged by the "boasting expressions" of the "free French mulattoes," including "their insolent behaviour," and he observed that their malevolent "designs were not kept secret." The "insurgents took their prisoners up to Fedon in the woods" and "they killed or wounded every white man they could meet."[87]

Grenada, a small island, represented larger trends that appeared to be extending. It was not solely a matter of armed Africans now pillaging and plundering settlers. As one mid-19th century analyst, Benjamin C. Clark, observed when scrutinizing this period: "the war between the whites and mulattoes was marked with atrocities even more revolting than that between the whites and blacks. The law of morality and nature were all outraged by it; fathers strangling their sons and sons plunging their bloody hands into the yet living vitals of their fathers."[88]

Slave society seemed to be decomposing—violently. Many slave-holding republicans in response dug in their heels, refusing to retreat—until they were compellingly obligated. Thus, one visiting Frenchman during this tempestuous decade encountered Ralph Izard, the prominent Carolinian, and a "zealous advocate for slavery." It was his "firm belief that a Free Negro is more indolent and vicious than a Negro slave,"[89] which was not the attitude needed for a system acutely in need of allies.

Meanwhile, a woman known simply as "Aunt Margaret," who too had ties to Massachusetts, found herself in the midst of an "'insurrection," just after arriving in Grenada. It was "occasioned by the coming of French Negroes from the other islands. They produced such an excitement," she said with amazement, "that one morning large parties of Negroes collected and went to different plantations seizing more than forty of the white inhabitants, carrying them into mountains, confining them in one room, and keeping constant guard over them"—with an unclear destiny intended.[90] Thus, it was possible for readers in Rhode Island to hear of "Mr. MacMahon," who "in the insurrection of 1795" was "placed in a room previously to being summoned to execution by the slaves. He saw all his companions taken out and shot one by one"—before managing to escape.[91]

What these Bay State residents experienced was hardly unforeseeable. It was in mid-1794 that Lord Stanley in London was told of the "extreme weak state" of "garrisons" in Grenada with "more regiments" needed, so as to better bolster Barbados, St. Vincent, Antigua, Dominica, etc.—and, it could have been added, the mainland too for as events displayed, if slavery was weakened in the islands, it could hardly hold in North America. "The Carolina Negros will be [dispatched] to the different islands" was the recommendation[92]—but was this the best guarantee for the survival of slavery on the mainland, given that these armed men had fled from there in the first instance?

The presence of toughened Carolina Corps soldiers[93] off the coast of New England also meant that unrest in Grenada would be even more menacing to the mainland than even the hair-raising events in St. Vincent and Dominica. All of these trends would stimulate abolitionism in London with similarly menacing consequences for the slave-holding republic.

At any rate, arming Africans and placing them in the Caribbean in order to police slavery was of doubtful usefulness in the long run. By 1795 London was said to have an encampment of Africans in Barbados who had been enlisted "from the revolted French islands"—just as the Carolina Corps had fled the mainland antagonist—but betting on their allegiance in the crunch may have been overly optimistic. There were 1600 of them near Bridgetown, whose mettle would be tested repeatedly in coming years as Africans revolted. Yet since other islands were ablaze and requiring maximum attention—especially Dominica,[94] St. Vincent, and Hispaniola—there were few good options,[95] especially since Maroons in Jamaica, as was their wont, were marauding.[96]

Supposedly, the analogous uprising on the tiny spice island of Grenada began with the arrival of French Jacobins, which, it was said, led to an "uproar of the Negroes in the streets" that "increased that confusion." The equivalent of General Toussaint there was referred to as General Julien Fedon and he was called "Commander of the French Republican Troops."[97] London was reaping the fruits of what was now easy to see as an uncertain victory in that Grenada too had been French territory, until London ousted its rivals in about 1762, but it still contained a significant percentage of those likely to be influenced by radicalizing Paris—or so it was thought.[98]

By March 1795, Whitehall was told of a "great concern" due to the "General Insurrection of the French Free Coloured people" that "broke out on the island," accompanied by a "massacre of the English white inhabitants" and a "seizure of the persons of the English white inhabitants." Even the Lieutenant Governor was "unfortunately captured by the insurgents" and "martial law" did little to calm things down. There were pitched battles involving hundreds on each side.[99] "Most horrid acts of savage barbarity" was the settler accusation.[100] That General Fedon communicated in French confirmed his incipient Jacobinism in the minds of many,[101] as did the fact that he had "white people with him"[102]—an indicator of an ideology inimical to the premise of racial slavery. That he was said to pledge to "put to death" each and "every one of the Prisoners" he held the "instant an attack" was launched against his forces confirmed the formidability of the foe faced.[103] That forces had to be hurried from Barbados to attack him ironically underscored the vulnerability of the British enterprise in the Caribbean.[104]

That "General Fedon" was described as a "mulatto" only enhanced the antipathy toward him on the mainland. By June of 1795, redcoats were arrayed to confront him. Grenada was said to be of "value and importance" to London, but these troops had to be diverted to Hispaniola to engage a perceived larger threat. In Grenada a British source described with undisguised contempt the "French white inhabitants," who had joined the "free coloured insurgents" of General Fedon, not to mention "four execrable traitors," who were "born of British parents yet joined in the unnatural insurrection."[105]

It was hard to say what the local authorities thought was worse: the "revolt among the slaves" or that this upsurge was "aided and abetted by many disaffected white French inhabitants," indicative of a trans-racial ideology contrary to then reigning slavery. This challenge had "brought a very heavy debt upon the colony" and the question was: for how long could the Exchequer bear this burden?[106]

Jacobinism was leaping forward and like any other ideology that seemed to be ascending was snowballing, attracting adherents that—minimally—challenged frontally the slave system. Statements posted island-wide in French proclaimed "liberté" and "égalité" and assailed British officials by name.[107] Bewildered officials wondered plaintively how those "delegated by the National Convention of France" could "claim alliance with the most barbarous and abandoned" of the island; how they could "arm the servant against the master and the son against his parent"; and how they could "insult common sense by a shameless appeal to the rights of humanity."[108]

Predictably, redcoats were defecting and disintegrating. Some of their forces, it was stressed, were "almost in a state of mutiny" and had "begun quarreling one with another." A man in the militia emphasized that he and his like "were volunteers," who were only interested in protecting their own "property," and were not up to the "Bush fighting" that was expected.[109]

Estates were going up in smoke. Fedon's forces were reportedly "overloaded with ammunition" and another Hispaniola seemed to be unfolding, accompanying like-minded revolts in Dominica and St. Vincent.[110] The Jacobins in nearby Trinidad were mobilizing too, leading to the unavoidable conclusion, thought one British leader, that the "misconduct and ingratitude" of these forces had to be stamped out and an "entire deliverance from all French connexion" must take place to restore "tranquility."[111] There was a "calamity," said local officialdom, a "general insurrection in the French Free Coloured people." The Brigadier General was slain and troops were hurried over from Martinique, leaving that island exposed similarly. "Many of the French inhabitants have joined the insurgents," it was added dismayingly, and a "very general spirit of revolt has shown itself among the slaves," as a "large proportion of the estates have been desolated by fire and pillage." The proposal for "arming a Black Corps of 300 men from the trusty slaves" at once illustrated the frailty of colonialism and the growing strength of Africans. But since it was thought that the insurgents sought to "rob you of your property and to extirpate you and your families" via "deliberate massacre," arming even more Africans was thought to be the best way to proceed.[112]

What was going on in Grenada, said local authorities, "can scarcely be paralleled in the history of mankind"—though settlers in Hispaniola and Louisiana could have responded similarly. The "refractory disposition of the slaves" and an "awful sense of the evils which surround us" rendered appeals to "Providence" as helpful as those to London.[113]

Some "rebels" involved in the "Horrid Rebellion," which had "existed for sixteen months," were placed on trial by July 1796, though their rising had "not yet [been] quelled." Still, "forty-seven of the Rebels" were slated for "execution,"[114] though the approaching "hurricane season" was heightening "how much we have to apprehend." Again, the remedies seemed worse than the illness: i.e. conscripting 300 Africans for the Royal Navy who "would be condemned to serve fourteen years without pay, which would be [a] saving to the public" and "would become very useful particularly in climates unhealthy to the whites."[115] But would more than a decade without compensation leave these unfortunates in the mood to serve London capably?

As the fall of 1796 crept closer, Whitehall was told that "the insurgents have done no mischief whatever. Their only object seems to have been to conceal themselves in the woods until they could get off from the island in canoes by night . . . many have been killed" and "we have now little to fear." But "fever" was spreading among the redcoats while a different kind of Jacobin fever had yet to be arrested in the region.[116]

For London's problem was that rebellion was not limited to Grenada. In 1796 the nation that was to become Guyana was also on fire. Among the rebels were "Maroons" or "Bush Negroes," who had escaped direct supervision by the Crown and its minions. One Londoner "discovered from fatal experience that the Bush-Negroes were more formidable than had been imagined" in confronting "regular European troops," who "were the best fitted for this kind of duty." The result was that the Crown "raised a corps of Blacks," but even though severe measures were adopted—"*a premium was offered for every right hand of a Bush-Negro that should be brought in*"[117]—this too proved unavailing.

Since slavery was less evident on the banks of the Thames—or the Seine—than the Potomac, it was possible for Londoners to assess the rapidly changing environment with more equanimity than their republican counterparts on the west bank of the Atlantic. Abolitionist debates were now accelerating in parliament, however, with far-reaching consequences for the United States. In fact, as one analyst put it with skepticism in 1796, the "example of the loss of America is held up to us by way of warning not to provoke the West India islands lest they should also be lost to Great Britain."[118] Yet more sober analysis would reveal that a bevy of planters—no matter how hearty—were not comparable to a mass of "white" mainland settlers in ability to secede from the empire; thus, maintaining the Caribbean colonies by way of abolition while buying off said planters seemed to be the optimal remedy to be pursued. This did not augur well for the slave-holding republic, however.

Mainlanders were also scrambling to keep up. By 1796, the influential Virginian St. George Tucker warned that by not giving rights to free Negroes, whose numbers had been augmented by the flow from the island, they possibly would find refuge elsewhere, since the message from Hispaniola was that this grouping was too dangerous to leave well enough alone.[119] The intellectual Tucker may have heard that policymakers in the nearby Bahamas had "resolved" that same year "to dispatch two or more fast sailing vessels to some of the Southern Ports of the United States of America and to the British ports in St. Domingo to notify [all of] the scarcity of provisions at present prevailing within these islands."[120] In short, the blaze of revolt had crept closer to the mainland, now licking the Bahamas, and imperiling the slave system to the point where London was now seeking aid from its mainland dueling partner.

What may have illuminated Tucker's thinking were the recurrent fires in Charleston that year of suspicious origin. Then this port city received credible information of now reviled "French Negroes" headed there to complete the task of reducing Charleston to ashes.[121] During the important year that was 1794, a man of European descent using the pen name "Rusticus" observed that Africans brought from the island to Carolina "gave the ideas to our slaves" and "opportunities of conversation with the newcomers" allowed these ideas to "ripen into mischief!"[122] The number of runaways there had been mounting since 1793 and showed little sign of surcease, providing signs of a society in decay.[123]

This spate of fires was not limited to Carolina and seemed to increase as the tumultuous century lurched to conclusion. One writer then found a similar outbreak in "several of the Southern States," lit by "wicked persons." The observer was unsure if the "cause or causes" of this "unusual commotion" could be ascribed to the "European nations," meaning France or the "West India islands"—i.e. most pointedly, Hispaniola. "Certain it is," nonetheless, "that American States have of late been exposed to threatening and unusual calamities from lawless and wicked men." Before the rise of Jacobinism in whatever guise, there were "but few instances of arson or house burning, attended with night robbing in this country," meaning Boston. "But of late," complained John Lathrop, "instances of perpetrating or of attempting to perpetrate those crimes, have become alarming," including "several daring attempts to set fire to Boston." This did not equal the troubling "desolation" that "spread . . . through the capital of Georgia and of South Carolina," the product of a "wicked design." There were "many attempts . . .made to set fire to buildings in New Jersey, in New York, in Connecticut, and in several towns in Massachusetts" of late. Lathrop emphasized—as did others—that a "black man" was "suspected" and this "unhappy creature" had "been confined for some crime in Nova Scotia" and was now "bound in chains." "For several weeks, almost every newspaper has given an account of fresh instances of setting fire to buildings of one kind or another, either in our neighborhood or in some parts of the country." This was attributable to "the political situation of the American States," then "peculiarly difficult" which in turn was due to "quarrels of the European quarter of the world."[124]

As if veritable biblical plagues were descending, the rise of Jacobinism and the attendant mass flight to the mainland, along with this wave of arson, were

accompanied by a malady that was perceived as not unconnected to the foregoing: a contagion of yellow fever that had a devastating impact most notably in the
place that French exiles found most congenial: Philadelphia. "The Negroes were
wholly free" from this disease, it was thought, and even the "French newly settled
in Philadelphia have been in a very remarkable degree exempt,"presumably due to
a built-up immunity.[125] What if the yellow fever cut a prodigious swath through the
mainland as armed Africans—perceived as immune—mounted an invasion? "The
mortality at St. Domingo," asserted an 18th century medic, speaking of the impact
of yellow fever on invaders, "has filled the minds of every one with terror and astonishment."[126] This was an untold weapon in the island's arsenal for as late as 1862,
the U.S. envoy in Port-au-Prince found it to be the "hottest and most enervating
city of the West Indies," with the "climate" being "debilitating." He was "quite
sure" that he would "not be able to go through the intense summer heat" and the
diseased environment that came along with it.[127] A few years earlier, the U.S. emissary there had been "very ill with the yellow fever," since "it has been very sickly
here this summer" and there have been "many deaths from yellow fever among the
foreigners"[128]—a direct deterrent to U.S. occupation.

It would have been understandable if the superstitious, if not the religiously
minded, had inferred that a kind of biblical revenge was being visited upon the
mainland as an outgrowth of countenancing slavery. The numerous French speakers now babbling in the streets of urban nodes was surely indicative of a transformation then only understood dimly. Island settlers were offering estates at fire sale
prices, but only the most courageous—or mad—investor would be so adventurous
as to accept such meretricious offers.[129]

Gloom and doom were ascending within the youthful republic, as Jacobinism
of various stripes seemed to be the wave of the future. Such was the case on a vessel
sailing between the then anxious ports of Charleston and Philadelphia. A hand-
ful of refugees from Hispaniola were aboard and they injected further melancholy
in the already depressed atmosphere by blubbering about their immense loss of
property. In the southern port, though these "unfortunate exiles" were treated in an
"obliging and hospitable" manner that "signalized" both "beneficence and generosity," the haughty royalists, quite typically, did not reciprocate with courtesy, perhaps at revulsion toward the bourgeois. Both sides could unite on the basis that "the
hatred against England" was "almost universal," said the Duke de la Rochefocauld
Liancourt,[130] but it was not clear how that would help to salvage the disintegrating
slave system.

Since by this juncture it was apparent that the mainland could not be quar-
antined from hemispheric trends, aware republican slaveholders should have been

paying attention to events as far afield as the northern coast of South America, where Africans had proven themselves capable already of being able to seize power altogether and where French and Dutch settlers clustered tremblingly. Once more, settlers were reduced to the questionable praxis of arming other Africans in defense of the slave system. The "Bush-Negroes" there, it was reported with a quiver, "if they should find themselves able to overpower us, would certainly take off our scalps, and perhaps not leave us our heads!"[131] Such petrifying thoughts had occurred to this observer, especially since his class was compelled—because of population deficits—to enlist one group of Africans to ride herd on another, expecting class interests to override all else in the manner of the vulgar economist. George Pinckard, instead, mused "whether it may not be employing a temporary convenience to establish what may hereafter become an extensive evil. May it not teach the slaves a fact," that had been established in Hispaniola, "which will not be readily forgotten: may they not learn that they are not only the most numerous, but also the strongest party." He knew about this volcanic island all too well and the "frightful horrors" there and was suitably impressed with an "American author" whose "popular works" had exposed these matters.[132]

What Pinckard apparently did not recognize was that by offering more enticements and inducements to Europeans in the form of liberties and land taken from indigenes, the slave-holding republicans had gained an insuperable advantage in the all-important realm of attracting those defined as "white" and, thus, thought they had fewer worries to mull over than those in South America.

The radicalizing of revolutionary processes in France and Hispaniola delivered an unmistakable bulletin to the slave-holding republic: their model of development based on mass enslavement of Africans would be receiving a stiffer external challenge. As Jamaica, Grenada, Dominica, and St. Vincent erupted, with settlers reduced to arming more Africans in response, it was crystal clear that a crisis had descended upon the hemisphere. The population ratios on the mainland that favored settlers provided a cushion, perhaps an insurance policy to divert the fate that Hispaniola had not escaped. Yet, since jousting with European powers from the hemisphere took precedence strategically over squashing Black Jacobins, it was evident that slave-holding republicans were relegated to the distasteful choice of being compelled to choose only between which poison to swallow.

It is "significant," argues historian David Brion Davis, "that in 1798 when Toussaint finally triumphed over the British in Saint-Domingue, Georgia became the last American state to close off the slave trade and even Southern Congressmen agreed to a prohibition of any slave from outside the United States into the Mississippi territory."[133] There was the "liveliest apprehension," argues another scholar, that the Africans arriving from the islands "might disseminate among the [mainland] slaves the revolutionary principles" of Black Jacobinism.[134] It would have been folly for slave-holding republicans to ignore the fiery lessons emerging from Hispaniola.

Nonetheless, like any earthshakingly radical trend, the rise of Black Jacobinism had a contradictory impact. Yes, it gave considerable pause to the slave-holding republicans, but, as noted, others felt compelled to retrench, sharpening their swords and hardening their shields for future battles they knew were sure to come. Any tide running against slavery in the Upper South at the end of the 18th century seemed to have reversed, driven not just by the invention of the cotton gin but also, precisely, due to the desire to somehow elude the logic of Black Jacobinism.[135]

3
—

Confronting the Surge of Black Jacobins
1797–1803

A S 1797 UNROLLED, LONDON WAS like a firefighter besieged by a roving band of arsonists, hurrying from one Caribbean island to another, vainly seeking to dampen the flames of revolt. How long could the Exchequer bear this brunt when priorities in India—not to mention Europe itself—beckoned? London could be excused for being confounded for the 1790s seemed like they would lead to His Majesty becoming the inheritor of France's Caribbean holdings—but then ended with a stinging setback in Hispaniola that seemed to suggest that Britain would be stripped of its own holdings.[1] "It was impolitic to grant a momentary independence to Toussaint," said Colonel Charles Chalmers of London, "which in its trivial advantages did not compensate for the dangerous precedent of a Black Empire almost in view of Jamaica."[2] So armed with a porous rhetorical defense, the redcoats suffered an ignominious defeat.

Per usual, the slave-holding republic was torn: delighted to see the British foe drained and—possibly—expelled from the hemisphere but frightened by the likely possibility that redcoats would be replaced by Black Jacobins. Eventually, this drove the two sparring partners into a kind of embrace. A similar outlook had governed the U.S. response to France. As matters evolved, the United States sought alliance with Britain in the face of a quasi-war with France, which in turn made the new republic amenable to engaging with the man referred to as General Toussaint.

Naturally, this conflict entered domestic party politics and Federalists had begun to circulate the credible rumor that an African uprising in Dixie was nigh, incited supposedly by the spread of Jacobin notions. Secretary of State Pickering argued that these radicals were "secretly fomenting a slave rebellion in the South and would launch an invasion of the Southern states" from Hispaniola. Appropriately alarmed, former secretary of war Henry Knox urged John Adams to raise an army—sooner rather than later—to guard against an attack by "ten thousand blacks." He feared that the invaders would land at "the defenceless ports of the Carolinas and Virginia"—where it just so happened that numerous enslaved Africans from Hispaniola had arrived only recently—and that these ebony marauders would be joined by the Dixie enslaved in a march of conquest. Rumors suggested that special African agents were already distributing arms among the local enslaved, as a Federalist pamphlet—in words that took on added meaning given their premonitory weight in the decades leading up to 1776—proclaimed that "your Negroes will probably be your masters." The fear of French radicals and Black Jacobins in turn spurred the Federalists to look longingly toward an entente with London, which invited opponents to see this party as a toady of the presumed eternal foe on the Thames.[3]

Also per usual, Jefferson reacted as if his flaming red hair was actually on fire. Hysteria unbound, he remarked in 1797 that the "first chapter" of a tragic history had "begun in St. Domingo and the next succeeding ones will recount how all the whites were driven from all the other islands"—and would it simply stop there? "If something is not done, and soon done," he advised darkly, "we shall be the murderers of our own children," as "the revolutionary storm now sweeping the globe will be upon us." Seemingly shedding copious tears, he found that "from the present stage of things in Europe and America the day which begins our combustion must be near at hand, and only a single spark is wanting to make that day tomorrow." Expecting aid from allies was a "delusion," as "insurrection" loomed evilly.[4] Though the security "threat" from the Caribbean has dissipated (though the continuing embargo of Cuba should remind us that it has not disappeared), readers today may have difficulty grasping what Jefferson intuited: that a central challenge to the security of the mainland was African rebelliousness in the Caribbean which could spread easily to Dixie.

To be fair, Jefferson was not the only mainland republican who appeared to be losing composure. Near that same time it was Pickering who told a U.S. envoy on the island about the "hostile proceedings of the French government and its agents" that were "bringing unparalleled distress" to "American commerce with St. Domingo," which had been formidable. "Their conduct will fill many dark pages in history," he counseled. More troubling still were the "American traitors, who impudently pretend to be patriots" and "have been taught to believe" that they could "throw a majority of our citizens into the arms of France." They, thus, had contributed immensely to the deteriorating status of "our suffering seamen" on the island;[5] these "traitors"were no more than members of the opposing political party. In an indication of the direction of political winds, Pickering had appointed a man with French and island roots—"Major Lewis Tousard"—as a leader "in the corps of artilleries and engineers" tasked with defending the republic.[6]

Pickering thought he had reason to believe that destabilization of his government was on the agenda. When vessels approached Philadelphia with "French passengers and their Negroes on board," he cautioned that "apprehensions are entertained of their attempting to land, in defiance of the regulations" devised and "force" would be deployed if their "wishes to land" were not aborted forthwith.[7] The next day the Secretary of the Navy instructed that the "Negroes" were "impatient to land" and noted their "disposition to outrage." Moreover, it was "expedient that they should be prevented from landing" and "if they should attempt it . . . without permission," then steely "force" should be employed. Perhaps unconsciously, he linked "keeping these people in subordination" and "preventing their landing"—"at all events the Negroes are not to be suffered to land,"[8] he repeatedly insisted.

From the vale of optimism about bilateral relations with Paris, the slave-holding republic had turned drastically toward thinking France had launched a none too covert war against it. With delicacy, a Parisian told the eminent Manigault family that the "political horizon of America & France is too much clouded at present to admit of your visiting with comfort the latter"[9]—which was devilishly accurate. Communicating from Paris, Mary Pinckney—also a member of a leading Dixie family—expressed her own unique concern about turmoil on the island, admonishing that what was occurring there "may be our own destruction," speaking of her native Carolina. "How hard upon our poor citizens to be always patrolling & guarding!" was her coda—which at once displayed typical disregard for the perpetual discomfort of Africans.[10]

Congressman Robert Goodloe Harper was among those who joined the growing chorus of voices in 1798 upbraiding France. His attack—published in London—was reported to have had "extensive sale."[11] The prolific Carolinian told his local constituents that the slave-holding republic needed to spend more on armaments, especially the navy, so necessary to confronting the alleged threat from the Caribbean. Raise taxes, even on sale of the enslaved, was another suggestion—all of "which would not have been necessary had not the conduct of France compelled us to arm."[12]

President Adams told Congress that French agents "claimed the privileges of arming and embodying the citizens of America within their own territory." No good deed went unpunished, he argued, since his nation had sought to "pay up the arrearages of their debt to France, which had been unavoidably permitted to accumulate, to make disinterested and liberal advances to the sufferers of St. Domingo."[13]

Ms. Pinckney herself was in Paris as 1797 approached, a city she found terribly expensive because of the "influx of foreign ministers" from "the Kingdoms & Principalities of Europe" which was driving up prices. As for herself, she was unsure about remaining there because of deteriorating relations with France, a disappointment since she reveled in the cultural magnetism of this city, notably "the freedom with regard to dress."[14]

Her fellow slave-holding republican, Charles Lee of Virginia, wanted to dress down Paris instead. As she was nattering, he was battering, apprising one and all of those who seemed to have "no sense of national honor," speaking of those "so infatuated as not to perceive how rapidly" his beloved Virginia was "meeting the horrors of St. Domingo." This meant that "in case of war, nothing can save her but the northern states and if Virginia prefers France to them"—well, there rested disaster. He sensed that with French emancipation, a new African—a Black Jacobin—had risen: "another war in America will not be conducted with regard to the blacks as the former was, and they who think so," he chided, "forget the change which has taken place of late years with respect to the rights of man."[15]

Others were not angry at Paris but London, blaming the British lion for the island rebellion, as payback to France for backing the 1776 revolt. As early as 1791, Pierce Butler was critiquing London sharply.[16] Yet, as suggested by the British attempt to douse the flames of Hispaniola, such a view—at least in its incipiency—was sufficiently far-fetched to suggest the fevered alarm and clouded thinking that had infected slave-holding republicans. Republicans had little difficulty aiding Londoners—even officials—in their many trade disputes on the island.[17] Rufus King, U.S. envoy in London, also knew better, rebuking a blind anti-British posture. Though he worried about General Toussaint's rise, he stressed to the Secretary of State in 1798 that London's "*Lord Grenville does not approve*" of tacit recognition of the regime headed by Black Jacobin Number One, "and that he sees the *pernicious effects* which it will have *upon our Trade, as well as upon the future security of their own Colonies*"[18]—an obvious reality that had driven Britain's failed island intervention.

King well knew that the island rebellion would "materially" impact "great interests" of his republic, requiring a "comprehensive as well as cautious Policy to protect those interests" and to "profit" from "the changes *of which the Independence of Saint Domingo* is the forerunner." So, he thought that London and the slave-holding republic, "*should act in concert*" and "*in Harmony with you.*" Yes, there were "inconveniences *from the influence of the example upon slaves in the Southern states*," notably the "*depredations and Piracy to be apprehended should St. Domingo become the Resort & Asylum of Buccaneers & rovers.*" But what could be done to upset this?

London hedged its bets in response, as King sought energetically to focus Britain's attention on the potentially calamitous effect of island sovereignty on Jamaica. *"Must it not be soon* followed," he forewarned perspicaciously, *"notwithstanding all your vigilance, by the abolition of the whole Colony System in that quarter of the world?"* Thus, "nothing remains but to *postpone it as* long as possible and to employ such measures as seem best adapted to diminish the *Evils of the event* when it arrives."[19]

Unity was a mainland prerequisite to confront a lengthening list of foes—the European powers including Spain, indigenes, and militant Africans—but the opposite was occurring. As early as December 1794, when the implications of emancipation in the Caribbean were beginning to dawn on the mainland, Ralph Izard—a Carolinian who had resided in France for years—observed that tension with both London and Paris was a must to avoid. And with emancipation in the Caribbean, "a joint war with France" could produce the "same horrid Tragedies among our Negroes . . . so fatally exhibited by the French islands."[20] In a sense, he anticipated the stormy happenings of 1797–1799.

For by the summer of 1798, one mainlander had detected what Izard had predicted. "Congress has almost in effect declared war," said Richard Creech and perhaps not coincidentally in Edgefield County, South Carolina—customarily wary of Negro intentions—"the Negroes collected together" with "two French Negroes" and with a malignant "result" apparently intended.[21]

Hence, by early 1799, there were sighs of relief on the mainland when Toussaint Louverture, denoted as "General in Chief of the Army of St. Domingo," sought to "form again bonds of friendship and good understanding with the United States." Still, his flourish—"I greet you in the name of Universal Liberty"[22]—may have been interpreted by slave-holding republicans as an intentionally dangerous provocation, intimating the ultimate horror: emancipation. General Toussaint gently scolded "Mr. President" for his "coldness" and offered to protect U.S. vessels in the ports where his jurisdiction obtained.[23] Battling France, then Spain, and then Britain had led the Black Jacobins to this diplomatic nimbleness.

Then there were the mainland's own exploding internal problems. Strikingly, also in 1799, a message from President Adams mentioned "the insurrection in Pennsylvania"—the "Whiskey Rebellion"—alongside the matter of the "renewal of commerce with St. Domingo and the Mission to France" in its title. The chief executive endorsed entrance of U.S. vessels to the island, including "Port Republicain, formerly called Port-au-Prince." He also discussed Shays' Rebellion in Massachusetts, suggesting that a beset republic thought the better part of wisdom was to seek commercial outlets in part to assuage the pain and drain of internal revolt.[24]

Displaying an ability to adapt to onrushing reality, the U.S. delegate in London, after meeting with his peers, exhorted about the "Dangers" to the Caribbean "as well *as to our Southern States from the numerous Inhabitants of St. Domingo.*" How to confront the "Danger" of Black Jacobins? Once again, choosing the "least bad" option, King urged "complete *Independence of the Island and of a free trade with it* as the best means of retaining *the Negroes in the state of* mere *Cultivators* and of guarding against the Dangers that are apprehended *from them.*"[25] That could possibly lock the island into a trade relationship that operated to its detriment.

This concession had a shattering downside for the slave-holding republic too: any kind of recognition of Black Jacobins—even informal—ate voraciously at the innards of the mainland regime. "Toussaint's clause," Jefferson told Madison in early 1799, referring to this parlous state of affairs, "was retained. Even South Carolinians" in the House "voted for it," suggestive of the corner into which the flesh peddlers had been forced. Thus, he added dejectedly, "we may expect therefore black crews, supercargoes & missionaries thence into the Southern states." Distraught, he concluded, "if this combustion can be introduced among us under any veil whatever, we have to fear it."[26] He was beside himself when considering that "Toussaint's subjects" might gain "free ingress & intercourse with their black brethren in these [Southern] states."[27] When Jefferson referred to the Black Jacobins as the "cannibals of the terrible republic," his fear of mastication may not have included his own marrow but, surely, that of the slave system over which he presided.[28]

For the very sight of Black Jacobin seafarers striding boldly through Norfolk and Charleston or Savannah, where not so long ago beleaguered French settlers had scuttled cravenly, was bound to be inspiring to the enslaved—but at this point, the slave-holding republic had been maneuvered into this difficult position.

A little over a week after Jefferson had penned these startling words, the Secretary of State was dickering to insure that "Genl [*sic*] Toussaint" through a "private merchant" in "partnership with the United States" could obtain "supplies of cloaths & provisions." This might be "inexpedient"—supplying Black Jacobins was hardly a priority for the slave-holding republic—"because a negotiation is contemplated to be commenced with France." Nonplussed, Charles Lee of Philadelphia said with a scoff, "I have no more confidence in the black Frenchmen than in the white"[29]— therein the dilemma was posed: of the two, the more populous, more developed France was seen as the larger threat.

Were slaveholders actually arming abolitionists? Mainland republicans did not have many attractive choices. Reporting from the Mississippi Territory, Winthrop Sargent informed Pickering in mid-1798 that "in case of hostility with France," his already perilous land would become a major "Theater of War," with all the past memories of Paris collaborating with indigenes flooding back into focus.[30] Governor Sargent, realized that a "few French troops with a cordial co-operation of the Spanish Creoles and arms put into the hands of the Negroes, would be to us formidable indeed"—which, if anything, downplayed the gravity of the matter. "The Indians," he added correctly, "(now I fear wavering) would be induced to join them"—creating a fiasco for the slave-holding republic.[31]

The quasi-war with France had concentrated the minds pointedly of the slave-holding republicans, leaving them with few choices beyond cutting a deal with General Toussaint—a deal that he could then leverage in favor of ultimate sovereignty for the island. Colonel Charles Chalmers, an inspector general of redcoats during the failed intervention on the island, blamed these republicans for this petard on which they were hoisted. Instead of viewing the British setback on Hispaniola with "contrition and horror," she reveled in the reversal handed to her old foe. "By such misconduct, apathy and, impolicy," he charged, "America is in much greater jeopardy from the power of France than in 1755, when that power carried ruin into her frontier settlements." More in anger than sorrow, he jabbed the republicans with the blow that "the passions of her rulers clouded their understanding."[32]

The initial mainland impulse was double-dealing, seeming to seek an entente with the Black Jacobins (and London), while not ruling out stabbing them both in the back. The problem was that since this kind of duplicity was normalized, as Black Jacobins entered the family of nations they could gain tactical advantage by seeming to lean in the same direction.

By 1798, London's island intervention was coming apart at the seams. A "blockade of St. Domingo" would not be opposed by the "North American states," said London's emissaries, "as if we were to blockade any other part of our enemies['] territories"—but what if the devious republicans sought to aid General Toussaint and also to undermine Jamaica? General Toussaint wanted control of Hispaniola and if Britain did "not stand in his way . . . he would not in the interim molest Jamaica," or so it was thought. Yes, his victory would place the "security of Jamaica . . . in his hands," which left the option of backing André Rigaud and the *gens de couleur*, which did not seem like a winning bet then. "Assisting any of Toussaint's chiefs who may rebel against him" was too considered, along with an "attack [on] his most defenceless positions on the coast," but that was just another toss of the dice.[33]

Rigaud who fought in Savannah during the anti-London revolt had good reason to believe that his labor would be rewarded, though he should have understood that there was growing disenchantment with those of his type on the mainland.[34] The confrontation between Rigaud and General Toussaint tended to serve the economic interests of the slave-holding republic and London to the extent that it served to maximize their trade with the island to the detriment of France. *Gens de couleur* were increasingly being viewed as blameworthy in the first instance for the ignition of August 1791, shedding light on the reports that in the end, the mainland republic and London secretly supported General Toussaint against Rigaud,[35] as the latter was viewed as too close to Paris. The absence of compelling options led to a U.S.-U.K. entente with General Toussaint.

By late 1799 this dilemma was exposed when a Massachusetts schooner—described by Pickering as "valuable"—was "capture[d]" on the island. "General Toussaint," said this diplomat, was about to "march with a considerable force" toward the area where this cargo was detained—near "Petit Goâve"; "it is not improbable that it is now in his hands" and not "subject to Rigaud's authority," and such facts on the ground dictated political arrangements.[36]

This also meant the slave-holding republicans could be accused of betraying the fabled founders by trucking not only with Black Jacobins but London too. In fact, a 1799 concord was brokered indicating that "no Frenchman or foreigner" would be allowed to sail on a U.S. or U.K. vessel "bound to St. Domingo" absent strict pre-conditions. Though dueling only recently, the two—following Rufus King—found "common interest in preventing the dissemination of dangerous principles among the slaves of their respective countries."[37]

To that end, the leading British military man—Thomas Maitland—journeyed from the island to the mainland to confer not only on mutual "security," but also what Pickering termed measures "necessary" for the "tranquility of our Southern States and of the British West Indies" which "would be endangered by an unrestrained intercourse with St. Domingo." Anomalously, both powers now recognized that the "political safety of the Dominions of each nation abounding in Negro population must depend for their establishment on the orders of General Toussaint."[38] When the "political safety" of Negro slavery depended on the good wishes of Black Jacobins, it was manifest that a crisis of the entire slave system had erupted.

Hence, by March 1799 Pickering was telling General Toussaint directly that he was unhappy about French harassment of U.S. ships, while, by way of contrast, he was pleased with the "good disposition manifested in your letter."[39] Pickering also was upset with British influence in Hispaniola and looked to counter it. "We have strong expectations that Toussaint will declare the island independent," he announced in April 1799, for "unquestionably he has long contemplated that event." It was "absolutely false" that the United States had "intrigued with Great Britain" against the rebellious Africans. "The Negroes and people of color of St.

Domingo formerly slaves," he added knowingly, "have become incurably jealous (and I believe with reason) that France intended in the end to bring them back to slavery or so destroy them and repeople [*sic*] the island from Africa. I have been well informed that [French officialdom] had declared that to be her intention."[40]

Pickering also communicated directly with the man he called "General Christophe," the African leader fluent in English, and through him arranged to "procure various articles for General Toussaint," including "large quantities of arms and ammunition" that, it was thought, "could not be exported from the United States." The "prohibition of our own laws," he said, "render it more important that Toussaint should keep on good terms with the British, who alone can insure him a supply," which was an incentive for the enslaving republic to emulate London. "I repeat," said Pickering, "that it is of the greatest importance for Gen'l Toussaint to be on good terms with the British."[41]

A good deal of Hispaniola had escaped the bonds of colonialism, increasing its importance to the Unites States since islands like Cuba and Jamaica faced restrictions in trading with the mainland. "The continuance and security of our commerce with St. Domingo," Pickering insisted, "is of such vast importance, it must not be hazarded for the sake of a few armed vessels from France trading to its ports."[42]

But from that juncture, the two powers embarked on differing paths in coming decades: the republic yearned and strained to break free from this dependence upon Black Jacobins, while the more far-sighted British monarchy now sensed that as to the slave trade (if not slavery), the jig was up.

General Toussaint did not make things easy for his erstwhile partners. There was a frequent plaint made, according to U.S. envoy Edward Stevens—whose birth in raucous Antigua and blood ties to the similarly born Alexander Hamilton[43] prepared him well for Hispaniola—that U.S. vessels were "forcibly put in requisition by the military Commanders in the different sea ports" held by Black Jacobins. Stevens "lost no time in remonstrating to General Toussaint against this arbitrary conduct," with little apparent effect, as mainland republicans were forced into an alien posture: trying to deal equitably with Africans and not necessarily from a position of strength.[44]

Of course, there were those who were aware of this subversion of mainland culture and were not pleased. One Charlestonian told the State Department that irrespective of views held by "mercantile" forces, he considered it "erroneous" to make so many concessions to Black Jacobins. "To avert such a dreadful calamity from [afflicting] the Southern States of the American Union," insisted this French surnamed individual, "will require the most prompt exertions" of the slave-holding republic against rebellious islanders, not conciliation of them.[45]

But at the time, the U.S-U.K. alliance was receiving the benefit—according to Stevens—of General Toussaint pulling back from a possible invasion of Jamaica and Dixie, which would have delivered ruination to both, even if the oppressors had prevailed.[46] Thus, even the most chauvinistic Charlestonians had to swallow their sturdiest doubts.

London thought that the general's plan was to send "half of his Army" to assault these vulnerable "Dominions" and the other toward his local foes, particularly—it was said—"the mulattoes," who "never will forgive him for the cruelties he has exacted upon their colour, and he is determined to exterminate them." Apparently, the general's comrade—and successor—Henri Christophe said "candidly" that they would put "every man of that colour to death." This leader was viewed as having "as much influence as . . . Dessalines" and General Toussaint's powerful's nephew—and he was also regarded to be "equally as ambitious and far superior to either of them in abilities [and] knowledge of the world." Thus, he had to be taken seriously. Christophe was also a "native of Grenada," where the embers of revolt still simmered in a palpable demonstration of what could occur if he—and the island leadership generally—were ignored or underestimated.[47]

This island conflict provided an opening for the mainland to exploit—except its own relentless targeting of *gens de couleur* complicated this approach mightily. The more flexible London—once again—was devising an opposing approach toward this influential grouping, which provided more leverage for the monarchy vis-à-vis the mainland, especially when it turned toward abolition.[48]

London was pushed in this direction for it had considered augmenting the Carolina Corps, i.e. "raise a company of Negroes" and "employ them on the protection of the back settlements" on the northern coast of South America "against the Bush Negroes." Yet when one ebony leader of this regiment "landed at Port Royal" in Jamaica, the "alarm was general amongst the principal inhabitants," as they cast a gaze upon "a Negro with the appearance and appointments of an officer." This produced a "dangerous effect on the mulattoes and Negroes; they saw in him the head of a future insurrection," particularly when this leader "entered into the grievances, real and imagined, of the Mulattoes and Negroes."[49] How could London continue to countenance slavery when it was forced to rely upon armed Africans to defend this peculiar institution? This was a question that the more farsighted mainlanders should have been posing.

This "dangerous effect" may have influenced Paris. So thought Colonel Charles Chalmers, who served with the redcoats in Hispaniola in 1797 during the failed intervention. "France in war with Great Britain," he said, "never regimented Negroes for defence of her colonies," though Paris was "aware of their insufficiency to oppose our troops" and the "danger" this meant. Only a "few Free Men of Colour on horses" were "armed and mounted," suggesting French skittishness.[50]

But if the Carolina Corps could not be safely augmented, an entente had to be forged with *gens de couleur* if slavery were to have a whisper of a chance of sustaining itself. If bronze soldiers could not be deployed, while the slave-holding republic was more successful at attracting those defined as "white," the Crown perforce had to be more flexible in attracting *gens de couleur*. Thus, London chose to confront that which the mainland was unable to engage frontally: "the whites," said a British delegate in the Caribbean knowingly, seemed to "fear the idea of the condition of Mulattoes or Negroes approaching theirs."[51]

Thus, as the bloodletting increased, mainlanders could at least realize that Black Jacobins were capable of inflicting great pain, an incentive to negotiate with them. "Whites" were "daily going to Cuba," fleeing Hispaniola, and "in the greatest misery" too said London's emissary, while "three thousand men of colour have been put to death—about thirty were tried and shot."[52]

General Toussaint also was disappointed with London since it was accused of not supplying him from Jamaica as had been pledged, while his opponent— Rigaud—reportedly "drew the greatest part of his supplies from Jamaica." Hugh Cathcart, London's man on the scene, explained that the latter supplying was unauthorized, an excuse the general found hard to accept.[53]

Though their island intervention had been rebuffed stingingly, the clear danger of having Black Jacobins as a neighbor continued to shape London's policy. In a "secret" missive, Whitehall while seeking to forge an accord with General Toussaint—"including security of Jamaica,"which involved coordination with the mainland too—had not excluded a possible "blockade" if the revolutionaries did not comply; this could implicate "vessels belonging to the American states" but would not work if the mainlanders balked.[54]

Despite the import of the Jay Treaty, which a few years earlier had seemed to seal a new era of amity between the once warring Crown and republicans, by 1800 the wounds were still raw to the point where trust between the United States and the United Kingdom was not easy, making it easier for both to deal with island revolutionaries in order to evade their mutual mistrust. Plus, all sides had to account for France and Spain, both of which claimed territory on the mainland that the slave-holding republicans desired, which enhanced the advantage held by island revolutionaries, who were similarly seeking to fend off these so-called "Catholic" powers.[55]

Hence, the U.S. representative in Hispaniola, Edward Stevens, still felt obliged then to make "arrangements with Genl Toussaint," even as the waters were roiled by "late disturbances at Jamaica" and "measures adopted" there to "prevent its tranquility from being disturbed by French emissaries."[56] Thus, Stevens continued to entertain "Genl Toussaint on the subject of supplies for his army in the South and of the assistance he requests to further his operations."[57] By the spring of 1800, Stevens remained in close "communication with Genl Toussaint," who "in very strong terms" expressed his "ardent desire to do everything which can preserve the existing harmony between this colony and the U. States."[58]

The following year the Norfolk businessman Christopher Tomkins made the ten-day voyage to the island. Despite Stevens's best efforts, he did not "find the markets here encouraging," though bilateral relations remained positive since the heralded "General Toussaint has given an answer to my petition."[59] Upon arrival, he was "introduced to General Toussaint" (slave-holding republicans may have been excused if they thought his first name was "general," an honorific to an African at a time when their mainland counterparts were referred to as "boys," though adults, well into the 20th century). "Amongst the many questions he asked me," said Tomkins, "was the reason so few American vessels came here now." As with any other regime, they discussed at length "the great duties" that visiting merchants like himself had to pay.[60]

But, again, the embrace of Black Jacobins by slave-holding republicans—even if it could only be a temporary marriage of convenience based on shared antipathy toward Madrid and Paris (and London intermittently)—was bound to deliver friction. One Philadelphian denounced, with emphasis, the "hundred endearing expressions" exchanged between the general and the diplomat. "The General writes" as a "lover would to his mistress." To make things worse, Stevens reportedly "does not possess, nor ever did possess General Toussaint's confidence"[61]—making the homeland a chump of sorts. The U.S. national, Jack Roche, who joined the navy in the late 18th century, was dismissive of the leading Black Jacobin, noting "we may shortly see the whole Island containing near a million of Inhabitants govern'd despotically by an ignorant Negro, formerly a slave"[62]—the latter image would haunt slave-holding republicans for decades to come.

These critics should have realized that slave-holding republicans were playing a double game: seeking to engage General Toussaint and undermine him too, as their discussion of a possible blockade of a recalcitrant island indicated. Black Jacobins may have been similarly inclined, aware that any forced friendliness toward slaveholders could not be permanent and thus, in 1798, settlers continued to be driven from the island to the mainland[63]—ditto for 1799.[64] This trend continued in 1801 when Lady Nugent found herself "very much shocked" by a "sad account of the massacre of three hundred and seventy white persons in St. Domingo. How dreadful," she cried, "and what [an] example to this island," speaking of her own Jamaica, which continued to be rocked by periodic disturbances fomented by Maroons.[65]

By 1801 one of these erstwhile French settlers was receiving the curt directive that the island had yet to "become calm" and "returning there to look after your interests" might be inadvisable. Why bother, Louis de Tousard was asked, when "you have all the facilities for living honourably in America?" Moreover, "why should you risk your life in an unfortunate country troubled by Revolutions?"[66] Was this Frenchman so blind that he could not see that his new homeland was seeking to pass special federal legislation to compensate him for his losses—so why even dream of returning to the island?[67]

Yet these critics might have connected the official friendliness toward the general to a bill also introduced in 1800 which sought to "prohibit the carrying of the slave trade from the United States to any foreign place or country," violation of which would mean a prison sentence of more than a decade.[68] Even if not passed, this was a dramatic gesture indicating the slave-holding republic might have to rethink its business model. The wiser slaveholder also might have thought that reducing the number of Africans in the hemisphere might be simple good sense.

These critics might have gotten the best of the argument among slave-holding republicans—except 1800 also witnessed an attempted insurrection by the enslaved in Virginia, led by those apparently inspired by Hispaniola. If the much-discussed "General Toussaint" did not have normalized relations with the mainland regime, it could easily have facilitated the kind of collaboration across borders that slaveholders so feared. As things stood, the revolt led by "Gabriel" was—according to the local press—aided by "two Frenchmen, said to be at the bottom of this horrid plot." Indeed, "the French principle of liberty and equality is the sole cause of the late alarms," said this journalist who declared himself emphatically to be *an American citizen from the heart, though born in France*."[69] Subsequently, the scholar William Drewry argued that the conspiracy was "due to French statements that the scenes of St. Domingo might be even more successfully executed in Virginia" and in "succeeding years rebellious slaves in various sections of Virginia confessed that they had been inspired by hopes that Gabriel's plans and those of the Negroes of Hayti might be successfully repeated."[70]

But were these conspirators French, as this correspondent suggested—or Black Jacobins? Splitting the difference, another observer was "very certain" that "this dreadful conspiracy originates with some vile French Jacobins," as "the horrors of St. Domingo have already proved"; this cabal "cannot fail of producing either a general insurrection or a general emancipation."[71] Was it more likely that this stunning eventuality could be forestalled if—at least—the patina of normalized relations was extended to General Toussaint? And if Paris could be credibly accused of stirring up mainland Africans, it could only be imagined what Black Jacobins could accomplish.

For the enormity of this plot was bound to produce inflamed reaction and even realistic thinking. A chief witness, an African known as Ben Woolfolk, testified in September 1800 that "all the whites were to be massacred, except the Quakers, the Methodists, and the Frenchmen, and they were to be spared on account of their being friendly to liberty and also [because] they had understood that the French were at war with this country"—the enemy of my enemy is my friend, a staple of diplomacy. And then "an army was [to be] landed," which they hoped would assist them; they also "intended to spare all the poor white women who had no slaves."[72] The future president, James Monroe, was told that "the Negroes were to rise" and "take possession of the arms and ammunition and then to take possession of the town"; for those immersed in denial, this correspondent insisted, there was "not a doubt in my mind but that my information is true."[73]

By all appearances, the plot stretched from the center of power that was Richmond to miles away in Petersburg, suggesting a network of communication more extensive than had been imagined.[74] A year later Monroe was told "with much regret and anxiety" of a "Negro insurrection" in "some parts of Virginia," that "might have been extensively injurious, even as far as our state," meaning South Carolina where there was a "like conspiracy."[75] The governor of the latter state thought he had reason to believe that Africans from the Caribbean were to land in South Carolina primed to fight.[76]

St. George Tucker had had enough. This jurist spoke at length about "the danger arising from domestic slavery" to the point where "no man denies its magnitude." The "late extraordinary conspiracy has set the public mind in motion; it has waked those who were asleep" since it was "an awful alarm of a future danger." Sure to evoke ire was his comparison of Gabriel's plot to "the revolt under Lord Dunmore" intended to squash the republican patriots. "The blacks who are far behind us, may be supposed to advance at a pace equal to our own; but, sir, the fact is they are likely to advance much faster." Slavery, he suggested, was creating its own undertakers, since "when you make one little tyrant more tyrannical," as this system tended to do, "you will make thousands of slaves impatient and vindictive"—make them Black Jacobins, in other words. For "fanaticism is spreading fast among the Negroes of this country," he advised, while in his home state, "the number of Blacks and Mulattoes in Virginia must now exceed three hundred thousand,"[77] which only magnified the peril at hand.

But where were these Africans to be sent? West of the Mississippi River? But what would that mean for republican expansionism? Back to Africa? That idea would gain traction later. This was a conundrum that was to occupy the sharpest minds in the slave-holding republic, including Jefferson's. Governor James Monroe of Virginia, who was presiding in the commonwealth at the time of Gabriel's conspiracy, drew a misleading lesson from Hispaniola—one that too would gain traction—when he pushed to secure a site of exile for *gens de couleur* too.[78]

Tench Coxe, on the other hand, had a broader view, instructing Jefferson that the disorder on the island "evince[s] the importance to *consumption* and *revenue* of the plan of promoting the sugar, coffee, and cocoa cultivation of China and other yet independent Asiatic states." Also, "ginger, pimento & molasses" should be produced in Asia too; this should be combined with an entente with the Turks to facilitate entry into their sprawling jurisdiction. He knew the "fate of Martinico is not certain. That of Guadeloupe probably unfavorable"[79]—with the possibility of a pan-Caribbean contagion. In sum, Hispaniola was not only sending forth ripples but waves of change that were to transform the ambitions of the slave-holding republic, compelling slaveholders to be globally minded.

More to the point, months after Gabriel's plot was uncovered, the Virginia House of Delegates passed with little dissent, a resolution urging the federal government to buy lands on which to deposit Negroes, especially, "persons obnoxious to the laws or dangerous to the peace," a spectacularly broad category.[80] Monroe made explicit what was evident when he told Jefferson that "resolution was produced by the conspiracy of the slaves."[81] The latter founder thought Hispaniola might be a good fit.[82] Hispaniola? Why bolster Black Jacobins? Jefferson backtracked on second thought, recalling the "possibility that these exiles might stimulate & conduct vindictive or predatory descents on our coasts & facilitate concert with their brethren remaining here"[83]—which was quite perceptive. This was one reason among many why far distant West Africa became the preferred site of expulsion. Soon it would be U.S. Negroes by the thousands who decided that buttressing the Black Republic was a nifty idea.

Meanwhile, back on the island the maximum leader was now being called "Governor General of the island of St. Domingo," as "commercial relations" between the slave-holding republic and the Black Jacobins continued,[84] according to Tobias Lear, a colleague of the now sainted George Washington. Nevertheless, when Lear met the governor general in mid-1801, he asked for a letter from the U.S. president addressed to him, which Lear did not have. "He immediately returned my commission without opening it," Lear recounted, expressing his disappointment and disgust in strong terms, saying that his colour was the cause of his being neglected or not thought worthy of the usual attention—a perceptive reading of mainland history. "He became more cool" and the following day he met with Lear again, this time accompanied by Christophe, the militant Grenadian. The governor general "repeated the observations which he had made the evening before"— but "notwithstanding the mortification he felt," he reasserted his "sincere desire to preserve harmony and cultivate a good understanding with the United States." There were then "32 American vessels now in this port" bringing "flour, fish & dry goods," a trade relationship hard to build in neighboring islands where "Imperial Preference" favoring Britain, France, and Spain hindered such ties.[85]

There were "numerous arrivals from the United States to all ports of this island," said Lear, to the point where "markets" were "entirely overstocked."[86] "There are many American vessels in this port," it was said in early 1802, referring to western Hispaniola.[87] But when U.S. vessels were found to be "proceeding to and from Jamaica" to Hispaniola "without the knowledge or authority of that Government," formal protest ensued.[88]

There was sufficient back-and-forth between the island and the mainland that detailed navigational instructions were distributed in Baltimore in 1802 to guide U.S. vessels. The traffic was such that, it was reported, there were "many losses occasioned to American and other vessels, from the want of a thorough knowledge of its navigation."[89]

Lear also sought to "cultivate a good understanding" with the governor general since, he "commands everything in this island." He was "an extraordinary man," he gushed. "He appears to be adored by all the inhabitants." And, most importantly, the "treasury of the island is very rich," featuring a sizeable "accumulation of money," which—truly—was "without precedent. What the object may be in collecting & keeping this sum is not for me to say—conjectures are various"[90]— though a fair inference would be that an island surrounded by antagonists should have a fund stashed away for a rainy day.

This cultivation was viewed with a jaundiced eye by London, which had thought the slave-holding republic was rather short-sighted in reveling in its devastating loss to General Toussaint. Even the man designated by London as "the British agent" on the island was "publickly [*sic*] known"—said another British agent—"only as an American," as he seemed to sense who was bound to receive favor from the general. "The Americans have such influence here," said this agent, that "they ought to be regarded with a jealous eye both with respect to their politicks and commerce neither of which I am fully convinced tend to promote the British Interests in this quarter"[91]—which was all too true.

What is remarkable about this squally era is how many of the major powers could be accused of being shortsighted. As Hispaniola was being bombarded, Napoleon Bonaparte came to power. This spelled retrenchment of Jacobinism in

Paris and a like result was intended for the island. It was the Corsican who was cited for a curious proposition: "I am for the whites because I am white. I have no other reason for that one is the good one."[92] This should have made him a soul-mate of the slave-holding republic: instead they were at each other's throats. This suggested both the artificiality of the historically recent racial category that was "whiteness" and its instrumentality, a tool to secure the real prize: national then international hegemony.

Back on the island, Lear continued to maneuver. He told Secretary of State Madison that he was pressing the revolutionaries for "paying the debts due from the Government of this island to the United States," though island attorneys could well have argued that satisfaction for such obligations should have been sought in Paris or Madrid. Lear knew that his "situation . . . [was] much different from what it would be in any other country," where the presence of Black Jacobins in power was not the norm. Moreover, there was "so much jealousy" among American merchants that the office of the U.S. Consul was not sufficiently "respected by our own citizens abroad . . . to give respectability to it in the eyes of the Government" of the island.[93] The fractiousness among U.S. nationals on the island facilitated the ability of the Black Jacobins to manipulate one against the other, keeping the slave-holding republic off balance.

What Lear did not bother to say was that a representative of a slave-holding republic, where Africans were at the bottom rung of society, was now engaging with Black Jacobins and from a subversive vantage point of relative equality. This experience abroad was preparing the United States for a future, which it resisted strenuously at home—a future in which at least formal equality had to be accorded to those of African descent.

As of 1801, Lear was picking up hints of island independence, which it seemed was the "wish and intention of the Governor." But an issue that would dog bilateral relations for decades to come diverted his attention: damage claims by expropriated U.S. nationals. The "expressions" of the "Governor" were "cordial and his determination to do justice very strong," but Lear's fellow U.S. nationals were providing "considerable sums" to islanders to lobby the authorities and planting the seeds of corruption that would hamper Haitian development for years to come. "In the end," Lear said with scorn, "nothing is done: bribery and corruption are declared to prevail in every department."[94]

Contradicting those who thought the island revolutionaries were all thinly disguised agents of British abolitionism, General Toussaint himself, in what he termed "year 8 of the French Republick," referred indirectly to "the English" as "deceivers."[95] Yet even Charles de Vincent, who was writing from Philadelphia, described excruciatingly the bigotry there against Africans and chided General Toussaint for—supposedly—allowing some to delude him into breaking with France and not with the slave-holding republic.[96] What this Philadelphian did not clasp firmly was that the island revolutionaries did not have an array of choices, given that their enemies were legion.

There were other problems for the United States on the island. "The late alarms," said Lear in late 1801, a veiled reference to ongoing warfare, massacres, and the like, have "operated greatly against the American commerce," giving this diplomat "anxiety," and obliging him to request "some advices or instructions" in order to defeat the "bad effects."[97]

By early 1802, tensions between the island and France were escalating, leading to the perceived harassment of French citizens heading to the mainland. Those of French origin who arrived were confined. According to Lear, one French "gentleman arrived here about 4 or 5 months ago from Charleston, S.C. to look after an estate which he has in the island. He was not received with cordiality," which was minimization writ large. In fact, he was "arrested by order of General Christophe." Yet another U.S. national, John Lemonier, who "resided in the island for some years past and never . . . declared himself a citizen of the United States," vainly sought his consular skills.

Lear "remonstrated against their being detained" to little avail for Paris was "coming out with a large force" in order to "reduce the blacks to slavery," unnerving islanders. This befuddled Lear since the official "declarations" insisted "that this is a French colony." But it was not so much colonialism that was at issue but slavery, and Lear well knew that seeking to bring back this monster would have "destructive effects." He also knew that those who "formerly held property in this island"—many of whom were now his countrymen—had "urged . . . violent and ill judged measures." These angry petitioners not only desired their property but also demanded that it be "restored to them again with all its appendages," including enslaved property. "Other nations who have colonies in the W. Indies," he declared, "will also urge by every means in their power, the reduction of the blacks here to slavery." Curiously, Lear did not include his own slave-holding republic in this lineup, perhaps because he thought—wrongly—a *cordon sanitaire* could be built to enclose the mainland.

There was a reason for this ellipsis. "I do not believe," he proclaimed in words that would echo through the ages and reverberate on the mainland too, that these Africans "ever again will submit to the yoke of slavery but before they could be extirpated they will kill all the whites in their power and lay waste all the property that could be destroyed."[98] Then there were fifty U.S. nationals residing in one key

port of western Hispaniola and they "met at my house," said Lear, "and agreed
to embody themselves accordingly." But whatever their level of organization, they
could readily fall victim if rampaging Africans chose to "kill all the whites" rather
than be reenslaved.[99]

The slave-holding republic drew the lesson from Hispaniola that since Africans
would not submit to enslavement readily, they needed to be overawed numeri-
cally—hence, increased emphasis on European immigration—and brutalized
(even more) physically. But when London drew an opposing lesson the United
States found itself cornered—but rather than retreat, this republic instead accentu-
ated this initial failed response.

"French coming here in force" were Lear's terse words in early 1802.[100] Soon
he was addressing formally "Citizen Le Clerc, General in Chief, Captain General
of the Island of Saint Domingo," the Frenchman now seeking to assume control.
Any impulse that Lear and his superiors might have had to ally with Le Clerc as a
class and racial comrade dissipated in the heat of inflammatory charges that Paris
had resumed the quasi-war but this time on the island against U.S. nationals. It
was "alarming" said Lear—one of his favored words to describe island events—
when U.S. citizens "arrived in this port" and quickly were separated from their
vessels, often by a "French frigate."[101] Then two U.S. nationals, said Lear, were
"most rigorously confined in the dungeon" of a local prison, "deprived of every
necessary," and "all access to them is forbidden"—and "Citizen Le Clerc" refused
to intervene.[102]

Soon Lear had returned to addressing General Toussaint in euphoric terms,[103]
though—continuing the sectional divide on the mainland—Jefferson reportedly
backed the French takeover spearheaded by Le Clerc. It hardly seemed coinciden-
tal that as the quasi-war waned and Jefferson ascended to the highest office in the
land, General Toussaint found his economic and political relations with the mainland in steep decline. On 30 September 1800, the Treaty of Mortefontaine effectively terminated the quasi-war—though aspects, like the beard continuing to grow
on the corpse, continued—causing Madison, a faithful Virginian, to assert: "the
United States would withdraw from Saint-Domingue rather than hurt relations
with France."[104] When France concluded the Peace of Amiens with Britain shortly
thereafter, it further reduced the leverage wielded by island Africans, setting the
stage for a massive French invasion.[105]

The slave-holding republic was walking a slippery tightrope, seeking simultaneously to avoid falling into the jaws of French revanchism and what would soon
become the claws of Haitian abolitionism. This became clear when slaveholder
George Hunter en route to Savannah arrived on the island in the spring of 1802

accompanied with what was described as a "certain coloured man named Joseph," his "property." Having an acute sense of time and place, "Joseph" managed to reach the "shore by means of swimming"—but was captured and wisely "claimed the protection of a French citizen to which he was entitled" and "that he was not at full liberty and no longer a slave." It was "incumbent" a U.S. agent was told with emphasis, to "protest" this bald attempt to "deprive Mr. Hunter of his property in the said Joseph"[106]—but he and other slaveholders were to find that once Haiti was established, the ramparts of slavery had been breached fatally, as cases like that of Joseph rose in profusion in coming decades.

But French troops kept arriving nonetheless. James Madison was told by a U.S. national in Aux Cayes about "the arrival of about twenty five or thirty thousand troops from France." Fighting raged. "The Cape was burnt & all of the white and mulatto inhabitants without exception were butchered by the Negroes before they left the city & that they had also destroyed the plantations & killed the white inhabitants throughout the whole country. The same was said to be the fate of Port Republicain & its vicinity." There was the "greatest anxiety among the whites for their safety of their lives & property"—a growing circle that decidedly included U.S. nationals who too were part of this growingly fragile racial category.[107] The press screamed about the "race war of 1802," with one outraged journal arguing that a "Black State in the Western Archipelago is utterly incompatible with the system of all European colonisation"[108]—which was certainly true in the long term.

Robert Livingston, who was to be the prime mover in snatching the Louisiana Territory from Paris's grasp, heard about this bloody conflict—though since his source was a New York "lady, it may not be very correct." Still, while ensconced in Paris, he passed on to Rufus King the news that "Le Clerc has not yet learned to fight the blacks—who contend with him in the manner of our savages, much blood has been shed, neither side bury their dead." That Paris had to divert "the troops in Italy," now "destined for St. Domingo,"[109] suggested the weakness of France's position and why they might have to reverse this course—i.e. retreat in the Americas so as to advance in Europe.

"Private letters from St. Domingo," he said, "make the destruction by the blacks much greater than the public accounts,"[110] which was good news for those dedicated to chasing France from the hemisphere but bad news for the future of slavery. By November 1802 he was riveted by the fact that "so melancholy are the accounts from St. Domingo" that "not a part of troops designed for Louisiana are now to go to St. Domingo." Things were so catastrophically bloody that Livingston mused that at "this moment under deliberation" was whether "the whole world should not go there."[111] What Livingston, quite typically, did not contemplate was the news from

Martinique: slavery had been abolished there in 1794 during the onset of Black Jacobinism—then returned with a thud in 1802.[112] Something similar occurred in the vast land then known as French Guiana on the northern coast of South America.[113] A straw in the wind materialized in New York in 1802 with the sudden death of an African from the island named Romain who committed suicide; he had been brought to the island in 1793 by his "master" and rather than return there he killed himself.[114] Island Africans had maximum motivation to fight, as enslavement to some was a fate worse than death.

Peter Chazotte's account of the early 19th century bloodshed on the island did not emerge in New York until 1840, but it only served to reinforce what many had heard already. He indicted General Toussaint specifically, as the leading Black Jacobin "flew into a raving passion" and "instantly ordered his guards (guides) to shoot" an accused "mulatto" thought to have "inflicted with a sword" a nasty wound on a "black man." The general reprimanded Chazotte to the point where the latter "felt very angry . . . my hands were clenched and I was near striking him" before his good sense returned. He too thought that the general had signed "secret articles" of a "treaty" with London, a sign of "duplicity" underlining a "shameful connection formed by [that] government with the black barbarians and cut-throats of St. Domingo." He dismissed Tobias Lear as a "middle sized, portly man, distant, and pompous," always bedecked in the "full costume of an American Commodore." He excoriated Lear's "unjustifiable and everywhere exhibited hatred of the name of France." In this dystopia, the only "white men" who survived were those who were "the declared enemies of France or the disreputable agents of . . . the Wilberforce Society."[115]

Some, like Chazotte, were struck by the fact that on 4 February 1801 General Toussaint was presiding over an assembly that was held on the island that reinforced the gathering reality of abolition, while, by October, African cultivators were reputedly shouting, "Death to all the whites!"[116] In other words, slavery and exploitation had been racialized to the point that when the material reality of the oppressed did not seem to alter materially with abolition, they struck back fiercely at their presumed oppressors who were thought to have profited so handsomely from enslavement.

Actually, the attempt to reenslave island Africans gave rise to a thundering counter-reaction. The early 19th century witnessed numerous press reports from the mainland detailing what was referred to loosely as "race hatred"[117]—which was somehow disconnected from enslavement (the term "class hatred" would have been similarly descriptive). In early 1802, Jefferson was told that the "whites in St. Domingo escaped a general Massacre" by a "mistake in the day it was to take place," as "some" were "going by the old & the others by the new calendar." General Toussaint's militant nephew, it was said, "vowed a general extirpation of the whole" settler population.[118]

Nevertheless, like a perplexed pianist at the keyboard, slave-holding republicans had difficulty in deciding whether to strike black or white. Paris held the vast and richly endowed Louisiana Territory and harassed this capitalist and republican mainland competitor besides; while those who would soon be known as Haitian promised abolition of a fabulously lucrative form of property. Jefferson was duty bound to keep a close eye on both, though the casual observer could be excused for thinking that it was the latter that was a preoccupation. Shortly after a hair-raising report from Aux Cayes, he wrung his hands about the "course of things in the neighboring islands of the West Indies," which, he said worryingly, "appears to have given a considerable impulse to the minds of the slaves in different parts of the U.S. A great disposition to insurgency has manifested among them, which in one instance, in the state of Virginia, broke out into actual insurrection." Was this a harbinger of things to come? And, if so, did this make the island more dangerous than Paris? The expulsion of these Negroes "out of the limits of the United States." was his soberest recommendation.[119]

Why such extremism? Thomas Newton of Norfolk, who had been shaken at the sight of untidy French refugees streaming onto his shores, reminded Jefferson of the "dreadful situation of the French in St. Domingo" where "no quarter is given." He noted as well "the accounts are that several white people have been found hanging, with labels fixed on their breasts that all taken would meet the same fate." He concluded, ironically, given the redhead's proximity to similarly inclined black slaves, "I am wishing you health."[120]

So prompted, Jefferson wailed about the "convulsions prevailing in the French West India islands." These convulsions, he observed, "place in a state of alarm all the nations . . . into which Blacks have been admitted"[121]—a capacious classification that could easily extend to Norfolk.

It could also include Charleston for it was in that state that the governor received the startling news that the dastardly French were sending vessels containing African prisoners from Hispaniola to their port in order—it was said exasperatedly—to "turn loose the French Negro incendiary prisoners upon us."[122] In 1802 French forces defeated African rebels in Guadeloupe—then expelled thousands to the coast of Florida[123]—which at once got rid of a "problem" while creating another for Spain. As well, the U.S. slave-holding republicans were in a familiar position, drifting into panic mode: a Federalist newspaper, with the largest circulation in the nation, warned that if island Africans imbued with Jacobin ideas came to the

United States—a distinct possibility—then slave revolts would ensue.[124] Whether these hyperventilating rumors were a probability or just the fumes of guilty fear, the larger point was that a deeper apprehension about both slavery and Africans was becoming imbedded in the minds of mainland republicans. In London this led to abolition, while in the slave-holding republic it fortified the idea that the chains of enslavement required tightening.

The well-connected Pennsylvanian Tench Coxe concurred, telling Jefferson that every attempt should be made to "subserve *the great end of checking, counterbalancing, and diffusing the blacks*." This meant not only island Africans but local ones too as Coxe's imperative became inured in the republic in a pattern that was replicated in succeeding decades. In 1776 the republicans had defeated an incipient alliance between Africans, indigenes, and their European patrons and now, just years later, Africans had refused to accept that defeat and were once more on the march. With its population mostly on the eastern seaboard, close to the Caribbean and still facing real or imagined enemies in Spanish Florida, Canada, Newfoundland, and Bermuda, the new republic was quite vulnerable. Coxe worried that Cuba might emulate "St. Domingo": "we are to remember that it is but 30 or 40 leagues from our continent" and "hardy, enterprising, and enthusiastic men, who might be disposed to introduce mischief among the black & red" could reach "our Southern ports" with ease. "The Spanish Government may revolutionize; the blacks daily increased by importation may rise; and, in the event of a crush of the French force in St. Domingo, the blacks might excite an insurrection in Cuba. These things," he proclaimed, "with possible events in Florida & Louisiana, ought to inspire us with prudence & forethought."[125]

Coxe's reference to Spanish Florida may not have been a slip of the tongue. For St. Augustine during the colonial era had long been the jumping off point for pulverizing raids on Georgia and points northward. By the turn of the 19th century, the fearsome island fighter Jorge Biassou, who at one point had actually outranked the more famous Toussaint, had decamped there. As things turned out, his brother-in-law, Juan Jorge Jacobo, married Rafaela Witten, daughter of Prince Witten, an escaped slave from South Carolina. Those described as "Anglo planters" seemed to be on the verge of a nervous breakdown when Biassou arrived in their backyard, giving sustenance to the idea that Black Jacobins were also expansionists. Surely, if the stirring news from Hispaniola had somehow eluded Florida Africans, the weighty presence of Biassou should have solved this problem.[126]

During the height of the 1830s wars in Florida that pitted Africans and indigenes against Washington, the authorities of the latter reprinted a letter from a Spanish official in 1802 worrying that "Free Blacks" might "become dissatisfied and probably go over to the Indians." More troops were requested to "check the progress of the savages."[127] This was likewise the mainland theme in the early 19th century.

By 1802, as the island remained enveloped in chaos and promiscuously smeared in corpuscles, Virginia continued to grapple with the aftermath of Gabriel's plot. Just as 1789 and 1791 had merged in many minds into a single stream of Black Jacobinism, by the early 19th century this flow was seen as manifesting uncontrollably on the mainland. The "alarming occasion of the Negroes rising" was the report from Petersburg on 2 January[128] (while another correspondent termed it the "intended insurrection").[129] The "designs" of the "people of colour"—allegedly abetting this "conspiracy"—were seen by a Norfolk resident as "inimical" to order by March. A "considerable impression on the minds of many respectable citizens" was the result, with "frequent meetings" of "from one to three and four hundred," along with "correspondence" with "similar ones in North Carolina."[130] Days later he hastened to assure that "the fears of the people have not yet subsided"—and such fears were not to do so for decades to come.[131]

Days after that came news from Halifax County in the commonwealth that an "insurrection among the Negroes was about to take place"; for doubters there was the "certainty that such a plot was formed." As for "insurgents" in Campbell County, "the alarm had been more serious"; it was reported that "several Negroes had been killed" and "many others [were] taken up and committed to prison." Miles away in Charlotte an uncovered "plot had been on hand about six months" led by "the eternal enemy" who intended "misfortune" for "our country."[132] In nearby Hanover County, there was simultaneously "an alarm of an insurrection of the Negroes."[133]

One scholar has argued that "by 1860 'St. Domingo' had become a byword for slave revolt in many American minds and had developed into a trope for the massacre of whites."[134] What needs to be pondered is the point that the island had leapt to this inflamed status much earlier—perhaps 1791, at least by 1802—helping to shape the contours of domestic enslavement and the republic itself, along with the tortured fate of the people that became known as "African-Americans."

That is not all. The relentless shedding of blood by settlers was so shocking to Euro-Americans to be seen as historically new, perhaps inaugurating a new stage in human development to their detriment. Lost in this phantasmagoria with concrete consequences was that the French invaders were bent on genocide—and then had the tables turned. The massacre of settlers was a merciless indication that the construction of an identity politics known as "whiteness" had reached the point of dire crisis. This artificial racial category had been instrumental in bonding Europeans across ethnic, class, religious, and gender lines and facilitating both the expropriation of indigenes and the degradation—and crass labor exploitation—of Africans.

But as London, Paris, Madrid, and mainland elites all squabbled, the identity politics that was "whiteness" was being battered beyond recognition in the nation that was to become Haiti.

One response was the revivification of an abolitionist movement; another was the recrudescence of the politics of class, which dueled with and at times was imbricated in "whiteness" itself. Sadly, this former politics unfolded too gradually on the mainland to save Haiti from almost being swallowed by the United States in the 1870s, nor suffering through a despotic military occupation beginning in 1915.

By 1804 Haiti was moving constitutionally toward a radically new concept of citizenship: that only those denoted as "black" could be citizens, revalorizing what had been stigmatized. Yet "black" was defined expansively—unlike "white"—to mean those that rejected both France and slavery, meaning that even a "white" could be defined as "black" as long as he or she repudiated the logic of racial slavery that intended that only "whites" should rule and Africans should serve.[135] In the long-term contest between the slave-holding—then apartheid—republic's "whiteness" and the revolutionary republic's "blackness," the former prevailed in the 19th century and the latter only began to gain momentum in the latter part of the 20th century.

4

Confronting the Triumph of Black Jacobins
1804–1819

THE BACCHANALIAN INDEPENDENCE DAY celebration in Philadelphia in 1804 was proceeding according to a decades-long script when suddenly the specter of violence reared its head. A feisty crowd of several hundred Africans interrupted the revelry by forming themselves into armed military formations with elected officers. They marched through the crowded streets of this metropolis in a display designed to exhibit what one observer termed, "damning the whites and saying they would show them St. Domingo."[1]

What came to be called the Haitian Revolution—formally proclaimed a few months earlier on the historic day of 1 January 1804—sent a frisson of nervousness coursing through the slave-holding republic, reminding those who may have forgotten that slavery was an inherently unstable, conflict-ridden system that inevitably gave rise to bloody rebellion. This dramatic news had noticeable impact in New Orleans, which was undergoing a similarly dislodging and transformative transition to U.S. rule at the same time.[2]

For it was on 22 December 1803 that Louisiana's new territorial governor accepted the formal transfer of authority to the federal union.[3] Alice Izard, member of a prominent slave-holding family, was among those delighted with the Louisiana Purchase. She announced with enthusiasm "the mania is Louisiana."[4] But soon "The history of the Mississippi Valley's Cotton Kingdom that has come to emblematize the word 'slavery,'" argues one recent observer, "was from the beginning, twinned with the history of the most successful slave revolt in the modern era."[5] It could also be added that delivered by the Haitian Revolution was a tradition of African militancy. For in rapid succession there were three slave plots in that vicinity during the 1804–1805 period with one involving a scheme to liquidate all city officials in New Orleans and seize power.[6]

Though the mouth of the Mississippi may have been ground zero for the effects felt on the mainland from the Caribbean detonation, it was hardly alone. For in St. Louis also recently detached from French control, many were uneasy and alarmed at the conduct of mere slaves. There was a felt desire to "preserve this New Territory of the United States from the horrors which different American colonies have lately experienced"; but since "there exist[ed] among the Blacks a fermentation which may become dangerous," it was not clear if a dire fate could be avoided.[7]

Such unrest was bound to have national ramifications. As for the event with which it was linked in a nearby Caribbean island, the opinion differed sharply. Certainly, there were not many U.S. citizens—apart from a number of Negroes whose nationality was questionable in any case—who would have saluted the Haitian constitution, adopted in 1806, which stated, "no white person of whatever nation shall set foot on this territory as a master or a proprietor."[8] This "explosive" combination of "race" and class was designed to serve as a rebuff, not just to the French but also to mainlanders who now saw the island as both an abolitionist threat and as a barrier to commercial expansion generally, not least in the long-desired goal of seizing Cuba.

The wider point was that Haiti and New Orleans were linked, not only because the loss of Hispaniola drove France to liquidate many of its vast mainland claims to the benefit of the slave-holding republic. It was also because settlers were fleeing the island for Louisiana often accompanied by Africans who had seen that their "masters" were often not masterful in confronting enraged bonded labor, providing delightful inspiration for revolt. Moreover, after 1 January 1804 and the ouster of France from much of North America, it became possible for the slave-holding republic to concentrate more directly on island revolutionaries.

For even if the enslaved were not able to overthrow racist rule on the mainland, they could still inflict painful damage, not least by allying with the republic's antagonists, be they indigenes, British, Spanish, or French—or the newly created Black Republic. "The French and the English are not satisfied with going to war themselves," asserted the slave-holding James Manigault, "but they pay other nations the compliment of inviting them to assist at the entertainment"[9]—or become a victim of same.

The takeover of the vast Louisiana Territory, which still contained masses of antagonists of the slave-holding republic of various means, also provided plenty of opportunity for the enslaved to direct mischievousness. As early as 1801, Governor Winthrop Sargent in the Mississippi Territory, addressing militia men, warned them that it was "more than probable" that soon "there will be more Blacks than Whites" where he ruled since "they can never forgive . . . that we deprive them of the sacred Boon of Liberty." He knew that "European"or "even Indian Power[s]

. . . irresistibly stimulated to Vengeance"would assist the enslaved. His approach then was to "impress [upon] the Negroes that we are never off our Guard."[10] The dilemma for the governor was that among the most prominent new arrivals in Vicksburg, Mississippi, were the Morancy family from Hispaniola, who barely escaped being massacred on the island and whose allegiances—despite their pro-slavery attitude—were uncertain.[11]

The island revolution, as Philadelphia demonstrated and Louisiana showed thereafter, was a beacon of inspiration for mainland Africans, reinforcing the idea that they were far from alone and, similarly important, they could prevail.

JUST BEFORE THIS COMBATIVE MANIFESTATION in Philadelphia, Tobias Lear recounted to his superiors what was occurring on the island. He had arrived there in May 1801 as a commercial agent but was greeted rudely on 22 October when—as he recalled—"an insurrection of the blacks took place; the object of which was to destroy all the white inhabitants of the island," which "spread universal terror and dismay among the whites." A "scene of destruction" unfolded, "which is too well known to be described"—which was accurate in that mainland journals had shaken their many readers with these tales of tribulation. Despite his attempt to establish warm relations with the revolutionary leadership, "the house of your memorialist was burnt in common with others and every article of furniture and other things to a considerable amount belonging to your memorialist was plundered or destroyed." Now he requested "indemnification" for his losses but such claims, which often went unfulfilled, were to complicate bilateral relations between mainland and island for decades to come.[12] Lear, closely associated with George Washington himself and a graduate of Harvard besides, also served the republic in Algiers and negotiated peace with Tripoli, but would have been excused if he had asserted that Hispaniola was his most troublesome assignment.[13]

Actually, Lear may have considered himself lucky to escape with his scalp intact. His memorial was prepared in 1803 and by the next year, the island leadership was being accused of rounding up settlers of various stripes—then executing them en masse.[14] When a popular mainland newspaper blared the headline—"Massacre of All Whites at Cape François"[15]—the question was if mainlanders had become inured and accustomed to such news from the island or whether they would finally be compelled to understand that the slave system was decomposing, perhaps even on the mainland itself. An early historian of the era argued in 1803 that "crews of Mulattoes and Negroes" were "let loose in St. Domingo by the frenzy of Jacobinism" and "committed great spoliations." A debate ensued in Jamaica concerning abolition as a direct result.[16]

The problem for those now operating from the new capital city, Washington, was that, even though it was mostly French settlers that were being slaughtered, strict solidarity with Paris remained more aspiration than reality. In fact, both London and Washington had reason to become anxious when it was also reported disconsolately in 1804 that on the similarly vexed island of Dominica that "many of the original inhabitants remain and . . . French seems still the prevailing language among the Negroes and people of colour."[17] Would dominoes begin to collapse from there leading northward to Antigua, then Cuba—then the mainland—perhaps inspired by a crafty Paris more interested in national grandeur than class and "race" solidarity? Not reassuring were the words of a self-described "French Counselor" who in Philadelphia derided the United States—in English: "they call themselves 'free,'" he spat out, "yet a fifth of their number are slaves. That proportion of the whole people are ground by a yoke more dreadful and debasing than the predial servitude of Poland and Russia."[18]

Fortunately for Washington, in the beginning of the 19th century, France was tied down in a round-robin of wars—against Austria, Prussia, Great Britain, the Dutch Republic, Spain, and Russia—giving the United States a desired breathing space. Napoleon Bonaparte—as he reeled from pulverizing Haitian blows—hardly had time for confrontations in the Americas.[19] This did not spare the Corsican from verbal harpoons from the mainland, such as those launched by the influential Carolinian, George Izard in 1807.[20]

Yet Peter Chazotte, writing from New York years later, recalled that as Haiti was emerging as an independent republic, it was the "Machiavellian and perfidious policy" of London that was responsible for the "horrors" of the island. This was part of a plan of "kindling the fire for a universal war" against the slave-holding republic. In 1804, he said, "the whole white population of Aux Cayes had been massacred and . . . Dessalines was on his way to Jeremie to visit that city with the same horrible deeds of carnage." When the imposing Dessalines arrived, "he surveyed the white people with the ferocious eyes of a famished tiger." Dessalines reportedly growled: "you white men of Jeremie, I know you hate me. I know you hated the law that made black men free." With emphasis he added, *the blood of you all should pay for* [this] *treacherous conduct!*" The shaken Chazotte thought Dessalines "had worked himself up to the extreme of a maniac's fury; his eyes were blood red" as "1436 white men" stared terrified, as the Haitian leader, in a "voice resembling the howling of famished wolf," said jail them promptly.

Chazotte also made note of a European woman who was told by a "mulatto" that "if she would listen to his proposals," he would spare her spouse. She submitted to his lascivious desires; her spouse was killed anyway. "Horrible! Horrible!"

said Chazotte, an observer who spoke frankly of his "former slaves." Chazotte knew from "authentic sources" of proposals by black officers to "young and handsome white females, to save their lives if they would consent to wed them," but "most all preferred death to such ignominy." Nonetheless, "the massacre of all the white women and children" was "ordered." Then "on the day appointed for this last and general extermination, those females who were supposed to have money were made prizes of by the officers and the rest were abandoned to the unrul[y] fury and brutish passions of the soldiery."

Chazotte also espied "four hundred white men, quite naked, dragged forcibly on the rough stones by soldiers. . . . I saw several fine and well brought up colored young men," he recalled, who "to save their own lives, were forced to plunge their swords in those whom they used to call by endearing names," like "father, brothers, uncles, friends." The distraught Chazotte "hid my eyes with my hands. I looked again; I saw the blood gushing out of the inflicted wounds. I could see no longer; I fainted and fell." When he shook himself out of his torpor, he saw "many corpses, besmeared with gore," a veritable "slaughter house of human bodies . . . upwards of 1400 corpses lay, heaped one upon another."

The fazed Chazotte had the nerve to confront the now reigning Black Jacobin— Dessalines, who "was undressed and wrapped in a morning gown and seated on a sofa." Agape, Chazotte "felt some rather strong pulsations in my heart." The leader allegedly said he was simply avenging the outrages of Bonaparte. Still, "not one single French white inhabitant remained . . . alive" and "those atrocious slaughters were advised, directed, and witnessed by the agents of the British Society for the Emancipation" of the enslaved. The purpose? "The ultimate object of the promulgation of this deceitful philanthropy," he offered with a shriek, was "to strike at, undermine, and impede the growing colossal march to power of the United States." This "blood doctrine," he proclaimed, "must cause the dissolution of the Union and as in St. Domingo the destruction of the white population, the desolation and entire subversion of the slave-holding states, which now furnish three fourths of the productive wealth of the whole nation." The British backed the other leading Black Jacobin, the English-speaking General Christophe, who by himself was responsible for "hanging three American citizens." As for Chazotte, like many of his then readers, this entire episode "so strongly excite[d] his indignation as to make him abhor even the sight of a Negro."[21]

Even if contemporary readers dismiss the veracity of Chazotte's overheated words, it is likely that slave-holding republicans did not. He helped to imprint in the consciousness of many mainlanders the idea of a British-Haitian alliance against U.S. slavery—an idea not without a scintilla of truth, which gave Chazotte's impassioned words added resonance. The lurid bloodthirstiness of the Black Jacobins that he depicted helped to undergird U.S. slavery—for if abolition produced such results, it would be foolhardy to take this dangerous path. This depiction also served to justify ever more brutal exploitation of mainland Africans. His anguished portrayal of ("white") damsels in distress was bound to excite emotions furiously. The reality was that giving sustenance to Chazotte's dark vision was the continuing arrival on mainland shores of disarranged and unkempt but once mighty settlers from Hispaniola.

Overall, Chazotte views reflected the historical consensus on Haiti—at least by Euro-Americans—which insured a rocky road ahead for island revolutionaries. For even before Chazotte, yet another New York-based historian painted an awful portrait of the Haitian Revolution, noting, in what is probably his mildest assessment, that "human blood was poured forth in torrents" during "this terrible war." "Within two months after the revolt first began, upwards of two thousand white persons of all conditions and ages had been massacred" and "one thousand two hundred Christian families reduced from opulence to such a state of misery as to depend altogether for their clothing and sustenance on public and private charity."[22] Literate mainland observers may have been excused if they thought the official name of Haiti—or Hayti—was "horrors."[23]

The "value" of such histories was that they rationalized the setback to white supremacy brought by the Haitian Revolution by blaming "Perfidious Albion" while portraying an uncommon, almost inhuman, outburst of cutthroat bloodiness by Africans, which again ratified supposed Negro Inhumanity—and justified enslavement.

The problem for the profoundly anti-Haitian and anti-British scenario of Chazotte and others was that—in the immediate sense—New Orleans and the Pan-Caribbean basin were not easy for the mainland republicans to engage, given the unfriendliness of a proliferating number of powers, who could easily collaborate with revenge seeking Africans. Even if Chazotte proved to be paranoid, the fact was that the slave-holding republicans had real enemies.

For during this chaotic era, even Britain contemplated taking New Orleans, which would have been a punishing blow for the slave-holding republic—even if unsuccessful.[24] But London would have had to stand in line for the local governor there carped not long after taking the reins of power from France that "hostilities" with Spain were imminent, with Madrid's "agents" calculating on a "speedy rupture."[25] The governor was not hallucinating for thereafter yet another source argued that the "principal Spanish officers are intriguing with the Indians, with views hostile to the United States" and collaborating with "some of the Indian chiefs, particularly the Choctaws" who were receiving from these Madrid agents a "considerable quality of military stores."[26]

It was Pierre M'Callum who confided, "I had the honour of being at the Court of the ill-fated Toussaint L'ouverture," before the Black Jacobin was illicitly captured by French forces and bundled off to Europe. Writing from Liverpool, he was in Trinidad shortly thereafter and was disturbed by what he saw. "There are two Negro Regiments stationed there," he recalled in 1805, "comprised of Negroes taken from the French colonies and commanded by French officers. The arming and training of so many of these hirelings," he wrote with grave concern, "after the mournful scenes and horrid barbarities of their committing we have witnessed in St. Domingo is surely not the prudent dictates of wisdom." He wondered "what tie is there to bind a black hireling to be faithful to his duty?" "The late ferocity of one of the Negro Corps in Dominica where they murdered their officers (mostly British, I believe) is a striking presage of their conduct." The distressed observer was clear: "I tremble for the fate of the colonies, if the evil is not removed, especially as the island of St. Domingo" was a role model and the hired guns "do not know the meaning of loyalty." Like others in the hemisphere, he demanded more of a "white population," but the package offered by the slave-holding republic was sufficiently inducing to gain a stranglehold on this precious grouping. He predicted that if this did not occur, Jamaica would be attacked from an independent Haiti. In "several conversations I had with General Christophe," a successor of General Toussaint, he "told me" of a plan to "send some small vessels to Jamaica to take away slaves who were willing to embrace freedom." The Haitian plan to "import emigrants (for he always avoided the term Negro) from Africa" was a "danger to the planters of Jamaica" too.[27]

The wider point is that Jefferson's dystopian fear of Africans taking control of the Caribbean as a prelude to a wider hemispheric domination did not seem like fantasy in the early 19th century.

London—and to a degree the United States too—was in a bind since there seemed to be a perpetual deficit of "whites" to overawe Africans, so that Chazotte's nightmare vision would not materialize. But London could appeal to the *gens de couleur*, now fleeing hither and yon from Haiti, in a way that exceeded the response of the slave-holding republicans, and which placed pressure on the latter to do the same. This only increased conflict on the mainland.[28] Haiti could pressure this group while Britain could embrace them, providing a combination of punches that left the slave-holding republicans woozy.

Predictably the decibel level of voices demanding abolition intensified in London. "The late changes in St. Domingo," said one Londoner, "and the continuance of the Slave Trade" needed to be conjoined, particularly when considering "the two important islands of Jamaica and Barbados," which "contain nearly three fourths of the . . . slaves in the British colonies." The "insurrection" in Haiti was "the natural consequence of the Negro importation" and the revolt was bound to direct attention to "the proud superiority" of Jamaican "free brethren on the opposite shore." The remaining remedy was evident: "when the enemy's forces are besieging you, is it prudent to excite mutiny in your garrison and to admit into the heart of your fortress the best allies that your enemy has?" Haiti showed that continuing the African Slave Trade "for another hour" was "worse than insanity." The "planters have now to chuse [sic] between the surrender of the Slave Trade and the sacrifice of their possessions." As for the United States, which sought to circumvent this dilemma by moving toward "breeding" Africans in Virginia, underscoring their "obedient conduct during the whole of the St. Domingo Revolution,"[29] it would be swept up in the African whirlwind nonetheless. This was not the conclusion reached in the slave-holding republic; instead, the decision was made to ride the tiger of slavery, replace London as the kingpin of flesh peddling—then reap the whirlwind with hundreds of thousands of dead in the 1860s Civil War.

Creative artists were reflecting and responding to this Londoner's grave admonitions. Heed Haiti or face certain death was the grim message. "Let Domingo's fate give warning ere it prove too late" was the word from 1805 by a U.S. national, with the emphasized coda: *Death to the Monster, Slavery.*" Before then, New Yorker William Foster asserted that "Equality has forc'd her way . . . . And drench'd their native hills with blood!" As well, the celebrated William Wordsworth addressed General Toussaint directly in fulsome praise.[30]

To be sure, there was nervous apprehension about continuing the African slave trade on the mainland. However, like hopelessly hooked addicts, the presumed euphoric profits were too extravagant to reject. As early as December 1802, there was a bill debated in South Carolina to reopen the odious commerce "from any part of the world, except the French West India islands," but it was defeated. In North Carolina opposition to the foreign slave trade centered around a like fear of Haitian inspired revolt. Interestingly, one of the key agents in Charleston importing Africans was the French surnamed Francis Depau.[31]

THE ATTEMPTED CHOKING OF SUPPLY gave rise to predictable complaints, virtually guaranteeing that smugglers of Africans would surge to the forefront. "Africans being so excessive[ly] high at present," groused David Fleming in Carolina in 1806, "in my opinion it would be the height of extravagance to think of purchasing just now."[32] The inquietude brought by Africans, particularly those who had revolted successfully, was reflected that same year when another Carolinian announced both wistfully and anxiously, "I hope your fears with respect to the Yanke[e]s setting [our] slaves against us will never be realized."[33]

Across the border in Wilmington, North Carolina, the official apprehension was directed at the arrival of Africans from Guadeloupe and the perception that there was "much danger to the peace and safety of the Southern States of the Union" as a result.[34] There was a general fear of "French Negroes" arising and two spooked Congressmen near the same time sought to ban the importation of Africans to Louisiana because they feared that "our slaves in the South will produce another St. Domingo."[35]

Similarly, in the interregnum between the end of French rule in Louisiana and the U.S. takeover, vessels were delivering hundreds of enslaved Africans and the designated U.S. governor did not seek to halt this commerce—though by March 1804 a measure was passed designed to curtail this traffic. But since most U.S. nationals complained bitterly about this measure, restrictions were unlikely to be effective—though Governor William C. C. Claiborne warned that the result could be another Haitian revolt.[36] Governor Claiborne felt himself trapped in a contradiction in that—as he put it—"the citizens of Louisiana are greatly apprehensive of the West India Negroes" but nothing could be done to halt their influx.[37] Another U.S. official of that time, James Watkins, felt that no subject was as important to citizens there than importing more Africans[38]—even from Hispaniola.

However, the U.S. Congress passed a law, signed by President Jefferson on 25 February 1806, prohibiting trade between the United States and Haiti that was renewed in 1807 to be effective until 1809. This measure backfired in that it allowed Britain to gain a good deal of trade that previously was controlled by the mainland, meaning the United States—though eventually developing a robust trade with the island—could have been even more successful. Albert Gallatin, a ranking U.S. official, conceded that this bill was enacted due to the "apprehension of the danger which at the time (immediately after the last massacre of the whites there) might on account of our numerous slaves, arise from an unrestricted intercourse with the black population of that island."[39] But again there was no unanimity on this bedrock issue, as Senator Samuel White of Delaware complained that "so extensive and valuable has our trade become in the West Indian seas, that it has excited and is daily increasing the jealousies of other nations."[40] In any event, mainlanders being masters of smuggling could easily defy such a ban.

This was another aspect of the conflicted U.S. relationship with Haiti. For it was well recognized in Washington that France could hardly regain control of Louisiana without reclaiming Haiti: this permitted U.S. merchants to send arms and ammunition southward, but this also raised the possibility that these rifles could then be pointed northward.[41]

Paris was staggered by this hypocrisy and shortsightedness of the slave-holding republic. "It was not enough," sputtered General Louis Marie Turreau, "for some citizens of the United States to convey munitions of every kind to the rebels of St. Domingo, to that race of African slaves, the reproach and the refuse of nature"—but provisions too?[42] Charles Talleyrand, likewise incensed, denounced the shipping of "objects of supply" and dismissed the idea that the federal government could "separate itself from the inhabitants of the United States" by arguing this was a matter that concerned only Carolina or Virginia—and not Washington. How could this be "when there is a question [of] unparalleled revolt, whose circumstances and whose horrible consequences must alarm all nations."[43] The leading French diplomat was irate, asserting that "the existence of an armed Negro people, occupying places that they have despoiled by the most criminal acts, is a horrible spectacle for all the white nations; all of them should feel that by allowing them to continue in that state, they are sparing incendiaries and assassins."[44] There were those in the southern quadrant of the mainland who shared Talleyrand's unease, heightening sectional tensions at a fraught moment.

Paris and Dixie had a point. Though the slave-holding republic condemned a Norfolk ship together with its cargo for allegedly trading with the revolutionaries in 1803, the larger point was that irrespective of stated policy, there was a praxis that was hard to squelch.[45] By 1805 Madison was incensed that the French, with a continuing foothold in Haitian waters, pledged to inflict "*death*" on "all persons on board vessels allied as well as neutral, bound to or *from* ports occupied by the blacks, *or* found within two leagues of any such port; and the trial in those cases is to be by *military commission*."[46] This deterred but did not squelch mutually profitable trade—though the Louisiana Purchase's consummation made it easier to accommodate Paris's wishes to the detriment of Haiti.

There were also those in Dixie who were disquieted by the influx of *gens de couleur*, though these were often class comrades quite comfortable with the project of enslaving Africans. Among them was a European gentleman, deported from New Orleans to France in 1803, who then returned to Manhattan by 1804. He despised *gens de couleur*, particularly those with an African mother and a European father since "in general all these creatures have a sovereign contempt for their mothers especially when the latter are black." Referring to "San Domingo" he recounted an episode which "horrifies the soul": the "Negress" often cuckolds the spouse and in this case the latter opted to sell her. "All mulatto women," he opined, "whether in Louisiana or elsewhere, have alike a sovereign contempt for their Negro mothers." He was gleeful that on the island "the whites and the blacks have in great part put them to death," meaning *gens de couleur*, since "they merited that terrible punishment."[47]

He was reflecting an attitude still murderously resentful toward this group for supposedly being the cause of the transformative events flowing from August 1791. Moreover, enslaving or at least oppressing them terribly on the mainland could be seen as a fitting punishment and widening the base of lucrative exploitation besides. At times, Dixie did not distinguish between Free Negroes and the overlapping category of *gens de couleur* and adopted rigid measures to expel both.[48]

For as one former French official put it, the island "was of all our colonies in the Antilles, the one whose mentality and customs influenced Louisiana the most" since "frequent intercourse existed between the two." And thus when settlers depicted as "white" and *gens de couleur* arrived in New Orleans, they often brought their island conflict with them. Moreover, as this official put it in November 1803, "one meets many former settlers from there who had been given shelter in Louisiana" and, "who, as a general rule, show neither affection nor kindness toward the blacks"[49]— which was somewhat understandable given the fire through which they had walked only recently. Yet delivering such noisomeness to a mainland that already had exceeded its quota, was bound to incite passions further.

By January 1804, the U.S. Secretary of War was told frantically that the "jealousies of the People of Colour & the Whites seem to be increasing," but, said James Wilkinson, "the former are most to be relied on by us for they universally mounted the Eagle in their Hats & avow their attachment to the United States" while the "latter" (mostly French and Spanish) "still demonstrate their love for the Mother Country and do not conceal the fond Hope, that some incident" would cause an erosion of U.S. influence. "The People of Colour are all armed," he noted, "and it [is] my Opinion, a single envious artful bold incendiary, by rousing their fears & exciting their Hopes, might produce those Horrible Scenes of Bloodshed & rapine, which have been so frequently noticed in St. Domingo."[50] The problem was that, though *gens de couleur* may have supported the United States, they were not seen as possessing the correct coloration.

Governor Claiborne also found a strong pro-Paris trend in his jurisdiction, which compromised security, but relying upon militia comprised of *gens de couleur*—presumably more loyal—was a non-starter. Though he was more aware than most of the unviable security situation faced in New Orleans, he too was skeptical of *gens de couleur*, associating them with privateering.[51] The problem was that discriminating against the *gens de couleur*—which inevitably followed—compromised security accordingly and with the growing importation of Africans was creating the basis for another Haitian-style revolt, which arrived accordingly in 1811.[52]

The question of what to do with the *gens de couleur* and the overlapping categories of "Mulattoes" and "Free People of Color" was a vexing issue for the slave-holding republic. There was a real fear that the preexisting policy of relentless oppression would create another Haitian-style revolt, but the history of the republic had provided few other options. Writing from Paris, Charles-Cesar Robin argued that the republic should be more forthcoming toward this group, rather than run the risk of driving them into the arms of the darker-skinned.[53]

The problem for such rancid attitudes was that in 1804 federal rule of Louisiana was tenuous with French settlers of uncertain allegiances continuing to arrive. On one day in April of that year, Madison was told that their "total apparently increases" with just then a "vessel with one hundred and fifty passengers" being "now in the river." Governor Claiborne added, "I fear a majority of them will be useless"[54]— though not apparently so for Paris's purposes.

Then the governor found that a "meeting of the Free People of Color . . . occasioned an inquietude among the white inhabitants," as the "Municipality of New Orleans expressed a wish that I should punish the Mulatto man" in charge of such organizing. However, Claiborne was reluctant since "in a country where the Negro population was so great the Less noise that was made about this occurrence the better." What did he mean? "I remembered," he said strikingly, "that the events which have spread blood and desolation in St. Domingo, originated in a dispute between the white and Mulatto inhabitants and that the too rigid treatment [by] the former, induced the Latter to seek the support & assistance of the Negroes." For the time being, he cautioned Madison, "I am well assured there is nothing to fear either from the Mulatto or Negro population—but at some future period," he added knowingly, "this quarter of the Union must (I fear) experience in some degree, the Misfortunes of St. Domingo and that *period* will be hastened if the people should be indulged by Congress with a continuance of the African Trade."

In short, one lesson of Haiti—intermittently realized *ab initio*—was the necessity of not replenishing the ranks of potential African combatants by flooding the zone of conflict with their presence. "African Negroes are thought here not to be dangerous," Claiborne clarified unsteadily, "but it ought to be recollected that those of St. Domingo were originally from Africa and that Slavery wherever it exists is a galling yoke." So he was adamant about the need to "prevent the bringing in of Slaves that have been concerned in the insurrection of St. Domingo," but he also knew that halting their arrival was futile.[55] "I am particularly desirous," said the governor days later, "to exclude those Slaves who (from Late habits) are accustomed to blood and devastation and whose counsel & communication with our present Black population may be pregnant with much future Mischief."[56]

It was evident that, in the early days of U.S. rule, Governor Claiborne was fearful that somehow Haitians would either inspire the enslaved to revolt—or lead it themselves. The "brigands from St. Domingo or the refuse of the Negroes of the West India islands" were his adamant preoccupation and already there were "many dangerous Characters" in his neighborhood.[57]

In sum, it was not only enslaved Africans that the authorities had to monitor. For soon Claiborne was alert to the presence of "dangerous Negroes" in the vicinity, i.e. "some of the Brigands from St. Domingo" who "landed below Plaquemine and [were] introduced Clandestinely into this City." The ubiquitous Hand of Haiti was suspected, particularly when "of late many Negroes of this City have escaped from the service of their Masters and the general opinion seems to be that they are secreted in vessels going to Sea," occasioning significant losses for slavery.[58] Just before then, Claiborne was told by a sea captain that "18 or 19" of his crew had "left him, several of which were Negroes from St. Domingo."[59] (It was not just the governor who kept a wary eye on unwelcome arrivals from Hispaniola. The Frenchman Pierre Clement Laussat did so too, warning about the arrival of seafarers from there and demanding that they be denied any contact with local Africans.[60])

By November 1804, the governor was losing whatever composure he held. "The late admission of foreign Negroes," he informed Jefferson, "has also been a Subject of Complaint against me." However, the "Searcher of all Hearts knows, how little I desire to see Another of that wretched Race, set his foot on the Shores of America!" What was involved was old news: hypocrisy. For "the People here have United as one man!" They insisted, he stressed, that "they must import more Slaves"[61] His reminders about the "Horrors of St. Domingo" fell on deaf ears.[62]

Predictably, a few months after the governor's remonstration, he received a petition from "Inhabitants & colonists" worriedly noting the "existence of a plot" by the "Slaves of this city," leading to a "fear" that this region was "prey to the same Events which have laid waste the French colonies & particularly the Proud and rich colony of San Domingo."[63] By the summer of 1805, a Frenchman known as "Le Grand" or "Grand Jean" was supposedly instigating an insurrection, reifying Claiborne's worst fears as he planned to enlist aid—it was reported—from *gens de couleur* and the Africans. Reputedly he planned to slay all those defined as "white."[64]

Claiborne, who was unable to speak French, was disadvantaged at a time of sharp contestation between (mostly) English-speaking U.S. nationals and those with roots in France.[65]

The response in Louisiana was draconian. Shortly after the U.S. takeover, a code was adopted to govern slaves. Its chief drafter—Louis Casimir Elisabeth Moreau Lislet—was a refugee from a Hispaniola slave-holding family. This new law was a broad retrenchment from earlier laws, particularly in terms of toughening requirements for manumission. Under the guise of separating church and state, these "Black Codes" eroded rights to baptism and marriage within the Church for the enslaved. There was an intense focus on public safety reflecting a society on high alert, guarding against the danger of uprisings. For the first time a special court was devised to handle slave crimes and there was also wider reliance upon the citizen as informer and vigilante—a U.S. trademark—which helped to enlist even non-slaveholders in defense of the peculiar institution. *Gens de couleur* were targeted in new discriminatory ways. As one recent historian observes, "in the wake of the Haitian rebellion free people of color were increasingly seen as natural allies of slaves and as potential leaders of slave revolts."[66] According to another recent historian, "it was the first modern code anywhere that contained such [draconian] provisions."[67] With the fear of France reduced, mainlanders were less queasy about cracking down on *gens de couleur* and, as one observer put it, this antipathy "conditioned the attitudes of Louisianans toward any Negro regardless of color from that island for the next half century."[68]

The drafter had an excuse: for worrisome to Washington was the report discussed by Monroe and Madison that the island revolutionaries were offering a "reward of 40 [dollars] to the commanders of our vessels for every one of its blacks now in the U. States whom they may bring back to the island." Quite wisely, Monroe concluded that "this is probably" a "policy intended to increase their strength to enable them to make a better resistance hereafter." This was not only incentivizing mainland Africans to reach the island by any means necessary but also capitalizing upon the mercantile instincts of ship commanders as well.[69] Yet mainland Africans required few incentives to fight—or resort to flight. By August 1804 in recently acquired Missouri, serious unrest was reported among the enslaved.[70]

Mainland leaders were so concerned about the real and imagined threat from Haiti that some of them too sought to expel a number of U.S. Negroes, which served to implant the idea that they should, perhaps, accept the island's invitation to migrate there. By late 1804, Jefferson again had returned to a preoccupation: ridding his republic of this troublesome population—perhaps "beyond the Mississippi," perhaps to the British colony of Sierra Leone, unwise in that it would bolster a continuing antagonist. "I will keep it under my constant attention," he said, an indication of his priorities.[71]

This was "delicate business," replied Governor John Page of Virginia, this matter of "desired asylum for Free Negroes and Mulattoes," who numbered "at least 19,000." A "distant country" was the preferred option—but where? He also wanted the "purchase, removal, and education of young slaves," which only complicated an already complex problem. Perhaps "St. Domingo" was the optimal site but that depended on Paris's recognition of Haiti as "free and independent," which was not then in the cards. This "perplexing subject," he instructed Jefferson in a "confidential" missive, had to be "discuss[ed] fully in a free conversation."[72]

By repelling Africans of whatever status and refusing to allow *gens de couleur* to return to the exalted status they once enjoyed in Haiti, the slave-holding republic was bestowing a gift to London, which then reaped dividends during the 1812 war.[73] It was in 1805 when Alice Izard, member of a prominent slave-holding family in Carolina, was in a tizzy about a "French gentleman formerly an Abbé, who is married to a Negresse, as black as ink & as fat as possible." Yes, he was "very polite & dressed very fine," but it was inescapable that "she is not visited by anybody"—and that their children would endure a worse fate,[74] not least because the Frenchman in question was said to be favorable toward General Toussaint.[75] His not being able to return to the island where he had many assets and possessions was also not held in his favor.[76] Ms. Izard, in her defense, could argue that she was sweeping in her bigotry—not targeting those with African ancestry alone—as she spoke of Irish migrants disparagingly as "poor wretches!"[77] Of course, many of these despised Irish would have been more than willing to oppose London, whose cruisers would soon be bombarding mainland shores.

Still, there was an abolitionist celebration on the mainland in 1808 when the hated African slave trade was outlawed—officially.[78] The historian, David Brion Davis argues that the "Haitian Revolution strengthened the political argument" for this epochal decision, though it is also true that expert mainland smugglers and entrepreneurs hardly ceased in dragging enchained Africans to Cuba and Brazil in coming years, where they quickly claimed leadership in this commerce of opprobrium.[79] Nonetheless, it remains noteworthy that the island revolt spared a countless number of Africans from the violent drudgery of enslavement while hastening the day when those entrapped in this hellish system would find liberation. To that end, it was also in 1808 that the antislavery "Angola Beneficial Society" was started in Philadelphia.[80]

As was the case generally during this era of insurgency, London set an example for its former colony to follow. It was in 1807 that the abolitionist James Stephen fretted about the "possible calamity" of "our falling under the yoke of France" and thus posited that a British-Haitian entente would be a fitting response, along with "immediate Abolition of the Slave Trade." This iniquity caused "mischief" and "evils" and was a "ruinous waste of our national wealth." He moaned about the "bankruptcies among our merchants and the losses among our manufacturers produced by the Slave Trade and by West India speculations in new lands" targeted for slavery. "War alas is now becoming a perennial evil," as this phenomenon stoked in Africa lubricated the path for slave sales, while competition among the powers for control of this commerce stoked even more conflict. This was happening though "sugar planting has long been, on an average, a losing business" and all this madness brings "danger in these colonies" besides. What was there to like?[81]

Hence, seeing this welcome 1808 ban as wholly an outgrowth of domestic progressivism would be an error—unless this progressive thinking is viewed globally, i.e. as an outgrowth of the Haitian Revolution, the growing strength of British abolitionism (where this trade was banned in 1807), and the linkage between the two. For to the contrary, the mainland continued to attract a vast array of disreputable refugees fleeing abolition in Haiti. This growing roster included Francesco Richard, a native of Florence, Italy, who wed Genevieve Bianna of French origin—she had barely escaped revolutionary justice in Haiti. By 1807 the two were controlling a plantation in Florida—soon to be under U.S. rule. There was also Francois-Didier Petit de Villers, a native of Lorraine province in France, who too barely eluded island revolutionaries before leaping to Philadelphia, then Savannah, and then Baltimore—where he too attained prominence.[82]

Such mainland denizens virtually guaranteed that the road to diplomatic recognition of Haiti would be difficult, given the continuing resentment toward the island harbored by so many refugees and, likewise, the related point that abolition would be associated in their minds—and that of others—with blood-red revolt. Indeed, two years after the official ban of this awful trade, an abolitionist confab in London concluded that "the persons" who are "by far the most deeply engaged in this nefarious traffic appear to be citizens" of the slave-holding republic. Four years after the ban abolitionists conferring in Trenton expressed "sorrow" and "shame" since "no meetings were held." There was an "abatement of zeal among the members in this state" since "generally speaking, the slaves in this state are clothed and fed decently and comfortably," while "too many of the free people of color do not exhibit that industry, economy, and temperance that was expected by many and wished by all."[83] And these were the "abolitionists" speaking. As was to be the case until the attack on Fort Sumter in 1861, abolitionism on the mainland was driven by external events—principally those engineered by Britain and Haiti.

These French refugees honored those on the mainland who rescued them from the clutches of revolutionaries, which helped to engrave the idea of their mutual dependence in a fight to the death with Africans. Eliza Boudinot was one of "2400," who Duncan McIntosh served as a "benefactor." At an elaborate ceremony in Baltimore in 1810 a grateful covey of refugees crowned McIntosh with a wreath of laurels and white satin on which was written in letters of gold, "the savior" of those rescued from Hispaniola. The grand swell of music and a cacophonous clapping of hands greeted him. "There was scarcely a dry eye in the room," according to Ms. Boudinot, as he was serenaded by a young girl "whom he had saved." A painting was also presented to him in gratitude. In this work, the now lost colony is symbolically represented by the figure of a woman described as "white," who, pressing two affrighted infants to her bosom, is rescued by a tutelary angel from the jaws of a monster described as "half Negro and half tiger." This was followed by the "most magnificent dinner you ever saw," which too was symbolic in its own way.[84]

Somehow, as hundreds awaited certain doom, McIntosh wielding "large sums of money," according to one escapee, "bribed the keepers and affected" an escape.[85] The ampler point was that those feasting had reason to pillory Haiti and resist vigorously any tentative steps toward normalizing relations with the island.

McIntosh became a kind of folk hero in France, a living symbol that slavery and colonialism could survive because of the heroism of those like him. The French legation in the United States requested that Paris assist this now suffering U.S. businessman then still residing on the island. He had lost all of his once substantial fortune but in compensation his story had also been spread throughout Europe, buoying those who might have had doubts about slavery and colonialism.[86] "In the darkest period in which crimes were committed in the colonies," it was said, McIntosh acted. "There was this man in Saint-Domingue, stranger to our country who had the courage to revenge the humanity for so many troubles and ignominy." He was rich. Now he is poor. He gave his gold in exchange for the lifeblood of France.[87] This was also a story that could easily strike a chord among Euro-Americans, bonding them further to slavery and settler colonialism.

Other mainland denizens emulated McIntosh. It was in July 1808 that Jacob Hart of New Orleans advertised three island Africans for sale, including a woman cook and two fishermen.[88] By 1809 there were so many refugees and enslaved persons arriving in New Orleans from Cuba by way of Hispaniola that at that time the population of that town was scarcely larger than the 10,000 arriving from the island itself.[89] About 10% of the enslaved Africans in the 1810 census in the Territory of Orleans were imported by Hispaniola planters who had fled to Cuba and were expelled from there in 1809.[90]

Their numbers were also filling another void: for after becoming a major sugar producer by the time of this latter arrival, Haiti's production had dropped precipitously so that by 1823 it was recorded as not providing a single ton with Cuba, Brazil—and especially Louisiana—assuming the pole position.[91]

Yet the increase in the population with island roots exacerbated the concern that the *gens de couleur* would duplicate in Louisiana what they had purportedly done in Hispaniola: ally with Africans to bring down the slave system. By the summer of 1809, New Orleans' mayor was eyeballing suspiciously "a few characters among the Free People of Color" who "have been presented to me as dangerous for the peace of this territory."[92] The concern about the threat from Haiti skyrocketed when a few days later a mariner commanding a vessel from Haiti—Jean Marie Arbeau—was arrested on a charge of piracy off the coast of New Orleans,[93] reminding those who had forgotten about Jefferson's caustic prediction that the island could easily become an "American Algiers." The "occasional discovery of Free Negroes" on the Gulf Coast, says one analyst, "who had fought on the rebel side" in Hispaniola "did nothing to assuage white anxiety" on the mainland, particularly since "southern whites were well aware that unrest among the Free People of Color had triggered the revolt which eventually established the Haitian Republic and they worried about restlessness among their own growing free black population."[94]

In short, Washington's rule in New Orleans was far from firm in 1809, but this was the time when the authorities chose to embark on a witchhunt, focused on those who supposedly had collaborated with island revolutionaries before arriving in Louisiana.[95] The parish priest in Point Coupee, still on edge because of the 1795 slave revolt, accused one prominent refugee of "traitorous" activity during the island war. His accusers launched a double-barreled assault, alleging that not only was he of African descent but also that his spouse was a "quadroon,"[96] as the heedless baiting of *gens de couleur* continued unabated.

Peter Dormenon was slated for punishment, accused of having "headed, aided, and assisted the Negroes of St. Domingo in their horrible massacres and other outrages against the whites, in and about the year of 1793." Was he not "a municipal officer" in that pivotal year "when the general freedom of the slaves was proclaimed? This Mr. Dormenon admits," said a Louisiana jurist. "It is proved also, that in that character, wearing a scarf, his badge of office, he marched at the heads of the brigands, whose sole purpose and employment was the indiscriminate murder and massacre of the whites who refused to conform to the orders" of his superiors. This was "unexampled cruelty and barbarity" in "the quarter of Jacmel, Jeremie, and its dependencies." The "safety of this country," it was proclaimed triumphantly, "requires that no person who has acted in concert with the Negroes and mulattoes of St. Domingo in destroying the whites, ought to hold any kind of office here," even as a member of the bar. It was their "duty to exclude him" and, by implication, to exclude peremptorily *gens de couleur* who were painted with the same brush.[97]

Unfortunately, New Orleans was not the only territory with perceived antagonists. As Haiti's sugar production declined, bringing a reduction of revenues, it was forced at the same time to spend more on the military since an abolitionist republic in the midst of slave-holding states was perceived correctly as a dangerously dire threat. There were splits in Hispaniola among the jurisdictions ruled by Haitians— represented by Christophe and Alexandre Pétion—and the eastern and largest portion of the island, which would become the Dominican Republic, ruled variously by Spanish and French colonialists. A visitor in 1810 found that Christophe's "population is the largest," compared to Pétion's—and the east too—and, most importantly, "his troops amount to about 10,000 men. His fleet is also the most numerous and consists of two corvettes, nine brigs, and a few schooners."[98]

Though draining the coffers of funds that could have been devoted profitably to the education of children, it would have been folly for the Haitian leadership to give military defense short shrift. In 1807 when a major plot emerged in Martinique to poison dozens of the wealthiest planters and, for good measure, assassinate a number of plantation managers, Haiti was suspected. A few years later there was angst about the possibility of a Pan-Caribbean revolt and it would have been understandable if the abolitionist republic had been fingered as a suspect since the very existence of Haiti was wholly incompatible with the slave-holding status quo. Then a female slave was boiled alive there for attempting to poison the mother of the former Empress Josephine. News of such terrifying events often reached the mainland, particularly since the local elite often educated their sons in the United States.[99]

And just as U.S. nationals had held substantial investments in Hispaniola, the same held true in other islands. In 1809 Carolinian George Izard arrived in Havana in the midst of a slave revolt. "You will probably in Charleston have [an] inundation of those worthy Creoles," fleeing in panic, as had happened in Hispaniola, it was said.[100] But those "worthy Creoles," or at least their relatives in Paris, continued to press for "re-establishment of the French Slave Trade," as if the Haitian Revolution carried no dispositive lessons.[101] Near the same time, slave traders in Manhattan— who had plied their ugly trade previously and murderously in Hispaniola—were organizing as if they were mechanics forming a guild, while their salaciously bitter sarcasm betrayed an understandable unease about the future of this profession in light of the Haitian Revolution.[102]

Sardonic musings could not hide the point that the revolution had wounded a lucrative—albeit barbarous—slavery, with the visionary now able to foresee the terminal phase of the entire system. Helping to illuminate this new reality were the frequent hemispheric flames now leaping more regularly at the behest of newly energized Africans. The 1811 revolt in Louisiana, generally viewed as one of the most significant and largest on the mainland, was seen as being stimulated by Haiti, not least since the presumed leaders were viewed as having participated in analogous rebellions in Hispaniola before arriving on the mainland. "Only by the narrowest of margins,"said one astute observer, "had the state escaped a repetition of the brutal and sanguinary scenes which had marked the servile revolt in Hayti."[103] Like a number of revolts of the enslaved, this one too was inspired by the island revolutionaries.[104] Also like many slave revolts, this one too was felt far away, St. Louis in this case,[105] and not surprisingly since the Mississippi River, replete with frequent boat traffic, was linked directly to New Orleans. Punctuating the impact of the island on the mainland was the curious occurrence that the man who ordered the execution by firing squad of the perpetrators of the 1811 rebellion was a refugee from the slave-holding class of Hispaniola.[106]

Feeding the anxiety about cross border plots of Africans was the fact that in the massive 1812 rebellion in Cuba, a key leader—Juan Barbier—had resided previously in Charleston and for a considerable period in Hispaniola. Literate in French, he was also a former leader of the Haitian military, which added weight to the notion that a simultaneous attack from Haiti would be launched in the midst of a slave revolt.[107] Since many enslaved Africans were beginning a decades-long trend of escaping from Cuba and Puerto Rico to the island of freedom, this did little to dampen a deepening dread among hemispheric slaveholders.[108]

Since enslaved Africans were commodities and could be shipped easily from Carolina to Cuba and Barbados,[109] it surely facilitated their ability to raise a ruckus across national borders. In 1812 Lewis Boah betrayed a slave conspiracy in Louisiana and then—presumably because of the blistering outrage of his fellow enslaved—petitioned to move to Virginia. He informed the authorities that on the Gulf Coast the Africans desired a "spectacle of ruin and desolation exceeding anything which formerly transpired in St. Domingo," an island with which he was apparently familiar.[110]

This betrayal, as the date suggests, came at a perilous moment for the slave-holding republic. For it was then that the blunder was made of declaring war on Britain, at a time when Napoleon seemed to have Perfidious Albion on the run. The prize would be Canada, a sanctuary for capital flight—i.e. Africans running away from the United States—perhaps Bermuda too. Weakening the gathering entente between the island of abolition and the Crown also had not evaded Washington's calculations.[111] In response, it was during this war that Haiti flexed its own muscles, imposing harsh duties on U.S. trade and bestowing special privileges on British shipping. The property of U.S. merchants in Haiti was seized as restitution for debts.[112]

In turn, as the *de facto* collaboration with Napoleon suggested, Washington was moving closer to Haiti's eternal foe: Paris. The 1812 war also involved London's collaboration with the indigenes of the North American heartland against the interests of Washington with Indiana being a battlefield. There in Vincennes were numerous French settlers still, remnants from an earlier era, and London's ally, the great indigenous warrior, Tecumseh, was also reported to speak French, suggesting the reach of Paris within the republic.[113] During this same era, it was reported that the Africans of St. Louis all spoke French or, as was tellingly said, "all the inhabitants used French to the Negroes, their horses, and their dogs."[114]

With the flexibility—or opportunism—for which it was becoming renowned, the slave-holding republic detoured temporarily from its hostility toward *gens de couleur* and allowed those from that community, e.g. Joseph Savary, to fight alongside slaveholder and future president Andrew Jackson in rescuing the United States from what seemed to be certain dismemberment.[115] A battalion of 210 men was organized from Savary's community.[116] Savary had earned a distinguished reputation as an officer in the French military during the losing battles in Hispaniola. It was Savary who raised a mighty battalion from among the émigrés from the island, most of whom had fought as loyalists under the French flag. Many were slaveholders themselves. Yet, despite their heroic service, their military units were seen as threatening and were disbanded after they handed the republic a smashing victory over the redcoats.[117]

This ability of the *gens de couleur* to be forgiving and embrace the nation that had rejected them was keenly needed since London took the opportunity of unleashing armed Africans in Louisiana, a strategy guaranteed to be intimidating.[118] "There can be no doubt," Jefferson was made aware, that during this war "the enemy will endeavor to use the black population against us. It is the policy of the British in every part of the globe." The evidence for this thesis was that "they arrayed the blacks of St. Domingo against the whites."[119] Madison thought that sponsoring rebellion among the enslaved was one of the strategies considered by Le Clerc during his ill-fated attempt to reclaim Hispaniola and this made the idea of deploying on the mainland anything but troops defined as "white" quite problematic.[120] Madison may have been familiar with the lurid stories that maintained that London had prepared a massive force of African troops from the Caribbean to invade Dixie during the spring of 1815 in order to excite insurrection among U.S. Negroes—and to ignite the now much ballyhooed "horrors" of Haiti.[121]

For just as these armed Africans in redcoats were descending upon New Orleans, the slave-holding republic was faced with an analogous problem on the porous border separating Georgia from Spanish Florida, where Madrid's rule had deteriorated sharply leading to a free-for-all. It was then that President James Madison was told breathlessly that "our slaves are excited to rebel, and we have an army of Negroes . . . brought from Cuba to contend with. Let us ask," pleaded this patriot, "if we are abandoned, what will be the situation of the Southern States with this body of black men in the neighborhood. St. Augustine, the whole Province, will be the refuge of fugitive slaves; and from thence emissaries can, and no doubt will be detached, to bring about a revolt of the black population of the United States." But what was really animating this furor was detailed finally when it was said, "a nation that can stir up the savages . . . will hesitate but little to introduce the horrors of St. Domingo into your Southern country."[122]

The slaveholders on the Georgia-Florida border desperately yearned for a U.S. takeover altogether, particularly since Madrid brought many African troops from Santo Domingo and Cuba to fight the so-called "patriots." Indeed, the sight of these soldiers frightened the Euro-Americans since it was thought that these ebony soldiers were there in part to sponsor an insurrection among their enslaved. That the indigenous—the Seminoles—also sided with the Spanish was both intimidating and prescient since these warriors went on to fight three bloody wars with Washington before 1860.[123]

The response was to drive Spain out of Florida, which—it was thought— reduced the possibility of marauding Africans from St. Augustine via Cuba crossing into Georgia or Alabama to rile the enslaved. But this response had the downside of bringing the slave-holding republic's borders even closer to the abolitionist island, bringing the alleged "horrors" closer too. Given such threats, it made sense at that moment for Washington to seek to embrace previously derided *gens de couleur*.

Many of the *gens de couleur* of New Orleans who rode to the rescue of the slave-holding republic at a time of menace, also spoke French, which was not unusual in Louisiana.[124] The same held true for South Carolina, where Huguenots had been arriving since the late 17th century. As redcoats were rampaging across the eastern seaboard of North America in 1814, French descendants in the Palmetto State were rejoicing at the restoring strength of monarchial forces in Paris. "I can now think with pleasure upon cette belle France which I loved & still love," said a member of the potent Manigault family there, which too had French roots. "All our French friends are in high spirits," as were Frenchmen in the slave-holding republic who with royalists rising could dream again of restoring their lost properties—perhaps even slaves—in Haiti.[125] "Who would have thought that the restoration of the Bourbons would have had such an effect upon Philadelphia," said M. I. Manigault, a revival that was fortifying "my old & smothered affection for France."[126] Lost sight of was the point that the Keystone State's leading city still retained a sizeable complement of refugees from Hispaniola and "affection for France" that in whatever guise was not good news for Haiti.

There had been an up and down relationship between Paris and Washington, but, with London in bad odor with both, the two former powers were driven closer together, not least given their hostility to the perception—and reality—of a British-Haitian entente. "Napoleon is no more the enemy of the human race than the present administration of Washington & their majority in Congress,"[127] said Henry Izard of yet another slave-holding dynasty in Carolina. This view was common wisdom among his class, at a time when the Corsican was lacerated continuously in Britain and Haiti.

"Our country is doomed to be the asylum for so many French characters," was the view of Alice Izard thereafter, but this too was nothing new.[128] She was then informed that a comrade had "become a thorough Royalist & a great admirer of the Bourbons."[129] This bond between feudalists and slaveholders was tailor made for those who sought counterrevolution in Haiti.

A debilitated Spain continued to exert influence in Hispaniola though it was being hammered by the slave-holding republic, as it was nudged out of Mexico and was in the process of being pushed out of Florida and California and—via the loss of Mexico—Texas too. Veritably supine in confronting Washington, Madrid was, thus, encouraged to be confrontational in engaging Haiti. Thus, when the 1812 war ended in a standoff, Madrid began to sell off some of its posh real estate holdings in the former capital that was Philadelphia, a parallel to their losses in the southern quadrant of the mainland. "Mama made a great purchase yesterday," said Harriet Manigault; "the house which she set her heart upon as soon as she saw it & which the Onis family have lived in for three years past." She concluded with emphasis that "the *King* of *Spain* it seems is very desirous of having an establishment near Philadelphia,"[130] though this prediction proved to be misleading.

By then the revolutionary island had survived for more than a decade despite being surrounded by slave-holding regimes of various strengths—including a continuing Spanish foothold just across an ill-defined border in what was to become the Dominican Republic. Continuing with the deft diplomacy of General Toussaint, Haiti had been able to survive by choosing not to take on all these powers at once. Instead, it pursued the equivalent of a divide-and-rule stratagem that involved currying favor with London while cultivating U.S. Negroes, which provided a toehold in the backyard of the ever-expanding slave-holding republic. This latter approach was soon to involve the migration of thousands of U.S. Negroes to the northeastern side of the island where by 1822 Haiti had managed to expel Spanish rule, uniting Hispaniola under revolutionary rule—a true landmark that was to come a cropper by 1844 in a true victory for the slave-holding republic. In the meantime, Haiti continued to be accused of spreading the abolitionist gospel throughout the hemisphere. This, to be sure, enraged the slave-holding republic, which had its own ambitions in the Americas that decidedly did not include antislavery—or an enhanced role for Haiti for that matter.

5

Hemispheric Africans and Black Jacobins
1820–1829

THE NEWS FROM BARBADOS WAS UNHAPPY—for slaveholders. Yet another slave revolt had erupted in 1816 and, seeking to reassure themselves as much as anything else, an official body spoke hesitantly of the "utter insensibility which the slaves generally have shown to the revolutions in the French islands, especially to that in St. Domingo." Indeed, it was added, "insurrections have been unprecedentedly rare" though the failure to detail a benchmark for this evaluation cast doubt on the proposition. There were no "torrents of blood," it was reported—though if that were the benchmark, it left plenty of room for unalloyed devastation.[1]

A specter continued to halt slaveholders, the specter of the "horrors of St. Domingo" being visited upon them. However, as time passed this was more than a specter, which placed inordinate pressure on all concerned to move to an alternative model of development. Haiti, which was not opposed to extending aid to the neighboring enslaved, was invoked even when it was not directly involved in spurring unrest. Haiti, the island of freedom, mocked the pretensions of slaveholders—those on the mainland not least—and inspired the enslaved to believe realistically that their plight was not divinely ordained, nor perpetual but could be overcome.

Haiti also inspired British abolitionism. This gave momentum to the gathering notion in London that the slave-holding republic—with which the Crown had just fought a bloody though inconclusive war—could be better subdued if slavery were to be destabilized. Since Caribbean planters were also thought to be sympathetic to their counterparts on the mainland, this gave impetus to the idea that abolition could forestall the arrival of yet another 1776 revolt, adorned in the finery of freedom while trumpeting bondage at the same time and spelling another destructive loss for the Crown. A telling sign of the times occurred during the same year as the Barbados revolt—1816—when Protestantism was introduced into Haiti by the Wesleyan Methodists of Britain at the special invitation of President Pétion,[2] which was also a rebuke of the original colonizers—predominantly Catholic France and Spain.

The Barbados revolt also occasioned frantic ship and troop movements in the region, leaving His Majesty's possessions vulnerable if jealous neighbors—the United States, Spain, France—chose to then pounce.[3] For the crisis then faced was sufficiently serious for even the sympathetic to suspect that British rule was far from invincible. "An insurrection having burst forth among the Negroes," it was said in May 1816, meant "sixteen plantations have been destroyed and that five hundred of the insurgents have been killed and about as many more taken prisoners by the Black Troops stationed at Barbados who"—it was added with haltingly misplaced relief—"behaved . . . well." St. Lucia was "in a similar state of insurrection" and even in the jewel in the crown that was Jamaica, Haiti's neighbor and little brother, "apprehensions are entertained of a rising amongst the Negroes" thought to be "rife for revolt." Blamed angrily were abolitionist debates in London: "universally masked discontent has pervaded the Blacks of this island," meaning Jamaica, "since the pernicious" discussions were launched in Parliament. Somehow the enslaved latched onto the idea that London wanted them to be set free, but that the "colonists alone are inimical thereto"—they believed those in the metropolis would have "applauded" their revolt,[4] a dangerous idea indeed.

Actually, the colonists—more precisely, the "Association of West India Merchant Planters"—had "unanimously resolved" that a bill in Parliament "preventing the unlawful importation of slaves and the holding [of] free persons in slavery" was inimical to their interests, especially since it "has excited the most serious alarm." The bill proceeded "on the assumption of a contraband trade," an "assumption without the shadow of proof," but anyone paying attention—particularly those in Haiti—knew that an illicit slave trade was then accelerating, leading to attendant ills, e.g. kidnapping free Africans in the region into slavery.[5] The latter practice was a mortal threat to the continued existence of the abolitionist republic.

As Africans were rebelling, London had reason to believe that mainlanders were seeking to take advantage of the resultant flux. British merchants were reportedly facing "great annoyance" from "privateers." These "piratical cruisers"—"no less than fourteen"—were "equipped in the ports of the United States," principally New Orleans and "all" were "provided with great guns, small arms, and ammunition from the government arsenal" in that Louisiana town. The "crews" too were "principally composed of Americans" for "predatory purposes."[6] By that point

Jean Lafitte, with roots in Bordeaux and now sited in Louisiana, had attained a measure of fame as a pirate.[7] He boasted a labor force of more than 6000 with a fleet of thirty vessels.[8]

Then one Joseph Pilland of New Orleans was somehow persuaded to testify in Haiti to the effect that he had sailed from near there to Maracaibo—though he claimed he was the victim of privateers himself.[9] Still, the point remained that—possibly—the island of freedom could be enlisted in London's battle with mainland predators. When Britain's Lord Castlereagh was told that "several members of the French government," who had "interests at St. Domingo," were now "emigrants from that colony to the island of Jamaica,"[10] it was easier to suspect that—once again—there was a confluence of interest between Paris and Washington in the mutually advantageous game of undermining London. Warmer relations with Haiti could help to derail this ambitious plan.

Such a postulate was taking flight since the revolt in Barbados was thought to have been inspired by an insurrection in Guadeloupe, where Haitian influence was known to persist. Indeed, when Alice Izard of Carolina was moved to write about "some excellent soup" prepared by an African cook from Guadeloupe, one wondered why she did not keel over instantly from poisoning, given this island's growing reputation for militancy inspired by the freedom isle.[11] "Martial law" was imposed in this French colony and "insurgents" were "suppressed," but this rebellion combined with parliamentary debates "inflamed" Barbados. The Earl of Bathurst was told that London's delegates in the region were contacting those "within . . . reach" to insure there was no contagion, but St. Vincent was already "under martial law" and in Dominica "some arms and ammunition" had been found.[12]

But—London was told—Barbados was where the "calamity" was centered. There the Africans asserted that "the island belonged to them and not to white men whom they proposed to destroy, reserving the females." Frighteningly, "among the flags used by these insurgents," said Sir James Leith's informant, was a "rude drawing served to inflame the passions, by representing the union of a black man with a white female."[13] The rhetoric and the imagery, it was thought, reflected the now fabled "horrors" of Hispaniola. By the time of this report, it was now estimated that "80 estates had been burned and upwards of 1000 of the insurgents killed or executed" in Barbados.[14]

As a direct result, settlers were settling into a state that could easily be diagnosed as clinical depression. The "disposition of the slaves in general is very bad," it was declared by June 1816; "they are sullen & sulky and seem to cherish deep feelings of revenge," no small matter since settlers were outnumbered greatly and their backup included armed Africans of uncertain allegiances. "We hold the West Indies by a very precarious tenure," said this informed correspondent, and that was due to "military strength only," a frail reed indeed in light of the reliance on ebony soldiers. "I would not give a year's purchase," he said, "for any island except Trinidad"[15]—and even that could be questioned.

Barbados 1816 caused London parliamentarians to relive a nightmare—yet another Haitian Revolution. Recounted were the near misses: an "insurrection" in 1760 in Jamaica that was attended with "every circumstance of terror and alarm" as the "scenes which had occurred at St. Domingo." Then "in 1766 there had been another; in 1767 another; and in 1795 another"—and "besides those greater insurrections," it was said with dismay, "there had been many others of a local nature,"[16] which was accurate. Why should fate be tempted so capriciously? Why run the risk of losing all—as occurred in Hispaniola—and not, instead, proceed methodically toward abolition? When this did occur during 1833–1834 it was a reflection of the tutelage of Haiti, which then was to strike the slave-holding republic a few decades later.[17]

Other Londoners begged to differ. Yes, Barbados, 1816 was a "great and deplorable calamity," but there were "only two white men . . . killed during the whole of the insurrection" and, moreover, "the whites" were "also peculiarly strong in numbers there." Don't be stampeded, it was said shakily, by a "ridiculous account" that a "Haytian fleet had been steering towards Barbados at the time the insurrection broke."[18]

Others were not as confident. They were not as confident because policymakers in Barbados itself concluded that "the example of Saint Domingo was held out to the Slaves as worthy of imitation and as exhibiting a prospect of success which they might reasonably hope to emulate." The enslaved concluded rightly, as one put it, "that the only way to get [freedom] was to fight for it" and "that the way they were to do [so] was to set fire, as that was the way they did at Saint Domingo." When an enslaved person named Cuffee Ned was interrogated, he said bluntly that when Africans were freed in the region, "[they] had fought for it and got it" and the island he mentioned specifically was "*Mingo*"—meaning Saint Domingo or Haiti. A comrade named Robert echoed his impassioned words. Indeed, so many of these witnesses used virtually identical words—"fight" and "Domingo"—to explicate their revolt that it was easy to speculate that they were all speaking from a script prepared in Port-au-Prince.[19]

Furthermore, Africans had the dueling inspiration of what was befalling Spanish colonies, which simultaneously were fighting for their freedom from Mexico through Venezuela to Argentina. Near the time of the testimony of Cuffee Ned and Robert was the report of sharp clashes in "Buenos Ayres" involving a lurch toward anti-colonial freedom.[20] It was in 1815 that Simon Bolivar arrived in Haiti where he received support and then pushed for abolition—a signal to the mainland once more that the model of development there did not have an infinite shelf life.[21]

For as this pot was boiling in the Caribbean, back on the mainland the worst fears of James Madison were being realized as newspapers were full of stories about slave insurrection and bloodshed. One Baltimore organ had passed along the rumor that Africans had destroyed Sierra Leone, a British colony where U.S. slave dealers were known to lurk, and had murdered all those defined as "white." Then there were the bloodcurdling stories from Barbados. And then on what was becoming a hallowed day of insurrection for the enslaved—the 4th of July, this time, 1816—an expansive slave plot was exposed in Camden, South Carolina. "I think it is time for us to leave the country," said one of those intended for slaying, "[since] we cannot go to bed in safety."[22]

But the Camden scare was a simple prelude to the unnerving fright brought by the plot led by Denmark Vesey in Carolina in 1822. "Little has been said of this conspiracy," said Alice Izard, "but it is supposed to have extended widely. Nothing is apprehended now," she maintained, "as everybody are [*sic*]on their guard now."[23] What had Izard and those like her upset was the allied idea that Vesey and company intended to liberate themselves from Charleston, with bloodshed inevitable. There were those who believed that Haitians were complicit in this conspiracy, especially since there was apparently a company of French Negroes among the rebels and purportedly a letter was sent to President Jean Boyer of Haiti urging support. One Carolinian said that the rebels felt that as soon as they began to fight Haitians would rally to their support. As John Adger put it at the time, it was felt that Haitians would "march an army" to Carolina and that as soon as the rebels robbed the banks and the King Street shops of their goods and got everything aboard a vessel, they would sail away to freedom in Haiti and enjoy their treasure.[24]

Intensifying the hysteria in Carolina was the concomitant allegation that—as one source put it—"the English were to come & help them—that the Americans could do nothing against the English & that the English would carry them off to St. Domingo."[25] Since pro-London sentiments were known to abound in Haiti, this supposition could not be easily dismissed.[26]

Indeed, even London's top diplomat in Haiti acknowledged that "black and Coloured subjects" of the Crown had a "similarity of language" and "pretensions to the same character" akin to U.S. Negroes, allowing the latter to pass "without much risk of detection" as the former.[27] This was in the context of "applications of relief" made in Haiti "by Black and Coloured People describing themselves as

British subjects" but now "distressed"[28]—who like U.S. Negroes had sought a better way of life in the Caribbean. What if U.S. Negroes committed depredations on the mainland and then escaped to the Caribbean disguised as British subjects?

John Adger, who was on the scene then, saw Vesey as being part of a larger Haitian plot against the slave-holding republic. Thus, when the embattled African leader approached the gallows where the conspirators were to be hung, he had a grim sense of satisfaction. "The whole city turned out" for this festive execution, suggesting that these Euro-Americans too felt relieved at dodging disaster. Yes, he said, Vesey and his comrades, "wanted their freedom, which is the natural desire of all men," but "he wanted also blood and booty that he might get off with a load of specie and other valuables to San Domingo."[29]

Giving heft to pro-slavery fears was that 1822 also saw the unveiling of a vast conspiracy of the enslaved in Martinique, intent on destroying the settlers through poisoning. Hundreds were tried, then summarily executed, with others sentenced to harsh punishment and deportation. Then three months after the Denmark Vesey plot in Carolina, scores of Africans revolted in the midst of poisoning outbreaks. This was followed by the execution of hundreds more and the punishment of about a thousand.[30] The specter of Haiti continued to haunt this French colony.

London was startled with this "conspiracy" to "cut the throats of the whites"; "all the militia" were called and "a great portion of the regular troops" too. Evidently "some of our craft," meaning those from Barbados with Africans aboard, had "gone to that country" and "others may go," adding to the insurrection. Others fled to St. Thomas and "not being allowed to return to Martinique, [they] will endeavour no doubt to disseminate themselves in the different islands." The unnamed correspondent in Barbados, asserted flutteringly that the "number of runaway Negroes is getting alarmingly great in the island and I am told that some of them are concealed by white men, nay even protected by the armed Negroes."[31]

The "total destruction of the white population" was at issue in Martinique, said J. R. Littlepage, Harbour Master of Trinidad. This was to commence "at the time of the church service, the Negroes in the south were to set it on fire at both ends and then to commence the bloody scene" by "butchering the inhabitants as they might hurry out of the place of worship." A "number of white planters & both women and children were butchered before assistance could be afforded . . . a great many prisoners have been made and a large quantity of powder . . . together with some arms . . . have been discovered concealed about the country & town." The slaveholders were heartened when "their General [was] taken" but saddened when "the King [eluded] all search." More awfully for the slaveholders, a "vessel had been seized at St. Pierre's from St. Domingo under very suspicious circumstances," while another "loaded with munitions of war and having upwards of 100 men on board" was nearby. Fortunately for the slaveholders, the suspicious "fleet was dispersed by a gale before reaching its destination," but there was still room for worry since "clandestine communication is kept up with [Trinidad] and St. Domingo." As these words were penned, within view were "two vessels now fitting out in this port under suspicious circumstances." One was "owned by a colored man named Edward Paul, commanded by a coloured man named Wm. Pass, and intended to clear out for Jamaica." The other "sloop" was owned by "Paul Dumaire also coloured," though "her sentiments [were] not yet declared"[32]—the French surname gave a hint of what might be in store.

From Puerto Rico came the report that as Martinique was exploding, a "military expedition," including a man named Ducoudray Holstein who was to receive a command in Cartagena, had departed to join Simon Bolívar. But the two parted on bad terms and Holstein moved to Curaçao where he taught piano—and French. Then he was off to the United States where he "intended expeditions" gaining him "350,000 dollars" and then it was from there to St. Barthélemy and St. Thomas where he was to recruit "200 more" men—but he was detained with "6000 muskets." Puerto Rican officialdom had made "necessary arrangements" to liquidate them if they arrived on their shores. The mastermind behind this peripatetic voyaging was none other than President Boyer of Haiti, it was said. Holstein was tasked with seeking to "gain the adherence of the Mulattoes and Negroes" and "the whole of the archipelago of the Antilles" was "threatened" as a result by "these ruffians without a home, without honour or a country they call their own," who were "attempting to establish another kingdom" under a "Government which has already been profaned by so many crimes and usurped by the most detestable perfidy"—meaning Haiti. This latter "piratical" regime was a regional threat. "How highly necessary," cried the Captain General of Puerto Rico, "it becomes to prevent on our territories the dreadful effects of a war carried on by the coloured and Negro inhabitants" as had beset Hispaniola.[33] As San Juan saw things, Haiti was moving aggressively to implant Jefferson's nightmare of regional hegemony of the Africans.

Joel Roberts Poinsett, a Carolinian with Huguenot roots and an architect of U.S. foreign policy in the Americas, had reason then to see Haiti as "lofty and broken." He passed by the island on his way to Puerto Rico in 1822 but could not escape its reverberations, i.e. "an intended insurrection of the slave population. Although the slaves are not numerous," he said with a wistful sigh, "the vicinity of the republic of Hayti renders such a movement a probable event." He was so overwhelmed by the looming specter of Haiti that, unlike his fellow Carolinians, he was not dismissive of the "Spaniard's being in the habit of mixing with the people of colour without those prejudices so common in the other West Indian colonies" since this "prevents any jealousy or bad feeling towards him on their part and forms a great security against the slave population and their neighbours of San Domingo." Illustrating the bonds between and among slave-holding regimes, the specter of Haiti in Puerto Rico induced this Carolinian to rethink bedrock precepts.[34]

This was of a piece with a general rebellion against European colonial rule in South America, a revolt that Haiti supported. On 18 August 1823—barely two scant decades after the eruption in Hispaniola—there was a similar outbreak in Demerara on the northern coast of South America. This was now a British colony, giving London further reason to contemplate that unless abolition took hold, all would be lost—including lives. But then martial law was imposed and a number of African rebels were decapitated; as was the custom, heads were affixed on poles in a vain attempt to intimidate. This was a mass rebellion with one witness testifying that "about 500" Africans were rebelling on one specific estate—but they were joined by others. Another still shaken European witness recalled that "about a thousand Negroes came to the door and demanded arms" and threatened to "set fire" to his house—then for good measure about 400 more arrived, "all armed."

The tumult occurred on a Monday morning at 6 a.m., as settlers groggily began a new week. Mainlanders petrified by the notion of treachery inflicted by *gens de couleur* chose to ignore that it was—according to reports—a "mulatto servant named Joseph" who foiled the rebellion by betraying the seditionists. Still, it was said, "the Negro Prince, a carpenter," who was the "principal ringleader of this multitude of insurgents, nearly 2000 in number" instilled dread in the marrow of settlers. The "1st West India Regiment" was sent to drown the revolt in blood—but how long could London depend upon armed Africans to police enslaved Africans, particularly when abolitionist Haiti lurked nearby?[35]

This thought was not animating the minds of all Britons, including Sir Charles Brisbane, Governor of St. Vincent—an island which had yet to shed its rollicking reputation for rebellion. As he—and others—saw things, there was no real alternative to slavery and the abolitionists who argued otherwise failed to detect that "their favourite country of Saint Domingo is an existing proof of the fallacy of their assertions."[36]

Sir Charles's detractors could well argue he was ignoring reality, particularly in neighboring Trinidad, which was at the center of an abolitionist debate in 1823. There resided, it was reported, "slaves enfranchised by desertion" from the mainland, who had fled the slave-holding republic at the behest of London and were "now universally regarded as a valuable acquisition to the colony." But those who thought Sir Charles had the better of the argument dissented, contending that the "dreadful . . . affairs in that abyss of anarchy" known as "St. Domingo" were a standing advertisement against abolition. Haitians were "relapsing into barbarism" and now abolitionists were demanding the same in the Caribbean. Recalled was the "Maroon War of 1795"—a harbinger of Haiti—and the losses incurred by the Crown. And now that "bloodthirsty brigand Christophe of St. Domingo was hailed in London by the humane Wilberforce"—where was the justice?[37]

Back and forth it went, as all sides sought to tease out the lessons of the Haitian Revolution with the prevailing side destined to either bolster the slave-holding republic—or join the growing legions opposing it. One Londoner wondered why "from the days of Las Casas," centuries earlier, "to the present," meaning the 1820s, "there have been fewer servile insurrections in the Spanish colonies than have taken place in the British West Indies within the last thirty years."[38] Why? Was British slavery more pernicious? Should it be abolished? Yes, argued a Londoner: Slavery breeds "insurrections" and, thus, was unsustainable.[39]

James Stephen claimed that it was London that was "enslaved by her own colonies." Evidence included "our treatment of *Hayti* from the moment of its first Revolution," which had led to "one continuous surrender of national interests to the narrow views and potent influence of the Colonial Party." Despite this capitulation to slaveholders, "our ships of war were received in their [Haitian] ports with every honour the government could possibly pay and our officers . . . were astonished at the elegance and splendour with which they were entertained on shore." Tariffs on British goods were half of those of other exporters. London's "bad policy" forced a Haitian indemnity to France, which weakened instead of strengthened a key anti-Paris ally because of undue influence of slaveholders. It was "conjectural" but not inaccurate to estimate that the "Sugar Colonies had cost us during the last thirty years at least a hundred and fifty millions in national debt incurred . . . and *fifty thousand lives.*"[40]

The "subordination of the Negroes," Henry Brougham posited, was "derived from the habitual conviction of the decided superiority of white men," now severely questioned in Haiti. How could slavery survive when Haiti undermined the racist rationale that undergirded this system? The "Negroes then," it was acknowledged, "are the enemies most to be dreaded in America by all Europeans; they are the natural foes of white men." For "with such a power as the new black republic no European colony can form a league against any other European colony or any other Negro state." For "if any power deserves the name of a natural enemy, it is the Negro commonwealth." Hence, "if the European powers value their colonial possessions, it becomes them to unite against this tremendous enemy" that was Haiti; i.e. "to forget all rivalry and to join in opposing the progress of this inevitable calamity."[41] There were those who wanted to circumscribe "intercourse" between

Haiti and "the West India Colonies belonging to European powers," but this was tricky since the freedom isle was accused repeatedly of seeking to subvert slavery.[42]

Still, Brougham's viewpoint had a certain logic in that Haiti did represent a breach in the system of slavery and the leading powers—if they wished to maintain this system—should have hung together against the abolitionist isle. The problem was that burying profound differences between and among the powers was easier said than done, as the War of 1812 and jousting over the centuries suggested. In reality as Londoners were maundering, Haiti was strengthening by ousting Spain from the vaster eastern portion of Hispaniola and then seeking to populate that rich region with thousands of migrating—and often talented—U.S. Negroes.

Anyway, if Brougham had paid attention to the recent revolt in Demerara, he would have noticed that a rebel was asked: "Did you ever hear of the French and English fighting?" The answer: "Yes, I have heard"—with the inference left that this was part of seditionist calculation, striking while colonialists were quarrelling, and indicating why colonialist unity had been breached fatally by the Haitian Revolution. A missionary was indicted for supposedly bringing this colonial disunity to the attention of the enslaved by dint of biblical stories. "That I have an aversion to slavery, I cannot deny," said this man of the cloth—who was convicted and sentenced "to be hanged by the neck until dead."[43] Not so easy to execute was a strategy of colonial unity that could exclude full consideration of Haiti.

BY 1823 THE "INSURRECTION AT MARTINIQUE" had yet to be calmed and,[44] as was typical of such restiveness, ripples of unrest spread inexorably outward to other islands.

Part of the problem was that Washington was in the process of ousting Madrid from ruling Florida. This would prove a weighty coup in the long term, but in the short term it brought the slave-holding republic's borders closer to unrest in Cuba, where its close neighbor—Haiti—was thought to wield influence. This was the backdrop for the first formal war between indigenes in Florida—known widely as the "Seminoles"—and the slave-holding republic. Africans in what was to become the Sunshine State were also known for their rambunctiousness and had allied with indigenes to that end, with many from both groups fleeing to Cuba where they found refuge. They also marketed timber and fish in Havana in exchange for rum— and firearms. Runaway slaves from the peninsula also found refuge in Cuba and from there could make it to the island of freedom.[45]

Instability from the Caribbean could now easily reach U.S. soil, as the epitome of slave-holding hawkishness—John C. Calhoun—was told. "Look at [Santo] Domingo & at the West India islands and at Cuba," he was informed on the twentieth anniversary of the onset of the Haitian Revolution. "The black monster encreases [*sic*] in size & terrifies," argued Thomas Law. Florida was destined to increase its already heavy share of Africans, as the enslaved from Georgia and points north fled there in order to try to make it to the Caribbean, he said. "Insurrections in modern times," he added philosophically, "are not partial but general & systematized. Say that it will cost 100,000 whites to suppress an insurrection & 50,000 dollars & the destruction of 1,000,000 blacks and of two harvests in the black States." This, he added ghoulishly, would be a heavy but unavoidable cost. Then there was the hardy perennial: "the number of mulattoes is becoming a serious cause of apprehension," particularly since "they are enlightened" and prone to think that they could ally with Africans and take power.[46] But with Haiti now aligned with Britain, even these estimated—macabre—costs may have been underestimated.

Some may have been leaving Dixie in fear of the costs sketched by Law but others were not, many of them of French origin. A Frenchman visiting Charleston in 1817, who had earlier participated in the anti-London revolt of 1776, heard "Creole French" on "every corner." With the roots of this population being evident, he noted that "it seems that the white and black population of Santo Domingo has been poured out on all the continental beaches from New York to the mouth of the Mississippi." He found that the "white families from Santo Domingo are languishing and ill-starred here as everywhere else," and he noticed that "there are three thousand French in Charleston." That some were not doing well was not good news for Haiti; for it might reawaken visions of reclaiming Haiti or—worse—reenslaving the denizens there.[47]

By 1818, James Madison was acknowledging that "the market of Baltimore has been much benefited in dry seasons by the irrigation introduced by exiles from St. Domingo."[48] A token of their presence was the proliferating idea among U.S. Negroes that their interests would be better-served if they were to abandon the mainland that French refugees had embraced. In fact, there was a dialectical connection between the contrasting realities that those who resisted abolition would be comfortable in the United States while those who were of an opposing viewpoint would not; i.e. as the French fled Hispaniola, their place was taken there by U.S. Negroes.

Thus, as Frenchmen huddled in Carolina, both Britain and Haiti—which had a mutual interest in opposing France and the United States—were brought together, notably on the platform of abolitionism. It was at this time that Thomas Clarkson, the noted British abolitionist, reached the man formerly known as General Christophe to discuss "the persons of colour who might be induced to leave the United States for Hayti." He prodded the man then known as King Henry with the notion that "such persons would be useful to Your Majesty. They would form that middle class in society which is the connecting medium between the rich and poor." Washington might be persuaded to "buy the Spanish part of your Island and cede it to you as indemnification or recompense for receiving the free people of colour into your Dominions." This was a dicey proposition—still, the slave-holding republic was fed up, suspecting that this group slated for ouster were too prone to aid the enslaved, as Hispaniola reputedly showed, and removing them would be worthwhile, even if sent to a nearby and putative British ally. King Henry was willing to provide "pecuniary assistance" to effectuate this objective.[49]

Clarkson knew and stressed that a "change of opinion has taken place" and now the conversation was focused on settling *gens de couleur* and Free Negroes generally not somewhere in North America but in Africa—e.g. Sierra Leone—or even Haiti. The War of 1812 with its repetitive scenes of enslaved Africans fleeing to redcoat banners, then moving on to Trinidad, indicated that the slave-holding republic's position was more perilous than thought. Surely, London was a more formidable foe than Port-au-Prince and the latter was the "least bad" alternative as a site for the despised. In 1819, as Spain was reeling from anti-colonial upsurges, the idea arose to move these disgruntled categories of U.S. denizens to the territory Madrid claimed in Hispaniola. The British abolitionist stressed that "Congress must buy the Spanish part of the island" and the duel sovereigns in Haiti could administer this land "cojointly under both." The wider point was that despite their atrocious maltreatment, the Free Negroes could be positioned as a stalking horse in Hispaniola for Washington and ultimately destabilize Haitian rule. The Haitian leadership showed courage by brushing aside this consideration. This emigration project was commenced when the island remained split, which increased even more the possibility that free Negroes could be deployed as a wedge by Washington.

"Calamities of war" could be the result, said Clarkson, if Free Negroes from the mainland were plopped in the middle of contesting island sovereigns. Washington was having difficulty as to which to favor. King Henry seemed to be disfavored though, it was said, "you may travel through" his territory "with safety and if you lose your purse, it will be returned, if found, to its right owner" while in the Pétion-Boyer land thievery was thought to reign. There were schools in the former, not the latter, it was also stated. Of course, Clarkson was "well acquainted" with King Henry and in "frequent communication" with him, which probably colored his opinion. This Haitian leader had sent to London "for professors of the language," meaning English, as yet another means to escape the French. The "fear of invasion," a la Le Clerc, was "still hanging over his head." Thus, said the influential Clarkson, dispatch the Free Negroes forthwith to Hispaniola with three sovereigns—King Henry, Boyer, and the United States—sharing jurisdiction over them.[50]

Clarkson, like others, had decided that Africa was "unfit" for "the free people of colour" and had hoped that Haiti would become their "asylum." However, "in consequence of the unpleasant feelings which the cession of the Floridas must have created" with Spain, "I regard any cession by the latter" as "highly improbable." This thought had occurred to Haiti too—which is why Boyer simply marched eastward in 1822 and took over. Yet something had to be done and quickly about the mainland crisis, said this abolitionist, for "the prevailing spirit in Georgia and the Carolinas at this moment is rather to rivet more strongly the chains of the oppressed, than to loosen them." Plus, Washington was seized with the idea of "getting rid of the whole of the free population of colour"—not a portion—which was complicating things further.

So Clarkson recommended to begin by sending a "few families consisting, let us say, of 10,000 individuals to Hayti from the United States." In any case, urgency was the watchword since "the poor people in question are liable to be kidnapped and sent into slavery in the Southern States." The acceleration of the "execrable" slave trade meant "they cannot but feel their degraded condition and be made unhappy on that account." King Henry would "give a very handsome sum toward the payment of their passage," though "he would take no Haytians who might be found among them because they had traitorously left their country and he could place no confidence in them for the future." Also, "he would take no idle farmers" or "none of bad or abandoned character." Thus, King Henry would take at least a "few thousand of the free people of colour," particularly since "he has lately too disbanded a part of his army that he may promote agriculture equally with letters."

On more sober reflection, Clarkson thought, rather than the United States alone, instead to be recommended was "the idea of the different powers of Europe guaranteeing the peace and security" of the migrants in eastern Hispaniola; i.e. not just the three previously noted sovereigns but adding to the mix Spain—and it was "highly probable both that England and Russia, nay even France itself, would have joined in the guarantee." London was reluctant to cross Paris by recognizing King Henry so what was needed was a "treaty" between the two and King Henry on migrants— which presupposed recognition of his regime. That France was now deploying "secret agents" to confer with King Henry was suggestive,[51] though Paris was relieved when he expired in 1820.[52] Certainly, U.S. Negroes would have benefited if their unsteady status had been guaranteed by an array of powers, including Russia.

The liaison in this vast scheme was Prince Sanders (also spelled Saunders). A U.S. Negro, he was born in New England and attended Moor's Charity at Dartmouth College in 1807 and 1808. At the suggestion of the British abolitionists, he came to Haiti to assist in organizing the schools, where he became an enthusiastic devotee of

King Henry. It was reported that Sanders introduced vaccination into Haiti and personally vaccinated King Henry's children. The ban against trade with Haiti, passed in 1806, renewed in 1807 and continued until 1809, hampered his ability to establish more fruitful bilateral relations between Haiti and his birthplace.[53] Yet Sanders's trajectory indicated why this new formalized relationship between U.S. Negroes and Haiti was so crucial for both: he died in 1839 as Attorney General of his new homeland,[54] a post that he could hardly aspire to in the land of his birth.

At any rate, by the time Clarkson reached his powerful Haitian correspondent, King Henry, things were looking up. Even if diplomatic recognition was not in the offing, the dexterous slave-holding republic was flexible enough to recognize that a presence in Haiti would allow monitoring of London's activity there. Moreover, trade restrictions hindered the ability of the United States to engage in commerce with colonized islands—a category that most definitely did not include Haiti. By 1817 merchants from the United States were busily surveying markets in Haiti.[55] That same year, Carolina's favorite son, John C. Calhoun, was mulling a "very large sum" that Congress "at two different times" had voted for "Saint Domingo refugees," an indication of past commercial ties that might yet have a payoff.[56]

By 1819 Haiti was seen as a major trade partner of the United States, ranking with Britain, France, Russia, Holland, and other leading powers.[57] By 1821 an official Haitian periodical encouraged trade with the United States,[58] a relationship that could also benefit from migration of U.S. Negroes to the island. Also by 1821 John Quincy Adams was told of the "growing importance of trade between this place and the U. States particularly since the Union of the northern with the southern departments," following the expiration of King Henry; hence, a "commercial agent" was desperately needed. Adams's correspondent had been "trading to this island more than eighteen years, the last three of which . . . as a commission merchant."[59] By 1822 U.S. exports to Haiti equaled those to Russia, Prussia, Sweden, Denmark, and Ireland combined.[60] No, said another source, U.S. exports to Haiti reportedly exceeded those to either Russia, Sweden, Norway, Italy, Denmark, Portugal, Prussia, Sicily, Greece, Colombia, or China.[61]

By 1826 Haitians were chortling about this increased commerce.[62] That same year a British merchant who had resided on the island since 1812 marveled that the "Americans have the greatest trade with Haiti."[63] "Trade with these blacks," claimed one mainland journal, "is more important in amount to us than that of many other countries to whom we have highly dignified ministries and agents."[64]

This too came with a steep price. For New England Federalists heavily invested in trade with the island of freedom thereby offended Dixie and quickened sectional conflict that eventuated in civil war.[65]

There was another price to pay that may been steeper than the sectional crisis. The slave-holding republic found it hard to accept when a U.S. sailor of British origin was reputedly bilked by Haitians after his ship was sold to them. Charles MacKenzie, London's envoy, somehow blamed "frauds practiced by the Americans on ignorant British subjects whom they abandon without ceremony when convenient." The slave-holding republicans were confronted not only by Black Jacobins but also by sharp dealing Haitians, at a time when most mainlanders thought those of such ancestry were fit only for cotton fields.[66] That MacKenzie was also a man of color only served to question the mainland model of development that presupposed unrelenting subordination for any not defined as "white."

U.S. trade with the island would have been even more lucrative but for the fact that Haiti was compelled to pay an indemnity—i.e. reparations—to France for alleged losses suffered during the revolutionary era. This massive payment of 150 million francs in 1826[67] was seen by London abolitionists, e.g. James Stephen—and many Haitians and U.S. Negroes—as outrageous, particularly given the enormous sums France had looted over the decades. At the same time, Washington and Paris were cuddling—the former seeking leverage against abolitionism and the latter seeking revenge against Haiti. Moreover, since so many planters from Hispaniola had fled to Louisiana, this meant that Haitian indemnities also were benefiting certain mainlanders.

Yet enhanced ties between Paris and Washington narrowly limited Haiti's options. In 1822 U.S. envoy Albert Gallatin assured the Viscount de Chateaubriand that his mission was to insure amicable and consolidated relations with France.[68] He then took leave for six months in order to repair to Le Havre for more pleasantries.[69] Just before that John T. Robinson of Charleston was gloating about cotton prices since "the manufactories have increased in Great Britain & to a much greater extent in France."[70] Joel Poinsett, a Carolinian of French extraction, busily transmitted agricultural intelligence—including seeds and alternatives to sperm oil for lamps—from the hexagonal state to his homeland. This alternative was also good for food preparation and painting, but the broader point was the tightened link between the two states represented by such intelligence, a link that was of no small import to Haiti.[71]

Paris kept a close eye on U.S. domestic issues and personalities—including navigation of the Mississippi River and the rise of the maniacally pro-slavery John C. Calhoun[72]—sensing that the slave-holding republic would be essential in the process of pressuring Britain and Haiti. But Haiti also kept watch on the mainland, particularly its allies, the abolitionists,[73] as well as mainland antagonists, e.g. Mexico.[74] When the fraught matter of Carolina arose—the epicenter of the slaveholders' realm and the home of numerous former slaveholders in Hispaniola—President Boyer discussed this region in terms of potential for trade, rather than the noxious question of slavery.[75]

Yet providing Haiti room for maneuver was the fact that Paris and Washington, which after all had fought a "quasi-war" years earlier, were also at odds at times. In 1819 the Carolinian Henry H. Coming was in a familiar position for a mainlander—in France and complaining about the absence of English speakers, making him a "Perfect Stranger." Worse, he thought, "in every part of France that I have been in, we were greatly annoyed by the insults of the lower People and frequently of the Soldiers, cursing us as Englishmen."[76] Those he was able to communicate with, he said disgustingly, were "excessively dull and stupid."[77] As for the celebrated Jean-Jacques Rousseau, he was "crack brained"; "with all his absurdities," he added damningly with feint praise, "[he] is a great favorite of mine."[78]

In 1825, when U.S. trade with the island was rising, Paris' Vice-Consul in Cap-Haïtien was reporting with seeming glee that mainland vessels were rarer with every passing day. The slave-holding republicans feared France, he argued.[79] Thus, he said, Paris should find a way to diminish the commercial influence in Haiti of not just London—but Washington too.[80] But such intentions were risible when France was imposing damaging indemnities on Haiti, causing even the Vice-Consul to refer to President Boyer as imprudent for making such sizeable payments.[81] The Vice-Consul was baffled in seeking to understand why London's relations with the island were closer than Paris's.[82]

However, despite their inroads in the Haitian marketplace—arguably at Paris' expense—the U.S. emissary on the island continued to complain. By November 1820, the issue was "no white man has been permitted" in certain areas and "an embargo" had "been laid on all vessels at the Cape in consequence of Christophe's Crown and Star [his emblems of sovereignty] having been stolen and reported to have been sold to foreigners"; besides, a "great many abuses of the American character in the other ports of the republic" were rife and "our flag prostituted to the purpose of cloaking the trade of other nations."[83]

The problem that was to bedevil the enslaving republicans in Hispaniola for years to come was that their white supremacist homeland ill disposed them to engage fruitfully with Haitians, placing Washington at a disadvantage in its ongoing competition for influence with other leading powers.

When Samuel Hambleton—who was to represent Maryland in Congress—arrived in Port-au-Prince in early 1823, he was unimpressed with its "desolate appearance," a result of a "great fire" that had just occurred with "about 200 houses in the most commercial part of the place" destroyed. He seemed similarly taken aback when "Black Officers visited the ship" transporting him.[84] When a scion of a prominent Carolina family arrived in Port-au-Prince in 1824, he was pleased to discover that "the place is not so sickly as one mite [*sic*] suppose for the time of the year," though "the heat appears to [be] about . . . hotter than Hell"—and the same could be said for his rude reception since the "Negroes about," unlike the enslaved he encountered in Charleston, were "saucier" than most and were, he added in what was thought to be a slap, "10 times blacker than the ace of spades."[85]

Washington was not singular in racial insensitivity, to a degree. For it was in the 1820s that Britain's leading diplomat on the island—Charles MacKenzie—was singing a similar blues. He happened to be a man of color and since a similar appointment would be hard to imagine in the slave-holding republic, this gives his remarks a notable poignancy. "Five hundred torches were prepared for the destruction of the Houses and Property (ostensibly) of all French but in reality of all white residents. The alarm was general" and "the whole country was in a very fever-ish state," a state that was "rooted [in] antipathy to everything European among all classes." Yes, he concluded, "though a temporary cry may be raised against Frenchmen and in favour of Englishmen, I am convinced that no distinction would be made, in case of any violence being committed against the former. We should all be indiscriminately classed together and extermination would be the order of the day"; i.e. there were "insults from which even the agents of friendly powers are not exempt."[86] Soon MacKenzie was urgently summoning a warship for his protection and that of other subjects.[87] One response would be to distinguish London more sharply by moving toward abolition.

London watched carefully what had bedeviled Haiti for years: the question of color, which was ultimately a question of national origin and class position. "Mulatto women were worse treated than the Blacks," said one commentator. "[I] saw mulatto women employed carrying stones to build a church driven by a black woman who had a whip with which she impelled them speed when she thought necessary. Many mulatto or coloured women complained to the British officers of the punishments which they received from the blacks." He was stunned to find that the "crews of the merchant vessels were white" and that "on shore they were fre-quently abused by the blacks and reproached as being white slaves."[88] Such reports were not easy for British colonialists to ignore, nor were they easy for "white" Americans to digest.

Worse for Haiti was the point that the unavoidable antagonist in Paris also mon-itored carefully the color equation in Haiti with an envoy asserting in 1826 that—ironically—the *gens de couleur* and those raised in France were more haughty toward the French than other Haitians, a reality that was befuddling to this emissary. The recommendation made was to stop sending Haitians to France for education but, instead, to send French teachers to the island.[89]

Yet despite the alleged antipathy of gens *de couleur* toward Paris, the latter's delegate in Cap-Haïtien felt that the former desired external support because they supposedly fretted that the African majority were conspiring against them. At the same time, this diplomat said that the *gens de couleur* had their own vexatious plans that they intended to inflict on the majority, causing the latter to suspect that lighter-skinned individuals were the ones conspiring with France. That this mutual suspicion of plotting was beneficial to France was exposed when the envoy suggested France send more troops to the vicinity to forestall bloodshed.[90] When the Vice-Consul concluded in 1827 that the two groups—*gens de couleur* and Africans—could not coexist peacefully in the same nation, this seemed like wishful thinking ripe for exploitation, as much as anything else.[91] When Alice Izard spoke glowingly of "high expectations" by her French colleagues in Charleston "of agreeable news from St. Domingo," it was easy to suspect that Paris had driven a deeper wedge between the citizens of the island.[92]

However, MacKenzie's and other animadversions could not obscure the point that London's relations with Haiti were much warmer than either Paris's—or Washington's—which was hardly a minor matter in light of the vast mineral wealth on the island, a point that was hardly secret.[93] Later, the U.S. agent, William Miles, enthusiastically asserted, "the Haitiens have the most beautiful spot on this earth." This was said after he had travelled through a good deal of the islands and the Americas. "I never saw such a country as St. Domingo," he observed dazedly, "cotton grows everywhere,"[94] which was bound to spur the interest of slave-holding republicans who had made fortunes in this field.

By early 1825, Joseph Webb was reporting from Fleet Street that "many English merchants" that "have resided in Haiti "for many years" felt that the regime "constantly favoured" them, "in a particularly distinguished manner," no less. Indeed, he told George Canning, a British statesman, it "would be advantageous to the commerce of England if Hayti were entirely independent of France." Webb was elated with the "independence of Hayti and the rapid progress which has [been] made," which "in the course of a few years [will] tend to remove more effectively the evil consequences attending the Foreign Slave Trade and slavery than any other means that can be adopted, not only in Africa but also in the West India islands, as well as in the United States of America," leading to "total abolition."[95] The idea that a successful Haiti would undermine slavery and the slave trade led to the contrasting idea on the mainland that it was crucial to make Haiti fail for precisely this reason.

This latter thought had occurred to Washington—or at least Dixie—which galvanized a movement to quarantine the island of freedom. Yet Washington too could not allow London to gain advantage by having unchallenged sway in Haiti, contributing to the idea that even the dispatching of dismayed U.S. Negroes to Haiti could serve U.S. interests. Paris too worried about London's growing influence in Haiti, even speculating that when Africans from the Caribbean basin began departing for this island, it was not due to the desire for freedom but part of a plot by Britain to gain influence in the freedom isle.[96]

Still, this was a fiendishly difficult course Haiti was seeking to walk: trying to counter a hostile Paris, a weakened though still dangerous Spain, and an enraged Dixie, replete with former slaveholders from Hispaniola, by improving relations with London, which contained a potent slave-holding lobby. An obvious cue was transmitted after Haitian troops marched eastward in 1822, took power—then banned slavery: Washington, Paris—and London—were united in discontent.[97] Former settlers in Hispaniola now residing in Louisiana feared—or at least circulated the story—that Puerto Rico and Cuba were next and urged London, Washington, and, presumably, Spain to unite to stop it from happening. Haiti had to wonder if its avid abolitionism could eventuate in uniting a formidable bloc of foes.[98]

But Haiti also had cards to play. When the British navy espied "movements of the French squadrons in these seas"—in possible "support of the Royal Cause of Spain in St. Domingo" in light of the 1822 reversion of the eastern part of the island to Haiti—France had to worry about being checkmated by London and Port-au-Prince, as opposed to being bolstered.[99] Then as now, a deft Haitian diplomacy could rely upon maneuvering within the interstices of hostility between and among the leading powers.

When Africans revolted in Martinique, some fled on craft from there while others—which was customary—fled to the site of unrest. Others seized upon the flux by fleeing to Hispaniola. "[President] Boyer receives all handy craft," said an unnamed Barbadian, and "those who have no trade are immediately enrolled in regiments and sent to that part of St. Domingo lately taken from the Spaniards"[100]—which in turn caused even more to flee various islands for a now larger Haiti. Colonial powers seeking to unseat Black Jacobins had to consider if, instead, their island regimes would collapse as "their" Africans fled to buttress Haiti. Surely this thought crossed the minds of Puerto Rican officialdom concerned that a recent plot against this Spanish colony had telltale signs of Haitian intrigue.

To that end, a British diplomat in Haiti encountered the man he called General Joseph Inginac, referring to President Boyer's right-hand man. This Haitian leader—who, it was reported, looked "white"—"asked me a number of questions about the state of affairs in Jamaica," a not so subtle hint at British weakness. As well, he "entertained us with an account of their military force," an ironic complement to London's debility. To that end, it was observed that the "number of regular troops of Hayti" was "about 20,000." This led this envoy to a meeting with President Boyer—"his complexion is that of a mulatto," it was noted, as London was not above playing upon color contradictions in Haiti. "He asked me a number of questions particularly about Sierra Leone and the Burmese War,"[101] indicating how Haiti was seeking to measure the global correlation of forces in order to develop a winning strategy.

Haiti's problem—-among others—was that Washington too was not above picking at the loose thread of color on the island, thus magnifying similar efforts by London and Paris. When William Miles was posted as a commercial agent in Aux Cayes, he was careful to inform John C. Calhoun that "the Negroes of Haiti have a common proverb," i.e. "the White man has a country, the Black man has a country (Africa), the Colored man has no country"[102]—making the latter noticeably vulnerable, it was thought, to foreign blandishments.

Yet as is so often the case in diplomacy, London too had a dual agenda. How could it not? It was seeking to gain leverage against Paris and Washington by warming relations with Haiti, but not so much as to lead to a challenge to its colonial rule in Jamaica and the vicinity. Thus, earlier a British envoy had noted menacingly that "all" the "military officers under Christophe" were "black but all the civil officers were coloured men" while "under Boyer he did not observe the same distinction."[103] Repeatedly, London crafted detailed analyses of the Haitian military with a focus on color composition.[104] This provided opportunity for sowing discord.

Still, by 1826 MacKenzie was busily conferring with Boyer and Inginac—the latter leaders, he said, sensing his own leverage, "professed great anxiety to proceed without delay to the formation of a Treaty of Amity and Commerce."[105] For this was during the tense time when, said MacKenzie, Paris was "assembling a force calculated to intimidate the Haitian government into compliance" with France's adamant demand for reparations,[106] raising the fearsome possibility of another Le Clerc reenslavement or genocidal mission. Boyer balked[107]—but could not withstand the pressure. He writhed in agony as he sought to rationalize why reparations were not streaming into the coffers of Port-au-Prince—rather than Paris.[108]

With Haiti yielding to Paris, London pressed its advantage against the island—which in a sense, was narrow-minded, insofar as this strengthened the slaveholders of the Caribbean who were friendly to their counterparts on the mainland and, thus, not necessarily patriotic. Still, MacKenzie demanded that Haiti "entirely . . . prohibit all intercourse between" Haiti and the British Caribbean. This was "not merely to lull the apprehensions of the British West India island proprietors; but also to check the illicit intercourse" that "takes place even at present." Of particular concern was London's desire "to restrain the escape of slaves from all the colonies to this place." For it was a "certain fact" that huge numbers of formerly enslaved Jamaicans, Antiguans, and the like were now living in freedom in Haiti. Haiti in turn was seeking advantage "by granting particular privileges in favour of our North American colonies," meaning Canada, in order to "mark" their "dissatisfaction" with the United States.[109]—flourishing trade notwithstanding.

Paris too feared that Haiti could ignite anti-colonial independence, though they banked on—if not encouraged—what they saw as antipathy between the freedom state and Martinique.[110] Similarly, Paris's policy leaned heavily upon the dubious counsel of those settlers who had escaped the island frantically during revolutionary times but instead of decamping to Charleston, wound up in Bordeaux.[111]

Nonetheless, soon MacKenzie was reporting that on the island "discontent is universal with [the] present order of things . . . in spite of the attempts of the government to divert the attention of the multitude from their real or imaginary evils, by raising a cry against France which in truth is against any white man in the country."[112] MacKenzie did not seem to realize that if London stopped backing those who enslaved Africans, relations could possibly improve. However, MacKenzie must have been doing something right since Paris was no fan of his,[113] nor was Washington,[114] probably a reflection of the fact that he was a man of color and that London was gaining advantage by employing him, forcing these two powers to act similarly to the consternation of domestic public opinion.

Sufficiently intimidated, in 1826 President Boyer issued a proclamation—in French—barring intercourse with all Caribbean colonies except St. Thomas and Curaçao.[115] Intense negotiations with General Inginac continued concerning a key clause that sought to "secure the admission into the provinces belonging to His Majesty in North America of all the produce of Haiti, on the same terms with similar protections of other Foreign countries"; there was "no difficulty in allowing to Haitians in Great Britain all that is claimed for British subjects in Haiti" and Haitian consuls would be allowed in Canada, not a welcome development in Washington's view. The same could be said for the strong provisions barring the slave trade, which surely were drafted with the slave-holding republic in mind.[116]

London was also looking to Haiti for guidance on the practical implementation of abolition, a maneuver that too would compromise the slave-holding republic. MacKenzie was asked "to ascertain in minute detail the different regulations issued by Toussaint L'Ouverture by which he was enabled to enforce Agricultural Industry among the Negroes of St. Domingo after slavery had been abolished."

MacKenzie was not altogether successful in this venture: "I was unable to find in Haiti," he conceded, "any documents referenced," though "in repeated conversations with Toussaint's surviving officers," he found that coercion was employed by the Haitian authorities. "A flogging of a woman by the order of Dessalines" was detailed, though "she was big with child and the punishment so severe that abortion took place on the spot." But, unlike in Dixie, there was "remuneration . . . one fourth of the net proceeds."[117]

Overall, London had more leeway in this bilateral relationship, not only because of its relative wealth and military strength. MacKenzie adjudged in 1827 that the island had a "small population (423,000)," so trade—even optimally—strained to be significant. But, he noted sagely, "as a military" ally "Haiti is more respectable. In the event of war, mischief might result from her ports being crowded with Privateers of the enemy" and "the pirates of all nations," which meant treading carefully.[118] Months later MacKenzie was to be found in the eastern end of the island and noticed several leading pirates resting offshore. He wondered what "intrigue" might be perpetrated by these buccaneers tied to "agents" of Port-au-Prince.[119] Washington had reason to wonder similarly.

THE TRICKLE OF U.S. NEGROES to Hispaniola began to gush after Clarkson's initiative and within a few weeks the mainland press was reporting that official Haiti was willing to pay passage for the damned of the mainland to migrate to the island.[120]

The fact of the matter was that the damned—overwhelmingly free Negroes—were being courted by others more impressed with their manifest skills. For at the same time, the colony then known as French Guiana—on the northern coast of South America—thought it could attract this group too, which would also deprive the enemy in Port-au-Prince of their talents. Passage too would be paid there, along with land grants and material support and the promise to return them to the mainland if they were dissatisfied.[121]

Cayenne was spurned in favor of Haiti. The census of 1820 showed that in New York state alone there were over 29,000 free Negroes and more than 10,000 enslaved persons. By that juncture the Haitian authorities had dispatched an official emissary to the mainland to attract more U.S. Negroes southward.[122] Among those packing their bags was M. Silvain Simonisse, a naturalized Haitian born in South Carolina; he and his two brothers had been sent by their French father to Britain to be educated. He then returned to Carolina but the reigning racism was repugnant to him. So he moved to Haiti,[123] with the support of Joseph Balthazar Inginac, Boyer's Secretary of State.[124]

He was not alone. From 1824 to 1826 at least 6000 Free Negroes departed the United States for Hispaniola. In 1822 Haitians successfully chased slavery from their eastern border and, to a degree, wounded the racist oppression that those defined as "white" visited upon those who were to become Dominicans. Many of these oppressors and a large number of skilled laborers fled—to Cuba and Puerto Rico, for example—leaving behind rich lands and increasing the need for able workers in agriculture and industry. President Boyer was also concerned with foreign invasions, which a more evenly spread population, he believed, would deter. So he instructed, "find artisans of African blood, such as carpenters, wood-sawyers, blacksmiths, caulkers, rope-makers, sail-makers."[125] So prompted, John Russwurm, a prominent Jamaican-American, sought thirty cultivators among U.S. Negroes to move to Haiti.[126]

Answering Boyer's call were thousands of U.S. Negroes, thirteen thousand by one estimate.[127] Echoing this departure, *Freedom's Journal*, the leading U.S. Negro periodical, sensed that "the vicinity of one or more independent black states would be dangerous to the internal tranquility of our country," while in fact Haiti "would naturally attract from among us the free blacks who are found in the slave-holding states to be troublesome members of society."[128]

There was push and pull involved. Free Negroes were viewed suspiciously for fear that they would join with the enslaved in a mainland version of the Haitian Revolution and getting rid of them by any means necessary was a priority. St. Louis, Missouri, was distant from Haiti, but even there in the 1820s there was deep apprehension of what one observer termed "riotous Negroes."[129] Vesey's revolt led to a tightening of slave patrols and arguments that another Haitian Revolution was nigh.[130] Yet these besieged U.S. Negroes—like many other Africans—were also attracted to the isle of freedom because of opportunity, liberty, and pride.

The "push" was well organized in the form of the American Colonization Society, hell-bent on stripping North America of a good deal of its population of Africans. The Richmond branch acknowledged in early 1825 that the "prevailing wish among the free persons of colour" was to head speedily to the abolitionist isle, particularly since "an agent was sent from Hayti with tempting offers for emigrants to St. Domingo. By many of the free persons of colour, the offer has been accepted." This was causing perturbation among some Euro-Americans who found the island "much more unpleasant than even in the wilds of Africa"[131]—the latter being their preferred site for mass deportation.

The "pull," in short, was embodied in residing in a sovereign African republic, as opposed to a slave-holding republic. President Boyer had made an enticing offer to U.S. Negroes, urging them to relocate en masse. "The hand of Providence," he proclaimed, "has destined Hayti for a land of promise, a sacred asylum, where our unfortunate brethren will in the end see their wounds healed by the balm of equality & their tears wiped away by the protecting hand of liberty."[132]

He made his sentiments clear again in April 1824 when he said of the beleaguered U.S. Negroes, "far from enjoying the rights of freemen, they have only an existence, precarious and full of humiliation," and this "entitles you to the gratitude of the Haytiens, who cannot see with indifference the calamities which afflict their brethren." Do not depart for Africa, he counseled. No, he announced, "I am about to send to New York funds and a confidential agent" with a "view to facilitate the emigration to Hayti of the descendants of Africans."[133]

This was a metronomic theme of Boyer's. A mainland journal trumpeted, "President Boyer is inviting the free blacks of the [United States] to emigrate to Hayti, in preference to Africa."[134] This was not the only vote of confidence in Haiti. In fact, this prominent mainland paper also said of the liberty isle in 1822 that the "population is rapidly increasing & knowledge is diffusing and, if the government shall remain stable & continue to be administered as it is now is, a powerful & wealthy nation will spring up in a few years."[135]

Enslaved Africans from Tortola accepted Boyer's generous offer and escaped to freedom in Haiti in 1822, as slaveholders contorted in discomposure.[136]

U.S. Negroes were also eagerly hopping on the Haitian bandwagon. The Reverend Thomas Paul was ordained in 1805 as Minister of Boston's "First African Baptist Church," but by 1823 he had spent six months in Haiti where he met President Boyer and months later published a letter urging his fellow Negroes to emigrate. Secretary of State Inginac told Reverend Paul directly that he was "offering the descendants of Africans who groan in the United States in misery and humiliation, an asylum."[137] Black New Yorkers saluted the "philanthropic offers of President Boyer" and his attempt to aid them to "remove . . . the prejudices which oppose the civil, intellectual, and moral advancement of men of colour in the United States." But now there was an alternative, "where a dark complexion will be no disadvantage," where one can join the "pioneers of a vast multitude," and where one will not be subject to "persecution" for failing to follow the "established religion."[138]

By 1824 a number of Haitian agents had arrived in New York, determined to attract an even larger portion of the Negro population southward. The potential emigrants were told to arrive in groups of twelve since "by going in large numbers in the same neighbourhood, they will form communities of themselves" and "their conversations will be one with another." Have no fear though since "all religious professions are tolerated"—unlike certain European nations.[139] The principal agent—Jonathan Granville—was bound to impress U.S. Negroes. He had studied in Paris at the College de La Marche, at the same time as the sons of the now sainted General Toussaint, before returning to Haiti in 1816.[140]

"Citizen Granville arrived some weeks since from Hayti," it was announced on the mainland in the summer of 1824. His "purpose" was "encouraging emigration of the free people of colour to that country." Yet, this correspondent worried that the "lands" slated for these emigrants were "still claimed by the Spanish authorities and may still be a source of contention," thus landing these U.S. Negroes in a hornet's nest of conflict.[141] Nevertheless, when one of the more affluent U.S. Negroes—James Forten—weighed in on the virtues of emigration, it was apparent why "Citizen Granville" would be greeted so warmly on the mainland.[142]

By the fall of 1824, fourteen-year-old Serena Baldwin of the mainland was among the thousands of U.S. Negroes who were to flock to freedom in Haiti. "If ever there was a country where Liberty dwells," she enthused, "it is here. It is a blessing enjoyed alike by all men, without respect to fortune or colour" and, "as respects our situation, it is a pleasant one."[143] Charles Fisher also had arrived in Haiti, telling his father happily, "I have received a plantation from the government and find the soil good for tillage." Though "we have plenty of vegetable food," meat was "not procured in such abundance here as in America," meaning some of the emigrants were "impatient" and "dissatisfied on that account." But Francis plodded on, reporting happily that "production of my land is in good order, yielding coffee, corn, sweet potatoes, yams, bananas, oranges, pineapples, cotton trees in abundance, and oil trees. I have two thousand bearing coffee trees, besides young ones, too numerous to mention. My plantation is eight miles from the City of Cape Hayti."[144]

Freedom's Journal, the Manhattan-based Negro journal, agreed with Fisher, pointing out that on the freedom isle, "the necessaries of life are abundant and cheap; and so fertile and productive is the soil that a Haytien farmer is not under the necessity of laboring more than one half the time, usually devoted to agriculture in New England"; the island was "compared to a Garden of Eden." So "if the laws permitted the settlement of Americans in Hayti, in twenty years we should see the soil completely occupied by them."[145] Hence, the migration was gaining even more traction, as "the editor of the Genius of Universal Emancipation" was on the verge of going to the island "with a number of emancipated slaves," a move that had sparked interest since "they will be emphatically free, the moment they touch the soil of Hayti."[146]

The editor Benjamin Lundy was enmeshed in this project by 1825. Subsequently, he recalled that after he had detailed an account of sending of "eleven slaves to Hayti," he was then approached to send "eighty-eight" more. He "complied with the request and they were all settled there, perfectly free." He then "persuaded" a group of North Carolinians "to send to Hayti one hundred and nineteen slaves who were under their care." Then in 1829 he went to the freedom isle for the second time, bringing along "twelve more emancipated slaves."[147]

In sum, the mass migration southward was matched by an effusion of praise for Haiti in the U.S. Negro press. The "energetic sway" of Boyer was hailed: "the cause of Education has always received firm support from the Executive of Hayti," said *Freedom's Journal*. "In no quarter of the globe are crimes less frequent." In fact, "so secure do the citizens consider themselves and [their] property that many never close their doors during the night"; even "the great capitalists of Europe consider the government as permanently fixed," giving migrants a sense of security too.[148] Believing this was so, this journal had "authorized agents" in Port-au-Prince.[149]

"The island of Hayti," said this journal, was "the only country on earth where the man of color walks in the plentitude of his rights"; it was the "cradle of hope" for "future generations."[150]

And that was the problem as far as Dixie was concerned. Haiti's existence incentivized enslaved Africans to escape southward by any means necessary. Fresh on the minds of many was a startling incident in mid-1826 when enslaved Africans en route from Baltimore to New Orleans revolted and sought to steer the vessel to Haiti—before being captured.[151] Haiti's existence compelled London to consider abolition more insistently and encouraged Spain's rebelling colonies to add abolition to the agenda. Thus it was in 1826 when future U.S. Secretary of State Edward Everett proclaimed passionately: "I would cede the whole continent to any one who would take it—to England, to France, to Spain. I would see it sunk to the bottom of the Ocean, before I would see any part of this America converted into Continental Hayti, by that awful process of blood and desolation by which alone such a catastrophe could be brought on."[152] During congressional debates that same year as to whether the United States would participate in a hemispheric conference in Panama in which Haiti would presumably participate, Senator Thomas Hart Benton was apoplectic, asserting forcefully that "no mulatto Consuls or black Ambassadors" from Haiti could ever engage with their counterparts from the slaveholding republic in Panama or elsewhere. Dixie "will not permit black Consuls and Ambassadors to establish themselves in our cities," he exhorted, and never would he countenance an effort "to parade them through the country and give their fellow blacks in the United States proof in hand of the honors which await them for a successful revolt on their part."[153] The Panama assembly was greeted with favor in Haiti, particularly since their sacred cause—abolition—would be discussed.[154]

The senator had a point. But trade with the island and the necessity of preventing

Haiti from becoming a citadel of British—and anti-Washington—influence suggested otherwise, as did the allied notion that failure to move toward abolition was hastening another revolution in which case all would be lost, lives not least. Yet this inclination was deepening a sectional rift. Indeed, John C. Calhoun concurred with his fellow representative of a slave-holding state, Missouri's Benton. Yes, said the Carolinian, "recognition of the independence of Hayti" was a "delicate subject" now "spoken of in Northern papers" and causing "great mischief." But what would occur to "our social relations" with the arrival of a "Black minister in Washington?" Calhoun was beyond outrage: "must he be received or excluded from our dinners, our dances, and our parties and must his daughters and sons participate in the society of our daughters and sons?" To even bruit the matter perforce "must involve the peace and perhaps the union of this nation,"[155] he declaimed thunderously.

The ampler point was that the very existence of Haiti was complicating Washington's relations with London and deepening an already wide sectional chasm. Both factors were to eventuate in civil war—and abolition.

6

U.S. Negroes and Black Jacobins
1830–1839

The bloodily transformative slave revolt led by Nat Turner in Virginia in 1831 persuaded some pro-slavery defenders to believe that the Haitian Revolution had descended on the shores of North America. One scholar argues that the mainstream press in the commonwealth inadvertently propelled this idea since it was easier to focus on bloodshed emerging from the Caribbean, than in its own backyard, even when obliquely referring to the charismatic leader of slave rebellion. Nat Turner remained unmentionable because of the Caribbean menace his very name was thought to have foreshadowed.[1]

One of the first accounts of this catalytic episode, published in 1831, evoked the specter of Haiti in its very first sentence. Sounding the tocsin, Samuel Warner warned that "in consequence of the alarming increase of the Black population of the South . . . fears have been long entertained that it might one day be the unhappy lot of the whites in that section, to witness scenes similar to those which but a few years since, nearly depopulated the once flourishing island of St. Domingo of its white inhabitants." Though it was Nat Turner that ostensibly drove Warner's concern, he returned like a magnet to metal to Haiti: "such were the horrors that attended the insurrection of the Blacks in St. Domingo," that it was easy to infer that "similar scenes of bloodshed and murder might our brethren at the South expect to witness, were the disaffected Slaves of that section of the Country but once to gain the ascendancy." He cautioned that in the case of "a 'General Nat,' they might then find a wretch not less disposed to shed innocent blood than was the perfidious Dessalines." That "General Nat" launched his rebellion virtually to the day that Hispaniola had erupted a mere four decades earlier gave added resonance to Warner's pained remarks.[2]

As abolition crept closer to reality in the Caribbean, the Black Jacobins had reason to believe that a strategic goal was coming to fruition. Concomitantly, their slave-holding foes on the mainland were thinking that—instead—the noose was tightening around the neck of their hated system, a perception that the audacity of "General Nat" did little to alleviate. Their fearful apprehension was exacerbated by an economic downturn that hit with a thunderclap in the mainland. Then there was the predictable dislocation presented by the triumph of British abolitionism, an epochal event difficult to keep away from the eager ears of the enslaved. "You seem to apprehend troubles from the Negro in the South," said F. S. Case in 1836. In fact, he added, "they will produce great trouble in all the slave states and [the] time is not far distant."[3]

Thus, a debate erupted in the Virginia legislature following the Turner massacre with the purpose of seeking to show the futility of abolition—with Haiti being an alleged case in point. In January 1832 in Richmond one policymaker pondered if the proposal from Haiti should be considered, i.e. as Philip A. Bolling averred, "their Chief offers to pay for their [Negroes'] passage, to receive them as free citizens."[4] Concurring with the underlying sentiment, a leader of the Colonization Society declared, "it is only necessary to cast a furtive glance at the scenes in St. Domingo and more recently in Jamaica and the various insurrections planned and attempted in this country" to glimpse the importance of ousting these Negroes.[5] On the other hand, Thomas Dew who taught, *inter alia*, "Metaphysics" at the College of William and Mary, when summarizing this spirited colloquy, was also keen to point to the growth of the African population as a condition precedent for mass revolt, an allegation that encouraged emigration of free Negroes. "During the ten years too immediately preceding the revolution," he said, "more than 200,000 Negroes were imported into the island from Africa. It is a well known fact that newly imported Negroes are always greatly more dangerous than those born among us" and a "very large proportion" of these islanders "consisted of Kormantyn [*sic*] slaves, from the Gold Coast, who have all the savage ferocity of the North American Indian." So, he concluded, study Haiti to avoid another "General Nat." The dazed metaphysician also projected the commonwealth's history a century into the future and assured "in 1929 . . . we shall be much more secure from plots and insurrections than we are at this moment."[6]

Africans in Greenville, South Carolina, weeks after General Turner's revolt sought to deliver a different, non-metaphysical, future. There were "horrible tales about insurrection" emerging and with some "in such a state," said one resident, "they had both near scared themselves into cocked hats."[7] This jitteriness was comprehensible given the fevered reporting that gripped post-Turner Dixie and touted the arrival of another Haitian Revolution.

Following on the heels of this fright was another in New Orleans. Captain J. E. Alexander of the 42nd Royal Highlanders happened to be there when "an alarm of a slave insurrection" occurred. "Hand-bills of an inflammatory nature were found, telling the slaves to rise and massacre the whites" and that the fabled "Hannibal was a Negro" and he too had defeated Europeans. Do "not leave one white proprietor alive" was the message. Punctuating the rhetoric were "several stand of arms, some said three hundred," which were "found in a coloured man's house; and the affair looked so serious," said this military man, "that five hundred of the citizens were under arms every night and the mayor solicited a detachment of four companies or regulars from the nearest garrison."[8] This was Louisiana, the place of choice for former settlers in Hispaniola, who were all too aware of what could befall slaveholders.

The professor's misplaced optimism notwithstanding, there was good reason for pessimism, beginning with abolition in the Caribbean, then moving on to the poetic salute of General Toussaint by the noted mainland writer, John Greenleaf Whittier[9]—this at a time when Haiti was being painted as a cataclysmic nightmare. Minimally, this reflected a sectional divergence. Then there was the debate in the Chamber of Deputies in France on abolition, which highlighted even more poisoning plots in Martinique. It appeared as if a mass movement was driving slaveholders from the colony—not the message that this class in the hemisphere sought to hear. The poisonings were also discouraging cattle-raising, according to Alexis de Tocqueville, who added that slavery meant the "idea of labor is inseparably connected with the idea of bondage" and this discouraged work itself. De Tocqueville, who was to garner a glowing reputation on the mainland, freely admitted that the debate in France was "preoccupied by the recollections of St. Domingo" and the "bloody collisions" there[10]—but the same could be said about post-Turner Virginia.

Revolutionary fervor swept France in 1830 and predictably, on 9 February 1831, 300 Africans attacked eleven plantations in Martinique. This reflected and fed the abolition in surrounding islands that in turn led to steps toward abolition in Saint Pierre.[11] Just as predictably, the same year that Martinique went up in flames, Jamaica witnessed the rebellion led by General Nat's island counterpart—Sam Sharpe. Both burned with the fervor of religion though the Jamaican was more overtly inspired by abolitionist debates in London. Settlers on the island feared they were all slated for liquidation.[12] As if it were hardly a coincidence, the U.S. agent, William Miles, instructed John C. Calhoun that "the Scottish Abolitionists sent an agent to Haiti in 1831 or thereabouts."[13]

The "spirit of insubordination" had also found its way to St. Lucia and Antigua too, said a Jamaican source in a position to know. "Any acts of insubordination contemplated by the Negroes," he said, "usually break out during the Christmas holidays, the season always considered to be that of the greatest danger." To be expected, thusly, were "simultaneous rising[s]" across the Caribbean since "all the buildings on more than one hundred and fifty estates" in Jamaica were only recently "burnt to the ground" and the "most frightful atrocities [were] committed on the persons of the white inhabitants."[14]

Jamaican planters were also grousing about stiffer competition from mainland plantations who gained an advantage since the latter's government was lethargic in the face of the "illicit traffic in Negroes"; their "labour [was] being directed at the cultivation of [sugar] cane" to the detriment of Jamaica itself. The bar on the slave trade may have, paradoxically, strengthened abolitionist Haiti and its mainland "rivals" simultaneously. One subject reached the opinion that Britian's policy exhibited "reckless disregard for [the] consequences" of abolition—a state of affairs that was pushing some Caribbean planters toward their mainland counterparts.[15] For the Foreign Office in London was then told that "overtures have been made to the government of the United States by disaffected individuals in Jamaica."[16] Surely, enslavement, wildly profitable, would continue under the Stars-and-Stripes. Britain's envoy in Washington recognized that these planters tended to "act in union with the citizens in the slave holding states of this Union" though their economic interests often clashed with those of competing sugar planters, e.g. in Louisiana.[17]

Just as these slaveholders' alignments traversed boundaries, these planters continued to have justification in fearing cross-border collaboration by enslaved Africans, a policy that often implicated Haiti. "What happened in places like Saint Pierre," proclaims one scholar sagaciously, "not only mattered to those in Martinique or Bordeaux or Paris but also potentially to those in Wilmington, North Carolina, or Portsmouth, England or even Venezuela." Thus, after British abolition, the equivalent movement in Martinique was turbo-charged, the United States was not unaffected, and Haiti was strengthened objectively.[18]

This was the essence of the message delivered to John C. Calhoun by William Miles, who was the commercial agent for the United States in Aux Cayes in 1833. Initially, he recalled later, "the prejudices of the people were not strongly sh[o]wn towards the whites." However, "as soon as the treaty [of] indemnity was settled with France" and Washington refused to "appoint Consuls" to Haiti, "there very soon arose considerable prejudices against us & in favor of the English & this feeling increased until after the British Emancipation Act." At that critical juncture, "the prejudices against all whites now commenced, were increased by the Mulattoes & lighter colored people, who were jealous of the whites," and "by the year 1836 & 1837 foreigners generally began to leave the island."

Providing a taste of the bitter medicine ingested regularly by mainland Africans, Miles was infuriated when his five-year old stated plaintively, "Father, I wish I was like Amelie Ligonde." The latter was "a colored child," he told Calhoun, still horrified. Thus, he said angrily, "the same repugnance exists in colored people toward us, we have for them." Thus, there was a fear that abolition also meant "equality" and miscegenation with incalculable consequences. Similarly, even with abolitionism, Miles detected a ray of hope for bondage in that "the greatest industry I saw was among the old men & women who had been slaves."[19]

Yet what was worrying the likes of Calhoun and those of his ilk was the reaction of Miles's daughter; that is, the existence of an abolitionist republic was profoundly incompatible with mainland slavery and inexorably eroded the rationale for the latter. Lieutenant Charles Steedman of the United States visited the liberty isle in the 1830s and immediately eyed "the step-daughter of Colonel Vehoe, a mulatto from Philadelphia." The military man was then "commanding President Boyer's guards," but what occupied Steedman's attention was the step-daughter. She was "as black as a Negress could be," but he added lasciviously, "had a most exquisite figure." The fact that she "had been educated in a convent in Paris" seemed to enhance his—and others'—interest for "notwithstanding her ebony color, all of us vied with each other in securing her hand for the waltz or quadrille."[20]

Abolition could mean miscegenation and what would that mean for the slaveholding republic's founding principle of white supremacy? Likewise, would abolition mean the formerly enslaved would seek revenge for centuries of bondage? The settler known as "Mrs. Carmichael" spent five years in St. Vincent and Trinidad and Tobago and was puzzled to notice "jackets belonging" to an "estate" of the former "with the stamp of property upon them, worn in Trinidad by Trinidad Negroes." She also knew that "there are many Free Negroes and coloured people who can, and who do read the English newspapers; and the very memorable debates in parliament upon the subject of slavery soon found their way" to "the Negroes—and the effect was instantly visible. There was a total change of conduct." Somehow, they began to look at her as "their enemy." Yet, despite this overt enmity, "generally speaking, Negroes do not regard England and Scotland in the same light,"[21] since the latter was seen as more commercially minded and, therefore, reprehensible—which by inference underscores how they likely viewed rapacious Yankees.

This was notably the case because in Trinidad where there was a complement of former U.S. Negroes who had fled the mainland during the War of 1812. Indeed, she was stunned to encounter "B.W., a free American Negro and a rich man, with fine grounds on Laurel-Hill," a "person of some consequence."[22]

The broader point is that stirrings of abolitionism were causing ripples of concern in the Caribbean colonies, including islands where former U.S. Negroes with grievances against the mainland resided. This was occurring as the uproar embodied in General Nat was causing concern about a Haitian style revolution descending on wary slaveholders. And as London moved toward abolition, it was able to seize the moral high ground and more readily align with abolitionists—Black Jacobins most directly—to the disadvantage of the slave-holding republic. William Lloyd, a Briton visiting the Caribbean just after abolition, upbraided the pretensions of Washington, describing its heralded "Declaration of Independence" as the "greatest outrage upon good sense ever palmed upon the world, when we estimate the sentiments expressed by the acts of the American people towards the blacks." He did not spare his own land for the "folly" it had created—though it was unclear if he meant the slave trade or being the progenitor of the United States itself.[23]

The feeling was mutual. Washington and London had fought a war roughly two decades before Caribbean abolition, an event that marked the latter's attempt to improve relations with Port-au-Prince. With abolition, bilateral relations between the two North Atlantic nations took a predictable downturn. The Carolina slaveholder James Hammond spoke warmly of spending three enchantingly enthralling weeks in Paris—though he confessed openly that he was "not much delighted with England or the English."[24] In contrast, he mused, France was "like sunshine after darkness" after setting foot in Britain.[25] Other slaveholders were seeking to elude London's snare; for example, James Kirkpatrick was exploring the option of sending more cotton to France rather than Britain.[26]

Frenzied delirium accompanied the Virginia rebellion—much of which focused on Hispaniola and the growth in numbers of Africans that provided the fuel for revolution in the run-up to 1831; however, ironically, there was a laissez-faire attitude toward the slave trade on the mainland—before and after the revolt led by General Nat. In discussing this issue with his French counterpart, Albert Gallatin of the United States acknowledged freely that "it is known that American built vessels" and "it is believed that American capital are still employed under the French flag in that infamous traffic." Yes, it was also "too notorious," he continued, "that many vessels bearing the flag of France are still engaged in the trade," but he was unwilling to concede that London should have the right to interdict slavers under any flag.[27] The Viscount de Chateaubriand was told—accurately—that U.S. laws meant to curtail the slave trade were "ineffectual." Attached to the correspondence was a resolution from the U.S. president authorized to negotiate a pact deeming this iniquitous commerce to be "piracy"—but no intelligent diplomat could take this seriously.[28]

For at the same time this resolution was making its way to Paris, a more seri-ous report was concluding that the leading powers were fomenting wars in order to generate prisoners-of-war that could then be sold into slavery. "These wars are not the consequence of a disposition naturally quarrelsome," it was said, "but are the immediate offspring of cupidity, sharpened up and roused to action by the arrival of a slave ship."[29]

As abolition approached in the Caribbean, slaving vessels were arriving with the regularity of nightfall to Haiti's west in Cuba, with most of these vessels bearing the Stars-and-Stripes.[30] In September 1834—just after abolition—U.S. officials awakened from their usual slumber and charged a seafarer with "having been engaged in the slave trade"; that he had been in and out of Haiti was worri-some to Port-au-Prince given the well-known tendency to kidnap free Negroes.[31] Just as the Haitian Revolution did not force abolition on the mainland, abolition in the Caribbean had a similar result. In both cases, remaining true to founding principles, the enslaving republic dug in its heels and sought to stem the tide of progress.

Yet slaveholders could understandably complain that abolition's approach was placing their human property—and themselves—in jeopardy. Thus, weeks before abolition, the governor in the Bahamas was told worryingly of "symptoms of insub-ordination among the Negroes" and that "slaves on some of the islands are resolved not to work after August 1," 1834, and this was "most general among the slaves at Exuma and Eleuthera,"[32] just hundreds of miles from Haiti. British planters were disconsolate to find that as abolition neared, Africans felt they were "under no obli-gation to work for their former owners" at all. This was "attended with the most serious consequences," necessitating the perceived need for a "vessel of war cal-culated most impressively to enforce obedience."[33] This development could not be embraced by most Haitians, just as it confirmed the perception of enslaving repub-licans that abolition could only mean financial disaster.

Perhaps if such trends could have been limited to the Bahamas, London—and mainland slaveholders for that matter—could have exhaled more easily. But that was not to be and, again, it was easier to blame the hand of Haiti than to look askance at slavery itself.

TO A DEGREE IT WAS FELT THAT one way for a free Negro on the mainland to avoid being kidnapped was to migrate to Haiti. And with the escalating fear that ensnared Dixie after General Turner's revolt, slave-holding republicans renewed their longtime objective of ousting as many of this group as possible on the premise that they were prone to ally with rebellious Africans.

At the same time, the slave-holding republicans in the wake of General Nat's rise were confounded—they wanted to increase the number of enslaved Africans because of the fabulous wealth their presence promised but were fearful that this was only creating the climate for another Haitian Revolution. Blocking the slave trade (or even circumscribing the similarly lucrative business of "slave breeding"[34]) was a bridge too far, but ousting free Negroes—who were seen as the culprits insti-gating the revolution in the first place—once again was the "least bad" option, a phony war against Black Jacobinism. Conditions were made so unappealing for this group—a "push"—while the beacon of Haiti loomed so luminously (the "pull") that thousands headed from the mainland to the Caribbean.

There was a burst of migration between 1824 and 1826 and a steady stream thereafter. North Carolina Quakers were noticeably busy in promoting this traffic[35] though there was some resistance from a group of about fifty free Negroes who, it was reported, were "mostly opposed to going either to Liberia or Hayti but many of them would [be] willing to be sent to a free state."[36] Others were delighted to arrive at Aux Cayes, Haiti.[37] The self-proclaimed "Emigration Committee" of the Manumission Society was seeking "to get as many of the people of colour as oppor-tunity will admit" to "embark for the island of Hayti."[38]

With the expansive new territory to the east and the continuing flight of many of the residents of Hispaniola unhappy with the abolition of slavery, Port-au-Prince also had reason to attract covey after covey of emigrants. Tellingly, after the reversion of the eastern part of the island to Haiti, an influx of Spaniards flowed into New Orleans, augmenting the revenge-seeking French settlers who had been arriving since 1804.[39]

As this important migration was taking place—Caribbean settlers to the main-land and mainland Negroes to the Caribbean—some of the former who had experi-enced the trauma of the Haitian Revolution were expiring, raising the possibility of an easing of tension with Haiti. Foremost in this category was Stephen Girard who, born in Bordeaux in 1750, had made a fortune by exchanging U.S. beef and flour for sugar and coffee from Hispaniola, where he had familial ties. He was quite upset with the sacking of towns where these family members lived; besides, abolition in Hispaniola soured a number of his key investments. This did not prevent him from becoming one of the wealthiest men on the mainland. Yet when he died in 1830, this man, described as "an earlier Andrew Carnegie," did not allow his toxic legacy to be buried with him. For his will—as his sympathetic biographer noted—"specifically discriminated against non-whites" in his hometown, Philadelphia in provisions that were not addressed until well into the 20th century.[40] This meant that the ghost of counterrevolution continued to haunt Africans, even as counterrevolutionaries were passing into history.

The obduracy of the likes of Girard sheds light on why Haiti embraced so many free Negroes from the mainland with alacrity. President Boyer, said the Manumission Society, "has offered to take any number of colored people the United States may think proper to send and to pay a considerable part of the expense of transporting them himself"—though the "Colonization Society rejected the proposal, as not consistent with their plan of sending missionaries to Africa."[41]

Haiti was too close for comfort. As the bridesmaid of leading U.S. politicians—Henry Clay—asserted, Haiti was not the preferred site for free Negro emigration. This "should not be the policy of the United States," he huffed, speaking of sending this group southward. Moreover, he observed, when one "consider[s] the predominant power of the island and its vicinity to the Southern States, to add strength to it" was ill-advised.[42]

While men of Dixie like Clay were castigating Haiti, abolitionists were singing a different song, indicative of a ripening sectional rift. Angelina Grimké, an abolitionist, wondered why "white Americans" yearned for a "demonstration of the colored man's capacity for elevation." And, she asked, "why has not the intelligence of the Haytian convinced them? *Their* free republic has grown up under the very eye of the slaveholder, and as a nation we have for many years been carrying on a lucrative trade with her merchants, and yet we have never recognized her independence, never sent a minister there, though we have sent ambassadors to European countries whose commerce is far less important to us than that of St. Domingo."[43]

Here the premature feminist not only exposed the contradictions in U.S. policy toward Haiti but also demonstrated how the very existence of the freedom isle weakened the ostensible rationale for slavery. For the slave-holding republicans—protestations aside—were enslaving Africans for naked profit, irrespective of these Negroes' estimable qualities. The slave-holding republicans would even seek to make profits by trading with their supposed inferiors and bending a knee to do so, with their reputed racialist philosophy supposedly banning the same set aside. As the contradictions sharpened, so did the sectional rift and the march toward civil war—but this march had been accelerated by the Haitian Revolution.

As the abolitionist Benjamin Lundy had exemplified, arranging for the taking of enslaved mainland Africans to Haiti where they could be freed was also becoming popular. Again, there were naysayers in the American Colonization Society though *Freedom's Journal* argued that the island would "suit the great mass of our colored people better, by far, than any other place, beyond the limits of this Continent." Contrary to prevailing opinion in certain circles, the newly freed were "doing exceedingly well. They stand completely 'redeemed, regenerated, and disenthralled' from the prejudices of the white race."[44]

Thus, the Quakers—Isaac Hatch and Thomas Kennedy—arrived on the freedom isle from Manhattan after procuring the manumission of "thirty coloured people" in their homeland, then deposited them in Haiti, and "furnished them with clothes and agricultural implements." Boyer himself was so pleased—as *Freedom's Journal* put it—that he "received them with his accustomed urbanity."[45]

Unsurprisingly, news of Haiti was a constant in this Manhattan periodical and, correspondingly, by the end of the 1820s the number of U.S. Negroes who had emigrated there had ballooned—by their calculation—to 13,000.[46]

Of course, all those who were fed up with the mainland did not head to Haiti. Many headed to a newly created state, Liberia. Then there were those like Victor Sejour. While his father was born in Hispaniola, he was born in New Orleans in 1817. But, as one commentator observed, "young Sejour found the racial prejudice of Louisiana unbearable and in 1836 at the age of nineteen" moved to France where he established himself as a writer of note.[47] Sejour, a son of *gens de couleur*, has been credited with having published the first short story of "the African American tradition, 'Le Mulatre,'" written in French, which concerned a slave revolt in Hispaniola.[48] Though his father was one of an estimated 10,000 who fled Hispaniola for Louisiana during the revolutionary era, Sejour died in France in 1874, yet another exile alienated from the land of his birth.[49]

But other migrants of means spurned France in favor of Haiti. These included the so-called "mixed race" offspring of the Florida slaveholder, Zephaniah Kingsley. His son, Osceola Kingsley, was born in 1837 just as his father was providing a grubstake in Hispaniola for his siblings. The younger Kingsley went on to become a national hero in the Dominican Republic during the early 1860s war against Spain and was buried at Bergantín. His father escaped Florida at a time when yet another war had erupted between indigenes—ably assisted by Africans: the Second Seminole War, 1835–1842, was said by a Jacksonville newspaper to be leading to the "tragic scenes of Hayti."[50]

The elder Kingsley had fought a losing battle to alter the calcification of white supremacy in Florida. In the 1820s he tried and failed to convince officialdom to adopt Spanish "race policies" that were less rigid than those of the slave-holding republic. Then in 1833 as abolition was brewing in the Bahamas and Florida indigenes were about to take to the warpath he and eleven other planters, all fathers of children defined as Free Negroes, petitioned Washington to revoke the state's ossified apartheid laws—to no avail. Kingsley previously had travelled to Haiti in line with his coffee business and in 1835 returned again for less mercantile reasons. He purchased 35,000 acres on the northern coast of what is now the Dominican Republic, near Puerto Plata, a region where numerous U.S. Negroes had flocked.

One of his spouses, known as Anna Kingsley—who happened to be of African descent—administered a plantation there and another 1000 acres along the St. John's River in Florida.[51] The locale of her original homeland was unclear, perhaps Madagascar, perhaps Senegal, indicative of the broad reach of the slave trade, of which she was a product. The elder Kingsley, for example, operated a slave station along the Congo River, from which Africans were brought to bondage in Florida and Georgia.[52]

By September 1835 he was back in Haiti, which, he said, "resembled the Catskill mountains" in New York, "only more extended." In Puerto Plata he found "American and foreign shipping anchored before a pretty, scattered-looking small town of one story houses, something about the size of St. Augustine," Florida. "Amidst logs [of] mahogany" and "tobacco in bales" headed for the mainland, "its inhabitants . . . received me, as a white stranger with great civility as well as hospitality." This was thought to be impossible among slave-holding republicans but was typical if one approached the Haitians with like civility and not the rapacious mindset of a slave dealer. Instead the "white and black (the latter predominated)," greeted him warmly, "speaking Spanish, French, and English" while the "Spanish [predominated] rather the most and the white part of the population very much resembled the Minorcan population of St. Augustine." Kingsley took the time to "hear an old style Methodist sermon by an English missionary, where most of . . . [the] colored emigrants were assembled."

His venom was reserved for "our pseudo republicans," who "openly abuse Haiti, its people, and government." He also discovered that the Haitians "read our newspapers and [have learned of] daily accounts of mobs and persecution of color," which the Haitians found far from enamoring. Unlike the mainland, he ascertained that "this government of Haiti approaches nearer to pure republicanism than any other, now in use or on record." It was "hardly possible to find a servant to hire," since "every colored person of good character is a citizen from the moment of his arrival" and thereby able to pull herself up by her bootstraps.[53]

It was in 1836 that he took his son, George, "a healthy colored man of uncorrupted morals," as he put it, and then "about thirty years of age" and "tolerably well educated" along with the "six prime African men, my own slaves, liberated for that express purpose," to the northern coast of Hispaniola. Then in October 1837 he brought his "son's wife and children" there, "together with the wives and children of his servants," and "two additional families of my slaves, all liberated for the express purpose of transportation to Haiti." He knew all too well that this was not increasing his own popularity in Florida. Indeed, there were "some objections" to Haiti, which "originated in the fear of having a free colored Government and powerful people, so near our own slave-holding States." Ultimately, Kingsley freed at least fifty-three of his former slaves and brought them to Haiti. He was influenced by the capacious plan of abolitionist Benjamin Lundy who as early as 1825 conceived the idea of sending 50,000 freed slaves to Haiti each year at a cost of $14.40 each.[54]

This goal was not met, but U.S. Negroes continued arriving steadily in Haiti. When in 1839, for example, a vessel from the mainland arrived from Kingsley's Florida neighborhood with 101 free Negro emigrants aboard, a U.S. Negro journal reported that "their lively demonstrations of joy on reaching that land of liberty and plenty" were boundless.[55] When "Emancipation Day" was marked in Port-au-Prince in 1838, French and British consuls were present—and, doubtlessly, U.S. Negro emigrants too.[56] Kingsley's words about the fear of a "free colored Government," which these emigrants were determined to support, were highlighted in the U.S. Negro press, underscoring their potency.[57]

The elder Kingsley was no stranger to the island, having resided there for three years during the 1790s. "His" Africans—not unlike those on the island who were free—had roots in today's Nigeria and the Rio Pongo basin in Guinea and the slave emporium that was Zanzibar.[58] They were among the more than fifty newly freed slaves he brought to the island.[59] Kingsley had—perhaps—four spouses and three of them and their children migrated to Haiti. The most prominent—Anna—was born Muslim but converted to Catholicism, then learned Spanish, and then English.[60]

Kingsley was unique for his broadmindedness or, alternatively, his understanding of the perils presented by a too rigid white supremacy. Yes, there were massacres during the revolutionary era on the island, he told the Florida legislature and revolts in Barbados and "Demara" [sic] too; and, yes, Africans in Hispaniola were accused of perpetrating "wanton acts of cruelty"—but what about the context and what had driven them to this point? This he knew since "after the Revolutionary Flame had subsided," he reminded, "I lived a long time at Petit Goâve." His experience there seemed to shape his new vision for Florida, remaking it in a racial image closer, for example, to Cuba, i.e. envisioning an ample role for free Negroes.[61]

Just as British abolitionism was marked indelibly by the Haitian Revolution, Kingsley was too. Unlike many of his countrymen he defended *gens de couleur* avidly and warned forebodingly that "a war of color would in our situation of all wars be the most dangerous" and "therefore the least advisable."[62] Kingsley also worried about the security of Florida in light of its hardened racist policies for such praxis had driven a number of enterprising young men from the mainland and into the Haitian navy where they could then ally with the British Royal Navy.[63]

The well-positioned Kingsley was able to wangle a "long and familiar interview with President Boyer," a "very intelligent man" with a "rather dark complexion."

Nearby he noticed "33 regiments of regular infantry and one regiment of cavalry, besides 4 regiments of artillery." Military spending was "caused, it is said, by the fear of enemies from without," who saw the abolitionist isle as antagonistic, but such expenditures unavoidably meant less spending on education and health care, thereby deforming the economy. "The navy is small and consists of a few vessels of war and revenue cutters," but they were capable of keeping slave ships at bay. "Militia troops are well armed" and "consist of one hundred thousand effective men." He was also able to wangle an extensive comment from President Boyer on prospects for emigration—intended for the consumption of mainland Negro audiences.[64]

Born in Scotland in 1764, Kingsley's departure for Haiti was an indication of the furor he caused in Florida.[65] His last will and testament was blunt: he sought to "solemnly enjoin" his "colored and natural children" and, since "the illiberal and inequitable laws of this Territory," meaning Florida, "will not afford to them and to their children that protection and justice which is due in civilized society," he instructed that they abandon the peninsula. They were enjoined further to "remove themselves and properties to some land of liberty and equal rights where the conditions of law are governed by some law less absurd than that of color"—meaning Haiti.[66] The idealistic Scot believed that the "amalgamation of the white and colored races is to the best interests of America"—but his similarly idealistic will, in the final insult, was challenged successfully as being "against the public policy" of the Sunshine State and, thus, his then widow—Flora—moved to Santo Domingo where she perished in 1875, bequeathing a sizeable inheritance to her heirs.[67] When his will was read, his sister Martha—grandmother to James McNeil Whistler and mother of the subject of this famed painter's honored portrait of his own mother—became livid and took her fight for vindication to the highest courts in the land.[68]

Kingsley believed, said Maria Child who interviewed him, that "the only distinction should be between slave and free—not between *white* and *colored*." But this conservative idealism was still too radical for the slave-holding republic, which continued to harbor a grudge against *gens de couleur* and was busily expelling free Negroes. Kingsley plodded on, averring to the contrary that "the free people of color, instead of being persecuted, and driven from the Southern States, ought to be made eligible to all offices and means of wealth." According to Child, he thought that such a social setup "would form" a "grand chain of security, by which the interests of the two castes would become united and the slaves be kept in permanent subordination." Such an arrangement allowed slavery in Cuba and Brazil to survive decades after it had collapsed in North America, but that was not how it was seen during Kingsley's stormy lifetime.[69]

Kingsley, who saw himself as benevolent, was willing to allow his enslaved Africans to purchase their freedom at half-price—if they chose to migrate to Haiti.[70] Kingsley's activity was noticeable, as indicated by the fact that the U.S. envoy in Aux Cayes spoke of a "gentleman from Florida" who "came here" with "many people formerly his slaves and obtained permission from Mr. Boyer to have them bound to himself for a term" of undetermined "years." "I shall ascertain," the envoy added, "whether the same privilege will be granted to any other person wishing to come here with their former slaves," a worrisome trend that could deprive the slave-holding republic of free labor and bolster an abolitionist isle besides.[71]

Thus, U.S. Secretary of State John Forsyth, a resolute son of Dixie (Georgia in his case) was then told of others like Kingsley arriving at Aux Cayes with "their former slaves and securing their services for nine years," or so it was thought and not necessarily accurately. This was hardly minor: "I hope you will agree with me," said the U.S. emissary, "in thinking that this subject promises to be one of great importance to the U. States. Colored persons would undoubtedly prefer coming here," it was noted morosely, "than to be sent to the settlement at Liberia." Haiti was not bowing down to Kingsley and those like him since "persons bringing [former slaves] here must make the best bargain they can with regard to compensation for their services either by an offering of wages or a share in the produce of the soil." The "soil" was rich too, which augured well for these former slaves.[72] Another mainlander spoke to a Haitian military man and concluded that the issue of the arrival of "former slaves" was indeed profound and "promises to be one of great importance."[73]

There were "privileges granted" to the "*colored* children" of Kingsley, said a U.S. representative on the island, as he acknowledged that the Haitian leadership "would be pleased to see settlers here from America and were they [to] come there is certainly a wide field for exertion and enterprise" and "comparatively small capital would be required." Clarifying earlier notions, Ralph Higginbotham asserted that "property can always be leased for nine years renewable at the expiration of that time, at a very low rate, and although a white person is not allowed to hold land, it can always be purchased in the name of a colored person and this can be done without any possible risk," it was said with relief.[74]

The heirs and former slaves of the elder Kingsley were "fixed," as the Floridian put it in, "in a fine rich valley, about thirty miles from Port Platte [*sic*]; heavily timbered with mahogany all round; well watered; flowers so beautiful; fruits in abundance." His son had "laid out good roads and built bridges and mills." Kingsley was "anxious to establish a good school there. I engaged a teacher," he said. And he insisted, "my labourers in Haiti are not slaves. They are a kind of indented apprentices. I give them land and they bind themselves to work for me," adding unnecessarily to his interlocutor, Maria Child, "you know very well I could not sell them there." The budding abolitionist asserted forcefully, "I should be the last man on earth to give up a runaway. If my own were to run away, I wouldn't go after them." Well, replied Child, with emphasis, "if these are your feelings, why [not] take *all* your slaves to Haiti?" Kingsley responded, "I have thought that subject all over ma'am," but "all we can do in this world is to balance evils. I want to do great things in Haiti; and in order to do them I must have money. If I have no Negroes to cultivate my Florida lands," he continued, "they will run to waste." As the affluent have insisted before and since, he stressed, "to do good in the world, we *must* have money. That's the way I reasoned," he continued damningly, "when I carried on the slave trade."

Kingsley was a Quaker and, said Child, "he still loves to attend Quaker meetings" and "to complete the circle of contradictions, he likes the abolitionists and is a prodigious admirer of George Thompson," a British abolitionist viewed as Public Enemy Number One in Dixie.[75] Still, it would be a mistake to see the slave dealing and slave-holding Kingsley as typical of his class. To the contrary, it would be more appropriate to see him as a man who had the advantage of being sited in Hispaniola in the 1790s and had a ringside seat from which to view what could occur on the mainland, unless transforming changes were made. In sum, Kingsley had sought to glean lessons from the Haitian Revolution that were not heeded by those of his class and, instead, a whirlwind in blood was then generated in civil war.

IN ANY CASE, THE 1830S WERE a decade of turmoil, not only featuring abolition but also searing conflict leading to disjointing population movements of various sorts. Typically, the slave-holding republic was in the forefront, e.g. their ouster of the indigenous in the southeast and their removal, hundreds of miles distant, on a "trail of tears." This occurred though they were more than willing to assimilate to Euro-American norms, up to and including owning enslaved Africans.[76] The fact that this did not spare them indicated a deepening and coarsening of anti-Negro racism that was bound to bash Haiti. Indicative of the expanse of bigotry was the 1838 order from Missouri's governor adjudging members of the adolescent Church of Latter Day Saints (or Mormons) as "enemies" who "must be exterminated or driven from the state."[77] This was said to be in response to a Mormon "war of extermination" against their own antagonists.[78] The religionists were said to have "hostile intentions," suggested by how they "ingratiated themselves with the Indians [to] assist them in their diabolical career." These "fanatics"[79] also "exercised" a reputed "corrupting influence" upon enslaved Africans because of their alleged abolitionism, which seemed to be the *casus belli*.[80] While Missourians were contemplating this atrocious conflict with a determined foe, the governor was informed that, in now tottery Florida, the "frontier" was "in danger," requiring "five hundred or if practicable six hundred" troops from the Show-Me State; this at a time when the Osage there had yet to be subjugated altogether.

On the one hand, this political buzzsaw could provide a breather for the freedom isle since Washington was so preoccupied; on the other hand, the cumulative chauvinist bile provided a clear and present danger to Haiti.[81] Haitians had endured hellish centuries of enslavement at the hands of Europeans and then decades of threats, then brutalization of those nearby in Jamaica and Cuba with a like maltreatment promised to them if they let their guard down. This did not predispose many Haitians to greet those from the slave-holding republic with bonhomie. Similarly, slave-holding republics marinating in the brine of white supremacy were hardly in a position to go against the grain of prevailing racism. This made for a combustible recipe of distaste, e.g. when in 1838 the crew of a Haitian vessel were to be found in Charleston, compelled by inclement weather to put into port—and then were jailed en masse and, said an outraged U.S. journalist, were subjected to "barbarous treatment."[82]

At the same time, Haiti was moving strategically closer to Britain, particularly after abolition put them in the same camp opposing continuation of the slave trade, which their mutual antagonist on the mainland was now spearheading. This culminated in an accord between London and Port-au-Prince to that end, which attracted the admiring attention of the U.S. Negro press.[83]

This relationship of convenience between London and Port-au-Prince had its limits, particularly since there were those in Haiti who would have felt even more comfortable if the settlers were ousted altogether from Jamaica. The systems of labor that replaced slavery continued to contain elements of coercion in any case. Even as slavery was on the verge of abolition, London spoke openly of continuing the "disposal of colonial convicts," who previously were dumped in the "Spanish Main." However, said London, "after the Colombian Emancipation measure, the South American Governments [*sic*] refused admittance of condemned slaves into their territories and their example seems to have been followed at Cuba and Porto Rico," complicating the handling of all forms of coerced labor. Perhaps they could be sent to the "Australian colonies"—still not sufficiently distant for Haiti to have been at ease and assure that yet another form of coerced labor would not be part of its destiny.[84]

Still, London had a decided advantage over Washington. While Haiti had to worry about U.S. vessels arriving and then departing with newly enslaved (former)

Black Jacobins aboard, when U.S. nationals—including the enslaved—washed up on the shores of the neighboring Bahamas, all were told that "they were free to stay . . . unmolested," which included freedom for the slaves.[85] Meanwhile William Dalzell of Texas was in the Bahamas just before freedom day, 1 August 1834. He had been "deputed" by Lone Star slaveholders to "ascertain what privileges are to be granted to the Negro population" after this momentous day. And considering that the enslaved owned by mainlanders would "have to leave these islands for that state," meaning Texas, he wanted assurance that this human property would not be jeopardized.[86] Weeks later a schooner with 205 manacled Africans aboard was detained near Haitian waters due to slave trade violations and Port-au-Prince was left to wonder how these flesh peddlers viewed the island of abolition.[87]

In the prelude to abolition, though trade between the island and the mainland continued apace, diplomatic relations were far from ideal, particularly since Dixie wielded disproportionate influence on foreign policy complicating an entente with Haiti.

There also continued to be complaints about alleged sharp dealings by Haitian merchants who—according to a U.S. envoy—"are in the habit of shipping American seamen and leaving them destitute."[88] The question of "destitute seamen" washing up in Haiti, for whatever cause, continued to roil bilateral relations and was an outgrowth of increased trade unaccompanied by normalized diplomatic relations.[89] "Our seamen," said the U.S. envoy in Aux Cayes in 1838, lack "proper protection" and, besides, "have to contend with the prejudices of the natives as well as the climate."[90]

The island was strategically situated and even distressed British subjects found it necessary at times to seek aid there, e.g. when a vessel bound from Liverpool to New Orleans in storm tossed seas wound up there having lost everything it possessed.[91] The flip side of this matter was the knotty issue of Haitian seamen in U.S. ports that were unaccustomed to confronting real or imagined Black Jacobins.[92]

Haitian entrepreneurs were upset when a formidable vessel that had been sent to New York for repair, after being purchased on the island, was seized, along with its valuable cargo, on the spurious charge that it was "illegally sold." The Haitian purchasers then pursued the U.S. commercial agent on the island responsible and he was jailed, outraging Washington. Then, said an apparently pleased British diplomat, "two American vessels of war" in Port-au-Prince refused to "salute" the "Haitian flag," bringing further recriminations.[93]

Haiti—and the United States too—knew that the island's position was strengthened after abolition. A more confident Port-au-Prince slapped extra duties on U.S. vessels at that point: "duties on the products" from the United States said the U.S.

delegate, were "increased about fifty percent and vessels arriving from the United States must now bring specie to pay their import duties"; the "operation of these laws will tend to diminish very much the trade from the United States to this country," the delegate also said.[94] William Miles acknowledged that this was a reaction to his nation failing to "recognize Haiti as an actual government." (Formal recognition of Haiti did not arrive until the United States, reeling from the hammer blows inflicted by traitors in 1861, chose to bend to reality.)

At that juncture there was worry that lucrative trade would "be soon lost" because of this U.S. stubbornness. Already by late 1835 "British provinces in North America" were looking to take advantage of the situation, i.e. "several British vessels" from Nova Scotia had arrived "loaded" with various goods including "flour . . . beef, pork," and the like. As well, "Hanseatic vessels from Bremen" were bearing "soap" that was "made to imitate American articles."

William Miles in Aux Cayes wanted more U.S. diplomats appointed though political realities in Dixie forbade him from requesting a change in policy. "I am perfectly aware of the delicacy of the question of our relations with this country," Miles said tactfully, but if the United States wanted to block the rise of European commercial rivals now bent on challenging the slave-holding republic in their areas of strength, including "lumber, rice, [and] tobacco," a change in diplomatic relations was paramount.[95] Haitian trade to the United States—which consisted primarily of coffee, cotton, cacao, tobacco, mahogany, logwood, tortoise shells, pita, aloe, oranges, limes, and old rags—was diminishing rapidly, as Canada was substituted as a partner.[96]

Aux Cayes was hardly singular. There was trepidation in Cap-Haïtien, as well, that a "branch of trade that portends much injury to our eastern commerce" was unfolding. The U.S. Secretary of State was told that Britain had "commenced running several vessels here from Halifax, the cargoes consist of several articles . . . from our country," which "they say they can undersell us as long as the Haytien Government exact from us the additional duty of ten percent."[97]

Yet with typical bullheadedness, Washington adamantly refused to recognize the reality of an abolitionist republic. "The word St. Domingo used in my commission instead of Haiti or Hayti," said Miles, "and the grade or title of Consular Commercial Agent instead of Consul were and are still considered be the intentional and unfriendly acts of the U.S. government." London and Paris were not as rigid with such things, "while our conduct is openly attributed to the prejudice of colour"—a point made to him "expressly" by a Haitian leader.[98] Haiti was notably sensitive about accepting U.S. commercial agents in the newly acquired port that was Santo Domingo on the southern coast. After all, if Washington did not recognize this relatively recently acquired port as Haitian soil, then why should a still potent Spain?[99] The U.S.-appointed commercial agent there found his "position" to be "embarrassing & disagreeable" as a result, though he should have added "understandable," too.[100]

Thus, by 1838 the U.S. emissary in Cap-Haïtien was raising the roof about the "repeated and almost daily mortifications" that beset him and his fellow "agents"; they were "continually the subjects of suspicion among the mercantile class" and "liable to every species of contempt from the powers that be in this place. The United States agent is not acknowledged in his official capacity unless his appointment is to the Republic of Hayti instead of St. Domingo"—with this failure to recognize the nation's formal name a not so subtle denial of sovereignty. "This government," Washington was reminded repeatedly, "is determined to be recognized as an Independent Republic by the United States before they pursue a different course toward their agents."[101]

But recognition of Haiti conceivably portended a disaster for Dixie: namely, the arrival in Washington of melanin-rich diplomats, a slippery slope imagined to entail the seduction of Euro-American women. Miles wailed that "there exists a special prejudice against this country on account of non-recognition," though he was "fearful of annoying the [State] Department with my letters" of complaint.[102]

"Trade with the United States has considerably declined from its former prosperity," Lord Palmerston was told in March 1838 in reference to Haiti. Moreover, there was "little desire on the part of the Government to encourage the trade with the United States: this feeling arises from a dislike to the policy of the American Government" and the comprehensible desire of Haiti to engage in import substitution, i.e. seek domestic alternatives to items routinely brought from the mainland antagonist. Haitian leaders had "repeatedly expressed a desire to see the trade of our North American colonies supplant that of the United States with Hayti," said London's man on the island, Thomas Ussher.[103]

By May 1838, Miles "closed . . . [his] affairs at Aux Cayes" and returned to Baltimore and since "no other American resides there," nor was there any "European House willing" to handle U.S. affairs, he also "closed the Commercial Agency" that he had headed for Washington; this was due to the decline in U.S.-Haitian trade, a dangerous trend for the island too for it gave Washington more flexibility to meddle and stir up dissidence in the still unsettled eastern part of the island, which eventuated in Dominican independence in 1844.[104]

This closure came with a cost. As the Aux Cayes delegate reported, "cotton goods can be shipped to this country from the United States cheaper than from Great Britain" and "it would appear that we lose annually the sale of more than a million dollars worth in consequence of not having an accredited commercial agent here." Yet "so strong is the feeling against Americans," the Haitian leadership was "disposed to do everything to favor the trade from the British North American provinces,"[105] which could strengthen London immeasurably in the case of a replay of the War of 1812 or an enhanced quasi-war with Paris. "From the proximity of Haiti to the United States," said a U.S. official in late 1838, "we have much in every way to gain by securing their friendship, instead of having as we do by their dislike to us. In the event of war between Great Britain or France, these seas would swarm with privateers which could as well be fitted out here by the subjects of those countries, assisted by the Haitians."[106] This was even more likely since it was already common wisdom, according to one U.S. observer, that Cap-Haïtien, in particular, was "without exception the healthiest port in the West Indies, the harbour is one of the safest."[107]

Although it would deepen the sectional rift that was to explode in civil war, this sage advice had to be ignored because of Dixie's demands. By early 1839, a London diplomat's arrival was eagerly awaited in Haiti as he was slated to ink a treaty. "There is great reason to fear," said the U.S. envoy worriedly, that this pact "will materially affect our commercial interest." Already, he repeated, Haiti seeks to "favor the trade" from Canada over the United States, which was leading to "an entire exclusion of our vessels,"[108] a catastrophic financial and security development. By July 1839, Lord Palmerston was told that "British trade rather exceeds on average" that of the "preceding three years" while "the American trade" was "much depressed."[109]

The remedy proposed was for "some of our Squadron in these seas occasionally calling here," albeit "not with the view of intimidating this Government but such is the fact that if our ships of war are not occasionally seen here they imagine that the United States do not care for the interests of its citizens engaged in this trade and they are led to do what they would be restrained from by the occasional appearance of ships of war."[110] Haitian leaders, however, were not as confident that battleships from the aggressive slave-holding republic, cruising regularly in Haitian waters, would be seen by their constituents as a peace offering.

Earlier, British officials were mulling the same issue, but since, it was said, no "depredations had been committed on the property of any British subject" in Haiti, why should a "ship of war" visit? Anyway, the "increased activity of the slave trade to Cuba employed all the disposable vessels" to combat this pestilence, a consideration beyond the ken of the slave-holding republic.[111]

Haitians were not inclined to see cruisers from the major powers as vessels of friendship. As France was undergoing political unrest in the early 1830s, waving the bloody flag of revenge on Haiti for the revolution could be a useful diversion. Even Washington was expecting a "blockading squadron" from Paris in league with Madrid, still smarting over the 1822 ouster from the eastern side of the island, in order to "compel the Haytiens to come to terms." It was thought that this would incite "Civil War" on the island since "the President being very unpopular" was no secret. In that case, the "interest of the Americans as well as the foreigners would be jeopardized." The suggested solution? The United States should send a "naval force" too, not the wisest suggestion.[112]

It seemed that the bellicose mainland republic thought a show of force was always the best way to approach the abolitionist republic. Just as Henry Clay was recommending the ouster of free Negroes, he was being told that the United States should have "an armed vessel" at Cap-Haïtien and Port-au-Prince as a brutal reminder to Haiti of threatening possibilities.

The problem between the two nations mirrored Haiti's problems with France that led to the punishing indemnity paid to Paris. In fact, U.S. nationals repeatedly demanded compensation for property supposedly expropriated during the revolutionary era and thereafter. One difficult claim arose in 1828 amidst complaints of "sequestrations during the government of Christophe," involving "considerable property . . . without any just cause."[113] Another claim in 1833 pursued captains of vessels reproved, as it was reported, "for the alleged traffic, or intention of traffic, with the insurgent blacks of the French colony of the island of Saint Domingo."[114]

Wiser U.S. nationals were well aware of the dilemma posed by the hegemonic influence of Dixie on foreign policy. Just as there was a series of resolutions passed by states in the United States continuing to carp about alleged French spoliations, as if the quasi-war had resumed,[115] there were companion resolutions directed to Congress demanding recognition of Haiti.[116] Thus, by 1838 hundreds of petitions were arriving in Washington demanding recognition of Haiti.[117]

As 1838 was ending, a furious debate unwound in Congress on this issue, pushed by Nantucket in particular and, thus, bound to inflame Dixie. Congressman Henry Wise, who was to serve as John Brown's executioner, rose to object and thundered against "the petition [that] asks that a white republic should amalgamate with a black." John Quincy Adams, liberated from the White House by then, cracked, "is there not enough of amalgamation" in Virginia already? "Let him go and look at the color of a part of the people of Virginia and indeed, of all the Southern states and then come here, if he can and object to amalgamation." Dixie, said the former president, thought it "right and proper" to have "commercial intercourse" with Africa, meaning the slave trade, "but with a land of freemen! No, no; it amounts to amalgamation." For years, U.S. citizens had been making "large claims for indemnification for spoliations by the former government of Hayti," particularly stemming from the Christophe era, when this leader "made free with vessels and cargoes of our citizens; he seized and confiscated without remorse." These compatriots appealed to Washington for aid. The reply from Haiti was that a U.S. court had "seized some property of . . . [the Haitian republic] and that he [Christophe] had taken American property only in the way of retaliation; and when the United States should restore to him what these courts in Maryland had taken away, he would restore our property."

Then the same issue was raised with President Boyer who promptly requested the credentials of these emissaries, but since the United States did not recognize Haiti, they had none. The issue of France calling Haitian leaders "rebels" had ended with Paris's recognition of the abolitionist isle in the wake of the indemnity accord. All that was now left as a fig leaf for Congressman Wise was to cry "amalgamation"—the last refuge of a (chauvinist) scoundrel.

Wise was irate and contended that the United States now intended "to recognize an insurrectionary republic on our Southern coast," which contravened the principle that the "ulterior object" of abolition was "unconstitutional and illegal" and condoned the fact that "a large portion of those now in power" in Haiti "are slaves who cut their masters' throats." It was hardly "consolatory to think, when we are threatened by abolitionists with having our throats cut in the South, that these slaves in St. Domingo, though ten to one in number, never could have succeeded in insurrection but for the aid of a British army," now in alignment with these Africans. "We never will be driven to say, in effect, to our own slaves," he maintained, "when you have cut the throats of your masters, you will be acknowledged by England and by the Northern states as republican freemen." Disgusted, he concluded by querying querulously as to why "we have no petitions from the same quarter to recognize the independence of Texas,"[118] which had broken away from Mexico recently on pro-slavery grounds.

This inflammatory dialogue only served to further incite Dixie and exacerbate the sectional rift, particularly since it was detailed in the Boston press. Hugh Swinton Legare was an exemplar of the abolitionist republic's worst nightmare in that he was of Huguenot ancestry, hailed from South Carolina, and had served respectively as attorney general, acting secretary of state, and congressman. His father had escaped to Carolina from Nantes—and, thus, he knew that the status quo could cause one to flee, a perception bolstered by the presence in his vicinity of often embittered Africans. The cosmopolitan congressman had studied in Paris and apparently spoke both French and Italian. Recognition of Haiti, he proclaimed, was just a backdoor to promoting abolition, which was "virtually an act of war against one portion of the Union." This was designed to "revolutionize the

South and to convulse the Union" and "if this course is permitted," he warned, "the sun of this Union will go down—it will go down in blood—and go down to rise no more." It would be simple "treason"—but the perpetrators would be "traitors not to their country only but to the whole human race,"[119] which presumably did not include Africans.

Congressman Waddy Thompson, also of South Carolina, advised his opponents that it was "dangerous" to even "discuss" this matter; actually, he continued, "it was worse than dangerous—it was dishonorable and degrading [to] any Southern man to discuss it." He knew that "in the event of war" the "enemy" would "most certainly [strike] at the Gulf of Mexico" and "where else but in the West Indies" could "any foreign nation congregate their fleets?" This was a veiled reference to London's Jamaica colony and Haiti, both of which were prone to attack the vulnerabilities of the slave-holding republic, where an enslaved African population would not be hostile to the notion of revolt in the face of invasion, a situation made worse by the "Florida war." Still, as if he had a death wish, he remained unyielding in refusing to contemplate recognition of Port-au-Prince.[120]

The question for Haiti in the 1830s was if the gathering alliance with London would be sufficient to overcome deteriorating relations with Madrid and Paris—and the slave-holding republic. The odds were unlikely. Haiti had sent a diplomat to France to negotiate, perhaps expecting a positive outcome in light of the decision to pay an indemnity, but Secretary Inginac found the resultant pact to be "obnoxious"—at least that is what the U.S. Secretary of State was told. The "'objectionable demands of the French,'" said the secretary, "are that French citizens on their arrival in Hayti shall be allowed all the rights and privileges of Haytiens; that they shall pay half duties only on all imports"; that French vessels would be "allowed in time of war to enter the ports of the island with their prizes for condemnation & sale"; and that "said privileges" were "to be refused to all other nations," particularly Britain. Haiti was a deadbeat it was charged hotly, failing to pay the indemnity payments on time; thus, it was demanded that Port-au-Prince cough up $400,000 annually, "until the entire payment of the debt, principal and interest," was liquidated—or otherwise, it might be the abolitionist republic that could face liquidation.[121]

Particularly after abolition, Bordeaux—possibly sensing the strengthened posture of Haiti—petitioned furiously for payment of the indemnity.[122] Yet at the same time it was reported that a "French brig from Bordeaux" was the source of "the most horrible screams," a possible slaver en route to Cuba near Haiti in a demonstration of what might await if demands were not met.[123] With metronomic zeal, the Chamber of Deputies was instructed that Haiti was failing to adhere to the 1820s indemnity accord: it was a "scandal," it was said, both "moral" and "political" that was without example in the civilized world.[124] In other words, there was an attempt to fashion Haiti as a premature example of what was to be called neo-colonialism—that is, independent in name only. "This country is in an agitated state," it was reported, just before British abolition, "owing to the affair not being settled with France."[125]

Haiti was under strain. The "indemnity to France" and the "financial crisis in the United States" hurt the island badly, contributing to a "stagnation of European trade and almost annihilation of that of the United States,"[126] said one commentator. Declining relations with more belligerent major powers combined with the latter's ability to play upon color contradictions on the island to create crisis—and looming perilously were ever more frazzled ties with the Colossus of the North. "Ingenac," the "Talleyrand of Haiti," was a "very fair quateroon"[*sic*], said a U.S. visitor knowingly in 1837.[127] London thought that the influential Inginac was their "steady friend & powerful advocate"—but not President Boyer, which provided an arbitrage opportunity (though this maximum leader too thought that Britain's emissary was a "sincere friend to the interests of Hayti").[128]

As Jamaica continued to reel from the machinations of Sam Sharpe and Virginia was stunned by General Nat, a huge fire was ignited in Port-au-Prince; it was an "irresistible fury," said the U.S. representative, with "sixteen square [miles] containing about 600 houses [destroyed] in four hours," though "not in the commercial part of the city." However, "depredations on property were most shamefully committed" in the aftermath and in the commotion the "lives" of U.S. nationals were in "imminent danger," just as their "property" was in "jeopardy."[129]

This decade, the 1830s, was not just tumultuous for the British Caribbean and Haiti—or France, for that matter, as the attempt to seize Algeria suggested. General Nat insured that the slave-holding republic would be immersed in disquiet too and Bordeaux—which preened contumaciously as the island's prime foe—was quick to report that Vicksburg and Mobile too were afflicted by incendiaries at a time when Haiti was erupting in flames.[130] "La revolution des noirs" (or Africans) was spoken of in Paris,[131] as if this was not France's issue alone—though, admittedly, it did not take much to tempt the slave-holding republic to seek allies against Africans.

If Port-au-Prince had been able to get hold of a lengthy "memorandum respecting Hayti" in 1836, even more concern would have been aroused. For in May 1814 London and Paris agreed in a secret accord that the former would not oppose the latter's recovery of the island, though this was putatively made null and void when France recognized Haiti in April 1825 on the condition of the payment of a hefty indemnity. Still, the accord said that France could "employ any means whatever, even those of arms" to recover the island "and to reduce the population of that colony to obedience." When Charles MacKenzie was sent there to serve London's interests, somehow this was interpreted, likewise, as making the accord null and void. Yet Paris continued to insist that "considering the colour of the people and the fact of their having massacred the white population, France could not enter into any treaty with Hayti." These words were made even more viable when disputes arose over whether Port-au-Prince was fulfilling the terms of the indemnity. Settlers in "Martinique and Guadeloupe felt strongly upon this point," it was said, realizing that Haiti was an inspiration to the enslaved in both colonies. Thereafter Paris threatened Haiti continuously with a "blockade," even after recognition was extended. London was willing to court Haiti as an ally to gain leverage against Paris, but, as the secret accord indicated, this support was often wafer-thin. London was uncomfortable with provisos of the Haitian Constitution, which were said to place restrictions on "blancs"[132]—i.e. those defined as "white."

MacKenzie, though a man of color, was not helpful in this regard, referring often to the "suspicious character of the Haitians, who, influenced by the bad faith of France, regard all approaches from Europeans with distrust." Thus, Denmark was wary of "renewed intercourse" with Haiti from its perch in St. Thomas and Haiti's neighbors viewed with their own suspicion the "formation of a Haitian Commercial Navy," as if the island were undeserving.[133]

As the 1840s approached, Haiti was ripe for dismantling, beginning with the much vaster eastern end of the island, which was to comprise the newly born Dominican Republic. The U.S. Negroes who had arrived in eastern Hispaniola by the thousands in previous years were to find themselves in a different nation where Black Jacobinism was far from the reigning creed.

7

Black Jacobins Weakened
1840–1849

THE NEWS FROM HISPANIOLA WAS reminiscent of the revolutionary era. But it was now the 1840s and the U.S. Secretary of State was being informed that "within two days march" of Santo Domingo—the recently proclaimed capital city of the former eastern part of Haiti now known as the Dominican Republic—was an army of "ten thousand blacks," whose aim was the "extermination of all whites and mulattoes" said to be in the vanguard of the new state.[1]

This was not a fortuitous moment for the slave-holding republic, now drunk with confidence over the impending swallowing of Texas. However, abolitionist Britain still hovered darkly over U.S. fortunes and the prospect of the former sponsoring slave rebellions was rarely absent. Not daring to even mention London's name, the leading slaveholder, James Hammond of Carolina, warned in early 1845 that "should any foreign nation be so lost to [the] sentiment of civilized humanity as to attempt to erect among us the standard of revolt, or to invade us with Black Troops for the base and barbarious [*sic*] purpose of stirring up servile war, their efforts would be signally rebuked."[2] Hammond may have known that from 1840 to 1850 his state had gained three times as many enslaved Africans as men defined as "white," increasing profitability and insecurity alike in a devolving spiral.[3]

And France too did not favor annexation of Texas, given its preexisting claims to the sprawling landmass, a point well recognized by Louisiana's own Judah P. Benjamin, who was soon to be the leading foreign envoy of the so-called Confederate States of America.[4] With the enslaving republic expanding westward, Russia— perched in Alaska and only recently in California—was seen too as a threat. The future rested in Asia, said the then leading scholar, William Henry Trescot; "the increasing power and growing antagonism of England and Russia in the direction of Asia" had to be accounted for, given colonial India and the recent seizure of

Hong Kong, "while the conquest and rapid settlement of California have brought us to the same plane." Thus, "France and Russia are natural allies," a supposition soon to be disproved in the Crimea. Amidst the diplomatic maneuvering, Trescot was rooted in old verities that slavery served to cement: "Asiatic inferiority" was a given, he said, while "the connection between the Anglo Saxon race and the Asiatic nations on a footing of perfect equality has never existed and we conscientiously believe [it] can never exist."[5]

Then there was the grim news brought by the glimmerings of war with Mexico: "we are in imminent danger of an invasion from Mexico or her allies," the governor of Missouri was told heatedly in 1845,[6] though this state, being far from the border, was thought to be secure. The "latest intelligence" as of August 1845, the chief executive was informed, was that "we shall shortly be at war with Mexico or her allies,"[7] requiring an expensive mobilization. "Ten thousand Mexicans are marching rapidly,"[8] it was then announced. The U.S. Senate discussed means to "prevent the white population from being exterminated or expelled from [the] Yucatan," just across the water from Haiti. John C. Calhoun—unnecessarily—declared, "if this be a war of races in reality," then "my sympathies are for the white race." For "if the white race be overthrown and Indian ascendancy established," another "Hayti" was in store. "The case of the Yucatan does not stand alone. All the causes operating there to produce the present stage of things are operating in all the portions of this continent south of us" and "all are in great danger of falling into the condition in which Yucatan is now placed."[9]

Actually, it was not just "this continent south of us" that was in presumed jeopardy. In the enslaving republic too a schooner only recently had escaped from Washington and was bound for the open seas with scores of desperate Africans aboard. If the enslaving republic was not careful, said Calhoun, "we shall have St. Domingo [all] over again."[10]

Though the Black Jacobins had triumphed decades earlier, by the time of Dominican secession there continued to be worry in Washington that the presumed contestation between Africans and Europeans for control of the Americas was not settled. Weeks after Dominican independence, the U.S. envoy in Caracas observed that the leader there had "just grounds" for the "apprehensions he entertains as to the possible consequences of a war of races" in Hispaniola. Recalled was "Farfan's Rebellion, the notorious object of which was to array the colored population against the whites"; it was "not a question between master and slave, but one of color only, which it is feared may one day or other arise in Venezuela." It was assumed that "in fifteen years" slavery "will be extinct in the Republic," a distressing signal for the mainland, though—reassuringly—"into the best circles of

Caracas society, mulattoes can no more gain admission, than they can into those of the United States." Yet, unlike the mainland, in Caracas "they appear to be entirely and helplessly unprepared for the horrible conditions of affairs which they fear *might* be produced here by the evil and contagious example of Hayti." Attached to the correspondence was a note from Juan Manuel Manrique, Foreign Minister of Venezuela, who feared that the Dominican revolt would be crushed by Haiti, leading to intensified racial conflict regionally that would spread to Caracas—with obvious implications for Washington.[11] Robert Harrison, U.S. emissary in Jamaica, felt that the "people of St. Domingo (that is to say the Mulattoes)"—by which he meant the Dominican Republic—"are disposed to put themselves under the protection of Great Britain." This was a further reason for Washington to scramble to take a firm position on what was thought to be a "race war."[12]

While expending blood and treasure to dismember Mexico, the slave-holding republic had yet to absorb Florida effectively. By the year of statehood—1845—enslaved Africans outnumbered their masters in five of the twenty-six counties and a significant minority existed in ten other counties. Not coincidentally, there were repeated stories about arsons perpetrated by Africans and slave conspiracies, while awesome stories of revolts in the Caribbean—where Haiti was implicated—circulated widely.[13]

The annexation of Texas (a template for what was to become the attempt to annex the Dominican Republic) did not improve relations with Mexico; then there were the ongoing conflicts with Native Americans, contestation with Spain for control of Cuba—and much more. Furthermore, such news was bound to enhance sectional conflicts, with abolitionists accused of preparing a similar plan for the "extermination of all whites and mulattoes" on the mainland, a dire prospect not assuaged by trends in Hispaniola. France recognized Haiti de jure in 1838; by 1840 Haiti had paid France 4.5 million francs, leaving it 55 million francs in arrears[14]—but forming the predicate for an improvement in bilateral relations. British and Haitian relations improved markedly when formal diplomatic recognition was established in early 1841,[15] though the inability of London's man to speak French or Kreyòl (or Creole), the Haitian language, was a handicap.[16]

Be it in Texas or Mexico, North America or South America, the 1840s indicated that slavery and its handmaiden, white supremacy, were generating murderous conflict effortlessly. Hence, the secession of the Dominican Republic and the war that it delivered came at an inopportune moment for Washington. There was the delightful prospect of weakening Black Jacobins by depriving them of the vaster portion of Hispaniola, but it was no secret that the enslaving republic was no fan of the "mulattoes" said to rule in Santo Domingo. The latter factor only served to provide an opening for Madrid and London, thus exacerbating—not resolving—the fraught matter of U.S. national security.

Moreover, London's growing ties with Port-au-Prince were not good news for Washington either, as they increased the breathing space for the abolitionist island, giving it more freedom of movement—e.g. the ability to sponsor abolitionist plots. When a leading Haitian appeared in London in 1842 for a major abolitionist conference, it was not reassuring to the enslaving republic. The same could be said for the fact that the Haitian deputation, as was reported casually, "had the pleasure of breakfasting with nearly thirty gentlemen of colour, resident in Paris."[17] Five years later the U.S. Negro press seemed pleased when Haiti's delegate to the London gathering affiliated with U.S. abolitionists.[18]

Similarly, near this same time in Puerto Plata—soon to be part of the Dominican Republic—a militant abolitionist society was formed. They defined slavery as a "sin against God and man" and "pledge[d] . . . to do all in our power for the attainment of that righteous object," meaning abolition. Reflecting the presence there of a goodly number of U.S. Negroes, targeted was the "stronghold of slavery," i.e. the United States itself; "our measures shall be like those of [William Lloyd] Garrison" and "in alliance with the American Anti-Slavery Society." Though their official documents penned in English, Spanish, and French downplayed "insurrection" and "violence," this boilerplate was also not assuring to enslavers. Any "sect, sex or color" was invited to join their ranks. For "as philanthropists," it was asserted, "our country is the world, our countrymen are all mankind; our watchword is 'Liberty and Equality.'" Pleadingly, it was declaimed, "cooperate with us, for the extinction of that great evil of Slavery, the existence of which, among other nations, is so unfavorable to the prosperity of Haiti"—which was all too true.[19]

Boston abolitionists were travelling to the island then. Maria Weston Chapman was told in 1841 about "the friends in this country" and the "warm reception and kind attention" after "safe arrival on the Haytian sail"; this embrace was "highly gratifying to your numerous friends" and "your [proposed] visit to Hayti will be a precious benefit to the Anti-Slavery cause." If an enslaver had been able to peek at this missive, eyes would have been drawn to the words about "the strong talk of war between Great Britain and the United States" then growing in obstreperousness.[20] Abolitionist materials were flooding into Puerto Plata from Boston with untoward consequences for those who sought slavery's expansion there.[21]

Correspondingly, Washington did not seem to be adapting to these maneuvers by their rivals, a trend partly driven by the shot of adrenalin delivered to the bloodstream of the enslaving republicans when Texas was taken from Mexico. A grudge against Free Negroes and *gens de couleur* continued to mark the slave-holding republic, though they could have been co-opted easily. In 1840 there were more than 500 Free Negroes in Mobile, nearly all of them described as "mulattoes." Very few of them were illiterate or could otherwise be deemed less than upstanding, but they were coming under increasing pressure to evacuate the premises.[22] In 1842 Louisiana debated a measure to bar this group from entering the state, a rude signal to those who had fled from Hispaniola since 1791. Typical was a Euro-American in Chicago who in 1844 announced brashly that he had his first encounter with a free Negro.[23] "I smashed a chair rung over his head,"[24] he said tersely.

On the centennial of Dominican independence a novel was published about New Orleans and Haiti—antipodes in essence. It features characters who, in the novelist's words, "had never hated Negroes before," but, driven by the assumed misdeeds of Black Jacobins, they develop a hatred of this kind. Is "the black man" the "eternal enemy"? This is the novel's rhetorical query. The reply: "God, yes! He represents the bloodstained machete and the torch." What about the "black inhabitants" of the island? Should they be "reenslaved"? The implied answer was, of course. In the case of the protagonist, "though he had been sympathetic toward the Haitian mulatto elite, his Louisiana upbringing rebelled against the idea of social drinking with a black man." Another character prates, "manifestly the United States must be involved in an expansionist policy—southward, my friends, always southward. If Haiti and Saint Domingue, for instance, were acquired and admitted as a state, or two states, who can doubt that men from Louisiana would quickly become the ruling element there?" "We are the natural inheritors of Saint Domingue," it was written. "If the old Spanish colony," meaning the Dominican Republic, "is ready to shake off Negro rule it should be aided, and if it wishes to join this country [it] should receive the same welcome that is on the point of being given to Texas."

There was much anti-Haitian plotting portrayed in New Orleans though potential plotters were advised that Haiti "would resist a conqueror even more savagely than their ancestors resisted the army sent by Napoleon. Nothing short of making slaves of all survivors," it was stressed, "would be effective and in bondage their resentment and vengeful spirit would know no bounds." The reply: "it could be done, however" for "slavery could be brought back gradually." Described in detail was a Louisiana-based conspiracy to destabilize Haiti in 1843—then 1844.[25]

The enslaving republicans had reason to fear that if Haiti were to overcome the Dominican Republic, the leadership would aggressively turn its attention to the perceived source of the problem on the mainland, leading to more covert—or overt—support for slave rebellions. "Increasing poverty of the country has driven away all the American merchants," said London's island envoy in mid-1840; "formerly there were five American houses in Port-au-Prince, at present there is not one," while "trade with Bordeaux" had "nearly ceased" and with Marseilles had "ceased entirely."[26] "American commerce is declining," was the message received from Aux Cayes by Secretary of State Daniel Webster in 1842; "only nine American vessels have entered here for the past three months. There is no American mercantile house in this city."[27]

Despite this absence, complaints continued to mount about the "abuse which American ship masters suffer from the authorities of this port, abuses which . . . the government of the United States will not submit from any nation."[28] "It is in vain to attempt to establish the innocence of an American white citizen against the testimony of a Haytien, however false the accusation" was the complaint—enunciated with shock—by the U.S. envoy in Port-au-Prince.[29] Perhaps worse, duties slapped on arriving U.S. vessels were "more than on any other nation" and were imposed on "all imports from the United States."[30] Days before the announcement of Dominican independence, it was reported that the United States had "no other [personnel] than commercial agents in Hayti"—"one at Port-au-Prince, one at Cape Haytien, and one at Aux Cayes."[31] Despite this deficiency, there was a reported "frequent resort of American vessels at the ports of Miragoane and Gonaives," requiring attention and also indicating that there might reside a base for subversion of Haiti.[32]

Still, deteriorating trade reflected an overall downturn. The U.S. agent in Aux Cayes found it hard to understand why there was a "large standing army embracing about one seventh of the male population"; this had "diminished labour and plantations" which once "yielded wealth" and were "now abandoned." "Thousands of tons of coffee are lost for want of labourers to harvest" it and then there were the "losses sustained by the [recent] earthquake and late fire at Port-au-Prince [that were] computed at one half the wealth of the island."[33]

Bilateral relations with Port-au-Prince were far from ideal, a reality that underscored why John C. Calhoun reportedly backed one of the more significant covert operations in U.S. history: according to the veteran fire-eater Edmund Ruffin, his comrade, the then Secretary of State, "used the secret service fund to supply arms" to the Dominican rebels against Haiti in order "to repel their more barbarous invaders." The idea banked on the "permanent hostility of the two populations"— Haitian and Dominican—"& the weakness of the Dominicans" to "get footing on their territory & ultimately annex that larger portion of the island." There were more than niggling problems, of course, e.g. a "mixed population." "They are too near to being white to be denied the equal rights of citizens," said the reflective Ruffin, "& yet it would not do to contaminate the purity of blood of Caucasian settlers, by intermarrying with the mixed blood." In any case, "this acquisition would soon & necessarily lead to the conquest of Hayti," ending for all time a base of subversion for U.S. Negroes and then reversing course by ousting this group from the mainland in favor of a new homeland—precisely in Hispaniola.[34]

Ruffin had little respect for Haiti and in the temper of the times blamed the "insane government" in Paris for the revolution by "declaring first in favor of equal political rights of the free mulattoes" and then supporting emancipation, which led to "unprecedented rapine and slaughter and unspeakable outrages and horrors." Definitely, "if there had been only white masters and negro slaves and no foreign and stronger power, although the whites were only one-tenth the number of their slaves, their mastership would never have been seriously disturbed."[35] Haiti was a failure and a return to enslavement was the only way out, it was thought.

A self-described "Colored American" in Philadelphia sensed this vast conspiracy was occurring as it was unwinding. It was "JCC"—or Calhoun—who was the culprit and not just because he was singularly responsible for a "very great cause of alarm at the present juncture for the safety of colored people." Why was Boyer "deposed," as he was—curiously enough—just before Dominican secession? "Look back at the unsuccessful attempt made to stir up rebellion in Canada, about 1837 or 1838": weakening this sanctuary for fleeing U.S. Negroes, was akin to the deposing of Boyer. "Colored people may meet up with actual loss of liberty in Texas, in consequence of annexation"[36]—a prospect now faced by the Dominican Republic, and, perhaps, Haiti too. This unnamed observer had reason to be concerned for in his own Philadelphia, only recently, Negroes marching in favor of temperance were attacked after Euro-American bystanders were angered by the sight of a flag showing a Negro breaking his chains in favor of freedom.[37] Surely, if this banner was deemed a provocation, the existence of an island that had broken its own chains was a *casus belli*. Moreover, it was suspected that enslaving republicans had yet to forget that one of the first measures adopted by the Boyer regime when it took over the eastern portion of the island in 1822 was to abolish slavery.[38]

To hear one pro-Haiti spokesman tell it, there was more than racism at play. B. C. Clark argued that the turning point for the island came on 30 December 1843 when a constitution affirming religious liberty was bruited in Haiti which led directly to the 1844 secession. As noted, Haiti was willing to embrace thousands of migrating U.S. Negroes—most of whom were not Catholic and the same held true for those arriving from its patron in London. Yet even Clark pointed the finger of accusation at Calhoun, the Marx of the slave-holding class. The "Hon. Secretary" Calhoun, said Clark, was concerned that "*one hundred and thirty thousand white Dominicans*" were unsafe on the island given that their fate was bound up with that of an African republic. The "war of color" was launched by Calhoun and Company as a result, he said, as those cowering in the east "claimed protection at the hands of the Government of the United States," which was facilitated when Calhoun's "secret agent" successfully sought to "disparage Haiti"—"springes to entrap the unwary" perpetrated by "pious frauds." It was even more of a fraud since those defined as "white" on the island would not be regarded as such on the mainland; the D.R. was a "mulatto republic and any sympathy awakened for it on the Negro-phobia principle is a sheer loss."[39] Dominicans, said the 20th century scholar, James Parthemos, "were sensitive of their racial background to a point approaching para-noia,"[40] a perception driven by their unique role as being born in revolt against an abolitionist republic while aided immeasurably by enslavers.

The self-proclaimed "Secret Mission to San Domingo" by U.S. emissary David Dixon Porter in 1847 was certainly bathed in illicitness. He was quick to locate the military man who "appeared to be the only pure white person" present (though "they all consider it an insult to be called any other color; black being applied to the Haytiens at the west end"). Although Dixon railed against "vindictive decrees issued by the Haytiens against an oppressed nation of whites," the implications for the mainland of the proposition that the Dominican Republic constituted an "oppressed nation of whites" were too ghastly to contemplate. He eviscerated Haiti since "their enmity to the *United States* and some of our *institutions* is well known, though from commercial interest, they preserve friendly relations." He thought, as well, that it was actually France that was responsible for D.R. secession in 1844, not his own homeland.[41]

Actually the founder of the Dominican Republic—Juan Pablo Duarte—was educated in the United States and the declaration of independence there echoed that of the mainland republic,[42] though it remained true, as had been the case for centuries, that the major European powers (Spain, France, and Britain in the first place) were preoccupied with Hispaniola.

Nevertheless, unrequited claims for compensation by U.S. nationals stretch-ing back decades continued to irritate relations with Port-au-Prince, providing an incentive to disrupt the status quo.[43] Unfortunately for Haiti, such claims also ani-mated France and, in fact, brought Paris and Washington together to the detriment of Port-au-Prince.[44]

At times the opposite was true, e.g. when William Berson of Tennessee made claims against France seeking to be compensated for his lost inheritance in Hispaniola. Baptized in the place he called "St. Francis, Grand Goave, Santo Domingo" in 1780 and educated in Paris, he learned the trade of jeweler or clock-maker on the advice of a wise uncle but by 1810 was in exile in Boston with his U.S. wife and four children. By 1830 he had moved to the bountiful frontier—Franklin, Tennessee, in his case. He made a claim pursuant to the "law of 1826, the result of a treaty between France and Haiti," claiming a piece of the indemnity in other words.[45]

The French consul in New Orleans was instructed that the "losses" he "sustained during the revolution" on the island were compensable, as he sought to "take benefit under the laws providing for the sufferers of St. Domingo." Port-au-Prince had "paid some two or three installments to the French Government for the purpose of indemnifying the French who lost their property—but as yet," he moaned, "I have received nothing," though he remained a "Frenchman in feeling as well as by birth."[46] This description could fit numerous descendants of the hexagon in the slave-holding republic, perpetually jeopardizing Haitian sovereignty. On the other hand, capital from Haiti via France poured into New Orleans, increasing the already formidable wealth of this city—and the nation. Berson hired a Paris attorney to recover at least a portion of his former property, which was worth—he estimated—"about one thousand francs."[47] Paris and Washington could now—potentially—unite to press Haiti for compensation.

A Bostonian also had claims against Haiti "for losses sustained and occasioned by the late revolutions of 1843 & 44." Angered to the quick, he charged that "all moral influence would be lost on that government without a demonstration of physical force," as he headed with vehemence toward "Jeremie, Hayti."[48]

Haiti appeared to be a duck worth plucking by the major powers. It was a kind of neo-colonialism in the sense that if it could not be subjugated directly, this could be done indirectly via indemnification. Step by step, Haiti had been marched to this precipice with Paris issuing threats of invasion as early as 1823 before an indemnity was voted under duress by Haiti in 1825. This was followed by a "revolution" in France in 1830, causing Haiti to argue that this vitiated the earlier vote, which led to a new accord in 1838; then Boyer was dislodged in 1843, causing the new regime to threaten repudiation of the 1838 pact, leading to yet another accord in May 1847. Meanwhile Spain was arguing that if France got reparations, then so should Madrid, and, barring that, the cession of the eastern portion of the island would suffice, which was the approach taken as early as 1830. By 1842 Cap-Haïtien was destroyed by earthquake, weakening Haiti materially and making it more susceptible to the blandishments of Paris and Madrid.[49]

Yet Paris did figure into Washington's calculations for by the 1840s relations, which had spiraled upward, were headed downward again. If France had gained a foothold on the island, this too could have jeopardized national security, providing opportunities to Paris for leverage by dint of allying with the British in Jamaica or the Spanish in Cuba—not to mention the Haitians. Since Paris-London relations had taken an uptick, this too was worrisome for keeping the two divided was the *ne plus ultra* of U.S. foreign policy. Strikingly, almost to the day that D.R. independence was proclaimed, the U.S. Congress passed a resolution "concerning French depredations on American commerce" that, like similar claims against Haiti, went back years.[50]

Just as the cession of Florida brought problems with an ever closer Britain offshore in the Bahamas, the dismembering of Mexico was thought to deliver a related problem—Paris and London moving closer together in response. So thought one Charleston resident, who felt the two European powers "have an immense stake in the present contest between us and Mexico," with both expected to "dispatch a fleet to the Gulph [*sic*] of Mexico" to "watch their . . . interests."[51] Hispaniola's proximity made it all the more important for the enslaving republicans to destabilize this island. Earlier the bellicose Congressman Waddy Thompson of the Palmetto State was instructed that "while war is always a dreadful alternative," the enslavers would "try it rather than let [London] meddle and rule in this hemisphere where the regulating place by right is ours." To be sure, Washington desired positive relations with "all . . . Europe and the rest of the world"[52]—but not at any cost, certainly not at the price of London establishing a foothold in all of Hispaniola. Already the possibility of a Mexico-Britain alliance aimed at independent Texas had—supposedly—driven annexation of the latter.[53]

Then there was the racial "danger of Indians on our frontier & of the Negroes," said one leading Carolinian, which mandated a "damned thrashing" of Mexico in response.[54] There too racism was not absent—which magnified the concern about Hispaniola—since the enslavers' top diplomat in the region, Joel Poinsett, speculated intently about the racial bona fides of Mexico's former leader, Vincente Guerrero, wondering if "he was a Mulatto. He appeared to me to be of Indian descent," it was reported anxiously.[55] Africans were "nearly extinct in Mexico," said Poinsett with evident satisfaction. "In the capital I saw only three or four, and have not seen more than twenty since I entered in country." This pro-colonial emissary wrote that "many respectable Creoles have declared to me that they regret having assisted to shake off the yoke of Spain"—an attitude that he could imagine existing in Hispaniola, particularly since he was "glad to find that every precaution will be used to prevent the black population from gaining an ascendancy" in Cuba.[56]

For Spain had been seeking satisfaction for what it perceived as an improper takeover of the eastern portion of the island in 1822. "The Haitians have *no title whatever* to the Spanish part of the island but occupancy," stressed William Miles of the United States in 1844.[57] Months after Dominican independence had been formalized, the U.S. Secretary of State was told by the Dominican authorities that the 1822 "union" between east and west violated the sacred principle that slavery was thought to embody. Then the "white Dominicans," after the fall of President Boyer, a victim in part of color contradictions and a deteriorating economic environment delivered by intensified tensions with neighbors—the mainland republic not least—pushed successfully for sovereignty. Boyer fell in 1843 and on 27 February 1844 independence was declared. It was followed by a Haitian invasion "by more than thirteen thousand men," but by mid-March "Spanish Dominicans gained the victory" with "only two killed and three wounded, whilst more than a thousand Haytians remained dead in the field." This initiated a series of similar victories, followed by bloody setbacks, and then an invitation by the Dominican Republic for Spain to return as a colonizing power by the early 1860s in order to blunt Haitian advances.

The Dominican Republic, said Santo Domingo, had "many mines of copper, gold, iron" and "two great bays" suitable for "formidable squadrons." Samaná, where U.S. Negroes had settled, also had lucrative "pearl fishing," mahogany, and tobacco—"although . . . agriculture decayed in consequence of the union with the Haytian Republic and the abolition of slavery." Puerto Plata, a similar site for U.S. Negro emigration, ranked with Santo Domingo as a port for trade, and already had significant trade with New York, Bordeaux, and London. Puerto Plata and Samaná both had to be "fortified" against "our enemies, the Haytians," but the "migration of foreign agriculturalists . . . by increasing the white population" would "produce greater security," notably for the United States. "All the white Dominicans," many of whom were in New Orleans, should return and property "not alienated by the Haytian government shall be restored."

This was a priority since an "unlawful invasion" was expected, given the "innate and unconstitutional hatred of the Haytians to all of the white race to whom the rights of holding property is denied throughout the whole of the Republic." In words assured to receive maximum attention in the slave-holding republic, Haiti was said to possess a maniacal obsession, a "thirst for vengeance" in "their interest in preventing the progress of prosperity and the increase of the white population" on "the island, though "the Haytian population is much greater amounting to more than half a million of persons." A U.S. intervention was demanded to block this alleged race-baiting nation. To that end, Spain was assailed for "insolence" and "indifference," no small issue given the tensions between Madrid and Washington over Cuba. Spain did not lift a finger "for twenty years" to save the east, which languished "under the oppression and vexations of the Negroes of Hayti" and suffered through the "consequent destruction of the white population" in the period after 1791.

U.S. aid was needed too, according to this official document from the Dominican Republic It was noted, as well, that the "black population must, however, be necessarily in the majority" in the Dominican Republic, "as the treatment received by the whites during the last 20 years . . . induced many to emigrate and . . . depressed others. It is, however, to be observed that the Spanish dominions in the island, as well as the continent, did not contain a larger population of Negroes [than] those of the English and French." This was reassuring, indubitably, to Washington.

But the Dominican Republic, conforming with the norms of its closest neighbor, mandated that slavery was "forever abolished," and, likewise, "there is not in the Constitution any . . . difference of color or race." Until the failed annexation of the early 1870s, suspicion still brewed on the mainland about the racial bona fides of the Dominican Republic, blocking closer union with the mainland.[58] Similarly, this abolitionist decree by the Dominican Republic did not enhance relations with the enslaving republicans.

To countervail this understandable suspicion, Santo Domingo resorted to history. Recalled was the earlier declaration of independence—30 November 1821— and the arrest of Madrid's men: the Governor and Captain General. A new state— "Spanish Hayti"—was initiated and "hoisting the Colombian flag" occurred; cooperation with Haiti was on tap, but Port-au-Prince balked, and a "civil war" flared in the east, while President Boyer was "threatening" the new regime. By 12 February 1822, President Boyer arrived in Santo Domingo "at the head of more than thirteen thousand men"—it was he who "abolished slavery" and then took over.[59]

Despite the remonstrations of Madrid, it did not retreat so easily. In 1826 Haitians were criticizing the Spanish residents of the eastern side of the island for their supposed laziness—and vice versa—which delighted the French envoy: "in one week they are not doing more than [the] French in one day," he sniffed. Abolition had brought dislocation, it was thought.[60] By November 1828, a U.S. agent reported that a "considerable" army "has been marched to the eastern front of the island" by Haiti "to protect it from an invasion of the Spanish."[61] By December 1828, Haiti urgently denied a report about the cession of the east to Spain and the island's U.S. Negro ally added portentously, "no other government will ever be suffered to retain any portion of this beautiful island."[62] The flux led to "much agitation" in Haiti,[63] undermining Boyer.

By January 1830, a Spanish frigate arrived in Haitian waters determined to restore Spanish sovereignty in the east and forces from Cuba were headed to Santo Domingo. The chance of Haiti holding on was deemed to be "poor" by the U.S. delegate.[64] By February 1830, Haiti was making extensive preparations in expectation of a Spanish invasion of Santo Domingo; naturally, the U.S. emissary, instead of peace talks, called for "one of our vessels" to arrive immediately, particularly since "the British and French are constantly about here."[65] By March 1830, Madrid

demanded that Haiti withdraw from the east.[66] Just before the Dominican secession, the U.S. agent in Aux Cayes had detected "late difficulties between this government and the Governor of Cuba," which did not augur well for Haiti.[67]

Those of Huguenot descent—e.g. Joel Poinsett, the enslavers' top diplomat
regionally—played a critical role in formulating U.S. policy. Some of them, like
Poinsett, were fluent in Spanish and, assuredly, favored fellow anti-abolitionist
Spaniards over Haitians in Hispaniola. (President William Henry Harrison too
spoke Spanish, which was not a good sign for Haiti.[68]) Louis Manigault was also of
Huguenot descent but now an elite Carolinian and he too—said his biographer—
had a "love of the Spanish language" to the point where he "preserved copies of letters in Spanish written to him by various persons he befriended in Spain and Latin
America." Of course, he spoke French too—he was born in Paris[69]—and had inher-
ited a distaste for Haiti that was seemingly part of his birthright. Charles Manigault
was of similar mind; his favorite vacation spot was Paris, described by him lovingly
as "the Place, after all—& before all!"[70] Similar sentiments drove Poinsett, whose
close ties to Emperor Alexander of Russia and Paris alike[71]—soon to clash in war in
the Crimea in the 1850s—was indicative of the uphill climb faced by Haiti.

Poinsett had managed to visit Samaná in 1822 on the island's northern coast, this
after visiting France repeatedly. Fortunately, he favored limitations on the African
slave trade—though he was far from being an abolitionist.[72] Still, the fact that one so
influential in Washington was so partial to Paris was of concern in Port-au-Prince.
When Commodore Jesse D. Elliot of Carlisle, Pennsylvania, sought to move to
France in 1841 in order to join its military, it was Poinsett who he consulted, in a
process that reached to the office of King Louis Philippe himself.[73] In that same
vein, U.S. nationals in Paris during this period sought to reach Secretary of State
Daniel Webster via Poinsett.[74] A chronic problem for Haiti was the persistent influence of those of French descent in Washington.

Thus, in early 1843 the U.S. envoy in Aux Cayes did not seem displeased with
the "late attempt to revolutionize the country," as "three or four thousands of the
revolutionists were to take possession of this place." In the uproar some who "were
formerly citizens of the United States claimed the protection of the American government," as they barely escaped being "molested," though "many arrests have
been made among the respectable."[75]

This snare did not elude the U.S. national, Dr. H. P. Lovell, who was "imprisoned" and then "tried by a military court and sentenced to be shot." The U.S. emissary was "treated with the greatest indignity & pointed to the door" when he sought
to visit him. A "black colonel who can neither read nor write," said Dr. Lovell, was
"condemned" and, thus, "received great abuse from the president of the court." The

medic's health was failing, but the request to have him removed to a "hospital" was "refused," though "American, English & French gentlemen in the city have taken a deep interest" in this case—"also many of the most respectable Haytiens." The consul had to "suffer indignities hard for an American to endure." For centuries "the soil of this island" had "been moistened with the blood of human victims" and it seemed now that this earth would "be watered with the blood of an American citizen" accused of seeking to destabilize the regime. William Gooch, the agent, demanded that his government send forthwith "sufficient armament" that "may be immediately ordered to this place for the protection of the prisoner."[76]

Gooch did manage to wrest a second trial for Dr. Lovell, but his conviction was affirmed and he was slated to be "executed," as the accusing Haitian general was bent on "wash[ing] his hands in the blood of this unfortunate man." It is striking that a "Mr. Davis" of Charleston, a citizen of Hayti —said to be "the only man in this country [who] has one drop of colored blood in his veins" and to have "taken an interest in foreigners" like the unfortunate Dr. Lovell[77]—was arrested on the orders of President Boyer himself on a charge of being involved in an attempted insurrection.[78]

But by March 1843, as Boyer's fortunes declined, those of Dr. Lovell—like a seesaw—rose, as a so-called "popular army," as Gooch termed it, "entered the city" and "opened the prison doors & released the prisoners & among them was Dr. H.P. Lovell." Thus, "the revolution" was "achieved but with little bloodshed" to the benefit of Lovell's homeland too, since "American commerce" would be "benefited" and duties on U.S. vessels would be "annulled."[79] This was in the context of "fruitless attempts" by the "blacks" to "gain the ascendance over the mulattoes," with the latter thought to favor Washington,[80] though they, in turn, were hardly favored on the mainland. A "certain party here composed chiefly of Blacks," said Thomas Ussher of London, aimed to "take the power into their own hands" and this could "terminate in a fearful struggle between the Mulattoes and the Blacks."[81]

By August 1843, Richmond Loring of the United States was describing an "outbreak between the black and colored classes of this island which may lead to disastrous results. The actual power of the country is in the hands of the colored," though of late "sixty two of the most influential & intelligent of the Blacks signed a petition" that in stringent terms was "complaining of the situation." The response was their arrest. But "the most influential escaped to a plantation three miles" from Aux Cayes "where they sounded the alarm & raised nearly the whole of the surrounding country,"[82] to the detriment of President Boyer who evidently had alienated the "influential" and Washington alike.

It was in 1843 that Secretary of State Webster was told that a "political revolution" had "commenced in the southwestern part of the island" with the "revolutionary parties" having "gained the ascendancy." Boyer—appropriately thought Washington—fled on a British vessel to Jamaica. "No Americans have in any way suffered," it was said, but conflict with Britain had not ceased since a ship flying the Union Jack sought to "deprive" a U.S. vessel of its "crew," as "two black men from shore" joined the Londoners in this armed confrontation,[83] according to a U.S. informant.[84]

Ironically, if Duff Green—the powerful U.S. leader—is to be believed, it was in 1843 that Buenaventura Baez, future president of the Dominican Republic, went to Port-au-Prince to meet with French agents who promised aid if he was to spearhead a revolt.[85] Such a viewpoint is consistent with the prevailing idea that the island being a rare piece of real estate not claimed by colonialists—and close enough to the United States to generate value—was attracting ravenous attention. The environment was so rife with unrest that it is possible that all of these conspiracies were unfolding simultaneously. Months later, U.S. nationals Samuel Thomas and J. R. Thomas were imprisoned in Haiti on a charge of murdering the captain of a British vessel that had just docked,[86] increasing the possibility that Washington too would like to see the island dismembered.

By late 1843, Paris was told of "fermentation" in Santo Domingo, along with anger toward the authorities. But there was also positive feeling toward France emerging, something alien to Haiti in recent decades.[87]

In the prelude to Dominican secession, official U.S. views of Haiti—never positive in the best of the times—were declining precipitously. William Miles was now safely back in Baltimore from Aux Cayes. He took time to reflect on his island tenure, concluding bluntly, that the "people are not prepared for self-government" and "civil war" was inevitable. "Their separation from France is a great misfortune," he opined, "& their withholding freehold rights to poor whites" was a most "erroneous policy." These alleged missteps were not due to a dearth of resources; there was "plenty of rain" and the "richest and most abundant forests," containing "plenty of birds" and "fine rivers." The "port of Nicholas Mole," which the United States was to control later, was superb. But "in the interior African languages do exist," a presumed measure of underdevelopment, where "they believe in the evil eye & adore idols." Still, most were "chiefly Catholic & very much attached to their faith. The influence of the clergy is [un]bounded," which sheds light on the commotion brought by an attempt to deliver religious freedom.[88]

France, thought to be a major beneficiary of secession, was predictably pleased in February 1844 when independence occurred. In fact, it was asserted that French nationals had taken part in the independence battle on the side of the Dominicans.[89] The French consul was elated to ascertain that weakening Haiti appeared to be a goal of the Dominicans. Scorned was the supposed overconfidence of the Haitian leadership taken by surprise by this loss of the majority of the territory they ruled. But now Dominicans were shrinking in fear and seeking asylum at the French legation in apprehension of what was said to be the well-known ferocity of the Haitians when pricked. Even General Desgrotte, a Dominican leader thought to be of French ancestry, had asked France's delegate for protection for himself and his family. In response, the French envoy convened a meeting at his residence of opposed Dominican camps in a bid for unity, which proved to be successful. A "beautiful day" it was, he beamed, as all sides seemed to place confidence in him, perhaps because it was felt that Paris's man would brook no compromise with Haiti.[90]

The leader of the Dominican rebels, Pedro Santana, hastened to assure the consul that the rumor that his constituents were willing to accede to Haitian sovereignty and abjure French protection was simply false[91]—though not denied was the support he received from Madrid and its representatives in Cuba and Puerto Rico. The latter, thought the French envoy, would alarm the Africans in the east, given Spain's penchant for enslavement.[92]

France was consulted when the Dominicans sought arms from Curaçao. Paris's man thought that the Dominican leaders were interested in becoming a protectorate of France.[93] The consul thought the Dominican leaders had confidence in him and he conceded that he tried to take advantage of the situation while avoiding intrusiveness. He took the lead in seeking to oust from Dominican soil 630 Haitians unwilling to accept the new order, dispatching them to Jacmel by sea.[94] Reported without comment were the stringent strictures against slavery in the founding documents of the Dominican Republic, including the death penalty for slave trading.[95] This rhetorical mettle was tested when a Puerto Rican slave trader arrived in Santo Domingo in mid-1844 in search of his "property" that had escaped and found asylum in the Dominican Republic.[96] Apparently he received no satisfaction.

In the early stages after the secession, Richmond Loring informed Calhoun that "the French part of the island" will "probably soon be under a black government," as opposed to the Boyer regime, perceived as dominated by *gens de couleur*. "The Spanish, I believe, will soon establish a separate government."As he saw it, the problem was that "there are very few blacks capable of conducting the affairs of the island and by what I know of their character I have not a doubt that they will soon commence fighting each other & separate themselves into clans & become like Africa." Loring's view harkened back to Jefferson's dark vision. As well, he noted that "navigation in the vicinity of the island becomes dangerous to foreigners on account of piracy" (again raising the specter of a regional Algiers). And he observed that in Aux Cayes "there is a large amount of American produce in this city remaining unsold & must remain so, as they have [no] specie."[97]

The problem faced by Haiti was that the Dominican independence struggle was portrayed as a "race war" with the fate of Europeans—or "whites"—at stake and at risk. Not coincidentally, this inflamed enslaving republicans and royalist Spaniards alike. By early April 1844, two U.S. vessels departed Aux Cayes, bearing the chilling news of the "vengeance of the Negroes, who had declared a war of extermination against the Browns"[98]—and others. "Vessels are constantly arriving from the unfortunate island," said the enslavers' typically hyperbolic emissary in Jamaica, Robert Harrison, all "crowded with refugees consisting mostly of white and brown persons."[99] In Aux Cayes, Thomas Freelon of the United States railed when U.S. property was seized—"and to make reprisals," he added, "would be the certain destruction not only of the property, but of the lives of every white in the Town," as a fearsome comrade of the late General Christophe had taken charge.[100]

Even the U.S. envoy, William Gooch, was not exempt. A "company of freebooters," the Haitian military in other words, "forcibly entered" his abode, "took possession of my trunk containing all my Official papers, as well as private letters & funds" and, to cap it off, "issued an order for our arrest"; so, he wanted to depart—pronto.[101] Before he departed Aux Cayes, he reported breathlessly about "Civil War—the contest is now between the mulattoes and blacks. This city is in possession of the blacks" and it was "heart rending to witness hundreds & hundreds of the coloured population, rushing to the seaside to go on board the vessels in harbour for protection from the Negroes."[102] Trade slowed to a trickle: there was a "large amount of American produce in this city remaining unsold," as the island was about to "become like Africa,"[103] words unintended as complimentary. The "American residents" in Aux Cayes, said Gooch, felt his "prolonged stay" there was "necessary to their protection," since "revolution" and "anarchy" were unfolding—but he sought a speedy exit.[104]

When the defrocked Boyer arrived in Kingston after a brief stay in France—the "climate" there was "too cold," in more ways than one, said Robert Harrison—anxiety rose. France had made encroachments in Samaná where U.S. Negroes had nested and, said Harrison, the "mulattos are favorably inclined to the English but as they are not the one twentieth part as strong as the negroes, they will have to succumb to the wishes of the latter, who it is said have no goodwill to either the English or French." Philippe Guerrier, then leading Haiti, was a "drunken old fellow" and "very illiterate" besides[105]—not boding well for what was to be termed race relations.

But President Guerrier was sufficiently sober to be "preparing and organizing the Black army to march on" Puerto Plata "or the eastern end of the island to reconquer it," said Francis Harrison, reporting from this town where numerous U.S. Negroes resided. They were now—as in Samaná—trapped in a racial conflict, precisely what they had hoped to avoid when they migrated. For now they were side by side with the likes of Harrison, who announced hubristically that what was involved was "a struggle of my own race to liberate themselves from the horrible bondage of the Blacks, as many of the people of the island are white, the population being similar to that of Mexico." The helpful Harrison chose to aid his racial comrades "by supplying" them as a "Merchant with powder, balls, muskets, and other munitions of war to liberate themselves from . . . [the] horrible oppression of the Blacks of the West." Since the regime in Port-au-Prince was "decidedly one of the Blacks," Harrison, inevitably, was "personally obnoxious to the Blacks of the West. First as a white man" and also as a "citizen of the United States."

This was October 1844, but earlier he was "attacked in the street by two of them," meaning Africans, and he "killed one of them in my own defense and put the other one to flight." He had "resided here as an American Merchant since 1836" and was uninterested in moving, but if his side lost, "my property and person and the persons of my family would be in jeopardy." Thus, he demanded that Secretary Calhoun dispatch a warship immediately and reminded him bluntly—"I am known to most of the Gentlemen of Charleston and Savannah"—i.e. the slaveholding elite.[106]

He got results: days later Secretary Calhoun moved to implement Harrison's urgent request.[107] The next day John Mason, Secretary of the Navy, sent "one of the vessels" to Hispaniola and no cannonballs had to be launched for Haitians to get the message.[108] By the spring of 1844, Washington was told by its envoy that there were "three ships of war in the harbor" of Aux Cayes, "two English & one French"; more troubling was that "one of the English captains informed me that if I considered the property or lives of any Americans in danger he would protect them." This was not good news for Port-au-Prince insofar as the regime counted on the tensions between London and Washington to survive. "As the United States has several armed vessels on the West India station," Richmond Loring continued, "I consider it important for some of them to call at different ports on this island, as there is so much American property and lives unprotected."[109] When a major British capitalist offered Santo Domingo a loan of 1.5 million pounds—and then sailed to the island to punctuate his generosity[110]—Haitians should have realized that the tides of history were not flowing in their direction. Opportunistically, London was hedging, unwilling to be outfoxed by Paris, Washington, or Madrid, in the event that secession was successful. For at the same time, Paris was warning Port-au-Prince that if it sought "extermination" of their opponents, all of Europe would mobilize against them and, not least, this would supposedly hasten the advent of unfavorable stereotypes.[111]

Madrid was hurrying ships to the Dominican Republic simultaneously. Haiti was falling off of the diplomatic tightrope it had been traversing for decades, as it had managed to galvanize a pro-Dominican coalition among the major powers.[112] The enslaving republic was a chief beneficiary though in the long term this only served to heighten the bravado of the slave-holding class, helping to push them toward a bruising confrontation with their sectional rivals over Kansas and Nebraska and Cuba.

Weeks later, Secretary Calhoun was informed from Aux Cayes that the "dispute" between U.S. seafarers and Haitians was becoming ever more "serious." The latter were acting as "aggressors" and tended to "increase the Insolence towards foreigners," meaning "lives have been endangered." The remedy? More warships were sent.[113] The Dominican envoy to Washington, Dr. Jose M. Caminero "expressed . . . great exultation" to Secretary Calhoun for his "aid & assistance" to his homeland, which was now busily "repressing Haitian Negroes['] usurpations & attacks"—a fact that was in their mutual interest. The "five armed vessels" sent to "blockade Porto Plata" were proving to be decisive and was a warning to France to steer clear of Samaná.[114]

Dr. Caminero assured Calhoun that the "sympathies of the whole Dominican people are in favour of the Government and citizens of the United States in preference to all . . . European Powers." Puerto Rico too wanted to revolt against Spain. So, when the United States aided the Dominican Republic, this served to "haste[n] their political change" in San Juan.[115] Caminero, the Dominican delegate, came to the enslaving republic with impeccable credentials. Aymar & Co., one of the largest commercial firms in Manhattan, with substantial trade in the Caribbean and Latin America, vouched for the Dominican, informing Calhoun that the "republic he represents being a republic of *white* men" was now "permanently and safely established in their independence of the negroes," meaning Haiti.[116]

Caminero told Calhoun that Dominicans had been unhappy with Haiti ever since the "Union" of 1822; the union, "together with the abolition of slavery at the same time, occasioned a general unsettlement of habits, as well as of the principles of social life," he said obliquely, but in words that the enslaver Calhoun could interpret favorably. Tellingly, he asserted that "our agriculture decayed in the consequence of the union with the Haytian Republic and the abolition of slavery in 1822." The "oppressions and vexations of the Negroes of Hayti" were condemned in a tone that enslavers found comforting. Then "white Dominicans" rebelled when Boyer fell, which was seen as a blow against *gens de couleur*; ironically, the United States, which had been persecuting *gens de couleur*, was now poised to take advantage of their surge. As had been the case since the late 15th century, Caminero pointed to the "many mines of copper, gold, iron, and coal," and "two great bays." In the numbers game, he said that "half" of the population in the Dominican Republic was "white, who hold the general administration. And two thirds of the other half are *mulattoes*" and "the remainder are negroes"; thus "the number of ancient slaves is small." To bolster the prevailing ratio, he wanted to "effect immediately, the immigration of foreign agriculturalists who by increasing the white population will not only produce greater security" but will also constitute a force for "attracting and augmenting trade." And, to that end, "the Government has recalled (and no doubt they will come) all the white Dominicans who emigrated in 1822."[117] This would also serve to marginalize the U.S. Negroes who had been flocking to the eastern side of the island since the 1822 takeover and prime the pump for a potential annexation.

Caminero too echoed the historical explanations proffered by others to justify secession. The break with Spain in 1821 allowed Port-au-Prince to manipulate all sides and win the entire island, as President Boyer triumphantly arrived in Santo Domingo in February 1822—and then promptly "abolished slavery," enraging many. Again and again, he reminded Calhoun that in his emergent nation, a "portion of the people of colour, that is mulattoes and samboes [*sic*]" were "free by birth" and were "all natives of the same Spanish Dominican soil and not of the French part" and, thus, had "always been in contact with the whites."[118]

So buoyed, those Dominicans defined as "white" criticized Santo Domingo in mid-1846 when a delegation was dispatched to Europe for support that—supposedly—was comprised exclusively of those defined as "colored."[119]

Calhoun also sent an agent to the Dominican Republic with the instructions, *inter alia*, to "determine the aggregate population of the country and the proportion of European, African, and mixed races"—in short: the racial correlation of forces.[120] After returning, John Hogan, in private correspondence, "urged" the "recognition of the Dominican Republic in order to have those people [act as] a barrier against the movements of *France*," though Haiti could easily have played this role but remained unrecognized. He was concerned that France was more committed to abolition than the enslaving republic and was "now endeavoring to unite the other (Negro) part of the Island & then through the aid of Spain get control of the whole island of St. Domingo holding out to all [as] an inducement to their submission the abolition of slavery," which the Dominican Republic had pledged to do in any case. "The Haytian Govt. will the more readily yield in consequence of our conquest in Mexico. They say that we wished to get possession of the island of St. Domingo in order to put the Negroes into slavery"—not an inaccurate supposition. The "Southern States" of the United States were committing a "blunder" by not "soon" acceding to "recognizing the independence of the Dominicans for as soon as their independence is acknowledged no power could make them submit to France. They have a deep seated hatred to the French," which was not wholly accurate. But, he worried, "as soon as France can lay her hand on her lost possessions of St. Domingo she will then turn the Bay of Samaná to a good purpose," which happened to be "the finest harbor in the world" and a current residence for recently emigrated U.S. Negroes, who may not have supported the United States.[121]

Hogan, who played an instrumental role in U.S. policy toward the island, held high-level meetings in Washington upon return from his visit to the Dominican Republic in the summer of 1845. "The city of Santo Domingo has about 9000, two thirds white," he assured, unlike Port-au-Prince. The Dominican Republic controlled "about three quarters of the whole island" and, in sum, "there are three Whites to two Blacks & mulattos." Despite that worrisome ratio, he advised that "the Spanish Black are a more civilize[d] race than either [the] French Black or our Black. They are peaceable, quiet, submissive creatures, entirely unassuming and obedient, they yield obedience to their White rulers & they have the utmost veneration & respect for their White masters." The rise of the Dominican Republic, in short, was a coup for the United States and a blow against Haiti. As well, "our Southern States are safe & England is sorely beaten in her wicked efforts,"[122] Hogan concluded, which brought fervent thanks from Santo Domingo.[123]

The Dominican leadership repeatedly reassured Washington that Santo Domingo was on the side of the enslaving republic in the "race war" that was thought to be unfolding in the hemisphere. For example, when their mainland agent, Dr. Caminero, met with President John Tyler, he emphasized the supposed "large proportion of Negro blood in Haiti" and how the "free people of color in the Spanish part of the island" had long resented "Haitian domination."[124]

So moved, John C. Calhoun recommended immediate recognition. He envisioned great things from the relationship: "should the Dominican Republick [*sic*] sustain itself, it opens a prospect of restoring the Island again to the Domains of commerce & civilization. It may one day or another be one of the great marts for our product."[125] This recommendation was made based in part on the recommendation of the "secret mission" he sent to the island, though the emissary—David Dixon Porter—cautioned that "the pure whites amount to not more than 150 or thereabouts" and "about two thirds of the population are composed of the mixed race"; in fact, it was a "difficult matter to find twenty females with pure white blood in them." Despite this supposed debility, there were security issues that were overriding, e.g. the "German colony" that had "settled near Aux Cayes" four decades earlier. Moreover, there was "perhaps no country in the world so abundant in water power as the island of Saint Domingo." The haul of mahogany was breathtaking. Samaná contained the "finest harbor in the West Indies and the key to the Gulf of Mexico," long seen as the Achilles heel of the enslaving republic. Yes, Cuba "may be the key to the Gulf, but Samaná . . . could be made the key to the entrance of it." Then there was the "most beautiful scenery" extant, perhaps "in the world." If these natural resources could be combined with the "energy and the liberal sentiments of the Anglo Americans stock," the heavens were the limit. In fact, if the enslaving republicans did not act, their European foes (notably the British mining interests)—now joined by Germans—would and the Dominican Republic could become a "dangerous foe" rather than a "strong friend."

This was of notable concern since in the strategically sited Samaná, with "not more than 1000 inhabitants," the "most conspicuous portion of the community is a colony of Negroes who left the United States in 1822." Still, in light of the devastation of war, they were now "in the utmost state of destitution," which curbed their enthusiasm for further conflict. They "seem to have lived for the last twenty years on scriptural phrases," he noted sarcastically, as "their conversation is continually interlarded" with such words. He contended that Boyer's "Code Rural" was "put in force with great severity against the American blacks."

But what drove this "secret" agent and his homeland was what he termed Haiti's "great prejudice," which "has always existed with them against the Americans and there is no greater proof of their hostility than the fact of their imposing an extra duty [of] ten per cent on all articles of commerce from the United States. This has driven all our cheap manufactures out of [the] market," he added blazingly. "Our cheap cottons," he moaned, "cannot compete with the English." The trend was evident: "about 15 more American vessels visit Port-au-Prince than visit Saint Domingo; but the number that visit the former port is stationary, while those at Saint Domingo are increasing every year." Anyway, he concluded, with a final insult, Haitians did not observe the incest taboo.[126]

What was to follow was intense jockeying between the enslaving republic, Spain, France, and Britain for influence in Santo Domingo.[127] This was not unlike what had befallen Cuba with a similar result:[128] growing U.S. influence tending toward annexation. For as Porter was sizing up the Dominican Republic, his comrade—Francis Harrison—found that "the French made extensive surveys of Samaná Bay" with "at times as many as six vessels of war being employed." Madrid was also in an advantageous position, at least that was the suggestion of Harrison. The Dominican Republic was "prospering" in the midst of conflict with Haiti since the "depreciation" of the "country has principally affected the foreign merchants" and was "benefiting the native shopkeepers, planters, and woodcutters" who had been wrong-footing the "merchants" with "depreciated paper."[129] But these local elites were heavily of Spanish origin.

But first Haiti had to be defeated, which would weaken the abolitionist republic and circumscribe its aid to enslaved Africans on the mainland. A backlash was developing against the partisan enslaving republic, perceived correctly by Haitians as being all too interested in splitting the island in two. Aux Cayes was "in a state of great excitement," it was reported in March 1845, as "lives and property of American subjects are in jeopardy."[130] By December 1845, the U.S. envoy in Aux Cayes was taken by the fact that "difficulties between the Haitians and Dominicans augment daily with no prospect of speedy termination. A general recruitment is taking place in order to form an army destined to proceed against the city of St. Domingo"; the problem, said Loring, was that "lower classes are in a complete state of demoralization," pointing to the "great importance of having occasional visits from a vessel of war" from the enslavers to further intimidate Haiti.[131]

Haiti was not without weapons. From Cap-Haïtien the U.S. emissary sketched the possibility of a conflict between the enslavers and the abolitionists. "There sailed from this port," said G.F. Usher, "a Haytian man of war bark, carrying ten guns; a schooner, formally . . . of Philadelphia" of a hefty "133 tons," carrying "six guns; and three small schooners of three guns each. Their object is to cruise against the Spanish," though it had just "destroyed the Dominican schooners. And their next object will be to blockade" Puerto Plata where U.S. Negroes resided in significant numbers. This conflict was empowering the military and draining the island: there was an "insatiable desire for military titles" with the military "appropriating to themselves the little that is produced."[132]

By December 1845, the Haitian fleet was being confronted by warhips from the enslaving republic; "a shot was fired," said the U.S. agent, and his nation's vessel "then hove to again" and was "detained for some time." Despite this setback, things were looking up for the U.S.-Dominican side since they were "expecting aid" from Spanish Cuba.[133] Nevertheless, a few years later alarm bells were sounded when a Haitian vessel headed to New York, sailing—reputedly—under the guise of Danish colors with unclear intentions.[134]

Haiti was not finished. Their militant navy seized a U.S. vessel and the captain was imprisoned for three months for what was termed a "pretended fraud." The U.S. delegate demanded that "at once" a "man of war" should be dispatched, along with "such measures" as would preclude a repetition of this presumed outrage.[135] The enslavers were now enmeshed in a war with Mexico, so President James Polk was told to "send a vessel of war" or "have one stop on the way to Mexico."[136] Intriguingly, the U.S. delegate then spotted "two privateers or pirates under Mexican colors."[137]

The United States was not finished either for it was able to cast the conflict in terms unfavorable to Haiti and—stunningly—allowed the enslaving republic to gain the moral high ground in certain circles over the abolitionist republic. "A war of color has declared itself at Port-au-Prince," it was blared by 1848. "Colored people" urgently met with the Haitian leadership in response, but—supposedly—the latter's top leader was insulted and "ordered his guard to shoot down the speaker and to clear the palace, which was done immediately." Because the "American interests in this island are so great," said John Wilson, "I earnestly hope that our Government will not quietly look on and permit such butcheries, without sending out a man of war," since "the blacks so far outnumber the colored" and, thus, "become easy victims." This was simple self-interest too for "while the citizens and subjects of France and England are treated with respect, Americans are obliged to submit to whatever may befall them." Just as it was a turnabout for Washington to be defending the "colored," it was likewise a reversal for the enslavers to now pose as the champion of U.S. Negroes who had fled the mainland in terror years earlier. "I have been applied to by respectable colored people," said Wilson, "claiming to be American citizens, to know if in case of emergency, I could grant them protection." Wilson asked plaintively as to "how far . . . [he] should be justified in interfering in their behalf," though the import of his query was unclear.[138]

The desperate "colored people" of Haiti, said Wilson, were "praying for the intervention of the French government in their behalf . . . they desire the French government should take possession of the country"—which, he thought, "will undoubtedly be of vast benefit to the country" and a comeuppance for Black Jacobins too. For "it is impossible for the colored people to remain [in] their present position, as they are liable to be arrested or assassinated at any moment."[139] Though *gens de couleur* were harassed on the mainland, the United States posed as their protector on the island; "nothing less than the extermination of the colored portion of the inhabitants of this island" was at stake, according to Wilson. "Murdering and plundering" was now the norm. He demanded that battleships be sent immediately to "different seaports" on the island to effectuate a rescue.[140]

Ironically, it was the very same Wilson who expressed his stern "surprise" when in August 1848 there was the appointment of "colored men" in the employ of the U.S. commercial agent in Port-au-Prince. Practically, he said, such men would not be "able to grant protection to American citizens in case of need," since they were not able to "take care" of themselves. Besides, this peremptory act "has met with the condemnation of every foreigner . . . in the capital and notice of the appointment was received with indignation by the American ship masters in port" since it tended to "diminish the respect in which we should be held."[141] Of course, this evaluation evaded the 1820s appointment of Charles MacKenzie, a man of color serving London's interest, though it suggested that Washington's engagement with the "colored" had strict limits.

Port-au-Prince was "the seat of an open and armed revolt," it was reported in 1847. "Rumors are in circulation too horrible to be executed except by savages" of "the most inhuman and bloodthirsty" nature. "A large percentage of the black population have formed plots to overturn the Government and place at the head of affairs partisans of their own who would not only permit but encourage any atrocity," as "they wish to massacre without distinction of age and pillage their property." If this were to occur, "foreigners would not be safe for the Negroes look on them with a jealous eye as friends and protect[o]rs of the colored class. The hatred which the Blacks bear the people of color is well known and they have always [intended] a general massacre." Thus, in 1844 the time "seemed opportune" and they moved to "execute their projects. All colored people and many Blacks unwilling to participate in crimes so revolting to human nature were compelled to save their lives by flight leaving their property to be pillaged and destroyed." He found the "Negroes" to be "uncivilized," with "constant meditations of massacre and plunder," an assessment with implications for the United States itself.

Thus, the "Foreign Consuls" urged the dispatching of "vessels of war to protect the lives and property of their countrymen. The author of this damning report, Thomas Usher, had "passed the last twenty-three years" on the island and purported to possess "perfect knowledge" of Haiti, though he was "an American citizen" yet "well considered and respected by those in power."[142]

Richmond Loring may not have been as respected, but he too shared the view that "unless some foreign power interfere effectually, Hayti will become a disgrace to the civilized world."[143] This was an opinion also held by "British merchants," who demanded "protection of their property exposed by political dissensions in the presence of an armed revolt." Loring was noticeably dyspeptic, asserting that "anarchy reigns" due to the "present ignorant and depraved administration," which was "deplorable."[144]

In Puerto Plata, where there was also a contingent of Negro migrants from the mainland, things by way of contrast appeared "tranquil" in early 1847 with no "offensive war measures" from Haiti detected by Francis Harrison, who had extensive commercial interests in the vicinity.[145] He found "but one American vessel in this port," he said a few months later.[146] Yet the "difficulty in procuring horses and the bad state of the roads" caused him to "go by sea to Samaná." It was "fortified" with significant enrollment in the military of armed men, though he did not say if this included U.S. Negro migrants. However, he did seem more pleased when he arrived in "Savannah La Mar, a small town on the opposite side of the bay inhabited by white immigrants from the Canary Islands," a population thought to be friendly toward Madrid. He went on to meet with the Dominican leadership who were elated to greet him, but "disappointed that I had not any letter" from Secretary of State James Buchanan.[147] As for the "frontier towns that are near to Port-au-Prince," Harrison ascertained "premonitory symptom[s] of an invasion by the Haytiens," who were "mustering on the northern frontier."[148]

This proved to be a false alarm but not inaccurate was Harrison's claim about "marauding parties of the Dominicans," who had "been carrying off some horses and cattle," and contributed to a state of dislocation.[149] The riotous anarchy that then prevailed may shed light on why Harrison fell victim to a spreading fever that took his life.[150]

As comments about marauders suggest, the enslaving republic was seeking to corral an increasingly bumptious Dominican ally. Because Haitians then had the larger population, Santo Domingo—according to Jonathan Elliot, a U.S. agent—"insist[ed] that they have the right to exact military duty from all foreigners," including mainlanders. There were other problems too, e.g. when Jacob Wood of Darien, Georgia, purchased 2000 acres of land in the Dominican Republic, then manumitted about 250 enslaved Africans for the purpose of their being located there (akin to the move by Zephaniah Kingsley in the previous decade). Brusquely, he was informed by an official that "the government cannot receive other than European Emigrants and then only in such proportion as they deem proper." On top of that, the authorities then sought to "illegally" seize "the property of the late Francis Harrison,"[151] which was considerable and represented one more conflict between the local and global elites. But Washington was constrained. Relations with Haiti were so bad that a warmth in ties with the Dominican Republic was unavoidable, a maneuver also driven by the fact that rivals—e.g. France, Spain, and Britain—were moving in that direction. Hence, even though Jonathan Elliot confessed that the "greatest distress and stagnation in business prevails here" in Santo Domingo, an alternative to the status quo was difficult to develop.[152]

For whatever problems existed with the Dominican Republic paled into insignificance when compared to those with neighboring Haiti. "The greatest consternation and alarms prevails here," said Elliot in the Dominican Republic, since the "President of Hayti, Soulouque," has "beaten the people of this Republic in every battle. My house is already filled with frightened females. As soon as the Haytian President arrives within half a day's march of this city—it is my intention to go out and meet him to know if American property and persons will be respected."[153]

"The Haytian army are close to us," wailed Elliot days later, writing from Santo Domingo in the spring of 1849. Virtually "all the extensive merchants have packed up their goods and shipped them to the neighboring islands and [are] leaving with their families. This town is filled with women and children from the country and famine" is stalking the land. "They have asked [for] the protection of the French," which led the United States to increase its own meddling, particularly since "large quantities of goods belonging to merchants in New York have been placed in my care" (though in the north U.S. commerce involved "not more than four or six vessels in a year," it was "greater" in the south, "near three vessels per month").

Britain too was upping its involvement. "The President has told me that it is the intention to set fire to the place in case they cannot hold out against the Haytiens. I have written to St. Thomas, Curaçao, and Jamaica for one of our men of war. The merchants of Puerto Plata have all shipped their goods and gone to Turks Island or St. Thomas." The "destruction" of leading towns was nigh. "I have abstained from all participation in this war," he said, not convincingly. "I have not even expressed an opinion, but I have been given to understand that [President Faustin] Soulouque who leads these [Haitian] men has a strong hatred to Americans," while Dominicans "afford us advantages and extend us privileges more than to other foreigners."[154]

The problem for Soulouque was that he was perceived as seeking to suffocate a neighboring "mulatto" republic at a time when a number of the major powers thought that splitting the island was not a bad idea, not least since it would weaken abolitionist and ambitious Haiti. Moreover, he was seen as suppressing "mulattos" in his own land at a time when some of these same powers thought that this was just a prelude to an attack on their own nationals—or racial group. By May 1848, in Port-au-Prince, "political demonstrations" were reported, while a "deadly revenge" was said to "rankle in the hearts of the blacks against the more enlightened and enterprising mulatto population," a tendency that was said to exist "since the days of Dessalines." Presumably, "under the sanction of the authorities," this "revenge" had "burst forth in open violence," said S. C. Luther of the United States. "Some fifty or more of the mulattos were massacred by the president's guard and the police" and a "general massacre was only prevented by the bold threats of the French Consul General" and the looming presence of an "American sloop of war." This "flame of destruction" will "spread throughout the southwest part of the island,"[155] it was added forebodingly.

Only recently, Luther had demanded the "presence of an American man-o-war" since "acts of oppression and injustice" were "daily" taking place at the hands of these "sable officials and citizens upon American citizens, seamen, and vessels" and this could "only be repelled by threats of defence and force of arms." Moreover, there were "unprovoked assaults and depredations of the numerous depraved wretches who watch [for] their opportunity for pillaging & insulting the officers and seamen of our vessels," with "unjust extortion of money from their innocent victims." It was "in vain to attempt to establish the innocence of an American white citizen, however false the accusation." There were "internal wars" then "raging" in Hispaniola, pitting—ostensibly—the darker against the lighter and the United States seemed to think that Euro-Americans had a stake in the outcome.[156]

WHEN THE ENSLAVING REPUBLIC GOBBLED up a good deal of Mexico in the 1840s, it provided impetus for further interference in the internal affairs of Haiti, leading to the secession that created the Dominican Republic. Interestingly, though alarm was raised in Washington when the perception arose that *gens de couleur* in Hispaniola were being persecuted, this had no noticeable impact on a similar mainland policy. Relations between Haiti and Britain were held hostage to London's intense involvement in Hong Kong and other parts of the empire, complicating matters further for Port-au-Prince. The resultant military clashes between the abolitionist isle and the enslaving republic were the inexorable result, setting the stage in the 1850s for mainland dreams to arise not only of annexing Hispaniola but also, perhaps, of enslaving its inhabitants and reversing the gains of the Black Jacobins.

8

Black Jacobins under Siege
1850–1859

Militant pro-slavery forces on the mainland were intoxicated with reveries of territorial expansion in the 1850s.

"Have you ever in your visions, dreamt of a great federation of West India islands, stimulated in their prosperity and advancement by African slavery as now existing in the Southern States? History has never recorded such a commercial and naval power as Cuba, St. Domingo, Porto Rico, and Jamaica united under one confederation, could rear up."

Such were the dreamy words of James Gadsden, whose very name signaled annexation; writing tellingly from Mexico, site of a recent triumph, he confided his concoction to a man who could actualize his words: Jefferson Davis, soon to be the leader of secession from the mainland republic on the basis of the expansion of slavery. A priority was Hispaniola, since—after all—it was the only island not already controlled by a European rival and the priority there was to "take the initiatory to protect the white race in St. Domingo and give them the opportunity of recovering their power in that Garden of Eden." Both "Hayti and Domingo would sing anthems to their deliverers from barbarism and her regeneration under the restoration of African slavery." It would also be a great boon to U.S. naval power, providing a launching pad for further expansion for, "as in Japan, to secure a coal station at Samaná" was too a must.[1]

Hours after Gadsden's impassioned words, the British envoy on the island spoke of being reminded of the recent debate in the U.S. Congress about Nebraska, where it was said unashamedly that "unmistakable indications appear of a purpose to annex the eastern part" of the island and "to subjugate the whole island, restoring it to the dominion of slavery; and this is to be followed by alliance with Brazil and the extension of slavery in the valley of the Amazon."[2] London also could not ignore that somehow Jamaica too was part of the U.S. expansionary project.

That domestic colonialism was merging with imperialism was glimpsed when a U.S. diplomat, Ben Green, charged that Haitians were "half savage" and "below the Comanche Indians" in development and, thus, merited a similar fate.[3] Such bigoted analyses were influenced by the bloody war between Haiti and the Dominican Republic that showed few signs of surcease in the 1850s, but what was dimly grasped at the time was that the Dominican Republic's refusal to pay a share of the indemnity owed to France placed even more of a burden on Port-au-Prince, driving the war.[4]

The migration of U.S. Negroes to the island too was at issue: Unsurprisingly, when the United States sought to lease Samaná in 1854, Spain suspected that the purpose was to forge "an immense den of filibusters" that would be speedily deployed for the purpose of wider territorial aggrandizement[5] and it was suspected that the grouping that came to be known as "African-American" would be part of U.S. ambitions.

This ambition was hardly a secret. It was in 1850 that a leading British official insisted that Washington could seize Hispaniola on the pretext of racial unity with the "whites" of the Dominican Republic against the presumed bloodthirstiness of the Haitians, a perception fueled by still regnant fears of what had been wrought by Black Jacobins decades earlier. Confirming this apprehension was the statement by a prominent Manhattan editor who chortled, "St. Domingo will be a State in a year, if our cabinet will authorize white volunteers to make slaves of every negro they can catch when they reach Hayti." It was "probable," said historian Rayford W. Logan, that "the whole [President Franklin] Pierce administration estimated the Haitian republic in terms of the value its inhabitants would have on the slave block."[6] By 1851, 2500 freebooters had amassed on the mainland, ready to depart for the Dominican Republic, supposedly as simple settlers but actually with the idea of conquest in mind.[7] Negro emigrants were menaced since Puerto Plata was their focus.[8] Martin Delany, the U.S. Negro leader, condemned the "deep seated scheme for the invasion of Hayti."[9] Meanwhile, abolitionists continued to congregate in London, issuing one castigation after another of the enslaving republic,[10] whose ambition to enslave the entirety of Hispaniola's darker denizens was no secret.

As the grand intent of the enslaving republic became evident, London reacted, particularly as it was not only Hispaniola that was at stake but Jamaica too. By 1850, the U.S. emissary in Cap-Haïtien thought that "the Emperor," speaking of Soulouque, was "making active preparation for another campaign" against the Dominican Republic and, as a result, "has contracted in England for the building of a war steamer to cost some eighty thousand Spanish dollars." He had also sent agents to New York for the purpose of obtaining a "brig of war and is daily expecting from there one of two corvettes" and had emissaries in France too for similar purposes.[11]

Frederick Douglass had gotten wind of this news about Jamaica and was highly displeased. This "Jamaica talk of separating from the mother country and annexing themselves" to the mainland was driven by "planters" and would mean the "re-establishment of slavery; to this they have been encouraged by Mr. Calhoun's proposition to re-establish slavery in Hayti" and the Florida elite's "proposition to annex Cuba for the purpose of preventing the abolition of slavery."[12] Douglass excoriated the "gigantic scheme of conquest and annexation [that] is in progress, involving Cuba" and "Hayti with its millions of free blacks to be reenslaved."[13]

The confluence of such tribulations—prospects of reenslavement on the island and the scent of civil war on the mainland—fueled the related idea of African rebellion in the United States aided and abetted by *gens de couleur*, which seemed as imminent in the 1850s as it did during the revolutionary era. That the *gens de couleur* were seen as being under assault in Haiti did not contradict this as the contradictory notion arose that this group was a firewall that needed protection in the Caribbean, lest their perishing signal the doomed fate of those defined as "white" on the mainland; at the same time this group continued to endure difficult sledding in New Orleans and elsewhere.[14]

As the enslaving republic sped toward civil war, the heady ambition of the mainland secessionists was fed by the idea that secession in Hispaniola could easily eventuate in a reversal of the abolitionist victory of the Black Jacobins, delivering more slaves. Before Gadsden spoke, the pro-Haiti B. C. Clark of Boston spoke dismayingly of the "war of color and the 130,000 white Dominicans" then backed by Washington,[15] with the latter having a capacious agenda than soared far beyond simple recognition of the Dominican Republic

The enslaving republic had been constructed on the basis of racist polarization with the darkest of us all at the bottom of the socioeconomic pyramid. That was the lens through which the struggle to form the Dominican Republic was envisioned and this did not redound to the benefit of Haiti. Dedicated U.S. visitors to the island, including Louis Henop in early 1855, found upon arriving in Santo Domingo that "there are very few white residents and the population is composed almost entirely of Negroes with a few mulattoes" and, not coincidentally, "the city seems to be gradually falling to decay." Then the ultimate indignity occurred when his vessel was "boarded by a negro lieutenant in full uniform to whom the same honors were paid" as "would have been paid to one of our own officers."[16]

The longtime fear of the mainland enslavers about being overrun by Africans seemed to reach new heights in the 1850s driven by sectional tensions and the growth in the African Slave Trade (to nearby Cuba notably). The so-called "Africanization" of Cuba led to nervousness about more Free Negroes across the Florida Straits, leading to a free Negro state on Dixie's border. This was "utterly abhorrent," said one U.S. national, who mused about "squatter sovereignty" taking flight in Cuba to the enslavers' detriment.[17] When Jefferson Davis was told about the possible "Africanization" of Hispaniola, it was hard to say if he was elated at the prospect of more potential slaves arriving or horrified at the thought that yet another Haitian Revolution was brewing.[18]

Ideologically, this loose talk about legalizing the African slave trade, seizing Hispaniola, and enslaving its residents led to the increased popularity of the philosophy of the Frenchman Arthur de Gobineau and his theories about African inferiority. "I have seldom perused a work which has afforded me so much pleasure and instruction as the one of Count Gobineau," said one of his followers in Mobile, a city that was a twin of New Orleans. Dr. Josiah C. Nott contended that the Dominican Republic was acceptable since its "population consists of mulattoes." As for Haiti, said Dr. Nott, it possessed "intellect of the lowest order"; thus, "we see the Haytien negroes energetically repel the white man from their territory and forbid him to enter it"—evidence of their alleged dearth in intellect.[19]

U.S. enslavers were becoming bolder about extending a supposedly illegal African slave trade. Carolina's favorite son, L. W. Spratt, chided abolitionists with the charge that measures to curb this odious commerce on the mainland only served to deliver more Africans to Brazil and Cuba. Anyway, he objected, abolitionists did not have "repugnance to slavery or *the extension of slavery* in the United States." No, he said, "they have repugnance to the power of the United States and to slavery as the source and condition of that power," a force that could easily be easily extended to Hispaniola.[20] His fellow Carolinian, C. W. Miller, was more explicit, asserting forcefully that the African slave trade should be legalized since "every attempt of the African at self-government has failed or sunk him lower in the scale of liberty." The evidence? "Hayti and Jamaica illustrate this," it was said. Thus, "the African Slave Trade must be opened to bring down the price of negroes. The demand for slaves in the Western States is so insatiable that [before] long the cotton growing region of the old Eastern States, South Carolina, North Carolina, Virginia, and Maryland will be exhausted." Yes, "fear has been expressed of insurrections if native Africans should be introduced," but a "successful insurrection would defeat the fiat of God which dooms the African to servitude," so there was little to worry about.[21]

U.S. nationals continued to press large claims against Port-au-Prince for losses ascribed to the revolutionary era. This may have aided in moderating Washington's policy toward the island since there was apprehension that if Haiti were to be destroyed, the possibility of compensation for claimants would evaporate. One high-ranking U.S. envoy fretted about Haiti "exhausting its resources" in conflict with the Dominican Republic and the United States alike, jeopardizing "some ultimate & hardy reparation to the American claimants."[22] Such considerations may shed light on why in early 1851 Secretary of State Daniel Webster suggested "reciprocal recognition" of Haiti—but only if the abolitionist isle "shall abandon its ambitious projects of foreign conquest," meaning subduing the Dominican Republic in the first place. The other closely linked demand was that any diplomat posted to Washington be a "person not of African extraction."[23] The latter point aside, the talk of recognition was driven by those like Gerrit Smith of what Frederick Douglass termed the "Free Democratic Party," which posited that "the independence of Hayti ought to be recognized by our government."[24]

By 1850 London detected a "paradox" in that Washington seemed to be favoring Haiti over the Dominican Republic since once the "extirpation of the Dominican race" occurred, "it would prove easy for American aggrandizement to annex the whole island to the States." The frequent broadcast of racist attitudes was souring Dominicans toward their potential mainland guardian. Besides, as long as Haiti and the Dominican Republic were draining each other in war, Hispaniola as a whole was weakened, making it more susceptible to annexation by the United States.[25]

In the late 1840s "cannons of war" being "fired" in Aux Cayes seemed to be a routine occurrence, said one U.S. observer. President Soulouque was accused of "imprisoning the most worthy citizens" and encouraging "disorderly blacks whose only object is pillage and massacre" and were "openly threatening" to set "fire" to "suburbs." Since—reputedly—"the commerce of the United States is so extensive and where so much property is at stake," there was only one course of action: "a vessel of war" should be dispatched.[26] In other words, as Secretary Webster was promising recognition on the basis of no "African" allowed in Washington, he was perusing reports from Aux Cayes about the "massacre of the colored people" and how "foreigners are looked upon invidiously" as their "protect[o]rs."[27] In fact, said Richmond Loring, these "semi-barbarians" had yet to be "convinced" that "American citizens are not to be trampled on with impunity," as they and those they were said to be protecting were "daily exposed to the mercy of bands of lawless & bloodthirsty negroes."[28]

There was an added reason for opposition to the man then known as Emperor Soulouque. He was charged with the ultimate sin: "operating directly against

American commerce." Goods from the United States were "required to be sold at fixed prices, causing great loss to the American merchant who shipped them, while but one or two articles brought from France are subject to this law," said George F. Usher. "Trade with the island is valuable to us," he cried and he demanded "equal footing" with France. The emperor was maneuvering, however, knowing that the Dominican Republic was easing closer to France and realizing that "the King of Belgium is exceedingly desirous" to partake of the Hispaniola bounty too. He was planning to escalate against the Dominican Republic and the United States currying favor with this regime was antithetical to his long-term aims.[29]

Though the enslaving republic was no slouch in persecuting *gens de couleur*, official Washington reacted with barely concealed outrage at reports of this group being demonized in Hispaniola. They connected this "successful crusade" on the island to the growth of "insolence" against "foreigners." This also took the form, it was said, of "religion trodden under feet & the Bible" too in the midst of "horrible" scenes of "murder, assassination & pillage."Again, battleships were demanded. In this instance, they were deemed necessary to provide "protection to the extensive American commerce & particularly to the unfortunate citizens of the United States whose lives and property are so imminently exposed to the insubordination of the lawless Negroes of Haiti" for "only very recently" a "citizen of the United States was assassinated." The victim was John Noel of South Carolina, a resident since 1821, who also had family in New Orleans.[30]

Finally, a U.S. sloop arrived. Her officer came ashore to greet Loring, but "to our great astonishment," said the irked envoy, he espied the tumult and departed swiftly to Pensacola, leaving U.S. nationals to the none too tender ire and "the feelings of hatred amongst the lower classes" that were "on the increase."[31] A "state of alarm" persisted, said the besieged emissary, since the "Black Authorities" have accelerated their "threats and abuse." As well, they sought, "with the grossest ignorance," to "accuse" the United States of "being confederates of the Dominicans." This was happening as "the most respectable colored people" were "seized and shipped as prisoners" into Haitian confinement. And this spelled "danger" for those like himself, as the United States was slowly beginning to view *gens de couleur* not as those to be persecuted but as harbingers of a possible destiny for those defined as "white." Since the Dominicans had "promised to burn Aux Cayes," this intensified the peril faced by U.S. nationals on the island.[32]

"Outrages often occur on U.S. citizens," was the considered opinion of U.S. envoy Ben Green. At Jeremie he encountered a U.S. merchant "who complains of [the] forcible sale of goods under Haytian monopoly & of the refusal to pay him coffee at stipulated prices." At Port-au-Prince he bumped into a U.S. commercial agent from Cap-Haïtien, who fled to the capital to escape imprisonment, and there he also found items from U.S. vessels that "had been illegally seized by customs officials." He too thought "imposing naval force" on Haiti would be necessary ultimately.[33]

Green's mission was more complex than he might have imagined. It was true that residents of the Cibao region of the Dominican Republic reputedly desired to be annexed by the United States,[34] but a good deal of the leadership in Santo Domingo was pro-Paris, which countervailed this desire. Thus, Green was received by them with a decided lack of warmth. Germans also had begun to intrude on the island and Spanish ships continued to cruise nearby.[35] Nonetheless, those Dominicans who longed for annexation invoked the Monroe Doctrine in order to substantiate their questionable claim: "we are worthy of the advantages of the 27 states of the Union," they said.[36] So influenced, a leading Dominican official broke ranks and asserted bluntly to Ben Green, "I am charged by my government to communicate to you that desirous of putting an end to the cruel war which we have sustained against the Haytians since the moment of our glorious separation, we would see with pleasure the intervention of the powerful Anglo-American nation, which you represent, to maintain peace."[37]

In a presentiment of future U.S. policy, Green asserted that his nation preferred an ersatz independence for the Dominican Republic, rather than a protectorate— i.e. neo-colonialism rather than colonialism. But since other powers—e.g. Paris and Spain—were offering the latter, he was forced to make other concessions to keep Santo Domingo on side. Dominican leadership asserted that Santo Domingo and Washington had a common foe in Port-au-Prince and should proceed accordingly. Moreover, if the enslaving republic demurred, then the Dominican Republic would simply turn to Paris or Madrid (or even London) for satisfaction. For Dominicans made it clear that they had had their fill of Haitian rule, alleging that with this advent a flourishing university was destroyed in the east, which was part and parcel of a war on knowledge generally—or so it was said. One enticement waved seductively before the enslaving republic was a reversal of migration policy, as the Dominican Republic made it evident they would "forbid blacks" from the United States while seeking to "offer every inducement to whites."And if the Dominican Republic did not receive more aid, there would be further reason for "white" Dominicans to flee, thereby strengthening Haiti and, perhaps, fortifying a rear base for U.S. Negroes beyond the northern side of the island. Green found it reassuring that "whites control and have nearly all the offices" in Santo Domingo, though—like others—he thought that concessions made to "people of color" in the face of Haitian "aggression" could cease as soon as the "threat" from Haiti dissipated.[38]

But what Green saw in the Dominican Republic stunned him, suggesting as it did a future prospect for his own nation, and underscoring why intervention was invited. Haiti intended to "exterminate the whites & mulattoes," he exclaimed:[39] "Souluque is at present engaged in putting to death and driving out all the mulattoes and 'browns'—within the last few weeks he has shot four of the principal mulattoes and declares his intention to do the same with eleven others."[40] Green was made to believe that Souluque felt "his oath of office" mandated "him to subdue the eastern end" of the island.[41] Yet Green was conflicted since—as ever for U.S. diplomats— he was pressing Port-au-Prince "to conclude & sign a convention satisfying claims of U.S. citizens against Hayti.[42] The question was whether this lust for compensation would overcome the competing wish to seize the Dominican Republic and, perhaps, save lives. Green maintained that his nation had "claims since 1805" that originated in the "arbitrary, illegal, and oppressive acts of the Haytian authorities"; he proposed "articles" that would "settle for $500,000 to be divided pro rata by United States" and "paid at New York in gold or silver."[43]

As Loring saw things, the aggressiveness of Haitians was emboldening others. Of late "two American Captains" were "walking peaceably" along the wharf when "they were attacked" by a "Captain of a Danish Schooner," a "Negro," but instead of arresting the perpetrators, the two victims were detained "as criminals" as the authorities paid "no attention to the Negro aggressor."[44]

In essence, as rumors began to fly about a U.S. takeover of the island in league with "white" Dominicans, followed by enslavement of denizens east and west, Haitians reacted violently and furiously—particularly those most likely to be enslaved.

Yet, since Washington had normalized the brutal process of the enslavement of Africans, this power had difficulty in absorbing why Haitians reacted the way they did. Thus, by 1849 Duff Green, a powerful Whig politico, was pondering the reality that in recent years Santo Domingo had warred against its closest neighbor repeatedly, though Haiti was "four times their number." The more populous republic was seeking to "exterminate the whites & mulattoes" with the resultant uproar creating diplomatic space for France, which sought to mediate then have the Dominican Republic assume a share of the indemnity still owed Paris and perhaps confederate the two. But if D.R. sovereignty were to be guaranteed by Washington, said Green, a "large white immigration" would ensue that would "establish white ascendancy" in Hispaniola. Thus, U.S. policy should aid the Dominican Republic against Haiti not only because of its vast natural wealth but also because "the real question at issue" was whether "the white race shall be permitted to enjoy any share in this island." The answer had to be yes for otherwise slavery on the mainland could be imperiled. For Haiti's intent, it was thought, was to "establish on this island [a] nation of pure blacks to be the nucleus of a black empire, which it is proposed, shall embrace the whole West Indies." The mirror image of Gadsden contemplating a U.S. seizure of Caribbean islands was Haiti contemplating the same—or so thought Green. For Port-au-Prince not only wanted to conquer Santo Domingo but was bent on "inciting the blacks of Cuba & Puerto Rico & if [a] French protectorate [arises]" in the Dominican Republic, the Haitians "may cause trouble even in the Southern United States."

Prefiguring the 21st century trend of "humanitarian intervention," Green proposed a right of intervention—e.g. in Greece years earlier—"when the general interests of humanity are infringed by the excesses of a barbarous & despotic government," e.g. that which purportedly existed in Port-au-Prince. There was a "duty" by the United States "not to be indifferent to the continuance of this war" between the Dominican Republic and Haiti.[45]

It was in "Santo Domingo's interest," Green insisted repetitively, "to remain independent & induce white immigration" from the United States.[46] Frederick Douglass's journal reported that a "thousand and one rumors are afloat at the intentions of our government," as reflected by the interest of Green in the Dominican Republic. Douglass reserved a particular scorn for the claims of compensation Green put forward, stretching back to the earliest decades of the century.[47] Another U.S. journal questioned Green's "ulterior objects," which included the "subjugation of Hayti, the reinstitution of Slavery, and ultimate annexation to the United States."[48] Green, it was reported, "figured somewhat prominently in the intrigues for the annexation of Texas" and since "slaveholders have always regarded [Haiti] with an evil eye," it was evident that creating a "new White Republic" was on his mind. All the headlines in New York about how a "quarter of a million whites may be massacred by the ferocious Negroes of Hayti" were propaganda driving annexation, it was stated. Still, "the masses of the American people are with the apparently helpless and devoted white race" of the D.R. Rallies "in the South, from Norfolk to New Orleans" were occurring "as fast as the news spreads of the critical situation of the whites."[49]

Then Green's son, Ben Green, was sent to the island in 1849–1850. He immediately proposed "introducing . . . spies" on the island with the purpose of seeking to "provide disturbance and disaffectation [sic] among the black population."[50] He arrived via Cuba and began conversations with the London envoy, who rapidly reported the substance and confirmed that the enslaving republic was disconcerted by the "colour" of the D.R. leadership. Green was "frequently in my house," said Robert Schomburgk; he "does, therefore, not hide to me" his feelings about "annexation," which was slated to follow once Cuba was "in their possession."[51]

Green was compelled to promote such diabolical schemes because what caught his eye in the Dominican Republic was the "number of American Negroes & descendants of American Negroes who came in [the] time of Boyer" and "stayed here because of privileges in not being compelled to military service." But now they were dispersing which was not necessarily good news for Washington since they were proceeding to "neighboring islands or [to the] Spanish main" to "get certificates from consuls or consular agents." With its own eye toward recruiting them, London proclaimed that "once [an] Englishman, always so, [you] never lose birthright" and, thus, they were welcomed in Jamaica. Now under pressure, Green wondered how far he should go in "protecting American Negroes who have once served either Hayti or Santo Domingo and also American Negroes who have never served either but reside here permanently."[52]

Green had apparent conflicts of interest. He was accused of pursuing self-aggrandizing land schemes and, like others, accused of a plot to "colonize" Samaná, while controlling whaling there. President Baez was charged with disfavoring him and the nation he represented. "Being a man of colour," said London's emissary speaking of the D.R. leader, "he is well too aware of the uncharitable spirit that prevails in the United States against his race."[53] The frequent reports about potential U.S. invaders were a cudgel held by Green, making his proposal for a steady stream of Euro-American emigrants and the cultivation of indigo and the working of mines seem reasonable by comparison, though this would be a kind of *de facto* annexation.[54]

Green was merely reflecting his homeland in that he was seeking to replicate in Hispaniola what had taken place in Texas earlier, though London continued to insist that he had a "wish for private gain" that was "unauthorized" by his superiors.[55]

Green thought he could turn to U.S. advantage the perception that London was the "peculiar friend of the blacks," which meant Santo Domingo viewed this power with "suspicion." London's offer to mediate was a trick, it was thought in the highest levels of the Dominican Republic, no more than a "pretext to favor Haytians." This too provided an opening for the United States, he thought. For given the balance of forces, Washington could "act alone & get pacification & payment of Haytian debts & protection to U.S. citizens & property" simply by placing "one warship continuously in these waters." Santo Domingo, elated about having a potent ally generally unwilling—unlike others—to make compromises with Haiti, was willing to relinquish control of Samaná: the tipping point was the assumed "duty" of the United States "to protect these whites."[56]

With Green's arrival, literature began to circulate in the Dominican Republic reviving the old charge that it was London that had played the instrumental role in ousting France from Hispaniola decades earlier. London was predictably irate and accused the French consul of circulating such "falsehoods."[57]

Prematurely, as things turned out, Jonathan Elliot in Santo Domingo reported in 1849 that "the Haytian army under Soulouque has been beaten and routed at all points" and worse for Port-au-Prince a revenge seeking Paris was "promising in the meantime to bring fifteen hundred men here from Martinique," though London's man on the scene sought to block this maneuver. This man, Robert Schomburgk, was seen as ineffectual since he was—allegedly—not "able to speak Spanish or the President here English." Elliot played the role of interpreter and "hence I was let into all the secrets," he said, chuckling. Both sides wanted the "Bay of Samaná, one of the finest in the West Indies, possessing coal, timber," and other "fine resources for a naval depot either in time of peace or war." The D.R. leader courted avidly by Paris and London, then turned to Washington; he "requested a private interview" with Elliot, "asking me for [the] protection of the United States and if I through the United States would allow this Republic to annex themselves"; it was "probable" as a result "that a delegation will be sent from here to Washington, whose object will be to obtain the recognition of their independence by our government." Elliot had been in the Dominican Republic for two years and considered himself to be "well acquainted with the country."[58]

That he may have been, but since less than eighteen months after pronouncing the Haitians defeated, Elliot then announced that Port-au-Prince was "expected" to "attack" soon, his powers of analysis could be questioned.[59] For Elliot then went on to sketch "more attacks and aggressions" against the Dominican Republic by Haiti, though the nation had "agreed to armistice . . . towards making a peace." He also continued to insist on the "confidence and respect in the highest degree" in which he was held, obviating the need for Washington to send a special representative, which too was rumored. "I shall lose much in their esteem," in this eventuality. "These people," he said of the Dominicans, "are all American in their feelings and as Republicans look to us for protection and aid"—and he could have added that they found inspiration from the mainland in the growingly important category of "race relations."[60]

Dominicans were fighting—at times "naked"—with "implements of agriculture in one hand" and a "sword in the other" in a desperate gambit to defeat the Haitians, according to Elliot. Once more Port-au-Prince had "purchased vessels and arms" from the "citizens of the United States" and was promising havoc: purportedly Haiti "threatens (and no doubt will do) to put to death all the whites and confiscate their properties," a perilous signal "almost within sight of our shores" and an ominous precedent for the mainland itself.[61] By the spring of 1850, this U.S. dystopia had crept closer, as Washington was told that Haiti was "making preparations for [an] overwhelming attack upon Dominicans" and, more problematically, abolitionists in Boston and New York were forwarding military aid to Port-au-Prince in "violation of U.S. neutrality laws."[62]

Aux Cayes was far from unique. Bilateral relations were so bad that the U.S. agent there wanted the "subject of our trade with this island brought before Congress." U.S. nationals were being "plundered," not being "paid in coffee"—or anything else.[63] And an official with an "imbecile brain" was harassing them. "The only way to remedy this evil," said John Wilson in a repetitive plea, was "to have our men of war, frequently visit the several ports of the island and by proper remonstrances, backed by a *show of power*" show who was boss. "Something should be done and speedily," he warned, "or our vessels will no longer be able to trade here, as their masters are subjected to the grossest insults and indignities."[64]

The list of the insulted included John Wilson, the U.S. official in Cap-Haïtien. By 1850 he was facing "criminal proceedings" with "imprisonment from three to six months" possible. His position was "unenviable," he confessed. He was reduced to seeking "the protection of the French Consul General" simply because he was pursuing "the protection of the interests of American citizens."[65]

This U.S. agent did not seem to recognize that placing him on the defensive was seen in Port-au-Prince as a condition precedent to what Wilson termed "marching against the Dominicans" and "attacking them." At that point in the fall of 1850 "three large barges or open transports" were "in [the] process of construction," which were "intended for conveying troops and supplies up the coast."[66] The "enlisting of recruits has been going on vigorously," as "every person capable of bearing arms has been taken up." There was a "large body of troops recently concentrated" with the "enrollment and arming of all the male population, together with the daily arrival of numerous regiments" from surrounding villages. The Haitian "intention" was "to march immediately against" the Dominican Republic, more precisely to Santiago "in the interior, distant only some four or five days march; that place is considered one of the richest held by the Dominicans, the least protected and easiest to be taken."[67]

There were corresponding "rumors of a French invasion" of Haiti in response, while U.S. activity was hampered in the wake of a "fatal fever which has carried off many foreign seamen," devastating to the mainland since "the number of American seamen visiting this port forms more than half the total number."[68] Wilson thought that these U.S. seafarers may have been ducking the island not only because of fever but also on account of the "brutal treatment" they generally received there; it was "severe in the extreme and totally unwarranted," he thought. Given the perception

that "so little energy" has been "exhibited" by the United States "at previous outrages to our citizens and flag at the hands of the Haytien authorities," the "latter
seem to be under the impression that they can act with impunity and without any
fear of the consequences." The remedy? Wilson "strongly and earnestly" demanded
that a "vessel of war be forthwith ordered to Port-au-Prince and Gonaives." Soon
Wilson too abandoned ship, taking an extended leave in New York.[69]

However, not abandoning Haiti were U.S. Negroes, who clung tenaciously
to Port-au-Prince. "Nothing is more annoying to American pride or to American
cupidity," said Frederick Douglass, "than the existence on our very borders of this
noble Republic of colored men"; it was "notorious" that "the slaveholders of this
country have a design to subvert this truly brave Republic."[70] He refused to believe
bad news about Haiti since "so much exaggeration generally characterizes Haytian
news, via New Orleans, that we must wait for definite intelligence."[71] Douglass also
seemed unhappy when 164 newly freed mainland Africans chose to flee to Liberia,
rather than take their strengths to Haiti since their previous owner "thought it
impolitic to send them there."[72]

For the United States, Faustin Soulouque was simply a *bête noire* while
Douglass's journal sought to give him a fair hearing. He was "entirely black," he
said admiringly, with a "very full chest, large shoulders, and broad hips" and "one
of the best horsemen I have ever seen." Like Douglass he was "born a slave" and,
reportedly, "fought against Christophe" and on behalf of Pétion. He was "favored
by the blacks on account of his ebony skin and by the Creoles because they hoped
to use him as their pliant tool"—but "they were mistaken. They had chosen a
master, not a servant."[73] But Douglass too was displeased by what he saw as a
"war of extermination between the Haytiens and Dominicans" that seemed to
unfold in the 1850s.[74]

Douglass was not unique in his views. "There is constant hostility between
the Government of Hayti and the eastern part of the island, styled the Dominican
Republic," scoffed one Negro journalist in 1852. "Is not this hostility," it was asked
rhetorically, "fomented by the white Americans who have obtained a foothold
there?" "This so-called Republic is about as much as reality as the Mosquito King"
since "two American gentlemen" were among those who "have made arrangements
with certain parties in the United States for the purchase of a steamer in which they
propose to take a large number of emigrants" to the Dominican Republic "Eight
hundred men" had "enlisted," it was added with suspicion.[75] As this periodical saw
things, the Dominican Republic was little more than a front for Dixie.[76] More than
that, this journal thought that "taking possession of the island of Hayti" was the
ultimate purpose of Dixie's backing of the Dominican Republic.[77]

For "secret emissaries from our own Government," it was added by this periodical, "have been busy" in the Dominican Republic "fomenting strife and defeating reconciliation." Indeed, "schemes for the conquest and subjugation of Hayti by gangs of southwestern crusaders, eager to [raise] on her soil the black banner of spoliation and Slavery, have been openly displayed in our Satanic journals." John C. Calhoun "had something to do with a secret mission to Hayti" to spark this unrest, though the "land pirates, spoliators, and propagandists would be glad to go still further" and "colonize the eastern part of the island and form an alliance offensive and defensive with that 'White Republic.'"[78] It was thought that the devilish Calhoun "regarded with some favor" the Dominican Republic, a suspicious trend in light of the Carolinian's curious "theories in regard to races" and his "unfailing watchfulness in seeking or seizing opportunities to extend Slavery."[79] To bolster Haiti, U.S. Negroes bent on emigration chose to make the island the center of their campaign.[80]

Another leading Negro abolitionist, William Wells Brown, spoke eloquently about the strategic importance of Haiti for his people. He juxtaposed invidiously the import of 1776 with that of 1804 (and 1789): "would that the fathers of the American Revolution had been as consistent," even as their French counterparts. As for the "waters dyed with the blood of the slain" on the island, his conclusion was to "let the slaveholders in our Southern States tremble when they call to mind these events" for "who knows but that a Toussaint, a Christophe, a Rigaud, a Clervaux, and a Dessalines may some day appear in the Southern States of this Union?" Yes, he exclaimed, "the day is not far distant when the revolution of St. Domingo will be reenacted in South Carolina and Louisiana" for "the American slaves are only waiting the opportunity of wiping out their wrongs in the blood of their oppressors." It was Brown who argued that "no revolution ever turned up greater heroes than that of St. Domingo," particularly when it came to inspiring the enslaved Africans of the mainland.[81]

Yet beyond the revolutionary example of the island, there was a further reason for U.S. Negroes to take heed of what was going on there. It was in 1851 that the U.S. authorities contacted their D.R. counterparts requesting a list of mainlanders residing in the east. "A large number of colored persons, born in the United States, emigrated to this part of the island," the Dominican Republic was reminded, "while it was under the government of the Haytians," having been "induced by certain rights"—rights they did not enjoy on the mainland, it could have been added.[82]

Why the United States wanted to monitor the presence of former U.S. Negroes was not clear, though it was hardly a secret that many of these emigrants were abolitionists and not necessarily friendly to the enslaving republic. The problem for these newly minted Dominicans was not only that they thought they had moved to Haiti—and, thus, carried a possible stain of a nation with which Santo Domingo was now in seeming perpetual conflict—but also that they had stumbled into a nation keen to be friendly toward slaving powers, including Madrid and Washington. By 1852 a Portuguese schooner had sailed close to Puerto Plata—where many of these emigrants resided—and was suspected of being engaged in the slave trade. Since these unscrupulous slave dealers were known to snatch any African within arm's length and send them into bondage, this was a further worry for these emigrants.[83]

London's agent knew that the "inhabitants of the northern provinces" of the Dominican Republic "were as a general mass opposed to American annexation" since "as a mass the Dominicans connect closely with annexation the idea of a return to slavery and a similar illiberal treatment as the coloured races receive in the Southern States of the Union."[84] Though slaveholders were pushing for territorial expansion, contradictorily, it was slavery that was hampering this trend.

After Boyer was deposed, the new leadership in Puerto Plata freed the Africans deposited there by Zephaniah Kingsley in the 1830s from contracts thought to be overly onerous. There these migrants earned a livelihood in the mahogany trade and were conspicuous in their upright conduct and the neat and comfortable state of the plots they sowed. They constructed a Protestant chapel built on land purchased by co-religionists in Britain and their reach was extended to Samaná. A schoolhouse and then a Protestant cemetery were established—but by 1844 they found themselves residing in a new nation, the Dominican Republic, which initially opted for religious tolerance. However, things seemed to be evolving in a different direction when the British envoy arrived on an inspection tour in 1851. There he met with the emigrants, along with a number of Her Majesty's subjects and several German Protestants too. Then President Baez arrived and decided—probably because it was felt this was not a bastion of support for Santo Domingo—that this community should be broken up and scattered into the interior of the island. This was also viewed—not incorrectly—as religious discrimination. Even the United States, not known to be a staunch defender of the rights of Negroes, objected. Santo Domingo relented—but only slightly since they also thought that this community was a citadel of support for Haiti.[85]

"Religion was the cause" of this disruption was the point argued by a British cleric, William Fowler, though Santo Domingo said the accused "refused to do [military] service as Dominicans."[86] Poignantly, these former slaves of Kingsley were now being persecuted on the erstwhile abolitionist isle. President Baez saw them as being *"Anglo* American" and, thus, even "woman and child" were to be displaced.[87]

The climate, in sum, was not only complicated for U.S. Negroes but also for the enslaving republic. For 1848 marked the year of revolution in Europe and the year that France returned to abolition, a decision that had immediate impact on Martinique and Guadeloupe whose fortunes had been yoked to those of Hispaniola for decades, if not longer.[88] At the same time, the anti-slavery novel of Harriet Beecher Stowe soared to popularity in Paris.[89] By 1849 there was angst in Washington when the perception arose that France might cut a deal with Haiti that would lead to at least tacit support for a continued attack on the Dominican Republic. The prize for Paris would be what all the powers yearned for—control of Samaná, perhaps, "in perpetuity." Of late "coal has been found" there "which has whetted English & French appetites," said Ben Green.[90] Green sought to counter Paris's attractiveness by pointing to the "state of poverty, decay & insurrection" in Martinique and Guadeloupe, which he also saw as featured in Jamaica, a demerit against London.[91]

In seeming response, by 1850 agents of New York and Ohio, along with the Chamber of Commerce of Philadelphia, the Board of Trade of Baltimore, and others started clamoring for payment of claims allegedly owed to them due to French "spoliations," demanding "that Indemnity to which we are justly enti-tled." Some of these claims stretched back to the late 18th century and implicated Hispaniola as the claimants demanded "our just dues" in order to "soothe the declining years of those original sufferers who still survive a half-century's denial of public justice."[92]

A scant year before this démarche, the U.S. State Department was told that Santo Domingo had "applied to France" to become a "protectorate" and to be "admitted as a French colony." London too offered "protection" to the Dominican Republic in the form of "troops and arms should they need them; but it was refused," said a startled U.S. envoy, "on the ground it might sometime or other bring them into difficulty with France." Of course, this was bad news for an increasingly isolated Haiti which now had been abandoned by its erstwhile British ally just as Santo Domingo was making "active preparations to invade & savage the Haytien frontiers in retaliation."[93] By 1853 the Dominican Republic, thoroughly intimidated by Haiti and worried about U.S. freebooters, was seeking to become a protectorate of Spain. London fretted that this would mean the "re-introduction of Slave Institutions," a thought that had occurred to affected Dominicans too.[94]

London's emissary also confirmed in 1852 that Santo Domingo sought to settle Samaná with "French emigrants" in the context of an elaborate plot to oust the U.S. Negro emigrants who thickly populated this strategic region.[95] That Paris craved to control Samaná was well known and confirmed once more.[96]

Port-au-Prince could seek to play upon remaining tensions between Paris and London, then reaching a boiling point in Mauritius and elsewhere, but this was a far cry from the halcyon days of the heyday of the Black Jacobins.[97]

Nonetheless, it was striking that when tensions flared between Washington and Port-au-Prince, Paris's delegate offered to mediate and rebuffed the mainland's "forcible renewal of . . . claims" against Haiti, though the purpose was not benign: the idea was that U.S. claims against the island "might tend to injure the claims of France against the Haytian government."[98] As matters evolved, the question of claims was a motive force, shaping the policy of all the powers. Ben Green said that "French consuls in both ends of [the] island were trying to arrange for Dominicans to pay part of [the] Haytians' French claims." The Dominicans averred that they "took no part in servile revolt in Hayti" and, therefore, were "not responsible for [its] excesses."[99]

Soon London and Paris were determined to blockade Haiti. France was driven by the fact that Haiti was behind on its indemnity and that as long as the Haitians were at war with the Dominican Republic, the chances of payment were slim. Ben Green of the United States also thought that his homeland should "demand of Soulouque payment" of claims "before he exhaust[ed the] treasury by invasion."[100] As Green viewed the landscape, he concluded in 1850 that "each new military expedition or expenditure by exhausting [Haitian] resources, diminishes the security for some ultimate tardy reparations to the American claimants." As well, he said, "the continuance of the war by sea or land is moreover a source of annoyance and injury to American commerce, placing in jeopardy the lives, no less than the property of American citizens, trading to this island or in the adjacent seas." Thus, the enslaving republic would "not view with indifference any further incursions" by Haiti into the Dominican Republic for "predatory purposes."[101] When Green concluded that "there is no prospect" for Haiti "making arrangements to pay citizen claims," that was equally a signal that Washington would increase its campaign to bolster the Dominican Republic—and destabilize Haiti.[102]

Jonathan Elliot felt that London's purpose was to save Haiti from itself; i.e. the conflict with the Dominican Republic spurred freebooting invasions from the mainland, which conflicted with Britain's attempt to "sustain the Negroes in the Antilles."[103] When Santo Domingo informed London in 1851 that its forces were "fortunate enough to conquer" the Haitians and, besides, already had "severely punished" them for "their temerity,"[104] concern could have arisen that the Dominican Republic—with its avid freebooting Yankee backing—was on the verge of vanquishing Haiti, a prospect that could then jeopardize Jamaica.

Santo Domingo accused Haitians of having "decapitate[d] their own coloured brethren," while promising worse for "their most strenuous enemies, the Dominicans, the majority of whom are of the proscribed and persecuted races in Hayti." Port-au-Prince, said the D.R. leadership, had a "barbarous system of restriction against all those that are not of their colour" and were of a maniacal "belief that the existence of the Dominican Republic is their grave."[105]

This was assuredly overheated rhetoric, but it was complemented by similarly impassioned words emanating from Port-au-Prince where it was thought that uniting the island was a sacred cause. London's emissary had "not found a single Dominican" in 1851 who concurred with this latter belief, but he found many a man who would "strain his last nerve and sacrifice his life" rather than "to submit again to the Haytian yoke." For "even among the black race of the Dominicans" there "exists no sympathy for the Haytian cause"; yet "families of Haytian origin" in the east strained likewise to "sow disunion among the Dominicans."[106] Port-au-Prince denied stridently that when their troops arrived in the east, the Spanish language was barred. Instead, Haitian leadership objected to the influx of Europeans at the behest of the Dominican Republic, which was a dire threat to what had been an abolitionist isle.[107]

Though the foothold of the enslaving republic was more secure in the east of the island—than the west—concerns remained in Washington about the nature of the Santo Domingo regime. President Buenaventura Baez was dismissed as a mere "mulatto" and "a great enemy to the United States" besides. Even his competitor, Pedro Santana, who was deemed a "much better man," was suspect. He was "called a white man," though Elliot felt he was "a little mixed with the Negro." And although Washington was particularly concerned about London and Paris, eyebrows were raised on the mainland when a "Spanish vessel of war . . . visited this part of the island." Despite these apparent threats to sovereignty, Santo Domingo "made large offers to emigrants," including U.S. nationals, "but on being put to the test they [quickly] revoked" the offers.[108]

Thus, by early 1853 Spain was offering to form an "alliance" with the Dominican Republic, pledging to deploy a "force of five thousand men, in case difficulties should arise with the United States." Wily Madrid also sent an agent to Haiti with a similar offer. "The French are also intriguing for favor here," said Elliot in Santo Domingo; "they are building a steamer for this government and are completely [determined] to man, equip, and furnish everything except the hull" and were close to making a "secret treaty of alliance" with the Dominican Republic. This would mean a "military force" from the hexagon "to be placed at Samaná." To have "European troops . . . garrisoned" on the island was worrisome, particularly "if difficulties should arise between the United States and Europe."[109] Of like concern was the thesis propounded by the U.S. agent, Ben Green, who thought that Paris and London "desire[d] to see the Haytians victorious."[110]

Spain was reputedly concerned about "large emigration" to the Dominican Republic from the United States, a step toward possible annexation. Yet, said Elliot, the "climate" there was so "very fatal to Europeans," if "thirty thousand were landed on the eastern part of this island, the probability is that there would not be five thousand alive at the end of twelve months."[111]

The forbidding climate did not halt the maneuvers by rivals of the United States, however. For soon there was "great excitement" in Santo Domingo after two French nationals arriving from Haiti were expelled because it was thought they were "spies" and in response a French "steamer of war" arrived. Then France demanded that the president oust the Secretary of the Treasury and other leading officials in satisfaction. Elliot thought Paris's ultimate intention was to oust "General Santana, a man of liberal principles and place ex-president Baez again in power," the aforementioned "mulatto who most cordially hates Americans and all that is American and is purely a Frenchman in his heart." The remedy? "Send immediately a vessel of war to this port." Elliot spoke to Santana trying to cheer him up, but he was "very downhearted" and full of "regret" at the dearth of support he was receiving from Washington.[112]

France, thought Elliot, remained focused on an ongoing effort to "overthrow or destroy" the Dominican Republic,[113] which put Paris in objective league with Haiti.

AS ADDUCED, AS MURDEROUS CONFLICT descended upon the island, the destiny of Negro emigrants from the mainland became ever more complicated. This was nothing new. It was in 1837 that a disturbing—and credible—report emerged that mainland soldiers of fortune planned an attack on Cuba while posing as emigrants from Santo Domingo—and then would move on to attack both Samaná and Puerto Plata. The project, as reported, was to "subjugate both Dominicans and Haytians" and "compel all the blacks to labour" under adverse conditions up to and including enslavement. Then, "after possessing themselves of the best lands to flood the country with a white population," it was reported as well; "the Americans thereby hope to establish a monopoly of tropical products, such as they now enjoy" in cotton. "No doubt great numbers of the blacks also would be transported" to Hispaniola, enslaved mainland Africans most likely, reversing the gains of the Black Jacobins. "They have already got the legislature of Georgia," it was noted unpropitiously, "to grant an act of incorporation in such a way that the sailing of these steamers with professed emigrants from any of the American parts cannot be interfered with."[114]

By 1852 there was a likeminded plot being prepared on the mainland, with the design of taking Cuba, Puerto Rico—and the Dominican Republic; Puerto Plata was a focal point but so was Santo Domingo. Madrid threatened to seize the latter city if the plot by these "American adventurers" was launched since Spain had yet to relinquish her claim to eastern Hispaniola, liquidated—unfairly in its estimation—in 1822. London and Paris also felt that this plot would jeopardize their own Caribbean holdings, which helped to nip this poisonous plant in the bud.[115]

But when a Spanish battleship arrived in Santo Domingo in late December 1852, after an interval of nearly thirty years, disquiet was stoked further. For now the issue seemed to be not only that Madrid was halting freebooters but also imitating them on behalf of His Catholic Majesty. Robert Schomburgk, the British consul, was stunned when this vessel refused to salute the Dominican flag and was similarly bothered when Santo Domingo did not seem to mind, adumbrating the Spanish takeover that emerged less than a decade later. Yet U.S. Negro migrants had the most to lose by this return of an enslaving Madrid, a worry that hardly dissipated when the vessel circled the island and headed toward Puerto Plata and Samaná.[116] All of this maneuvering by the major powers—warships had crowded the waters surrounding Hispaniola to the point of risking collision—threatened that a terrible miscalculation could easily have occurred. Thus, London pondered if it should preemptively attack the United States.[117] It was a thought never far from British minds, which would have been a boon to Haiti—and the U.S. migrants too.

Thus, the presence of U.S. Negroes in northern Hispaniola seemed to throw down the gauntlet to slaveholders generally. Enslaving them seemed to be a general goal too. Yet, by July 1852, even Africans from the British controlled Turks Islands were arriving there in search of employment. This was due in part to the industry and energy of the U.S. Negro emigrants who had built a jewel of a community that attracted attention far and wide. Yet Santo Domingo was suspicious, thinking—as London's consul was told—"that being black, they must naturally have a sympathy for Soulouque." The fact that a number of these erstwhile U.S. Negroes were now seeking to register as British nationals[118] suggests one reason why the enslaving republic often linked London and Port-au-Prince. There was a great deal of intercourse between the Turks Islands and Puerto Plata, which are separated by a mere 100 miles of sea, and this proximity was a kind of security blanket for the Negro emigrants of all types. Or so it seemed until reports emerged about freebooters from New Orleans amassing in the Turks Islands with potential designs on Puerto Plata—and, given the temper of the times, reenslavement was likely on their agenda.[119]

By February 1852, these U.S. Negro emigrants, who were mostly Protestant, had been residing relatively unmolested for years near Puerto Plata, but then Santo Domingo chose the path of religious intolerance, consistent with their ever closer ties to His Catholic Majesty in Madrid. They were ousted from some of their thriving sinecures and expelled to different parts of the nation with their pastor, William Fowler, a Wesleyan missionary, objecting stoutly.[120] The Dominican Republic was gaining a reputation for religious bigotry. Even its burial grounds were circumscribed.[121]

By September 1852, suspicious mainlanders had arrived in northern Hispaniola seeking to locate, according to London's envoy, "from four to five thousand American emigrants" with the reasons for their interest unarticulated. The consul, Robert Schomburgk, felt that these visitors' unexplained purpose would be "injurious," as long as their "ulterior plans" and "real object" remained murky. The underlying suspicion was that reenslavement was their plan and object.[122]

Propelling this impending crisis was a related economic one. After the revolution, commodities, e.g. sugar and coffee, fell in production while exports of mahogany and logwood multiplied. But with the post-Boyer convulsions an economic crisis followed that also had impact upon the wood trade, plunging the island into further misery and paving the path for outside intervention. London thought it was the winner in the sense that the "finest mahogany" wound up in their elite salons while "wood of inferior quality" wound up in New York and Paris—but more to the point: the plains and people of Hispaniola were the losers.[123]

Despite these losses, delivered by unequal trade practices and war wounds alike, Haiti was far from being a failed state in the 1850s. N. Parker Willis of New York was visiting there then and as he was tasting "the best claret I ever had," in walks an African "brought up in Charleston." This signifies at once why Haiti was able to survive: it could benefit from the talents of U.S. Negroes who continued to view it as a beacon of liberty.[124]

It was the fabulous natural wealth on the island that attracted these curious visitors eager to sample the wares on offer. One visitor in 1851 raved about the "great mountains of Cibao, rich in copper, iron, and gold"; he saw a "piece of pure gold weighing two ounces and a half" and another "twice as large," along with "much gold dust." There were bountiful plantations groaning with loads of coffee and tobacco. There were coal mines near Almacen. The population, it was said comfortingly, "consists almost entirely of whites" with "very few coloured people and much less blacks among them." In San Jose de las Matas there was the "pleasure" of seeing "the white complexion and rosy cheeks of the children." He found plenty of districts ready for increased "European immigration." In the north there were more

Germans, who countervailed the sizeable Negro migrant population, especially in Samaná, which "from east to west" stretched "about 40 miles long and 10 miles broad" with "sugar, coffee, and cacao" aplenty.

The center there was the "small town" called Santa Barbara. It had "about 90 houses and huts" and about 1721 in population, including "about 300 . . . American emigrants and their descendants." They were "garrisoned by 200 men." Santo Domingo had "made it a place of banishment for political and other criminals," a fact which, combined with the Negro emigrant population, had converted the area into a hotbed of dissidence. Samaná rivaled Guiana "in the luxuriance of the vegetation" with a similarly fabled "fertility" of the "soil." Samaná bay was protected by a reef, about thirty-five miles in extent and from ten to fifteen miles in breadth, that afforded "shelter during storms to whole fleets." There were "60 rivers and rivulets" that "empty themselves into the bay of Samaná," indicative of the perception that "perhaps not three places can be found in the globe similar to that of Samaná. It is to the Gulf of Mexico what Mayotte is to the Indian Ocean," which naturally attracted Paris.[125]

But London, unlike Paris and Madrid, had not colonized Hispaniola and, unlike the United States, it was now abolitionist. Thus, by 1851, 75% of imports to the Dominican Republic consisted mostly of British goods, giving this empire a tremendous advantage.[126] However, given the immense resources of the island, which had attracted mercantile interests since the late 15th century, Hispaniola found it difficult to avoid intrigue driven by the major powers.

Indicative of the intensified interest taken by the never-say-die enslaving republic in Hispaniola was the arrival on the fraught isle of Jane and William Cazneau. They were fresh from a successful campaign to push Texas into the federal union, a massive victory for bondage that pushed Washington to take ever greater risks. Their purpose was to bring the Dominican Republic closer to the United States, but this ignoble campaign was blocked by competing powers—led by London—that reminded all who would listen that Dominican elites were not seen in Washington as being "quite white" and, thus, would face all manner of personal insults there.

It was the Foreign Office in London that waved frantically the flag of distress when the scheming couple arrived. Angrily, it was proclaimed that whatever concessions were granted to the United States should be automatically granted to the United Kingdom—and France too—particularly rights in Samaná.[127] Prompted, their envoy leapt into action, speaking of the "lady . . . whose intrigues" were notorious. Concord between the Dominican Republic and the United States would "remove the apprehensions regarding Filibusters" which would "endanger" the entire Caribbean basin. Already "settling" in Santo Domingo were "a number of adventurers" with unclear intentions. The couple had the effrontery to tell him that mediation between the two sides of the island was no longer needed, since shortly a "sufficient number of Americans" would arrive to resolve matters fully.[128]

Indeed, Robert Schomburgk "ascertained that at the moment the treaty" between the United States and the Dominican Republic was signed, "a large body of American emigrants will be thrown into the Republic" in order to alter the "natural character" of the island. Fortunately, the proposed treaty was "unpopular" in the Dominican Republic, as the appearance of a U.S. "sloop of war" already had "produced alarm."[129]

Supposedly, the United States was offering "ten thousand American volunteers," as Schomburgk put it, "both to colonize and defend the country." There was "an expedition fitting out in New York," with the aim of taking the Dominican Republic, then moving on to Cuba and Puerto Rico. Puerto Plata was aghast at the notion, said the London emissary who found "few adherents" to this project there. "I have encouraged this aversion," he confessed, which was not difficult since "the majority" there were "colored" and predisposed to anti-Yankee sentiments given "the manner in which their race is treated in the United States and that a similar fate would probably await them if their Republic were to be annexed." Ironically, those residing in the Turks Islands, a London possession, had a "striking predilection for American manners and constitutions," unlike those who had experienced the same. If the filibusters did land, he was already positioning London to intervene too, along with Paris, to "prevent annexation."[130]

This fear about the fate of the island was not farfetched. Jane Cazneau confessed her collaboration with a Cuban "filibuster" who was "in intimate friendship with the chief men of this republic," meaning the Dominican Republic He was "about to purchase a small press" and, as she saw it, would aid in helping to "stand by the Dominicans, the Monroe Doctrine, and American interests in general in the bold, firm old-fashioned way."[131] The crusading Cazneau was conspiring with the Manhattan press, seeking to block "European interference . . . editorially." The editor, Moses Beach, was instructed to "give the folks at Washington a lecture"; Cazneau knew something about lectures, lecturing Beach about the "Jewish merchants here" in Santo Domingo and the "French & English steamers" too who refused to "take Yankee letters" to their destination "or if they do they meet with 'accidents' and are lost."[132]

A salient reason why this closer tie with the enslaving republic was unpopular was the revulsion generated in the north of the island. "The coloured and black population, to whom the prejudices of the Americans to their race are not unknown," had exemplified "in consequence great alarm," it was reported. The sly Cazneau couple had "disbursed considerable sums of money" to "Government members" who were now reveling in the "large quantity of American coin now afloat." The fate that befell the Lone Star State was now descending on Hispaniola since Cazneau, who "figured already in such a capacity in Texas and Mexico," had proven to be a master in producing "disaffectation [sic], confusion, and misery to force the people to annexation at American discretion."[133]

Santo Domingo feared "opposition" from the "coloured population" and leading figures were—reportedly—plotting a "coup" to garner "dictatorial powers" in order to prevail.[134] As noted, there had been migration to the northern side of the island from the Turks Islands, a British colony, and now these "coloured" subjects were complaining that mistreatment had ensnared them too, exacerbating the crisis.[135]

Santo Domingo was now facing stern opposition from a good deal of its own populace, backed by an adamant London and Paris. Cazneau, as a result, was said to find "his chances of success in his mission considerably lessened," which meant that he was "losing that equanimity which is becoming to an agent of a great power," an understatement of the fury that was engulfing this U.S. agent.

What may have inflamed Cazneau's ire was language in the proposed treaty that pledged non-discrimination and would spare "citizens that are of colour or black" the indignities routinely heaped on this group in Washington and elsewhere.[136] Schomburgk may have suggested these subversive words, but it was Cazneau who upbraided London for the "menacing display of armed force" recently displayed of late in Santo Domingo, which was designed to intimidate and derail the proposed treaty.[137]

This apparent menace seemed to be unavailing when in November 1854 the treaty was signed—but London did not retreat. The British reminded all who lent an ear that there was no "reciprocity" in the accord and it was, thereby, "subjecting" Dominicans "who are black [and] are of colour to great grievances, should they land in any of the States in the Union where slaves still exist." Such grievances would ensnare "nine tenths of the population" of the Dominican Republic and, understandably, have "caused great excitement among the coloured and black." In the leading parliamentary body in Santo Domingo "a great number of the members . . . [were] near of colour" and were bound to be restricted—at best—on the mainland, if not kidnapped into slavery. Cazneau would not budge because of objections in "Carolina and other Slave States"; thus the accord was bound to be "rejected."[138]

It was rejected and Schomburgk took credit, immodestly: "I used whatever influence I possessed," he proclaimed, to highlight the "humiliating" accord "by which nine tenths of their population were rendered liable of arrest and imprisonment . . . should they land in Charleston." The furious Cazneau began "threatening" the Dominican Republic so London and Paris replied by sending their own "vessels of war" to Santo Domingo.[139]

But Cazneau was not only opposed by London. Frederick Douglass looked askance at his efforts, particularly his attempting to secure "military and naval depots upon the northern coast of the island" that were deemed "necessary for insuring the acquisition of Cuba and Porto Rico by force of arms." To that end, the Dominican Republic was to be "colonized and annexed to the Union as a slave state," Cuba too (it would be "divided into two states"), and "St. Domingo and Porto Rico will form four additional slave-holding states."Douglass was taken aback by both the "shrewd and insinuating talents of his diplomatic lady," meaning Cazneau's spouse, and the "lavish bribery" that was doled out.[140]

Douglass was slightly bemused when the accord was turned down due to the sudden "discovery that the Dominicans are mostly of African descent" and the refusal to accept "Cazneau's standard of a white man." Douglass did not accept D.R. secession, arguing that Port-au-Prince was the "sovereign of the whole island," as the Santo Domingo regime was "probably transient." He was willing to concede that Haiti could send "white" envoys to Washington to assuage this racist concern.[141]

Even the dimmest could now see that the mossback policies undergirding slavery were hampering the extension of U.S. influence and providing an opening for antagonists, new and old, besides. This hastened sectional tensions, bringing civil war closer and, ultimately, the Black Jacobins were responsible for this crisis that brought abolition closer.

Britain and France coming together was an emblem of their stance in the Crimea and also may have been a savior for Haiti, since it was difficult to see how the U.S. takeover of the Dominican Republic would have been blocked otherwise and it could easily have led to reenslavement.[142]

Still, London was preoccupied with India, Jamaica, Hong Kong, and its lengthening list of colonial possessions, but, said one Briton, "the communication" with Haiti was "direct and frequent," involving a "large and lucrative trade with each other, as many English merchants are able to testify." F. W. Chesson saw "cabinet making" with Haiti's desirable wood as the product of this bilateral tie. Yes, there were those in London who "naturally regarded" Haiti "with an unfriendly eye, because she is a standing protest against the system of negro slavery," but this should not obscure larger strategic concerns, e.g. the United States seeking a toehold in the Dominican Republic so as "more effectually to attack the independence of Hayti." Santo Domingo was accused of trying to "promote the intrigues of American agents." Like others, Chesson "deplore[d] as a calamity the continued disunion subsisting between Hayti and St. Domingo," which served the interests of mainlanders. "The island ought not to be ruled by two distinct governments," he insisted, a result which "has enabled foreign intrigue" and all kinds of arbitrage opportunities for them. To this end, he said, "no country has been more grossly calumniated" than Haiti and no nation was more responsible for this than its antipode: the enslaving republic.[143]

Hence, by 1855 Port-au-Prince was in a familiar position—on war footing—while the intrigues of mainland freebooters in league with Santo Domingo had surged. This was contributing to an overheated atmosphere of combustible disorder.[144] Lord Palmerston, a key formulator of British foreign policy, warned Haiti that if it proceeded on this basis, Santo Domingo would increase ties with the enslaving republic. Santo Domingo would also "probably apply for and receive assistance from the United States and the known distance which the people of the United States feel for the Black Race would insure a result utterly disastrous" for Port-au-Prince, which would "of course expect no assistance" from London and "probably none" from Paris since Haiti "would have been the aggressor."[145]

London thought that the U.S. emissary, Jonathan Elliot, was conspiring with these freebooters on the promise that such aid to Santo Domingo would be tendered in return for control of Samaná. As a sign of good faith, he presented President Santana with a splendid pistol, a gift from President Franklin Pierce.[146] Elliot reportedly offered Santo Domingo $150,000 for the fight against Haiti—if Samaná were ceded forthwith.[147]

By 1856 yet another accord between the two had been proposed whereby the United States was said to have agreed to "end . . . all Filibusteros . . . saving [Santo Domingo] the fate of Nicaragua,"[148] which was then reeling from the depredations of U.S. national William Walker. But London again intervened, warning sternly of the "danger [that] existed of a war between the United States and England" with the further complexity that part of the D.R. leadership was bamboozled by the rise of a "Spanish party" that would actually take power a few years later.[149]

It was not easy to drive a stake through the heart of what was called the "Cazneaus" treaty because it spoke to a certain racial logic. Besides, Samaná was too lush a prize to relinquish easily. Elliot concluded that the "Haytians publicly accuse[d] Santana of wishing to give this island to the Americans," while Paris, London, and Madrid were all firm "in opposition to our having a naval station here."[150] But the stumbling block remained, i.e. nothing in the accord "could be construed to the prejudice of the local laws" of the Southern States, which—in turn—was a complicating factor in Santo Domingo.[151]

This time it was Madrid which was raising a ruckus, offering to pressure Haiti to vacate territory claimed by the Dominican Republic and offering to push for a "purely Spanish emigration" to transform the perceived racial imbalance. Also offered were a "protectorate, a quantity of troops, and a good navy"—and backup in "making opposition to the United States." The irate U.S. agent lambasted Madrid for—supposedly—pressuring Santo Domingo by backing Haitian incursions, leaving the east "to the butchery of the Negroes" and "Haytian invasion," besides. Derided was Baez, "a mulatto who hates Americans."[152]

Baez, it was reported, was "an ambitious Negro," backed by Madrid. The U.S. agent warned that the "majority of the people, particularly all the whites," would "suffer the loss of all they have and probably their lives," if they did not swiftly execute a course correction. This was the possible cost of not seeking a U.S. accord. Elliot added proudly that "the Dominican Government (who are all whites) will stand firm" even if he did not succeed in his goal of insuring the ouster of the nettlesome Spanish legation.[153] But by November 1856, the United States was again grousing since the "mulatto," Baez, "was made president" and in the process "put . . .down the white government [with] Spanish assistance."[154] What Washington called the "white government" in Santo Domingo was toppled, despite U.S. backing, while Baez was denigrated for allowing the "most gross insults to our flag" and "citizens."[155] "This country is in a most miserable state," said the U.S. agent, "and [with] no prospect of it improving. The Government here is made up of Negroes and rowdies," with hardly a distinction between the two.

Haiti was now working with France against the United States—or so Washington was told—as Paris was seeking to "excite these people against Americans," who were seen by all as the major threat, including London and Madrid.[156] London sought to block a loan from the United States to the Dominican Republic for fear that it "would hasten the Americanization of Santo Domingo at a rate more rapid than the [proposed] Treaty of the settlement of American emigrants in the Republic."[157] Spain's reconquest of Santo Domingo would not be easy either since the rumor was now aloft in the Dominican Republic that Madrid was seeking hegemony for the purpose of reintroducing slavery in complement with Cuba.[158]

In the midst of this squabbling among the powers for domination of Santo Domingo, Haiti continued to assert forcefully its own claims; those from the west taken prisoner in the east had been told they would be greeted as brothers in the Dominican Republic and that, it was reported, "they were [there] to fight their common enemy, the Americans."[159]

Things had gotten so bad that Washington was led to believe that the U.S. office in Santo Domingo was about "to be stormed" by pro-Madrid elements: "my person and family, as Americans, are in danger," cried the U.S. envoy. "I walk the streets with danger [to] my life" as there was "bloodshed [and] slaughter and waste of life, particularly among our citizens."[160] He blamed "a mob of matriculated Spanish Negroes" who "assembled in front of my house with the intention of pulling down my flagstaff and coat of arms," and "constantly" shouted: "death to the Yankee fili-busters." They had the idea that "all Americans are filibusters and enemies of the Spanish race." "Several stones were thrown at my house,"[161] said the envoy, just as the U.S. consulate "was to be stormed."[162] What had befallen this agent was "one of the most extraordinary events that has ever happened to any American representa-tive abroad," cried Jonathan Elliot. Moreover, he added, "the people here are still in a state of discord and revolution and there is no knowing what the result may be."[163] Not just this agent but U.S. citizens as a whole, he said as well, "are in the greatest danger, as this President Baez has an implacable hatred to all that is American."[164]

This apparent antipathy in the Dominican Republic toward the United States rested uneasily with a competing trend of demonizing Haiti and a longing for a larger "white" population. The good news, however, was that London was pressur-ing Santo Domingo to sign a treaty that would compel the latter to make the slave trade piracy under domestic law, combined with a right to search challenged ships by the Royal Navy.[165] This was preceded by a treaty between newly abolitionist France and the Dominican Republic.[166]

Thus, the Dixie scheme to facilitate the splitting of Hispaniola was only partially successful. Yes, it weakened Haiti and may have weakened the abolitionist move-ment—but it was not a fatal blow. The failure to ratify a treaty between the United States and the Dominican Republic because of racial recalcitrance in Washington indicated that retrograde Dixie policies were hampering national expansion, thereby exacerbating sectional tensions. And when Madrid moved to snatch the Dominican Republic, as the mainland was plunged into civil war, it seemed, in retrospect, that the lengthy quest to split Hispaniola had simply served to split the mainland and weaken Washington generally.

9

The U.S. Civil War, the Spanish Takeover of the Dominican Republic, and U.S. Negro Emigrants in Haiti, 1860–1863

A CCORDING TO THE NOTED HISTORIAN Rayford W. Logan, the "voluntary submission" by Santo Domingo "to the restoration of Spanish sovereignty is probably unique in the history of modern colonialism." This was just one of a number of startling events in the early 1860s, including the attempt by Jane and William Cazneau—who were foiled in their effort to forge a U.S. treaty with the Dominican Republic—to organize the "American West Indian Company" for the purpose of developing large cotton plantations on which they planned to deploy in Hispaniola enslaved Africans from the mainland—and elsewhere. Presumably, this could have meant that U.S. Negro emigrants now residing uneasily on the north side of the island might have found themselves trapped by what they thought they had escaped: bondage. An inauspicious signal emerged when the ruling Spanish authorities closed what were viewed as "heretical" Methodist churches, which catered to these emigrants.[1]

Not accidentally, as Fort Sumter was about to be assaulted, Puerto Plata too was about to come under siege. This bastion for U.S. Negro migrants was agog when in late March 1861 the British envoy there saw the Dominican flag "replaced by the Spanish flag," so "that the Dominican Republic will cease or has ceased to exist" as an "independent nation and become an annexed province of Spain!" His view was that "the people" were neither "satisfied or contented" by this annexation and all were "rather apprehensive of an outbreak of the lower classes" with "disturbances" expected.[2] For as the Spanish flag was hoisted throughout the land, there was not a cheer, not a groan, not a gun was fired; there was silence and melancholy and astonishment—though this turned out to be calm before the storm.[3] Another British agent found that the "mass of the population" viewed "with great uneasiness the contemplated transfer" to Spain of the Dominican Republic He noted as well that an "attempt at rebellion" was inevitable not to mention a "threatened Haitian invasion."[4]

The onset of the U.S. Civil War in early 1861 was a clear signal to Spain to take advantage of Washington's preoccupations. By the following April, Washington found that "trouble is again brewing between Hayti and Spain" with the latter demanding the "ancient boundaries" of the Dominican Republic, i.e. more Haitian territory, and promising "grave trouble" if this did not occur. There was a "desire & intention to pick a quarrel with Hayti . . . bringing the whole island under either the Spanish or French rule"—but, ironically, this was a prod for the United States to recognize Haiti so as to foil rivals. Though the United States was amidst civil war, its emissary demanded that a "half dozen" warships be sent to Haitian waters immediately.[5]

What had prompted the Spanish takeover was what had been the obsession of Santo Domingo since secession in 1844—the fear of a Haitian takeover. Spain too found it hard to accept that numerous enslaved Africans continued to escape from Cuba and Puerto Rico to Haiti and believed that establishing a presence on Hispaniola could possibly help to stanch the flow.[6] Spain may have heard what one historian subsequently wrote: that the Haitian agent of British origin, James Redpath, sought to "organize a John Brown raid on Cuba if Haiti would support it."[7]

Rather quickly, Madrid sent a formal claim to Port-au-Prince demanding a good deal of Haitian territory.[8] These were the plains in the center of the island, replete with natural resources.[9] Spain's claims were seen then as a prelude to a takeover of the entire island—including Haiti—and reversing the gains of the Black Jacobins.[10]

Haiti was not without friends. It took a while for the United States to realize that a strong Haiti was an antidote to secessionist plots. Instability in Haiti itself—fueled by external conflict with Washington—did not facilitate this realization. By 1859, the U.S. Secretary of State was told that Haiti was "threatened with a revolution."[11] "Ambition is at the highest pitch," said Richmond Loring, as "the greater portion of the most influential and intelligent blacks are conspiring to overthrow the government to have a chief of their own and if another revolution breaks out, not only our properties but our lives are greatly exposed."[12]

As mainland emigrants poured into Haiti—often not speaking the principal languages—at times they got caught up in this instability, with many opposing Soulouque and supporting the man who replaced him: Fabre Geffrard. The fact that one noteworthy emigrant, James Theodore Holly, named his son Joseph Geffrard is indicative of this support.[13] It was an emblem of the fact that President Geffrard in August 1860 heartily endorsed the project to bring more U.S. Negroes to Haiti,[14] a measure backed by parliamentarians.[15] Perhaps it is worth mentioning that the lighter-skinned Geffrard replaced a darker skinned man: the real and imagined conflict of color on the island sucked these emigrants into the maelstrom of the Haitian color question, which was bound to alienate one side or another. For example, Haiti still contained at least one plantation owner who purportedly told U.S. emigrant James Rapier, Jr. that this landowner was a carrier of color bias and that "like all mixed bloods . . . [he too] hates the blacks to death."[16] Moreover, members of one Louisiana family comprised of *gens de couleur*, formerly of Hispaniola, were enthusiastic supporters of the slave-holding secessionists; their perspicacity was unmasked when after the defeat of the enslavers, a number committed suicide, while others sought exile. "The blacks hate the mulattoes and the mulattoes look down upon the blacks," was the pithy assessment of Frederick Douglass, though such a parallel elides the unavoidable fact that one group in this neat equation was often implicated in enslavement of the other.[17]

A U.S. agent was also elated when Geffrard's predecessor was overthrown, which meant, it was said, "restoration of a Republican Government." Haiti had been "as ridiculous as it was despotic and during the past ten years the entire resources of this island have been a source of profit to the Emperor and some of his favorites."[18] "We are also surely under some obligation to watch over the interests of the neighbouring Republic of Hayti," said London abolitionists, "which under the intelligent and patriotic administration of General Geffrard, has established for itself an indubitable claim to the friendship of England." To that end, a protest meeting had been held in Kingston, Jamaica, reproving Spanish actions since taking Samaná—in particular—could threaten British interests regionally.[19]

As ever, the United States—and now the so-called Confederate States of America—thought they had a decisive advantage in Haiti because of these real—and imagined—color conflicts that seemed to preoccupy eastern Hispaniola too. "The population of Hayti is divided into two classes," said a U.S. observer: these were "the colored and the pure blacks, between which classes a deep-rooted antipathy exists. When the head of the government is a black man, then the pride of all the black people is gratified, and the colored people feel humbled. And so, vice versa. As the blacks are far the most numerous and can more readily be acted upon by designing men"—including an "immense number of generals and colonels" ("more generals and colonels than there are private soldiers")—they generally had the whip hand.[20]

In the previous decade Washington had rallied to the side of those who seemed to represent the lighter skinned on the basis that this was the least bad option. Now there was an opinion afloat, according to Benjamin S. Hunt, writing in 1860, that "the mulatto has no vitality of race; that after three or four generations he dies out." But the "tropics" refuted this since "for more than a century" the Dominican Republic—and its predecessor—had survived though it was "virtually a nation of mulattoes," even after being "put to death in great numbers." Hunt spoke to a "Haytien mulatto" who heard with "surprise and mortification" the notion that on the mainland "persons of all degrees of color are confounded together, and popularly called Negroes." In St. Domingo, he said, "the French have been destroyed by the blacks; in Jamaica, the English are being peacefully absorbed by them," and there was a lesson there for the United States.[21] Unfortunately, another lesson grasped was that—sometimes unbeknownst to these emigrants—lighter-skinned U.S. Negroes arriving in Haiti were perceived as weighing in the color conflict then unfolding. This along with a language barrier and the promise delivered by the end of the U.S. Civil War helps shed light on why a number chose to return to the mainland.

It did seem that the onrush of civil war on the mainland was bringing a reevaluation of the often despised *gens de couleur* or mulattoes as they were sometimes called. The Haitian agent, James Redpath, had spoken to Senator James Doolittle of Wisconsin who told him that other than the heralded "Anglo-Saxon," those denoted as "mulattoes" were the only ones with a future in the hemisphere and thus able to block the "grand slave-holding Confederacy" of "sugar, cotton"—and expansionism. While the Senator endorsed the notion of sending U.S. Negroes en masse to Central America, Redpath—who was more attuned to the wishes of this group slated for ouster—wanted to strengthen Haiti against Dixie by arranging emigration there. This would block the Dixie plan to seize Cuba and then threaten Haiti. Redpath had in mind what he called a "delicate question"—establishing a "secret fund for politicians" to enable his ambitious plans.[22]

IN THE PRELUDE TO GEFFRARD'S 1859 elevation, though the number of U.S. vessels in Cap Haïtien was "unusually small," trade between this port and the mainland was deemed to be "in a prosperous state" with a "large quantity of American provisions . . . imported here yearly," said the U.S. delegate.[23] Despite this commerce, relations were far from ideal; Port-au-Prince was accused of having "insulted the national flag" of the enslaving republic and it was advised that Haitians be taught a punishing lesson; the naval squadron that was supposed to seek slavers was advised to now watch the abolitionist republic for another alleged miscue.[24]

Then there was the lingering apprehension—held by both Spain and the Dominican Republic—that it was a U.S. takeover of Santo Domingo that was to be feared; Madrid thought that after taking the Dominican Republic, the United States would then move to take Cuba and Puerto Rico also.[25] Madrid did not look kindly when, in the spring of 1860, U.S. freebooters landed at a small island claimed by Santo Domingo—and planted the U.S. flag. Ironically, though slave-holding expansionists were the driving force behind such aggression, this was precisely the force favored by Madrid.[26] As late as September 1860, U.S. citizens—allegedly in search of guano—had occupied the island of Navasa, Haitian soil.[27] Not only this island but Tortuga, Île-à-Vache, Les Cayemites, and Gonâve Island were also points of contention between the two republics.[28]

Madrid's own intentions became clear in July 1861 when six Spanish warships sailed into Port-au-Prince, causing—said the U.S. agent—"the greatest excitement." They demanded indemnification and the Haitians "at first positively refused to comply, saying in the strongest terms that they would rather die than to submit" and Spain responded by threatening to "bombard" the port, causing an intervention by British and French diplomats. Still the general opinion was that Madrid did "intend to take possession of the whole island as soon as possible," sparking mass unrest in Haiti. Even the U.S. envoy, representative of a nation that had its own designs on Hispaniola, confessed that Haiti "will never do any good until some foreign power takes possession" of it.[29]

The mainland enslavers had mixed feelings about enhanced European activity in the Caribbean. "Spain would not have dared to attempt this conquest if the U.S. power had remained entire & as strong as before the disruption," said one fire-eater. Thus, when Madrid took Santo Domingo, Edmund Ruffin of Dixie thought it would mean that France—with Spain's assistance—would bring "great benefit to civilization, to the world, & especially to the slave-holding interests of these C. [Confederate] States, that the mongrel race of Dominica [*sic*] shall be overcome & finally eradicated, by the intrusion of white conquerors & colonists. Still better will it be for the like results to be produced in the barbarous negro government & territory of Hayti"; this would, thankfully, mean a successful effort to "reconquer & subdue Hayti."[30]

Mainlanders were torn, pulled in a racial direction of solidarity with the European powers against Haiti but also pushed toward their own dream of hemispheric hegemony, which meant undermining these same powers. Ultimately, however, Washington had to scramble to ally with Haiti for to do otherwise would have jeopardized the United States itself. Just as the Emancipation Proclamation came into effect, one mainlander was musing that Paris "will probably interfere west of the Miss[issippi] under the guarantees of the Treaty by which France ceded [the] Louisiana Territory. If so," it was said sagely, "our affairs may become complicated."[31] Coastal Virginians, Carolinans, and Georgians (and to a degree Louisianans) were far closer to Europe in custom and language than to their New England compatriots, which too created an opening for Paris to the detriment of Haiti.[32] By 1863 press accounts revealed that France was dickering with the secessionists to either take Texas or guarantee its independence.[33]

The leading Confederate, Judah P. Benjamin, had a thorough acquaintance with the French language and literature and his spouse, says his sympathetic biographer, was a "refugee from the black horror of St. Domingo"; he was an attorney in Louisiana in important cases of slave revolt—including a notably contentious episode in 1841–1842. His father-in-law told thrilling tales of the insurrection in Hispaniola and the family was among those that felt that the example of Haiti was a living advertisement of the mistake of abolition. Such attitudes made Benjamin, the secessionists' leading diplomat, willing to listen to French revanchist plots in Hispaniola—and elsewhere.[34]

Benjamin was personally close to the influential Erlanger family in Paris, which proved helpful when the time came to arrange loans for the secessionist plot.[35] Both sides shared antipathy toward Black Jacobins. Though there were repeated accusations that Paris was collaborating with Port-au-Prince against Santo Domingo, the record reveals continuing animosity harbored by France toward Haiti. "Noirs et Mulatres"—Blacks and Mulattoes—were incapable of governing, it was said by a Parisian in 1857, as Haiti was said to be regressing to barbarism.[36]

A 20th century novelist captured the prevailing sentiment in Confederate Louisiana, deeply influenced by "refugees from the black horror of Santo Domingo." New Orleans "had no dearth of those who were familiar with the terrible slave uprising and the tales were all alike." The "family had lived in a marble-terraced plantation home. Always there had been flight with bloodthirsty blacks in pursuit. Always a hiding place in the jungle" was sought. The Benjamin family was foremost in that regard and it was Benjamin himself who was hailed as "an Israelite with Egyptian principles."[37]

The same might have been said about yet another top secessionist diplomat: Pierre Rost was born in France in 1797, fought alongside Napoleon in 1814, then moved to the United States, and worked alongside the family of Jefferson Davis himself. In Louisiana regiments known as "Zouaves"—some of whom had fought in Algeria alongside Parisians—were prominent, as was the "French Legion." There were 30,000 French nationals in New Orleans alone,[38] many of whom had profited handsomely from Haitian indemnities that created a fabulously wealthy class. They were eager to perpetuate slavery on the mainland and to resume it in Hispaniola too.

Another son of Dixie spoke glowingly of Louis Napoleon as "by far the shrewdest monarch in Europe" and "he is entitled to gratitude of France."[39] Yet while France took advantage of the Civil War to make encroachments in Mexico, it was Haiti whose ports became coaling stations for Washington.[40] The support of Haiti and the crass opportunism of France and its Louisiana advocates were both ironic and inexorable results of a distorted policy whose roots extended to earlier in the century.

Paris monitored the Civil War carefully. A high level official was in Richmond conferring—supposedly about tobacco—in early 1863.[41] Actually, cotton was the commodity that Dixie banked on to turn the tide of diplomatic recognition, though this was not sufficient to sway the man Washington called "Emperor of the French."[42] Paris was courted by the secessionists nonetheless with pointed references to French investments in coal in Virginia and their kind regard of French intervention in Mexico.[43] U.S. Secretary of State William Seward in response praised his nation's "traditional friendship" with France and rued the possibility of "compromise" with Dixie.[44] Seward denounced the idea of the "recognition of the insurgents" and groused that "this civil war owes the length and severity it has already attained mainly to foreign influences and aid"; thus, "recognition of the insurgents by any of the great powers would bring with it only new complications and aggravations."[45]

The traitors fired back, counseling that their opponents' goal was "abolition" not just union and calling into question Washington's credibility. Unctuously the secessionists lavished praise on the "powerful" hexagon and the "prestige" of the Emperor and posed as an "old ally" of France. London was privately dismissed: "I need not point out," Paris was told, "the advantages which a friendly position of the Government of the Emperor must secure" if the slave-holding secession was recognized and this would not be to the advantage of Perfidious Albion.[46] With a final flourish John Slidell told the Foreign Ministry that Washington's policy "looks to nothing short of the extermination or exile of the white population,"[47] a none too veiled challenge to France in Mexico City and a revival of the "black scare" bruited by Jefferson decades earlier. Slidell thought that the "sentiment against slavery in the abstract" was "quite widespread in France as it is in England," but he did not find a "considerable class of people" in Paris "who consider that its existence" should "control or even modify the policy of the nation in its relation with our Confederacy"; as he saw it, "the Emperor, the members of his Cabinet, and the higher functionaries of his government generally are quite indifferent on the subject of slavery."[48]

By the fall of 1862, Slidell in Paris was eagerly expecting "something definite as to the Emperor's intentions respecting our affairs"—but then "complications in the Italian Question" intervened and "entirely absorbed the attention of the government."[49]

The Spanish takeover of the Dominican Republic and Madrid's coddling of mainland secessionists also influenced a reappraisal in Washington. By 1862 B.F. Sanford, U.S. envoy in Aux Cayes, had noticed that "Spain has opened her capacious maw to swallow this end," meaning Haiti, "as she already has the other end of the island," meaning the Dominican Republic. Hence, a "true republic under the protectorate of the United States would be far superior to the disposition of Spanish rule." Moreover, since "for many years to come" the United States would maintain a standing army, "why not then quarter portions of this army in the different distracted countries of America that need our aid"—Haiti, in short.[50] Thus, in Congress there was prompt protest of the "insolent and aggressive conduct of the Spanish government."[51]

The momentum of events was pushing Washington toward an entente with Haiti, including diplomatic recognition. Seth Webb, the U.S. envoy, thought European rivals were seeking to push U.S. interests from Hispaniola and wanted to "destroy the influence" of his nation there too. Britain, Spain, and France were now "acting in unison whenever they can to cripple the power & interests" of Washington. Webb was "embarrassed" that his nation had yet to recognize Haiti and expressed "bitter disappointment that nothing has yet been done." Already, irritated Haitians were reacting, as the U.S. agent at Gonaïves was compelled to take down the U.S. flag. This was "significant," he declared, and "would not have happened three months ago." Hence, the United States should "lose no time in acknowledging the independence of Hayti" by "sending a diplomatic legation here to counteract the schemes of foreign powers."[52]

By late 1861, Seth Webb in Haiti had received "the English news threatening war with the United States" and, it was thought, this prompted Washington to flash its abolitionist credentials in response by moving toward recognizing Haiti, so as to sharply distinguish itself from the Confederates and win abolitionist backing in London. This move also meant, he said, that there were now "hardly any limits" that should "be put to the closeness" of Washington and Port-au-Prince.[53]

Dixie did not take Haiti—but under the sledgehammer blows of the pressure of public opinion and the blood sacrifice of the United States' own Black Jacobins then in a death match with the traitorous slaveholders, Washington was compelled to extend diplomatic recognition to Haiti, after an immense struggle lasting decades. Earlier Duff Green had contended that his nation did not recognize Haiti "any more than we recognize the ourang [sic] monkey chiefs and their tribes of chatterers at Sumatra or Borneo"[54]—though the press of war helped to dissolve this pigheadedness. Congressman D. W. Gooch of Massachusetts echoed a gathering consensus when he proclaimed in mid-1862—with the outcome of the war then unclear—that "we cannot afford to be indifferent to anything which pertains to this continent. The geographical position of Hayti is such that our Government cannot, without disregarding its own interest, be indifferent to the future of that island." In fact, if the United States had been more alert and acted earlier, Santo Domingo might not have been under Spanish control, then jeopardizing national security. "The objection principally urged against this bill," he said dismissively, "is that these republics may send here black men as their representatives." So what? This was the essence of his response. "They have sent them to England and France"; others argued that recognition meant racial equality, which he equally denied.[55] The abolitionist solon, Charles Sumner, carried the day for recognition.[56]

He had help from politicians in 1862 who were still unsure as to how the titanic civil war would unfold. Haiti, said Congressman Robert McKnight of Pennsylvania, though its population was less than a million, could be an effective buffer against "European nations" seeking a "foothold on our continent." Yes, some objected since the nation "might be represented at this republican court by . . . a full blooded Negro"; but this was untrue since "white agents" were likely appointees. "Liberia has always been represented in London by Gerard Ralston, Esq., a highly respected gentleman from Philadelphia." Anyway, why not follow the praxis of Britain and Brazil who do not mandate the color of foreign diplomats?[57] Webb, the U.S. agent in Haiti, told Washington that the refusal to recognize Haiti was "disastrous" for their nation. President Lincoln agreed that recognition would have a "salutary" impact on "foreign nations," notably abolitionist London pondering if secession should be recognized.[58]

By May 1862, Secretary of State Seward was told of the "festivities" and "universal satisfaction" among "Haytians and Americans alike," all of whom "rejoiced" at the imminent prospect of diplomatic recognition. Madrid was enmeshed in "boundary claims" with Port-au-Prince though recognition probably had weakened Spain's posture, particularly—as the U.S. envoy argued—because "the Haytian government shows considerable skill in protracting the negotiations."[59] By 1864 there was an extradition treaty between the two focused on "fugitive criminals" and promoting "amity, commerce, and navigation."[60]

Madrid may also have realized that U.S. Negroes had their own agenda, i.e. if a sufficient number of this group migrated to the island, they could then take advantage of the Madrid-Santo Domingo conflict to weigh in to the disadvantage of enslavers, then move on to Cuba and Puerto Rico to settle scores further. Thus, between 1859 and 1862 it has been estimated that roughly 2000 emigrants left the United States for Haiti.[61]

Again, there was push and pull: Even after the Emancipation Proclamation, certain Euro-Americans—as the failure of Reconstruction suggests—were not reconciled to the Negro presence on the mainland. "There still remains to be set-tled," said one with doubts about this presence, "(not the Slavery but) the Negro question, to which the rebellion has but opened the door."[62] What did that mean? A new disguised form of slavery? Mass deportation? Many U.S. Negroes thought that wisdom dictated self-determination, which meant to many hurrying to Haiti.

Apparently, Port-au-Prince had even more ambitious plans, thinking of trying to attract—according to one with reason to know—"seven or eight millions of the descendants of Africa in the new world," even though many might be only conver-sant in "speaking the English language." This was an abrupt departure from the 1820s venture when, it was said, the plan was to bring "20,000 such persons" to Haiti. "Nothing can be more natural," said this spokesman, "than that Hayti should [look] favorably towards the colored people of the States or that they should look with great interest toward Hayti. This mutual interest," it was said with confidence, "will doubtless increase; in fact, nothing could be more natural." Hence, in the immediate years preceding the U.S. Civil War, numerous agents were therefore employed by Haiti to hold public meetings amongst U.S. Negroes and lecture on the general subject of emigration. By this means thousands heard of Haiti and some moved to the island and, as a result, it was announced, the "English language has already made great way in Hayti."[63]

More than this, when spurious questions were raised about the fighting ability of mainland Africans, this shaky concern was doused by invocation of the martial capability of island Africans, with the caveat added that if abolition was the goal, these mainlanders would fight with even more brio.[64]

Tellingly, there was an overlap between Haitian emigration and the supporters of John Brown's 1859 raid in Virginia, which portended the armed overthrow of slavery on the mainland and was thought by some to bear the fingerprints of Haiti. Some of Brown's most avid backers founded an agrarian colony of Negro exiles from the United States and Canada in Saint-Marc at the mouth of the Artibonite River—near an existing colony of Africans from Louisiana. John Brown, Jr., him-self recruited settlers for Haiti in Canada. George Stearns, who helped to bankroll Brown's father, sought Haitian support for the assault on Dixie.[65]

The Secretary of State of the Interior and Agriculture in Port-au-Prince was giddy, asserting ecstatically that the "reception given at St. Marc to one hundred and twenty emigrants from Louisiana is proof of the good-will of the country people as regards these persons."[66] The U.S. legation in St. Marc reported that by late 1861 there were "about 1000 Americans and Canadian emigrants at and near this place."[67]

The legation may have underestimated the number of emigrants there for another source reported that there were "two or three hundred Louisiana exiles" there and "among them" were "some of the richest colored planters" of that woebe-gone state. They had chosen this site over Port-au-Prince, with a reported popu-lation of 26,000, and Cap-Haïtien, described as the "Little Paris of the Antilles" but in need of aid since the 1842 earthquake which occasioned the death of almost 6000. St. Marc was said to have almost 3000 residents and opened its arms to emigrants. All of these cities were to be preferred over Monrovia, another site of exile for U.S. Negroes, since, said one pro-Haiti writer, "Liberia, if a success will be [a] white man's victory, for he called it into being, and has fostered it from its birth." Strengthening Haiti was touted as a blow against the enslavers. "Would you [inflict] on the Carolinas the punishment that they have often inflicted on your friends?" Well, "the way is open. Tar and cotton them in England. Hayti will enable you to do it by producing both staples and hemp enough to hang every friend of slavery in Missouri and Kentucky." "Hayti . . . could produce sugar enough to drive Louisiana out of every market in the world" and "could raise rice enough to bury Wilmington, Charleston, and Savannah out of sight."[68]

Haiti had a strong argument, particularly in that while it was zealously trying to curtail the iniquitous slave trade, there were credible reports that emigrants arriving in Liberia were promptly detained, then sold into slavery.[69]

John Tyler, Jr., scion of a presidential family, was beyond rage in his response to Haiti's gumption, as suggested by its presumed alliance with John Brown. "Neither the invasion of the Low countries by the Spanish General Avila, nor the French Revolution of 1789–90, nor the conquest of Algeria, nor the late rebellion in India, either in its progress or suppression, nor the slaughterings of Cortez and Pizarro in Mexico and Peru, terrible as they are admitted to have been, were attended with monstrosities approached to those perpetrated by the Negroes of San Domingo"—and the Brown raid was intended as a replay.[70]

White supremacists who paid attention may have noticed the reverential funeral held in Port-au-Prince for the heroic Brown. He was hailed as a "martyr for the blacks" and a lengthy procession of leading Haitians hailed him unreservedly. Brown was convinced—apparently—to launch his crusade because of the success of the Haitian Revolution in toppling slavery through violence.[71] Those who sought to reopen the slave trade legally had good reason to fear Haiti's response.[72]

There was a repetitive and wounded cry from Dixie that the courage of Brown and his comrades was not only a replay of the revolutionary era but also a product of contemporary Haiti. "Brown's foray was nothing more and nothing less than an attempt to do on a vast scale what was done in St. Domingo in 1791, where the col-ored population was about equal to that of Virginia." The irate Louis Schade asked rhetorically, "are the people of the United States prepared for such horrid scenes of devastation, atrocities, and bloodshed"; i.e. "will they follow the teachings of those philanthropical fools, some of them perhaps under pay from England?" Why, he fumed, "such massacre and rapine as those committed in the revolution of St. Domingo are almost unequaled in the annals of atrocity." This was no surprise, he proclaimed, since "the Negro is incapable of self-government" and "if left to himself, he always will fall back into his former state of African barbarism." The lesson? U.S. slavery had to be maintained: not because it was liked, but because it was the only alternative when dealing with Africans. For, as leading politicos in Charleston affirmed, the "blood stains of St. Domingo" discredited abolitionism for all time; the "barbarism of Hayti and Jamaica" combined with the "frenzy and folly of France and of England" to create a catastrophe. In fact, not only should slavery be perpetuated, but the African slave trade should be re-opened so as to insure this outcome.

Yet the Republican Party was then "using the very same arguments and employing the very same means by which through the French and English philanthropical societies, the revolution in St. Domingo was originated"; they didn't seem to realize that a "rebellion in the Southern States of the slaves against the whites would not only result in the entire devastation and ruin of the country and all its relations but also end in the total destruction or expulsion of the Negroes, after terrible scenes of bloodshed." The writer, Louis Schade of Iowa, drew a strict parallel between what John Brown had attempted and what Black Jacobins succeeded in doing—violently overthrowing slavery.[73] The premier Confederate, Jefferson Davis, found talk of the Haitian Revolution and slave rebellion in the context of discussion of secession as "exceedingly offensive." Contrary to what he was hearing, what happened there was "not a case where black heroes rose and acquired a government."[74] But John Brown—hailed in Haiti to this very day—showed that there was a tendency in slavery to produce bloody revolution.

Despite such inflamed rhetoric, Madrid often saw the Negro emigrants as agents of Washington—though they had fled in terror from that republic. Still, as was their wont, barely after unpacking their bags upon arrival on the island, they launched churches, often powerful Methodist ones. "Wherever I have found, far back in the interior, a little knot for our Americans," said Benjamin Hunt, "there I have also found some semblance at least of religious exercises."[75]

Some Dominican elites may have thought that unless they aligned with Madrid, they would be overrun by Port-au-Prince, in league with these U.S. Negro emigrants and thought—correctly—to be sympathetic to Haiti. The Haitians were "greatly superior in numbers and resources" to their eastern neighbors and the latter "would willingly let the Haytiens alone, if the latter were equally forbearing," said Benjamin S. Hunt, a pro-Haitian writer, in 1860.[76]

The Civil War on the mainland interrupted the more capacious U.S. (and U.S. Negro) plans—only to reappear at the end of the decade in the form of an attempted annexation of the Dominican Republic, which barely failed. A closely related plan to annex Haiti too and deport the newly freed mainland slaves to a new homeland perished as well. However, Dixie was defeated militarily—though not politically—and the mean-spirited policy toward Africans that had characterized the (formerly) enslaving republic since its inception continued.

This was a policy that handicapped, in the first instance, U.S. Negroes themselves, which caused many of them to continue heading due south toward Haiti. Thus, the leading Negro journal in Canada seemed elated when the man then known as "Emperor Soulouque" formed an association called "Maison Centrale" with the task of "instructing youth in mechanical occupations." It was "under the direction of Baron Nathaniel Montgomery, an intelligent colored man from Baltimore whose father emigrated to Hayti" from the United States "during the latter part of the last century. He is described as possessing extensive chemical and mechanical" experience, useful for his present shop which "contains a foundry, smith shop, and a sawmill."[77]

According to Frederick Douglass, Montgomery's father was a Haitian who migrated to the United States during the revolutionary years. Other Baltimoreans in Haiti included a man named "Grice" who too was said to have a superior knowledge of engineering and mechanics; one son was a "daguerreotypist" and photographer and another was a dentist. Like others, these Baltimoreans arrived with a sour attitude toward those defined as "white" and, according to Douglass, were motivated by the slogan *"To cheat a white man makes God laugh."*[78]

Increasingly, these emigrants were playing a prominent role in the Haitian economy, fulfilling the promise that they would reinforce Port-au-Prince, providing a protective membrane that would shield the nation from the lances of the enslaving republic. The best tailors in the capital city were two young Negroes from Dixie. One of the most prosperous bakers was a Negro from New Orleans. The principal sail-maker of Cap-Haïtien and his counterpart in the capital had arrived from Philadelphia. One of the best cabinet-makers hailed from Philadelphia (but when unrest crept closer, he moved to Jamaica). Benjamin S. Hunt, who wrote of their accomplishments in 1860, asserted that they were among the most prominent of the "thirteen thousand American immigrants of 1824–1827." Although some had departed, unable to cope with conditions that at times included war, he concluded optimistically that "on the whole this class of people is better off in Hayti than in the United States."[79]

For the Minister of Interior in Port-au-Prince was from Maryland, the chief of police was from South Carolina, and the commander of the port was from Alabama.

It is unclear if this latter leader was from Mobile, but, if so, he was among those fleeing a policy that suggested that the state's *gens de couleur* and free Negroes were about to be sold into slavery or forced to emigrate.[80] It is possible that those from Mobile adapted more easily to Haiti since the French influence continued to predominate there to such a degree that many Africans there spoke French.[81]

By 1860 this onerous policy had reached beyond Mobile. "Free colored people of Arkansas," said the pro-Haiti James Redpath, "have been required by law to leave the state"—or "go into slavery." The "effect of this disgraceful law," he said angrily, "has been to compel hundreds of poor colored persons to remove" themselves and besides Haiti there were not that many places to alight.[82]

Redpath received "news" in January 1861 that "the colored class had been ordered to leave Mobile" and the "rumor" that the "free colored people of Opelousas," Louisiana, were mandated similarly. Some were "inclined to emigrate to France or Mexico" or "Salvador, Chile, and Peru"—but "everywhere" there was a "great interest manifested in Hayti," meaning that "next spring there will undoubtedly be a good emigration."[83]

Redpath somehow wangled a meeting in Charleston with potential emigrants. He told his Haitian contact in December 1860 that "all are decided upon going to Hayti, as soon as they can settle their affairs, many are ready to go within a month. The richest families," he said instructively, "are not Black but colored generally" and "among the free, colored men are the most numerous; so that the Southern emigration to Hayti will be men of color chiefly." He knew all too well that "it makes a certain impression [in Haiti] if the mulatto emigrants prevail in number." As the drumbeats of war sounded terribly, Redpath announced, "I have numerous applications from whites desiring to know what chance there is for them in Hayti, I encourage none of them to go," he said curtly. Meanwhile, from U.S. Negroes he got "never less than thirty or forty letters of inquiry every week" and, thus, had "made arrangements at New York by which all the escaped slaves of good character that pass through that state or city will be sent" to him. As for this group, he said, with little fear of contradiction, that they "will never be troubled by homesickness." In any case, he was "in indirect correspondence" with the highest level in Port-au-Prince on this matter, indicative of its importance to Haiti.[84]

Of course, these emigrants—whether lighter or darker—too were associated with a nation that had tormented Haiti for decades and it was not easy for all to see that these recent arrivals may have shared the same distaste for the mainland that many Haitians did. Thus, by 1862 the U.S. emissary in Aux Cayes was raging about his office being invaded by officialdom, a complication made worse by the fact that—like so many mainlanders—he was "unable to converse in French."

Whatever the case, the Haitian official in charge "posted men with guns" at the "street entrance" and snarled, "the Americans have never been very friendly to the Haytian people," alluding probably to the fact that the United States had not yet acknowledged the independence of Hayti.[85]

The U.S. envoy in St. Marc, Haiti, professed in early 1862, "I know of no subject more interesting to the United States at the present time than that of the immigrant movement from the United States and the Canadas to this island of the Free Colored People. The movement is set on foot and carried on solely and at its own expense by this Government," meaning Haiti. "Each head of family" was accorded "about sixteen acres" and, resultantly, a "large number of immigrants, over twelve hundred, have arrived during the past year and are at work on their land and they are still arriving in large numbers." The enthused Thomas Miller, who was born in New York and had never been to Haiti before his appointment, declared, "I have no doubt satisfactory arrangements could be made with this Government for the reception of all the colored persons which the United States might desire to colonize. The Government now pays the whole expense of each immigrant & his family" and perhaps could be persuaded to offload this subsidy to Washington.[86]

Days later Miller was trying to contact Redpath about a "mutual" plan of emigration and Auguste Elie of Haiti assured the envoy that "our Government" owned "immense and very fertile lands" and was willing to entertain "any overture" regarding such a plan.[87]

The mainland Civil War ignited a dramatic change in racial dynamics and this led to a concomitant change in how emigration was viewed—at least, it caused a reappraisal by the U.S. envoy in Aux Cayes, B. F. Sanford. For it was he who was "more and more impressed with the idea that it would be good policy" for the United States "to encourage a flow of emigration to Hayti of the religious, moral, and industrious colored people." Suddenly, it was acknowledged that "there are in our country a large number of colored people possessing characters worthy of high respect"—yet this group was facing an uphill climb on the mainland. "They can become the means of being an immense benefit to Hayti; and they will reflect back credit on America besides adding greatly to its material prosperity." For "on the plains of Aux Cayes," was "some of the finest sugar land in the world" at a time when this commodity was "needed in the United States." Why not "encourage this desirable emigration" by opening "regular steam communication with Hayti" from Charleston? This town was "not more than four days distance from this island by steam" and Haitian influence in turn would aid border towns like Cincinnati in "winning the people of that city back to a love of the Union" more than the "presence of an army"—or the "presence" of Negroes, he could have added candidly.[88]

Aux Cayes alone could "absorb 100,000 easily"; plus, "the whole southern portion of Hayti may be regarded as healthy, owing to the influence of the Trade Winds," making it "one of the most delightful and healthy places in the world." Haiti was "offering 16 acres of land to each family of emigrants as soon as they arrive" and "the profits of this increased commerce that will thus spring up will be reaped almost wholly by the United States. Three fourths at least of the entire commerce of Hayti will continue to flow to the American seaport towns as naturally as water flows downhill." Moreover, there was an added bonus in that the emigrants will enforce "that degree of civilization to which they have already attained"—but this point was subordinate to flowing profits.[89]

Haiti desired U.S. Negroes and Dixie wanted to get rid of them, creating an ironic confluence. There was an "exodus" from South Carolina, reported Redpath.[90] By February 1861, he found that a "large number of men are preparing to leave New Orleans where the condition of affairs looks threatening to men of African descent." The jumpy governor of South Carolina thought that the "true design" of those like Redpath was "to make a descent on the plantations to liberate the slaves" and, thus, "sent out a war steamer along the coast." This was heightening panic on all sides. So Redpath wanted Port-au-Prince to provide "free passage including board" to emigrants, in order to match similar offers from Liberia that should extend for "six months after arrival."[91] A. Jean Simon of Haiti, from what became the Foreign Ministry, told Redpath that emigrants who were "agriculturalists" would be subsidized, including "passage," along with "board and lodge" for "eight days"; also he said that "they can have the same civil and political rights as the Haytians."[92]

It was in early March 1861 that a well-connected Chicago periodical asserted that there was an "army of 8000 Negroes, armed, equipped, and well drilled" that was "ready" to march southward from Canada "at a moment's warning." Radicals on the mainland wanted to discuss this with President Geffrard and charge the Africans in Haiti with the task of "raising an army there" too. They would head "directly for the Gulf through the portion of the South most thickly populated with slaves to join them" and then "pillage, plunder, murder, and burn"; they should "pass through Texas, skirt along the Mexican coast, and make themselves at home in Central America where they are prospecting for the location of a colony."[93]

As civil war crept closer, nerves jangled accordingly, particularly as purported plans of invasion of Dixie from Haiti garnered attention. Redpath, backed by the Haitians, was seeking to start a journal to rally his forces—"in the interests of Hayti and the colored races in America," as he put it.[94] As Fort Sumter was assaulted, friends of Haiti on the mainland launched their own broadside. Redpath was among the editors and the contributors included such stalwarts as John Brown, Jr., and William Wells Brown. Ambitiously, it was "devoted to the interests of freedom and of the colored races in the Americas" and insisted that slavery be abolished if need be by "John Brown expeditions and simultaneous and extended Negro insurrections"—which were to unwind in coming months—and also by "the building up of Hayti" via emigration. This would convert the abolitionist republic "into the rank of a great American Power," essentially fulfilling Jefferson's most troublesome fear. The cry was placed insistently: *We must create a great Negro Nation* in Haiti. Punctuating this charge was a sizeable drawing of General Toussaint.[95] The Haytian law on emigration, it was said, was intent on "making Hayti to the black race what England is and has been to the proscribed and persecuted classes of Europe, a safe place of refuge, not only but a free and a powerful fatherland." An 1846 formulation proclaimed, "all Africans or Indians and their descendants are able to become Haytians."[96]

Also featured, revealingly, was a large drawing of Louis S. Leary, described as "one of the colored martyrs" of the raid led by John Brown in 1859.[97] And with every issue there was sizeable attention paid to emigration[98] and, tellingly, "Indian" or Native American, emigration was also touted.[99] On the other hand, the provision from the Haitian constitution stating that "no white man . . . shall be permitted to land on the Haytian Territory"[100] was underlined, a provision that should be interpreted as both anti-slavery and anti-colonialist. A premature understanding of the late 20th century concept of affirmative action was also part of the conversation about Haiti then. "The invitation of the Haytian Government" to emigrate, it was said, was "extended only to persons of African or Indian descent. In Hayti, the tables are turned upon the white man; he cannot become a citizen or hold real estate," but "we cannot much blame that people considering what they suffered at the hands of the white man before the Revolution."[101]

In a world where white supremacy predominated, it was not easy—perhaps not wise given prevailing attitudes and the prevalence of espionage—for Haiti to adopt 21st century norms of racial egalitarianism.

"The legal rights of the white race in Hayti are not very numerous," said an official Haitian document, though "exemplary conduct on their part always enables them to overcome the social disadvantages attaching to their unfortunate color." Still, they were not allowed to possess real estate nor hold mortgages for longer than nine years. They were allowed to be wholesale merchants, artists, mechanics, professors, teachers, clerks, engineers, and the lessees of estates; but the retail trade, the bar and the bench, military honors, and the like were not as open to them.[102] According to Frederick Douglass, the "whites" in Haiti were "composed chiefly of merchants and their clerks, with some servants, a limited number of professors of mathematics and of languages, and a few artisans, as bakers and shoemakers. The whole number of them may be estimated at four hundred, of whom two hundred reside in Port-au-Prince" and "a good number of them are married to or live with mulatto women."[103]

Despite the restrictions they faced, London thought that—in some ways—their subjects faced fewer penalties in Haiti than they did in the Dominican Republic, where harassment was routine. After cattle of London's subjects were "plundered" by "certain Dominican citizens," the British envoy observed that it was "true" that "no foreigner can hold landed property or real estate in Hayti, but there is no law that prevents their professing moveable property, such as horses, cattle, etc. or to purchase anything on the land whether coffee, cotton, mahogany, or any other wood."[104]

This antipathy toward Euro-Americans generally did not unduly hamper the ability of Port-au-Prince to see that the defeat of the so-called Confederate States of America was in its best interest. However, said antipathy helps explain why there was a spurt of U.S. Negro emigration to Haiti in the early 1860s. This included a large body of South Carolinians[105] and among them were "quite intelligent men,"[106] said one observer. The literate may have been influenced by the fact that the Negro press—notably the weekly, *Anglo-African*—chose to publish what was described as a "large amount of information on Hayti and Emigration [*sic*] each week."[107] Among those so influenced was the Proctor family, which left Dixie in 1840 for Ohio, then moved on to Canada by 1860, and had landed in Haiti by 1861. The patriarch, Alexander Proctor, was a Baptist minister, who died there in 1865, and then his spouse reversed sail and returned to Kalamazoo.[108]

Dismissed by Redpath was the enslavers' insistence that abolition would mean the introduction of the so-called "horrors of St. Domingo."[109] In part, this stern reaction was a response to events across the border where Santo Domingo was pursuing an opposite policy, straining to attract emigrants that could be defined as "white." One New York writer insisted that those "who fancy that no skin but a black one can cover the firm muscle and endurance of a perfect and hardy manhood" were "mistaken." Richard Kimball, instead, stressed that "*the most manly workers I have seen in this country,*" speaking of the Dominican Republic, "*are white men.*" For "the few who have good farms of their own tilling are mostly white men."[110] At that point, said Redpath, there were 120,000 residing in the Dominican Republic and 800,000 in Haiti—but there were "not five hundred whites in Hayti."[111] This ratio might have been even more skewed in Haiti but for reported missteps by Redpath who—according to one source—engaged in "bad faith" with Negro emigrants: "most of them were deceived and forced to work two days in the week for the Government in order to contribute to the money for their passage out."[112]

The atmosphere was seething with tension as a result. Eager to "allay" the "apprehensions" of these emigrants not interested in joining a marauding army but seeking simple emigration instead, Redpath insisted that it was "necessary" to transport these "fugitives from slavery," i.e. the "greater number of the Canadian emigrants from a British port and under the British flag," lest they suspect that a Stars-and-Stripes slaving plot was at hand. Hence, a "charter vessel from Quebec" was arranged. "Distinguished men," he assured his Haitian liaison, "many of them British officials, have given this movement support. This is a victory for us," he added beamingly, "as Jamaica needs emigrants."[113]

Hispaniola was a beacon for U.S. Negroes, even setting aside the yeoman efforts of Redpath and his comrades. A Negro from South Carolina named "Smith" was residing in Puerto Plata by 1860, though he spoke no Spanish and was even deficient in English too. Still, with the gritty energy that had difficulty in finding a productive outlet on the mainland, he became a successful farmer (though he had never practiced this trade previously), which was not tremendously difficult since the soil was so fertile. He used a steel plow imported from the mainland to turn the soil and soon was regarded as the most successful agriculturalist in the region.[114]

With the arrival of U.S. Negroes came U.S. goods—as the plow exemplified. The coasting trade was conducted by small U.S. vessels and codfish from mainland waters was a chief food item among the working class and poor of the island. Lard from the mainland, rather than butter, was used in cooking. Still, Hunt was distraught at the plight of a number of emigrants. For "seventeen years" he had been "resident in or conversant with Hayti" and could only think of "thirteen Americans of African blood, who have been what might be called 'successful'" and "several" of that number were only moderately so. Six of these immigrants were from New Orleans, or parts adjacent, and of course "spoke French on arrival," while "seven of them were merchants or traders, four were mechanics, two were lawyers, and all were men of color or mulattoes." He did know "one black man and one man of color from the free States, who acquired a little property as carters; and four others, two black men and two men of color, also from the free States, who cultivated in a poor way, a little land which they called their own. All the other Afric-Americans [sic]," he lamented, were "day laborers" or "rag-pick[ers]." Despite this, Hunt remained upbeat about Haiti's—and the emigrants'—prospects.[115]

There were others who likely would have agreed with Hunt on the relative satisfaction of residing on the island, including a former slave from South Carolina, who had made his way to Key West before escaping to the Bahamas and then Puerto Plata. J. Dennis Harris, who had encountered him, also validated skepticism about the bona fides of Euro-Americans: "there is of course," he said, "and it is certainly natural enough—a lingering prejudice against white Americans," a widespread opinion that complicated relations with Washington.[116]

Despite this animosity, when a man described as "white" who had a "colored" wife inquired about emigration, he was told that they would not be "excluded from the advantages offered to emigrants by the Haytian Government"; of course, "white men cannot hold real estate in the island yet their colored wives can if of African descent."[117] This policy may have derived from a kind of affirmative action. For, as one Bay State resident was told, "females who emigrate to Hayti are equally eligible to grants of land with males. It is now common there for females to cultivate the soil and it is much more easily done than in this country."[118] One woman was told that it was "entirely proper for single persons to emigrate to Hayti."[119]

Essential to propelling emigrants southward was a British activist and journalist who resided on the mainland: James Redpath. It was in the early fall of 1860 that the mustachioed man with a receding hairline was to be found in Philadelphia where, it was noted, he "addressed a congregation of colored people" and "obtained a list of names of the leading colored men of the city and vicinity" with the goal of enticing them to Haiti. A "distinguished clergyman of great influence" agreed to "favor the project and be one of my agents. He is a black," it was said knowingly, while a leading journalist agreed to "publish articles favorable to Hayti"; then Redpath "ordered 10,000 copies" of these pro-Haitians articles "for distribution by agents" on the mainland. The latter included a "man of color," he added with sensitivity to the dynamics of Haiti. Redpath's audacious plan sought to "reach the entire free colored population of America." A Negro leader from Connecticut, he noted, "promises a colony of picked men" from the Nutmeg State.[120]

But Redpath had plenty of help from Haiti, which—once more—was decidedly interested in attracting U.S. Negroes, perhaps because it was being menaced by Spain nearby—not just in Havana and San Juan but now Santo Domingo. Just months before John Brown's epic raid, the Secretary of State in Port-au-Prince, F. E. Du Bois, issued a call to the "Men of our race dispersed in the United States" for emigration. He emphasized that "your fate, your social position, instead of ameliorating, daily becomes worse" as the United States has "invented a new slavery for the free"; "contempt and hatred increase against you," which was all too true. "Come, then to us! The doors of Hayti are open to you," he declared. For those "not able to pay the expenses of your passage, aid will be given from the public treasury" and said emigrants "will be exempt from military service." With magnanimity, he concluded, "our sympathies are equally extended to all those of our origin who, throughout the world, are bowed down under the weight of the same sufferings. Let them come to us!"[121]

Beyond marketable skills, these U.S. Negro emigrants were bringing to Haiti other capabilities. Speaking of U.S. Negroes generally, one journalist remarked that it was "by no means an uncommon thing for such men to 'talk French and English' sensibly and grammatically. It is a fact that they acquire languages with peculiar facility; and we have met with many colored persons whose acquisitions as linguists were so respectable that they could converse fluently in from two to six different languages. One of the persons alluded to was a cook on a steamboat well acquainted with English, French, Spanish, Danish, Swedish, Portuguese, and German," while a "colored girl in St. Louis could converse in four different languages. For colored men in Louisiana to speak English, French, Spanish, and Portuguese is by no means uncommon."[122]

Redpath was also maneuvering against Santo Domingo. "I have succeeded," he boasted, "in dissuading one large capitalist from investing money in the Dominican Republic gold schemes" and also was seeking to "prevent any abolitionists from encouraging the project of a white emigration to the eastern part." Still, the "president" of the Dominican Republic was "taking vigorous although quiet measures" in opposing him: this leader was enmeshed in "encouragement of white emigration" in response.[123] Redpath was a mortal foe of what he described as "a white emigration to the Dominican Republic—a purpose which it is impossible to accomplish peacefully." He was determined to block their exploitation of "iron, sulphur, copper, antimony . . . mercury, gold, cobalt, manganese."[124]

What was impelling this acidulous attitude was no mystery: the enslaving republic was also a kingpin in the illicit African slave trade, the existence of which placed Haitians in perpetual jeopardy. The 1850 census had shown that there were a little more than three million enslaved Africans in the United States, worth more than $1.5 billion, and by 1860 there had been a leap to about four million with even more wealth embodied in these bodies.[125] What accompanied such wealth was—inexorably—a debased attitude toward Africans that could not help but ensnare Haiti too. Traveling from Hot Springs, Arkansas to St. Louis, Sarah Glasgow spoke of arriving in the land of the "heathens," where "they think no more of niggers than of dogs"—actually, the latter were seen as being favored over the former.[126] Thus, even before the Emancipation Proclamation, President Abraham Lincoln had sought a treaty—finally—with London to undermine the African Slave Trade, the lifeblood of secessionists; strikingly, in addition to the "coasts of Madagascar," to be patrolled were the waters of "Puerto Rico and San Domingo," in addition to "those of Africa and of Cuba."[127]

This was welcome news in Port-au-Prince for by early 1862 slave ships were spotted in Haiti's northern waters at the behest of Spain. There were about 150

enslaved persons all told—all "in chains" and "treated very cruelly," according to
W. R. Inglis, in the Turks Islands. This bestiality was preceded by the presence of
a mainland vessel full of Africans that had landed in Puerto Rico; then a cargo of
300 Africans was expected to land in Samaná—disguised as apprentices. In Puerto
Plata, where U.S. Negro emigrants continued to reside, a proclamation of equality
had been enunciated by Spain, but slavery went curiously unmentioned, suggesting
to some that restoration of this savage institution was on the way.[128]

By May 1861, on the northern side of the island of Hispaniola there were acts
of piracy ascribed to U.S. vessels, leading to seizures by the Haitian authorities.[129]
There was a consensus in the Turks Islands that Spain would re-introduce slavery
in the Dominican Republic This was the "firm belief of all who are acquainted"
with the subject, since—as Inglis put it—"no class exists as agricultural laborers for
hire."[130] Already there had been reports of attempts to sell Africans from Jamaica to
mainlanders.[131] Britain sought to "guard against any such occurrences," but with an
energized slave-holding class on the mainland and a fortified slave-holding Spain,
this would not be easy to attain.[132]

Dixie's idea of seizing the entirety of Hispaniola and reenslaving most, if not all,
was part of a campaign that predated secession and, indeed, was seen as a necessary
strengthening before the attack on Fort Sumter. Edmund Ruffin, one of Dixie's
most hawkish proponents, also saw disrupting the "cordial alliance" between Paris
and London and supplanting it with "mutual suspicion & fear" as a necessity. He
noted that this would put an end "to their combined efforts to impede the progress
of & to injure the United States . . . & leave us free to settle our own business,
whether foreign or internal without the interference of always hostile England or
France"—for example, taking Hispaniola without muss or fuss. Both leading abolitionist powers were determined to "crush Negro slavery"—which he was just as
determined to sustain and expand.[133]

His comrade, Wade Hampton, thought that key to Dixie's ambition was precisely the reopening of the African slave trade. He thought it was the "surest means
to accomplish their desires" and a project that should be pursued with measures
both "earnest and zealous."[134] Simultaneously, hundreds of Africans—fresh from
the continent—were turning up in Charleston harbor.[135] But why travel across the
Atlantic when it was felt there were vulnerable Africans to be seized in Hispaniola?

By 1861 the secessionist naval commander, Raphael Semmes, was off the coast of
Hispaniola and complaining that his mainland opponents "would gladly see another
San Domingo revolution in our unhappy country." By early 1862 he was "dropping
anchor" in Santo Domingo, as he claimed a victory in "having thus displayed for
the first time" on this site of slavery's defeat "the flag of the young republic."[136] He

recalled vividly sailing the Mona Passage separating Hispaniola from Puerto Rico before arriving in Samaná. He had "approached" this passage "with much caution, fully expecting to find so important a thoroughfare guarded by the enemy," but was gleeful to find that he was wrong and that the island was vulnerable. After a pleasing sojourn in Santo Domingo, Semmes "could not but moralize on the spectacle. Sixty years before the negro had cut the throat of the white man, ravished his wife and daughters, and burned his dwelling in the island of St. Domingo, now in sight. The white man in another country"—i.e. Washington—"was now inciting the negro to the perpetration of the same crimes against another white man."

He sailed close to Cap-Haïtien with such thoughts firmly in mind. He encountered U.S. ships which he and his crew torched: "the islands of St. Domingo and Jamaica were both sufficiently near for their inhabitants to witness the splendid bonfire, which lighted up the heavens far and near," he said gloatingly. Then he was "still steaming to the eastward, along the Haytian coast" before returning to Santo Domingo. A Spanish naval commander "came on board to visit me. I had no difficulty in arranging with him for the landing of my prisoners," unfortunates from the torched vessels. Santo Domingo was lovely, he thought—"the most interesting city in all the Americas." Still, he observed that that the "negro and the mulatto in this oldest of American cities are thought rather more of than the white man and the Yankee skipper finds in it, a congenial mart, in which to vend his cheese and his codfish and distribute his tracts—political and moral—and put forth his patent medicines!" While there he scrutinized a "specimen of the Haytian paper money, worth five cents on the dollar. Like the American greenback," he said sneeringly, "it is the offshoot of revolution and political corruption." Then he had a "picturesque run along the Haytian coast for the rest of the day." He was happy to see that "the coasts of Hayti abound in fish and as there is a succession of fruits all the year round, it is the paradise of the negro," he wailed.[137]

He also visited Martinique finding it "remarkably pleasant," with "the inhabitants"—presumably the settlers—"showing us every mark of respect and politeness and the officers of the garrison, and of a couple of small French vessels of war, in the port, extending to us the courtesies of their clubs and mess-rooms." Naturally, the "war was frequently the topic of conversation, when such expressions as 'les barbares du Nord!' would escape, not unmusically, from the prettiest of pouting lips."[138] He was delighted to find that "no social admixture" of "the whites and blacks" was "visible." Fortunately, pews in churches were segregated.[139]

Sadly for Haiti, Semmes was not alone in lurking offshore. During the summer of 1861, there was detected near the Mona Passage a privateer of the secessionists, with twenty guns mounted, and thought to have been fitted out in Europe.[140]

By early 1863, more than half of the trade between Port-au-Prince and the United States was carried on under the U.S. flag, "owing to the fear of capture by rebel privateers," according to the U.S. envoy.[141] The United States was worried that "combatants in the war now raging in the eastern part of the island" could have impact on their vessels. According to Rear Admiral J. L. Lardner of the U.S. Navy, "the complaints and calls for assistance have been made, I believe, in all instances by our colored countrymen who have settled and become domiciliated [sic] among the Dominicans." Madrid thought that "our Government is interested in the success of the revolutionists and probably assisting them"—which was accurate in all senses. Still, the admiral asked the Spanish military leadership to employ their "good offices" and direct "those under his command" to aid his U.S. "countrymen—consuls and also colored immigrants—which he cordially promised."[142]

This was an obviously dire threat to emigrants and a damper on further plans to emigrate from the mainland. By October 1863, refugees from the Dominican Republic were arriving in the Turks, though it was unclear if U.S. emigrants were among them.[143] The next month anti-Spain outbreaks in Puerto Plata led to the town's destruction, creating even more refugees,[144] as Spanish troops were accused of committing "outrages."[145] What a London agent called "political intrigue" in the Dominican Republic was rippling outward, causing concern in Britain, and, as a result, London could reinforce ties to Haiti.[146]

Nonetheless, in 1862 there was yet another "attempted revolution." Martial law was declared and there was a "universal reign of terror" with "blacks . . . gathering together in the mountains in large numbers." The U.S. envoy, B. F. Sanford, journeyed to a prison to visit a former U.S. consul who had been swept up in the commotion and arrested. He bemoaned that "they not only refused me permission to go in and see my friend, but with . . . menacing language they ordered me away." Since his friend Ernest Dentertte claimed French nationality, this could have provided "Louis Napoleon his coveted opportunity to interfere with the affairs of Hayti." And this, he observed, "would be decidedly against the interest of the United States."[147]

This more understanding approach was also reflected in a more nuanced attitude toward Haiti. By early 1862, Secretary of State Seward was apprised that because the United States itself had "a population of over 4 ½ millions of the African race," perforce "everything concerning the nature and habits of this people, their capability of rising, their desire for improvement"—all of it— "becomes of interest to the American statesman." In that vein, Haiti had to be scrutinized—and was acquitting itself well for Port-au-Prince had met the "first duty of government," i.e. to "render life and property secure"; Haiti "accomplished this," and did so "as well as the most civilized governments of the world. Great crimes on the part of individuals are seldom heard of here. Deliberate and premeditated murder is exceedingly uncommon, as well as also highway robbery"; yes, "petit larceny is very common," along with "excess of indulgence in sexual intercourse and promiscuous embracings" and "such bad habits" had become "ingrained in the whole of society." But here morality met policy for this perceived decline could "soon be regenerated by the influence of a large Christian emigration," i.e. more U.S. Negroes. This was imperative since "men who give all their strength to women, can have little for anything else." Moreover, it was thought that these U.S. Negroes could alter the policy of the "upper classes," who were seeking "lives of slothful indulgence by becoming recipients of governmental patronage" and were contributing to an "aversion to work" itself.[148]

Nevertheless, the above perception was corroborated by a man from Alabama who arrived in Haiti in the 1860s and was stunned by the "remarkable politeness" he encountered; after he "spent some weeks on the island," he remarked that "he should have to be very careful when he reached home, or he should find himself tipping his hat to every Negro he met on his plantation."[149]

But these favorable perceptions were contradicted by the U.S. emissary, James de Long, who spat out angrily that "this country is no place for emigration." He added—revealingly—that "no more should be permitted to embark for this island, unless it is the only object of our govt. to get rid of them." For the "character of the people" included those who were "ignorant, immoral, and lazy"—and all were presided over by "absolute despotism."[150] Mr. de Long, who had resided in Aux Cayes since 1850 and spoke French, thought he was in a better position than Sanford to judge events.[151]

But de Long apparently did not take into account commercial considerations, not a trivial point given how colonialism blocked the expansion of U.S. trade in Cuba, Jamaica, and elsewhere in the region. "Formerly" there was "considerable lumber" arriving on the island from Wilmington, but with British encroachments in recent decades this Carolina town had been supplanted by Nova Scotia. "The absence of any American Mercantile House here," he moaned, "and the fact that the English, German, and French houses lend all their energies to promote the consumption of goods from their respective countries" both needed to be corrected.[152]

Given the transformative change on the mainland with slavery in the process of being abolished and the commercial horizons then arising, Haiti—yet to be colonized—loomed as a tantalizingly profitable opportunity. One mainland writer observed that Hispaniola was "so near the coast of the United States, its capabilities are so manifest, and its staple products are [so] necessary, that we cannot remain indifferent to its fate"—so, what to do? *"Colonize it with the free blacks of the United States"* was the answer. This must be made "compulsory," i.e. "forced colonization." But it was "objected that the success of this enterprise would be to build up a black government, so near our Southern States, as to affect injuriously the slave population." This was a risk worth taking, since "we of the Southern States" were "specially interested" in Hispaniola.[153]

One entrepreneur, Bernard Kock, received $50,000 for his aid in forming a colony of freed mainland slaves on an island near Haiti. Hundreds were shipped there by Kock, who was related by marriage to Pierre Soule, a hawkish politico of French descent.[154] However, by April 1863, President Lincoln was seeking to cancel Kock's lucrative contract.[155] Thus, Secretary of War Edwin Stanton was discussing in "confidential" terms in 1864 the "colored colony" on "the Island of Vache on the coast of San Domingo" and the particulars of the repatriation of this population.[156] It was not long before these migrants were discussed as "destitute and suffering." James de Long said that the "country is very sickly" and has "no hospital or other accommodations"—so, send these "poor unfortunate, neglected and destitute people" back to the mainland.[157]

This turmoil on the island that was compelling emigrants to return to the mainland had wider consequences. Jonathan Elliott, U.S. delegate in Santo Domingo, found himself under siege with a carbine pointed menacingly at his spouse.[158] Things got so bad that the United States was led to believe that the French consul was secretly collaborating with Haiti to forge a marriage with the Dominican Republic—and was spreading "false calumnies" against the United States in the bargain.[159] Washington got hold of a French message musing—before secession—of the disadvantage suffered by the enslaving republic which "consider[ed] as an insult the sending of consuls of mixed blood to their ports."[160]

Once the Dominican Republic seceded from Haiti, the latter's laws that tended to restrict the nationals of the major powers from owning land in the abolitionist republic were weakened. The flow of new investment and capital to Santo Domingo placed pressure on Port-au-Prince to alter the restrictive status quo. "Dominicans are certainly a superior race to the Haytians," said the U.S. consul, pointing to the reality that "their laws are liberal in the extreme for foreigners, they occupy three fourths of the island, the richest in land, timber, and minerals of all the West Indies."[161]

But Spain was seizing control of the Dominican Republic and the open door for investment by the United States and the other powers was—if not already slammed shut—quickly closing, creating an opening in Haiti, which France was thought to enter. Even before the seizure, the U.S. emissary was complaining that "the Spanish

. . . opposed everything having connection with the U.S. government or its citizens."[162] At the same time, while roughly 70% of U.S. emigrants to the Dominican Republic were returning home, they were being replaced by emigrants from Venezuela, Puerto Rico, the Canary Islands, and other sites deemed to be friendlier to Madrid.[163] "A large number of persons, principally foreigners, have arrived here since the annexation," was the report by London's envoy in Santo Domingo in late October 1861.[164]

This development did not seem to deter Jane Cazneau who by 1862 was busily seeking to attract U.S. emigrants, admittedly on a segmented basis: "the Haytien Republic is likely to be the most agreeable to a colored man," she conceded, while those defined as "white" were deemed suitable for the Dominican Republic[165] The ambitious plans of Cazneau and her spouse included organizing a company to fund cotton plantations in eastern Hispaniola that would deploy slave labor. This was a dire threat not just to Haiti but also to the U.S. Negro emigrants who now—in 1862—found they might have stumbled into a situation worse than that which they had abandoned on the mainland. Surely, this was a threat to many within in the Dominican Republic too.[166]

Nonetheless, even the Spanish seizure did not disrupt her sangfroid. She conceded that annexation made it appear that the Dominican Republic "is not the country for a poor white man" from the United States and "still less for a colored man." However, Cazneau still saw the Dominican Republic "to be the best, if not the only place in this world for the happy solution of the great problem of races. Those who think that the whites will be given up exclusively to the blacks are utterly mistaken. It is the Eden of the earth for educated labor." As for Haiti, it was warned that "the thirty millions of whites will not suffer the ten millions of blacks and Indians to exclude them from the most desirable portion of the Western Hemisphere. It is not human nature to consent to it."

Haiti's "experiment of exclusionism," she continued, would have to be ditched soon and Port-au-Prince would "have to give it up and take the Dominican position." This supposedly involved "perfect equality," where "the blacks" had been "forced to be thrifty, industrious, and progressive to keep up with . . . white competitors." The "social equality of races has been so long established here," she said of the Dominican Republic, "that there is no danger of a war between them." Yet at that time—1862—in the United States such a so-called "race war" was "now hatching" and it would "shock the world by its ferocity." As a result, she thought, "a large emigration from the ruined cotton states is looking this way" and "so long as he keeps out of politics," such an emigrant would fare well. She urged further emigration to the Dominican Republic given the "imminence or possible magnitude of the war of races now incubating," which was the "inevitable sequence" of the "government [having] passed into the hands of the Republicans."[167]

Her husband, William Cazneau—a Texan of French descent, a Catholic, and a staunch man of Dixie—was well-positioned to enact the most far-reaching plans for the island. They were investing heavily in Dominican real estate while pushing diplomatic levers—including the promotion of annexation by the United States—to insure their investments would pay off handsomely.[168] His spouse, also known as Cora Montgomery, was the preeminent female filibuster and had been a secret agent in Mexico during the war with that nation. A distant relative of James Buchanan and a close friend of William Marcy, who had served as Secretary of State, she and her spouse were suspected not only of designs on the Dominican Republic but also Cuba and Latin America as a whole. The Cazneaus represented a dangerous trend in U.S. foreign policy—i.e. the merger of imperialism with private greed—in that they would benefit tremendously if Hispaniola were to be annexed by dint of their immense real estate investments there.[169]

The problem in the execution of their scheme was the color quotient of the Dominican population, which was viewed with both skepticism and hostility on the mainland. One Manhattan journal looked askance at the melanin content of the population, a viewpoint bound to be expanded upon beyond this cosmopolitan center.[170] On the other hand, Dominicans thought their homeland was destined to return to slavery under U.S. domination,[171] an opinion that stood as a stumbling block to annexation. London did not help matters by floating the rumor that the United States would work with Haiti—somehow—to liquidate the lighter-skinned within the Dominican Republic.[172]

As things evolved, the Spanish takeover was short-lived. Dominicans—assisted by Haiti—rose in revolt to chase out the invaders from Madrid. At the same time, the emigration of U.S. Negroes to Haiti did not go as well as it could have, with many being forced to return to the mainland. The mainland secessionists too were defeated and the enslaving republic perished. Emerging from the ashes of defeat was a now resurgent mainland republic, quite ready to replace a Spanish annexation with one of its own.

10

Haiti to Be Annexed and Reenslaved?
1863–1870

The island endured a head-spinning turn of events between 1860 and 1870—from the Spanish annexation of the D.R. that ultimately failed to the attempted U.S. annexation that also failed. Haiti opposed both of these efforts not only because of the undesirability of having such powerful neighbors so nearby but also because there were many in Port-au-Prince who had not been reconciled to the 1844 secession and longed to reunite the two nations. As one Haitian editorialist wrote, the Spanish cession meant "slavery within seven leagues of the capital of the republic."[1] This challenge to Haitian sovereignty, this Spanish control of two-thirds of Hispaniola, was to last—not coincidentally—for a good deal of the length of the U.S. Civil War.[2]

Dominican patriot Ulises Espaillat was among those who denounced the Spanish takeover, a maneuver—from Santo Domingo's side—that was driven by "anti-Haytian feeling." He argued that "four fifths of the territory which comprised" his nation wanted "independence" instead. He demanded that the United States "interpose its good offices with the Spanish" to restore Dominican "autonomy"[3]—but the mainland, then convulsed in civil war, was hardly in an advantageous position to intervene, which is precisely why Spain moved when it did.

Britain too tended to oppose both annexations, while France leaned inconsistently in that direction. In the prelude to the first failed annexation, Santo Domingo's policy was insufficiently nimble to the point where acceding to a Spanish takeover seemed to be the only alternative to acceding to a Haitian takeover. British subjects from the Turks and Caicos Islands continued arriving in Puerto Plata—and continued to complain about "depredations" visited upon them.[4] Why, complained the British envoy in Santo Domingo, on the anniversary of Dominican independence, was "the French national flag" hoisted "above the flags" of his nation and the United States' too?[5] When tariffs were increased on foreign imports, redress was provided to those from France—but not Britain.[6] This was a slap at abolitionist London, still perceived as pro-Haiti, and a slap at Washington because of its color-obsessed policy that seemed to preclude a warming tie with Santo Domingo.

Thus, the U.S. State Department was forced to apologize for the real and imagined misdeeds of its Santo Domingo envoy and the "just displeasure" and "improper conduct" he had perpetrated.[7] The envoy, Jonathan Elliot, responded by bemoaning the "personal violence" and "insults" that had been inflicted upon him.[8] Elliot declared that his "wife" was "attacked" and "threatened" by "the most insulting language." Elliot also requested documents for passage for his family and "servants"[9]—and it was unclear if the latter term was simply a euphemism for slaves, which was part of the problem he had with Santo Domingo.

D.R. forces were accused repeatedly of such transgressions. "A great outrage has been committed" near Samaná and Puerto Plata, it was said in 1857, as "lives were threatened by the lawless mob," and Her Majesty's subjects were "thankful to escape with their lives."[10] This was followed by a D.R. "vessel of war" detaining a British schooner near Samaná that reputedly carried "munitions of war."[11] By 1858 there was yet another accusation of British "ships of war" carrying "contraband of war," leading to the "imprisonment of the master and crew."[12] U.S. vessels were detained too.[13] British vessels were also charged with receiving on board deserters from the Dominican Republic[14] and there were complaints of British mail being intercepted.[15] Though London's delegate argued that a Jamaican detained in the Dominican Republic was actually campaigning against Haiti, Santo Domingo was unconvinced.[16] At the same time, the states that were to comprise Germany were increasingly seeking to exhibit their own unique influence.[17]

Either for humanitarian reasons or to halt the weakening of the island, which would have made it more susceptible to being annexed by a competitor, London pressed repeatedly for an end to the hostilities between the Dominican Republic and Haiti. "A cessation of Civil War"—a concept that seemed to suggest that this was not a conflict between competing sovereigns—was demanded by London, along with an end to the "horrors" and "unnecessary bloodshed."[18] Both Haiti and the Dominican Republic were said by London's envoys to have "committed . . . depredations . . . on the frontiers." Yet, perhaps since Santo Domingo was more prone to enter the embrace of a major power—Spain—it was that nation that was at the receiving end of Britain's choicest barbs.[19]

Why was there so much contestation and contention over a relatively small nation, the Dominican Republic and the island itself? A New Yorker, W. S.

Courtney, provides one answer. He had arrived in the Dominican Republic in 1860 in order to promote an annexation that was seen as following that of Texas. "The island of St. Domingo," he remarked rhapsodically, "is *one immense gold field* from one extremity to the other," a massive lode made all the more valuable since the population then was estimated to be a mere 120,000. It seemed "scarcely credible," said the bedazzled writer, that "such vast wealth, and especially mineral wealth, should have lain there so easily attainable for so many years" without "exciting at least the cupidity, if not the enterprise of the Yankee." He peremptorily dismissed the idea "that the Government and people are jealous of foreigners, especially from the United States," though there was considerable evidence pointing in an opposing direction. Taking Samaná was a goal of his: "here all the navies of the world could lay at anchor in safety," he mused.[20] Another eager U.S. investor seemed to salivate when contemplating the "quicksilver mine" and "salt mine" of the Dominican Republic; the "natural resources of this country," said A. K. Shepard, "afford numerous avenues to wealth." With satisfaction, he concluded, "nothing is wanting to render St. Domingo the 'Queen of the Antilles.'"[21] Petroleum was also said to be sited in the Dominican Republic.[22] Unfortunately for abolitionist islanders, George Bickley, a leader of the maniacally pro-slavery Knights of the Golden Circle, had substantial investments in mines on the island.[23]

It was not just the notorious Bickley who chose to pay attention to the Dominican Republic. The fire-eating Edmund Ruffin sought an audience with William Cazneau in 1858, calling on him at his hotel and remembering darkly about the revolutionary era when "all the whites were either killed or fled the country." Like his compatriots, Ruffin was suspicious of Dominican leaders: Buenaventura Báez was a "dark mulatto" and Pedro Santana was "mostly white but part Indian"—discrediting characteristics in his view. "Social equality" reigned there, he said with a huff, adding, opportunistically, "no doubt the whites, & even the colored population, would be very glad to have Americans to settle there, or even to be annexed to this country, for protection against the Haytian blacks." Lest Santo Domingo get too excited with this idea, he asserted, "amalgamation with this black and mongrel race is out of the question." He scorned Paris and London, which "have systematically and shamefully aided the Black power by their influence," and have "as much as possible worked to produce internal dissensions among the Dominicans to promote the Negro ascendancy." "These glorious portions of the earth," he insisted, "cannot always remain as they are under Negro population & power." Looking ahead to the advent of secession, this Dixie patriot predicted that with this eventuality, "it would not be difficult to extend our power & our race, as masters, over Hayti." As for the Africans there, "all having property, or other means for the purpose, might be permitted to leave the island—& all of the destitute, who are in fact now slaves to their rulers, might be made slaves to individuals." Sure, there would be objection to this "reenslavement"—but he shrugged off this concern.[24]

Nonetheless, while London and Santo Domingo (and the United States and the Dominican Republic) were trading accusations, relations between Madrid and Santo Domingo were steadily improving. Spain had little hesitation in referring to the "enemies," meaning Haitians; besides, Spain and the Dominican Republic were said to be united in "blood" and "language" as well as in "customs" and "religion." Spain defending the Dominican Republic was said to be the equivalent of defending its own interests.[25] This entente did not please London and the same could be said for a similar attempt to improve relations with Washington.[26] Still, Britain— and Haiti too—had more to fret about when it came to Santo Domingo and Spain for it remained difficult for the color-obsessed enslaving republic to improve relations with the Dominican Republic.[27]

Thus, though Washington and Santo Domingo both had problems with Port- au-Prince, it was hard for the two to unite on that basis when—as occurred in 1858—the U.S. delegate denounced "insults" that had been "offered not only to its Commercial Agent but to its Flag"; such "complaints . . . existed for a long period," involving "injuries" and "acts of violence." It was demanded that the U.S. flag "be saluted with . . . twenty one guns."[28] Santo Domingo did not agree and "night after night" there were "serious demonstrations" in front of the U.S. legation "by a collection of persons with abuse and threats," said the U.S. envoy.[29]

Not coincidentally, it was in the spring of 1861—when mainland secession was proclaimed—that Eustis Hubbard, who represented the United States in Port-au- Prince, told the Secretary of State that "on the 18th [of] March the Dominican government hoisted the Spanish flag and delivered the country to Spain." Hubbard observed that "Porto Plata and St. Iago are reported to be indignant and rebellious" and Haiti was irate, "inciting the Dominican people to revolt and promising them aid and arms." Spain, he said, acted with the "silent assent of England and France"—though this was not the consensus view.[30] Still, this is what Washington was told more than once: "The deliver of the country to the Spaniards," said Arthur Folsom, "was brought about by English & French machinations."[31]

The conflict between London and Santo Domingo seemed to be made to order for an encroachment by Washington on the island, but the reputation garnered by the United States—justifiably—for racism or worse (including the possibility of reenslaving the island) complicated bilateral relations mightily. Still, as civil war was about to rock the mainland, the more aggressive elements in Washington were inebriated with dreams that soared beyond an improvement in bilateral relations:

first taking Cuba, then the Dominican Republic, and incorporating both as slave states. A self-described "White man" observed that the "breeding slave states of America might possibly for a time prove sufficient to provide the newly-acquired state with slave labour; for it is no less notorious than true, that existing treaties with the United States, although forbidding the importation of slaves from 'the coast' do not discountenance the traffic amongst Americans in their own states."[32]

In short, the seizure of these islands—which particularly in the case of Cuba had a well-developed infrastructure for slave trading—would allow a wide-open back door through which more enslaved Africans could be brought to the mainland itself and to Hispaniola too. When the newly appointed Captain General in Santo Domingo was compelled in March 1863 to deny the charge that "Spain intended to make you slaves," he reflected an unease amongst the populace that would also make a U.S. annexation problematic.[33]

This plot to take Hispaniola first had to contend with ousting Spain from Hispaniola. By early 1863 London was objecting to the policy of barring "celebration" of "any religion which is not the Roman Catholic," a mandate that was noticeably unpopular in Puerto Plata and Samaná, where U.S. Negro emigrants proliferated.[34] John Horne Darrell, a Wesleyan missionary there, recounted how Negro Protestants from the mainland had arrived with the assurance that religious liberty would reign. When other missionaries arrived in the 1830s, they too enjoyed a tolerant atmosphere and this continued even after the 1844 secession. Freedom of belief was then confirmed in a treaty between the England and the Dominican Republic in 1850. By 1863 there were at least 1200 Protestants in the vicinity who felt threatened when the authorities vowed to "employ armed force" to shut down their churches.[35] Days later the Dominican Republic was in an uproar of revolt, with many fleeing to Haiti, and Samaná particularly faced "disturbance."[36] Soon there were stories emerging about the "total destruction" of Puerto Plata by the Spaniards, who "pillaged the town and shot several coloured people."[37]

There were also reports of a "serious fire" on the island that "completely destroyed the Custom House and the principal mercantile establishments." There was a lack of clarity as to whether this was an "intentional and premeditated act of incendiarism" with a "political purpose." The alternative explanation—that what was involved was simple "plunder"—was not assuring either.[38]

Tellingly, it was London—not Washington—that looked after the interests of U.S. Negro emigrants. These emigrants, it was said, "always have been considered natives of the country" since their arrival; this was evidenced by the fact that since 1844 "they all served either in the Army or Navy." Yes, they were "Protestants," who "have regularly attended worship at the British Chapel." But since the annexation by Spain, they were all "disenfranchised." In fact, it was ruled that "no Protestant can be a subject of the Queen of Spain." Now as their former homeland was wracked with the bloodletting of civil war, they were "in the extraordinary position of having no country at all."³⁹

While Spain was engaging in religious intolerance, Frederick Douglass saluted the "religious toleration" of Haiti. It was "Dessalines," he pointed out with a lack of irony, who "completed the extinction of the whites" and "first proclaimed the doctrine of religious toleration."⁴⁰

Unfortunately, religious intolerance was not limited to Madrid. Martin Hood, the British envoy on the island, thought that his predecessor, David Leon— "formerly a merchant" but "now in a hopeless state of bankruptcy"—was also a "very vain man . . . striving always to please." It was "this failing" which "induced him to make himself most agreeable to the Spanish authorities since the annexation" of the Dominican Republic. This might have been influenced by his being "of the Hebrew persuasion" and, thus, "willing to sacrifice" the "interests" of Protestants.⁴¹

Though anti-Madrid attitudes may have been most intense among these U.S. Negro emigrants, this mindset had spread from there. Agriculturalists, whose numbers overlapped with emigrants, were upset when Madrid mandated the relinquishing of the ubiquitous machete, which was viewed as a third arm on the island. Hood reported that their discontent was magnified by the rumor that this disarmament was part of a larger plot to "make slaves of the Blacks."⁴² Over and over again, Spain had to proclaim that it was not "possible to re-establish slavery" for "Her Majesty has declared this system abolished forever in this Province."⁴³

When the story emerged that U.S. agents had arrived on the island to destabilize Spanish rule, it was unclear if these emigrants should celebrate their impending liberation—or, alternatively, worry that they had moved closer to re-enslavement. "There will be a revolution provoked by these agents," said Hood in July 1862, "followed by an appeal from the Dominicans to the Federal Government" demanding "annexation" by the United States. Then "American ships of war" will appear to seal the deal. Hood was unsure if their activity was actually sanctioned by Washington, then in a death match for survival. And, since at this juncture neither side in the war was explicitly abolitionist, emigrants on the island had more reason to worry.⁴⁴

London thought that Santo Domingo was so disgusted with Spanish misrule and so fearful of a Haitian return that it would be more than willing to bow to Washington. With a rare prescience, Hood foresaw that a victorious United States would seek to "throw into this island all the Blacks of whom they wish to rid themselves" in order "to outnumber the native population" and "that in the course of a few years it will be in reality an American state." Port-au-Prince was on board with this project, he said—a mistaken assumption. It was true that the United States lusted for "the Bay and Town of 'Le Mole St. Nicholas,'" which were a "direct menace to the Spanish colonies of Cuba and Puerto Rico." Then there was the "startling intelligence" that at a time when it was not clear that Washington would prevail militarily during the Civil War, it was arming anti-Madrid rebels in the Dominican Republic.[45]

It was "startling" that, just as France took advantage of the Civil War to seize Mexico and Spain to seize the Dominican Republic, Washington itself too had yet to abandon plans of territorial expansion though its very existence was then threatened, as if some kind of deep-seated instinct was operative. For, according to a close colleague of Hood, the U.S. plan was to take "all the West Indies" as "soon as they have done with their own troubles in the Southern States"; at that point, "they will give immediate attention with their large military and naval forces to Mexico and the West Indies." Dominicans were so disgusted with Spain that they were willing to welcome Washington—"or even [a] Haitian" return.[46]

Perhaps because of the fright that Spain would seek to make the Dominican Republic an enslaved twin of Cuba, Dominicans were said to fight like "supernatural fiends" with a "desperate" intensity. It would require "complete and absolute extermination" by Spain to put down the rebellion; it was a "war of races and colour" and a civil war besides, "in evidence of which" is "the fact that many Dominicans have been put to death by the insurgents themselves," said Hood.[47] Adding to the complexity was the point that, by December 1863, Hood was mulling the possibility that Spain should retain control of the Dominican Republic as "an effectual check on American ambition."[48] What may have motivated this surprising turnabout was Hood's realization that a leader of the insurgents, "with a large sum of money," was headed to Manhattan to purchase "arms and ammunition,"[49] which doubtlessly was destined to bring increased U.S. influence.

This also seemed to be prophecy when by early 1864 a U.S. diplomat, who was "actively engaged in American propaganda," was headed to the Dominican Republic with the "avowed intention" of forming a liaison with the anti-Madrid rebels. If they agreed to U.S. terms, said Hood, the United States would provide "money, men, and arms"; a U.S. "schooner destined to become a Dominican privateer . . . actually left New York laden with arms and ammunition" and was headed for the island—with official "sanction."[50]

By 1864 it appeared that Dixie would not prevail, which further emboldened its opponents. France was preoccupied in Mexico,[51] though it cocked an eye to the attack on Vermont launched from its former colony, Quebec.[52] Britain was tied up with a revolt in Jamaica that Paris also monitored.[53] And Spain was bleeding profusely in the Dominican Republic All of this should have been good news for Haiti—except it was undergoing severe political strain too.

As Spanish rule was decomposing, Jane Cazneau continued to gloat about the "many immigrants" expected in Santo Domingo and the timber there that could be useful in designing a small town. Hoping against hope, she continued to contend that "liberty of conscience" would obtain on the island, as the lack of which would serve as a disincentive to emigration. She maintained that "the Bethel Church, a congregation of respectable and well-to-do colored people from the United States, has had its building made over [by] the Spanish Government. The house was an old government office and until now was only lent to the congregation, but henceforth it will belong to it in absolute property." She concluded by observing that "Santo Domingo has been very sickly this summer, but the country is healthy"[54]—but that did not seem to apply in her description of Puerto Plata, where U.S. Negro emigrants had flocked.

She continued to prepare propaganda hyping emigration "for circulation among [those] in the border states." Cazneau was optimistic about success in this regard since "Spain is on her very best behavior in St. Domingo" with "all sorts of liberal encouragements and ample toleration for farmers & mechanics." Spanish annexation, she contended, had caused a five-fold increase in land prices. Whereas "well situated sugar and coffee lands bring from $30 to $50 an acre in Cuba, this island has more good cotton tracts up among the hills [than] Cuba & Porto Rico put together. That item is what has settled us here."[55]

Though the Cazneaus were ostensibly U.S. agents, they proved to be quite comfortable with the new status quo inaugurated by Spanish annexation. This was due largely to the fact that this couple gave priority to profiteering, which could be accommodated by Washington—or Madrid. "I know better than the State Department itself many of the most important and controlling facts" about the region, which also meant that she did not feel duty-bound to follow the rules as articulated in Washington. "I handled the preliminaries of the Texas annexation movement," she boasted, and "would like to do the same with the new issue of the Antilles now looming." She added that it should be done in league with the Manhattan press, which would be able to "run up its own circulation at the same time" in the bargain.[56] William Cazneau was her match as an adventurer, but she had an advantage. When Randolph Keim met him en route to the Dominican Republic, he found the freelance diplomat had "extreme deafness—quite a convenience for confidential consultation."[57]

By the time she had penned this previous message, Spain had been ousted and the Cazneaus pivoted smoothly toward backing annexation by the United

States. The Dixie secessionists were scrambling to avoid Spain's fate and thought they could continue to play upon Gallic sentiments still smarting over the loss of Hispaniola decades earlier. For it was in early 1865, when Confederate defeat seemed just a matter of time, that Louisiana governor Henry Allen contacted "His Majesty the Emperor of the French." Allen told him that "my state was once a portion of France" and, now, "all look to you" in our "hour of need." For the "descendants of those daring Frenchmen who brought the flag of France to Louisiana & settled this state now appeal to you as did the Christians of Syria, as did Turkey, as did Italy, as did Mexico." Now "if the armies of the North are permitted to overrun the Southern States, they will march triumphantly over the ruins of the Confederacy to the conquest of Mexico. The destiny of these states is deeply interwoven with the integrity of the Mexican Empire. They are coterminous for a thousand miles" after all and Washington "seeks the destruction of both." "I know we have your sympathy," he added unnecessarily. He did not add, however, that if France had come to his rescue, this would have preserved slavery and further portended revanchist policies toward Hispaniola.[58] For even before Allen's démarche, a Savannah journal had suggested that Haiti be brought into the Union and this was before slavery was abolished.[59] It was in 1855 that Martin R. Delany scorned the "deep seated scheme for the invasion of Hayti."[60]

Allen's appeal reaped no immediate dividends though Delany's fear remained real by 1865. Chasing Spain from the Dominican Republic only returned Santo Domingo to the *status quo ante*, i.e. what to do about Haiti? One leader in eastern Hispaniola feared that the restoration of local rule in this vast territory would only serve to "throw the Dominicans into the arms of the Negroes," meaning the Haitians. "I announce it here," he said, "that in that land which we were the first to discover, the European race, the white race, the Spanish race will be destroyed" as a result.[61] This marked the heightening of the movement to save Santo Domingo from Haiti with yet another annexation: this one by the United States.

Spain's ouster and the military defeat of Dixie secessionists reanimated long-held plans of a U.S. takeover of the Dominican Republic It was not just the Cazneaus who stood to benefit for also poised to profit was another U.S. national, Joseph Fabens, who was accorded certain ill-defined "mineralogical" rights. His compatriot, John O'Sullivan, got a concession for "mail steamers" and another mainlander received guano and railway rights.[62]

This is the backdrop for one of the more troubling incidents of that entire era: the evident attempt by Franco-American Antonio Pelletier to land a vessel illicitly in Haiti for the purpose of capturing Africans for enslavement in Cuba—or perhaps the mainland itself.

The accused, a native of France, was naturalized in the United States in 1852. By March 1861, he was in Haitian waters and would be tried and imprisoned because of his effort to effectuate Haiti's worst nightmare: reenslavement. He was sentenced to be shot, along with his crew, but the high court in Haiti reversed the judgment and he was retried and sentenced to five years' imprisonment.

In 1860 Pelletier bought a vessel at Key West, which happened to be a condemned slaver. He sailed to Mobile, where he loaded lumber, and then to Cartagena by November. Pelletier was a partner in a cotton merchant firm, which made him seem even more suspicious. In any case, a revolt was in progress so he was detained there for two weeks. Upon departure, he took aboard Juan Cortez and his family and others, but wind blew them off course to the Caymans where they arrived by mid-December. Also taken aboard was Binar, a "colored man, a political refugee" from Cartagena, who became a principal witness against him. Then he sailed for Haiti to dispose of goods but encountered difficulty. He also claimed later that he was headed to Navassa for guano. He left for New Orleans before landing at Puerto Plata—or, at least, that's where he thought he had landed. He raised a small French flag as a signal for help, then entered the port where he was stunned to see a Haitian flag flying. Apparently, he thought he was in Puerto Plata, raising the tantalizing possibility that he was bent on snatching U.S. Negro emigrants. (Yes, said Pelletier, there were "single instances of successfully kidnapping free persons" and selling them—but this would be "utterly impossible" with Haitians.)

He then thought that he should feign that his vessel was French (he spoke this language, among others)—though why he thought this would provide protection (instead of savaging) was not apparent. A member of his crew later testified that "there is hardly a vessel that sails out of the United States that does not carry three or four different flags." However, this same witness said when the Haitian authorities boarded the vessel and saw a U.S. flag, one of their number "spoke in English" and said, "S—t [sic] on your American flag." There Pelletier's problems accelerated, culminating in the verdict of guilty. Subsequently he argued that a crew member suggested that he fly the French flag and to tell the Haitians who inquired that he was bound from Havana to Le Havre but encountered distress.

Upon being detained, outraged Haitians expressed their wrath by pelting him with dirt and stones. Like an exhibit, he was paraded—and lacerated with knives. There was a "savage multitude of thousands surrounding us" and "we left a trail of blood."

This was in Cap-Haïtien, though it was repeated in Port-au-Prince. He was marched the lengthy distance between the two cities, being beaten and mangled during the entire course. He claimed that there was an attempt to poison him. He

refused to eat after a while since an African jailed with him consumed offered food—
"and in half an hour he was dead." He claimed that he was tortured and subjected
to "insults and violence from the populace." Thrown in a dungeon, he asserted
that "small boys were permitted to beat out" his "eyes with sticks for their amuse-
ment." He was tied to a tree and "about a dozen soldiers with muskets" menaced
him. Tellingly, the U.S. crew members were treated worse than others, subjected to
torture and bound in irons.

Benjamin Whidden, appointed by President Lincoln as consul to Haiti in 1862
found Pelletier to be in "wretched, miserable condition; his flesh had been eaten"
by "maggots" and there were "sores on his body." He was "emaciated," "pallid,"
and "ghostly." But damagingly, he also conceded that aboard Pelletier's vessel were
documents indicating that he was "bound for a place on the African coast" and also
planned to journey to Cuba.

The Haitian side asked pointedly why his vessel contained at least twenty pairs
of handcuffs, a sizeable quantity of arms and ammunition, empty casks, provisions in abundance, woolen blankets in great number, and a false deck suitable for
blocking prying eyes. (The accused said there were only "eight pairs" of handcuffs
aboard and a mere "eight water casks," not "over a hundred" as charged.) "I have
no doubt," said Haiti's consul, "that the intention of Captain Pelletier was to induce
a number of Haytiens to go on board of his vessel . . . and then make his escape
with them and sell them into slavery." This was not conjecture since a member of
his crew, his chief mate, said as much. His goal was to grab 150 men to sell in Cuba.
Haiti was not prone to be merciful. By 1823 Haitian courts, acting upon a similar
question, had laid down the general principle that there should be no mercy in suppressing piracy.

A disappointed Pelletier was distraught at what he perceived as a lack of effort
by his government to rescue him. That "white men," his "own race," were "to
be sacrificed by the colored race" was the dilemma he felt he faced. He appealed
for protection from the representatives of "all civilized governments," as he "was
suffering in behalf of all white men." The United States, distracted by civil war
and desiring access to Haitian ports, was reluctant to intervene and the so-called
Confederate States of America were unwilling to be seen as aiding a slave dealer.
Moreover, Britain, France, the Netherlands, Spain, Prussia, Austria, Norway, and
Sweden all turned their backs on him. In fact, Seth Webb, the U.S. envoy, suspected that Pelletier was an agent of the Confederacy and suspected further that
a plan was afoot to seize his vessel by stealth and convert it into a privateer to be
wielded against the United States. In any case, the U.S. consul was said to be compromised since he was married to the "mulatto" [*sic*] daughter of a Haitian official.

By November 1862, Haiti had been recognized by the United States and Pelletier thought his plight would improve. It was at that point that a crew member wrote President Lincoln. "I got my letter smuggled out," he said later. By then, Thomas Collar was "about naked" and "barefooted and bareheaded" besides in a dank cell. This gambit worked. He was released, arriving in Manhattan by December 1862, but he had difficulty adjusting: "I could not stand it; I had not seen cold weather for ten years." He had returned to Haiti by early January where he espied Pelletier who was "nothing but skin and bones. I took him some tobacco; I knew he was a great smoker."

But as the Emancipation Proclamation was signaling a new birth of freedom on the mainland, Pelletier chose to emulate that example. For on 11 November 1863 at 10 p.m. he scaled the wall of the hospital where he was confined and fled to the French legation where he stayed for thirty-six hours, before repairing to the British legation for a similar length of time. And by 14 November he was on a Spanish steamer headed to Kingston, Jamaica, arriving two days later. By 1864 he was in the United States where he launched a lawsuit that would last decades and poison the well of bilateral relations.

Pelletier, who was born in Fontainebleau, was a man of affluence, having been involved in the Australian trade previously. Most of his crew were born in France and, given the charges and Haitian history, this was an uncomfortable combination. At the trial in Port-au-Prince, lines of inquiry suggested that after snatching Haitians, the vessel would then sail to the slave emporium that was New Orleans. One crew member confessed that he sought to use his "influence to dissuade Pelletier from his intended slave trade." This trial—from 26–30 August 1861—culminated in jurists conferring for four hours before pronouncing a death sentence.

The chief defendant was also damaged when a carpenter on board confirmed that their purpose was to kidnap Haitians and sell them in Dixie. That the vessel in question had formerly been engaged in the slave trade, including voyages to Africa, did not help the case of the accused. That his arrival in Hispaniola also coincided with an ongoing dispute of the accused with the son-in-law of Haiti's president did not help his cause either.

Pelletier was a man of means, the owner of several patents for the manufacture of shoes by machinery. This work was conducted in Troy, New York, though he was pushing to move this business to Cuba. In 1860 he was in Havana in pursuit of this goal—though it was not manifest if he planned to use slave labor there. In Chicago he had investments in distilleries. While imprisoned in Haiti he forfeited many of these holdings, including land in Iowa.

The affluent Pelletier was also a currency trader, obtaining silver coins from France and, as the Iowa example suggested, a major landowner, confessing to owning "650,000 acres of land" in western Virginia. He was also a major stockholder in the "Panama Telegraph Company," had coal interests in Central America too, and speculated in gold besides. He had an office at 98 Wall Street in Manhattan and a residence in New Rochelle. He also conducted major business with "cotton brokers" and that was a connection that convinced many Haitians of his ill intent.[63]

Ernest Roumain, newly installed at the Haitian legation in Washington, declared that the "real object" of the Pelletier "expedition" was the "slave trade and piracy in the seas & on the coast of Africa." Upon arriving in Haiti, Pelletier gave his name as "Jules Latelleir" and pretended to be recruiting crew—but actually those so duped were "destined to be taken off and sold in Cuba." This was not "conjecture" and it was confirmed by his crew, who said the goal was to dragoon 150 enslaved men for Cuba.[64] Victorin Pleasance, Haiti's leading diplomat, was told that while in Cartagena, Pelletier had engaged in fraud and other sharp practices, adding to the image that he would not be above human trafficking.[65] Pelletier's lack of support was ratified when Haitian-based envoys from France, Holland, Denmark, Italy, Austria, and Norway concurred that Pelletier should face punishment.[66]

The U.S. envoy, Eustis Hubbard, was similarly dismissive of Pelletier, referring contemptuously to his "illegitimate voyage." The "proof" was "strong" that he was a "slaver." Indeed, "in consequence of his highly suspicious activities," Hubbard did "not deem it . . . [his] duty to interfere with the Haitian authorities" and, besides, "his assertions are notoriously untrue." "I have no doubt," said the emissary, that Pelletier planned to "sell [Haitians] into slavery." As for his crew, they too were suspect and were "composed of the refuse of all nations."[67] Addressing Pelletier directly with venom, Hubbard said that the would-be enslaver was "perfectly aware" that he was on the coast of Haiti and that he had seen Pelletier's ships with his "own eyes."[68]

Henry Byron of the British legation in Haiti viewed Pelletier's claims with skepticism, pointing to the "slave deck" on his vessel and the "suspicious circumstances" of his arrival in Hispaniola. Byron also noted the fact that "his vessel was here denounced as a slaver by the crew and passengers on board of her" and his general "temerity."[69]

This case, says the historian Rayford Logan, "occasioned the longest dispute in the history of the relations between the United States and Haiti." It concluded ironically with Pelletier—a presumptive slave trader—being defended aggressively by the U.S. envoy to Haiti (the African-American John Mercer Langston) who pledged in 1879 that "no effort on my part shall be spared to bring his case to a speedy and just settlement." In a manner redolent of the Haitian indemnity paid to France, Pelletier was awarded compensation.[70]

The news got worse for Haiti, as far as the United States was concerned. In 1868 the Negro-phobic Andrew Johnson stated in his annual address to Congress that the "annexation of the two republics of the island of St. Domingo" was his goal.[71] This ambition, which would have effectively liquidated the sovereignty established by Black Jacobins, was barely checked by Congress—though it effectively helped to squash the promise of revolution. Many Haitians mourned the passing of Abraham Lincoln and Johnson gave them further reason for doing so.[72]

President Johnson's anti-Negro policies had external backing. Though Spain had been ousted from the Dominican Republic, Madrid continued to pose a problem for Negroes in that credible reports emerged of arms being distributed from its consulate in New Orleans to ultra-conservatives determined to block Negro voting and political activism.[73] That may shed light on why the soon-to-be Negro congressman John Willis Menard visited Haiti.[74] Perhaps, as a result, Negro solidarity with Haiti did not cease after the deposing of Geffrard. In fact, one periodical proclaimed that his successor, Sylvain Salnave, was "without any exception, the most popular ruler in the world"; doubters were told bluntly, "the fact is beyond question" since "even [George] Washington was not made president with such universal spontaneity of choice."[75]

For those who cited Haiti as a negative example of abolition, another Negro journal asserted that "with all her civil contentions and internal revolution," Haiti "cannot compare for anarchy, changes of government, and periodic rebellions with Mexico and the South American republics."[76] Negro pride was bursting when a Haitian battleship—"with a colored commander and crew," it was noted pointedly—arrived in Norfolk and "attracted general attention."[77] There was a material basis for this interest for, it was noted in May 1865, that "two-thirds of all the commerce of this island" was "American trade."[78]

Yet despite this evident enthusiasm for Haiti among U.S. Negroes—a fervor that had begun decades earlier—these beneficiaries of the Civil War did not stand united in opposition to annexation, which in President Johnson's own words could incorporate Haiti. This was even more striking in light of the mass opposition to annexation on the island—and not just in Haiti.[79] What was occurring was that the population to be known as "African American" was learning an early and bitter lesson of citizenship: support imperial ventures or run the risk of being demonized as unpatriotic, a charge not easily dismissed. After all, it was only recently that, as slaves, this group had become well-known for its backing of abolitionist London, a certified foe for decades of enslaving Washington.

Haiti, by way of contrast, was unreserved in its hostility to annexation, reminding the United States that it had "the freedmen question" to deal with. This should occupy its attention and, thus, "leave to the island of Hayti its whole territory. It is necessary to the men of African race who, perhaps soon, will not be able any longer to reside in the territory of the United States [to have] a refuge which Haiti alone can offer them"—so, leave the island "intact." Washington should recognize, said Port-au-Prince, that "not only justice but self interest" dictated such a result.[80]

Samaná, again, was at issue and numerous Dominicans too were not favorable to giving up this valuable site. Samaná, forty-five miles in length and twelve miles wide at its greatest width, was a prize that the United States desired to hold in a lease arrangement for up to fifty years—or in perpetuity—for the sum of one million silver coins annually—plus armament, which could be used to menace Haiti.[81] (Another proposal was a lease of Samaná at an annual cost of $100,000.[82]) The importance of Samaná was clearly signaled when Secretary of State Seward journeyed there in 1866 in pursuit of this potential base.[83]

London was told that the United States not only wanted "acquisition" of Samaná but also "annexation" of the whole of the Dominican Republic—which was an accurate perception.[84] In a "confidential" report, the Foreign Office in London was informed that "Samaná is to the Gulf of Mexico what Mayotte is to the Indian Ocean. It is not only the military but also the commercial key of the Gulf." Hence, London wanted—minimally—"neutrality" for Samaná.[85]

Washington was determined to disappoint London. It was in early 1868 that the U.S. president requested "transfer of the peninsula and bay of Samaná to the United States." In return Santo Domingo wanted "munitions of war" so as to better confront Haiti. Besides, said Secretary of State Seward, the Dominican Republic was "very liberal in granting privileges to parties desiring to explore and work the numerous and valuable mines" there and, as well, had "a soil unsurpassed in the West Indies." There were "coal mines" in Samaná too, just waiting to be exploited. The "naval station" there commanded "the transit from Europe to the Gulf of Mexico through the Mona Passage." It was not irrelevant that during the recent Spanish occupation "the adjacent Republic of Hayti was menaced." And given Port-au-Prince's historic tendency to see itself as a kind of defender of Africans in the hemisphere, this potential challenge to U.S. sovereignty could not be ignored either. It was only recently that the Dominican Republic and Haiti agreed that neither would "alienate any portion of its territories"—that the proposed Samaná cession contravened—but that treaty was "not absolutely concluded" in Seward's estimation.[86] Seward had fewer qualms about the legality of what Santo Domingo had told him, i.e. "the fulfillment of this Treaty" between the Dominican Republic and the United States on

Samaná "shall be determined by the Supreme Court" of the United States to which the Dominican Republic "will delegate . . . full powers"[87]—an effective liquidation of sovereignty and a precursor to annexation.

Prominent residents of Cibao renounced the authority of those in Santo Domingo in opposition to the Samaná deal.[88] The leading Dominican personality, Gregorio Luperón, objected to giving up Samaná. He argued that the "majority of our people" agreed that the proposal should be made "null and void" and that it would "threaten the Republic of Hayti" if enacted.[89] This Santo Domingo well knew. In fact, days before Luperón's warning, his Dominican opponent, M. M. Gautier, told a U.S. investor, Joseph Fabens, that "already the Haytians . . . [have begun] to be alarmed in consequences of the report that you have powers to treat for annexation."[90]

Yet by late 1869, U.S. agents were satisfied that all was "quiet" in Samaná, as "both native and those of American descent," meaning U.S. Negroes, "are well satisfied with the proposed change of sovereignty." After the American flag was raised there, a confident Joseph Fabens strolled to the Wesleyan Chapel, where these U.S. Negroes congregated. They had "suffered much," he said unctuously, but were now recovering from the Spanish scourge. As he counted, the "population of the town is about 300" with "1500 on the peninsula" and of those "about 600 are colored persons of American descent."[91]

This list of opponents also included J. B. Zafra, who told his fellow politicos that the constitution of their homeland "forbids the alienation of territory." Ironically, this principle was sanctified in the "treaty of peace concluded" with Haiti—in which it was pledged "not to cede to any nation the smallest particle of territory." For "to introduce a very powerful foreign state into our very weak Republic is to attack [our] independence and put our nationality in danger." This would be an "act of treason." And what of the "flood of men who will invade us through Samaná"? What would ensue would be a "war of caste from the day when a stranger to our language"—as well as our "color" and "religion"—"shall have come among us." Even a cursory glance at U.S. history suggested that "wherever there are whites, who hold the blacks in sovereign contempt, or blacks, who are just freed from slavery," the latter would be looked at with an "evil eye" by "those who are not of the same color." It was also a "declaration of war against the Haytien people" and would "deem us ever as traitors to our nationality." And it was "to declare war against European nations who hold possessions in America." It was already known that annexation would be followed by the mass expulsion of the newly freed mainland slave population. It was asked plaintively, "what then will [be] the future in a few years only of the three hundred thousand Dominicans of mixed breed who are neither white nor black?" Even if the entire island were not gobbled up, but simply Samaná, this latter site would become a "school of immorality" and a "place of refuge of all conspirators, the open door to the denationalization of the entire Republic and the supreme retaliation of the Spanish party"—i.e. a replay of 1861 when Madrid took over.[92]

What was stiffening the spine of those like Zafra was the adamant objection emanating from Haiti. Louis Achille de Pitti Fernandie, Haiti's consul in Manhattan, stridently protested the "selling" of island soil to the United States, agreeing that his nation's treaty with the Dominican Republic strictly forbade such a measure.[93] Yet undermining Haiti's stridency was a spate of reports that echoed events in recent decades. Attacks on U.S. nationals in Haiti were reported, though denied as "false" and "scandalous accusations invented by the enemies" of Port-au-Prince; those assaulted were said to be "naturalized Haytians," but this did little to curb the growing notion that at least a U.S. takeover would forestall such unwelcome attacks.[94]

But Haiti would have difficulty standing up to the United States given the instability there. Moreover, Haiti—as had been its historic pattern—was hardly opposed to an influx of U.S. Negroes, though harboring qualms about their being expelled from the mainland. One official from Haiti expressed "readiness to make amends to a race formerly oppressed," with the pending emigration thought to express "those noble principles" said to animate Washington. Port-au-Prince was pleased that in a rare gesture, a Negro had been posted to Haiti as an envoy to "represent the great and powerful" United States.[95] This conciliation may have been influenced by the fact that at the same time in Jacmel there was "protest" against a hostile act "committed by a ship of war under the American flag."[96]

In a pattern that would increase in coming decades, the United States had begun to play a more active role in Haitian affairs and, with the U.S. Negro population now nursing its tenuous citizenship, the latter was reluctant to object. Evariste La Roche of Haiti pointed accusingly to vessels then "repairing at Chester," Pennsylvania, that were "intended for the rebels in Haiti." He demanded this pro-rebel interference be stopped since the United States, which had "borne the ravages of civil war," i.e. the "Southern Rebellion," should be more sensitive to such blatant interference in the island's internal affairs.[97]

But these words fell on deaf ears and soon he was complaining again. This time it was about "F. W. Clapp," a merchant in Saint-Marc, who "fitted out the 'Mount Vernon' in one of the ports of Rhode Island" and then "sent the steamer to the rebels of St. Marc." Since the United States had just passed through "a terrible civil war," how could it tolerate this behavior? "Were they glad of the moral or material aid," La Roche asked, that "the whole of the South" was "receiving from Allied Powers"?[98]

No, the United States was not "glad" about past European aid to the secessionists, but it did not equate the island republic with the mainland republic. Besides, pressure on Haiti hampered the ability of Port-au-Prince to object too strenuously to the attempted seizure of Samaná or the entire island for that matter. Then there was the ongoing turmoil in Cuba that was washing over Haiti. One vessel had just changed her name and diverted from Cuba to Hispaniola in order, said the Haitian consul, to "aid the rebels in Haiti" and, to that end, was "equipped for warfare."[99]

Haiti also charged that in addition to its political aims, this aid to rebels was simple profiteering. "The profits made out of us by foreign brokers" for vessels and arms, said one Haitian leader, were "enormous"—"no wonder they want to see the contest keep up as long as possible & they benefit and we suffer." The vessels were old secessionist models, of which there were quite a few. Yes, the appointment of "some colored men to office" on the mainland was welcomed, but this kind of interference was eroding whatever goodwill had accrued.[100]

Then there was the ongoing problem of mainland profiteers flooding Haiti with counterfeit currency. There was a "vast organization abroad," said Haiti's delegate in Washington, centered on the mainland, that operated with impunity due to the nonfeasance of U.S. authorities. This corrupt praxis was "carried on" on a "grand scale" in the United States, as if it were a "legitimate branch of industry." This "piracy of a new kind" was "mainly carried on by American citizens on American soil," allowing the perpetrators to elude the long arm of the law in Haiti. This "does as much harm to my country," it was said, "as was done a few years ago by Southern privateers." This was a cruel payback. Indeed, during the Civil War, "while all the ports of the Antilles were, in a manner, closed to the United States, while a kind of hospitality was extended to the Confederate cruisers," Haiti—in virtual isolation—refused to go along.[101]

As Haiti saw things, while it had hastened to rebuff the secessionists, Port-au-Prince was now being treated shabbily, as if it had been an arm of Dixie. The proposed annexation, said Stephen Preston, Haiti's man in Washington, "has caused me deep and painful surprise" and was a "formal menace to the independence of Hayti." The United States had been "considered as our ally and as one that would, in case of necessity, protect us against the aggressions of European Powers." This, however, was not panning out: please "calm" our "legitimate anxieties," he implored.[102]

Washington proceeded otherwise. Preston noted nervously that Washington's "treaty to annex the *Island of San Domingo* (the name formerly given to Hayti by Europeans and still commonly used in the United States)" left the impression that his nation's sovereignty was up for grabs. This was a "formal menace to the independence of Hayti," he said accurately. Secretary of State Hamilton Fish did not assuage matters when he told Preston that the proposed treaty was "strictly and exclusively a domestic document" and, thus, his complaint was "premature"[103]— should Preston have waited until the treaty was a *fait accompli* and Haitian sovereignty was being strangled before objecting? Secretary of State Fish insisted that, since the United States was now abolitionist, there was little basis for Haitian objections to annexation.[104]

Other U.S. nationals were not as circumspect. Amandus Meyer of New York was already speculating on the island's "close connection" with the United States and its "willingness" to "acquiesce in a change of nationality." Haiti alone, he said, "would give us a foothold in the very center of the West Indies, commanding them all, better even than the larger island of Cuba, and offering in case of war a self supplying position." This would erode "English, French, and German competition" in a "perfect paradise on earth, however it may have been . . . ridiculed." This was reciprocal since, before the Civil War, the very name of the United States "had a bad sound to the ear of a Haytian." It was "under the softening influence of French mannerism" and accustomed to the "well mannered and unprejudiced French" and "German." Both powers, he noted, had become hostile to the United States and the latter barely contained the "rudest class of seamen," creating a "disagreeable impression." This was "further increased by the often undisguised dislike of the Negro as a race, expressed by degrading epithets and allusions to slavery." And this was "further increased by the general low moral standing of the official representative[s] of our government in that country," mere "pothouse politicians whom the government wished to get rid of and whom it was thought [were] good enough for the niggers."

But with the Civil War there had been a readjustment of the "domestic policy with regard to the Negro and slavery." Continued restiveness in Haiti itself and the "considerable influx of dissatisfied Jamaican emigrants settling in Hayti . . . [was] spontaneously aiding in disseminating the belief that the final destiny of all the islands of the West Indies . . . [was to be] annexation to the United States sooner or later." It was true that Haitians were "extremely jealous of their nationality and their history gives them a certain reason to be proud of the deeds of their ancestors. They mention with mature satisfaction Toussaint L'Ouverture and Alexander Dumas." For Washington's ample plans in the Caribbean, a special approach toward Haiti in particular was required. The "worst feature in the Haytian character" was the inclination for "political intrigue and consequent revolution." And this, Meyer said, had to be addressed. They disdain farming and seek cities; and when flummoxed, they look to "politics" as a salve. As for the masses, "their wants are very small and a transfer to American citizenship could only be of benefit to them"; many of them would be "relieved, among other burdens," of having to perform "military service." The "wealthiest young men," he observed, were "exempted by joining the national guard," which was akin to "performing a duty of mere child's play in times of peace." Addressing this inequity, Meyer added, would bring instant credibility to the U.S. occupiers. Abolition was a plus in that there had been a "want of capital, which was kept out of the country by laws against whites," but the "removal of slavery" had now "satisfied the Haytians that no danger to their freedom would arise from a change of those exclusion laws." Though this writer knew Haiti better than the Dominican Republic, he was convinced that "the same remarks apply with more [or] less variation" to the Dominicans too: "they are among the same people as regards their Negro parentage, contain a larger number of lighter shade mulattoes, allow whites to immigrate and own real estate, and are certainly readier to accept the Stars and Stripes" than the "Haytians." Hence, if the United States could only avoid the snare of "secret intriguing," an entire island was theirs for the taking.[105]

Haiti continued to strain to placate Washington, seeking to avoid offending delicate sensibilities by seeking to avoid appointing envoys whose color might offend. The former enslaving republic restrained itself too and occasionally appointed envoys who were perceived as having high level access back home. Thus, one of the top emissaries to the island republic was Arthur Folsom, a resident of Jérémie for a half-century though he was a native of Exeter, New Hampshire. He was the grandson of Nathan Folsom, who had commanded troops in Boston in 1775, and then served as a congressman before expiring in 1790.[106] Yet his pedigree did not spare him when in 1865, as he reported anxiously, "four young men congregated near my home with the . . . intent to assassinate me."[107]

The threat to Folsom was a reflection of the fierce reaction to U.S. maneuvers in Hispaniola. By 1868 a revolt had erupted in Santo Domingo that one Dominican described as "calamitous" and inducing "misery." This was in response to the gathering idea of a Spanish return, liquidating Dominican Republic sovereignty once more. The culprit was said to be Buenaventura Báez whose "principal object" was the "introduction of European influence," the "cause of the convulsions and continual civil war."[108] It was true that Báez told one chief U.S. investor in the Dominican Republic that "the country needs the importation of every class of the elements of civilization whether coming from America or from Europe—and it cannot be otherwise."[109] Gregorio Luperón was the leader of the revolt and he was said to have purchased a steamer, pretending it was for Haiti, then hoisting the Haitian flag before sailing into combat. He was headed to Puerto Plata "to make war," it was said disconsolately. This was an "insult" to Washington, "offered by the very man who reproached" Santo Domingo "for sympathy" with the United States.[110] The peripatetic Luperón was spotted with a Venezuelan flag on his embattled vessel before heading to Samaná. There he and his crew were said to have "plundered," but were "energetically expelled by the loyalty of the inhabitants, who without order or aid from the Government, fought them on shore and forced them to embark." A "North American citizen trading at Samaná," advised M. M. Gautier of the Dominican Republic, "was under arrest for 26 hours on board" Luperón's vessel. It was an affair—it was thought—that demanded a U.S. intervention to halt this "bandit."[111]

Gautier sought to appeal to Washington's basest racial instincts, asserting that Luperón was "very much behind the times." How so? He "declared that the African race must rule and that it should be united in favor of the extermination of the others"; to that end, he had been "plundering"—including the taking of an "American steamer"—and had committed other "acts of piracy," all of which was quite "shameless."[112]

Washington thought that Luperón was backed by Haiti. By early 1870, Port-au-Prince was said to have "ordered" about "2500 men with arms, ammunition, and provisions" to Santo Domingo to "assist" in "warfare against Báez," formerly scorned by the United States as a feckless "mulatto" but now seen as a savior. Problematically, Washington was not seen as a savior by many in Santo Domingo: "Americans are very much disliked," said U.S. naval leader E. K. Owens, and "the American Minister has been occasionally insulted by the people" and the vaunted U.S. flag too. The "supposed acquisition of Samaná has greatly aroused the people against us," he said, "backed, as I believe, by the English Minister and merchants who desire the control of the trade of the island."[113] This was the contention, though Washington also had evidence that Luperón and his comrades crafted a stern "protest" of the proposed Samaná deal, which drove them to take up arms.[114] Still, London was unsupportive of annexation of the Dominican Republic and perceived it as just one more way to keep Haiti at bay.[115]

Whatever the case, though Haitians and Dominicans had been fighting intermittently since secession in 1844, now they were uniting to fight a Santo Domingo regime said to be in the pocket of Washington. Haitian leader Sylvain Salnave was reportedly captured on Dominican soil, along with 180 others, including twenty-seven generals. Gautier said that Haiti was sending vessels to "bombard" Santo Domingo. Salnave reportedly confessed that his emissaries in Philadelphia had bought an "ironclad war vessel" for further attacks on the Dominican Republic, which caused Gautier to demand U.S. "protection." Santo Domingo forces could fight well "on land," but "at sea, with the naval resources" of Haiti, they were "weak" and thus, he demanded, U.S. "naval forces in these seas."[116] Secretary of State Fish, engaging in coercive diplomacy toward Santo Domingo, confessed that an "ironclad" that was "full armed" would be delivered soon to Haiti.[117]

While this conflict was escalating, Báez reputedly garnered a loan from London, which was displeasing to Washington. At the same time, a U.S. national, David Hatch, accused this Dominican leader of looting his property in the Dominican Republic Adding to the complexity, Hatch was about to be executed, before being pardoned.[118] Hatch was charged with being hostile to annexation, a posture inconsistent with demanding consular aid from the United States.[119] This fracas sounded an uncertain trumpet. The Cazneaus were seeking to bring "immigrants" to the Dominican Republic, but "political disturbances" delivered by Luperón hindered "peace on our frontier," according to Gautier. And these disturbances made it difficult to "oppose [the] pretensions" of Haiti, which he saw as Luperón's puppeteer. Now it was recommended that these settlers be armed, but it was unclear how many would arrive in light of what had befallen Hatch.[120] On the other hand, the ubiquitous investor, Joseph Fabens, was appointed by Báez and Gautier as their envoy in Washington and was given "full powers to arrange and negotiate" deals.[121]

These deals likely would include military aid to the Dominican Republic, particularly as Cazneau was frantically denouncing "guerilla forays" from Haiti that "drained" Santo Domingo. This suggested that a U.S. annexation would entail the dreaded "war of the races," jeopardizing "self-protecting American settlements." Partially responsible was a U.S. national, Raymond Perry, who "aroused the fears and suspicions of a number of political refugees from Hayti" due to "old prejudices of race and Mr. Perry's rough contempt for the colored citizens who he does to surprise with a blow when they displease him." As a result, those struck were "preparing their minds for a deadly collision and it will not surprise me," Cazneau noted, "to hear of their heading guerilla bands on the frontier within three months. It is giving the rulers of Hayti an excuse for appealing to their friends in the United States for at least the vocal support of public opinion against annexation"—not to mention heightening racial tensions that were already flowing due to an incomplete Reconstruction.[122] Cazneau had reason to worry. In fact, his lengthy campaign to annex the Dominican Republic, which would have benefited his narrow mercantile interests, was attracting more negative attention. One critic spoke to him directly, objecting to "grants of public lands—amongst them one to yourself of some 200,000 . . . acres of land."[123] In seeking to deny self-interest, Cazneau conceded the main point, i.e. that "no one American has been more intimately connected with the Samaná and annexation negotiations from their inception to their close than myself."[124]

To be sure, the conflict between Perry and Cazneau was hardly one between an angel and a devil. Gautier sputtered about a "scandalous incident" in which a U.S. national, sued in the Dominican Republic by a man from neighboring St. Thomas, "slapped" his court opponent "in the face." Gautier remarked that "unfortunately the man who received the blow is a Negro. The painful sensation produced by this occurrence in society here could not well be exaggerated" and it was all Perry's fault since he makes "more injury than could have been done by the most open enemy" because of the "irritability of his temper."[125] In the presence of Báez, Perry termed Cazneau a "trickster and a dishonest man."[126] Indeed, such bickering was hardly conducive to building confidence in Washington's stance.

Yet it continued. As noted, Cazneau claimed that "no one American has been more intimately connected with the annexation negotiations" than himself. Well, said the spluttering Perry, "I am well aware of the design yourself and Fabens" constructed and of your "intrigue." As for President Ulysses S. Grant, "I have every reason to fear [he] has already been used by [a] financial ring,"[127] i.e. he was part of the profiteering, an opinion held by others. A flabbergasted Cazneau hotly denied the "absurd insinuation" that the president "has been used by me or any associates of mine for private speculation"; this was "too ridiculous for serious notice" and the "wild fancy of a distempered brain"—though such inflamed rhetoric conveniently evaded a specific denial.[128]

Perry, the U.S. commercial agent in Santo Domingo, countered persuasively that "there are some who are taking a very active interest" in the Dominican Republic and "would jeopardize their flag or friends to gain it," a thinly veiled reference to Cazneau. Yet with all these clashes, Washington was moving steadily to seize Samaná—if not the Dominican Republic as a whole—even as Haiti, Luperón, and other opponents objected. By late 1869, the U.S. flag had been "hoisted" in Samaná and was "saluted . . . by the Governor." "The whole country is anxious for annexation," said Perry—though by "anxious" he may not have meant "eager" but "nervous."[129] The U.S. Navy was told that unanimity in favor of annexation did not attend to Puerto Plata, where ample funds to back Luperón were then being collected—though there was no word as to whether this grouping included U.S. Negro emigrants.[130]

While Perry and Cazneau were squabbling, Haitians were fighting vigorously against annexation. Haitian soldiers, said Gautier, were "captured by us in the ranks of the enemy."[131] According to Perry, the Dominican allies of Haiti were not only backed by Port-au-Prince but also the feared "Cacos [that is, militant patriots], who are enemies to the Haytian and Dominican" governments alike and were "very strong at present on the frontier." Cacos, he said, "bombarded" the border.

London was accused of fishing in troubled waters by trying to buy the allegiances of Dominican Republic military leaders. All the while, Perry was being assured by Santo Domingo that there was a "very strong majority in favor of annexation throughout the island" and his antagonist, Cazneau, may have been assured by his concluding words: "real estate is going up rapidly."[132] Spencer St. John, the London emissary, thought annexation was "not thoroughly understood" in the Dominican Republic. Moreover, in the case of "those who do understand the project it is generally condemned," while "others" felt they could "expel the Americans," just as they did the Spaniards, if annexation did not work out well.[133] London was also told that annexation—in addition to being a project in land speculation by the Cazneaus and their ilk—was, as well, a crafty way for Santo Domingo to avoid bond repayments.[134]

U.S. Negro emigrants, also a factor that had to be accounted for, had their own preoccupations, at least in Haiti, where some seemed to be objecting to mandates to serve in the army and labor on public roads. As a result, they were forced to turn to the U.S. consulate for protection—an ironic turnabout from recent decades.[135] This desire for U.S. protection may explain why so many of this group were said to back annexation; insidiously, annexation may have enhanced their personal position in that Washington would have been desirous of having forces on the scene who were English speakers and presumably not hostile to the United States.[136] These emigrants were taking their newly found citizenship seriously. One, said G. H. Harding in Saint-Marc, "flatters himself" that he is "as capable as any other man of fulfilling the duties of consul for that country which he has the honor of claiming as his own." However, this man was "in great danger of being supplanted by an unprincipled individual," who "has no other recommendation [than] that of being *white*." Harding also observed that a "great many of the American immigrants at this point are from the state of New York and are personally acquainted with the Secretary of State," i.e. Seward, and sought to capitalize upon this connection. There were about "four hundred" of this group in Saint-Marc and they now felt themselves able to reverse the previous consular policies which "did not pay sufficient attention to the complaints of the poor col'd Americans; they protected the white Americans only."

These emigrants were arbitraging: for it was Haiti that had placed pressure on the United States by, it was said, having "shown its entire want of prejudice of color by conferring upon a citizen of the United States the most lucrative Haytian consulate . . . in America, that of Boston, worth from three to four thousand dollars a year." This was in marked contrast to the consulate contested in St. Marc that was worth one hundred dollars a year.[137]

In short, the defeat of the enslavers during the U.S. Civil War brought an uncertain benefit to Haiti: a different result would have meant increased pressure to reenslave Haitians while Washington's victory "only" meant increased pressure to terminate Haitian sovereignty.

In other words, the decades following Haitian independence involved continuous efforts by the United States and U.S. nationals to reenslave the entire island and liquidate independence. This was followed in the 20th century by U.S. occupations of both Haiti and the Dominican Republic, which realized dreams that had been harbored in Washington for years. The 21st century then brought another kind of U.S. occupation in the wake of the devastating earthquake in 2010.[138] Still, the spirit of Black Jacobins has yet to be quelled, not least since the revolutionary example of Haiti spread throughout the Americas and created a general crisis of the slave system that could only be resolved—thankfully—with its collapse. As a result, Africans in particular and the international working class in general owe a massive debt of gratitude to the Black Jacobins of Hispaniola.

II

Annex Hispaniola and Deport U.S. Negroes There?
1870–1871

W as there a Haitian plan to fire upon Frederick Douglass during his visit to Hispaniola in early 1871?
This was the controversial contention of Santo Domingo when a U.S. delegation, which included Douglass, arrived on the island. The delegation was dispatched by President Grant to examine the modalities of annexation. It was well known that Port-au-Prince and its Dominican allies were firmly opposed to annexation and it was equally notorious that Luperón and others had taken up arms against this prospect, reputedly backed by Port-au-Prince. If Haitians and their island allies could be credibly accused of firing upon Douglass, still the reigning symbol of U.S. Negro freedom, it was a troubling sign that both this beset mainland grouping, which had just escaped enslavement, and those thought to be their comrades in Hispaniola were in more danger than either seemed to acknowledge.

PRESIDENT GRANT DESIRED TO SEE the "valuable timbers" of the Dominican Republic in U.S. hands. Moreover, it was the "gate to the Caribbean Sea" and, most importantly, "capable of supporting the entire colored population of the United States"; since "the present difficulty in bringing all parts of the United States to a happy unity and love of country grows out of the prejudice to color," he was eager to see the mass deportation of the newly freed to Hispaniola. Only "space" was needed and a "refuge" like the Dominican Republic was where the U.S. Negro would find that his "worth . . . would soon be discovered." For "if Providence designed that the two races should not live together, he would find a home in the Antilles." This interest dovetailed with security concerns since "in case of war between England and the United States, New York and New Orleans would be as much severed as would be New York and Calais, France," due to the string of British islands surrounding the mainland—Bermuda and the Bahamas not least. And this increased the value of Hispaniola. "San Domingo is weak," he said with frankness, "and must go somewhere for protection. Is the United States willing that she should go elsewhere than to herself? Such a confession would be to abandon our oft repeated 'Monroe Doctrine.'" Grabbing the isle would be "carrying out Manifest Destiny"; anyway, "can anyone favor rejecting so valuable a gift who voted $7,200,000 for the icebergs of Alaska?"[1]

Territorial aggrandizement had seized the now abolitionist republic. One Grant supporter, Samuel G. Howe, likewise maintained that "the Emperor of Russia had far less right to convey Alaska to the United States than the government of Santo Domingo has to convey its territory."[2] According to Congressman Oliver Morton of Indiana, "San Domingo alone" was "worth to us commercially, socially, and in every other way fifty Alaskas." The Dominican Republic would be "consolidated and absorbed" into the United States "long before the people of Canada will be converted to annexation," referring to that other sizeable land that had resisted U.S. charms.[3]

Samuel Howe, told the president that "foreign powers which disfavor the growth of our political influence in the West India islands" opposed annexation. They "also stirred up the anger of that party in Haiti which covets the domination of the whole island even at the price of extermination . . . of white or mixed blood"—which necessitated a robust response from Washington, lest this project gain momentum and head northward to the mainland.[4] Annexation failed in Congress; however, indicative of its importance was Grant sending to the Dominican Republic the commission which included Douglass—a purpose of which was to revive this defeated proposal.

As annexation was going down to congressional defeat in Washington, the U.S. consul in Cap-Haïtien, who employed a "secret" agent, conveyed "intelligence that the Haytien man-of-war 'L'Union'" had departed Port-au-Prince "for this city and Fort Liberty" and had "on board arms and ammunition, destined for the Dominican insurgents." Worse, the consul noted, "we have no way of preventing it. They have sent ammunition in empty soap boxes" in order to evade shipboard search.[5] Thus, General Nord Alexis of Haiti was warned that "a large majority of the Dominican people [have] asked to be annexed to the United States" and Port-au-Prince would be well-advised to curtail its backing of opposing forces, e.g. Luperón.[6] General Alexis was dumbfounded, maintaining stoutly that his nation enforced the "strictest neutrality" with regard to Santo Domingo and that aid to Luperón was simply "incomprehensible."[7]

Still, this was an ironic coda to mainland abolition and what had helped to inspire it—the rise of Black Jacobins on the island. This was too a signal that abolition was not without cost, i.e. the formal adoption of U.S. nationality by the formerly enslaved meant that these newly formed "African Americans" would feel constrained to go along with the more noxious aspects of U.S. imperialism as a way to avoid an even steeper decline of their now routinely degraded status. Yet, breaking with Haiti and coddling imperialism were not the surest route to equality of any sort; along with the contemporaneous enlisting of U.S. Negro soldiers in the military and their involvement in leading attacks against Native American polities, these were clear signs that the destiny of the newly freed slaves would be precarious at best. Fortunately for the island, annexation failed[8]—and this, ironically, saved African Americans from being shipped to Hispaniola, a paradoxical conclusion to the decades-long trend of solidarity with Haiti and Black Jacobins.

The failure of annexation also had other consequences. It drove a wedge between President Grant and Senator Charles Sumner—or perhaps deepened it—and, thus, reduced the potential of conflict with London, which would have ensued if annexation had succeeded. Whether the reduction in tension between London and Washington was of benefit to U.S. Negroes is questionable, particularly in light of this group having been able to engage in fruitful arbitrage between the two capitals for decades previously.[9] When the Haitian regime presented Senator Sumner with a richly ornamented and exquisitely wrought gold medal for his staunch opposition to annexation—and this was then praised in certain U.S. Negro newspapers—it also deepened a wedge among African Americans,[10] which pitted those who backed Douglass's mission against those who did not. When President Grant said of Sumner's unyielding opposition to annexation—"I think he is mad"—some U.S. Negroes were inclined to apply that descriptor to the occupant of the White House.[11]

By December 1870, one friend of Sumner proclaimed that "little has been talked of but San Domingo." As for Sumner, he felt that initially there were not "more than six senators . . . in favor of annexation at first," which indicated the effectiveness of Grant's arm-twisting.[12]

Though Senator Sumner was certainly influential,[13] the anti-annexation posture of U.S. Negroes—who presumably would have been sent en masse to the Dominican Republic if the pact had been ratified—was also reflected among other congressional stalwarts. Fernando Wood of New York thought the project was designed to "overawe" Haiti and "protect American interests," which was why the United States had dispatched "three ships of war of our small Navy" to "Samaná bay."[14] Yet it was Senator Sumner who argued passionately that the annexation resolution was simply a "dance of blood" since "Báez has been and is now maintained in power by the naval force of the United States. Deny it, if you can," he taunted, but instead of annexation, the two republics—Haiti and the Dominican Republic—should be one.[15] Sumner did not note what his adversary Samuel Howe did, namely that President Báez was willing to relinquish sovereignty if the United States assumed his nation's debt and made D.R. nationals U.S. citizens.[16]

Joseph Fabens, the land speculator and investor who stood to profit from annexation, confirmed Sumner's—and many Negroes'—worst fears when he confessed openly that taking the Dominican Republic was just the first step: we "must have Hayti too," he demanded. Proponents of annexation were displeased when word leaked that the jowly, bearded, and balding Haitian envoy, Stephen Preston, had spent a hefty $20,000 to sink the treaty and had helped to disseminate stories of shabby land deals between Báez and his mainland backers—stories that alienated potential backers. In any case, the avenue named after Sumner in Port-au-Prince was an emblem of the appreciation for him in Haiti.[17]

Carl Schurz, another potent force in Washington, proclaimed that annexation *"ipso facto"* was "the most flagrant threat against Hayti that can possibly be uttered. Is there a man on the floor of the Senate," he asked, "who thinks that when we have the one half of that island we shall stop before we have the other?" The "very nature of our customs service would oblige us to take the territory of the Haytian republic too" and, like falling dominoes, this would inexorably lead to taking Cuba too. Spain lost 10,000 soldiers and $40 million in trying to take the Dominican Republic—and the United States with folly was seeking to emulate Madrid, he said.[18]

This was hardly the consensus view in Washington. Samuel Howe argued that the Dominican Republic "is worth more to us than even Cuba would be," since "it has no slaves. More than half of its population are [*sic*] of the white race (in the Southern sense of the word)."[19] Congressman Job Stevens of Ohio argued with similar intensity that Samaná was the key "to the Gulf of Mexico, the mouths of Mississippi, and the route across the Isthmus." This was no small matter in a time before the Panama Canal and given the necessity to reach California from the eastern seaboard so as to avoid combative Native Americans on overland routes. The annexation "will give us the mastery of the West India islands," said the congressman. Yes, "gentlemen say the population of this West Indian republic is inferior." And, yes, there were those who thought the United States had enough Negroes, thank you very much. But, "sir," he asserted, "it is the same blood as that of five million American citizens" whereas "there are less than one hundred and fifty thousand of them" in the Dominican Republic. Anyway, many of those who objected to taking the Dominican Republic still lusted for Cuba—"bond and free, a million and more, slavery and slave trade, coolie and coolie trade, all and all." And if the United States rejected the Dominican Republic, could the United States credibly object if the Dominican Republic requested annexation by Spain—again—and at what cost to U.S. national security?[20]

Congressman Oliver P. Morton of Indiana was of like mind. He denied that annexation of the Dominican Republic would lead to a similar fate for Haiti. Anyway, his sources told him that "the people of Hayti, the great majority, were in favor of annexation" because "they hoped that it would be the precursor of their own annexation." Anyway, "the annexation of San Domingo will come" sooner or later "and with it too the annexation of Cuba and Porto Rico"—this was "destiny not to be averted." Yet the Dominican Republic "is the key to the West Indies. It contains the finest harbor in the world. It commands the great Mona Passage from the Atlantic Ocean to the Caribbean Sea." "San Domingo is the richest piece of earth" extant, a "great natural cabinet of all the choicest productions of the world."[21]

Senator Zachariah Chandler of Michigan felt that annexation meant an "increase" in "commerce" by "enlarging our borders. Take in the islands of the Gulf; take in the Sandwich Islands" and, yes, "take in the Dominion of Canada; take in Colombia" too. Given this, "why should we not take San Domingo in?" For "in 1789 the commerce of San Domingo was immensely greater than the commerce of Cuba at the present day" and "the island of San Domingo is several hundred miles nearer by water to New York than New Orleans." Like others, he thought that controlling Hispaniola "gives us the key to the Gulf; and once possessing the key to the Gulf, we make all the world tributary to us." This would open a vast cornucopia, i.e. "the commercial relations of this nation will be entirely changed at the moment we take possession of the West India islands." Unlike some, the Michigander was "not afraid of representatives from the island of San Domingo, although they may be black." The Dominican Republic was a stepping-stone since "it will not be . . . five years before the island of Cuba will be ours, if we raise our flag in the island of San Domingo."[22]

Senator Cornelius Cole of California was not opposed to the idea of acquiring "some property in the tropics suitable for the emigration of the freed population." He was grateful that the United States was able to "obtain the Dominican portion of that large island almost for the taking." Visiting Puerto Plata he found "many of the buildings" to be "comparatively new, the town having been entirely destroyed . . . almost three years before by the Spaniards," presumably taking vengeance against U.S. Negro emigrants known to be hostile to the occupation. Actually, it was not just the emigrants, for the Spaniards "on leaving," with "unheard of malignity, burned and destroyed as much property as possible," costing "thousands of lives and millions in money." He denounced Sumner as a "man of remarkable egotism" and claimed that his opposition to annexation came from "European sources." He bumped into the former Mexican foe of the United States, General Santa Anna, reminding him of the national security importance of the Dominican Republic. He too was struck by Báez, a "rather small man, with a tincture of African blood," who "understood English better than he spoke it."[23]

Instead of praising Senator Sumner, Benjamin Wade "ascertained" that the "source" of his "delusion upon the subject of annexation" was a supporter of the solon with "large interests" on the island; indeed, said Wade, "the most important and essential papers used by Mr. Sumner were made up in Washington to deceive him—forged for the purpose."[24]

President Grant was pleading by this juncture, openly expressing "an unusual anxiety for the ratification of this treaty." This pact would uphold the Monroe Doctrine, he said, but—it was added—"I now deem it proper to assert the equally important principle that hereafter no territory on this continent shall be regarded as subject of transfer to a European power." It was Santo Domingo, he claimed, that "has voluntarily sought this annexation. It is a weak power, numbering probably less than 120,000 souls and yet possessing one of the richest territories under the sun." The issue was blocking other powers, e.g. the unnamed one that "stands ready now to offer $2,000,000 for the possession of Samaná bay alone."[25] Grant compromised his already tenuous position when he was forced to issue a curious denial. "You have doubtless noticed hints in Congress," he said, "and charges in various newspapers that I am financially interested in the acquisition of Santo Domingo." He denied the allegation, but mere words could not vitiate the accompanying claim that some of his more affluent supporters surely stood to profit.[26]

Báez was at issue and the image he conveyed was not necessarily appealing, even to pro-annexation forces. When the U.S. national Samuel Hazard encountered him he remarked that Báez "would never be taken for other than a Spaniard were it not that his hair, as he turns his head, shows just a little of the character of the hair of the African." Still, he noticed that "the Dominican people differ widely in this particular from the Haytians, among whom the black race is in complete ascendancy." This was not a minor matter since, said Hazard, the "masses of the people of the United States [were] watching with great interest the action of their representatives in Congress on the question of the admission of St. Domingo into the Union."[27] Andrew D. White, who served alongside Douglass as a commissioner, also found that Báez was a "man of force" and "though a light mulatto, he had none of the characteristics generally attributed in the United States to men of mixed blood."[28]

Howe, was keen to assure that a "large proportion of the Dominican people are of a high type of physical organization and may be properly classed with the white race"—a view that stretched this privileged category beyond all meaning and recognition. He pleaded that "the people of all ranks" in the Dominican Republic "do earnestly and almost unanimously desire annexation," which too was an exaggeration. He knew that this project had "important bearing upon the subject of West Indian and Brazilian slavery," which was accurate insofar as the newly abolitionist United States could more credibly threaten Cuba if it annexed Hispaniola.[29]

Despite the strenuous ministrations of Douglass and others, President Grant had to write President Báez to inform him with regret of "the failure of the treaty for the annexation of San Domingo to the United States" and of the fact that he "had hoped [for] a different result." Still, he remained ready to fight. "I believe now," Grant said, "that if the subject was submitted to a popular vote of the people, it would carry by an overwhelming majority."[30] As his successor, Rutherford B. Hayes, confided when speaking of Grant, "San Domingo was his pet topic."[31]

Do not blame Grant, said Samuel Howe, for this failure since "annexation was an old project," extending back to the creation of the Dominican Republic. He went on to associate anti-annexationists with foreign foes, especially "European traders." The proposal also "angered" Haiti, "which represents the aggressive Negro party that came into power by murdering the preceding president, Salnave, who was suspected of being an annexationist. This party has ever coveted possession of the whole island and incited the several attempts made by the government to subdue by force and arms the Dominican territory and to drive out, or exterminate, all of Spanish descent." Thus, the U.S. patriot Benjamin Wade announced that he would go to "Hayti and tell that black prince that he must call off his dogs immediately or take severe consequences." If the United States did not act against Haiti forthwith, it would be "execrated, as was England for her shameful abandonment of Parga in 1819" (a reference to a tragic episode in Greek history). For Haitians "are vastly superior in numbers" and "in wealth and warlike resources. They have, naturally enough, ever coveted and never ceased their effort to get possession of the whole island and"—most critically—"dominate the whites." Howe seemed perturbed to observe that "it is not very strange that our people should have believed the mistaken statements" of anti-annexationists "because popular sympathy is now turning in favor of Negroes, so long and cruelly oppressed."[32]

Since the lengthy tie between London and Port-au-Prince had not disintegrated, it had become easier to associate opposition to annexation with foreign foes. As the commission dispatched by Grant was returning from Santo Domingo, Haitians were arranging to visit the "Royal Arsenal" and "other Military Establishments" in London[33]—including "Her Majesty's Dockyards"[34]—for purposes that would not be reassuring to Washington. The same could be said of a highly desirable invitation to the London International Exhibit of 1871 to be opened by His Royal Highness the Prince of Wales Himself.[35] A Haitian emissary was present when the celebrated Benjamin Disraeli spoke at the installation of the Lord Mayor of London, providing an opportunity for sharing notes on mutual foes. The difficulties then faced by France, reeling from conflict with Prussia, were duly noted.[36] Port-au-Prince surely hoped that municipal elections in France would lead to a new type of politics.[37] For when London agreed to a substantial loan to Haiti with ironclad guarantees, Port-au-Prince was looking over its shoulder to gauge Paris's reaction, fearing that France would seek to scuttle this deal in light of debts owed to the hexagonal nation.[38] Haiti was seeking a $2 million loan—with $300,000 to be directed immediately to pay debts to Paris.[39] Paris was also monitoring the aftermath of the failed annexation with the United States still scrambling to take charge of Samaná.[40] By 1873 the French delegate was closely monitoring an "insurrection" in Puerto Plata that involved "les Americains." It is unclear, however, if he was concerned that U.S. emigrants were in an uproar or if this provided an opening for Paris.[41]

Wade, who was part of the commission that visited the Dominican Republic, returned "as strong for annexation" as upon his departure. "Nothing can redound as much to the honor and glory of our country as to plant our flag on this beautiful island, and lay the foundation of one of the most wealthy and prosperous states of the Union. By its location it belongs to us," he exclaimed. For "it is but the eastern boundary of our continent and must not and shall not fall into other hands. Its annexation," Wade cried, "will be the crowning glory of your administration. For God's and humanity's sake, do not give it up," he told the president.[42]

M. M. Gautier of the Dominican Republic was irate because of attacks that coincided with the visit of Douglass and his fellow commissioners, which left many dead and wounded. It was "planned" by Haitians, he asserted accusingly, "for the sole purpose of surprising the U.S. Commissioners" and causing them "to believe that there was some legitimate opposition to the plan of annexation."[43] Soon he was arranging to meet President Grant himself on a "confidential" mission with a murky agenda.[44] There was "not a shadow of a doubt," contended the U.S. envoy, Stanislaus Goutier, "that something serious is taking place to defeat the intentions of our Government in the annexation." There were, he added, "certain leaders" that desired "to cause an uprising in several sections of the country" while the U.S. commission was present.[45] One thing was certain: Luperón had made it translucently clear that he opposed annexation and that just as Santana turned over the nation to Spain, Báez was doing the same with an even more formidable antagonist—the United States.[46]

The visiting commissioners made it similarly pellucid that their mission was to investigate the mining and agricultural capacities of the island, along with the harbors and even the meteorology. They departed on 17 January 1871 and, said one commissioner, Andrew D. White, upon completion of their mission, it was possible to say that it was "doubtful whether any country was ever so thoroughly examined in so short a time." White was unimpressed with certain aspects of the Dominican Republic: "I never in its entire domain saw a bridge, a plow, a spade, a shovel, or a hoe," he said wondrously—though he did notice "magnificent squared logs of the beautiful mahogany of the country," begging to be exploited. "Under the natural law of increase the population of the republic should have been numbered in millions," but "there were not two hundred thousand inhabitants left and that of these about half were mulattoes, the other half being about equally divided between blacks and whites." He did not say which group backed annexation, though he did say that there was support from the clergy. Like others, he thought that the island had a "curse" from "which it had never recovered," stretching back decades to the abolitionist revolution. This seemed to strike him when he arrived in Port-au-Prince—"few things could be more dispiriting. The city had been burned again and again." These "revolutionists of 1793, imitating those [of] 1793 in France, as apes imitate men, had torn the corpses" out of a mausoleum "and had them scattered." His view of Douglass, his fellow commissioner, was a limited accolade, calling him "one of the two or three most talented men of color I have ever known." This opinion was apparently substantiated when the Negro leader found that Santo Domingo "discouraged and depressed him. He said to one of us, 'if this is the outcome of self-government by my race, Heaven help us!'"

White visited Geffrard, the former Haitian leader, in Jamaica. He was a "light mulatto," who "calmly discussed with us the condition of the island, and evidently believed that the only way to save it from utter barbarism was to put it under the control of some civilized power"—like the United States, perhaps. Like others, he was eager to grab Samaná but accepted, philosophically, the setback to annexation since the United States felt that "with the new duties imposed on them" by the newly freed slaves, "they had quite enough to do without assuming the responsibility of governing and developing this new region peopled by blacks and mulattoes."[47] Before departing the commissioners were told that their mission was "to feel the pulse of the colored community of two hundred thousand" and to "ascertain how that enlightened community is disposed toward us."[48] However, since they could not be altogether open about an underlying purpose—depositing tens of thousands of U.S. Negroes in their midst—taking the pulse was problematic at best. Still, Samuel Howe felt compelled to argue that the "canvass of the people" in the Dominican Republic was "minute and extensive."⁴⁹

So buoyed, U.S. Negroes resumed their decades-long effort to move to Haiti—though this was now happening in the wake of abolition, indicating that the terror of the Ku Klux Klan was taking a toll and, similarly, that the attraction to Haiti had yet to abate,⁵⁰ though it was far from being idyllic. "The whole country is a state of anarchy, East and West," said the U.S. envoy in late 1867. "Never was Hayti in such a deplorable condition since the [advent of the] Republic."⁵¹

Nissage Saget had succeeded Sylvain Salnave as president in Port-au-Prince in 1869 and, in the months preceding the latter's departure, Haiti was in an uproar. It was early in that fateful year that the "Southern State of Hayti, Council of State" mandated and did "solemnly declare that it places itself under the protection of the Government of the United States of America, as its natural ally"⁵²—which simultaneously inflamed a good deal of public sentiment. Weeks after this provocation, foreign consuls were promised that their quarters would not be assaulted—so, "women and children, sick and infirm" promptly moved to said quarters, with about "357 persons" in the U.S. consulate alone. The consul, James de Long, visited the outskirts of Aux Cayes and was overcome by the "stench emitted by dead bodies," which had been "left for food for the hogs and other animals. Hats and shoes" were "scattered" all about. He spoke to two elders, who had been hiding in the woods: "it made my blood chill," said the shaken consul, "to hear them relate the murders." "My life as well as that of all the foreigners and nations are in the most eminent danger," with "horrors" too macabre to detail, though "surpassing anything recorded in the history of the most barbarian country." A "steamer under the American flag came into the harbor towing a [barge] laden with arms, ammunition, and provisions" for Salnave. However, de Long fingered the latter as being responsible for most of the atrocities. This "open assistance rendered to Salnave created considerable excitement and a strong feeling of resentment against foreigners generally and especially Americans," which was justified—though he was shortly to be victimized by these passions. "Speculators" were responsible for this influx of arms, seeking to profit from restiveness; "officers of the U.S. Navy" were "resigning their positions and allowed the command of Salnave's privateers" and it was "these same officers" who were "committing acts of cruelty and barbarity unknown to civilized countries." The "hands" of these once beribboned officers were "stained with the blood of innocent women and children"; he resolutely confirmed that "none of these acts of cruelty or vengeance have ever been practiced by the rebels."⁵³

"My life as well as that of others are in as much danger as on a field of battle," wailed de Long in May 1869; "we are hemmed in on all sides like cattle in a slaughter pen."⁵⁴

Salnave was perceived as more favorable to U.S. interests, a realization ratified when in December 1869 the U.S. intervened to insure the safe passage of his
mother, wife, and children from Saint-Marc.[55] Luperón, on the other hand, leader
of the anti-annexation forces, was perceived in Washington as being pro-London,
a sentiment confirmed when in early 1870 the U.S. consul in Cap-Haïtien noticed
that a "small British schooner" was headed to the Turks and Caicos Islands with
Luperón aboard, bringing him "nearer" to the "revolution at Puerto Plata."[56] Thus,
when Douglass and his fellow commissioners visited, Saget and his cabinet were
cold and formal,[57] a cul-de-sac for U.S. Negroes then under siege by Ku Klux Klan
terrorists on the mainland and now seen as turning away from their global backer.
Douglass was portrayed as being equally dismissive of Haitians, purportedly telling
an inquiring reporter that "in his judgment the Dominicans are a far superior people to the Haytians, that there is no republicanism whatever in Hayti, and that the
Government there is an absolute despotism of the most oppressive character." For
good measure, the Negro leader reprimanded Senator Sumner's backing of Port-au-
Prince.[58] This was not Douglass's finest hour: apparently he was chosen for this delegation with the idea that his imprimatur would encourage U.S. Negroes to emigrate
en masse to Hispaniola, ridding the mainland of a presumed intractable problem.[59]

When President Grant held a dinner at the White House for the commissioners—excepting Douglass—it became more difficult for the masses of U.S. Negroes
to accept annexation or the counsel of this Negro leader for that matter. When a
steward on the return voyage from Santo Domingo refused to serve him in the main
dining room, Douglass's luster was tarnished further.[60] The indignity continued
when, upon arriving in Charleston, Douglass was refused service on a train heading north and his fellow commissioners in solidarity refused to enter the dining car,
meaning they all returned to Washington famished.[61] Douglass seemed a tad too
proud to be traveling as a U.S. representative on an important mission with members of the elite. However, this was not just a personal flaw, it was symptomatic of
a larger trend: when a form of citizenship was thrust upon U.S. Negroes, the price
of the ticket was seen as going along with imperial projects, even if it meant those
inimical to a nation that had sacrificed so much for abolition: namely, Haiti. Thus,
the Negro leader preened about the "spectacle presented by a colored man seated at
the captain's table" since it "was not only unusual but had never before occurred in
the history of the United States Navy." He was baffled as to why "my presence and
position seemed to trouble" the "colored waiters" aboard, seemingly unaware that
their unease might have reflected their opposition to annexation.[62]

But it was not just Douglass who had to bend preexisting views in order to
fit the new annexation consensus. Samuel Howe considered James Redpath a

"worthy friend," but this progressive voice denounced annexation—unlike Howe. In fact, Howe confessed that "one of the most painful episodes of my life was a short sojourn in Haiti," a nation he otherwise supported. He "had always felt a deep interest in the experiment of a Negro republic. I came a warm friend," he confided. "I wanted to be an indulgent admirer; but I had seen too many countries not to feel instinctively on landing that I was no longer among a democratic people, as I had been in the eastern end of the island" since a "reign of terror" existed. "Mulattoes, especially, seemed in fear for their lives" and "after a few days, Frederick Douglass, meeting me on the quay, said sadly, 'if this is all my poor colored fellow-men have been able to do in seventy years,'" then "'God Help the race!'"

Even a cursory reading suggests that Howe—and Douglass too—were indicting Haiti in order to propel annexation. However, neither seemed to consider that even if their allegations about Port-au-Prince were accurate, this still did not justify liquidating island sovereignty. In any case, Howe was reputedly told that "if we mulattoes should shout our wishes about annexation, the Negroes would murder us and our children." Howe's confidantes there "all looked to the annexation of Santo Domingo to the United States as a step toward the annexation of Hayti"— and "their deliverance," which helps to explicate why this group may have faced a bit of hostility from those who continued to subscribe to Black Jacobinism. Howe was willing to sink to great depths in order to indict Haiti, contending that "where they are left to themselves," the "Negroes of Hayti, as in other West India islands" tend to "revert toward barbarism." Thus, "witness the sacrifice of infants and the eating of their flesh." Hence, "avoid the scheme of building up a great Negro confederacy in the tropics. That implies the converse, to wit, a white republic in the temperate zone. . . . it implies segregation based on color and the world has had too much of that." After all, "of all races the Negro can least flourish under such disadvantages. He needs contact with more highly developed races" since "he imitates rather than originates."

Perhaps the color difference illuminated why President Báez "walks about freely among his people, without parade and without guards, in striking contrast with the president of the neighboring Negro republic, who seldom appears except on horseback, bedizened, and befeathered and surrounded by armed guards." The drive to annex Hispaniola perforce led to a sharp devaluation of Haiti, which opposed this maneuver that complicated its future.[63] Of course, when Howe became involved in land speculation in Samaná, it called into question his selfrighteous approach to Haiti.[64]

Still, the influential Gerrit Smith took issue with Howe when he said that the "tropics belong to the sable races" while "the temperate zones" were the "natural dwelling place of the pale races of men." Thus, annexation would be "robbery." Not only was Santo Domingo just a step toward taking Haiti, it was also the "first step toward our getting possession of all the West India islands" and, besides, "an important and even indispensable means for paying our national debt." How could the United States, a nation which has "surely . . . surpassed every other country in wronging Africa," commit such "further injury to her children"? Yes, Smith confessed, "I was wrong" about taking Mexican soil and trying to take Cuba and was now repenting.[65]

When Douglass visited Port-au-Prince in 1870, he supped with John Bell Hepburn, formerly of the United States, who introduced him to the nation's president. But Hepburn then was in conflict with his new homeland and was lobbying President Grant for support. "When I was in the United States," he told the U.S. leader, "as a man of color, I was considered a *chattel and by judicial election* had *no rights that a white man ought to respect*. Being a man of sensibility and honor," he said pleadingly to Grant, "could I be blamed for VOLUNTARILY EXPATRIATING myself to another country"—even one where he found difficulty?[66] It was Hepburn, who described himself in 1869 as a "mulatto and native of Virginia, sixty four years old, and thirty five years absent from my native country."[67] Also weighing in during Douglass's sojourn was Ed Horton, a Negro "born eight miles from Plimoth (North Carolina) in 1825"; his "mother and father" were "still living" there.[68] Like Hepburn, Henry Allen, then in Port-au-Prince, was lobbying Grant. Born in Maryland in March 1800, he left in September 1824 for Haiti where he had resided for "46 years." Allen added, "I have brought property and built a large two stories [*sic*] house of two apartments," but it had been destroyed and he was bereft; so he invoked the U.S. Constitution and a "treat[y]" with Haiti to bolster his claim against Port-au-Prince.[69] Such difficulties made these emigrants more prone to back annexation.

Just as the Dominican Republic had invited the return of Spain in 1861 because of the fear of Haiti, a decade later Santo Domingo was making a similar invitation to the U.S. president. Báez was unequivocal in his charge that Haiti was backing the Luperón-led rebels with "arms and ammunition" that—at least—was "brought" to these forces "through Haitian territory." It was, he said, no more than a "Machiavellian policy."[70] U.S. naval leaders, poised to bombard Haiti in league with Santo Domingo, heartily concurred. "There is a large party in Haiti in favor [of] annexing" the Dominican Republic, said John Irwin. "They are composed of the followers of the late President Salnave and they are doubtless causing the present Government much anxiety"; Báez was eager to "capture some Haitien [*sic*] officers in order to prove the complicity of the Haitien [*sic*] Government."[71] Downplayed in this regard was the Dominican insurgency led by Luperón, which Washington knew was opposed to the "cession of Samaná."[72]

Haiti was infuriating Washington because of its opposition to annexation. Secretary of State Fish made it plain that Washington was "peculiarly interested" in "exemptions" of the Dominican Republic from "internal commotion and from invasions from abroad."[73] The man of color serving as U.S. envoy in Haiti—Ebenezer Bassett—cautioned that there was "much excitement here just now in reference to the annexation" and "ruling sentiment" was "opposed to any and everything looking to a possibility of giving up the nationality of Hayti." These forces had aligned with Senator Sumner, though he thought the support squishy since the presumed leader of this bloc had "over and over again assured me that he is in favor" of annexation.[74] Nevertheless, Bassett well knew that when Grant was reelected as president in 1872, the reception in Haiti was—at best—mixed with the annexation scheme accounting for the negative reaction.[75]

Washington was thinking that it could parlay the alleged Haitian attacks on the Dominican Republic into an overall effort to annex the entire island. The Cacos, or militant Haitians, were just as determined to undermine the Port-au-Prince regime, another U.S. commander asserted. Since "American influence decidedly preponderates amongst the adherents of Salnave," which had "embittered" the Cacos, this created a set of circumstances ripe for U.S. intervention. The U.S. Secretary of the Navy was informed that "without some outside assistance Salnave will be overthrown and the influence which the United States has acquired through him will be lost"—and the despised Cacos could surge to power in Haiti. The solution? Fund Salnave in return for access to Môle-Saint-Nicolas, a key Haitian port. Of course, Paris and London were "extremely inimical to our possession" of this port which—at least—"would cut off the approach to Jamaica." In annexing Haiti altogether "would be found an elephant both costly in money and lives"—but this was becoming a minority viewpoint in Washington.[76]

For there were potent merchant forces in Haiti—with U.S. roots—that found the status quo unacceptable; for example, there was "Sumner & Brooks" in Gonaïves which, it was said, "carries on a large business at that port," but now the lives—and perhaps more importantly—the "property" of businessmen were "unsafe."[77] Thus, the press reported then that "Big Business" was the driving force behind annexation of the island.[78] Dozens of U.S. nationals had lost property or investments during the Salnave years and the resultant conflict. About a half-million dollars in claims by U.S. citizens were posited with little headway toward resolution and they were piled upon preexisting claims from previous years.[79]

Haiti's agony had continued during the Salnave years with reports of "unabated violence and barbarity unknown in any country professing civilization," according to the U.S. consul, whose own nation's experience with mass enslavement provided a tutorial on barbarism. "Tyranny exists in its worst shape," said James de Long, "and I may say it is nothing less than a 'Reign of Terror.'" He recalled a distressing episode when "all the *mulattoes* were shot in cold blood and their bodies frightfully mutilated. The *black* prisoners taken were liberated, their only punishment being a good thrashing"; this was an emblem, he observed, of the "war of caste—class or colour—a conflict between the black and coloured races." Anyway, the country was "full of thieves and murderers," who deployed color as a cover for plunder. The unrest had taken a toll on the economy since "labourers are scarce and what little field work is done by women." This had an effect on the United States too with "Hayti being one of the principal consumers of American produce." The consul was exasperated, having been in Haiti for "almost six years" and having "passed through some four or five revolutions." The frightened de Long worried that "were it not for the awe which natives" held for "the power" of "the whites," this latter group "would be taken and killed" and were "ill treated" in any case.[80]

The U.S. consul in Gonaïves found "complete anarchy" there that also was intimidating to the French—who were receiving a stream of "insults"—while, strikingly, the British seemed to be "intimate friends" of local leaders.[81] Former Haitian leader Geffrard—according to the U.S. Negro press—was rumored to be in Jamaica in the late 1860s and was considering becoming a naturalized British national.[82] Hence, annexing the entire island could have extinguished this developing trend.

In the prelude to annexation being debated in the U.S. Congress, U.S. relations with Haiti were undergoing the usual strain with abolition not eliminating underlying tensions. The U.S. delegate in Aux Cayes found it "very unhealthy," compelling him to reside "six miles" away from the city where he had a "small farm and sugar mill." (Other foreign consuls too found it necessary to move away from the center of the city.) That did not keep his property from being stolen regularly; the most recent case had "caused considerable excitement amongst the natives and caused quite a crowd to assemble." Then, quite typically, a "Captain" approached and after a spirited exchange of words, "deliberately got off his horse and knocked me down," said a startled James de Long, "and commenced beating me." He was comprehensibly upset, angry that "nothing" had "been done for me (being a white man I suppose) to punish this man for the outrage & assault of which I was the victim." That was not the end of his misery for when he subsequently went for a ride on his horse, he was "surrounded by eight or ten Negroes, headed by the commander of the district, who pulled me from my horse, throwing me heavily on the ground, and commenced beating me with clubs"; then "they took my horse" and "one of the men mounted him [*sic*]" and rode away. The indignity continued when they marched him home, "continuing always beating me with their clubs." While this pummeling was unfolding, "the commander of the district was present all the time ordering the men to beat and kill me. After I got into the house the commander left, but returned in a short time with several other natives and by his orders they broke open all the doors and windows and entered the house." While this was occurring, the "commander during this time [was] calling out 'beat him,' 'kill him'! 'Get a rope and bind him and take the d---d [*sic*] white man to Aux Cayes." At this point, de Long was "exhausted" and for days following "could neither walk, sleep, nor eat, vomiting almost constantly and sore from head to foot"; he had "not yet recovered and probably I never shall," he confided. Why was this "outrage" committed? The consul "had caused the commander's son to be arrested for stealing money and he [the commander] was determined to have satisfaction in some way. My son was so disgusted and mortified that he left for the States on board the first vessel" heading north. As for de Long, he was beset with injury: "I would prefer being shot at once and put out of misery and disgrace, rather than re-pass through what I have" and "were it not for my friends I could not live."[83] When he appealed to a judge, de Long's words were unheeded,[84] despite evidence of "violent language and threats"—and worse—raining down upon him, including threats to "shoot" him by a Haitian who "drew a pistol."[85] Like others, de Long did not connect the hostility that he personally experienced with the hostility felt by many Haitians toward his government. This was an immediate product of the proposed annexation, but the fury toward annexation should be seen as a culminating vehemence toward a lengthy and hostile U.S. policy toward Black Jacobinism.

By late 1869, Paris had gotten hold of a U.S. message penned near Jacmel, warning Haitian forces to halt their "acts of hostility" against the Dominican Republic and their aid to rebels in the east, consisting of "men, money, arms, and ammunitions of war." Haiti was warned that unless this ceased, the United States would deem this to be a hostile act against itself.[86] Paris also conferred with Spencer St. John, the British representative, who had spoken with Báez, but found him reluctant to engage with Haiti since he felt he held a trump card: U.S. support. Yet he also dismissed the idea of widespread backing for annexation, alleging that "no one but Báez and his Ministers are heartily in favor of annexation; the majority of people are averse to it but are kept down by terror, while the others, somewhat indifferent, believe that they will be able to expel the Americans with the same ease they did the Spaniards, if they find their new masters troublesome"; and, he concluded, "very little encouragement would induce them to insist on their Government abandoning the thought of annexation to the United States." Paris and London should "act together" on this "to preserve the independence" of the Dominican Republic.[87]

By early 1870, de Long had been replaced—but similar results obtained. "Much of the property of the United States at this Consulate has been stolen or lost," complained the new consul, W. A. Gould, in early 1870. There was "no flag at present," nary a "bookcase nor any proper place to keep papers on file," and "no stationery of any kind"; moreover, "nothing of this sort can be bought in this place," which severely hampered communication and normal operations.[88] Shortly however, the "war" had "virtually ceased," said Gould, "though armed bands" marauded "occasionally."[89] Nonetheless, as late as May 1872—after annexation had been squelched—the United States delivered a howitzer to its allies in Haiti, which even Secretary of State Fish acknowledged "caused considerable excitement at that place."[90]

Gould's view of Haiti was as malignant as de Long's. To be sure, he had not "observed any hatred of Americans, as distinguished from other foreigners." However, the "governing class" was "bitterly opposed to all foreigners without respect to their nationality. There are but two parties here," he said, "the party of the blacks and the party of the browns" (he had crossed out "whites"). There were "no public schools of any kind" and "the insane run wild in the streets," while "the poor Negro of the mountain is the only one whom you can at all trust."Aux Cayes, which had an estimated "population of over ten thousand," had "not more than one hundred votes" that were "cast at an election."[91] The problem was that Port-au-Prince knew "nothing about what is taking place" in Aux Cayes—and vice versa. Still, he suspected that what was obtaining in Aux Cayes was not peculiar. "Threats of assassination are openly made against persons who have incurred the displeasure of the authorities and they say, 'if we kill a white man, the government will have to pay a few thousand dollars and that is all they can do to us.'" Meanwhile, "the chief merchant in the American trade" there was suffering "persecution." This strife may have affected his judgment negatively since he also thought that the prospect of "annexation" meant that Haitians' "respect for and fear of America is very much increased thereby. All the foreigners here," Gould noted, "say that when San Domingo is fairly annexed to the United States, they will feel perfectly safe in Haiti."[92]

Maybe so—though the U.S. consul in Cap-Haïtien was enduring similar harassment at that precise moment. By early 1870, as the annexation debate was waxing, this agent found that the "military authorities" had become "riotous and menacing" and engaged in "unpleasant surveillance" that included "forcible entrance into my consulate." Haiti, he said haughtily, was "semi-civilized" at best; besides, the domestic upheaval meant a "heavy expense for the support of so many refugees," which was a "terrible infliction on one with my small salary."[93] His ordeal was just beginning. Soon there was a "large military force" that "surrounded this consulate" with the "most impertinent scrutiny"; "during the whole of the night" they "indulged in the most abusive, riotous, and barbarous orgies." They threatened, the consul said, to break in and shoot him on account of the refugees he housed, forcing him to retreat to his "balcony, revolver in hand."[94] Vice Consul Charles Brody was accosted too: "two soldiers advanced on him," General Nord Alexis was informed, and "one of them dealt his horse a heavy stroke with his bayonet, whilst the other fired" at him; "the ball pass[ed] . . . near his head," creating a "flagrant outrage."[95] General Alexis again issued a blanket denial—but his words were not taken seriously in Washington.[96] Unfortunately, Washington did not connect the growing problems experienced by U.S. envoys in Haiti with the vociferous opposition to annexation of the island; nor did Washington tie this opposition to the long and troubled relationship between Black Jacobinism and the former enslaving republic.

Problematic for the United States was that—Douglass and Haitian problems of biblical proportion notwithstanding—U.S. Negroes often disagreed with Gould's assessment: they were hardly monolithic in their backing for annexation, bringing rifts at a time when wars with Native American polities were ascendant and necessitated a kind of national unity. Henry Highland Garnet, for example, was among those in opposition. *The Weekly Louisianan* was among the periodicals in this beleaguered community that assailed Douglass for having accepted the position of "a mere attaché on the Santo Domingo Commission after his name had been mentioned as a probable Commissioner." The "colored people everywhere," said this journal, "felt that a man who is always and everywhere mentioned as the representative *par excellence* of the Negro race [had] compromised his dignity and belittled the colored man's claims to consideration and where the interests of a Negro nationality were most at stake by going as a sort of nondescript official."[97] This pro-Haitian sentiment reached a new zenith when a Negro congressman was touted as being a "native of Hayti"—though he was born in South Carolina.[98]

Successful U.S. Negro emigrants in Haiti continued to be touted by this press. Theodore Holly, a cleric born in Washington, D.C., was one of these emigrants.[99] There was also Hezekiah Grice, a native of Baltimore, who was a "tolerable French scholar—speaking that language with great fluency." A veteran, as early as 1832, he presented a report to a mainland convention on voluntary emigration; by 1834 Grice, having taken his own advice, had migrated and promptly found a high-level post as a machinist and inventor. He survived the dislodging of Boyer and acquired the confidence of Soloque; the Emperor sent him to Manhattan to obtain machinery for sugar manufacturing. He died in 1863, but left behind a family of six sons and five daughters, all of whom were born in Haiti: "they are all good French scholars," it was said proudly. However, three of his sons returned to reside in the United States, leaving their siblings behind.[100]

Both sides in the annexation debate had to take account of the U.S. Negro emigrant population on the island. This included Samuel Hazard, who visited Port-au-Prince in the early 1870s, and "found a good many English-speaking people and amongst them some coloured people who settled here years ago, established themselves in business, and are now doing well." It was unclear if this cohort were among those who felt that annexation was "the only salvation for the island." However, he met one individual who declared that if annexation occurred, the response would be chilling: "there won't be a white man left alive in the island." Despite this reservation, Hazard found "an almost universal wish of the people, high and low," in Santo Domingo "to come into the American Union."[101]

Such an opinion was shared by some of the U.S. Negro emigrants—but the extent to which such a view took root is not clear. One mainland visitor arrived near the time of Hazard's visit and made his way to Samaná, where he detailed the "arrival" in 1824 of "a few free colored people from the American states of Pennsylvania and Maryland. About 300 of these people and their children are still living, the majority at Samaná. They rank among the most intelligent and industrious on the island. In 1851 the population of the town of Samaná was about 1800 souls, of which 300 were colored Americans," and it grew even larger in the 1870s, propelled by "commerce" with the "Turks Island."[102]

President Grant also was the recipient of a fusillade of criticism and his Haitian policy was termed an "outrage." With barely contained rage, one journalist said that the White House "proceeded to strike at the independence of the black republic in an open menace of war." How could the United States be involved in "threatening to . . .capture the Haytien ships" and other acts of aggression? The newly abolitionist republic "would have done no such thing to any white ruler, nor would our country have tolerated such a menace." Why was the U.S. Navy "hovering on the coast keeping that insulted people in constant anxiety"? How could the United States collaborate with Báez, who "immured" a U.S. national—David Hatch—"because it was feared he would write against the treaty [of] annexation"? This was enough to call for the replacement of Grant with Horace Greeley on the Republican Party ticket.[103]

This steadfastness in support of Haiti was all the more remarkable given the parlous condition to which so many U.S. Negro emigrants had descended in Haiti. As early as 1863, there were reports of "destitute coloured emigrants," notably those "located on Isle a Vache." A statute had been passed to subsidize Negroes in Washington, D.C., who wished to emigrate to the tune of $100,000;

this was in addition to an earlier $500,000 subsidy. But, by the late 1860s, many were still streaming back to the mainland and the terrible portrait of their misery no doubt influenced those U.S. Negroes who longed for annexation by a richer power, i.e. the United States.[104] Of course, some of those returning—at least before 1865—were doing so in order to join the fight to rout the secessionists.[105] Consider Edouard Tinchant, for example. He was born in France in 1841, but both of his parents hailed from Gonaïves during the revolutionary era and settled in New Orleans thereafter. Tinchant fought in the U.S. Civil War and played a role in crafting the Reconstruction Constitution, which was adjudged to be quite radical.

For good reason there were those who sought to abandon the mainland for Haiti—or elsewhere. (Tinchant became a cigar merchant in Antwerp, for example.[106]) It was in late 1868 that Judge David Irvin in Texas was told that the hue and cry about the Negro would soon die—and a kind of terrorism against him could easily resume.[107] R. J. Lackland of St. Louis said that the Negro had fulfilled his destiny in building the productive forces of the mainland and now could be ushered off stage as bonded labor from China would proceed to hold sway.[108]

Yet those U.S. Negroes who opposed Washington's foreign policy were pursuing a dangerous course. The United States continued to challenge Haitian sovereignty over Navassa, the small island replete with guano, and was willing to back up this claim with armed force.[109]

Yet Secretary of State Fish continued to be befuddled by the downturn in relations with Haiti: in 1870, as annexation hung in the balance, he "learned with regret that a sentiment hostile to the United States prevails among" a good number of Haitians, despite "what the United States has done for the African race within the past ten years."[110] The sanctimonious secretary understood why Haiti might view Spain with disdain, but "this feeling should not however include the United States," especially "in view of the fact that the equality of races here before the law is signally exemplified in the person of our diplomatic representative accredited to them"[111]—namely, the U.S. Negro, Ebenezer Don Carlos Bassett.

What might be called the "Bassett Card," or underscoring the ancestry of U.S. diplomats, was played repeatedly by Washington to establish the allegedly progressive credentials of the recently enslaving republic (and in a pattern that was to extend for decades, in the absence of concrete policies to highlight). When Stanislaus Goutier of the United States met President Saget, he gushed about Bassett, telling the Haitian leader that the United States, "having abolished slavery at an enormous sacrifice," was now "striving to obliterate its last vestige—prejudice of color" and to that end "has sent a gentleman of your race to represent" the United States. "These remarks had the intended effect"—or so thought Goutier.[112] The United States even thought the fact that it was now officially abolitionist should disarm Haiti and compel the nation to back annexation.[113]

Appointed by Grant in 1869, Bassett was the son of a "mulatto" and an indigene (Pequot), which pursuant to the typical U.S. calculation made him a Negro. He had studied French and, given these characteristics, it should not be deemed surprising that from 1879 to 1888 he served as Consul General of Haiti in Manhattan. It is likely that Haiti did not want to "insult" mainstream Euro-American opinion by sending a darker man as its agent. This may explain the appointment of its Washington emissary, Stephen Preston, the grandson of a British officer, who had settled on the island after the failed occupation by London. He served for two decades in Washington as ambassador.[114] Bassett, however, was reproved by the U.S. consul in Cap-Haïtien, who resigned in early 1870, though it is unclear if his melanin content was the reason.[115] John Bell Hepburn, a U.S. Negro emigrant then residing in Haiti, did not shrink from making a racial reprimand, stressing to President Grant that the "interests" of the United States "would be better served in Hayti by a *White* Representative rather than a *Black* one."[116] Secretary of State Hamilton Fish too was upset with Bassett after he allowed asylum seekers to enter the legation, contrary to instructions. He was "inclined to recommend his recall" though he objected to the typical Haitian tactic of "surrounding his legation with a military force," an "indignity which cannot be allowed"; thus, he said, a "vessel of war will be sent there."[117]

Ultimately, it was Bassett who played the larger role in bilateral relations. He was a "highly educated colored man and for years . . . [had] been the chief of the faculty of the Philadelphia Colored High School," said one confidant of President Grant.[118] Bassett himself said, "[I] was born and educated in New England—partly at Yale."[119] A post in the diplomatic service—even in a place that was scorned like Haiti—was deemed to be a plum position and there was competition for the assignment. George Vashon told Grant, "I resided in the island for nearly three years, during the latter portion of which I held the professorship of the Greek and English languages in the *College Faustin*, which enabled me to attain an extended familiarity with the French language."[120] But it was Bassett who got the job.

This sourness was an aspect of a larger ennui that gripped the island in the aftermath of a failed annexation. Stanislaus Goutier, the newly appointed U.S. consul in Cap-Haïtien in 1871, found it "very gloomy" and wracked with an "uneasiness which has been severely felt in business circles for some time past"; this was worsened by the "unfortunate Franco-Prussian war," which "completely paralyzed commerce" and harmed U.S. interests too.[121] Surely, U.S. maritime interests were threatened when David Williams, described as a "black man," emulated many from his mainland group and "deserted" his navy vessel in Haiti; "although a reward of $20 was offered," Goutier noted, "he was not apprehended."[122]

Though London was elated with the foiling of annexation, it was displeased with what it saw as "communistic assassins," who were supposedly proliferating in Haiti. These forces seemed to "answer the call of any agitators who cry out against the proprietors that they are intriguing to sell the country to the foreigner and who propose a division of the property of the wealthy." Perhaps strengthening the Catholic Church would flummox these forces, it was said.[123] London, then worrying over a typical spate of insurrectionary unrest in Jamaica,[124] had reason to fear that any contagion from Haiti could have easily spread to Kingston, just as it was fretting over spreading unrest from Cuba.[125]

President Saget was unhappy too, sternly rebutting claims by the United States and the major powers "for losses sustained by them during our last civil war" and the "considerable arrears [that] were due to France." While clamoring for payments, U.S. forces "occupied" the "island of Navaza [*sic*] situated but a short distance from our coast" and did so "without having entered into any contract with the Government," Saget noted. All the while, they were conducting a "considerable commerce with the guano"—the proceeds of which rightly belonged to Port-au-Prince since, President Saget reminded, his nation had "incontestable rights to this island." Such aggression meant "bankruptcy stares us in the face" though "we still have immense resources," as the "line of steamers" steadily plying the waters between New York and Haiti suggested.[126] Nonplussed, the United States steadily pressed claims and, just as steadily, Saget sought to rebut them.[127] When "American silver" became the "circulating coin of the country," which was the U.S. contention in 1873, and the indigenous "filthy currency" was sidelined, the prospect for Haiti satisfying claims became even more complicated.[128] This difficulty compelled Port-au-Prince to apply to a London bank for a loan[129]—even a successful deal would have made for more complex relations with its powerful mainland neighbor.[130] This possibility of economic distress seemed to be realized when, weeks later, Haiti found it difficult to pay its London envoy[131]—and key personnel in Port-au-Prince too.

The news for Haiti was getting worse with the rise of Germany—or Prussia—indicated by its recent triumph over France. There was now yet another power interested in plundering Haiti. By 1872, the United States resorted to appointing a "Mr. Herberlein," an "American citizen," to the post of consul in Gonaïves; he was both a "partner in an American house"—and "a Prussian" and also "German consul at Gonaïves." But it seemed his allegiance rested with Berlin, particularly since another U.S. consul thought that "he might raise the German flag above the glorious stars and stripes."[132]

Joseph Fabens was disconsolate too. The failure of annexation had scuttled his ambitious real estate visions for Hispaniola and seemed to inflame his ire toward Haiti accordingly. By 1873 U.S. warships still hovered near the island, which he endorsed, since it deterred "filibustering expeditions" and "invasion by land and sea" from Haiti. Why was the Dominican Republic so despotic? It was Haiti's fault. The fear of their western neighbor was of justifiable concern since the "Dominicans are of the white race and mixed breeds" too, with "few pure blacks," whereas "the Haytians are almost all Negroes." Thus, "all intelligent Dominicans perceive that their existence as a people is constantly threatened by the Blacks of Hayti." In fact, "mothers frighten their children by threatening to call a black Haytian to come and gobble them up." This was not, Fabens maintained, pure fantasy since "five times in forty years, the Negroes of Hayti, who although possessing only the western end of the island and about a fifth of its territory, are five times as numerous and rich as the Dominicans, have crossed the mountains in open war and in large numbers."[133] More pressure on Haiti was needed, a proposal that would have been supported by William Cazneau, whose American West India Company, founded in 1862, was designed to exploit annexation but now had to turn to other schemes.[134]

While Fabens was licking his wounds, Santo Domingo remained in an uproar. Rebellion rocked Puerto Plata, purportedly led by those still concerned about annexation. A Dominican general was killed and two of his sons rebelled in response; they then fled to the British consulate after committing an assassination of their own. They were granted asylum and strident resistance was accorded to those who sought to capture them. These were "humiliations" claimed the U.S. envoy.[135] If it had the opportunity, Washington would have looked with grave suspicion on the seemingly congratulatory message to Haiti's London envoy from Port-au-Prince, cheering the revolt in Puerto Plata and awaiting eagerly the downfall of Báez.[136] By January 1874, Port-au-Prince seemed to have been gloating when it reported that Báez had departed unceremoniously and was headed to the United States. Now was the time for an entente with Santo Domingo, it was said. The agents of the president's demise had been placed on a steamer, apparently at Haiti's behest, headed for the capital to form a provisional government.[137] That was in January and in June there was enthusiasm at the eclipse of Báez and his annexationist plan,[138] but by August the news was discouraging in terms of bilateral relations on the island;[139] there seemed to be much bad blood and too much interference from external forces to bring the two republics together. In any case, a story—possibly false—was circulated that Haiti was seeking ammunition, arms, and steamers from the United States in order to better confront what had become a perpetual antagonist.[140] Still, Port-au-Prince continued to speak optimistically about an "entente,"[141] though right after that U.S. gunboat diplomacy continued to operate when Secretary of State Fish requested a battleship to be sent to the island and virtually demanded that Haiti take no offense;[142] almost two decades later, Haiti's envoy in Washington was informed that "the welfare of Haiti is again threatened by [the] very likely real negotiations for the partition of St. Domingo."[143]

This perception was confirmed when in 1874 the British consul in Port-au-Prince was trying to negotiate a treaty between Haiti and the Dominican Republic, the completion of which would involve a bailout of Port-au-Prince and annulment of foreign concessions in Samaná; the latter decision would be contrary to Washington's interests and entail its possible replacement by Her Majesty's minions—and, thus, was receiving pushback in Samaná.[144] Nonetheless, soon official Haiti was satisfied by improving relations with its immediate neighbor to the east and the apparent decline of U.S. influence that inexorably accompanied this development. Vigilance was counseled and the mandate to unite the two populations of the island was the watchword—while guarding against outside meddling.[145]

This rosy scenario was not easy to realize as evidenced from reports emerging from Puerto Plata. There were a "considerable number of American vessels trading in wood, honey, and other products of this island at the port of Monte Cristy [*sic*], Santo Domingo and near the Haitian frontier."[146] But soon there was a predictable event—a "revolution was pronounced" and "strangers have been the main sufferers," it was reported. Cubans who were "naturalized American citizens" were "the greatest sufferers," while even "children of American citizens" were "forced to bear arms." The city, which still contained a number of U.S. Negro emigrants, was besieged, but it was not evident if the "outrages" that were "daily being committed upon American citizens as well as other foreigners" included these migrants from decades earlier.[147]

Evidently, one of those so affected was not Jane Cazneau. Even after the unsuccessful annexation—perhaps to fulfill the promise of her real estate speculation—she continued to expound on the island. By 1878 she was in Samaná — the "Gibraltar of the Antilles" was her phrase—where she took careful note of "a widow, the daughter of a colored emigrant from Virginia." There were other "colored Americans" all about, a "band of freedmen and their children" was "in many respects the most remarkable missionary congregation I ever had the good fortune to encounter. They deserve honorable mention as industrious Christians, but it is especially of their qualities as reliable sailors that I wish to offer this certificate of merit." These "colored American settlers" owned and cultivated "some of the prettiest little homesteads in this region. They all speak English as well as Spanish," which made them valuable interlocutors regionally—though "they are almost a state unto themselves." This "state" involved "fifty homesteads—each a picture in itself—each tidy cottage nestling in its own grove of coffee and fruit trees, scattered in irregular profusion over a rich upland, sometimes expanding into level savannas and sometimes swelling up into romantic eminences." Many "claimed descent from a party of liberated slaves sent out from Virginia while Boyer was president of the whole of Hayti. The newcomers received a generous welcome from that wonderful man." They controlled "several small vessels, ranging from twenty to forty tons" that plied "constantly between Samaná bay" and the Turks and Caicos "in the fruit trade." These "colored Americans," effused the adventurer, "have surprised me more profoundly and more agreeably than anything else I have met in this land of surprises." Their "small estancias—seldom reaching ten acres in extent" featured "more care and, of course, more profit also, than those of the average of their Dominican neighbors." She was impressed with this setting and lamented that it was "no wonder that England and France forbade the cession" to the United States. Yet she was disturbed that Haiti "still clings to the doctrine of Negro supremacy," but not the Dominican Republic. "A white man, though just as wise and well-behaved as the most exemplary Negro, is denied citizenship alike in Ashantee and Hayti." Looking back, she recalled how she was "twice present in the library of the White House, when the project of a free port at Samaná was explained and defended" by her spouse. Secretary of State Lewis Cass was present during this briefing, where Mr. Cazneau warned about a Spanish takeover—a warning ignored—and now Samaná was in the hands of mere U.S. Negroes.[148]

Despite the setback, Jane Cazneau had fared well in the region, with an estate in Jamaica and another near Santo Domingo of about twenty acres; she had controlling interest in a wharf in the latter city and a square of land nearby with four homes sited. She was still pursuing a claim of $10,000 against Madrid in the wake of the occupation and owned a tract of forty acres near Samaná.[149] In December 1878, she left there for New York City—but her vessel was lost at sea,[150] an ignominious end for her and for this chapter in the history of Hispaniola.

Though wracked with instability, Haiti in succeeding years continued to maintain legations—not just in key ports, e.g. Hamburg[151]—but also in flashpoints, e.g. Wilmington, North Carolina.[152] Port-au-Prince also continued to maintain an acute interest in mainland trends, notably the struggle for equality.[153]

And the mainland continued to reciprocate. In his final message to Congress in December 1876, President Grant continued to complain that the newly "emancipated race of the South would have found" a "congenial home" on the island; "whole communities would have sought refuge in Santo Domingo." Yes, "the whole race would [not] have gone," but enough to fulfill the dreams of those who longed for a land free of Africans.[154] Grant seemed to be obsessed with the failed annexation, speaking in 1878 in harsh terms about the abolitionist Wendell Phillips who had spoken with contempt of the "treachery to the black race" involved in this pro-annexation effort. Yet, countered Grant, Douglass was "among the most enthusiastic supporters of the treaty" that "would have given a new home for the blacks." For "if two or three hundred thousand blacks were to emigrate to St. Domingo under our Republic, the Southern people would learn the crime of Ku Kluxism." And, he said with regret, "we [would] have made of St. Domingo a new Texas or a new California."[155]

Taking this into account, the militant U.S. Negro journalist, T. Thomas Fortune sought funding from Port-au-Prince to establish a mainland newspaper. "I believe," he told Haiti's U.S. envoy, "that a newspaper devoted to the interests of the Government and the people of Haiti, printed in the English language at New York, and properly circulated here and elsewhere throughout the country, would serve an important and useful purpose," not least "in correcting the misleading and often malicious and damaging statements which constantly appear in the American journals concerning Haiti, its Government, its people, its social life, and the admin-istration of its laws." Said Fortune, "I understand that the Haitian Government has already a paper of that character issued at Paris in the French language"—so why not one published in Manhattan? Was it not true that "the desirability or the neces-sity of having such an organ in the United States is much greater than . . . in France or elsewhere in Europe"? Was not Haiti sensitive to the impact of "the prevailing contemptuous feeling existing in the United States, but not in Europe, toward the African race"? He was willing to concede that the "matter appearing in the columns should be approved by the representatives of the Haytien Government," though "it would weaken rather than strengthen the force of the paper, if it should be known to be in any way a Government organ. I would name the paper *The West Indian Trade Journal*"—indicative of regional ambition—and it should be "free of charge to all persons engaged in the import and export trade between America and Haiti." Start-up costs would be a mere "four hundred . . . dollars per month." But Haiti, then pressed on all sides, was hardly in a position to embark in this potentially attractive direction.[156] For example, the Haitian legation in the United States was—perhaps understandably—more concerned with "illegal practices," e.g. U.S. ves-sels' "supposed transmission of correspondence with political refugees from Haiti" with the aim of destabilizing a government that was unsteady in the best of times.[157] Understandably, Haiti too was consumed with unraveling the often convoluted problems that ensued from a massive emigration of U.S. Negroes, who left rela-tives—and at times property—behind.[158] Moreover, Haiti continued to be dogged by claims stemming from the revolution and the massive indemnity paid to Paris.[159] In 1888 Haiti was forced in Washington to hand to Charles Adrien van Bokkelen $60,000, funds that would have been better allocated to health and education in Port-au-Prince.[160]

Nonetheless, Fortune's project, which envisioned mutually beneficial trade relations with Haiti, would have been a boon for both sides,[161] as suggested by the fact of a surfeit of applications for presumably lucrative Haitian consular posts in ports like Mobile[162] and Norfolk.[163]

The point is that the failed annexation did not squelch continuing interest by U.S. Negroes in the fate of Haiti.[164] Perhaps seeking to redeem himself, Douglass speaking in Chicago in 1893 saluted the Haitian Revolution as "one of the most wonderful events in the history of this eventful century and I may also say in the history of mankind." Rather than castigate the Haitians, as he did during his mission, he acknowledged that they "met deception with deception, arms with arms, harassing warfare with harassing warfare, fire with fire, blood with blood, and they would never have gained their freedom and independence if they had not thus matched the French at all points."[165]

In Samaná and Puerto Plata, the U.S. Negro emigrants continued to play a major role on the island—and this remains true today. During the dictatorship of Rafael Trujillo in the mid-20th century, this community suffered. Still, they persevered and, like their relatives on the mainland, they valued education; they built many schools and their children often returned to the United States for study, including at the Tuskegee Institute of Booker T. Washington. Some of the first engineers in the Dominican Republic emerged from this community.[166]

The influence went in the other direction too: Haitian-Americans have left an indelible mark on the mainland. The growing list includes Jelly Roll Morton, the famed musician and composer,[167] and Septima Clark, who has justifiably been compared with the legendary Rosa Parks as a heroine of the anti–Jim Crow movement from her perch in South Carolina.[168] Of course, perhaps the leading light of Black America—W. E. B. Du Bois—had roots in Haiti.[169] Unfortunately, this mutuality is not always recognized; for example, the contemporary Haitian-American artist Wyclef Jean who grew to maturity in the U.S. Northeast, has been troubled by conflict between this largely immigrant grouping and those now designated as "African American"—an ironic counterpart to the 19th century emigration to "Hayti" of U.S. Negroes.[170]

By the same token, African Americans today have not fully digested the implications of the failed annexation of the island. Indeed, the assumption of U.S. citizenship has come at a steep price: namely, presumed—or coaxed—support for imperial ventures that are harmful to longtime allies and are, ultimately, detrimental to the true interests of African Americans themselves. Nevertheless, the ultimate legacy of Haiti on the mainland is the penetrating impression left by Black Jacobinism, which inspired abolition and helped to generate a spirit of militancy among African Americans that has yet to be extinguished.

Notes

INTRODUCTION

1. George Washington to John Vaughan, 29 December 1791 and George Washington to "Sir," 2 October 1791 in Philander D. Chase, ed., *The Papers of George Washington, Presidential Series, Volume 9, September 1791-February 1792* (Charlottesville: University Press of Virginia, 2000). The island of Hispaniola was referred to by many—when a colony—as Saint Domingue or San Domingue or San Domingo or even Santo Domingo, the latter also being the name of the leading city in today's Dominican Republic. To avoid confusion, when referring to the entire island, I will use the term "Hispaniola." When referring to the post-1803 republic that dominated the western portion of the island (though it too at times was split along a north-south axis), I will use the term "Haiti" (though those I cite often use the term "Hayti"). Note: for about two decades concluding in 1844, the entire island was united as "Haiti."

2. George D. Terry, "A Study of the Impact of the French Revolution and the Insurrections in Saint-Domingue upon South Carolina: 1790-1805" (M.A. thesis, University of South Carolina, 1975), 40–41. See also Robert J. Alderson, *This Bright Era of Happy Revolutions: French Consul Michel-Ange Bernard Mangourit and International Republicanism in Charleston, 1792-1794* (Columbia: University of South Carolina Press, 2008), 179, 104–106: During this era it was "probable that South Carolina slaves influenced by the Haitian example . . . prepared a well-organized attempt to secure for themselves some measure of liberty." Typically crossing borders, a "rumored slave insurrection in 1793 had inter-state connections." It was on 20 July 1793 that the influential John Randolph in Richmond heard Africans stating, "the blacks were to kill the white people soon in this place. . . . the one who seemed to be chief speaker said, you see how the blacks . . . killed the whites in the French island and took it a little while ago . . . the date for the revolt was 15 October."

3. Emily Clark, *The Strange History of the American Quadroon: Free Women of Color in the Revolutionary Atlantic World* (Chapel Hill: University of North Carolina Press, 2013), 27. See also Robert Louis Stein, *The French Slave Trade in the Eighteenth Century: An Old Regime Business* (Madison: University of Wisconsin Press, 1979).

4. George Washington to Charles Pinckney, 17 March 1792, in Philander D. Chase, ed., *The Papers of George Washington, Presidential Series, Volume X, March-August 1792* (Charlottesville: University Press of Virginia, 1983), 128–129. See David Brion Davis, *The Problem of Slavery in the Age of Emancipation* (New York: Knopf, 2014), 48: "The Haitian Revolution strengthened the political argument for outlawing the American Slave Trade in 1808."

5. Rayford W. Logan, *The Diplomatic Relations of the United States with Haiti, 1776–1891* (Chapel Hill: University of North Carolina Press, 1941), 46.

6.   H. Knox to U.S. President, 20 June 1798, in Dudley Knox, ed., *Naval Documents Related to the Quasi-War Between the United States and France: Naval Operations from April 1799 to July 1799* (Washington, D.C.: Government Printing Office, 1936), 235–236. In 1798 the French governor of Guadeloupe reportedly said that if French-U.S. tensions eventuated in war, then Negro troops—viewed properly as especially intimidating on the mainland—would invade. John Adams contemplated this possibility and envisioned South Carolina—with its boisterous Negro majority—as the point of embarkation: See Terry, "A Study of the Impact of the French Revolution," 111, 117.

7.   Edward E. Baptist, *The Half Has Never Been Told: Slavery and the Making of American Capitalism* (New York: Basic, 2014), 44: Bonded labor was a drag on wage labor, pulling it downward and when bonded labor began to crumble, this downward drag began to dissipate.

8.   Francois Furstenberg, *When the United States Spoke French: The Refugees who Shaped a Nation* (New York: Penguin, 2014), 55: During the heyday of the slave trade to the island, an annual average of 37,000 Africans—a number approaching the total population of Philadelphia at that moment or greater than that of New York City—were transported from 1783 to 1792. For more on the role of North Americans in this trade, see—passim—the book by Horne referenced in the following footnote.

9.   Gerald Horne, *The Counter-Revolution of 1776: Slave Resistance and the Origins of the United States of America* (New York: New York University Press), 2014.

10.   Gerald Horne, *Race to Revolution: The United States and Cuba During Slavery and Jim Crow* (New York: Monthly Review Press), 2014.

11.   *City Gazette and Daily Advertiser* [Philadelphia], 12 August 1799.

12.   Gerald Horne, *Negro Comrades of the Crown: African-Americans and the British Empire Fight the United States before Emancipation* (New York: New York University Press), 2013.

13.   T. Lothrop Stoddard, *The French Revolution in San Domingo* (Boston: Houghton Mifflin, 1914), vii.

14.   Nick Nesbitt, *Universal Emancipation: The Haitian Revolution and the Radical Enlightenment* (Charlottesville: University of Virginia Press, 2008), 194. See also Logan, *The Diplomatic Relations*, 72: the "specter of a free Negro republic that owed its independence to a successful slave revolt frightened slave-holding countries as much as the shadow of Bolshevist Russia alarmed capitalistic countries in 1917."

15.   Logan, *The Diplomatic Relations*, 122.

16.   James Alexander Dun, "Dangerous Intelligence: Slavery, Race and St. Domingue in the Early American Republic" (Ph.D. diss., Princeton University, 2004), 168.

17.   Abraham Booth, Pastor of a Baptist Church, "Commerce in the Human Species, and the Enslaving of Innocent Persons Inimical to the Law of Moses and the Gospel of Christ, a Sermon . . . , London, January 29, 1791" (Philadelphia: Lawrence, 1792), Brown University, Providence, Rhode Island.

18.   James Stephen, *New Reasons for Abolishing the Slave Trade; Being the Last Section of a Larger Work, Now First Published Entitled 'the Dangers of the Country'* (London: Butterworth, 1807), Brown University.

19.   Quoted in Ralph Korngold, *Citizen Toussaint* (London: Victor Gollancz, 1945), 5. Stevens believed that there was a plan afoot during this time to invade both Dixie and Jamaica from Hispaniola. See Arthur Scherr, *Thomas Jefferson's Haitian Policy: Myths and Realities* (Lanham, Maryland: Rowman & Littlefield, 2011), 92.

20. Edward Stevens to General Thomas Maitland, 23 May 1799, in Dudley Knox, ed., *Naval Documents Related to the Quasi-War Between the United States and France: Naval Operations from April 1799 to July 1799* (Washington, D.C.: Government Printing Office, 1936), 235–236. Cf. James O. Jackson, "The Origins of Pan-African Nationalism: Afro-American & Haytien Relations, 1800–1863" (Ph.D. diss., Northwestern University, 1976), 145: "Evidence suggests that professional revolutionaries entered Jamaica from Hayti and participated in the Second Maroon War of 1795."

21. Timothy Pickering to John Adams, 5 June 1799, in Knox, *Naval Documents Related to the Quasi-War*, 301–303.

22. Hugh Cathcart to Thomas Maitland, 26 November 1799, CO245/1, National Archives of United Kingdom, London. Hereafter denoted as NAUK.

23. R.C. Dallas, *The History of the Maroons . . . , Volume II* (London: Strahan, 1803), 388, 291.

24. Thomas Jefferson to Rufus King, 13 July 1802, in Barbara Oberg et al., eds., *The Papers of Thomas Jefferson, Volume 38, 1 July to 12 November 1802* (Princeton: Princeton University Press, 2011), 54–56.

25. Winston Babb, "French Refugees from Saint Domingue to the Southern United States, 1791–1810" (Ph.D. diss., University of Virginia, 1954, 220).

26. Thomas Jefferson to William Moultrie, 23 December 1793, in John Catanzariti, ed., *The Papers of Thomas Jefferson, Volume 27, September to December 1793* (Princeton: Princeton University Press, 1997), 614.

27. Terry, "A Study of the Impact of the French Revolution," 3–4. France's emissary in Charleston "worked hard to carry out his orders to spread international revolution." See Alderson, *This Bright Era of Happy Revolutions*, 36.

28. Scherr, *Thomas Jefferson's Haitian Policy*, 290–291. See also John Adams to Abigail Adams, 26 September 1802, Reel 118, *Adams Family Papers*, Massachusetts Historical Society-Boston: "The prisoners from Saint-Domingue will be dangerous settlers in the Southern States . . . .the French care very little whether turning them loose is an insult or injury."

29. Edmond Charles Genet to French Consuls in the United States, 11 November 1793, in John Catanzariti, ed., *The Papers of Thomas Jefferson, Volume 27, 1 September to 31 December 1793* (Princeton: Princeton University Press, 1997), 405.

30. Furstenberg, 392. In other words, a timely reconciliation could have obviated the perceived need for the Louisiana Purchase.

31. David Barry Gaspar, "Slavery, War, and Revolution in the Greater Caribbean, 1789–1815," in Gaspar et al., eds., *A Turbulent Time: The French Revolution and the Greater Caribbean* (Bloomington: Indiana University Press, 1997), 1–50.

32. Kimberly S. Hanger, "Conflicting Loyalties: The French Revolution and Free People of Color in Spanish New Orleans" in Gaspar et al., *A Turbulent Time*, 178–203.

33. Roland McConnell, *Negro Troops of Antebellum Louisiana: A History of the Battalion of Free Men of Color* (Baton Rouge: Louisiana State University Press, 1968), 27.

34. David Barry Gaspar, "La Guerre des Bois: Revolution, War, and Slavery in Saint Lucia, 1793–1838," in Gaspar et al., *A Turbulent Time*, 102–130.

35. Raphael Dalleo, "Introduction," in Carla Calarge et al., eds., *Haiti and the Americas* (Jackson: University Press of Mississippi, 2013), 3–22.

36. Alexander Houston to Rear Admiral Harvey, 16 July 1796, CO101/34, NAUK.

37. Henry Hamilton to Henry Dundas, 18 December 1791, CO37/43, ibid.

38. John Harvey, President of the Council to Henry Harvey, 17 January 1792, CO37/43, ibid.

39. Henry Harvey to Henry Dundas, 12 January 1792, CO37/43, ibid.

40. Dalleo, *Haiti and the Americas*, 7.

41. Jose Morales, "The Hispaniola Diaspora, 1791–1850: Puerto Rico, Cuba, Louisiana, and Other Societies" (Ph.D. diss., University of Connecticut, 1986), 82.

42. Robert J. Cottrol, *The Long, Lingering Shadow: Slavery, Race, and Law in the American Hemisphere* (Athens: University of Georgia Press, 2013), 63.

43. Morales, "The Hispaniola Diaspora," 267.

44. Report, "Of the Carolina or Black Corps Serving in the Leeward Islands . . . ," circa 1791, CO101/31, NAUK.

45. Alfred Nathaniel Hunt, "The Influence of Haiti on the Antebellum South, 1791–1865" (Ph.D. diss., University of Texas, 1975), 38. See also Alfred N. Hunt, *Haiti's Influence on Antebellum America: Slumbering Volcano in the Caribbean* (Baton Rouge: Louisiana State University Press, 1988). But see *The Colored American*, 2 October 1841: This U.S. Negro journal stated that the "servile war" of Spartacus, "71 years before the Christian Era," led to the death of "40,000 Roman soldiers" while the "servile war" on the island meant "only 2000 whites were slain by the insurgents" and "nearly 10,000" of the latter "were slain by the whites." However, a leading U.S. Negro claimed during this era that "60,000 white men" were killed during the uprising of 1791–1804; see Jackson, "The Origins of Pan-African Nationalism," 178.

46. See also J.R. Oldfield, *Transatlantic Abolitionism: The Age of Revolution, 1787–1820* (New York: Cambridge University Press, 2013), 4–5: The Haitian Revolution "and the Caribbean region generally . . . played an important role in the slave-trade debates of 1804–1807. Indeed, for many activists, chief among them Henry Brougham, Haiti posed a simple choice: either to give up the slave trade or to risk losing everything—slaves, property, livelihoods—in a wave of violence orchestrated by Haiti's military leaders or, at the very least, patterned after their example."

47. Philippe R. Girard, "Caribbean Genocide: Racial War in Haiti, 1802–1804," *Patterns of Prejudice*, 39 (Number 2, 2005): 138–161, 139. See also Jeremy D. Popkin, ed., *Facing Racial Revolution: Eyewitness Accounts of the Haitian Insurrection* (Chicago: University of Chicago Press, 2007).

48. T. Lothrop Stoddard, *The French Revolution in San Domingo* (Honolulu: University Press of the Pacific, 2003), 348. The premier chronicler of the revolution, the Trinidadian intellectual C.L.R. James, argued that "these anti-white feelings" expressed on the island "were no infringement of liberty and equality but were in reality the soundest revolutionary policy. It was fear of counter-revolution." C.L.R. James, *The Black Jacobins: Toussaint L'Ouverture and the San Domingo Revolution* (New York: Vintage, 1989), 261. See also James's words in Britain's *New Statesman*, 28 March 1936; here he points to "the fact that the murder of all the whites in San Domingo (a tragedy from which the Haitians suffered ultimately) was instigated by white men and Englishmen. Cathcart, the English agent, warned Dessalines [the Haitian leader] that the English would neither trade with him nor support the independence of Haiti until every white man in the island was killed." See also Christian Hogsbjerg, ed., *Toussaint Louverture: The Story of the Only Successful Slave Revolt in History: A Play in Three Acts by C.L.R. James* (Durham: Duke University Press, 2013), 176–177.

49. See e.g. Ashli White, *Encountering Revolution: Haiti and the Making of the Early Republic* (Baltimore: Johns Hopkins University Press, 2010).

50. Pierce Butler, *Judah P. Benjamin* (Philadelphia: Jacobs, 1906), 59. See also Robert Douthat Meade, *Judah P. Benjamin: Confederate Statesman* (New York: Oxford University Press, 1943), 14, 76.

51. Colonel Tousard to Alexander Hamilton, 7 August 1798, Box 3, Anne-Louis de Tousard Papers, University of Michigan-Ann Arbor.

52. Mary Lilla McLure, *Louisiana Leaders, 1850–1860* (Shreveport: Journal, 1935), 22, 63. Protestants were found heavily in the southwest of France—e.g. Bordeaux—a region which supplied a goodly number of "white Americans." See Timothy Baycroft, *France: Inventing the Nation* (London: Hodder, 2008), 197.

53. Jon Butler, *The Huguenots in America: A Refugee People in New World Society* (Cambridge: Harvard University Press, 1983), 100–101, 121–122, 150.

54. Sally Edwards, *James Louis Petigru, 1789–1863* (McCormick, South Carolina: McCormick County Historical Commission, 1977), 25. See also Francois Lagarde, ed., *The French in Texas: History, Migration, Culture* (Austin: University of Texas Press, 2003).

55. Gerard Colby Zilg, *DuPont: Behind the Nylon Curtain* (Englewood Cliffs: Prentice Hall, 1974), 33. This family with French roots owned Africans in South Carolina and also leaned toward royalist and anti-Jacobin factions in the homeland.

56. Tench Coxe to Aaron Burr, 17 January 1802, in Mary-Jo Kline, ed., *Political Correspondence and Public Papers of Aaron Burr, Volume II* (Princeton: Princeton University Press, 1983), 656–657.

57. Faye Felterman Tydlaska, "Between Nation and Empire: Representations of the Haitian Revolution in Antebellum Literary Culture" (Ph.D. diss., Tulane University, 2007), 138.

58. Timothy Baycroft, *France: Inventing the Nation* (London: Hodder, 2008), 16.

59. Letter from U.S. Legation, 23 October 1819, File 6, Affaires Diverses Politiques/Etats Unis, 1814–1896, Ministere des Affaires Etrangers-Paris. Hereafter denoted as MAE-Paris. At the same site in Annex 1, see also correspondence from the legation beginning 12 August 1818 and in Annex 2 (from which the quotations are taken), *Collection de differents discourse et pieces de poesie prononces le jour de la fête donnée à Mr. Duncan McIntosh par les Francais refugies de Saint Domingue auxquels se sont Joints Beaucoup d'Americains. Amis de la Bienfaisance.* Tribut de Reconnaissance. Baltimore, 9 January 1809. Impressed for Coale and Thomas by Jean W. Butler, 1809. All translations are by the author unless indicated otherwise.

60. Peter Stephen Chazotte, *Historical Sketches of the Revolutions and the Foreign and Civil Wars in the Island of St. Domingo* (New York: Applegate, 1840). The version of this book that I read at the New-York Historical Society does not contain page numbers.

61. Hunt, "The Influence of Haiti," 146; Arthur Gobineau, *Comte de Gobineau and Orientalism: Selected Eastern Writings* (New York: Routledge, 2009).

62. Terry, "A Study of the Impact of the French Revolution," 111: In May 1797, the French Consul in Charleston "protested vigorously against the action of the city in forcing the French mulatto general, Martial Resse, to put up a bond to remain in the state."

63. Edmund Ruffin, "Equality of the Races—Haytien and British Experiments," *De Bow's Review*, 1 (July 1859): 27–38.

64. Morales, "The Hispaniola Diaspora."

65. William Sidney Drewry, *The Southampton Insurrection* (Washington: Neale, 1900), 121–
     123: He notes that "recollections of St. Domingo were still vivid in 1831" and points to an
     enslaved African named "Philip," who "may have had communication with some of those
     who were in ringleaders" in Turner's revolt; he "came from St. Domingo" before arriving
     in the commonwealth. The judge presiding in the trial of the conspirators had similar
     ties to the island via marriage and Africans owned by this family came from the island.
     See also Jackson, "The Origins of Pan-African Nationalism," 127–128: "Fragmentary
     evidence . . . suggested the Nat Turner rebellion may have been influenced by the Haitian
     Revolution. Many Haytian refugees and their black slaves settled in the South Hampton
     area." Apparently following the revolt, an African named—impressively—"Nero" came to
     this still shaken area and told slaveholders there of his plan to "educate blacks, to spy upon
     the whites of the South, to disseminate insurrectionistic [*sic*] pamphlets," and, generally,
     to wreak ruination. He also detailed the role Haiti "was to play as a site for training the
     leaders of the approaching insurrection and in raising money for a black college to be built
     in Boston. Finally, after the rebellion, Haiti would offer 'an asylum for those who survive
     the approaching carnage.'"

66. Larry Koger, *Black Slaveowners: Free Black Slave Masters in South Carolina, 1790–1860*
     (Jefferson, North Carolina: McFarland, 1985), 122. See also Lois A. Walker and Susan
     R. Silverman, eds., *A Documented History of Gullah Jack Pritchard and the Denmark
     Vesey Slave Insurrection of 1822* (Lewiston: Mellen, 2000), 91, 169, 183: Haiti was "almost
     certainly a factor" in this uprising; "there was a company of French Negroes" among the
     Vesey rebels. A contemporary source said the conspirators "were even made to believe that
     as soon as they began to fight . . . that the San Domingo people . . . would 'march an army'
     to aid their struggle; and Vesey had proclaimed amongst them that as soon as they robbed
     the banks of their specie and the King Street shops of their goods and got everything
     on board ship, they should then sail away to San Domingo to enjoy their treasure." In
     this volume, see also the "Intendant's Report," 295–337, 300; here an enslaved African
     repeats this story of Haitian involvement in the plot. Contemporaneous sources took quite
     seriously the claim of Haitian involvement and even if exaggerated—a point stressed by
     many historians today—what needs to be considered here is to what extent did these claims
     influence ongoing policy and what was the impact of so many Africans then perceiving
     that they would be backed by Haiti? See *Report of the Minority of the Special Committee
     of Seven and Whom was Referred so Much of his Late Excellency's Message No. 1 as Relates
     to Slavery and the Slave Trade* (Columbia: Steam Power Press, 1857); the Vesey revolt, it
     is noted here, "was entirely owing to emissaries from the West Indies." Henry Bibb, *Slave
     Insurrections in Southampton County, Virginia headed by Nat Turner with an Interesting
     Letter from a Fugitive Slave to His Old Master* . . . (New York: Wesleyan Book Room,
     1850): A witness to the Vesey revolt, who was an enslaved African, was informed by "one of
     his companions" that "in the event of . . . [a] rising they would not be without help, as the
     people from San Domingo and Africa would assist them in obtaining their liberty, if they
     only made the motion first themselves." *The Late Contemplated Insurrection in Charleston
     . . . with the Execution of Thirty-Six of the Patriots: The Death of William Irving, the
     Provoked Husband, and Joe Devaul for Refusing to be the Slave* . . . (New York: Publisher,
     1850). The latter three sources were all viewed at the University of South Carolina. See
     also Babb, "French Refugees from St. Domingue to the Southern United States," 401: The

revolution "influenced American slaves to consider insurrections and American whites for a generation attributed all revolts to Santo Domingo." See as well Jackson, "The Origins," 126: A co-conspirator in the 1822 plot said that Vesey "was in the habit of reading to me all the passages in the newspapers that related to St. Domingo."

67. David Brion Davis, *The Problem of Slavery in the Age of Emancipation* (New York: Knopf), 82.

68. Sylvia Frey, *Water from the Rock: Black Resistance in a Revolutionary Age* (Princeton: Princeton University Press, 1991), 226, 132; Chris Dixon, *African America and Haiti: Emigration and Black Nationalism* (Westport: Greenwood, 2000), 27–28.

69. Petition to Governor William Claiborne, 9 November 1804, in Clarence Edwin Carter, ed., *The Territorial Papers of the United States, Volume IX: The Territory of New Orleans, 1803–1812* (Washington, D.C.: Government Printing Office, 1940), 326.

70. Lachance, "The Politics of Fear," 171.

71. John Watkins, Mayor of New Orleans, to Secretary Graham, 6 September 1805, in Carter, *The Territorial Papers*.

72. Robert Livingston to Rufus King, 7 May 1803, in Edward Alexander Parsons, ed., *The Original Letters of Robert R. Livingston, 1801–1803, with a Brief History of the Louisiana Purchase* (New Orleans: Louisiana Historical Society, 1953), 120–122. The flux introduced in this sensitive region was not only detected by Haiti. By 1807, Aaron Burr—a leading U.S. official—was said to have noticed that "many boats were under preparation," featuring "an unusual number of suspicious characters," adding weight to his plan to subvert the United States: "this enterprise is to receive aid from certain foreign powers." See "Message from the President of the United States Transmitting Information Touching an Illegal Combination of Private Individuals Against the Peace and Safety of the Union and a Military Expedition Planned by Them Against the Territories of a Power in Amity with the United States with Measures Pursued for Suppressing the Same . . . ," 22 January 1807, The Historic New Orleans Collection, Williams Research Center, New Orleans.

73. Rebecca Hartkopf Schloss, *Sweet Liberty: The Final Days of Slavery in Martinique* (Philadelphia: University of Pennsylvania Press, 2009), 56–57. See also William Omer Foster, *James Jackson, Duelist, and Militant Statesman, 1757–1806* (Athens: University of Georgia Press, 2009), 181: In 1805, said Jackson, "in a private [conversation] . . . a French general had remarked that plans had been made, on the expectation of French victory, to send the rebellious slaves to the southern parts of the United States," which was a "melancholy subject for South Carolina and Georgia . . . .one of those brigands introduced into the Southern States was worse than an hundred . . . blacks from Africa and more dangerous in the United States."

74. Albert Thrasher, *On to New Orleans! Louisiana's Heroic 1811 Slave Revolt; A Brief History and Documents Relating to the Rising of Slaves in January 1811 in the Territory of Orleans* (New Orleans: Cypress, 1995), 70; see also Daniel Rasmussen, *American Uprising: The Untold Story of America's Largest Slave Revolt* (New York: Harper, 2011). Strikingly, Deslondes shared a surname with the spouse of the state's preeminent ante-bellum politician, John Slidell; see McLure, *Louisiana Leaders*, 35. She spoke fluent French.

75. Timothy Dwight, "Triumph of Democracy," in James G. Basker, ed., *An Anthology of Poems about Slavery, 1660–1810* (New Haven: Yale University Press, 2002), 488.

76. "Testimony of Ben," 1800, in Robert Starobin, ed., *Blacks in Bondage: Letters of American Slaves* (New York: New Viewpoints, 1974), 133–135. See also James Sidbury, "Saint Domingue in Virginia: Ideology, Local Meanings, and Resistance to Slavery, 1790–1800," *Journal of Southern History* (Number 3, August 1997): 531–552.

77. "Circular Letter to Slave Holders" from Governor Winthrop Sargent, 16 November 1800, in Dunbar Rowland, ed., *The Mississippi Territorial Archives, 1798–1803: Executive Journals of Governor Winthrop Sargent and Governor William Charles Cole Claiborne, Volume I* (Nashville: Brandon, 1905), 311–312.

78. Faye Felterman Tydlaska, "Between Nation and Empire: Representations of the Haitian Revolution in Antebellum Literary Culture" (Ph.D. diss., Tulane University, 2007), 18.

79. Uriah Derrick D'Arcy, *The Black Vampire: A Legend of St. Domingo* (New York: Author, 1819).

80. Thomas Jefferson to James Madison, 5 February 1799, in Barbara Oberg, ed., *The Papers of Thomas Jefferson, Volume 31, February 1799 to 31 May 1800* (Princeton: Princeton University Press, 2004), 9–11. See also Logan, *The Diplomatic Relations*, 70: By the late 1790s, in the United States, there was "fear both of a new piratical nation like those in North Africa and of the danger to the institution of slavery"—both were "uppermost in the mind" of the slave-holding republic.

81. Albert Gallatin to Thomas Jefferson, 25 July 1801, in Barbara Oberg et al., eds., *The Papers of Thomas Jefferson, Volume 34, 1 May to 31 July 1801* (Princeton: Princeton University Press, 2007), 637.

82. Thomas Jefferson to Albert Gallatin, 26 July 1801, in Oberg, *Volume 34*, 644.

83. Report by Mayor James Watkins, 2 February 1804, in Dunbar Rowland, ed., *Official Letter Books of William C.C. Claiborne, 1801–1816, Volume II* (Jackson, Mississippi: State Department of Archives and History, 1917), 3–13, 5. See also Thrasher, *On to New Orleans!*, 44: In June 1804 "revolutionary Africans from St. Domingue had in fact penetrated the city" of New Orleans; an African "named Marseille" who had served in the insurgent army on the island was "inside the city gates." Weeks later a "colored man named Dutque accused of having taken a very active part in the revolt of St. Domingo was aboard a ship in the river." See also Governor Claiborne to Captain Johnson, 18 July 1804, in ibid., 256–258: New Orleans was "instructed to visit every vessel entering the mouth of the river and to ascertain the number of Negroes on board"; the authorities were "particularly desirous to prevent the introduction of any of the brigands of St. Domingo"; though, sadly, the "vigilance heretofore observed has been evaded and speculators and others have found means to bring hither many dangerous Characters."

84. Daniel L. Schafer, *Zephaniah Kingsley, Jr. and the Atlantic World* (Gainesville: University Press of Florida, 2013).

85. William Omer Foster, *James Jackson, Duelist, and Militant Statesman, 1757–1806* (Athens: University of Georgia Press, 2009), 182.

86. Logan, *The Diplomatic Relations*, 114.

87. Frederic Bancroft, *Slave Trading in the Old South* (New York: Ungar, 1959), 41.

88. Sara E. Johnson, *The Fear of French Negroes: Trans-Colonial Collaboration in the Revolutionary Americas* (Berkeley: University of California Press, 2012), 92.

89. Matthew Joseph Karp, "This Vast Southern Empire: The South and the Foreign Policy of Slavery, 1833–1861" (Ph.D. diss., University of Pennsylvania, 2011), 190.

90. Letter from Vice Consul, Cap-Haïtien, 19 December 1825, Tome 1, Correspondance Consulaire et Commerciale (1793–1901)/Le Cap (Haiti) et Gonaives, 1825–1837, Cote 163CCC/1, p. 6, MAE-Paris.

91. Letter to "My Dear Sir," 22 October 1822, CO28/91, NAUK.

92. Colonel A. William Young to "My Dear Sir," 28 October 1822, ibid.

93. Report of Harbour Master of Trinidad, 20 October 1822, ibid.

94. Miguel de la Torre, Captain General, and Francisco Gonsalvez de Dinares, Jefe Superior Politico to the Governor of Barbados, 14 October 1822, ibid. Haitian assistance to Simon Bolivar's national liberation struggles is well-known. See A. James Arnold, "Recuperating the Haitian Revolution in Literature: From Victor Hugo to Derek Walcott," in Doris L. Garraway, ed., *Tree of Liberty: Cultural Legacies of the Haitian Revolution in the Atlantic World* (Charlottesville: University of Virginia Press, 2008), 179–199: Apparently the Haitian leadership "asked Bolivar not to liberate the slaves in South America in [their] name" in order to "avoid the wrath of the United States," the leading enslaving power. See also David Patrick Geggus and Norman Fiering, *The World of the Haitian Revolution* (Bloomington: Indiana University Press, 2009) and Brian Ward et al., eds., *The American South and the Atlantic World* (Tallahassee: University Press of Florida, 2013).

95. Joseph C. Dorsey, *Slave Traffic in the Age of Abolition: Puerto Rico, West Africa, and the Non-Hispanic Caribbean, 1815–1859* (Gainesville: University Press of Florida, 2003), 71–72.

96. Rachel Hope Cleves, *The Reign of Terror in America: Visions of Violence from Anti-Jacobinism to Antislavery* (New York: Cambridge University Press, 2009), 113. Holland's conception of Black Jacobins may have been influenced by the fact that as early as 1799 one observer found that "Charleston is full of Frenchmen from St. Domingo" and, thus, "the principles of the French demagogues predominated long" there. "For several years a Jacobin club existed in this town." See Duke de la Rochefoucault Liancourt, *Travels Through the United States of North America, the Country of the Iroquois, and Upper Canada in the Year 1795, 1796 and 179 . . . , Volume I* (London: Phillips, 1799), 584. See also Hunt, "The Influence of Haiti on the Antebellum South," 121, 127: "The French Revolution, Jacobinism, and black revolt became synonymous to many Americans," notably since "there is ample evidence to suggest that the efforts of Toussaint Louverture, Jean Jacques Dessalines, Henri Christophe, and other leaders did not go unnoticed by American slaves."

97. U.S. Consul to Secretary of State, 30 July 1821, Roll 1, T330, *Despatches from U.S. Consuls in Aux Cayes*, National Archives and Records Administration, College Park, Maryland. Hereafter denoted as NARA-CP.

98. W. Jeffrey Bolster, *Black Jacks: African American Sailors in the Age of Sail* (Cambridge: Harvard University Press, 1997), 145–147.

99. Charles McKenzie to George Canning, 2 June 1826, FO35/3, NAUK.

100. Letter from Dessalines, 14 January 1804, in Daniel Supplice, ed., *Pages D'Histoire* (Port-au-Prince: Presses Nationales d'Haiti, 2012), 110.

101. President Jean P. Boyer to Charles Collins, 25 May 1824, in *Correspondence Relative to the Emigration to Hayti of the Free People of Color in the United States, Together with the Instructions to the Agent Sent out by President Boyer* (New York: Mahlon Day, 1824).

102. *Freedom's Journal*, 16 January 1829.

103. William Lloyd Garrison to H.E. Benson, 18 August 1836, Ms. A.1.1., Boston Public

Library. This archive has some of the richest material on Haiti during this era. Also at this site see Ms. A.9.21, p. 13: letters to Garrison from the island.

104. P. Treadwell to Mr. and Mrs. Chapman, circa 1840s, Ms. A.9.2.15, p. 45, Boston Public Library.

105. See, e.g., "Instructions pour Les Croiseurs . . . Annexe à La Convention Supplementaire Relative à La Represion de la Traite des Noirs . . . ," 22 March 1833, and "Traite Signe a Port-au-Prince avec La France Pour Assurer La Represion de la Traite des Esclaves," 29 August 1840, in *Recueil des Traites de la République D'Haiti . . . Tome Premier, 1804–1904 . . . ,*" Publication de la Secretaire d'Etat des Relations Exterieures, Imprimerie de L'Etat, 1945, Ministere des Affaires Etrangers, Port-au-Prince. Hereafter, MAE-Port-au-Prince.

106. Entry, 22 June 1858, in William Kauffman Scarborough, ed., *The Diary of Edmund Ruffin, Volume I, Toward Independence, October 1856–April 1856* (Baton Rouge: Louisiana State University Press, 1972), 149–150.

107. *A Colored American, A Brief Inquiry into the Prospective Results that Might Follow the Secret Mission to Dominico and Hayti, with Its Probable Effects on Colored Americans* (Philadelphia: John Coates, 1852), Historical Society of Pennsylvania, Philadelphia.

108. Report from Consulate of France in Santo Domingo, 1 July 1844, Secretario de Estado de Relaciones Exteriores, Institucion de Procedencia, Consulado de Francia en Santo Domingo, 1844–1846, Caja/Legajo/Libro 4, Archivo General de la Nacion, Santo Domingo. Hereafter, AGN-Santo Domingo. A "Massacre of the whites" was said to be intended by Haiti, which caused the secessionists to "desire the protection and intervention of France." Report in French.

109. Memorandum on Treaty between the D.R. and Spain, 18 February 1854, Relaciones Exteriores, Legajo 6, Expediente 1–7, 1853, ibid.; Legajo 7, Expediente 1–13, 1854, ibid. Report in Spanish; translations by author unless otherwise indicated.

110. John Wilson to Secretary of State John Clayton, 30 March 1850, Roll 8, T8, *Despatches from U.S. Consuls in Cap-Haïtien,* NARA-CP: "The English Vice Consul at Port-au-Prince has long been the influential advisor of the Emperor and exercises considerable influence over him."

111. Robert Schomburgk to Earl of Clarendon, 18 December 1854, FO23/19, NAUK.

112. Robert Schomburgk to Earl of Clarendon, 6 November 1853, FO23/16, ibid.

113. John Wilson to Secretary of State Daniel Webster, 7 August 1851, Roll 8, T8, *Despatches from U.S. Consuls in Cap-Haïtien.*

114. Report from D.R. Consulate in Curaçao, 8 December 1857, Relaciones Exteriores, Legajo 10, 1857, Expediente 1–23, AGN-Santo Domingo.

115. Davis, *The Problem of Slavery in the Age of Emancipation,* 326.

116. Richmond Loring to Secretary of State Lewis Cass, 30 November 1860, Roll 3, T330, *Despatches from U.S. Consuls in Aux Cayes.*

117. John Tyler article in *De Bow's Review,* April 1860, Edward Everett Remarks at Faneuil Hall, 8 December 1859, and *Feuille du Commerce* [Haiti], 21 January 1860, in John Stauffer and Zoe Trod, eds., *The Tribunal: Responses to John Brown and the Harpers Ferry Raid* (Cambridge: Harvard University Press, 2012), 329–330, 400–401, 178–181.

118. David C. Keehn, *Knights of the Golden Circle: Secret Empire, Southern Secession, Civil War* (Baton Rouge: Louisiana State University Press, 2013), 67.

119. James Redpath to Hon. M. Pleasance, 2 March 1861, *Bureau of Emigration (Haiti), Reports and Correspondence*, Boston Public Library. See also *Chicago Times*, 21 February 1861.

120. Stephen Preston to U.S. Secretary of State, 30 June 1870, Roll 2, *Notes from the Haitian Legation in the U.S. to the Department of State*, 1861–1906, NARA-CP.

121. See "Traite Haitiano-Americain," 3 November 1864, in *Recueil des Traites*, MAE-Port-au-Prince.

122. Gabriel Manigault, *The Signs of the Times* (New York: Blelock, circa 1860s).

123. President W.R. Inglis to "Sir," 17 January 1862, CO301/33, NAUK.

124. See, e.g., Soraya Aracena, *Los Immigrantes Norteamericanos de Samana* (Dominican Republic: Helvetas, 2000).

125. "The American and Haytien Claims Commission; the United States vs. the Republic of Hayti in the Matter of the Claim of Antonio Pelletier; Record," Washington, D.C., 1885, Harvard Law School Library, Cambridge, Massachusetts.

126. Report, 8 July 1862, Despatches from Haiti, Ministerio de Asuntos Exteriores-Madrid. Hereinafter designated as MAE-Madrid. For more on this anxiety about links between U.S. Negroes and Haiti, see Memorandum, 23 October 1860, Box 5, *Papers of Spanish Consulate in Charleston*, Duke University.

127. Martin Hood to Earl Russell, 8 September 1863, FO23/48, NAUK.

128. Interview with U.S. Grant, 6 July 1878 in John Y. Simon, ed., *The Papers of U.S. Grant, Volume 24: 1873* (Carbondale: Southern Illinois University Press, 2000), 430–432.

129. Daniel Payne, *Recollections of Seventy Years*, New York: Arno, 1969, 14–15.

130. Robert S. Levine, "Circulating the Nation: David Walker, the Missouri Compromise, and the Rise of the Black Press," in Todd Vogel, ed., *The Black Press: New Literary and Historical Essays* (New Brunswick: Rutgers University Press, 2001), 17–36, 26–27.

131. See, e.g., Julian Stohlman to Clement Haentjens, Haiti's envoy in the United States, 24 March 1894 and L. Edgar Frost to Clement Haentjens, 9 June 1894, Départment des Relations Extérieures, 740, Légation d'Haiti a New York et a Washington, Archive Nationale d'Haiti, Port-au-Prince. Hereinafter, ANH. Stohlman wrote from Brooklyn: "I am desirous of serving in the Haytian army as a commissioned officer"; he had "several years experience in military affairs. I am 26 years of age, [a] graduate from military school." Frost wrote from Lansing, asking "would it be possible for a graduate of a military academy, now [an] officer in the National Guard, to obtain a commission in the army of Hayti." At the same site and in the same file, see Sarah Jones, New York, to Haitian Consul, 18 October 1892: She writes about "Armand Willy Jones, who was sergeant in the 10th Regiment for Apache," and who presumably was then residing in Haiti. The question of U.S. Negro soldiers who emigrated to Haiti and joined the military needs more investigation.

132. Frederick Douglass, "Lecture on Haiti," Chicago, 2 January 1893, in Philiip S. Foner, ed., *The Life and Writings of Frederick Douglass, Volume IV, Reconstruction and After* (New York: International Publishers, 1955), 478–490.

133. W.E.B. Du Bois, *The Suppression of the African Slave Trade to the United States of America, 1638–1870* (New York: Social Science Press, 1954), 70.

134. Letter to Charles Villervaleix, 9 September 1874, Département des Affaires Etranger, 828, Légation d'Haiti à Londres, 1871–1874, ANH.

135. Foreign Office to Charles Villervaleix, Légation à Londres.

136. E.A. Keeling of American Expedition Association of New York to Clement Haentjens, 7

December 1895, Departement des Relations Exterieures, 740, Legation d'Haiti a New York et a Washington, ANH.

137. B. Waddington to Clement Haentjens, 2 January 1896, in Legation d'Haiti a New York et a Washington, ANH.

138. Gerald Horne, *Race War! White Supremacy and the Japanese Attack on the British Empire* (New York: New York University Press, 2003).

139. U.S. Department of State to Clement Haentjens, 23 October 1895, in Legation d'Haiti a New York et a Washington, ANH.

140. Robert J. Cottrol, *The Long, Lingering Shadow: Slavery, Race, and Law in the American Hemisphere* (Athens: University of Georgia Press, 2013), 67.

141. Sergei N. Durylin, *Ira Aldridge* (Trenton: Africa World Press, 2014), 24.

142. William Wells Brown, *St. Domingo: Its Revolutions and its Patriots, a Lecture. Delivered Before the Metropolitan Atheneum, London May 16 and St. Thomas Church, Philadelphia. December 20, 1854* (Boston: Bela March, 1855). See also Ezra Greenspan, *William Wells Brown: An African American Life* (New York: Norton, 2014).

143. "Sketch of a Journey through the Northern Provinces of the Dominican Republic and the Peninsula of Samana," 25 August 1851, FO23/11, NAUK.

1. CONFRONTING THE RISE OF BLACK JACOBINS, 1791–1793

1. George Washington to "Sir," 24 September 1791, in Philander D. Chase, ed., *The Papers of George Washington, Presidential Series, Volume 9, September 1791 to February 1792* (Charlottesville: University Press of Virginia, 2000), 15–16.

2. Morales, "The Hispaniola Diaspora, 1791–1850," 33. See also Donald Hickey, "America's Response to the Slave Revolt in Haiti, 1791–1806," *Journal of the Early Republic*, 9 (Winter 1982): 361–379. See also Tom Reiss *The Black Count: Glory, Revolution, Betrayal, and the Real Count of Monte Cristo* (New York: Crown, 2012), 75: "In 1781 alone, the Crown spent 227 million livres, a huge portion of its budget, on the American cause; its naval costs alone were five times their normal peacetime levels" fueled by "borrowing on a massive scale."

3. Dun, "Dangerous Intelligence," 122.

4. Hunt, "The Influence of Haiti on the Antebellum South, 1791–1865," 125. See Gabriel Manigault to Mrs. Manigault, 7 December 1792, *Manigault Family Papers*, University of South Carolina: Writing from Columbia, South Carolina, he reports on a "most tedious debate" on "stopping the importation of Negroes for four years"; while the House is receptive, the Senate is not.

5. Mary Treudley, "The United States and Santo Domingo, 1789–1866," *Journal of Race Development*, 7 (1916): 83–274, 103. See also George Washington to Charles Pinckney, 17 March 1792, in Philander D. Chase, ed., *The Papers of George Washington, Presidential Series, Volume 10, March–August 1792* (Charlottesville: University Press of Virginia, 2002), 128–129: While referencing the island, it is observed that the "direful effects of Slavery which at this moment are presented, would have operated to produce a total prohibition of the importation of Slaves."

6. Carolyn Fick, *The Making of Haiti: The Saint Domingue Revolution from Below* (Knoxville: University of Tennessee Press, 2004), 105.

7. Jacob Mayer to Thomas Allen, 17 October 1791, Box 5, Folder 5, *Allen Family Papers*, American Antiquarian Society, Worcester, Massachusetts: "Our land is at present greatly

disturbed by the Negroes who have again revolted and destroyed the plantations . . . little or no business is done."

8. Davis, *The Problem of Slavery in the Age of Emancipation*, 349.

9. Account of William Brown, U.S. Navy, 10 October 1800 in Dudley Knox, ed., *Naval Documents Related to the Quasi-War Between the United States and France: Naval Operations from June 1800 to November 1800* (Washington, D.C.: Government Printing Office, 1938), 484.

10. Thomas Jefferson to Albert Gallatin, 26 July 1801, in Barbara Oberg, ed., *The Papers of Thomas Jefferson, Volume 34, 1 May to 31 July 1801* (Princeton: Princeton University Press, 2007), 644.

11. Entry, 21 September 1791, in Elaine Forman Crane, ed., *The Diary of Elizabeth Drinker, Volume I* (Boston: Northeastern University Press, 1991), 471.

12. Charleston Merchants to George Washington, 9 November 1793 in Theodore J. Crackel, ed., *The Papers of George Washington, Volume 14, 1 September to 31 December 1793* (Charlottesville: University Press of Virginia, 2008), 347.

13. William Walton, *Present State of the Spanish Colonies Including a Particular Report on Hispaniola or the Spanish Part of Santo Domingo with a General Survey . . .* , Volume I (London: Longman, Hurst, 1810), 16, 123.

14. Lawrence N. Powell, *The Accidental City: Improvising New Orleans* (Cambridge: Harvard University Press, 2012), 73.

15. Horne, *The Counter-Revolution of 1776*, passim.

16. William R. Nester, *George Rogers Clark: 'I Glory in War'* (Norman: University of Oklahoma Press, 2012), 100–101.

17. Lachance, "The Politics of Fear," 162.

18. Alfred E. Lemmon and John H. Lawrence, "Common Routes: St. Domingue and Louisiana," in *Common Routes: St. Domingue/Louisiana* (New Orleans: Historic New Orleans Collection, 2006), 85–120, 86. See, e.g., Father Mathurin Let Petit, S.J., *The Natchez Massacre: A Full and Authoritative Relation Derived from Eye-Witnesses of the Massacre at the Post of the Natchez on October 28th 1729, in which More than Two Hundred French Men, Women, and Children Were Treacherously Murdered* (New Orleans: Poor Rich Press, 1950).

19. Gerard LaFleur and Lucien Abenon, "The Protestants and the Colonization of the French West Indies," in Bertrand Van Ruymbeke and Randy J. Sparks, eds., *Memory and Identity: The Huguenots in France and the Atlantic Diaspora* (Columbia: University of South Carolina Press, 2003), 267–284: "The Huguenots played a crucial role in the French Antilles during the first years of colonization"—ditto for Carolina. In the same volume, see R.C. Nash, "Huguenot Merchants and the Development of South Carolina's Slave Population and Atlantic Trading Economy, 1680–1775," 208–240. See also Bernard Van Ruymbeke, *From New Babylon to Eden: The Huguenots and their Migration to Colonial South Carolina* (Columbia: University of South Carolina Press, 2006).

20. Tom Reiss, *The Black Count: Glory, Revolution, Betrayal, and the Real Count of Monte Cristo* (New York: Crown, 2012), 69.

21. "Strangres [*sic*]," no date, Box 2, *Illinois Writers Project. 'Negro in Illinois' Papers*, Vivian Harsh Research Collection of Afro-American History and Literature, Carter G. Woodson Regional Library, Chicago Public Library. See also Lawrence Cortesi, *Jean Du Sable:*

Father of Chicago (Philadelphia: Chilton, 1972); Joseph Jeremie, *Jean Baptiste Dessables: An Emancipated Haitian Negro Slave Founder of Chicago*, circa 1950, Chicago History Museum. At this latter site, see also Joseph Jeremie, "Haiti and Chicago: From Saint-Marc to Saint Charles, Missouri," 1953. Mr. Bossu, *Travels Through that Part of North America Formerly Called Louisiana* (London: Davies, 1771), University of North Carolina, Chapel Hill.

22.   Marquis de Lafayette to Benjamin Franklin, 20 March 1779, in Barbara Oberg, ed., *The Papers of Benjamin Franklin, Volume 29, March 1 through June 30, 1779* (New Haven: Yale University Press, 1992), 171–172.

23.   See, e.g., J.P. Brissot de Warville, *Oration Upon the Necessity of Establishing, at Paris, a Society to Promote the Abolition of the Trade and Slavery of the Negroes* (Philadelphia: Francis Bailey, 1788). See also *Mémoire Sure Les Noirs de L'Amérique Septentrionale Lu à L'Assemblée de la Société des Amis des Noirs, le 9 Février 1789* (Paris: Calliau et De Senne, 1789).

24.   Eugene Parker Chase, ed., *Our Revolutionary Forefathers: The Letters of Francois, Marquis de Barbe-Marbois, During his Residence in the United States as Secretary of the French Legation, 1779–1785* (New York: Duffield, 1929), 46–48, Letter, 29 June 1779: On his way to the mainland, the writer was eating dinner "peacefully" when he noticed an "American vessel . . . we saw something black falling from the top of the yards into the sea . . . .we looked with our glasses and saw that it was a miserable Negro, entirely naked, whom they were giving a keel-hauling. Since this punishment is very severe," he rationalized unconvincingly, "it must have been a grave offense."

25.   "Slavery Legislation in Missouri," no date, Vertical File, Missouri State Archives, Jefferson City. See also Eugene Morrow Violette, *A History of Missouri* (Washington, D.C.: Heath, 1918), 80.

26.   See, e.g., Jacob M. Price, *France and the Chesapeake: A History of the French Tobacco Monopoly, 1674–1791, and of its Relationship to the British and American Tobacco Trades*, Two Volumes (Ann Arbor: University of Michigan Press, 1973).

27.   Horne, *The Counter-Revolution of 1776*, passim.

28.   See *A State of the Trade Carried on by the French on the Island of Hispaniola, by the Merchants in North America, Under Colour of Flags of Truce . . . by a Merchant of London* (London: Owen, 1760); this rare document can be found both at Columbia University and the New-York Historical Society.

29.   Mary Treudley, "The United States and Santo Domingo, 1789–1866," *Journal of Race Development*, 7 (1916): 83–274, 91.

30.   Fred Rumble, "The Life of Ralph Izard, 1742–1804" (M.A. thesis, Indiana University, 1935), 10–11, 22.

31.   Frank Moya Pons, *The Dominican Republic: A National History* (Princeton: Markus Wiener, 2010), 92.

32.   Charles Pettigrew to "My Dear Polly," 11 March 1785, Box 1, *Pettigrew Family Papers*, University of North Carolina, Chapel Hill.

33.   Richard J. Follett, "The Sugar Masters: Slavery, Economic Development, and Modernization on Louisiana Sugar Plantations, 1820–1860" (Ph.D. diss., Louisiana State University, 1997), 62–63.

34.   Francis Alexander Stanislaus, Baron de Wimpeffen, *A Voyage to Saint Domingo in the Years 1788, 1789, and 1790* (London: Cadell and Davies, 1797).

35. Clark, *The Strange History of the American Quadroon*, 12. See Dun, "Dangerous Intelligence," 28: "Between August 1789 and the end of 1793, vessels coming from the island made up between 18% and 25% of all arrivals" to Philadelphia "from foreign ports." See also Walton, *Present State of the Spanish Colonies*, 167: "A very extensive trade was carried on by the United States of America to the French ports in St. Domingo. In the year 1789, six hundred and eighty-four [U.S.] built vessels . . . entered the different ports of St. Domingo. Their cargoes, brought from the [United States] consisted of barrels of flour, salted provisions of all kinds, as beef, pork, butter, etc., salted herrings and other salt fish in great quantities . . . such vessels carried back in payment to the United States, cotton, wool, indigo, cochineal, coffee, sugars, rum, molasses, ginger, black pepper, cordials, gums of various kinds, sweetmeats, segars [cigars] in great quantities, Nicaragua wood, logwood, fustic, lignum vitae ebon[y] . . . mahogonies of all sixes in great quantities."

36. John Kearnes to Governor Beverly Randolph, 10 August 1789 in William Palmer and Sherwin McRae, eds., *Calendar of Virginia State Papers and Other Manuscripts, from July 2, 1790 to August 10, 1792, Preserved in the Capitol at Richmond, Volume 5* (Richmond: Derr, 1885), 17.

37. Henry Adams, "The Importance of Saint Domingue," in Mercer Cook and Dantes Bellegarde, eds., *The Haitian American Anthology: Haitian Readings from American Authors* (Port-au-Prince: Imprimerie de L'eta, 1944), 4–5.

38. William A. McCorkle, *The Monroe Doctrine in its Relation to the Republic of Haiti* (New York: Neale, 1915), 24–28.

39. James, *The Black Jacobins*, 31.

40. William Walton, *Present State of the Spanish Colonies including a Particular Report on Hispaniola or the Spanish Part of San Domingo with a General Survey . . . , Volume I* (London: Longman, Hurst, 1810), 36, 38.

41. Samuel G. Perkins, *Reminiscences of the Insurrection in St. Domingo* (Cambridge: Wilson, 1886), 3.

42. Scherr, *Thomas Jefferson's Haitian Policy*, 387.

43. Dun, "Dangerous Intelligence," 9.

44. Pierce Butler to George Mason, 25 July 1790, *Pierce Butler Letter Books*, University of South Carolina.

45. Babb, "French Refugees from St. Domingue to the Southern United States, 1791–1810," 168. See also Ashli White, *Encountering Revolution: Haiti and the Making of the Early Republic* (Baltimore: Johns Hopkins University Press, 2010).

46. Peter N. Moore, *World of Toil and Strife: Community Transformation in Backcountry South Carolina, 1750–1805* (Columbia: University of South Carolina Press, 2007).

47. Powell, *The Accidental City*, 261.

48. Logan, *The Diplomatic Relations of the United States with Haiti*, 49.

49. "Chapron, Senior" to Mr. Dortenil, 28 March 1803, *Jean Marie Chapron Letter Book*, Alabama Department of Archives and History-Montgomery. Original in French, translated by the Works Progress Administration in 1937.

50. Mederic-Louis-Elie Moreau de Saint-Mery, *A Civilization that Perished: The Last Years of White Colonial Rule in Haiti* (Lanham, Maryland: University Press of America, 1985), translated and abridged by Ivor D. Spencer, Introduction, viii.

51. Pamphlet [designated as "PAM" in the archive], 11, 201, *Baltimore Sun*, 1 September 1929,

and *Maryland Gazette and Baltimore Advertiser*, 12 July 1793, Maryland Historical Society, Baltimore.

52. *An Inquiry into the Causes of the Insurrection of the Negroes in the Island of St. Domingo. to which are Added Observations of M. Garran-Coulon on the Same Subject. Read in His Absence by M. Guadet, Before the National Assembly*, 29 February *1792* (London: Johnson, 1792), Maryland Historical Society. At the same site, see also *A Particular Account of the Commencement and Progress of the Insurrection of the Negroes in St. Domingo, which Began in August 1791: Being a Translation of the Speech Made to the National Assembly, the 3rd of November 1791, by the Deputies from the General Assembly of the French Part of St. Domingo* (London, circa 1792) and *An Historick [sic] Recital of the Different Occurrences in the Camps of Grande-Reviere, Dondon, Sanite-Suzanne, and Others from the 26th of October 1791 to the 24th of December of the Same Year, by Mr. Gros* (Baltimore, circa 1792). See also Thomas Somerville, *A Discourse on our Obligation to Thanksgiving for the Prospect of the Abolition of the African Slave Trade with a Prayer, Delivered in the Church of Jedburgh on April 15* (Scotland: Kelso, 1792,) Boston Public Library. See also, Granville Sharp, *Letter from Granville Sharp, Esq. of London to the Maryland Society for Promoting the Abolition of Slavery, and the Relief of Free Negroes and Others, Unlawfully Held in Bondage. Published by Order of the Society* (Baltimore: Yundt and Patton, 1793).

53. *A Particular Account of the Insurrection of the Negroes of St. Domingo Begun in August 1791, Translated from the French. Speech Made to the National Assembly the Third of November 1791. By Deputies from the General Assembly of the French Part of St. Domingo*, Huntington Library, San Marino, California.

54. *A Short Account of the African Slave Trade and an Address to the People of Great Britain on the Propriety of abstaining from West India Sugar and Rum*, 1791, Boston Public Library. At the same site, see also *A Short Sketch of the Evidence for the Abolition of the Slave Trade Delivered before a Committee of the House of Commons. To Which is Added a Recommendations of the Subject to the Serious Attention of People in General* (London: Lawrence 1792): "war is made on purpose to procure slaves, the King's soldiers set fire to villages in the night and seize the wretched inhabitants as they attempt to escape from the flames."

55. "A Letter from Percival Stockdale to Granville Sharp, Esq . . . [On] the Present Insurrection of the Negroes in the Island of St. Domingo . . . " (Durham: Pennington, 1791), New-York Historical Society, Manhattan.

56. *Remarks on a Speech Made to the National Assembly of France by the Deputies from the General Assembly of the French Port of St. Domingo with Observations on the Evidence Delivered Before a Select Committee of the House of Commons in 1790 and 1791. On the Part of the Petitioners for the Abolition of the Slave Trade* (London: Philip Mallet, 1792), Columbia University.

57. William Patten, "On the Inhumanity of the Slave Trade and the Importance of Correcting It. A Sermon Delivered in the Second Congregational Church, Newport, Rhode Island. August 12, 1792" (Providence: Carter, 1793), New-York Historical Society Manhattan. Emphasis original. See also David Rice, *Slavery Inconsistent with Justice, and Good Policy; Proved by a Speech Delivered in the Convention, Held at Danville, Kentucky by Philanthropos* (Philadelphia: J. Bradford, 1792).

58. *Daily Advertiser* [Jamaica], 1 September 1791. I viewed this newspaper at the American Antiquarian Society in Worcester, Massachusetts.

59. *Proceedings of the National Assembly of France Upon the Proposed Abolition of the Slave Trade* (London, 1790), Columbia University. At the same site, see also, *An Address to the Inhabitants of Glasgow, Paisley, and the Neighbourhood Concerning the African Slave Trade by a Society in Glasgow* (Glasgow: Alex Adam, January 1791).

60. *The Abstract of the Evidence Delivered before a Select Committee of the House of Commons in the years 1790 and 1791 on the Part of the Petitioners for the Abolition of the Slave Trade* (London: Phillips, 1791), Boston Public Library.

61. *An Inquiry into the Causes of the Insurrection of the Negroes in the Island of St. Domingo, to which are Added Observations of M. Garran-Coulon on the Same Subject, read in his Absence by M. Guadet, Before the National Assembly, 29th February 1792* (London and Philadelphia: Cruikshank, 1792), Boston Public Library.

62. Lord Grenville to Major General Williamson, 21 April 1791, CO137/89, NAUK.

63. Brian J. Costello, *A History of Pointe Coupee Parish, Louisiana* (Donaldsville, Louisiana: Margaret Media, 2010), 44–45.

64. Philip J. Schwarz, ed., *Gabriel's Conspiracy: A Documentary History* (Charlottesville: University of Virginia Press, 2012), Introduction, xxiv. Peter Chazotte arrived in Baltimore in mid-1804 from the island, barely escaping with his life. "I remembered well," he said, what had occurred in 1799 when in Charleston, "the Southern Federal Party papers violently opposed the election" of Jefferson "on the ground that he was too much of a philanthropist—that he had taken a black wife—was the best friend of the blacks . . . and that if elected President of the United States he would at once destroy slavery." He was influenced unduly by Jefferson's maneuvering to oust France from the hemisphere, which meant in part ousting France from Hispaniola—an ungracious payback for Paris's aid to the mainland revolt against London. See Peter Stephen Chazotte, *Historical Sketches of the Revolutions and the Foreign and Civil Wars in the Island of St. Domingo* (New York: Applegate, 1840).

65. Tommy L. Bogger, *Free Blacks in Norfolk, Virginia, 1790–1860* (Charlottesville: University Press of Virginia, 1997), 135.

66. See, e.g., Brook Thomas, *Plessy v. Ferguson: A Brief History with Documents* (Boston: Bedford, 1997).

67. David C. Rankin, "The Forgotten People: Free People of Color in New Orleans, 1850–1870" (Ph.D. diss., Johns Hopkins University, 1976), 164. See Clark, *The Strange History of the American Quadroon*: "By 1788 on the eve of the Haitian Revolution, 21,813 free people of color approached demographic parity with some 27,723 whites." On the rude reception of men of color in Philadelphia in 1793, see Laurent Dubois, *Avengers of the New World: The Story of the Haitian Revolution* (Cambridge: Harvard University Press, 2004), 168–169.

68. *An Inquiry into the Causes of the Insurrection of the Negroes in the Island of St. Domingo, to which are Added Observations of M. Garran-Coulon on the Same Subject, Read in his Absence by M. Guadet, Before the National Assembly, 19th Feb. 1792* (London: Johnson, 1792), Columbia University.

69. Letter to Elias Ball, 6 October 1790, *Ball Family Papers*, University of South Carolina.

70. Pierce Butler to Don Diego de Gardoqui, 17 February 1791, *Pierce Butler Letter Books*, University of South Carolina. For more on Spain in Louisiana during this era see, e.g., Box 14, *Gwen Midlo Hall Papers*, Tulane University.

71. Brian J. Costello, *The Life, Family, and Legacy of Julien Poydras* (2001), The Historic New

Orleans Collection,Williams Research Center. See also Julie Eshelman-Lee, ed., *The Selected Writings of Julien Poydras* (Fort Collins: Creole West, 2004) and Mary Flower Pugh Russell, "The Life of Julien Poydras" (M.A. thesis, Louisiana State University, 1940).

72. Erica Robin Johnson, "Louisiana Identity on Trial: The Superior Court Case of Pierre Benonime Dormenon, 1790–1812" (M.A. thesis, University of Texas-Arlington, 2007), 23. See also E. Wilson Lyon, *Louisiana in French Diplomacy, 1759–1804* (Norman: University of Oklahoma Press, 1934) and William Henry Truscot, *The Diplomatic History of the Administrations of Washington and Adams, 1789–1801* (Boston: Little Brown, 1857).

73. Frances Pirotte Zink, *Julien Poydras: Statesman, Philanthropist, Educator* (Lafayette: University of Southwest Louisiana, 1968), 4.

74. Evelyn Byrd Crump, "Governor Carondelet's 'Reglement,'" *Missouri Historical Society Bulletin*, 6 (Number 2, January 1950): 167–71.

75. Anonymous, "Ode, the Insurrection of the Slaves at St. Domingo," in Basker, ed., *Amazing Grace*, written 1792, 439. See also Edward Alexander Parsons, ed., *The Letters of Robert R. Livingston: The Diplomatic Story of the Louisiana Purchase* (Worcester: American Antiquarian Society, 1943); and Arthur Preston Whitaker, *The Mississippi Question, 1795–1803: A Study in Trade, Politics, and Diplomacy* (Gloucester, Massachusetts: Smith, 1962).

76. Eva Sheppard Wolf, *Race and Liberty in the New Nation: Emancipation in Virginia from the Revolution to Nat Turner's Rebellion* (Baton Rouge: Louisiana State University Press, 2006), 115.

77. Smith Snead to "Sir," 5 May 1792, Reel 5048, *Governor's Office, Henry Lee Executive Papers*, Virginia State Library, Richmond.

78. Henry Guy to "Dear Sir," 9 May 1792, Reel 5048. This letter can also be found in Palmer and McRae, *Calendar of Virginia State Papers*, Volume 5,541; the letter from Thomas Newton—below—can also be found on the same page.

79. W. Wilson to "Sir," 10 May 1792, Reel 5048, *Governor's Office, Henry Lee Executive Papers*.

80. Thomas Newton to "Sir," 10 May 1792, Reel 5048, ibid.

81. Holt Richardson to Governor, 5 June 1792, in Palmer and McRae, *Calendar of Virginia State Papers*, Volume 5, 571.

82. Letter from Smith Snead, 21 July 1792, Reel 5049, *Governor's Office, Executive Papers*.

83. James Madison to Edmund Pendleton, 25 March 1792, in *Letters and Other Writings of James Madison, Fourth President of the United States, Volume I, 1769–1793* (Philadelphia: Lippincott, 1867, 550).

84. Treudley, "The United States and Santo Domingo, 1789–1866," 110.

85. Auguste de Grasse to George Washington, 24 August 1793, in Theodore J. Crackel, ed., *The Papers of George Washington, Volume 13, 1 June to 31 August 1793* (Charlottesville: University Press of Virginia, 2007), 532–535.

86. See, e.g., Letter from M. de Cadaschy, President of the General Assembly, St. Domingue, to the Members of the Congress of the United States of North America, 24 August 1791, p. 7; Extract from the Register of Deliberation of the General Assembly of St. Domingue, 24 August 1791, p. 8; Letter from Mr. Polony, Deputy in St. Domingue, 12 September 1791, p.18; and Mr. Blanchelande to Mr. Cernan, Minister of France in the United States, 40CP/36, *Affaires de Saint-Domingue: Correspondance entre la légation et les Autorités de la Colonie, Documents Divers, 1791–1793*, Microfilm, n P/4670, MAE-Paris.

87. See, e.g., "Oster" to "Thevenard," 2 October 1791, Number 97, in "Correspondance Consulaires" in "Affaires Etrangères," BI 927, Folio 286, Norfolk, Volume I, 1787–1791, in Abraham P. Nasatir and Gary Elwyn Monell, eds., *French Consuls in the United States: A Calendar of their Correspondence in the Archives Nationales* (Washington, D.C.: Government Printing Office, 1967), 122: A newspaper column from Baltimore containing news of the insurrection of Africans on the island is referenced here—as well, aid is requested and promply provided by Pennsylvania. In the same volume see Petry to Bertrand, 26 October 1791, FI 372, Folios 371–372, 79: An official body from the island sent a delegate to South Carolina to solicit aid to halt the uprising of the Africans.

88. Dun, "Dangerous Intelligence," 176.

89. Ronald Angelo Johnson, *Diplomacy in Black and White: John Adams, Toussaint Louverture, and Their Atlantic World Alliance* (Athens: University of Georgia Press, 2011), 23.

90. Horne, *The Counter-Revolution of 1776*, passim.

91. James, *The Black Jacobins*, 54, 73–74.

92. Melanie Randolph Miller, *Envoy to the Terror: Gouverneur Morris & the French Revolution* (Washington, D.C.: Potomac, 2006), 13–14. Like others, this Founding Father realized that Paris's support for North American rebels led directly to a fiscal crisis in France and, ultimately, to the ousting of the monarchy—and, resultantly, the Haitian Revolution.

93. Alderson, *This Bright Era of Happy Revolutions*, 22.

94. See, e.g., Robert J. Alderson, "Charleston's Rumored Slave Revolt of 1793," in David Geggus, ed., *The Impact of the Haitian Revolution in the Atlantic World* (Columbia: University of South Carolina Press, 2001), 93–111.

95. "Petry" to "La Coste," 14 June 1792, No. 80, Charleston, Folios 387–388, in Nasatir et al., eds., *French Consuls in the United States*, 80.

96. David Brion Davis, "The Impact of the French and Haitian Revolutions," in David Geggus, ed., *The Impact of the Haitian Revolution in the Atlantic World* (Columbia: University of South Carolina Press, 2001), 3–9.

97. Samuel G. Perkins, *Reminiscences of the Insurrection in St. Domingo* (Cambridge: Wilson, 1886), 3, 32, 52–54. See also E.W. Gilliam, *1791: A Tale of San Domingo* (Baltimore: Murphy, 1890.)

98. Letter to Sylvanus Bourne, 14 July 1791, Box 1, *Sylvanus Bourne Papers*, Library of Congress, Washington, D.C.

99. Jacob Mayer to Thomas Allen, 28 February 1792, Box 6, Folder 1, *Allen Family Papers*, American Antiquarian Society, Worcester, Massachusetts.

100. B.M. Mumford to Thomas Allen, 7 April 1792, ibid.

101. Pons, *The Dominican Republic*, 95.

102. Dun, "Dangerous Intelligence," 94, 112, 122, 163. See also George C. Rogers, Jr., *The Evolution of a Federalist: William Loughton Smith of Charleston, 1758–1812* (Columbia: University of South Carolina, 1962), 249.

103. *Daily Advertiser* [Jamaica], 17 September 1791.

104. Edwin Wolf and Maxwell Whiteman, *The History of the Jews of Philadelphia* (Philadelphia: Jewish Publishing Society of America, 1975), 191. On the substantial commerce between Philadelphia and the island, see, e.g., *James McCurrach & Company Accounts*, Historical Society of Pennsylvania, Philadelphia. See also Jane Campbell, compiler, "San Domingo Refugees in Philadelphia: Compiled from the Original

D'Orilic-Rodrigue Papers," *Records of the American Catholic Historical Society*, 28 (Number 2, June 1917): 97–379.

105. Edward Matthew to William Wyndham Grenville, 27 November 1790, CO101/31, NAUK.

106. Edward Matthew to William Wyndham Grenville, 28 November 1790, ibid.

107. Edward Matthew to William W. Grenville, 27 January 1791, ibid.

108. Edward Matthew to Lord Grenville, 31 January 1791, ibid.

109. Edward Matthew to Lord Damas, 22 December 1790, ibid.

110. Michael Duffy, "The French Revolution and British Attitudes to the West Indian Colonies," in Gaspar and Geggus, *A Turbulent Time*, 78–101.

111. Thomas Atwood, *The History of the Island of Dominica* (London: Johnson, 1791), 227–230, 243, 250, 271.

112. Major General Adam Williamson to Lord Grenville, 4 July 1791, CO137/89, NAUK.

113. Lord Grenville to Major General Williamson, 21 April 1791, CO137/89, ibid.

114. Letter to Earl of Effingham, 6 July 1790, CO137/89, ibid.

115. Henry Hamilton to Edward Matthew, 11 July 1790, CO101/31, ibid.

116. Letter, 7 June 1792, CO37.43, ibid.

117. Edward Matthew to Lord Grenville, 13 February 1791, CO101/31, ibid.

118. Lord Granville to Earl of Effingham, 7 January 1791, CO137/89, ibid.

119. Edward Matthew to Lord Grenville, 4 June 1791, CO101/31, ibid.

120. Edward Matthew to Lord Grenville, 29 June 1791, CO101/31, ibid.

121. Edward Matthew to Henry Dundas, 30 July 1791, CO101/31, ibid.

122. Earl of Effingham to Henry Dundas, 9 September 1791, CO137/89, ibid.

123. Earl of Effingham to Henry Dundas, 17 September 1791, CO137/89, ibid.

124. Lord Grenville to Earl of Effingham, 11 September 1791, CO137/89, ibid.

125. Dubois, *Avengers of the New World*, 304. See also Philippe Girard, *The Slaves who Defeated Napoleon: Toussaint Louverture and the Haitian War of Independence, 1801–1804* (Tuscaloosa: University of Alabama Press, 2011).

126. Stephen Fuller to Henry Dundas, 30 October 1791, CO137/89, NAUK. Emphasis original.

127. Letter from Spanish Town, Jamaica, 6 November 1791, CO137/89, ibid.

128. Edward Matthew to Henry Dundas, 1 November 1791, CO101/31, ibid.

129. Major General Adam Williamson to Henry Dundas, 6 November 1791, CO137/89, ibid.

130. Stephen Fuller to Henry Dundas, 16 November 1791, CO137/89, ibid.

131. Whitehall to Edward Matthew, 22 December 1791, CO101/31, ibid.

132. Report, Circa 1791, CO101/31, ibid.

133. Adam Williamson to "Sir," 19 December 1790, CO137/89, ibid.

134. Henry Dundas to Earl of Effingham, 8 August 1791, CO137/89, ibid.

135. *Consideration of the Slave Trade; and the Consumption of West Indian Produce* (London: Darton & Harvey, 8 October 1791), TS24/3/113, NAUK. See also Philip Francis, ed., *Proceedings in the House of Commons on the Slave Trade and State of Negroes in the West India Islands* (London: Ridgway, 1796), Missouri Historical Society, St. Louis.

136. Resolution, 2 April 1792, CO260/12, NAUK.

137. *The Debate on a Motion for the Abolition of the Slave Trade in the House of Commons, on Monday the Second of April 1792, Reported in Detail* (London: Woodfall, 1792) 83, 100, Columbia University.

138. Stephen Fuller to Henry Dundas, 16 November 1791, CO137/89, NAUK.

139. "Extract of a Letter" from Kingston, Jamaica, 18 November 1791, ibid.
140. David Patrick Geggus, *Slavery, War, and Revolution: The British Occupation of Saint Domingue, 1793–1798* (New York: Oxford University Press, 1982).

2. CONFRONTING BLACK JACOBINS ON THE MARCH, 1793–1797

1. Pierce Butler to G.C. Richards, 19 November 1791, *Pierce Butler Letter Books*, University of South Carolina: "I congratulate you . . . and the benevolent of all Nations on the Completion of the French Revolution . . . .the difficulties that the American Revolutionaries had to encounter were trifling when compared to those of the French."
2. Pierce Butler to G.C. Richards, 5 February 1791, ibid.: "If the French succeed, and I trust they will, they will give a benevolent and useful lesson to Rulers & the Ruled . . . .they will teach Princes that there is a reciprocity in all compacts; that Kings can not with impunity treat their Fellow Men as tho' they were worse than horses."
3. Pierce Butler to John Leckey, 5 February 1791, ibid.
4. Terry W. Lipscomb, ed., *The Letters of Pierce Butler, 1790–1794: Nation Building and Enterprise in the New American Republic* (Columbia: University of South Carolina), 2007.
5. Pierce Butler to G.C. Richards, 27 August 1791, *Pierce Butler Letter Books*. See also Joseph Manigault to Gabriel Manigault, 22 September 1791, *Manigault Family Papers*, University of South Carolina: As to the monarch of France it was said, "some pity him and others curse him for a hypocrite."
6. Lipscomb, 265, 266, 254–255.
7. Pierce Butler to Thomas Young, 28 October 1793, *Pierce Butler Letter Books*.
8. Pierce Butler to John Bee Holmes, 5 November 1793, ibid. The fascination with all things French was hard to shake, however. See, e.g., Letter from Mrs. Izard, 4 December 1794, *Ralph Izard Papers*, University of South Carolina: Of Daniel Blake she said that he dresses so much like the French leader, Talleyrand, "that I am often going to address him in French." See also Mary Pinckney to Mrs. Manigault, 19 February 1797, *Manigault Family Papers*: "The terror caused by Robespierre has been a fine thing . . . .people had rather submit . . . than risk the same horrors."
9. *Essays on the Subject of the Slave Trade . . . Extracts from an Address of the Abolition Society in Paris, to the National Assembly . . .* (Philadelphia: Oswald, 1791), Brown University, Providence, Rhode Island. See also *Report of the Committee to Whom was Referred the Several Petitions of the Quakers of New England, of the Providence Society for the Abolition of the Slave Trade and the Petitions from the Delegates of the Several Societies for the Same Purpose, in Convention Assembled in Philadelphia, January 1794* (Philadelphia: Childs and Swaine, 1794).
10. Daniel Kilbride, *An American Aristocracy: Southern Planters in Antebellum Philadelphia* (Columbia: University of South Carolina Press), 58.
11. Ibid., 21.
12. "A Letter from a Gentleman in Switzerland to His Friend in America," 24 February 1794, Lausanne, Switzerland, Brown University, Providence. Emphasis original. See also *Commission Civile. Au nom de la Republique. Leger-Felicite Sonthonax, Commissaire-Civil . . . a tous les Francais de Saint-Domingue. Saint Marc . . .* , (De L'Imprimerie de Francois Lamothe, 1793), Boston Public Library; See this attack on Adrien Nicolas La Salle, affirming the freedom from slavery of Africans and their descendants.

13. Carl Ludwig Lokke, "The Trumbull Episode: A Prelude to the 'XYZ' Affair," *New England Quarterly*, 7 (Number 1, March 1934): 100–114.

14. William Howard Adams, *Gouverneur Morris: An Independent Life* (New Haven: Yale University Press, 2003), 4.

15. Horne, *The Counter-Revolution of 1776*, passim.

16. Reiss, *The Black Count*, 185–186, 308.

17. P. J. Laborie, *The Coffee Planter of Saint Domingo* . . . (London: Cadell and Davies, 1797), 157.

18. C. Peter Ripley, ed., *The Black Abolitionist Papers* (Chapel Hill: University of North Carolina Press, 1985–1992), five volumes.

19. J.F. Mace and 36 colonists, "Addresse. Messiers, No oligations envers nos commettans," circa 1790s, Boston Public Library.

20. Commission Nationale Civile-Aux Iles Sout le vent. Proclamation. Au nom de la Republique, 1793, Boston Public Library.

21. Report by Thomas Jefferson, 3 December 1792 in John Catanzariti, ed., *The Papers of Thomas Jefferson, Volume 24, 1 June to 31 December 1792* (Princeton: Princeton University Press), 693–695.

22. Transcriptions from French, 5 September 1792, Volume 4, *Anne-Louis de Tousard Papers*, University of Michigan-Ann Arbor.

23. Treudley, "The United States and Santo Domingo, 1789–1866," 113. See also Letter to Joseph Smith on the revolt, 6 July 1793, *Gratz Collection*, Historical Society of Pennsylvania, Philadelphia. At the same site, see also the *Diary of Tobias Lear*, a U.S. representative on the island and comrade of George Washington.

24. Thomas Newton to "Dear Sir," 6 July 1793, in Sherwin McRae, ed., *Calendar of Virginia State Papers and Other Manuscripts, From August 11, 1792 to December 31, 1793, Preserved in the State Capitol at Richmond, Volume VI* (Richmond: Micou, 1886), 437. For more on settlers from Hispaniola arriving in Virginia, post-August 1791, see Reel 5, *Records of the Virginia Assembly. House Journals, 1790–1807*, Virginia State Library, Richmond.

25. "A True and Particular Account of the Cruel Massacre," circa 1793, New York Historical Society.

26. On the massacre of settlers in Fort Dauphin, Hispaniola, see Report, 13 August 1794, *James McHenry Papers*, University of Michigan, Ann Arbor.

27. Captain Thomas Powars to Arnold Welles, 12 July 1793, MS3890, Boston Public Library.

28. Thomas Powars to Arnold Welles, 5 July 1793, ibid.

29. Thomas Newton to the Governor, 9 July 1793, in McRae, *Calendar of Virginia State Papers*, Volume VI, 443.

30. Joseph Jones to "Sir," 17 August 1793, Reel 5051, *Governor's Office, Henry Lee Executive Papers*, Virginia State Library, Richmond.

31. Multiple Signatories to Governor, 17 August 1793, *Governor's Office, Henry Lee Executive Papers*.

32. Editor's Note, in Charles T. Cullen et al., eds., *The Papers of John Marshall, Volume II, Correspondence and Papers, July 1788–December 1795. Account Book, July 1788–December 1795* (Chapel Hill: University of North Carolina Press, 1977), 201. The note refers to a report filed by the Council of State in Virginia on 15 August 1793.

33. Babb, "French Refugees from St. Domingue to the Southern United States," 222.

34. Terry, "A Study of the Impact of the French Revolution and the Insurrection in Saint-Domingue upon South Carolina," 6–7.

35. Quoted in Babb, "French Refugees from St. Domingue to the Southern United States," 219–220.

36. James Monroe to Secretary of State, 15 September 1794, in Stanislaus Murray Hamilton, ed., *The Writings of James Monroe, Including a Collection of His Public and Private Papers and Correspondence Now for the First Time Printed, Volume II, 1794–1796* (New York: Putnam's, 1899), 55–56, 59; the bill noted can be found on the latter page. See also Miles King to the Governor, 6 July 1793, in Sherwin McRae, *Calendar of Virginia State Papers, Volume VI*, 436: "Melancholy account of the distress'd French" now arriving in droves. On French abolitionism see "Société de Amis de L'Abbé Grégoire, 1789–1939. The French Revolution-Negro Emancipation," Paris, 1939, Huntington Library, San Marino, California.

37. Letter to Governor, 30 July 1795, in H.W. Flournoy, ed., *Calendar of Virginia State Papers and Other Manuscripts from May 16, 1795 to December 31, 1798, Embracing the Letters and Proceedings of the Committee of Correspondence and Inquiry of Virginia and the Other Colonies . . . , Volume XIII*, Richmond, 1890, Virginia State Library, Richmond.

38. Report, circa 1794, in Elizabeth Donnan, ed., *Documents Illustrative of the History of the Slave Trade to America, Volume IV, the Border Colonies and the Southern Colonies* (Washington, D.C.: Carnegie, 1935), 240.

39. William MacCreery to James McHenry, 13 August 1794, *James McHenry Papers*, University of Michigan, Ann Arbor.

40. Perkins, *Reminiscences of the Insurrection in St. Domingo*, 54, 58–59. See also J.G. Hopkins, *An Account of the Insurrection in St. Domingo Begun in August 1791, taken from Authentic Sources* (Edinburgh: Blackwood, 1833).

41. Thomas Newton to the Governor, 9 July 1793, in McRae, *Calendar of Virginia State Papers, Volume VI*, 443.

42. Proposals, 25 February 1793, 40CP/36, Affaires de Saint-Domingue: Correspondance entre le legation et les autorités de la colonie, Documents Divers, 1791–1793, Microfilm nP/4670, p. 155, MAE-Paris.

43. James S. Seton to Henry Dundas, 14 January 1793, CO260/12, NAUK.

44. "Planters and Merchants" of St. Vincent to Duke of Portland, 9 May 1795, CO260/13, ibid.

45. *Notes on Attaining Peace through Massacre*, circa 1790s, MS Haiti, 66–210, Boston Public Library.

46. *The Laws of the Island [of] St. Vincent and its Dependencies from the First Establishment of a Legislature to the End of the Year 1787*, 1788, Brown University.

47. Schloss, *Sweet Liberty*, 10.

48. James Seton to Henry Dundas, 8 March 1793, CO260/12, NAUK.

49. Resolution, 14 February 1793, ibid.

50. James Seton to Henry Dundas, 11 June 1793, ibid.

51. Minutes of Privy Council Meeting, 30 April 1793, ibid.

52. Proclamation, circa 1793, CO260/12, ibid.

53. James Seton to Henry Dundas, 13 July 1793, ibid.

54. Privy Council Minutes, 27 June 1793, ibid.

55. James Seton to Henry Dundas, 1 July 1793, ibid.

56. James Seton to Henry Dundas, 13 July 1793, ibid.

57. James Seton to Henry Dundas, 1 July 1793, ibid. In the same file, see also Seton to Dundas, 13 July 1793: He had just absorbed "between seventy and eighty of those unfortunate colored people who escaped from Martinico and . . . made an offer of them to be employed on the same footing as the Negroes on the fortification . . . at Martinico and St. Lucia."

58. Privy Council Minutes, 1 October 1793, ibid.

59. James Seton to Henry Dundas, 30 July 1794, ibid.

60. George Lowman, Speaker to His Honor, the President & Council, 4 June 1794, ibid. See also Privy Council to Governor Seton, 4 June 1794, ibid.: Here, a complaint is made about the influx of "French Negroes & mulattoes" who arrived from "neighbouring French islands" and the "Negroes & coloured people from the British islands, who are or pretend to be free," destabilizing St. Vincent.

61. J.B. Petry to Gabriel Manigault, 24 August 1794, *Manigault Family Papers*, University of South Carolina.

62. Schloss, *Sweet Liberty*, 37–38.

63. "Friendship with Britain the True Interest of America. The Speech of Mr. Smith of South Carolina Delivered in the House of Representatives of the United States in January 1794 on the Subject of Certain Commercial Regulations Proposed by Mr. Madison . . ." (Philadelphia: Bell and Bradfute, 1794), *University of South Carolina*.

64. Drewry Ottley to "Sir," 14 February 1793, CO260/12, NAUK.

65. James Seton to Duke of Portland, 16 March 1795, CO260/13, NAUK. In the same file, see also Duke of Portland to James Seton, 5 August 1795: Reference is made to the "conduct of the French inhabitants in fomenting the insurrection of the Charib."

66. James Seton to Duke of Portland, 8 May 1795, ibid.

67. Duke of Portland to James Seton, July 1795, ibid.

68. James Seton to Duke of Portland, 23 June 1795, ibid.

69. Letter from James Seton, 11 July 1795, ibid.

70. Letter to James Seton, 26 July 1795, ibid.

71. Powell, *The Accidental City*, 254.

72. McConnell, *Negro Troops of Antebellum Louisiana*, 27.

73. David Barry Gaspar, "La Guerre des Bois: Revolution, War, and Slavery in St. Lucia, 1793–1838," in Gaspar et al., *A Turbulent Time*, 102–130, 107.

74. *An Account of the Black Charaibs in the Island of St. Vincent with the Charaib Treaty of 1773 and Other Original Documents, Compiled from the Papers of the Late Sir William Young* (London: J. Sewell, 1795), Brown University. Emphasis original.

75. Thomas Newton to Robert Brooke, 9 June 1795, Reel 5212, *Governor's Office, Robert Brooke Executive Papers*, Virginia State Library, Richmond.

76. Letter, 11 June 1795, ibid.

77. Thomas Newton to "Sir," 23 June 1795, ibid.

78. Thomas Newton to "Sir," 29 June 1795, ibid. See Hunt, "The Influence of Haiti Upon the Antebellum South," 57: "Philippe S. Noisette and his family were long-standing free black landowners of Charleston who arrived in the state from St. Domingue in 1794."

79. Letter signed by numerous arriving French refugees, 29 June 1795, Reel 5212, *Governor's Office, Robert Brooke Executive Papers*.

80. "Decisions Under the Convention with France of 1831," Box 218, *Caleb Cushing Papers,* Library of Congress, Washington, D.C.

81. "Special Joint Committee," "Report" on "French Claims," "Senate . . . No. 12 . . . Commonwealth of Massachusetts," 24 January 1841, Box 218, ibid.

82. Roger Norman Buckley, *Slaves in Redcoats: The British West India Regiments* (New Haven: Yale University Press, 1979), 4, 28.

83. Letter to Duke of Portland, 3 February 1795, CO101/34, NAUK.

84. Pinckard, *Notes on the West Indies,* 234.

85. Kit Candlin, *The Last Caribbean Frontier, 1795–1815* (New York: Palgrave, 2012), 1, 6, 8.

86. Letter, 18 November 1795, Box 1, *Cary Family Papers,* Massachusetts Historical Society, Boston.

87. Letter, 30 May 1795, Box 1, *Cary Family Papers.*

88. Benjamin C. Clark, *Plea for Hayti with a Glance at Her Relations with France, England, and the United States for the Last Sixty Years* (Boston: Eastburn, 1853), 9.

89. Duke de la Rochefoucault Liancourt, *Travels Through the United States of North America, the Country of the Iroquois and Upper Canada in the Year[s] 1795, 1796 and 1797 . . . ,* Volume I (London: Phillips, 1799), 587.

90. Words of "Aunt Margaret," circa 1795, and Caroline Gardiner Curtis, circa 1891, in Caroline Gardiner Curtis, ed., *The Cary Letters: Edited at the Request of the Family* (Cambridge, Massachusetts: Riverside Press, 1891), 49, 51.

91. *Six Months in the West Indies in 1825* (London: Murray, 1826), 163.

92. Letter to Lord Stanley, 22 June 1794, CO101/25, NAUK.

93. *Six Months in the West Indies in 1825* (London: Murray, 1826), 163, Brown University.

94. See *A Diary of the Defense of the Island of Dominica Against Invasion of the French Republicans & the Revolt of the Dominicans of the Quarter of Colybaut in June 1795,* Brown University.

95. George Pinckard, *Notes on the West Indies, Including Observations Relative to the Creoles and Slaves of the Western Colonies . . . ,* Volume I (London: Baldwin, Craddock and Joy, 1816) [mostly written in 1795–1796], 208, 233, 234. See also, The Reverend Cooper Willyams, *An Account of the Campaign in the West Indies in the Year 1794, Under the Command of their Excellencies General Sir Charles Grey, KB and Vice Admiral Sir John Jervis, KB . . . with the Reduction of the Islands of Martinique, St. Lucia, Guadeloupe, Marigalante, Desiada . . .* (London: Bensley, 1796): Note the "detachment of black light dragoons" involved in the attack on Martinique.

96. *Proceedings of the Honourable House of Assembly Relative to the Maroons, Including the Correspondence . . .* (St. Jago de la Vega: Aikman, 1796), Brown University.

97. Thomas Turner Wise, *A Review of the Events Which Have Happened in Grenada,* St. George, 1795, 2, 23, American Antiquarian Society, Worcester, Massachusetts.

98. "A Grenada Planter to a Merchant in London," *A Brief Enquiry into the Causes of and Conduct Pursued by the Colonial Government for Quelling the Insurrection in Grenada; From its Commencement on the Night of the 2nd of March, to the Arrival of General Nichols on the 14th of April 1795 . . .* (London: Faulder, 1796), Brown University.

99. K.F. MacKenzie to Duke of Portland, 28 March 1795, CO101/34, NAUK.

100. "A Proclamation . . . by the King," 4 March 1795, ibid.

101. "Copy of a Declaration of Julien Fedon . . . containing a Summons to the Island of Grenada to Surrender . . . Rec'd by a Flag of Truce the Same Day," 4 March 1795, ibid.

102. Charles Este to "Sir," 9 April 1795, ibid.
103. Letter to "Gentlemen," 6 March 1795, ibid.
104. K.F. MacKenzie to "Sir," 31 March 1795, ibid.
105. "An Eye-Witness," *A Narrative of the Revolt and Insurrection of the French Inhabitants in the Island of Grenada* (Edinburgh: Arch Constable, 1795), 15, 132, 160, 161.
106. Statement by Ben Webster, 1 March 1795, CO101/34, NAUK.
107. Statement by Victor Hugues, circa 1795, ibid.
108. Statement, no date, ibid.
109. Statement from Philip Gordon and James Park, 11 March 1795, ibid. Emphasis original.
110. H. Wright to "Sir," no date, ibid.
111. L. Mitchel to "My Lord and Duke," 22 January 1796, ibid.
112. K.F. MacKenzie to Council, 12 May 1795, ibid.
113. Statement by "We the Members of the Majesties Council for the Island of Grenada and Much of the Grenadines," circa May 1795, ibid.
114. Ben Webster et al. to "Sir," 2 July 1796, ibid.
115. Alexander Houston to Rear Admiral Harvey, 16 July 1796, ibid.
116. Alexander Houston to Duke of Portland, 16 September 1796, ibid.
117. *West Indian Sketches. Drawn from Authentic Sources. No. 1, Punishment of the Maroons of Demerara from Pinckard's Notes on the West Indies* (London: Ellerton, 1816). Emphasis original. The revolt reached its height on 16 May 1796.
118. Philip Francis, Esq., ed., *Proceedings of the House of Commons on the Slave Trade and the State of the Negroes in the West India Islands* (London: Ridgway, 1796), Boston Public Library.
119. Dun, "Dangerous Intelligence," 296.
120. Broadside, Resolution of the House of Assembly, Bahamas, 15 November 1796, New-York Historical Society.
121. Terry, "A Study of the Impact of the French Revolution and the Insurrections in Saint-Domingue upon South Carolina," 105.
122. Comment in Lois A. Walker and Susan R. Silverman, eds., *A Documented History of Gullah Jack Pritchard and the Denmark Vesey Slave Insurrection of 1822* (Lewiston: Mellen, 2000), 91.
123. Alderson, *This Bright Era of Happy Revolutions*, 107.
124. John Lathrop, "God Our Protector and Refuge in Danger and Trouble; A Discourse Delivered at the Public Lecture in Boston, on Thursday, March 16, 1797" (Boston: Manning & Loring, 1797), The Historic New Orleans Collection, Williams Research Center. Emphasis original.
125. "Select Pamphlets Respecting the Yellow Fever" (Philadelphia: Carey, circa 1795), D 799, s464p, Brown University. See also J.H. Powell, *Bring out Your Dead: The Great Plague of Yellow Fever in Philadelphia in 1793* (Philadelphia: University of Pennsylvania Press, 1949).
126. Hector McLean, *An Enquiry into the Nature and Causes of the Great Mortality Among the Troops at St. Domingo* (London: Cadell, 1797), vii.
127. Seth Webb to William Seward, 16 April 1862, Reel 4, T346, *Despatches from U.S. Consuls in Port-au-Prince*, NARA-CP.
128. Joseph Lewis to William Marcy, 10 August 1855, Roll 3, T346, ibid.

129. "Description of a Plantation Situated at Petit St. Louis, Near Port-de-Paix in the Northern Part of Hispaniola; with all the Buildings, Belonging to the Same and Necessary to Carry on the Cultivation . . . Now offered to be exchanged by J.B. & L. Samoual, Proprietors," 1797, American Antiquarian Society.

130. Duke de la Rochefoucault Liancourt, *Travels Through the United States of North America, the Country of the Iroquois, and Upper Canada in the Year[s] 1795, 1796 and 1797 . . .*, Volume I (London: Phillips, 1799), 553, 557–558.

131. Pinckard, *Notes on the West Indies*, 357, 458. See also Volume II, 121: The author espied a "gang of Negroes" that was laboring while "a female driver [was wielding] . . . whips at their backs"; he notes, with emphasis, that *"women drivers were sometimes particularly severe"* in administering punishments.

132. Pinckard, *Notes on the West Indies*, Volume II, 130, 404.

133. Davis, *The Problem of Slavery in the Age of Emancipation*, 354. Cf. Liancourt, *Travels Through the United States*, 605: In Georgia "the law of the land permits the importation of Negroes and this is the only state, the ports of which are not yet shut up against this odious trade . . . . Savannah employs no ship in the slave trade; but it is carried on in ships belonging to New England and especially to Rhode Island . . . a third of those who are imported are, in spite of the prohibition, every year smuggled into Carolina. These African Negroes cost three hundred dollars each; those of the Gold Coast are the best of all and next to them are those of the Congo and Ibo. The latter are the best labourers but frequently perish within the first two years. I witnessed an auction of Negroes in Savannah." It did appear that with the 1790s and the rise of Black Jacobins, manumission of the enslaved increased in certain precincts of the mainland. See, e.g., New Jersey Supreme Court, *Cases Adjudged in the Supreme Court of New Jersey Relative to the Manumission of Negroes . . .* (Burlington: I. Neale, 1794), Columbia University.

134. Treudley, "The United States and Santo Domingo, 1789–1866," 124.

135. Donald L. Robinson, *Slavery in the Structure of American Politics, 1765–1820* (New York: Harcourt Brace, 1971), 362.

3. CONFRONTING THE SURGE OF BLACK JACOBINS, 1797–1803

1. Michael Duffy, "The French Revolution and British Attitudes to the West Indian Colonies," in Gaspar et al., *A Turbulent Time*, 78–101, 85.

2. Colonel Charles Chalmers, *Brief Remarks on the Late War in St. Domingo* (London: Nichols and Son, 1802), 28.

3. Alexander De Conde, *The Quasi-War: The Politics and Diplomacy of the Undeclared War with France, 1797–1801* (New York: Scribner's, 1966), 84–85. For more on the lingering hostility to France, see William Henry Trescot, *The Diplomatic History of the Administrations of Washington and Adams, 1789–1801* (Boston: Little Brown, 1857).

4. Thomas Jefferson to St. George Tucker, 28 August 1797, in Barbara Oberg, *The Papers of Thomas Jefferson, Volume 29, 1 March 1796 to 31 December 1797* (Princeton: Princeton University Press, 2002), 519. See also Johnson, *Diplomacy in Black and White*, 79: During the late 1790s, Congressman Robert Goodloe Harper said that islanders were plotting an invasion with an "army of blacks" in order "to excite insurrection among the Negroes."

5. Timothy Pickering to "Sir," 22 September 1797, Roll 1, M9, *Despatches from United States Consuls in Cap-Haïtien*, NARA-CP.

6. Timothy Pickering to "Major Lewis Tousard," 27 February 1795, Box 3, *Anne-Louis de Tousard Papers*, University of Michigan, Ann Arbor.

7. Timothy Pickering to "Sir," 27 June 1798, ibid.

8. Secretary of the Navy to Stephen Decatur, 28 June 1798, ibid.

9. Letter from Paris to Mrs. Manigault, 11 January 1797, *Manigault Family Papers*. On the eminent Manigault family and others in that state of French origins, see, e.g., E.L. Manigault and H.F. Prioleau, eds., *Register of Carolina Huguenots, Partial Listing of 81 Refugee Families, Four Volumes* (Charleston: South Carolina Huguenot Society, 2007).

10. Mary Pinckney to Mrs. Manigault, 5 February 1798, *Manigault Family Papers*.

11. Robert Goodloe Harper, *Observations on the Dispute Between the United States and France* (London: Philanthropic Press, 1798), University of South Carolina.

12. "A Letter from Robert G. Harper of South Carolina to one of his Constituents . . . A Short Account of the Principal Proceedings of Congress in the Late Session and a Sketch of the State of Affairs Between the United States and France in July 1798" (Philadelphia: Cobbett, August 1798), New-York Historical Society, Manhattan.

13. "Message of the President of the United States to Both Houses of Congress," 4 May 1798, New York Historical Society. At the same site, see also *Instructions to the Envoys Extraordinary and Ministers Plenipotentiary From the United States of America to the French Republic, Their Letters of Credence and Full Powers and the Dispatches Received from them Relative to their Mission, Published by the Secretary of State . . .* (Philadelphia: Ross, 1798).

14. Mary Pinckney to Mrs. Manigault, 13 December 1796, *Manigault Family Papers*.

15. Extract from *Virginia Argus* [Richmond], 9 May 1797, in William C. Stinchcombe et al., eds., *The Papers of John Marshall, Volume III, January 1796 to December 1796* (Chapel Hill: University of North Carolina Press, 1979).

16. Pierce Butler to G.C. Richard, 19 November 1791, *Pierce Butler Letter Books*.

17. "Receipt," signed by John Marshall, "received from John Hamilton," British consul in Virginia, 30 November 1796, in Stinchcombe et al., *The Papers of John Marshall, Volume III*, 55: "The sum of two hundred & thirty three & one third dollars, as a fee for conducting a Suit" against two men "for there having detained . . . certain Horses shipped and about to be shipped from thence to the island of Santo Domingo for the Service of His Brittanick Majesty therein."

18. Rufus King to Secretary of State, 7 December 1798, in Charles R. King, ed., *The Life and Correspondence of Rufus King, Volume II, 1795–1799* (New York: Putnam's, 1895), 475–477. Emphasis original.

19. Rufus King to Secretary of State, 10 January 1799, in ibid., 499–503. Emphasis original.

20. Ralph Izard to Mathias Hutchinson, 20 November 1794, *Ralph Izard Papers*, University of South Carolina.

21. Richard Creech to Lewis Malone Ayer, 14 July 1798, *Lewis Malone Ayer Papers*, University of South Carolina.

22. Toussaint Louverture to John Hollingsworth, 6 January 1799, in Claude Swanson, ed., *Naval Documents Related to the Quasi-War Between the United States and France: Naval Operations from November 1798 to March 1799* (Washington, D.C.: Government Printing Office, 1935), 216–217.

23. General Toussaint to "Mr. President," circa 1799, Roll 1, M9, *Despatches from United States Consuls in Cap-Haïtien*.

24. "Message from the President of the United States, Transmitting Certain Documents on the Subjects of the Insurrection in Pennsylvania; the Renewal of Commerce with St. Domingo and the Mission to France," 5 December 1799, New-York Historical Society.

25. Rufus King to Secretary of State, 14 June 1799, in King, *The Life and Correspondence of Rufus King, Volume II*, 43–46. Emphasis original.

26. Thomas Jefferson to James Madison, 12 February 1799, in Barbara Oberg, ed., *The Papers of Thomas Jefferson, Volume 31, 1 February 1799 to 31 May 1800* (Princeton: Princeton University Press, 2004), 9–10.

27. Thomas Jefferson to Aaron Burr, 11 February 1799, in ibid., 22.

28. Arthur Scherr, "Jefferson's 'Cannibals' Revisited: A Closer Look at his Notorious Phrase," *Journal of Southern History*, 77 (Number 2, May 2011): 252–282, 253.

29. Charles Lee to Secretary of State, 20 February 1799 Roll 1, M9, *Despatches from United States Consuls in Cap-Haïtien*. Hugh Cathcart to Thomas Maitland, 26 November 1799, CO245/1, NAUK: "The American Consul" on the island intends to "supply ammunition and arms" to General Toussaint's forces.

30. Winthrop Sargent to Timothy Pickering, 16 June 1798, in *Correspondence, 1798–1819, Ms. (Territory) Governor*, SG3114, Alabama Department of Archives and History, Montgomery.

31. Winthrop Sargent to Timothy Pickering, 18 September 1798, in ibid.

32. Chalmers, *Brief Remarks on the Late War in St. Domingo*, 67–68.

33. Correspondents unclear, probably from Lord Balcames to the Duke of Portland, March 1798, CO245/1, NAUK.

34. Treudley, "The United States and Santo Domingo," 131.

35. Carolyn Fick, *The Making of Haiti: The Saint Domingue Revolution from Below* (Knoxville: University of Tennessee Press, 2004), 201–202.

36. Timothy Pickering to Peter G. Brooks, 20 December 1799, MS. Am. 2237, Boston Public Library.

37. Agreement, 20 April 1799, Roll 1, M9, *Despatches from United States Consuls in Cap-Haïtien*.

38. Timothy Pickering to Edward Stevens, 20 April 1799, ibid.

39. Timothy Pickering to General Toussaint, 4 March 1799, Roll 5, M28, *Diplomatic & Consular Instructions of the Department of State*, NARA-CP.

40. Thomas Pickering to Rufus King, 22 April 1799, ibid.

41. Timothy Pickering to Edward Stevens, 5 September 1799, ibid.

42. Timothy Pickering to Edward Stevens, 2 November 1799, ibid.

43. Treudley, "The United States and Santo Domingo," 134.

44. Edward Stevens to "Sir," 2 February 1799, Roll 2, M9, *Despatches from United States Consuls in Cap-Haïtien*. See also Edward Stevens to "Dear Sir," 29 January 1800, Roll 2, M9, ibid.: General Toussaint "transmitted to him the claims of several American citizens whose vessels were put in requisition by the military commander of Port-au-Prince, the Mole & Gonaives."

45. T. Delaire to "Sir," 11 January 1799, Roll 1, M9, ibid.

46. Korngold, *Citizen Toussaint*, 5.

47. Hugh Cathcart to Thomas Maitland, 26 November 1799, CO245/1, NAUK. London was also negotiating with the island rebel leader "Captain Jean Kina," hailing his "constant theme," which was "his attachment to the English, whom he always placed as his friend,

the French as his enemies. He was always saying the English lost St. Domingo from allowing the French to [do] as they pleased." The plan was to send him to London: "he is a man government must reflect upon. He might render great service." For something had to be done since the "political weakness of our colonial government exposes to danger" London's holdings. See Fred Maitland to "Dear Browning," 18 December 1800, CO166/1, ibid. For more on this matter, see Letter to "Dear Sir," 20 December 1800 in the same file as the previous letter.

48. CO166/1, ibid.: Reporting from Martinique, then undergoing a kind of political disruption that mirrored events in Hispaniola, London's operative committed to paper "thoughts on the situation of the Free Coloured People in the West Indies and those who have Pretensions to Freedom . . . .the conduct which Government should adopt towards this class of people is of the utmost importance to the colonies. They form a link between the whites and the slaves. If this tye [*sic*] is broken or not preserved by the former, the colored people must necessarily join their interest with the slaves—and the whites become the common enemy of each. This race risen originally from the intercourse of white men with black women—and also from the freedom granted to deserving Negroes." This grouping was "extremely numerous and increases daily." Reproved was the order of Sir Charles Grey in August 1794, mandating—with emphasis—that it would be "impossible that any man not free in" Martinique, St. Lucia & Guadeloupe "should legally become so."

49. Lt. General Trigge to "Dear Sir," 20 December 1800, CO166/1, ibid.: "the slave trade and the condition of the slaves in the West Indies has been much discussed, but I believe the state of free mulattoes and Negroes and the question with respect to the policy of granting or withholding freedoms, have been less considered and yet the number of free people of this description is so great; that on the measures taken with respect to them, may depend the preservation or loss of the colonies . . . .free Mulattoes and Negroes are numerous, many of them intelligent; if they should veer from and direct the slaves, the situation of the colonies will be critical indeed . . . .the law which appears to [hit] hardest and to occasion the greatest discontent, is that which subject[s] a free Mulatto or a Negro to punishment if he lifts his hand against a white man, however wantonly attacked or severely beaten . . . .in some colonies it goes to the loss of the right hand, here [Martinique] it is standing in the pillory."

50. Colonel Charles Chalmers, *Brief Remarks on the Late War in St. Domingo* (London: Nichols and Son, 1802), 28: He added, "no country seems so unfit for horses as Saint Domingo, where forage is often scarce and where European and American horses perish like their riders by disease."

51. Lt. General Trigge to "Dear Sir," 20 December 1800, CO166/1, NAUK.

52. Hugh Cathcart to Thomas Maitland, 31 October 1799, CO245/1, ibid.

53. Hugh Cathcart to Earl of Balcarres, 21 November 1799, CO245/1, ibid.

54. Whitehall to Earl of Balcarres, March 1800, CO245/1, ibid.

55. See, e.g., M.L.E. Moreau de Sal Mery, *A Topographical and Political Description of the Spanish Part of Saint-Domingo* (Philadelphia: Author, circa 1798), Boston Public Library.

56. Edward Stevens to "Dear Sir," 29 January 1800, Roll 2, M9, *Despatches from United States Consuls in Cap-Haïtien*.

57. Edward Stevens to "Dear Sir," 29 March 1800, ibid.

58. Edward Stevens to "Dear Sir," 24 April 1800, ibid.

59. Christopher Tomkins to "Dear Sir," 29 May 1801, *Christopher Tomkins Letter Book*, Virginia Historical Society, Richmond.

60. Christopher Tomkins to "Gentlemen," 29 May 1801, ibid.

61. Letter to "Sir," 20 December 1800, Roll 2, M9, *Despatches from United States Consuls in Cap-Haïtien*. Emphasis original.

62. Letter from Jack Roche, 20 January 1801, *Rogers-Roche Collection*, University of Michigan, Ann Arbor.

63. R.A. Hanrick to "Dear Friends," 15 September 1947, Box 2, *Hanrick Papers*, New York Historical Society: "My great grandfather, Dr. Pierre Elizabeth Benjamin Raynal of Charleston . . . who was born in France and lived for a while in Santo Domingo, from [which] place the French were driven out by the Insurrection of 1798."

64. Account, 25 October 1799, *African American History Collection*, University of Michigan, Ann Arbor.

65. Frank Cundall, ed., *Lady Nugent's Journal: Jamaica One Hundred Years Ago* (London: Black, 1907), 56.

66. Letter, 26 April 1801, *Tousard Transcriptions*, Volume 4, University of Michigan, Ann Arbor.

67. A Bill for the Relief of Louis de Tousard, 12 April 1802, ibid.

68. A Bill "to prohibit the carrying on the slave trade . . . ," 15 April 1800, New-York Historical Society.

69. *Virginia Gazette*, 19 September 1800, in Philip J. Schwarz, ed., *Gabriel's Conspiracy: A Documentary History* (Charlottesville: University of Virginia Press, 2012, 87.

70. William Sidney Drewry, *The Southampton Insurrection* (Washington: Seale, 1900), 120.

71. *Virginia Herald*, 23 September 1800, in Schwarz, *Gabriel's Conspiracy*, 97.

72. Confessions of Ben, alias Ben Woolfolk, 17 September 1800, in H.W. Flournoy, ed., *Calendar of Virginia State Papers and Other Manuscripts, January 1, 1799 to December 31, 1807 . . .* , Volume IX (Richmond, 1890), 150–152, Virginia State Library, Richmond. See also Joseph Jones to "Sir," 9 September 1800, Reel 5349, *Governor's Office, James Monroe Executive Papers*, Virginia State Library: A "diabolical plot" was intended in Petersburg involving the enslaved, free Negroes, and "Mulattoes."

73. Sheppard to James Monroe, 30 August 1800, Reel 5334, *Governor's Office, James Monroe Executive Papers*.

74. McClurg to James Monroe, 10 August 1800, ibid.

75. Letter to James Monroe, 27 September 1801, ibid.

76. Terry, "A Study of the Impact of the French Revolution," 136.

77. St. George Tucker, "A Letter to a Member of the General Assembly of Virginia on the Subject of the Late Conspiracy of the Slaves; with a Proposal for their Colonization" (Baltimore: Bonsal & Niles, 1801), New York Historical Society.

78. Babb, "French Refugees from St. Domingue," 247.

79. Tench Coxe to Thomas Jefferson, Circa March 1802, in Barbara Oberg et al., eds., *The Papers of Thomas Jefferson, Volume 37, 4 March to 30 June 1802* (Princeton: Princeton University Press, 2010), 25. Emphasis original.

80. "A History of the Legislation of Virginia and the Opinions of Some of Her Eminent Delegates Upon the Subject of African Colonization" in *Documents of the Colonization Society of Virginia* (Richmond: MacFarlane & Fergusson, 1853), 9, University of Virginia.

81. James Monroe to Thomas Jefferson, 15 June 1801, in ibid.
82. Thomas Jefferson to James Monroe and Thomas Jefferson to Governor Page, December 1804, in ibid.
83. Thomas Jefferson to James Monroe, 24 November 1801, in Merrill D. Peterson, ed., *Thomas Jefferson: Writings* (New York: Library of America, 1984), 1096–1099.
84. Tobias Lear to Governor General Toussaint, 13 July 1801, Roll 3, M9, *Despatches from United States Consuls in Cap-Haïtien.*
85. Tobias Lear to "Sir," 17 July 1801, ibid.
86. Tobias Lear to James Madison, 21 November 1801, ibid.
87. Tobias Lear to "Boyer, Commandante," 18 February 1802, ibid.
88. William Corbet, U.K. agent, to Tobias Lear, 8 October 1801, ibid.
89. *A Treatise Upon the Navigation of St. Domingo: with Sailing Directions from the Whole Extent of its Coasts, Channels, Bays, and Harbours Undertaken by Order of the King by M. de Chastenet Puysegur* (Baltimore: W. Pechin, 1802), translated by the Maryland Historical Society from the French.
90. Tobias Lear to James Madison, 20 July 1801, Roll 3, M9, *Despatches from United States Consuls in Cap-Haïtien.*
91. W. Whitfield to Edward Corbet, 21 January 1801, CO245/1, NAUK.
92. Logan, *The Diplomatic Relations of the United States with Haiti*, 122.
93. Tobias Lear to James Madison, 4 August 1801, Roll 3, M9, *Despatches from United States Consuls in Cap-Haïtien.*
94. Tobias Lear to James Madison, 30 August 1801, Roll 3, ibid. On U.S. claims, see Tobias Lear to "Citizen Le Clerc," 10 February 1802, Roll 4, M9, ibid: "Jonathan F. Law and William Furlong" of the United States complained about a "large sum of money which was recovered from the store" of the former citizen "after the burning of the Cape." This "respected American merchant" had "resided several years in this city and transacted considerable business and . . . Citizen Furlong arrived here some time since with a very valuable cargo," now distressed.
95. General Toussaint to Hugh Cathcart, "Year 8 of the French Republick," CO245/1. NAUK.
96. Charles de Vincent to General Toussaint, 17 August 1801, MS. Hait. 8(2), Boston Public Library.
97. Tobias Lear to James Madison, 21 November 1801, Roll 3, M9, *Despatches from United States Consuls in Cap-Haïtien.*
98. Tobias Lear to James Madison, 17 January 1802, Roll 4, M9, ibid.
99. Tobias Lear to "Commandant of this Place," 19 February 1802, Roll 4, M9, ibid.
100. Tobias Lear to James Madison, 21 January 1802, Roll 4, M9, ibid.
101. Tobias Lear to Citizen Le Clerc, 15 February 1802, Roll 4, M9, ibid.
102. Tobias Lear to Citizen Le Clerc, 13 April 1802, Roll 4, M9, ibid. For more on U.S. business in Hispaniola, see, e.g., *Accounts of James McCurrach & Company, 1790–1800*, Historical Society of Pennsylvania, Philadelphia. At this site, see also the *Diary of Tobias Lear.*
103. Tobias Lear to Toussaint Louverture, circa 1802, Roll 4, M9, *Despatches from United States Consuls in Cap–Haïtien*: "I will always seize with pleasure all the opportunities you will offer to me for strengthening the ties which are to unite your Government with that of St. Domingo and for consolidating the commercial relations existing between St. Domingo and the United States."

104. Thomas Ott, *The Haitian Revolution, 1789–1804* (Knoxville: University of Tennessee Press, 1973), 162–163.

105. Baptist, *The Half Has Never Been Told*, 41.

106. John Leonard to Commercial Agent of the United States, April 1802, Roll 4, M9, *Despatches from United States Consuls in Cap-Haïtien*.

107. Ben Dandridge to James Madison, 5 March 1802, ibid.

108. Davis, *The Problem of Slavery in the Age of Emancipation*, 76.

109. Robert Livingston to Rufus King, 8 June 1802, in Edward Alexander Parsons, ed., *The Original Letters of Robert R. Livingston, 1801–1803, with a Brief History of the Louisiana Purchase* (New Orleans: Louisiana Historical Society, 1953), 33–34.

110. Robert Livingston to Rufus King, 27 March 1802, in ibid., 83–85.

111. Robert Livingston to Rufus King, 17 November 1802, in ibid., 101–102.

112. Schloss, *Sweet Liberty*, 18.

113. Miranda Frances Spieler, *Empire and Underworld: Captivity in French Guiana* (Cambridge: Harvard Univesity Press, 2012), 76–80.

114. Johnson, *The Fear of French Negroes*, 1.

115. Peter Stephen Chazotte, *Historical Sketches of the Revolutions and the Foreign and Civil Wars in the Island of St. Domingo . . .* (New York: Applegate, 1840). The version of this book I read at the New-York Historical Society did not contain page numbers.

116. Johnson, *Diplomacy in Black and White*, 177.

117. *Philadelphia Gazette*, 31 December 1801; *Georgia Gazette* [Savannah], 24 December 1801.

118. Thomas Newton to Thomas Jefferson, 6 January 1802, in Barbara Oberg et al., eds., *The Papers of Thomas Jefferson, Volume 34, 1 May to 31 July 1801* (Princeton: Princeton University Press, 2007), 308.

119. Thomas Jefferson to Rufus King, 13 July 1802, in Schwarz, *Gabriel's Conspiracy*, 235–236. This letter can also be found in Barbara Oberg, ed., *The Papers of Thomas Jefferson, Volume 38, 1 July to 12 November 1802* (Princeton: Princeton University Press, 2011), 54.

120. Thomas Newton to Thomas Jefferson, 10 February 1803, in Barbara Oberg, ed., *The Papers of Thomas Jefferson, Volume 39* (Princeton: Princeton University Press), 2012, 491.

121. Thomas Jefferson to James Monroe, 24 November 1802, in Oberg, *The Papers of Thomas Jefferson, Volume 39*, 335. Cf. Malick Ghachem, "A Constitution of Slavery: A Comparative History of Virginia and Saint-Domingue," 14 September 1999, Virginia Historical Society, Richmond.

122. Terry, "A Study of the Impact of the French Revolution," 153.

123. Laurent Dubois, *A Colony of Citizens: Revolution and Slave Emancipation in the French Caribbean, 1787–1804* (Chapel Hill: University of North Carolina Press, 2004), 404–407, 411–412.

124. *Boston Columbian Centinel*, 9 October 1802. See also Scherr, *Thomas Jefferson's Haitian Policy*, 25.

125. Tench Coxe to Thomas Jefferson, 20 March 1802, in Oberg, *The Papers of Thomas Jefferson, Volume 37*, 92–93. Emphasis original.

126. Jane B. Landers, "Rebellion and Royalism in Spanish Florida: The French Revolution in Spain's Northern Colonial Frontier," in Gaspar et al., *A Turbulent Time*, 156–177, 168, 158. See also Gene Allen Smith, *The Slaves' Gamble: Choosing Sides in the War of 1812* (New York: Palgrave, 2013), 25–26: Biassou, a "caudillo of Charles IV's Black Auxiliaries in St.

Domingo, and twenty five of his followers relocated to St. Augustine. These men, who revolted against slavery in Haiti before [*sic*] joining with the Spanish, had bravely fought against French planters, British and French soldiers, and other black Haitians . . . . [Their arrival] heightened tensions along the Georgia-Florida border."

127. His Lordship the Marquis of Someremlos, Governor of East Florida, to Captain General of Cuba, 1 February 1802, in Report, 25th Congress, 3rd Session, Doc. No. 225, House of Representatives, War Department, "Negroes . . . Captured from Indians in Florida . . . Letter from The Secretary of War," 27 February 1839, University of South Florida.

128. Letter to Governor Monroe, 2 January 1802, Reel 5342, *Governor's Office, James Monroe Executive Papers.*

129. Rich Jones to "Dear Sir," 2 January 1802, ibid.

130. Letter to Governor Monroe, 10 March 1802, Reel 5343, *Governor's Office, James Monroe Executive Papers.*

131. Letter to Governor Monroe, 13 March 1802, ibid.

132. Letter to Governor Monroe, 21 April 1802, ibid.

133. Letter to Governor Monroe, 30 April 1802, ibid.

134. Dun, 26.

135. Baptist, *The Half Has Never Been Told*, 47. Laurent Dubois, *Haiti: The Aftershocks of History* (New York: Holt, 2012), 43.

4. CONFRONTING THE TRIUMPH OF BLACK JACOBINS, 1804–1819

1. Clark, *The Strange History of the American Quadroon*, 28.

2. Alfred C. Lemmon and John H. Lawrence, *Common Routes: St. Domingue and Louisiana* (New Orleans: The Historic New Orleans Collection, 2006), 85–120, 88, 94: "News of the [Haitian] revolution terrified Louisiana's influential planter class." See also Winston De Ville, *St. Domingue: Census Records and Military Lists, 1688–1720*, Ville Platte (Louisiana: Provincial Press, 1973), no page numbers: "From the earliest days of European settlement in [Louisiana], traffic between that island [Hispaniola] and the Franco-Hispano South was intense."

3. Baptist, *The Half Has Never Been Told*, 48. Cf. Sylvestris, "Reflections on the Cession of Louisiana to the United States" (Washington City: Smith, 1803), Virginia Historical Society, Richmond.

4. Alice Izard to Henry Izard, 15 October 1806, *Francis Lieber Collection*, University of South Carolina.

5. Walter Johnson, *Rivers of Dark Dreams: Slavery and Empire in the Cotton Kingdom* (Cambridge: Harvard University Press, 2013), 75: The Haitian Revolution "drastically diminished the value of the Mississippi Valley to Napoleon."

6. Vernon Valentine Palmer, *Through the Codes Darkly: Slave Law and Civil Law in Louisiana* (Clark, New Jersey: Lawbook Exchange, 2012), 117. See also Scott P. Marler, *The Merchants' Capital: New Orleans and the Political Economy of the Nineteenth-Century South* (New York: Cambridge University Press, 2013).

7. Alex Yard et al., eds., *Documents in St. Louis History*, 1993, Missouri Historical Society, St. Louis.

8. *The Constitution of the Republic of Hayti: To Which is Added Documents Relating to the Correspondence of His Most Christian Majesty with the President of Hayti: Preceded as a Proclamation to the People and the Army* (New York: Tredwell, 1818).

9.   Joseph Manigault to Gabriel Manigault, 21 December 1806, *Francis Lieber Collection*.

10. Address by Governor Sargent, 12 January 1801 in Rowland, *The Mississippi Territorial Archives, 1798–1803*, 324–326.

11. J.F.H. Claiborne, *Mississippi as a Province, Territory, and State, with Biographical Notices of Eminent Citizens, Volume I* (Jackson, Mississippi: Power & Barksdale, 1880), 535.

12. "Letter from the Secretary of State, Enclosing His Report on the Memorial of Tobias Lear, Made in Pursuance of an Order of the House of the 12th Instant" (Washington City: Duane & Son, 1803), New York Historical Society.

13. *Letters from George Washington to Tobias Lear with an Appendix . . .* (Rochester: Genesee Press, 1905), New-York Historical Society.

14. Girard, "Caribbean Genocide," 139.

15. *National Intelligencer*, 8 June 1804. See also Scherr, *Thomas Jefferson's Haitian Policy*, 388.

16. R.C. Dallas, *The History of the Maroons . . . , Volume II* (London: Strahan, 1803), 316, 388.

17. Daniel McKinnen, Esq., *A Tour Through the British West Indies in the Years 1802 and 1803 . . .* (London: White, 1804), 50.

18. "An Address to the Government of the United States, on the Cession of Louisiana to the French, and on the Late Breach of Treaty by the Spaniards: Including the Translation of a Memorial on the War of St. Domingo and Cession of the Mississippi to France Drawn up by a French Counselor of State" (Philadelphia: Conrad, 1803), University of North Carolina, Chapel Hill.

19. Timothy Baycroft, *France: Inventing the Nation* (London: Hodder, 2008), 112.

20. George Izard to Henry Izard, 13 December 1807, *Ralph Izard Papers*, University of South Carolina.

21. Chazotte, *Historical Sketches of the Revolutions and the Foreign and Civil Wars in the Island of St. Domingo*.

22. James Barsket, *History of the Island of St. Domingo from its First Discovery by Columbus to the Present Period* (New York: Mahlon Day, 1824). See also Richard Bingham Davis, "From Le Malheureux de St. Domingo," in James G. Basker, ed., *Amazing Grace: An Anthology of Poems about Slavery, 1660–1810* (New Haven: Yale University Press, 2002), 484–485: This graduate of Columbia University depicts a "white" refugee from the Haitian Revolution and writes of "dread scenes" and the "sable myriads" who "crush'd . . . beneath their steps *humanity*." This was published in 1807.

23. See, e.g., *Secret History or the Horrors of St. Domingo in a Series of Letters Written by a Lady at Cape Francois to Colonel Burr . . .* (Philadelphia: Bradford & Inskeep, 1808).

24. Duffy, "The French Revolution and British Attitudes to the West Indian Colonies," in David Barry Gaspar et al., *A Turbulent Time*, 86.

25. Governor William C.C. Claiborne to James Madison, 24 October 1805, SG3105, *General Correspondence, Mississippi Territory*, Alabama Department of Archives and History, Montgomery.

26. Robert Williams to Joseph Chambers, 27 March 1806, SG3114, *Correspondence 1798–1819, Mississippi (Territory) Governor*, Alabama Department of Archives and History.

27. Pierre F. M'Callum, *Travels in Trinidad During the Months of February, March, and April 1803 in a Series of Letters Addressed to a Member of the Imperial Parliament of Great Britain* (Liverpool: Longman, Hurst, 1805), 9, 26–28, 115–118.

28. See, e.g., William James Nelson, Jr., "The Free Negro in the Ante-bellum New Orleans Press" (Ph.D. diss., Duke University, 1977).

29. *A Concise Statement of the Questions Regarding the Abolition of the Slave Trade* (London: Hatchard, 1804), Boston Public Library.

30. "Anonymous," no title, 1805; William Foster, "An Address," 1803; and William Wordsworth, "To Toussaint L'Ouverture," 1802, in Baker, *Amazing Grace*, 596, 588–589, 583–584.

31. Carl Harrison Brown, Jr., *The Reopening of the Foreign Slave Trade in South Carolina, 1803–1807* (M.A. thesis, University of South Carolina, 1968), 3, 9, 33: 40,000 Africans arrived in Charleston in 1803 despite qualms about Hispaniola. Congo provided the most, but also weighing in heavily were Gambia, Senegal, Mozambique, Sierra Leone, Guinea, and Zanzibar, among others. Charleston was also supplying Cuba.

32. David Fleming to Mordecai Cohen, 22 September 1806, *Lewis Malone Ayer Papers*.

33. Letter to Isaac Ball, 24 November 1806, *Ball Family Papers*, University of South Carolina.

34. W.E.B. Du Bois, *Suppression of the African Slave Trade to the United States of America, 1638–1870* (London: Longman, Green, 1896), 72.

35. Julien Vernet, *Strangers on their Native Soil: Opposition to United States' Governance in Louisiana's Orleans Territory, 1803–1809* (Jackson: University Press of Mississippi, 2013), 44.

36. Joseph T. Hatfield, *William Claiborne: Jeffersonian Centurion in the American Southwest* (Lafayette, Louisiana: University of Southwest Louisiana, 1976), 176. See also Ausie L. Porter, "W.C.C. Claiborne's Administrations in Louisiana, Provincial, Territorial and State" (M.A. thesis, Tulane University, 1932).

37. Governor Claiborne to James Madison, 12 July 1804, in Rowland, *Official Letter Books of William C.C. Claiborne, 1801–1816, Volume II,* 244–246.

38. Nadia Rae Venable Calvert, "Establishment of Territorial Government in Orleans Territory, 1803–1804" (M.A. thesis, Tulane University, 1958), 21.

39. Scherr, *Thomas Jefferson's Haitian Policy*, 587. See also Albert Gallatin to John Quincy Adams, 26 September 1822, Reel 35, *Albert Gallatin Papers*, New York University.

40. Speech by Senator Samuel White, circa 1806, Columbia University.

41. Rayford W. Logan, *Haiti and the Dominican Republic* (New York: Oxford University Press, 1967), 99, 93.

42. General Louis Marie Turreau to Secretary of State, 14 October 1805, in "Message from the President of the United States Transmitting Documents & Papers Relative to Complaints Made by the Government of France Against the Commerce Carried on by American Citizens to the French Island of Saint Domingo in Senate of the United States, January 10, 1806," University of Virginia.

43. Charles Maurice de Talleyrand-Perigord to General Armstrong, circa August 1805, in ibid.

44. Jackson, "The Origins of Pan-African Nationalism," 36–37.

45. *New York Republican Watch Tower*, 12 March 1803, in Mary A. Hackett et al., eds., *The Papers of James Madison, Secretary of State Series, Volume 9, 1 February 1805–30 June 1805* (Charlottesville: University Press of Virginia), 1962, 335.

46. James Madison to Thomas Jefferson, 1 April 1805, in ibid. Emphasis original.

47. James Alexander Robertson, ed., *Louisiana under the Rule of Spain, France, and the United States, 1785–1807, as Portrayed in Hitherto Unpublished Contemporary Accounts by Dr. Paul Alliot and Various Spanish, French, English, and American Officials, Volume I* (Cleveland: Clark, 1911), 87–88.

48. Comment in Clyde N. Wilson, ed., *The Papers of John C. Calhoun, Volume XIII, 1835–1837* (Columbia: University of South Carolina Press, 1980), 155.

49. Pierre Clement de Laussat, *Memoirs of My Life to my Son During the Years 1803 and After, which I Spent in the Public Service in Louisiana as Commissioner of the French Government for the Retrocession to France of that Colony and for its Transfer to the United States* (Baton Rouge: Louisiana State University Press, 1978), 55.

50. James Wilkinson to U.S. Secretary of War, 11 January 1804, in Carter, *The Territorial Papers of the United States, Volume IX*, 159–161.

51. Johnson, *The Fear of French Negroes*, 102.

52. Calvert, "Establishment of Territorial Government in Orleans Territory," 41, 43.

53. Charles Cesar-Robin, *Voyage to Louisiana, 1803–1805* (New Orleans: Pelican, 1966) [originally published in French in 1807].

54. William Claiborne to James Madison, 13 April 1804, in Rowland, *Official Letter Books of William C.C. Claiborne, 1801–1816, Volume II*, 95.

55. Governor Claiborne to James Madison, 12 July 1804, in ibid., 244–246. Emphasis original.

56. Governor Claiborne to Colonel Freeman, 17 July 1804, in ibid., 254–255.

57. Governor Claiborne to Captain Johnson, 18 July 1804, in ibid., 256–258.

58. Governor Claiborne to Captain Nicoll, 25 July 1804, in ibid., 262–263.

59. John Watkins to Governor Claiborne, 24 April 1804, in Carter, *The Territorial Papers of the United States, Volume IX*, 234.

60. Pierre Clement Laussat to Manuel de Salcedo, 18 August 1803, *Pierre Clement Laussat Papers*, The Historic New Orleans Collection, Williams Research Center.

61. Governor Claiborne to Thomas Jefferson, 25 November 1804, in Carter, *The Territorial Papers of the United States, Volume IX*, 338–341.

62. Governor Claiborne to Thomas Jefferson in ibid., 221–223.

63. Petition, 17 September 1804, in Carter, 297. See also Jared William Bradley, ed., *Interim Appointment: William C.C. Claiborne Letter Book, 1804–1805* (Baton Rouge: Louisiana State University Press, 2002).

64. Babb, "French Refugees from St. Domingue," 236.

65. Elvina Marguerite Echezabal, "The Public Career of W.C.C. Claiborne from 1795–1804" (M.A. thesis, Tulane University, 1935), 110.

66. Palmer, *Through the Codes Darkly*, 109, 111, 117, 119, 121.

67. Lawrence N. Powell, *The Accidental City*, 333.

68. H.E. Sterrkx, *The Free Negro in Ante-Bellum Louisiana* (Rutherford, New Jersey: Fairleigh Dickinson University Press, 1972), 92.

69. James Monroe to James Madison, 6 May 1804, in Stanislaus Murray Hamilton, ed., *The Writings of James Monroe, Volume IV, 1803–1806* (New York: Putnam's, 1900), 184–188.

70. J. Hankins to Amos Stoddard, 4 August 1804, *Amos Stoddard Papers*, Missouri Historical Society, St. Louis.

71. Thomas Jefferson to John Page, 27 December 1804, Misc. Reel 5956, *Governor's Office, John Page Executive Papers*, Virginia State Library.

72. John Page to Thomas Jefferson, 1804, ibid.

73. Gerald Horne, *Negro Comrades of the Crown: African Americans and the British Empire Fight the United States before Emancipation* (New York: New York University Press, 2012).

74. Alice Izard to Mrs. Manigault, 15 September 1805, *Manigault Family Papers*, University of South Carolina.

75. Alice Izard to Mrs. Manigault, 20 September 1805, ibid.

76. Alice Izard to Mrs. Manigault, 17 February 1808, ibid.

77. Alice Izard to Mrs. Manigault, 22 July 1801, ibid.

78. Jedidiah Morse, "A Discourse Delivered at the African Meeting House in Boston, July 14, 1808 in Grateful Celebration of the Abolition of the African Slave Trade by the Governments of the United States, Great Britain, and Denmark" (Boston: Lincoln & Edmands, 1808), Columbia University.

79. David Brion Davis, *The Problem of Slavery in the Age of Emancipation*, 48. See also Gerald Horne, *The Deepest South: The United States, Brazil, and the African Slave Trade* (New York: New York University Press, 2007).

80. "The Present State and Condition of the Free People of Color of The City of Philadelphia and Adjoining Districts, as Exhibited by the Report of a Committee on the Pennsylvania Society for Promoting the Abolition of Slavery" (Philadelphia: Society, 1808), Columbia University.

81. James Stephen, *New Reasons for Abolishing the Slave Trade; Being the Last Section of a Larger Work, now First Published Entitled 'The Dangers of the Country'* (London: Butterworth, 1807).

82. Note in Walter Charlton Hartridge, ed., *The Letters of Don Juan McQueen to His Family Written from Spanish East Florida, 1791–1807* (Columbia, South Carolina: Bostick & Thornley, 1943), 51.

83. "Fourth Report of the Directors of the African Institution, Read at the Annual General Meeting, Held in London, on the 28th of March 1810," in "Minutes of the Proceedings of the Thirteenth American Convention for Promoting the Abolition of Slavery and Improving the Condition of the African Race, Assembled in Philadelphia" (Hamilton-ville: Bouvier, 1812), Brown University.

84. Eliza Boudinot to Sarah Colt and to "My Dear Friend," 15–25 January 1810 and 15 January 1810, Vertical File, Maryland Historical Society, Baltimore.

85. Eliza Boudinot to "My Dear Friend," 27 January 1810, Vertical File, ibid.

86. Letter from Mr. de Neuville, French Legation in United States to His Excellency, Monsieur le duc de Richelieu, 23 October 1819, Affaires Diverses Politiques/Etat Unis, 1814–1896, File 6, MAE-Paris.

87. Letter from Mr. de Neuville, 12 August 1818, File 6, ibid.

88. Bertram Wallace Korn, *The Early Jews of New Orleans* (Waltham, Massachusetts: American Jewish Historical Society, 1969), 94–95.

89. Paul F. Lachance, "The 1809 Immigration of Saint-Domingue Refugees to New Orleans: Reception, Integration, and Impact," in Robert B. Holman and Glenn R. Conrad, eds., *French Louisiana: A Commemoration of the French Revolution Bicentennial* (Lafayette: Center for Louisiana Studies, 1989), 252–278. See also *Federal Census of 1810, Territory of Orleans, Excluding the Parish of Orleans* (Baton Rouge: Louisiana Genealogical and Historical Society, 1961), Tulane University.

90. Vernet, *Strangers on their Native Soil*, 185. Cf. Babb, "French Refugees from St. Domingue," 381: Virginia and Maryland were said to have received 3000 migrants each during this period from Hispaniola; South Carolina—1000; Delaware and Georgia—about 300 each.

Out of a total of about 18,000 migrants, about 3000 were *gens de couleur* and the rest enslaved persons.

91.   Richard J. Follett, "The Sugar Masters: Slavery, Economic Development, and Modernization on Louisiana Sugar Plantations, 1820–1860" (Ph.D. diss., Louisiana State University, 1997), 62–63.

92.   James Mather to Sir, 18 July 1809, in Dunbar Rowland, ed., *Official Letter Books of William C.C. Claiborne, Volume IV* (Jackson, Mississippi: State Department of Archives and History, 1917), 387–389.

93.   Governor Claiborne to French Consul, 27 July 1809, in ibid., 393–395.

94.   Ira Berlin, *Slaves Without Masters: The Free Negro in the Antebellum South* (New York: Pantheon, 1974), 89.

95.   See "Observations on the Trial of Peter Dormenon, Esquire, Judge of the Parish Court of Point Coupee, who was Lately Held to Answer before Judge Lewis in the Superior Court of the Territory of New Orleans, for his Conduct in St. Domingo, During the Year 1793" (New Orleans: Author, 1809), New-York Historical Society.

96.   Erica Robin Johnson, "Louisiana Identity on Trial: The Superior Court Case of Pierre Benonime Dormenon, 1790–1812" (M.A. thesis, University of Texas-Arlington, 2007), 2, 26, 61–62.

97.   Francois-Xavier Martin, Compiler, *Orleans Terms Reports or Cases Argued and Adjudicated in the Superior Court of the Territory of Orleans, Volume I* (New Orleans: Dacqueny, 1811), 129–132, The Historic New Orleans Collection, Williams Research Center.

98.   Walton, *Present State of the Spanish Colonies*, 23. See also Henri Christophe, "The Formation of the New Dynasty of the Kingdom of Hayti, Formerly the Island of Saint Domingo" (Philadelphia, 1811), University of Florida, Gainesville.

99.   Schloss, *Sweet Liberty*, 37–38, 90.

100. George Izard to Henry Izard, 16 May 1809, *Ralph Izard Papers*.

101. "Remarks on the Ordonnance [*sic*] Issued at Paris the 29th August 1814; for the Re-Establishment of the French Slave Trade . . . and on the Proposition Submitted to the Chamber of Deputies by General Desfourneaux on the Subject of St. Domingo . . . " (London: Hatchard, 1814), New-York Historical Society.

102. Broadside, 5 June 1809, "At a General Meeting of the Traders of Slaves, Formerly Inhabitants of the Islands of Cuba and of St. Domingo, Now of New York, Convened at the Sanctum Sanctorum . . . Charles Collet, Chairman . . . ," New-York Historical Society: " . . . resolved unanimously that in order to deceive all the good Citizens of the United States and particularly our *great enemy*, known by the appellation of *Quaker*, we shall in future give to our meeting . . . the title *Club de Amis des Noires* . . . .resolved unanimously that in consideration of very great service, well known in the old and new worlds, when he being commander in chief of the Gendarmerie of St. Domingo, executed with zeal and punctuality, all orders in killing, shooting, drowning, strangling, and assassinating thousands of *whites, Negroes, Mulattoes,* people of color . . . he shall be from and after this day our *President* in perpetuity . . . .that it shall be lawful for the *President* to continue to keep two black women for such purpose as to him seems proper at his palace . . . .resolved unanimously that five thousand copies of the proceedings of this meeting be printed and distributed through the city."

103. Nathan A. Buman, "Historiographical Examinations of the 1811 Slave Insurrection," *Louisiana History*, 53 (Number 3, Summer 2012): 318–337, 321.

104. Robert I. Pquette, "Revolutionary Saint Domingue in the Making of Territorial Louisiana," in Gaspar et al., *A Turbulent Time*, 204–225, 219.

105. Maximillian Reichard, "Black and White on the Urban Frontier: The St. Louis Community in Transition, 1800–1830," *Missouri Historical Society Bulletin*, 33 (Number 1, October 1976): 3–17, 6.

106. Powell, *The Accidental City*, 345.

107. Matt D. Childs, *The 1812 Aponte Rebellion in Cuba and the Struggle against Atlantic Slavery* (Chapel Hill: University of North Carolina Press, 2006), 21–22, 83, 3–4.

108. Comment in John Blassingame, ed., *Slave Testimony: Two Centuries of Letters, Speeches, Interviews, and Autobiographies* (Baton Rouge: Louisiana State University Press, 1977), 259.

109. See, e.g., Gerald Horne, *Race to Revolution: The United States and Cuba during Slavery and Jim Crow* (New York: Monthly Review Press, 2014), passim.

110. Petition to Virginia Legislature, 6 December 1824, in Robert Starobin, ed., *Blacks in Bondage: Letters of American Slaves* (New York: New Viewpoints, 1974), 137–138.

111. Horne, *Negro Comrades of the Crown*, (New York, New York University Press).

112. Scherr, *Thomas Jefferson's Haitian Policy*, 621.

113. Gail Collins, *William Henry Harrison* (New York: Times Books, 2012), 26–27.

114. Reichard, "Black and White on the Urban Frontier," 4.

115. Johnson, *The Fear of French Negroes*, 104.

116. James E. Winston, "The Free Negro in New Orleans, 1803–1860," *Louisiana Historical Quarterly*, 21 (Number 4, October 1938): 3–13.

117. Charles Isidore Nero, "To Develop our Manhood: Free Black Leadership and the Rhetoric of the New Orleans Tribune" (Ph.D. diss., Indiana University, 1991), 47–48.

118. Roger Norman Buckley, *Slaves in Redcoats: The British West India Regiments* (New Haven: Yale University Press), 179.

119. "William Duane's Notes on the Expediency of Using Black Troops," 11 August 1814, in J. Jefferson Looney, ed., *The Papers of Thomas Jefferson, Retirement Series, Volume 7, 28 November 1813 to 30 September 1814* (Princeton: Princeton University Press, 2010), 533.

120. Clark, *The Strange History of the American Quadroon*, 86.

121. Alan Taylor, *The Internal Enemy: Slavery and the War in Virginia, 1772–1832* (New York: Norton, 2013), 346.

122. Rembert W. Patrick, *Florida Fiasco: Rampant Rebels on the Georgia-Florida Border, 1810–1815* (Athens: University of Georgia Press, 1954), 155.

123. Carita Doggett Corse, "Excerpts from *The Key to the Golden Islands*," Chapter V, manuscript, circa 1931, University of Florida, Gainesville.

124. Babb, "French Refugees from St. Domingue," 280: the Tulane family, prominent Huguenots in Hispaniola, was said to own 2000 enslaved persons, which made them quite wealthy. Forced to escape in an open boat, taking nothing with them, they wound up in New Orleans, where they founded a leading research university.

125. M.I. Manigault to Mrs. Allen Smith, 12 June 1814, *Manigault Family Papers*.

126. M.I. Manigault to Mrs. Allen Smith, 18 June 1814, ibid.

127. Henry Izard to Mrs. Manigault, 28 February 1813, ibid.

128. Alice Izard to Mrs. Manigault, 18 April 1816, ibid.

129. M.I. Manigault to Mrs. Alice Izard, 8 September 1816, ibid.

130. Entry, 10 April 1816, Harriet Manigault, *The Diary of Harriet Manigault, 1813–1816* (Rockland, Maine: Colonial Dames of America, 1976), 132.

5. HEMISPHERIC AFRICANS AND BLACK JACOBINS, 1820–1829

1. *Remarks on the Insurrection in Barbados and the Bill for the Registration of Slaves* (London: Ellerton, 1816), Brown University.
2. Note in James Redpath, ed., *Guide to Hayti* (Boston: Haytian Bureau of Emigration, 1861), 91.
3. J. Fuller to "Sir," 3 July 1816, CO137/143, NAUK.
4. L.E. Douglas to "Sir," 2 May 1816, ibid.
5. Account of Meeting of the "Association of West India Merchant Planters," 5 March 1816, ibid.
6. L.E. Douglas to "Sir," 19 October 1816, ibid.
7. William C. Davis, *The Pirates Lafitte: The Treacherous World of the Corsairs of the Gulf* (New York: Harcourt, 2005), 1–2. Cf. *Reflexions* [sic] *on the Blacks and Whites. Remarks Upon a Letter Addressed to M. Mazeres. A French Ex-Colonist to J.C.L. Sismonde de Dismondik Containing Observations on the Blacks and Whites, the Civilization of Africa, the Kingdom of Hayti . . .* , Translated from the French by Baron De Vasty (London: Hatchard, circa 1817), New York Historical Society.
8. Powell, *The Accidental City*, 226.
9. Joseph Pilland testimony, 3 May 1816, CO 137/143, NAUK.
10. W. Stuart to Lord Castlereagh, 12 August 1816, ibid.
11. Alice Izard to Mrs. Manigault, 20 August 1820, *Manigault Family Papers*, University of South Carolina.
12. Sir James Leith to Earl of Bathurst, 30 April 1816, CO28/85, NAUK.
13. Letter to Sir James Leith, 25 April 1816, ibid.
14. Report from St. Vincent, 25 April 1816, ibid.
15. Letter, 6 June 1816, ibid.
16. *Debate in the House of Commons on the 16th Day of March 1824 on the Measures Adopted by His Majesty's Government for the Amelioration of the Condition of the Slave Population in His Majesty's Dominions in the West Indies* (London: Hatchard, 1824), Boston Public Library.
17. Horne, *Negro Comrades of the Crown*.
18. *Remarks on the Insurrection in Barbados and the Bill for the Registration of Slaves* (London: Ellerton and Henderson, 1816), Boston Public Library.
19. Barbados Legislature, House of Assembly, "The Report from a Select Committee of the House of Assembly, Appointed to Inquire into the Origin, Causes, and Progress of the Late Insurrection" (Bridgetown: Walker, Murphy, and Gazette, 1818), American Antiquarian Society, Worcester, Massachusetts.
20. Letter from Jonathan, October 1817, *Abraham Falconar Papers*, Maryland Historical Society, Baltimore.
21. Dubois, *Haiti: The Aftershocks of History*, 60.
22. Kevin G. Lowther, *The African American Odyssey of John Kizell: A South Carolina Slave Returns to Fight the Slave Trade in His African Homeland* (Columbia: University of South Carolina Press, 2011), 205.

23. Alice Izard to Mrs. Manigault, 14 July 1822, *Manigault Family Papers*.

24. Intendant's Report; Testimony of Enslaved African; Comments in Lois A. Walker and Susan R. Silverman, eds., *A Documented History of Gullah Jack Pritchard and the Denmark Vesey Slave Insurrection of 1822* (Lewiston: Mellen, 2000), 169–170, 295–337, 300.

25. Taylor, *The Internal Enemy*, 349.

26. William W. Harvey, *Sketches of Hayti: From the Expulsion of the French to the Death of Christophe* (London: Seeley, 1827), 334.

27. Charles MacKenzie to John Bidwell, 26 June 1826, FO35/6, NAUK.

28. Memorandum, 31 August 1826, FO35/1, ibid.

29. John D. Adger, *My Life and Times, 1810–1899* (Richmond: Presbyterian Committee, 1899), 52–53.

30. Schloss, *Sweet Liberty*, 90–91, 95.

31. Letter to "My Dear Sir," 22 October 1822, CO28/91, NAUK.

32. Report of Harbour Master of Trinidad, 20 October 1822, ibid.

33. Report of Miguel de la Torre and Francisco Gonsalvez de Dinares, 14 October 1822, ibid.

34. Joel Roberts Poinsett, *Notes on Mexico, Made in the Autumn of 1822* (New York: Praeger, 1969), 2–5, 9.

35. Joshua Bryant, *Account of Insurrection of the Negro Slaves in the Colony of Demerara which Broke out on the 18th of August 1823* (Demerara: A. Stevenson, 1824) 1, 109. In the same volume, *Report of the Trials of Insurgent Negroes Before a General Court-Martial Held at Georgetown, Demerara on the 25th August 1823*, 3, 107. See also *Report on Debate in Council on a Despatch from Lord Bathurst to His Excellency Sir Henry Warde, Governor of Barbados* (Barbados: Barbadian Office, 1823). Both are in the collection at Brown University.

36. *A Communication from Sir Charles Brisbane, KCB Governor of Saint Vincent, to the House of Assembly of that Colony, Enclosing Lord Bathurst's Dispatch of the 9th of July with the Joint Reply of the Council and Assembly and a Letter Depicting the Alarm and Danger Excited by the Insurrection in Demerara* (London: Willich, 1823), 60, Brown University.

37. *An Official Letter from the Commissioners of Correspondence of the Bahama Islands to George Chalmers, Esq., Colonial Agent, Concerning the Proposed Abolition of Slavery in the West Indies* (Nassau: Royal Gazette, 1823), Brown University.

38. *Six Months in the West Indies in 1825* (London: Murray, 1826), 317, Brown University. Cf. Carrie Gibson, "There Is no Doubt that We Are under Threat by the Negroes of Santo Domingo: The Specter of Haiti in the Spanish Caribbean in the 1820s," in Matthew Brown and Gabriel Paquette, eds., *Connections After Colonialism: Europe and Latin America in the 1820s* (Tuscaloosa: University of Alabama, 2013).

39. *Negro Emancipation: A Dialogue Between Mr. Ebenezer Eastlove and Giles Homespun* (London: Thomas and George Underwood, 1824), Boston Public Library.

40. James Stephen, "England Enslaved by Her Own Colonies: An Address to the Electors and People of the United Kingdom" (London: Taylor, 1826), Massachusetts Historical Society, Boston. Emphasis original.

41. *Opinions of Henry Brougham, Esq. on Negro Slavery with Remarks* (London: Whitmore, 1826), Brown University.

42. Charles MacKenzie to John Bidwell, 26 June 1826, FO35/6, NAUK.

43. *An Authentic Copy of the Minutes of Evidence on the Trial of John Smith, a Missionary in*

Demerara . . . on a Charge of Exciting the Negroes to Rebellion (London: Burton, 1824), Brown University.

44.   Henry Warde to Earl of Bathurst, 30 January 1823, CO28/91, NAUK.

45.   George Klos, "Blacks and the Seminole Removal Debate, 1821–1835," *Florida Historical Quarterly*, 68 (Number 1, July 1989): 55–78, 60, Vertical File, *Florida Collection*, Jacksonville Public Library, Florida.

46.   Thomas Law to John C. Calhoun, 10 August 1821 in W. Edwin Hemphill, ed., *The Papers of John C. Calhoun, Volume VI, 1821–1822* (Columbia: University of South Carolina Press, 1972), 329.

47.   Lucius Gaston Moffatt and Joseph Medard Carriere, eds., "A Frenchman visits Charleston, 1817," *South Carolina Historical and Genealogical Magazine*, 49 (Number 3, July 1948): 131–154, 132.

48.   Address by James Madison to Agricultural Society of Albermarle (Virginia), 12 May 1818, in *Letters and Other Writings of James Madison, Fourth President of the United States, Volume III* (Philadelphia: Lippincott, 1867), 88.

49.   Thomas Clarkson to King Henry, 28 September 1819, in Earl Leslie Griggs and Clifford H. Prator, eds., *Henry Christophe and Thomas Clarkson: A Correspondence* (Berkeley: University of California Press, 1952), 161–163. See also J.S. Birt, *The Haytian Revolution, 1820*, Boston Public Library. This handwritten, though bound, volume was penned by Christophe's physician, a native of England, who died in Haiti at the age of 36 in 1825 and is further suggestive of "King Henry's" closeness to London.

50.   Thomas Clarkson to Robert Vaux, 8 March 1819, *Vaux Family Papers*, Historical Society of Pennsylvania. Cf. Henri Christophe, *A Correct Translation from the Original. The Formation of the New Dynasty of the Kingdom of Hayti . . . by a Near Relation to Bonaparte . . .* (Philadelphia, 1811), Historical Society of Pennsylvania.

51.   Thomas Clarkson to Robert Vaux, 31 January 1820, *Vaux Family Papers*. Emphasis original.

52.   Report by Mr. Mollier, circa 1820, Correspondance Commerciale, Le Cap (Haiti), 1825–1837, Tome 1, 53, MAE-Paris.

53.   Note in Griggs and Prator, *Henry Christophe and Thomas Clarkson*, 45.

54.   Hunt, "The Influence of Haiti on the Antebellum South," 197. See also Prince Sanders, *Haytian Papers: A Collection of the Very Interesting Proclamations and other Official Documents Together with Some Account of the Rise, Progress, and Present State of the Kingdom of Hayti* (Boston: Bingham, 1818), Huntington Library. At the same site, see also *The Rural Code of Haiti, Literally Translated from a Publication by the Government Press, Together with Letters from that Country Concerning its Present Condition by a Southern Planter* (Middletown, New Jersey: Evans, 1837).

55.   George Hockley to William Cramond, 28 July 1817, *Claude Unger Collection*, Historical Society of Pennsylvania, Philadelphia.

56.   Speech by John C. Calhoun, 4 February 1817, in Robert L. Merriwether, ed., *The Papers of John C. Calhoun, Volume VI, 1801–1817* (Columbia: University of South Carolina Press, 1959), 404.

57.   *Commercial Regulations of the Foreign Countries with Which the United States Have Commercial Intercourse, Collected, Digested, and Printed under the Direction of the President of the United States . . .* (Washington: Gales and Seaton, 1819), New York Historical Society.

58.   Jackson, "The Origins of Pan-African Nationalism," 45.

59. J. Boothroyd to John Quincy Adams, 5 December 1821, Roll 5, *Despatches from U.S. Consuls in Cap-Haïtien*. For more on U.S. trade with Haiti, see Letter from "Bibby" to Thomas Stagg, 23 April 1821, *Thomas Stagg Papers*, New York Historical Society.

60. Fritz Daguillard, *A Jewel in the Crown: Charles Sumner and the Struggle for Haiti's Recognition* (Washington, D.C.: Kalou, 1899), ix.

61. Clipping, no date, Box 218, *Caleb Cushing Papers*, Library of Congress, Washington, D.C.

62. *Feuille du Commerce*, October 1826, Correspondance Commerciale, Port-au-Prince, 1825–1826, 359, MAE-Paris.

63. Memorandum of James Franklin, circa 1826, FO35/1, NAUK.

64. *Niles Weekly Register*, 23 March 1822.

65. Alan Taylor, *The Internal Enemy: Slavery and War in Virginia, 1772–1832* (New York: Norton, 2013), 103.

66. Charles MacKenzie to John Bidwell, 3 March 1827, FO35/6, NAUK.

67. Indemnity Law, 26 February 1826, Correspondance Commerciale, Port-au-Prince, 1826–1826, 27, MAE-Paris.

68. Albert Gallatin to Viscount de Chateaubriand, 10 May 1823, Etat-Unis, 1817–1823, 7, MAE-Paris: "relations amicales qui subsistent . . . et a consolider les relations . . . entre le Gouvernement de La Majesté et celdi des Etats Unis."

69. Albert Gallatin to Viscount de Chateaubriand, 10 May 1823, ibid.

70. Letter from John T. Robinson, 10 September 1821, *Lewis Malone Ayer Papers*, University of South Carolina.

71. Joel Poinsett to Dr. Joseph Johnson, 11 August 1821, in Grace E. Heilman and Bernard S. Levin, eds., *Calendar of Joel Poinsett, Papers in the Henry D. Gilpin Collection* (Philadelphia: Gilpin Library, 1941), 3.

72. French Legation in Washington to Foreign Ministry, 25 October 1822, Etat-Unis, 1817–1823, 8, MAE-Paris.

73. *Le Telegraphe* [Haiti], 25 December 1825, Correspondance Commerciale, Port-Au-Prince, 1825–1826, MAE-Paris.

74. *Le Telegraphe*, 13 November 1825.

75. *Le Telegraphe*, 4 June 1826.

76. Henry H. Coming to Thomas Cumming, 22 February 1819, *Hammond, Bryan, and Cumming Papers*, University of South Carolina.

77. Henry H. Coming to Thomas Cumming, 7 April 1820, ibid.

78. Henry H. Coming to Julia Bryan, 17 May 1823, ibid. Emphasis original.

79. Report from Mr. Mollier, Vice Consul, 12 January 1826, Correspondance Commerciale, Le Cap (Haiti), 1825–1837, Tome 1, 6, MAE-Paris.

80. Report from Mr. Mollier, Vice Consul, 8 March 1826, Correspondance Commerciale, Le Cap, 16, ibid.

81. Report from Mr. Mollier, 12 March 1826, ibid.

82. Rerport from Mollier, 11 March 1826, ibid.

83. Andrew Armstrong to John Quincy Adams, 14 November 1820, Roll 5, *Despatches from U.S. Consuls in Cap-Haïtien*, NARA-CP.

84. Entry, circa January 1823, *Samuel Hambleton Diary*, Maryland Historical Society, Baltimore.

85. Letter to Mary, "Sunday the 14th 1824," *Ball Family Papers*, New York Historical Society.

86. Charles MacKenzie to George Canning, 17 January 1827, FO35/5, NAUK.

87. Memorandum, 16 January 1827, FO35/7, ibid.

88. Letter from William H. Geary, 24 August 1826, FO35/1, ibid.

89. Report from Vice-Consul, 1826, Correspondance Commerciale, Le Cap (Haiti), 1825–1837, Tome 1, 88, MAE-Paris.

90. Report from Vice-Consul, 1826, Affaires Commerciales, Cap-Haïtien, 144, MAE-Paris.

91. Report from Vice Consul, 5 August 1827, Affaires Commerciales, 155–158.

92. Alice Izard to Mrs. Manigault, no date, *Manigault Family Papers*.

93. William Walton, *Report on the Mines Known in the Eastern Division of Hayti and the Facities of Working Them* (London: Ridgway, Piccadilly, 1825).

94. William Miles to John C. Calhoun, 27 May 1844 in Clyde N. Wilson, ed., *The Papers of John C. Calhoun, Volume XX, 1844* (Columbia: University of South Carolina Press, 1991), 628–630.

95. Joseph Webb to George Canning, 19 January 1825, FO35/1, NAUK.

96. Report, 12 August 1826, Affaires Commerciales, Correspondance between Mr. Mollier, Vice Consul of France with the Minister of Foreign Affairs, 96, MAE-Paris.

97. Faye Felterman Tydlaska, "Between Nation and Empire: Representations of the Haitian Revolution in Antebellum Literary Culture" (Ph.D. diss., Tulane University, 2007), 208.

98. Scherr, *Thomas Jefferson's Haitian Policy*, 631.

99. Henry Warde to Earl of Bathurst, 7 March 1822, CO28/91, NAUK.

100. Letter to "My Dear Sir," 22 October 1822, CO28/91, ibid.

101. Memorandum, circa 1826, FO35/1, ibid.

102. William Miles to John C. Calhoun, 27 May 1844 in Clyde N. Wilson, ed., *The Papers of John C. Calhoun, Volume XX, 1844* (Columbia: University of South Carolina Press, 1991), 628–630.

103. Memorandum from William Geary, 24 August 1826, FO35/1, NAUK.

104. Charles Elliott to Sir Lawrence Halsted, 16 December 1826, FO35/7, ibid.

105. Charles MacKenzie to George Canning, 28 May 1826, FO35/3, ibid.

106. Charles MacKenzie to George Canning, 2 June 1826, FO35/3, ibid.

107. Printed Proclamation in French of Boyer, announcing non-ratification of 31 October 1825 treaty with France, FO35/3, ibid.

108. Proclamation of President Jean Boyer, 5 March 1826, Correspondance Commerciale, Le Cap (Haiti), 1825–1837, Tome 1, 25, MAE-Paris.

109. Charles MacKenzie to George Canning, 2 June 1826, FO35/3, NAUK.

110. Report by Mr. Mollier, 12 April 1826, Correspondance Commerciale, Le Cap (Haiti), 1825–1837, Tome 1, 61, MAE-Paris.

111. See Petitions by former "Colons," 1828, Haiti, Affaires Diverses Politiques, 1814–1896, MAE-Paris.

112. Charles MacKenzie to L.W. Halsted, 11 July 1827, FO35/7, NAUK.

113. Memorandum, 19 September 1826, Correspondance Commerciale, Port-au-Prince, 1825–1826, 354, MAE-Paris: Paris also paid significant attention to MacKenzie's arrival, as if London were seeking to gain unfair advantage by posting him in Haiti.

114. Charles MacKenzie to John Bidwell, 3 March 1827, FO35/6, NAUK.

115. Printed Proclamation, 1826, FO35/3, ibid.

116. Charles MacKenzie to General Inginac, 31 July 1826, FO35/3, ibid.

117. Charles MacKenzie to "the Earl Dudley," 10 March 1828, FO35/8, ibid.
118. Charles MacKenzie to George Canning, 5 March 1827, FO35/5, ibid.
119. Memorandum from Charles MacKenzie, 2 July 1827, FO35/5, ibid.
120. *Niles Weekly Register*, 17 October 1818. See also Scherr, *Thomas Jefferson's Haitian Policy*, 402.
121. *Baltimore Gazette*, circa 1819, *Benjamin Brand Papers*, Virginia Historical Society, Richmond.
122. Clipping, "Emigration to Hayti," circa 1820s, *Benjamin Brand Papers*.
123. Jackson, "The Origins of Pan-African Nationalism," 52–53.
124. Fritz Daguillard, *A Jewel in the Crown: Charles Sumner and the Struggle for Haiti's Recognition* (Washington, D.C.: Kalou, 1899). See also Julie Winch, "American Free Blacks and Emigration to Haiti," no. 33, Centro de Investigaciones del Caribe y America Latina, Universidad Interamericana de Puerto Rico, 1988, American Antiquarian Society, Worcester. This work is based heavily on the scholarship of the Haitian historian Beaubrun Ardouin.
125. Dennis B. Hidalgo, "From North America to Hispaniola: First Free Black Emigration and Settlements in Hispaniola" (Ph.D. diss., Central Michigan University, 2001), viii, 139, 82.
126. *Freedom's Journal*, 8 August 1828.
127. Laurent Dubois, *Haiti: The Aftershocks of History* (New York: Metropolitan, 2012), 94.
128. *Freedom's Journal*, 27 July 1827.
129. Reichard, "Black and White on the Urban Frontier: The St. Louis Community in Transition," 11.
130. Barbara Layenette Green, "The Slavery Debate in Missouri, 1831–1855" (Ph.D. diss., University of Missouri, Columbia, 1980), 30, 45.
131. Minutes of the Virginia Branch, American Colonization Society, General Meeting of the Richmond and Manchester Society Auxiliary to ACS, 17 January 1825, Virginia Historical Society, Richmond.
132. Letter from President Boyer, July 1820 in Benjamin P. Hunt, ed., *Notes Relating Directly or Indirectly to French St. Domingo & Hayti, Volume I*, no date, Boston Public Library: "Our past sufferings—our exampled efforts to regain our primitive rights, our solemn oath to live free & independent—the happy situation of our island, which may justly be called the Queen of the Antilles, & our wise constitution which insures a free country to Africans & their descendants."
133. President Jean Pierre Boyer to Loring Dewey, 30 April 1824, in *Correspondence Relative to the Emigration to Hayti of the Free People of Colour in the United States, Together with the Instructions to the Agent Sent out by President Boyer* (New York: Mahlon Day, 1824), Huntington Library, San Marino, California.
134. *Niles Weekly Register*, 1 July 1820.
135. 7 September 1822, ibid.
136. 3 August 1822, ibid.
137. Daguillard, *A Jewel in the Crown*, 5.
138. *Address of the Board of Managers of the Haitian Emigration Society of Coloured People, to the Emigrants Intending to Sail to the Island of Haiti in the Brig De Witt Clinton* (New York: Mahlon Day, 1824), New-York Historical Society.
139. *Information for the Free People of Colour who are Inclined to Emigrate to Hayti* (New York:

Samuel Wood & Son, 1824), Boston Public Library. The agents included Peter Barker, "Citizen Granville," John B. Platt, and Hugh McCormick—all of New York. At the same site, see also James Franklin, *The Present State of Hayti (Santo Domingo)* . . . (London: Murray, 1828).

140. Daguillard, *A Jewel in the Crown*, 5.

141. Letter from Jeremiah Warden, 18 August 1824, *George Flower Family Collection*, Chicago History Museum.

142. James Forten to "Dear Sir," 25 September 1824, ibid.

143. Serena Baldwin to "Dear Teacher," 29 September 1824 and Serena Baldwin to "Dear Teacher," 30 June 1825, in Abigail Mott, ed., *Biographical Sketches and Interesting Anecdotes of Persons of Color* (York, U.K.: Alexander & Son, 1826), 230, 232–233.

144. Charles W. Fisher to Father, 13 February 1825 and Charles W. Fisher to Father, 16 April 1826, in Mott, *Biographical Sketches*, 234–235.

145. *Freedom's Journal*, 12 October 1827.

146. 21 December 1827, ibid.

147. *The Travels and Opinions of Benjamin Lundy Including His Journeys to Texas and Mexico; with a Sketch of Contemporary Events and Notice of the Revolution in Hayti* (Philadelphia: W.D. Parrish, 1847), 29, 194, Huntington Library.

148. *Freedom's Journal*, 29 June 1827.

149. 31 August 1827, ibid.

150. 24 October 1828, ibid.

151. Note in Charles M. Wiltse, ed., *The Papers of Daniel Webster, Correspondence, Volume 2, 1825–1829* (Hanover, New Hampshire: University Press of New England, 1976), 128. See also Frederic Bancroft, *Slave Trading in the Old South* (Baltimore: Furst, 1931), 39–42.

152. Logan, *The Diplomatic Relations of the United States with Haiti*, 225.

153. Rayford W. Logan, *Haiti and the Dominican Republic* (New York: Oxford University Press, 1967), 101. See also Ken S. Mueller, *Senator Benton and the People: Master Race Democracy on the Early American Frontier* (De Kalb: Northern Illinois University Press, 2014), 126–127.

154. *Le Telegraphe*, 16 April 1826.

155. John C. Calhoun to Samuel L. Southard, 16 August 1825, in Clyde N. Wilson and W. Edwin Hemphill, eds., *The Papers of John C. Calhoun, Volume X, 1825–1829* (Columbia: University of South Carolina Press, 1977), 39. For a reference to Haiti by the U.S. president, see *New York Evening Post*, 20 March 1826.

6. U.S. NEGROES AND BLACK JACOBINS, 1830–1839

1. Tydlaska, "Between Nation and Empire," 18.

2. Samuel Warner, *Authentic and Impartial Narrative of the Tragical Scene Which was Witnessed in Southampton County (Virginia) on Monday the 22nd of August Last, When Fifty-five of its Inhabitants (Mostly Women and Children) were inhumanly Massacred by the Blacks!*, Special Collections, University of Virginia, Charlottesville.

3. F.S. Read to "Dear Marble," 26 January 1836, *Case Family Papers*, Missouri Historical Society, St. Louis.

4. " . . . Philip A. Bolling in the House of Delegates of Virginia on the Policy of the State in Relation to her Colored Population," Delivered on the 11th and 12th of January 1832 (Richmond: White, 1832), 20–22, Virginia Historical Society, Richmond.

5.   "Letter IV," circa 1832, in M. Carey, ed., *Letters of the Colonization Society and on the Probable Results . . .* (Philadelphia: Carey & Hart, 1834), 12–13, University of Virginia, Charlottesville.

6.   *Review of the Debate in the Virginia Legislature of 1831 and 1832 by Thomas R. Dew, Professor of History, Metaphysics, and Political Law, William and Mary College* (Richmond: White, 1832), Columbia University.

7.   S.A. Townes to George Franklin Townes, 8 October 1831, *Townes Family Papers*, University of South Carolina. Emphasis original.

8.   J.E. Alexander, *Transatlantic Sketches, Comprising Visits to the Most Interesting Scenes in North and South America and the West Indies . . .*, Volume 2 (London: Bentley, 1833), 19, 20.

9.   John Greenleaf Whittier, *Poems Written During the Progress of the Abolition Question in the United States Between the Years 1830 and 1838* (Boston: Knapp, 1837), 73–82.

10.   *Report Made to the Chamber of Deputies on the Abolition of Slavery in the French Colonies by Alexis de Tocqueville* (Boston: Munroe, 1840), Columbia University.

11.   Schloss, *Sweet Liberty*, 135.

12.   Bernard Martin, Sr., *Jamaica, As it Was, As it Is, and As it May Be . . .* (London: Hurst, 1835).

13.   William Miles to John C. Calhoun, 27 May 1844, in Clyde N. Wilson, ed., *The Papers of John C. Calhoun, Volume XX, 1844*, 628–630.

14.   Letter from Port Royal, Jamaica, 14 February 1832, CO137/186, NAUK.

15.   Abraham Hodgson et al. to Earl Grey of H.M. Treasury, circa 1832, ibid.

16.   Letter to "My Lord," 30 May 1832, ibid.

17.   Charles Bankhead to "My Lord," 28 April 1832, ibid.

18.   Ibid., Rebecca Hartkopf Schloss, *Sweet Liberty*, 229.

19.   William Miles to John C. Calhoun, 27 May 1844, in Wilson, *The Papers of John C. Calhoun, Volume XX*.

20.   Logan, *The Diplomatic Relations of the United States with Haiti*, 233.

21.   Mrs. Carmichael, *Domestic Manners and Social Conditions of the White, Coloured, and Negro Population of the West Indies*, Volume I (London: Whittaker, Treacher, 1833), 157, 244–245, 321.

22.   Mrs. Carmichael, *Domestic Manners and Social Conditions . . .*, Volume II (London: Whittaker, Treacher, 1833), 157.

23.   William Lloyd, *Letters from the West Indies During a Visit . . .* (London: Darton and Harvey, 1836), 175.

24.   James H. Hammond to Milledge Galphin, 8 January 1837, *Hammond, Bryan, and Cumming Papers*, University of South Carolina.

25.   Comment, 1836, in Carol Bleser, ed., *Secret and Sacred: The Diaries of James Henry Hammond, A Southern Slaveholder* (Columbia: University of South Carolina Press, 1988), 3–23, 13.

26.   John Kirkpatrick to Richard Singleton, 21 January 1832, *Singleton Family Papers*.

27.   Albert Gallatin to Viscount de Chateaubriand, 18 January 1823, Etats-Unis, Affaires Diverses, 1817–1823, MAE-Paris. In the same file, see also the letters and correspondence from 1818 on the slave trade.

28.   Letter to Viscount de Chateaubriand, 15 October 1823, ibid.

29.   *Information Concerning the Present State of the Slave Trade*, 1824, Boston Public Library.

30.   See, e.g., Charles Miner to Enoch Lewis, 25 January 1828, *African American Collection*, University of Michigan, Ann Arbor and Gerald Horne, *Race to Revolution*, passim.

31.   William Prince to John Forsyth, Secretary of State, 17 September 1834, Roll 1, T330, *Despatches from U.S. Consuls in Aux Cayes*, NARA-CP.

32.   Governor Balfour to "Sir," 14 July 1834, CO23/91, NAUK.

33.   John Arthur et al. to Governor Balfour, 28 June 1834, ibid.

34.   Gregory D. Smithers, *Slave Breeding: Sex, Violence, and Memory in African American History* (Tallahassee: University Press of Florida, 2012).

35.   Report, 19 May 1826, Box 1, *Manumission Society Papers*, University of North Carolina, Chapel Hill: Phineas Nixon headed to Haiti to supervise "the emigration of some peoples of color to that island." In the same file, see also: Report, 6 May 1826: An accord to send Negroes to Haiti from Guilford County, North Carolina.

36.   Report, 1826, ibid.

37.   Letter to Richard Mendenhall, 15 September 1826, ibid.

38.   Report by T. Stuart, Clerk of the Emigration Committee, 14 May 1828, ibid.

39.   Charles R. Maduell, ed., *Index of Spanish Citizens Entering New Orleans from 1820–1840* (New Orleans, 1968), i, Alabama Department of Archives and History, Montgomery. At the same site, see also Charles R. Maduell, ed., *Index of Spanish Citizens Entering New Orleans Mid-Nineteenth Century* (New Orleans, 1966).

40.   Reed Russell Eaton, "The Public Life of Stephen Girard" (Ph.D. diss., Kent State University, 1971), 1, 4, 15, 25, 59, 214, 217, 219.

41.   Minutes of Manumission Society, 27 September 1824, Box 1, *Manumission Society Papers*.

42.   Henry Clay to Colonization Society of Kentucky, 17 December 1829, in Robert Seager, ed., *The Papers of Henry Clay, Volume 8, Candidate, Compromiser, Whig, March 5, 1829– December 31, 1836* (Lexington: University Press of Kentucky, 1984), 152–153.

43.   Angelina Grimké to "Dear Friend," 20 July 1837, in Angelina Grimke, *Letters to Catherine E. Beecher* (New York: Arno, 1969), 35–41, 37. Emphasis original.

44.   *Freedom's Journal*, 16 January 1829.

45.   14 February 1829, ibid.

46.   Jacqueline Bacon, *Freedom's Journal: The First African-American Newspaper* (Lanham, Maryland: Lexington, 2007), 169, 34.

47.   Note in Edward Maceo Coleman, ed., *Creole Voices: Poems in French by Free Men of Color First Published in 1845* (Washington, D.C.: Associated Publishers, 1945), xxv.

48.   Anna Brickhouse, *Transamerican Literary Relations and the Nineteenth Century Public Sphere* (New York: Cambridge University Press, 2004), 24. See also James R. Frisby, Jr., "New Orleans Writers and the Negro: George Washington Cable, Grace King, Ruth McEnery Stuart, Kate Chopin, and Lafcadio Hearn, 1870–1900" (Ph.D. diss., Emory University, 1972).

49.   Charles Edwards O'Neill, *Sejour: Parisian Playwright from Louisiana* (Lafayette: Center for Louisiana Studies, University of Southwest Louisiana, 1995), vii.

50.   Daniel L. Schafer, *Zephaniah Kingsley, Jr. and the Atlantic World* (Gainesville: University Press of Florida, 2013), 199, 206.

51.   *Florida Times-Union*, 11 December 1993, Vertical File, Jacksonville Historical Society, Florida.

52. Carita Doggett Corse, "Excerpts from The Key to Golden Islands," Chapter V, University of Florida, Gainesville.

53. Zephaniah Kingsley, "The Rural Code of Haiti," 1837, *Zephaniah Kingsley Collection, University of Florida, Gainesville.*

54. Zephaniah Kingsley to Editor, 30 June 1838, and Notes in Daniel W. Stowell, editor, *Balancing Evils Judiciously: The Proslavery Writings of Zephaniah Kingsley* (Gainesville: University Press of Florida, 2000), 102–106, 53, 23, 73. See Zephaniah Kingsley to "Editor of the Christian Statesman," 20 June 1837, Box 218, *Caleb Cushing Papers,* Lib. of Congress, Washington, D.C.

55. *The Colored American,* 28 September 1839.

56. 22 September 1838, ibid.

57. 11 August 1838, ibid.

58. Daniel L. Schaffer, "Notes on the Life of Anna Kingsley," no date, Vertical File, Jacksonville Historical Society.

59. T.D. Allman, *Finding Florida: The True History of the Sunshine State* (New York: Atlantic Monthly Press, 2013), 194.

60. Interview with Daniel Schaffer, 19 May 2003, Vertical File, Jacksonville Historical Society.

61. Copy of Manuscript in Florida State Library of "Speech of Zephaniah Kingsley to the Florida Legislature," no date, Box 1, Zephaniah Kingsley Collection.

62. Zephaniah Kingsley, "A Treatise on the Patriarchal or Co-Operative System of Society as it Exists, in Some Governments and Colonies in America and in the United States Under the Name of Slavery with its Necessity and Advantages," 1829, Box 1,ibid.

63. Frank Marotti, *Heaven's Soldiers: Free People of Color and the Spanish Legacy in Antebellum Florida* (Tuscaloosa: University of Alabama Press, 2013), 43.

64. Zephaniah Kingsley to George Evans, 12 October 1835, "The Rural Code of Haiti," *Zephaniah Kingsley Collection.*

65. Genealogy and Death Certificate of Zephaniah Kingsley, Box 1, ibid.

66. "Copy of Will," 20 July 1843, ibid.

67. *Jacksonville Sunday-Times Union,* 8 June 1924.

68. *Folio Weekly,* 1 August 1889, Box 1, *Zephaniah Kingsley Collection.*

69. "Letters from New York," 7 July 1842, ibid. Emphasis original.

70. Philip S. May, Article on Kingsley, no date, ibid.

71. Letter to Secretary of State John Forsyth, 26 October 1838, Roll 1, T330, *Despatches from U.S. Consuls in Aux Cayes,* NARA-CP.

72. Letter to Secretary of State John Forsyth, 12 November 1838, ibid.

73. Letter, 12 November 1838, ibid.

74. Letter from Ralph Higginbotham, 15 December 1838, ibid. Emphasis original.

75. Typescript of Maria Child interview with Zephaniah Kingsley, 7 July 1842, Box 1, *Zephaniah Kingsley Collection.*

76. Theda Perdue and Michael D. Green, *The Cherokee Nation and the Trail of Tears* (New York: Viking, 2007).

77. Order from Governor Boggs, 27 October 1838, in Vertical File, "Mormons in Missouri, 1831–1839," Missouri State Archives, Jefferson City.

78. G.F. Pritchard et al. to Governor of Missouri, 12 September 1836, in ibid.

79. "Documents Containing the Correspondence, Orders . . . in Relation to the Disturbances with the Mormons; and the Evidence," 1836–1841, in ibid.

80. "The Mormon Occupation," in *History of Caldwell County, Missouri*, circa 1833, in ibid.

81. Edmund P. Gaines to "Sir," 27 September 1837, *Lilburn Williams Boggs Papers*, Missouri State Archives, Jefferson City.

82. *The Colored American*, 15 September 1838.

83. 9 March 1839, ibid.

84. Memorandum on "Disposal of Colonial Convicts," 18 May 1834, CO23/91, NAUK.

85. Memorandum, 18 February 1834, ibid.

86. William Dalzell to His Excellency, 4 April 1834, ibid.

87. Letter to Governor B.T. Balfour, 25 June 1834, ibid.

88. Letter to State Department, 10 June 1831, Roll 6, *Despatches from U.S. Consuls in Cap-Haïtien*, NARA-CP.

89. Memorandum, circa 1835, Roll 7, ibid. See also Report by William Miles, 1 January 1837, Roll 1, T330, *Despatches from U.S. Consuls in Aux Cayes*, NARA-CP.

90. William Miles to Secretary of State John Forsyth, 25 May 1838, Roll 1, T330, *Despatches from U.S. Consuls in Aux Cayes*, NARA-CP.

91. Thomas Ussher to Lord Palmerston, 23 October 1838, FO35/20, NAUK.

92. Memorandum, circa 1835, Roll 7, *Despatches from U.S. Consuls in Cap-Haïtien*, NARA-CP.

93. Thomas Ussher to Lord Palmerston, 20 March 1838, FO35/20, NAUK.

94. William Miles to Secretary of State John Forsyth, 26 October 1835, Roll 1, T330, *Despatches from U.S. Consuls in Aux Cayes*, NARA-CP.

95. William Miles to Secretary of State John Forsythe, 9 December 1835, ibid.

96. G.W.C. Courtenay to Lord Palmerston, 18 April 1837, FO35/18., NAUK.

97. Letter to Secretary of State Louis McLane, 29 January 1834, Roll 6, M9, *Despatches from U.S. Consuls in Cap-Haïtien*, NARA-CP.

98. William Miles to Secretary of State John Forsythe, 10 December 1835, Roll 1, T330, *Despatches from U.S. Consuls in Aux Cayes*, NARA-CP.

99. Letter to John Forsythe, Secretary of State, 26 September 1837, Roll 1, T56, *Despatches from U.S. Consuls in Santo Domingo*, NARA-CP.

100. Daniel Carney to John Forsythe, 26 March 1838, ibid.

101. Letter to John Forsythe, Secretary of State, 14 June 1838, Roll 7, *Despatches from U.S. Consuls in Cap-Haïtien*, NARA-CP.

102. William Miles to Secretary of State John Forsythe, 25 May 1838, Roll 1, T330, *Despatches from U.S. Consuls in Aux Cayes*, NARA-CP. Emphasis original.

103. Thomas Ussher to Lord Palmerston, 24 March 1838, FO35/20, NAUK.

104. William Miles to "Sir," 24 May 1838, Roll 1, T330, *Despatches from U.S. Consuls in Aux Cayes*, NARA-CP.

105. Letter to Secretary of State John Forsythe, 12 November 1838, ibid. Emphasis original.

106. Letter from Ralph Higginbotham, 15 December 1838, ibid.

107. Letter to State Department, 10 June 1831, Roll 6, M9, *Despatches from U.S. Consuls in Cap-Haïtien*, NARA-CP.

108. Ralph Higginbotham to Secretary of State John Forsythe, 7 January 1839, Roll 2, T330, *Despatches from U.S. Consuls in Aux Cayes*, NARA-CP. Emphasis original.

109. G.W. Courtenay to Lord Palmerston, 1 July 1839, FO35/20, NAUK.

110. Ralph Higginbotham to Secretary of State John Forsythe, 4 December 1839, Roll 2, T330, *Despatches from U.S. Consuls in Aux Cayes*, NARA-CP.

111.   W.O. Pell to Captain Courtenay, circa 1836, FO35/18, NAUK.

112.   Letter to State Department, 10 June 1831, Roll 6, M9, *Despatches from U.S. Consuls in Cap-Haïtien*, NARA-CP.

113.   Letter to Henry Clay, 5 May 1828, Roll 6, ibid.

114.   Claim, 1833, Box 253, *Caleb Cushing Papers*, Library of Congress, Washington, D.C.

115.   Resolutions including Maryland, December 1835; Connecticut, 25 May 1838; Maine, 18 March 1840; and Pennsylvania, 8 June 1840, Box 218, *Caleb Cushing Papers.*

116.   Resolution on Haiti, circa 1835, Box 218, *Caleb Cushing Papers*: "there are many weighty reasons why this Republic of Hayti should be placed in political & improved commercial relations with the Government of the United States. . . . difficulties that have until recently existed between this Republic & France are now settled & most if not all the states & nations of Europe have acknowledged its independence. Before the year 1827 more than ten thousand emigrants had gone from this country to find a home in that island. . . . six thousand of which that Government defrayed the expense & should friendly political & commercial relations be established between it & our Government, it is believed that many free persons of color from the United States would seek a settlement on its soil."

117.   Treudley, "The United States and Santo Domingo, 1789–1866," 230.

118.   *Boston Courier*, 22 December 1838, Box 218, *Caleb Cushing Papers.*

119.   Speech in the House of Representatives, 18 December 1838, in *Writings of Hugh Swinton Legare, Late Attorney General and Acting Secretary of State of the United States . . . , Volume I* (Charlston: Burges & James, 1846), 124, 322. See also "Speeches of the Hon. H.S. Legare of South Carolina on the Recognition of Hayti; in Favor of a Southern Naval Depot" (Washington, 1839), New-York Historical Society.

120.   "Remarks of the Hon. Waddy Thompson on the Proposition to recognize the Republic of Hayti . . . House of Representatives, 22 and 28 December 1838 and 10 January 1839" (Washington: Gales and Seaton, 1839), Library of Congress.

121.   Letter to Secretary of State, 11 June 1831, Roll 6, M9, *Despatches from U.S. Consuls in Cap-Haïtien*, NARA-CP.

122.   See Bordeaux Petition, 1836, Haiti. Affaires Diverses Politiques, 1814–1896, MAE-Paris.

123.   Letter, 28 November 1836, FO35/18, NAUK.

124.   Petition to Chamber of Deputies, 1834, Haiti. Affaires Diverses, 1833–1845, MAE-Paris.

125.   Letter to Secretary of State, 29 January 1834, Roll 6, M9, *Despatches from U.S. Consuls in Cap-Haïtien*, NARA-CP.

126.   G.W. C. Courtenay to Lord Palmerston, 12 June 1837, FO35/19, NAUK.

127.   Jonathan Brown, *The History and Present Condition of St. Domingo, Volume II* (Philadelphia: Marshall, 1837), 262.

128.   Thomas Ussher to Lord Palmerston, 21 December 1838, FO35/20, NAUK.

129.   Letter to Secretary of State Edward Livingston, 19 July 1832, Roll 6, M9, *Despatches from U.S. Consuls in Cap-Haïtien*, NARA-CP.

130.   "Memorial Bordelais," circa 19 April 1838, Haiti. Affaires Diverses, 1833–1845, MAE-Paris.

131.   "Monsieur Le Comte" [Paris], 3 September 1838, Haiti. Affaires Diverses, 1833–1845. See also Document, 1831, 29 ADP, Marge 3, Numero 13, P18002, Microfilm, Haiti Memoires & Documents, MAE-Paris. Here the possibility of the abolition of the death penalty in Louisiana is addressed.

132.   Memorandum, October 1836, FO35/18, NAUK.

133. Charles MacKenzie to George Canning, 30 November 1836, FO36/6, ibid.

7. BLACK JACOBINS WEAKENED, 1840–1849

1.   Jonathan Elliot to U.S. Secretary of State, 13 April 1849, Roll 1, T56, *Despatches from United States Consuls in Santo Domingo*, NARA-CP.

2.   Letter, 28 January 1845, in *Selections from the Letters and Speeches of the Hon. James H. Hammond of South Carolina* (New York: Trow, 1866), 129.

3.   Robert Nicholas Olsberg, "A Government of Class and Race: William Henry Trescot and the South Carolina Chivalry, 1860–1865" (Ph.D. diss., University of South Carolina, 1972), 36.

4.   Pierce Butler, *Judah P. Benjamin* (Philadelphia: Jacobs, 1906), 296.

5.   William Henry Trescot, *A Few Thoughts on the Foreign Policy of the United States* (Charleston: Russell, 1849), 12; William Henry Trescot, *An American View of the Eastern Question* (Charleston: Russell, 1854).

6.   Elliott Lee to the governor, 21 August 1845, *John C. Edwards Papers*, Missouri State Archives, Jefferson City.

7.   Letter to the governor, 14 August 1845, ibid.

8.   Elliott Lee to the governor, 23 August 1845, ibid.

9.   Remarks by John C. Calhoun, 15 May 1848, in Clyde N. Wilson and Shirley Bright Cook, eds., *The Papers of John C. Calhoun, Volume XXV, 1847–1848* (Columbia: University of South Carolina Press, 1999), 414–415.

10. Remarks by John C. Calhoun, 20 April 1848, in ibid., 347.

11. Allen Hall to John C. Calhoun, 25 May 1844, in Clyde N. Wilson, ed., *The Papers of John C. Calhoun, Volume XVIII, 1844* (Columbia: University of South Carolina Press, 1993), 611. Emphasis original.

12. Robert Harrison to John C. Calhoun, 13 May 1844, in ibid., 500.

13. Ray Grenada, "Slave Unrest in Florida," *Florida Historical Quarterly* 55 (July 1976): 18–36. Vertical File, Jacksonville Public Library, Florida.

14. Scherr, *Thomas Jefferson's Haitian Policy*, 238, 683.

15. *The Colored American*, 23 January 1841.

16. G.W. C. McCourtneay, 10 June 1840, FO35/101, NAUK.

17. *The Third Annual Report of British and Foreign Anti-Slavery Society for the Abolition of Slavery and the Slave Trade Throughout the World Presented to the General Meeting Held in Exeter Hall on Friday May 13th 1842* (London: British and Foreign Anti-Slavery Society, 1842), Cornell University, Ithaca, New York.

18. *The National Era*, 20 November 1847.

19. *Constitution of the Port-Plate Philanthropic Society*, circa 1841, Boston Public Library.

20. John Telemachus Hilton to Henry Grafton and Maria Weston Chapman, 30 April 1841, MS. A.9.15, Boston Public Library.

21. William Griffin to Maria Weston Chapman, 21 September 1841, M.A. 9.2.a5, p. 70, Boston Public Library. At the same site, see also William P. Griffin to Maria Weston Chapman, 14 May 1843, MS. A.9.2.18, p. 38.

22. Reginald Horsman, *Josiah Nott of Mobile: Southerner, Physician, and Racial Theorist* (Baton Rouge: Louisiana State University Press, 1987), 57.

23. "An Act More Effectually to Prevent Free Persons of Color from Entering into this State

and For Other Purposes," 1842, The Historic New Orleans Collection, Williams Research Center.

24. M.C. Field to St. Louis Reveille Staff, 8 September 1844, *Ludlow Field Maury Collection*, Missouri Historical Society, St. Louis.

25. W. Adolphe Robert, *Royal Street: A Novel of Old New Orleans* (New York: Bobbs-Merrill, 1944), 24, 186–187, 198, 216, 222, 255, 270, 292.

26. G.W. C. Courtenay to Lord Palmerston, 10 June 1840, RO35/23, NAUK.

27. Letter to Daniel Webster, 12 August 1842, Roll 2, T330, *Despatches from U.S. Consuls in Aux Cayes*, NARA-CP.

28. Letter to Daniel Webster, 5 August 1842, ibid.

29. Joseph C. Luther to Abel Upshur, 26 March 1844 in Wilson, *The Papers of John C. Calhoun, Volume XVIII*, 89–90.

30. Report, Circa 1842, Roll 2, T330, *Despatches from U.S. Consuls in Aux Cayes*.

31. A.P. Upshur to C.J. Ingersoll, 24 February 1844, in 28th Congress, 1st Session, Rep. No. 428, House Diplomatic Relations with Hayti, 10 April 1844, University of Texas, Austin.

32. S.C. Luther to James Buchanan, 1 July 1845, Reel 2, T346, *Despatches of U.S. Consuls in Port-au-Prince*, NARA-CP. On the same reel with the same correspondents, see the 1 January 1847 letter: "my semi-annual statement . . . of the number of arrivals and departures of American vessels at and from this port," from 1 July to 31 December 1846, reveals "forty one arrivals with an aggregate tonnage of five thousand and six hundred sixty three & 66/95 tons."

33. Report, circa 1842, Roll 2, T330, *Despatches from U.S. Consuls in Aux Cayes*.

34. Entry, 22 June 1858, William Kaufman Scarborough, ed., *The Diary of Edmund Ruffin, Volume I, Toward Independence, October 1856–April 1861* (Baton Rouge: Louisiana State University Press, 1972), 149–150.

35. Edmund Ruffin, *The Political Economy of Slavery; or the Institution Considered in Regard to its Influence on Public Wealth and the General Welfare*, no date, unclear provenance, University of South Carolina.

36. *A Brief Inquiry into the Prospective Results that Might Follow the Secret Mission to Dominico and Hayti with the Probable Results on Colored Americans* (Philadelphia: Coates, 1952), Historical Society of Pennsylvania, Philadelphia. See also Horace Pauleus Sannon, *Essai Historique sur La Revolution de 1843* (Port-au-Prince: BNH, 2013).

37. Article, 1 August 1842, in John Blassingame, ed., *The Frederick Douglass Papers, Series One: Speeches, Debates, and Interviews, Volume I: 1841–1846* (New Haven: Yale University Press, 1979), 206.

38. Christina Violeta Jones, "Revolution and Reaction: Santo Domingo during the Haitian Revolution and Beyond, 1791–1844" (Ph.D. dissertation, Howard University, 2008), 203.

39. B.C. Clark, "Remarks Upon United States Intervention in Hayti with Comments Upon the Correspondence Connected with It" (Boston: Easturn's Press, 1853), Massachusetts Historical Society, Boston. Emphasis original.

40. James Parthemos, "Santo Domingo and the Monroe Doctrine, 1903–1907: A Study in Receivership Diplomacy" (M.A. thesis, University of South Carolina, 1949), 3.

41. "Diary of Secret Mission to San Domingo, 1847–1848," Box 1, *David Dixon Porter Papers*, Duke University, Durham, North Carolina. Emphasis original.

42. Comment, in Eric Paul Roorda et al., eds., *The Dominican Republic Reader: History, Culture, Politics* (Durham: Duke University Press, 2014), 136.

43. Martin Van Buren to John Forsyth, 2 March 1841, in "2nd Congress, Doc. No. 107, House of Representatives, Claims of Citizens of the United States on Hayti. Message from the President of the United States in Reply to a Resolution of the House of Representatives of the 12th Ultimo, in Relation to Claims of Citizens of the United States on the Government of Hayti, 8 March 1841," University of Texas, Austin. See also Jacob Lewis to John C. Calhoun, 28 March 1821 in W. Edwin Hemphill, ed., *The Papers of John C. Calhoun, Volume V, 1820–1821* (Columbia: University of South Carolina Press, 1971), 703: "My claim on the Haytian [government] requires my presents [*sic*] at home."

44. Correspondence between Michael Tesson family and attorneys in France, 1838–1881, Box 2, Folder 14, *Tesson Collection,* Missouri Historical Society, St. Louis: This concerns indemnities for property taken by the Haitian government after the revolution.

45. Accession File, circa 1955, *William Berson Papers,* University of North Carolina, Chapel Hill.

46. William Berson to "Dear Sir," 27 July 1841, ibid.

47. Contract between William Berson and Charles Regnault, no date, ibid.

48. A. Folsom to John C. Calhoun, 20 September 1844, in Clyde N. Wilson, ed., *The Papers of John C. Calhoun, Volume XIX, 1844* (Columbia: University of South Carolina Press, 1990), 812–813.

49. "Memoir on Dominican Republic in Reference to Her Relation to Hayti," 18 February 1851, FO23/10, NAUK.

50. Resolution, 24 February 1844, *Meredith Miles Marmaduke Papers,* Missouri State Archives, Jefferson City.

51. John Kirkpatrick to Richard Singleton, 27 May 1846, *Singleton Family Papers,* University of South Carolina.

52. Leslie Combs to Waddy Thompson, 8 October 1842, *Thompson-Jones Family Papers,* University of South Carolina.

53. James Harvey to Waddy Thompson, 18 October 1842, ibid.

54. Leslie Combs to Waddy Thompson, 14 October 1842, ibid.

55. Joel Poinsett to Waddy Thompson, 29 May 1843, ibid.

56. Joel Roberts Poinsett, *Notes on Mexico, made in the Autumn of 1822* (New York: Praeger, 1969), 141, 185.

57. William Miles to John C. Calhoun, 27 May 1844, in Wilson, *The Papers of John C. Calhoun, Volume XVIII,* 628–630.

58. Statement from the D.R. to U.S. Secretary of State, 8 January 1845, Roll 1, T801, *Notes from the Legation of the Dominican Republic in the United States to the Department of State,* NARA-CP.

59. Dominican Republic to John Calhoun, 25 January 1845, ibid. See also "Memo Respecting the 'Spanish Part' of the Island of Hayti," November 1836, FO35/19, NAUK.

60. Vice Consul of France to Ministry of Foreign Affairs, circa 1826, Tome 1, Correspondance Consulaire et commerciale (1793–1901), Le Cap (Haiti) et Gonaives, 1825–1837, Cote 163CCC/1, 86, MAE-Paris.

61. Sam Israel to Henry Clay, 11 November 1828, Roll 6, *Despatches from U.S. Consuls in Cap-Haïtien.*

62. *Freedom's Journal,* 12 December 1828.

63. Sam Israel to Henry Clay, 15 January 1829, Roll 6, *Despatches from U.S. Consuls in Cap-Haïtien.*

64. F.M. Dimond to Martin Van Buren, 30 January 1830, ibid.

65. F.M. Dimond to Martin Van Buren, 14 February 1830, ibid.

66. *L'Abeille* [New Orleans], 24 March 1830.

67. Letter to Daniel Webster, 7 February 1843, Roll 2, T330, *Despatches from U.S. Consuls in Aux Cayes*.

68. Gail Collins, *William Henry Harrison* (New York: Times Books, 2012), 69.

69. Anne Jenkins Batson, *Louis Manigault: Gentleman from South Carolina* (Roswell, Georgia: Wolfe, 1995), 14, 3, 163.

70. Comment in James M. Clifton, ed., *Life and Labor on Argyle Island: Letters and Documents of a Savannah River Plantation, 1833–1867* (Savannah: Beehive Press, 1978), xxviii.

71. G. Manigault, *A Biographical Sketch of the Hon. Joel R. Poinsett of South Carolina*, 1888, University of South Carolina. See also Dorothy M. Parton, "The Diplomatic Career of Joel Roberts Poinsett" (Ph.D. diss., Catholic University, 1934).

72. J. Fred Rippy, *Joel R. Poinsett, Versatile American* (New York: Greenwood, 1968), 91, 72, 10–11.

73. Commodore Jesse D. Elliot to Joel Poinsett, 31 January 1841, in Grace E. Heilman and Bernard S. Levin, eds., *Calendar of Joel R. Poinsett Papers in the Henry D. Gilpin Collection* (Philadelphia: Gilpin Library, 1941), 141.

74. Alexander Vattemare to Joel Poinsett, 5 May 1843, in ibid., 170.

75. Letter to Daniel Webster, 7 February 1843, Roll 2, T330, *Despatches from U.S. Consuls in Aux Cayes*.

76. William Gooch to Daniel Webster, 25 February 1843, ibid.

77. William Gooch to Daniel Webster, 28 February 1843, ibid.

78. Michael Lovell, to Daniel Webster, 22 March 1843, ibid.

79. William Gooch to Daniel Webster, 25 March 1843, ibid.

80. Letter, circa 1843, ibid.

81. Thomas Ussher to Correspondent in Jamaica, no date, circa 1843, FO35/23, NAUK.

82. Richmond Loring to Secretary of State, 8 August 1843, Roll 2, T330, *Despatches from U.S. Consuls in Aux Cayes*.

83. Thomas Curtis to Secretary of State, 22 September 1843, Roll 7, M9, *Despatches from U.S. Consuls in Cap-Haïtien*.

84. G.H. Usher to Daniel Webster, 5 April 1843, ibid.

85. Duff Green to John Clayton, 28 January 1850, Folder 399, *Duff Green Papers*, University of North Carolina, Chapel Hill.

86. Walker Anderson, U.S. Attorney, Pensacola, to State Department, 18 July 1844, in Clyde N. Wilson, ed., *The Papers of John C. Calhoun, Volume XIX, 1844* (Columbia: University of South Carolina Press, 1990), 383.

87. Mr. Juchereau de St. Denys to Mr. Guizot, Minister of Foreign Affairs, 20 November 1843, Correspondance Commerciale/Saint Domingue (1843–1850), Tome 1, Code: 584 fos 22.12.33, MAE-Paris.

88. William Miles to Sir, 28 March 1843, Roll 2, T330, *Despatches from U.S. Consuls in Aux Cayes*.

89. Mr. Juchereau de St. Denys to Mr. Guizot, 13 June 1844, Direction Communale et du Contention, Correspondance Commerciale/Saint Domingue (1843–1850), Tome 1, Code 584 fos. 22.12.13.

90. Mr. Juchereau de St. Denys to Mr. Guizot, 3 March 1844, ibid. See also attached documents and letters.
91. Letter from Pedro Santana, 1 June 1844, ibid.
92. Mr. Juchereau de St. Denys to Mr. Guizot, 10 February 1846, ibid.
93. Mr. Juchereau de St. Denys to Mr. Guizot, 6 March 1844, ibid.
94. Mr. Juchereau de St. Denys to Mr. Guizot, 11 March 1844, ibid. See also Jonathan Elliot to James Buchanan, 28 January 1849, Roll 1, T56, *Despatches from United States Consuls in Santo Domingo*: "French Consul General of Port-au-Prince left here in the French Corvette . . . convoying . . . with 180 Haytien prisoners . . . for Jacmel."
95. Official Declaration of the Junta and President Pedro Santana, 17 June 1844, Correspondance Commerciale/Saint Domingue (1843–1850), Tome 1, Code: 584, Fos. 22.12.33, p. 115. See also Translation of Dominican founding documents, 17 July 1844, FO23/7, NAUK.
96. Mr. Juchereau de St. Denys to Mr. Guizot, 29 July 1844, in Correspondance Commerciale/ Saint Domingue (1843–1850).
97. Richmond Loring to John C. Calhoun, 29 April 1844, T330, *Despatches from U.S. Consuls in Aux Cayes.*
98. Robert Harrison to John C. Calhoun, 25 April 1844, in Wilson, ed., *The Papers of John C. Calhoun, Volume XVIII,* 189.
99. Robert Harrison to John C. Calhoun in ibid., 331.
100. Thomas Freelon to Robert Harrison, 15 May 1844, in ibid., 566–567.
101. William Gooch to John C. Calhoun, 24 May 1844, in ibid., 600–601.
102. William Gooch to John C. Calhoun, 11 April 1844, in ibid., 201.
103. William Gooch to John C. Calhoun, 9 April 1844, in ibid., 359.
104. William Gooch to John C. Calhoun, 30 May 1844, Roll 2, T801, *Notes from the Legation of the Dominican Republic in the United States to the Department of State,* NARA-CP.
105. Robert Harrison to John C. Calhoun, 1844, in Clyde N. Wilson, ed., *The Papers of John C. Calhoun, Volume XIX, 1844* (Columbia: University of South Carolina Press, 1990), 112.
106. Francis Harrison to John C. Calhoun, 21 October 1844, in Clyde N. Wilson, ed., *The Papers of John C. Calhoun, Volume XX, 1844* (Columbia: University of South Carolina Press, 1991), 109–111.
107. John C. Calhoun to John Mason, 13 November 1844, in ibid., 280.
108. John C. Calhoun to John Mason, 14 November 1844, in ibid., 297.
109. Richmond Loring to John C. Calhoun, 29 April 1844, Roll 2, T330, *Despatches from U.S. Consuls in Aux Cayes.*
110. Mr. Juchereau de St. Denys to Mr. Guizot, 9 October 1844, in Correspondance Commerciale/Saint Domingue (1843–1850).
111. Letter to the President of the Haitian Republic, 31 March 1844, in ibid.
112. Mr. Juchereau de St. Denys to Mr. Guizot, 27 February 1846, in ibid.
113. Richmond Loring to John C. Calhoun, 31 December 1844, in Wilson, *The Papers of John C. Calhoun, Volume XX,* 673–674.
114. Dr. José M. Carminero to John C. Calhoun, 27 January 1846, in Clyde N. Wilson, ed., *The Papers of John C. Calhoun, Volume XXII, 1845–1846* (Columbia: University of South Carolina Press, 1995), 523–525.
115. Remarks by Dr. José M. Carminero, 16 July 1845, in ibid.
116. Letter to John C. Calhoun, 30 December 1844, in Clyde N. Wilson, ed., *The Papers of*

John C. Calhoun, Volume XXI, 1845 (Columbia: University of South Carolina Press, 1993), 663–664.

117. Jose Caminero to John C. Calhoun, 8 January 1845, in ibid., 60–67.

118. Jose Caminero to John C. Calhoun, 25 January 1845, in ibid., 193–196.

119. Mr. Juchereau de St. Denys to Mr. Guizot, 3 June 1846, in Commerciale Correspondance/ Saint Domingue.

120. John C. Calhoun to John Hogan, 22 February 1845, in Wilson, *The Papers of John C. Calhoun, Volume XXI*, 342–343.

121. John Hogan to John C. Calhoun, 10 November 1846, in Clyde N. Wilson and Shirley Bright Cook, eds., *The Papers of John C. Calhoun, Volume XXIII, 1846* (Columbia: University of South Carolina Press, 1996), 546–547. Emphasis original.

122. John Hogan to John C. Calhoun, 22 September 1845 in Clyde N. Wilson, ed., *The Papers of John C. Calhoun, Volume XXII, 1845–1846* (Columbia: University of South Carolina Press, 1995), 160–161.

123. Letter to John C. Calhoun, 22 February 1845, T801, *Notes from the Legation of the Dominican Republic in the United States to the Department of State*, NARA-CP.

124. Logan, *The Diplomatic Relations of the United States with Haiti*, 238.

125. John C. Calhoun to James Buchanan, 30 August 1845 in Wilson, *The Papers of John C. Calhoun, Volume XXII*, 97–98.

126. "Diary of Secret Mission in San Domingo, 1847–1848," *David Dixon Porter Papers*. Emphasis original.

127. Treudley, "The United States and Santo Domingo, 1789–1866," 232.

128. Gerald Horne, *Race to Revolution: The United States and Cuba During Slavery and Jim Crow* (New York: Monthly Review Press, 2014).

129. Francis Harrison to James Buchanan, 30 March 1847, Roll 1, T56, *Despatches from United States Consuls in Santo Domingo*.

130. Richmond Loring to Secretary of State James Buchanan, 10 March 1845, Roll 2, T801, *Notes from the Legation of the Dominican Republic in the U.S. to the Department of State*, NARA-CP.

131. Richmond Loring to Secretary of State James Buchanan, 31 December 1845, ibid.

132. G.F. Usher to James Buchanan, 9 September 1845, Roll 7, M9, *Despatches from U.S. Consuls in Cap-Haïtien*.

133. G.F. Usher to James Buchanan, 30 December 1845, ibid.

134. James Wilson to James Buchanan, 7 November 1848, ibid.

135. A.G. Lewis to James Buchanan, 22 April 1847, ibid.

136. A.G. Lewis to President James Polk, 23 September 1847, ibid.

137. John Wilson to James Buchanan, 28 April 1848, ibid.

138. John Wilson to James Buchanan, 28 April 1848, ibid.

139. John Wilson to James Buchanan, 9 May 1848, ibid.

140. John Wilson to James Buchanan, 2 August 1848, ibid.

141. John Wilson to James Buchanan, 30 August 1848, ibid.

142. Thomas Usher to James Buchanan, 29 August 1847, Roll 2, T330, *Despatches from U.S. Consuls in Aux Cayes*.

143. Letter from Richmond Loring, 26 August 1847, ibid.

144. Richmond Loring to James Buchanan, 31 December 1847, ibid.

145. Francis Harrison to James Buchanan, 25 February 1847, Roll 1, T56, *Despatches from United States Consuls in Santo Domingo.*

146. Francis Harrison to James Buchanan, 1 July 1847, ibid.

147. Francis Harrison to James Buchanan, 30 March 1847, ibid.

148. Francis Harrison to James Buchanan, 26 April 1847, ibid.

149. Francis Harrison to James Buchanan, 1 July 1847, ibid.

150. Harrison Parker to James Buchanan, 26 August 1847, ibid.

151. Jonathan Elliot to James Buchanan, 18 July 1848, ibid.

152. Jonathan Elliot to James Buchanan, 28 January 1849, ibid.

153. Jonathan Elliot to Secretary of State, 13 April 1849, ibid.

154. Jonathan Elliot to Secretary of State, 24 April 1849, ibid.

155. S.C. Luther to James Buchanan, 6 May 1848, Reel 2, T346, *Despatches of U.S. Consuls in Port-au-Prince,* NARA-CP.

156. S.C. Luther to Abel Upshur, 27 April 1844, ibid.

8. BLACK JACOBINS UNDER SIEGE, 1850–1859

1. James Gadsden to Jefferson Davis, 19 July 1854, in Lynda Lasswell Crist, ed., *The Papers of Jefferson Davis, Volume V, 1853–1855* (Baton Rouge: Louisiana State University Press), 1985, 79–80. The press chimed in: see *New York Herald,* 20 July 1850, and the reference to the "Dingy Emperor" of Haiti.

2. Robert Schomburgk to Earl of Clarendon, 20 July 1854, FO23/19, NAUK.

3. Ben Green to John Clayton, 27 August 1849, Folder 399, *Duff Green Papers,* University of North Carolina, Chapel Hill. See also W. Stephen Belko, *The Invincible Duff Green: Whig of the West* (Columbia: University of Missouri Press, 2006).

4. Robert Schomburgk to Lord Palmerston, 15 November 1850, FO23/8, NAUK.

5. Robert E. May, "The United States as Rogue State: Gunboat Persuasion, Citizen Marauders, and the Limits of Antebellum American Imperialism," in Lawrence Sondhaus and A. James Fuller, eds., *America, War and Power: Defining the State, 1775–2005* (New York: Routledge, 2007), 29–63, 42.

6. Logan, *The Diplomatic Relations of the United States with Haiti, 1776–1891,* 254, 255. See also *A Glimpse of Hayti and the Negro Chief* (Liverpool: Howell, 1850, University of Miami).

7. Charles Gallan Tansill, *The United States and Santo Domingo, 1798–1873* (Baltimore: Johns Hopkins University Press, 1938), 153.

8. Robert Schomburgk to Lord Palmerston, 6 February 1851, FO23/10, NAUK.

9. Martin R. Delany, "Political Aspects of the Colored People of the United States," in Robert S. Levine, ed., *Martin R. Delany: A Documentary Reader* (Chapel Hill: University of North Carolina Press, 2003), 280–290, 286.

10. *Report and Proceedings of the London Emancipation Committee,* 1850, Boston Public Library.

11. John Wilson to John Clayton, 30 March 1850, Roll 8, M9, *Despatches from U.S. Consuls in Cap-Haïtien,* NARA-CP.

12. *The North Star,* 2 March 1849.

13. *Frederick Douglass' Paper,* 14 April 1854.

14. Clark, *The Strange History of the American Quadroon,* 120.

15. B.C. Clark, *Remarks Upon United States Intervention in Hayti. The Comments Upon the Correspondence* (Boston: Easturn's Press, 1853), New-York Historical Society, Manhattan.

16. Entry, 9 February 1855, in Louis P. Henop, "Journal of a Cruise in Europe, Cuba, and Key West Aboard the U.S.S. San Jacinto," 9 August 1854 to 8 May 1855, University of Florida, Gainesville.

17. Letter, 16 May 1854, *Solomon G. Havens Papers*, University of Michigan, Ann Arbor.

18. Ben Green to Jefferson Davis, 6 May 1854, in Crist, *The Papers of Jefferson Davis, Volume V*, 339.

19. Appendix of J.C. Nott in *The Moral and Intellectual Diversity of Races with Particular Reference to their Respective Influence in the Civil and Political History of Mankind from the French of Count A. de Gobineau* (Philadelphia: Lippincott, 1856), 192.

20. L.W. Spratt, *The Foreign Slave Trade: The Source of Political Power, of Material Progress, of Social Integrity, and of Social Emancipation to the South* (Charleston: Steam Power Press, 1858). Emphasis original.

21. "C.W. Miller, Esq. of South Carolina to the Citizens of Barnwell at Wylde-Moore, Address on Re-Opening the Slave Trade, August 29, 1857" (Columbia, South Carolina: Steam Power Press, 1857), Boston Public Library.

22. Ben Green to "The Duc de Tiburon," 8 May 1850, in Kenneth Shewmaker and Kenneth Stevens, ed., *The Papers of Daniel Webster: Diplomatic Papers, Volume 2, 1850–1852* (Hanover, New Hampshire: University Press of New England, 1987), 316–317.

23. Daniel Webster to Robert Walsh, 18 January 1851, in ibid., 329.

24. *Frederick Douglass' Paper*, 27 August 1852.

25. Robert Schomburgk to Lord Palmerston, 5 September 1850, FO23/8, NAUK.

26. Richmond Loring to James Buchanan, 19 April 1848, Roll 2, T330, *Despatches from U.S. Consuls in Aux Cayes*, NARA-CP.

27. Letter from Richmond Loring, 20 May 1848, ibid.

28. Richmond Loring to James Buchanan, 13 June 1848, ibid.

29. George F. Usher and John Clayton, 2 September 1849, Reel 2, T346, *Despatches from U.S. Consuls in Port-au-Prince*, NARA-CP.

30. Richmond Loring to Sir, 31 December 1848, Roll 2, T330, *Despatches from U.S. Consuls in Aux Cayes*.

31. Richmond Loring to James Buchanan, 28 March 1849, ibid.

32. Richmond Loring to Secretary of State, 9 December 1849, ibid.

33. Ben Green to John Clayton, 15 June 1850, Folder 399, *Duff Green Papers*.

34. Petition from Cibao, 22 September 1849, FO23/7, NAUK: "the name of Americans is that of the inhabitants of the whole new world who no doubt would form in the course of time only one government and one nation."

35. Robert Schomburgk to Viscount Palmerston, 28 January 1850, ibid.

36. Letter from Dominican nationals, 22 September 1849, Folder 399, *Duff Green Papers*.

37. M.T. Del Monte to Ben Green, 23 January 1850, Folder 399, ibid.

38. Memorandum from Ben Green, no date, Folder 399, ibid.

39. Ben Green to John Clayton, 24 October 1849, Folder 399, ibid.

40. Ben Green to John Clayton, 20 August 1849, Folder 362, ibid.

41. Letter to Ben Green, 13 June 1852, Folder 399, ibid.

42. Ben Green to Minister of Foreign Affairs of Haiti, 27 April 1850, Folder 399, ibid.

43. Ben Green to Duke of Tiburon, 29 April 1850, Folder 399, ibid.

44. Richmond Loring to John Clayton, 31 December 1849, Roll 2, T330, *Despatches from U.S. Consuls in Aux Cayes.*

45. Duff Green to John Clayton, 24 October 1849, Folder 399, *Duff Green Papers.*

46. Duff Green to John Clayton, 28 January 1850, ibid.

47. *The North Star,* 30 May 1850.

48. *The National Era,* 26 June 1851.

49. 4 July 1850, ibid.

50. Ben Green to John Clayton, 15 February 1850, Folder 399, *Duff Green Papers.*

51. Robert Schomburgk to Lord Palmerston, 27 September 1849, FO23/4, NAUK.

52. Ben Green to John Clayton, 16 February 1850, Folder 399, *Duff Green Papers.*

53. Robert Schomburgk to Lord Palmerston, 27 May 1850, FO23/7, NAUK.

54. Robert Schomburgk to Lord Palmerston, 15 November 1850, FO23/8, ibid. See also Robert Schomburgk to Lord Palmerston, 3 July 1849, FO23/4, ibid.: Here is a proposal for increased Irish migration to the D.R.

55. Robert Schomburgk to Lord Palmerston, 27 May 1850, FO23/7, ibid.

56. Ben Green to John Clayton, 19 February 1850, February 399, *Duff Green Papers.*

57. Robert Schomburgk to French Consul, 26 March 1850, FO23/7, NAUK. The propaganda can be found appended thereto.

58. Jonathan Elliot to Secretary of State, 2 May 1849, Roll 1, T56, *Despatches from U.S. Consuls in Santo Domingo,* NARA-CP. See Robert Schomburgk to Lord Palmerston, 27 December 1851, FO23/11, NAUK: Here it is said that Schomburgk has knowledge of French, Spanish, and Portuguese. See also Robert Schomburgk to Earl of Clarendon, 3 July 1853, FO23/16, NAUK: Schomburgk had become alienated by the "sickly climate" of the island and his "small salary"; now 50 years of age, he had spent 8 years "in the exploration of the unknown regions of Guiana" and "I am now as poor as when I commenced my career." He was alienated further by the "famine" and "intrigues" of the D.R. and the "anti-English feeling" of the leadership there. See also Robert Schomburgk to Lord Palmerston, 27 September 1849, FO23/4, NAUK: While Minister of Foreign Affairs, Baez was "violently opposed to England." What may have influenced Baez was the lingering perception that abolitionist London was pro-Haiti. The proposal for U.K. "recognition" of the D.R. was a "mere mask in order to bring" Santo Domingo "back under Haytian yoke." See Robert Schomburgk to Lord Palmerston, 27 September 1849, FO23/4, NAUK.

59. Jonathan Elliot to Secretary of State, 16 September 1850, Roll 1, T56, *Despatches from U.S. Consuls in Santo Domingo.*

60. Jonathan Elliot to Daniel Webster, 28 September 1850, ibid.

61. Jonathan Elliot to Daniel Webster, 29 September 1850, ibid.

62. Ben Green to John Clayton, 9 May 1850, Folder 399, *Duff Green Papers.*

63. John Wilson to John Clayton, 15 January 1859, Roll 8, M9, *Despatches from U.S. Consuls in Cap-Haïtien.*

64. John Wilson to John Clayton, 23 February 1850, ibid. Emphasis original.

65. John Wilson to John Clayton, 20 April 1850, ibid.

66. John Wilson to Daniel Webster, 30 September 1850, ibid.

67. John Wilson to Daniel Webster, 31 April 1851, ibid.

68. John Wilson to Daniel Webster, 4 August 1852, ibid. See also Jonathan Elliot to Acting

Secretary of State, 18 January 1853, Roll 1, T56, *Despatches from U.S. Consuls in Santo Domingo*: In Santo Domingo, "yellow fever or black vomit is still prevailing here" and "some French and Italian vessels here have lost nearly all their crews."

69.   John Wilson to William Marcy, 26 July 1854, Roll 8, M9, *Despatches from U.S. Consuls in Cap-Haïtien*.

70.   *The North Star*, 21 April 1848.

71.   25 May 1848, ibid.

72.   1 March 1850, ibid.

73.   13 June 1850, ibid.

74.   31 October 1850, ibid.

75.   *The National Era*, 4 November 1852.

76.   1 June 1854, ibid.

77.   15 August 1850, ibid.

78.   2 January 1851, ibid.

79.   24 May 1849, ibid.

80.   James Theodore Holly and J. Dennis Harris, *Black Separatism and the Caribbean, 1860*, edited by Howard Bell (Ann Arbor: University of Michigan Press, 1970), 2.

81.   William Wells Brown, *St. Domingo: Its Revolution and Its Patriots. A Lecture. Delivered Before the Metropolitan Atheneum, London, May 16 and at St. Thomas Church Philadelphia, December 20, 1854* (Boston: Bela Marsh, 1855), New-York Historical Society.

82.   Commercial Agent of the United States to Minister of Foreign Affairs, 16 December 1851, Expediente 4, Relaciones Exteriores, 1851, Correspondencia Official, AGN-Santo Domingo.

83.   Robert Schomburgk to Foreign Minister, 29 November 1852, Expediente 4, ibid.

84.   Robert Schomburgk to Lord Palmerston, 26 August 1851, FO23/11, NAUK.

85.   Robert Schomburgk to Lord Palmerston, 27 December 1851, ibid.

86.   William Fowler to Consul, 2 December 1851, ibid.

87.   William Breffit to Robert Schomburgk, 5 September 1851, ibid. Emphasis original.

88.   Schloss, *Sweet Liberty*, 227.

89.   William B. Cohen, *The French Encounter with Africans: White Response to Blacks, 1530–1880* (Bloomington: Indiana University Press, 1980), 207.

90.   Ben Green to John Clayton, 27 August 1849, Folder 399, *Duff Green Papers*.

91.   Ben Green to John Clayton, 24 October 1849, ibid.

92.   Letter, 1 July 1850, Box 218, *Caleb Cushing Papers*, Library of Congress.

93.   John Wilson to John Clayton, 6 August 1849, Roll 7, M9, *Despatches from U.S. Consuls in Cap-Haïtien*. See also Robert Schomburgk to Lord John Russell, 5 February 1853, FO23/16, NAUK: Here it is said that the D.R. turned for protection to France because relying on Spain brought "too many difficulties" while the "profound" differences between London and Washington forestalled alliance with either. This led to an 1843 treaty with France—before D.R. independence—whereby Samaná was promised in return for aid in seceding. Attached is the *New York Herald* of 12 December 1852 and the *St. Thomas Tidende* of 8 January 1853, which confirm the above. See also Robert Schomburgk to Lord Palmerston, 10 July 1849, FO23/4, NAUK: The offer for the D.R. to become a British "protectorate" is declined. See also Robert Schomburgk to Lord Palmerston, 14 July 1849, FO23/4, NAUK: "General Santana is surrounded by the French Party who strain every nerve to obtain the Protectorate

or, asserted by others, to convert the [D.R.] into a French colony"; a large "amount of Secret Service money" from Paris was found in coffers in Santo Domingo. The French consul was a "secret advisor" to Santana. Maneuvering adroitly among the powers to gain leverage against Haiti, Santo Domingo requested protectorate status from Paris—and added that if it was not granted, their next application for this status would be to Washington; see Statement by Foreign Minister of the D.R., 18 October 1849, FO23/4, NAUK.

94. Robert Schomburgk to Earl of Clarendon, 31 December 1853, FO23/16, NAUK.
95. Robert Schomburgk to Earl of Malmesbury, 6 September 1852, FO23/14, NAUK.
96. Robert Schomburgk to Earl of Grenville, 4 March 1852, FO23/13, NAUK.
97. Correspondence, 1848, Angleterre, 1840A, MAE-Paris.
98. John Wilson to John Clayton, 14 June 1850, Roll 8, M9, *Despatches from U.S. Consuls in Cap-Haïtien*.
99. Ben Green to John Clayton, 15 June 1850, Folder 399, *Duff Green Papers*.
100. Ben Green to John Clayton, 19 February 1850, ibid.
101. Ben Green to Duke of Tiburon, 8 May 1850, ibid.
102. Ben Green to John Clayton, 27 August 1849, ibid.
103. Letter, 30 November 1850, Roll 1, T56, *Despatches from U.S. Consuls in Santo Domingo*.
104. Ministry of Foreign Relations, Santo Domingo to Britain, France, and the United States, 6 June 1851, ibid.
105. Translation of Dominican Statement, 10 June 1851, FO23/10, NAUK.
106. Robert Schomburgk to Lord Palmerston, 29 September 1851, FO23/11, ibid.
107. Robert Schomburgk to Lord Palmerston, 29 September 1851, FO23/11, ibid.
108. Jonathan Elliot to Acting Secretary of State, 17 January 1853, Roll 1, T56, *Despatches from U.S. Consuls in Santo Domingo*.
109. Jonathan Elliot to Secretary of State, 7 March 1853, ibid.
110. Ben Green to John Clayton, 15 February 1850, Folder 399, *Duff Green Papers*.
111. Jonathan Elliot to Secretary of State, 3 May 1853, Roll 1, T56, *Despatches from U.S. Consuls in Santo Domingo*.
112. Jonathan Elliot to William Marcy, 27 November 1853, ibid.
113. Jonathan Elliot to William Marcy, 30 November 1853, ibid.
114. Extract of a letter from Theodore Henderson to Robert Schomburgk, 29 June 1837, FO23/14, NAUK.
115. Robert Schomburgk to Earl of Malmesbury, 20 July 1852, FO23/14, ibid.
116. Robert Schomburgk to Earl of Malmesbury, 30 December 1852, FO23/14, ibid.
117. Robert Schomburgk to Foreign Office, 15 February 1855, FO23/14, ibid.
118. William Breffit to Robert Schomburgk, 5 July 1852, FO23/14, ibid.
119. Fred Forth, President of Turks Islands, to Robert Schomburgk, 12 October 1850, FO23/8, ibid.
120. Robert Schomburgk to Foreign Office, 12 February 1852, FO23/14, ibid.
121. Robert Schomburgk to Earl of Clarendon, 5 October 1853, FO23/16, ibid.
122. Robert Schomburgk to Earl of Malmesbury, 6 September 1852, FO23/14, ibid.
123. Letter to Earl of Grenville, 20 February 1852, FO23/13, ibid.
124. N. Parker Willis, *Health Trip to the Tropics* (New York: Scribner's, 1853).
125. "Sketch of a Journey Through the Northern Provinces of the Dominican Republic and the Peninsula of Samaná," 25 August 1851, FO23/11, NAUK.

126. Robert Schomburgk to Lord Palmerston, 25 September 1851, FO23/11, ibid.
127. Foreign Office to Robert Schomburgk, "Confidential," 22 August 1854, and Foreign Office to Robert Schomburgk, 4 November 1854, FO23/19, ibid.
128. Robert Schomburgk to Earl of Clarendon, 20 July 1854, FO23/19, ibid.
129. Robert Schomburgk to Earl of Clarendon, 7 August 1854, FO23/19, ibid.
130. Robert Schomburgk to Lord Palmerston, 30 May 1851, FO23/10, ibid. See *Boston Daily Courier*, 29 April 1851, on filibusters.
131. Jane Cazneau to Moses Beach, 27 December 1854, *Jane McManus Storms Cazneau Papers*, University of Texas, Austin.
132. Jane Cazneau to Moses Beach, 28 December 1854, ibid.
133. Robert Schomburgk to Earl of Clarendon, 20 September 1854, FO23/19, NAUK.
134. Robert Schomburgk to John Crampton, 20 September 1854, ibid.
135. Robert Schomburgk to Earl of Clarendon, 3 October 1854, ibid.
136. Proposed language, circa 1854, FO23/19, ibid.
137. William Cazneau to Robert Schomburgk, 17 November 1854, ibid.
138. Robert Schomburgk to John Crampton, 20 November 1854, ibid.
139. Robert Schomburgk to Earl of Clarendon, 18 December 1854, ibid. See also Logan, *Haiti and the Dominican Republic*, 38: Schomburgk, in order to ensure defeat of the accord, "prevailed on the Dominican government to insert a clause to the effect that coloured Dominicans travelling in the United States would be accorded the same treatment as white Americans. The Dominican government ratified the treaty," but the U.S. Secretary of State "did not submit it to the United States for ratification." Santo Domingo proposed that "all Dominicans, without any distinction of race or color, shall enjoy in all the states of the American Union the same and equal rights and prerogatives that the citizens of those states enjoy." Statement, 6 December 1854, Roll 1, T801, *Notes from the Legation of the Dominican Republic to the United States to the Department of State*, NARA-CP.
140. *Frederick Douglass' Paper*, 27 October 1854.
141. 2 February 1855, ibid.
142. Robert Schomburgk to Earl of Clarendon, 21 December 1854, FO23/19, NAUK.
143. F.W. Chesson, *A Few Words about Hayti*, Great Britain, 1856, Columbia University.
144. Robert Schomburgk to Earl of Clarendon, 22 November 1855, FO23/23, NAUK.
145. Lord Palmerston to Earl of Clarendon, 22 November 1855, FO23/23, ibid.
146. Letter from Robert Schomburgk, 24 November 1855, FO23/23, ibid.
147. Robert Schomburgk to Earl of Clarendon, 20 December 1855, FO23/23, ibid.
148. Robert Schomburgk to Earl of Clarendon, 21 March 1856, FO23/19, ibid.
149. Robert Schomburgk to John Crampton, 21 March 1856, FO23/19, ibid.
150. Jonathan Elliot to William Marcy, 16 January 1856, Roll 2, T56, *Despatches from U.S. Consuls in Santo Domingo*.
151. Jonathan Elliot to William Marcy, 22 March 1856, ibid.
152. Jonathan Elliot to William Marcy, 10 September 1856, ibid. Emphasis original.
153. Jonathan Elliot to William Marcy, 10 September 1856, ibid.
154. Jonathan Elliot to William Marcy, 11 November 1856, ibid.
155. Jonathan Elliot to Lewis Cass, 11 July 1857, ibid.
156. Jonathan Elliot to Lewis Cass, 27 April 1857, ibid.
157. Robert Schomburgk to Earl of Clarendon, 19 May 1856, FO23/26, NAUK.

158. Robert Schomburgk to Earl of Clarendon, 26 June 1856, ibid.
159. Robert Schomburgk to Earl of Clarendon, 7 January 1856, ibid.
160. Jacob Pereira to William Marcy, 6 November 1856, Roll 2, T56, *Despatches from U.S. Consuls in Santo Domingo*.
161. Jonathan Elliot to William Marcy, 11 November 1856, ibid.
162. Jacob Periera to Captain Dunlop, 10 November 1856, FO23/27, NAUK.
163. Jonathan Elliot to Secretary of State, 31 May 1849, Roll 1, T56, *Despatches from U.S. Consuls in Santo Domingo*.
164. Jonathan Elliot to Lewis Cass, 11 July 1857, Roll 2, T56, ibid.
165. Notes on UK–D.R. Treaty, circa 1850, Folder 399, *Duff Green Papers*.
166. Treaty of Commerce between France and the Dominican Republic, Negociations Comerciales, 1849–1884, Dominican Republic, MAE-Paris.

9. THE U.S. CIVIL WAR, THE SPANISH TAKEOVER OF THE DOMINICAN REPUBLIC, AND U.S. NEGRO EMIGRANTS IN HAITI, 1860–1863

1. Logan, *Haiti and the Dominican Republic*, 43, 40. Madrid, presumably, was displeased when Duff Green contemplated working with the Church of Latter Day Saints—the Mormons—to spur U.S. settlement on the island. See Belko, *The Invincible Duff Green*, 431–432.
2. L. Cheesman to President Fred Inglis, 26 March 1861, CO301/31, NAUK.
3. Letter from L. Cheesman, 27 March 1861, CO301/31, ibid.
4. Algernon Lyons to Commodore Dunlop, 11 March 1861, FO23/59, ibid.
5. Seth Webb to William Seward, 7 April 1862, Reel 4, T346, *Despatches from U.S. Consuls in Port-au-Prince*, NARA-CP.
6. Comment, in John Blassingame, ed., *Slave Testimony: Two Centuries of Letters, Speeches, Interviews, and Autobiographies* (Baton Rouge: Louisiana State University Press, 1977), 259.
7. Ludwell Lee Montague, *Haiti and the United States, 1714–1938* (Durham: Duke University Press, 1940), 84.
8. Richard Hill, *Haiti and Spain: A Memorial Dedicated to the Honorable W.H. Seward, Secretary of State at Washington* (Kingston, Jamaica: de Cordova, 1862), Boston Public Library.
9. Ibid.
10. *The Christian Recorder*, 6 April 1861.
11. Richmond Loring to Secretary of State, 16 January 1859, Roll 3, T330, *Despatches from U.S. Consuls in Aux Cayes*, NARA-CP.
12. Richmond Loring to Lewis Cass, 22 September 1859, ibid.
13. David M. Dean, *Defender of the Race: James Theodore Holly, Black Nationalist Bishop* (Boston: Lambeth, 1979), 44.
14. Decree by President Fabre Geffrard, 14 August 1860, in Redpath, *Guide to Hayti*, 79.
15. Official Record of the Legislative Chambers of Hayti, September 1860, in ibid., 80.
16. Franklin and Schweninger, *In Search of the Promised Land*, 181.
17. David C. Rankin, "The Forgotten People: Free People of Color in New Orleans, 1850–1870" (Ph.D. diss., Johns Hopkins University, 1976), 172, 277, 283. See also Carl A. Brasseaux and Katherine-Carmines Mooney, ed., *Ruined by this Miserable War: The*

Dispatches of Charles Prosper Fauconnet, A French Diplomat in New Orleans, 1863–1868 (Knoxville: University of Tennessee Press, 2012), 41, 125: Those with ties to Paris—including *gens de couleur*—had a difficult time during the war, compelling many to move to France, Mexico—and Hispaniola: "The position of the French has become quite difficult, worse perhaps than that of other foreigners, even in the city of New Orleans. . . . poverty has become widespread among them. . . . more than 2000 have already departed, some for France, others for Mexico. . . . the intention of completely eliminating from judicial and legal proceedings the French language, which, until now . . . [had] enjoyed equal footing with the English language" was also present.

18. Eustis Hubbard to Lewis Cass, 8 January 1859, Roll 9, M9, *Despatches from U.S. Consuls in Cap-Haïtien*, NARA-CP.

19. *London Emancipation Committee's Tract No. 6, The Annexation of San Domingo to Spain. A Memorial to Lord Russell* . . . (London: Watts, 1861), Boston Public Library.

20. B.F. Sanford to William Seward, 30 April 1862, Roll 3, T330, *Despatches from U.S. Consuls in Aux Cayes.*

21. Hunt, *Remarks on Hayti*, 6, 11.

22. James Redpath to Hon. M. Pleasance, 7 December 1860, *Bureau of Emigration (Haiti)*, Boston Public Library.

23. Eustis Hubbard to Lewis Cass, 15 April 1857, Roll 9, M9, *Despatches from U.S. Consuls in Cap-Haïtien.*

24. Eustis Hubbard to Lewis Cass, 15 September 1857, ibid.

25. Comment, David G. Yuengling, ed., *Highlights in the Debates in the Spanish Chamber of Deputies Relative to the Abandonment of Santo Domingo* (Washington, D.C.: Murray & Heister, 1941), 1. See also M. de J. Troncoso de la Concha, *La Ocupacion de Santo Domingo por Haiti* (Ciudad Trujillo: La Nacion, 1942).

26. Frank Moya Pons, *The Dominican Republic: A National History* (Princeton: Markus Wiener), 2010, 201.

27. C. Fortescu to "Sir," 6 September 1860, CO137/352, NAUK.

28. "Message of the President of the United States," 36th Congress. Senate Ex. Doc. No. 27, circa 1860, CO137/352, ibid.

29. Joseph Lewis to William Seward, 15 July 1861, Reel 4, T346, *Despatches from U.S. Consuls in Port-au-Prince*, NARA-CP.

30. Entry, 4 April 1861, in Scarborough, *The Diary of Edmund Ruffin, Volume I*, 577. See also *Free Negroism: Results of Emancipation in the North and the West India Islands, with Statistics of the Decay of Commerce, Idleness of the Negro, His Return to Savagism, and the Effect of Emancipation Upon the Farming, Mechanical, and Laboring Classes* (New York: Van Evrie, 1862), Columbia University: "if the Negro has any capacity for self-government, any of the inherent abilities or energies of the white man, surely he ought to have shown them during this time. . . . how fearfully the island has retrograded. . . . [The] degraded, barbarous condition of the Negroes in Hayti" proves this, as it was a "disgusting picture of savagism and heathenism. . . . Negroes themselves returning to their original African heathenism!" Edmund Ruffin, "Equality of the Races—Haytian and British Experiments," *De Bow's Review*, 1 (Number 1, July 1859): 27–38, 32: The "mad declaration of equal rights to the slaves" in Haiti was the problem at the turn of the century. "If there had been only whites, masters, and negro slaves and no foreign and stronger power, although the whites

were only one-tenth the number of their slaves, their mastership would never have been seriously disturbed."

31. Letter to Milledge Luke Bonham, 24 January 1863, *Milledge Luke Bonham Collection,* University of South Carolina. Many Euro-Americans were similarly divided in their view of Europeans generally. See, e.g., James Hammond to Harry Hammond, 23 November 1855, *Hammond, Bryan, and Cumming Papers,* University of South Carolina: The writer was learning to speak French, Spanish, and German and advised that Europeans "will cheat you of your *last* Sous & see you starved without consoling glance. . . . there is more genuine sympathy & conscientious scrupulousness in one average negro's heart, than in any 10,000 European hearts high & low save perhaps the *poor* Irish." Emphasis original.

32. Sally Edwards, *James Louis Petrigru, 1789–1863* (McCormick County Historical Commission, 1977), University of South Carolina.

33. *New York Times,* 1 January 1863. Pierce Butler, *Judah P. Benjamin* (Philadelphia: Jacobs, 1906), 294.

34. Butler, *Judah P. Benjamin,* 294, 296, 35, 42, 148, 266. See also William Henry Trescot, "The Confederacy and the Declaration of Paris," *American Historical Review,* 23 (Number 4, July 1918): 826–835.

35. Max J. Kohler, "Judah P. Benjamin: Statesman and Jurist," reprint from "Publications of the American Jewish Historical Society, No. 12," 1905, 63–85, 78, Tulane University.

36. Letter to Ministry of Foreign Affairs, 18 March 1857, F18002, Microfilm, Haiti Memoires & Documents, MAE-Paris.

37. Viña Delmar, *Beloved* (New York: Harcourt Brace, 1956), 57.

38. Ella Lonn, *Foreigners in the Confederacy* (Chapel Hill: University of North Carolina Press, 2002), 7, 67, 112, 144, 148, 167, 190–191, 411. Nevertheless, note the comment in footnote 17 of Lonn's work.

39. *Letters to the Southern People Concerning the Acts of Congress and the Treaties with Great Britain in Relation to the African Slave Trade* (Charleston: Steam Power Press, 1858).

40. Scherr, *Thomas Jefferson's Haitian Policy,* 631. See also Andrew Rolle, *The Lost Cause: The Confederate Exodus to Mexico* (Norman: University of Oklahoma Press, 1965).

41. Speech by Hon. M.F. Conway of Kansas, House of Representatives, 27 January 1863, Etats-Unis, Affaires Diverses, 30–32, 1861–1864, MAE-Paris.

42. "Concurrent Resolutions of Congress Concerning Foreign Intervention in the Existing Rebellion," 1863, ibid.

43. John Slidell to Foreign Ministry, 8 June 1863, ibid.

44. William Seward to William Dayton, 6 July 1863, ibid.

45. William Seward to William Dayton, 29 July 1863, ibid.

46. Letter to "My Dear Baron," circa 1861, ibid.

47. John Slidell to Foreign Ministry, 8 June 1863, ibid.

48. John Slidell to "Sir," 11 February 1862, Reel 3, *Confederate States of America Records,* Library of Congress.

49. John Slidell to Judah Benjamin, 20 October 1862, ibid.

50. B.F. Sanford to William Seward, 30 April 1862, Roll 3, T330, *Despatches from U.S. Consuls in Aux Cayes.*

51. Remark, 9 July 1861 in Roy B. Basler, ed., *The Collected Works of Abraham Lincoln, Volume IV, 1860–1861* (New Brunswick: Rutgers University Press, 1953), 446.

52. Seth Webb to William Seward, 12 December 1861, Reel 4, T346, *Despatches from U.S. Consuls in Port-au-Prince*, NARA-CP.

53. Seth Webb to William Seward, 25 December 1861, ibid.

54. *The National Era*, 4 July 1850.

55. Speech of Hon. D.W. Gooch, Delivered in the House of Representatives, 2 June 1862, Huntington Library, San Marino, California. At the same site, see also Speech of Hon. Robert McKnight of Pennsylvania, Delivered in the House, 3 June 1862 and Speech of Hon. William Kelley, Delivered in the House, 3 June 1862.

56. Speech of Hon. Charles Sumner of Massachusetts on the Bill to Authorize the Appointment of Diplomatic Representatives to the Republics of Hayti and Liberia, in the U.S. Senate, 23–24 April, 1862 (Washington, D.C.: Congressional Globe, 1862), Huntington Library.

57. Speech of Hon. Robert McKnight of Pennsylvania, Delivered in the House of Representatives, Tuesday, June 3, 1862. Recognition of Liberia and Hayti-Rights of Consuls, Columbia University.

58. Rayford Logan, "The United States Recognizes Haiti," in Mercer Cook and Dantes Bellegarde, eds., *The Haitian American Anthology: Haitian Readings from American Authors* (Port-au-Prince: Imprimerie de L'Eta, 1944), 29–30.

59. Seth Webb to William Seward, 27 May 1862, Reel 4, T346, *Despatches from U.S. Consuls in Port-au-Prince*, NARA-CP.

60. Abraham Lincoln to Senate, 13 December 1864, in Roy P. Basler, ed., *The Collected Works of Abraham Lincoln, Volume VIIII, 1864–1865* (New Brunswick: Rutgers University Press, 1953), 166–167.

61. Jackson, "The Origins of Pan-African Nationalism," 209.

62. Henry Hitchcock to Francis Lieber, 13 July 1863, *Francis Lieber Collection*, University of South Carolina. Emphasis original.

63. M.B. Bird, *The Republic of Hayti and its Struggles from Historical Notes Issued Under the Auspices of the Haytian Government* (London: Stock, 1867), 6, 94, 239, 36.

64. "Will the Blacks Fight," originally in "New Bedford Mercury," circa 1861, Massachusetts Historical Society, Boston. At the same site, see also Elizur Wright, "The Lesson of St. Domingo: How to Make the War Short and the Peace Righteous" (Boston: Williams, 1861).

65. David Cecelski, *The Fire of Freedom: Abraham Galloway & the Slaves' Civil War* (Chapel Hill: University of North Carolina Press, 2012), 28–30, 35–37. In the latter pages, see the reference to the "Black Strings" secret society that had Mississippi as a "probable target."

66. Comment by Secretary of State of the Interior and of Agriculture, 26 March 1860, in Redpath, *Guide to Hayti*, 68.

67. Thomas Miller to William Seward, 19 November 1861, Roll 1, T486, *Despatches from U.S. Consuls in St. Marc, Haiti*, NARA-CP.

68. Comment in Redpath, *Guide to Hayti*, 102.

69. James Hammond to James Latrobe, 27 November 1858, in *The Regina Coeli Correspondence between the Hon. James H. Hammond and John L.R. Latrobe, Esq.* (Baltimore: Toy, 1858).

70. Remarks by John Tyler, Jr., April 1860 in John Stauffer and Zoe Trod, eds., *The Tribunal: Responses to John Brown and the Harpers Ferry Raid* (Cambridge: Harvard University Press, 2012), 329–330.

71. Laurent Dubois, *Haiti: The Aftershocks of History* (New York: Metropolitan, 2012), 135.

72. *Report of the Special Committee of the House of Representatives of South Carolina on so Much of the Message his Excellency Governor James H. Adams as Relates to Slavery and the Slave Trade* (Charleston: Steam Power Press, 1857).

73. Louis Schade, *A Book for the 'Impending Crisis!' Appeal to the Common Sense and Patriotism of the People of the United States, 'Helperism' Annihilated! 'The Irrepressible Conflict' and its Consequences!* (Washington, D.C.: Little, Morris, 1860), Huntington Library.

74. Speech by Jefferson Davis, 10 January 1861, in Lynda Lasswell Crist, ed., *The Papers of Jefferson Davis, Volume VII, 1861* (Baton Rouge: Louisiana State University Press, 1992), 9.

75. Benjamin S. Hunt, *Remarks on Hayti as a Place of Settlement for Afric-Americans and on the Mulatto as a Race for the Tropics* (Philadelphia: Pugh, 1860).

76. Ibid., 3, 11.

77. *Provincial Freeman*, 10 November 1855.

78. *Frederick Douglass' Paper*, 28 September 1855. Emphasis original.

79. Benjamin S. Hunt, *Remarks on Hayti as a Place of Settlement for Afric-Americans: And the Mulatto as a Race for the Tropics* (Philadelphia: Pugh, 1860), 3, 6, 11. See also Hesketh Prichard, *Where Black Rules White: A Journey Across and About Hayti* (New York: Scribner's, 1900); and Mark Baker Bird, *The Black Man; or Haytien Independence. Deduced from the Historical Notes and Dedicated to the Government and People of Hayti* (New York: Author, 1869).

80. John Hope Franklin and Loren Schweninger, *In Search of the Promised Land: A Slave Family in the Old South* (New York: Oxford University Press, 2006), 181, 183.

81. Ella Lonn, *Foreigners in the Confederacy* (Chapel Hill: University of North Carolina Press, 2002), 7.

82. James Redpath to Hon. M. Pleasance, 17 November 1860, *Bureau of Emigration (Haiti)*, Boston Public Library. See also John R. McKivigan, *Forgotten Firebrand: James Redpath and the Making of Nineteenth Century America* (Ithaca: Cornell University Press, 2008).

83. James Redpath to Hon. M. Pleasance, 12 January 1861, *Bureau of Emigration (Haiti)*.

84. James Redpath to Hon. M. Pleasance, 18 December 1860, ibid.

85. B.F. Sanford to Seth Webb, 15 April 1862, Roll 3, T330, *Despatches from U.S. Consuls in Aux Cayes*.

86. Thomas Miller to William Seward, 20 January 1862, Roll 1, T486, *Despatches from U.S. Consuls in St. Marc, Haiti*, NARA-CP.

87. Thomas Miller to William Seward, 30 January 1862, and Auguste Elie, Solicitor General of the Bureau of Immigration, Haiti, to Thomas Miller, no date, ibid.

88. B.F. Sanford to William Seward, 20 March 1862, Roll 3, T330, *Despatches from U.S. Consuls in Aux Cayes*.

89. B.F. Sanford to William Seward, 20 March 1862, ibid.

90. James Redpath to Hon. M. Pleasance, 21 January 1861, *Bureau of Emigration (Haiti)*.

91. James Redpath to Hon. M. Pleasance, 2 February 1861, ibid.

92. A. Jean Simon to James Redpath, 17 August 1859, in Redpath, *Guide to Hayti*, 62.

93. *Chicago Times*, 2 March 1861.

94. James Redpath to Hon. M. Pleasance, 9 February 1861, *Bureau of Emigration (Haiti)*.

95. *The Pine and Palm*, Boston and New York, 18 May 1861, Boston Public Library. See also John Beard, *The Life of Toussaint Louverture* (London: Ingram, 1853).

96. Law and 1846 Constitution in Redpath, *Guide to Hayti*, 43.

97. *The Pine and Palm*, 27 June 1861.

98. 7 September 1861, ibid.

99. October 1861, ibid.

100. 27 February 1862, ibid.

101. Letter to Richard Gaines, 27 March circa 1861, *James Redpath Papers*.

102. Comment in Redpath, *Guide to Hayti*, 157, 102.

103. *Frederick Douglass' Monthly*, December 1860.

104. Robert Schomburgk to Ministry of Foreign Affairs, 29 January 1853, Relaciones Exteriores. Legajo 6. Expediente 1–7, 1853, AGN-Santo Domingo.

105. A.E. Newton to Reverend John Taylor, 15 February circa 1861, *James Redpath Papers*, Duke University.

106. A.E. Newton to Morrison, 28 February circa 1861, ibid.

107. A.E. Newton to J. Holland, 20 March circa 1861, ibid.

108. Emigration Document, 16 June 1861 and Guide, *Alexander Proctor Papers*, Duke University.

109. *The Pine and Palm*, 19 June 1862.

110. *In the Tropics by a Settler in Santo Domingo*, with an Introductory notice by Richard B. Kimball (New York: Carleton, 1863), 143, Huntington Library.

111. Comment, 1860, in Redpath, *Guide to Hayti*, 89.

112. Samuel Hazard, *Santo Domingo, Past and Present, with a Glance at Hayti* (New York: Harper & Bros., 1873), 461.

113. James Redpath to Hon. M. Pleasance, 2 March 1861, *Bureau of Emigration (Haiti)*.

114. Enoch P. Waters, *American Diary: A Personal History of the Black Press* (Chicago: Path Press, 1987), 95.

115. Hunt, *Remarks on Hayti*, 11.

116. J. Dennis Harris, *A Summer on the Borders of the Caribbean Sea* (New York: Burdick, 1865), 33, 57. See also Julie Winch, "American Free Blacks and Emigration to Haiti," no. 33, Centro de Investigaciones del Caribe y America Latina, Universidad Interamericana de Puerto Rico, 1988.

117. A.E. Newton to James T. Newman, 19 February circa 1861, *James Redpath Papers*, Duke University.

118. Letter to Mrs. Lewis, 14 March circa 1861, ibid.

119. A.E. Newton to Delia Burr, 9 April circa 1861, ibid.

120. James Redpath to Hon. M. Pleasance, 3 November 1860, *Bureau of Emigration (Haiti)*.

121. Comment, 22 August 1859, in Redpath, *Guide to Hayti*, 97–99.

122. *The Colored Citizen*, Cincinnati, 19 May 1866.

123. James Redpath to Hon. M. Pleasance, 1 December 1860, *Bureau of Emigration (Haiti)*.

124. Redpath, *Guide to Hayti*, 38, 39.

125. Entry, 25 June 1855, *William B. Napton Diary*, Missouri Historical Society, St. Louis.

126. Sarah Glasgow to Ann Lane, 9 November 1858, *William Carr Lane Collection*, Missouri Historical Society.

127. Abraham Lincoln to Senate, 18 February 1863, in Roy P. Basler, ed., *The Collected Works of Abraham Lincoln, Volume VI, 1862–1863* (New Brunswick: Rutgers University Press, 1953), 110.

128. President W.R. Inglis to "Sir," 17 January 1862, CO331/33, NAUK.

129. Letter to C.H. Darling, 20 May 1861, CO301/31, ibid.

130. W.R. Inglis to Governor Darling, 18 February 1862, CO331/33, ibid.

131. Letter from Foreign Office, 7 May 1860, CO137/352, ibid.

132. Letter from F. Rogers, Downing Street, 26 May 1860, CO137/352, ibid.

133. Entry, 25 July 1859, in Scarborough, *The Diary of Edmund Ruffin, Volume I*, 325.

134. *Speech of Hon. Wade Hampton on the Constitutionality of the Slave Trade Laws. Delivered in the Senate of South Carolina, December 10th 1859* (Columbia, South Carolina: Steam Power Press, 1860). See also *Letters to the Southern People Concerning the Acts of Congress and the Treaties with Great Britain in Relation to the African Slave Trade* (Charleston: Steam Power Press, 1858), 52: "neither the 'horrors of St. Domingo' nor the treachery of the 'Sicilian Vespers' will ever be imported from Africa, if they impend at all, they are fostered much nearer home."

135. Oscar to Parents, 7 September 1858, *Francis Lieber Collection, University of South Carolina*. See also *The Slave Trade not Declared Piracy by the Act of 1820. The United States vs. William C. Corrie. Presentiment for Piracy. Opinion of the Hon. A.G. Magrath* (Charleston: Courtenay, 1860).

136. Raphael Semmes, *The Cruise of the Alabama and the Sumter* (New York: Carleton, 1864), 133. See also Raphael Semmes, *The Confederate Raider Alabama: Selections from Memoirs of Service Afloat During the War between the States* (Bloomington: Indiana University Press, 1962).

137. Raphael Semmes, *Memoirs of Service Afloat During the War Between the States* (Baltimore: Kelly, Piet, 1869), 521, 523, 527, 566, 567, 568, 569, 573, 574.

138. Harpur Allen Gosnell, ed., *Rebel Raider: Being an Account of Raphael Semmes's Cruise in the CSS Sumter* (Chapel Hill: University of North Carolina Press, 1948), 123.

139. Raphael Semmes, *Memoirs of Service Afloat During the War Between the States* (Baltimore: Kelly, Piet, 1869), 234.

140. Letter, 4 August 1861, Roll 9, M9, *Despatches from U.S. Consuls in Cap-Haïtien.*

141. Henry Conard to William Seward, 5 January 1863, Reel 4, T346, *Despatches from U.S. Consuls in Port-au-Prince, NARA-CP.*

142. Report of Acting Rear Admiral J.L. Lardner, 6 November 1863 in *Official Records of the Union and Confederate Navies in the War of the Rebellion, Published Under the Direction of the Hon. H.A. Herbert, Secretary of the Navy B. Lieut. Commander Richard Navy, U.S. Navy et al., Series I-Volume 2* (Washington, D.C.: Government Printing Office, 1895), 492–493.

143. Lt. Governor Eyre to Commodore Cracraft, 6 October 1863, CO301/37, NAUK.

144. Lt. Governor Eyre to Duke of Newcastle, 23 November 1863, CO301/37, ibid.

145. President of Turks Islands to Lt. Governor Eyre, 17 October 1863, CO301/37, ibid.

146. Report of Mr. Hinson, Acting Special Justice, Turks and Caicos, 31 December 1860, CO301/31, ibid.

147. B.F. Sanford to William Seward, 3 May 1862, Roll 3, T330, *Despatches from U.S. Consuls in Aux Cayes.*

148. B.F. Sanford to William Seward, 19 March 1862, ibid.

149. *Maga Excursion Papers* (New York: Putnam, 1867), American Antiquarian Society-Worcester, Massachusetts.

150. James de Long to William Seward, 3 October 1863, Roll 3, T330, *Despatches from U.S. Consuls in Aux Cayes.*

151. James de Long to William Seward, 21 March 1868, ibid.
152. B.F. Sanford to William Seward, 31 March 1862, ibid.
153. Gustave D'Alaux, *Soulouque and His Empire* (Richmond: Randolph, 1861 [Translated and Edited by John H. Parkhill]), vii, ix, xii, xiii. Emphasis original.
154. William C. Edwards and Edward Steers, Jr., eds., *The Lincoln Assassination: The Evidence* (Urbana: University of Illinois Press, 2009), 1296–1297.
155. Letter from Abraham Lincoln, 16 April 1863, in Roy P. Basler, ed., *The Collected Works of Abraham Lincoln, Volume VI*, 178.
156. Edwin Stanton to "Sir," 3 February 1864, *Edward Hartz Papers, Duke University*.
157. James de Long to Edward L. Hartz, 1 March 1864, ibid.
158. Jonathan Elliot to Lewis Cass, 21 April 1858, Roll 3, T56, *Despatches from U.S. Consuls in Santo Domingo*.
159. Jonathan Elliot to Lewis Cass, 21 October 1858, ibid.
160. Translated letter from French envoy, 21 October 1858, ibid.
161. Jonathan Elliot to Lewis Cass, 22 October 1858, ibid.
162. Jonathan Elliot to Lewis Cass, 17 December 1859, ibid.
163. Jonathan Elliot to Lewis Cass, 20 July 1860, ibid.
164. Martin Hood to Earl Russell, 30 October 1861, FO23/44, NAUK.
165. Jane Cazneau to Moses Beach, 24 April 1862, *Jane McManus Storms Cazneau Papers*.
166. Logan, *Haiti and the Dominican Republic*, 43.
167. Jane Cazneau to Moses Beach, 7 June 1862, *Cazneau Papers*. Emphasis original.
168. Treudley, "The United States and Santo Domingo, 1789–1866," 246.
169. Alejandro Bolanos-Geyer, *William Walker: The Gray-Eyed Man of Destiny, Volume IV* (Lake Saint Louis, Missouri: AB-G, 1990), 60.
170. *New York Evening Post*, 2 September 1854.
171. Tansill, *The United States and Santo Domingo, 1798–1873*, 188.
172. *New York Evening Post*, 25 October 1854.

10. HAITI TO BE ANNEXED AND REENSLAVED? 1863–1870

1. *L'Opinion Nationale*, 16 April 1861.
2. Memorandum from M.M. Gautier, circa 1869, Roll 1, *Notes from the Legation of the Dominican Republic to the United States*, NARA-CP.
3. Ulisses Espaillat to the United States, 1 November 1863, ibid.
4. Robert Schomburgk to Foreign Ministry, 11 September 1852, Relaciones Exteriores, 1851, Correspondencia Official, Expediente 4, AGN-Santo Domingo. See also Robert Schomburgk to Foreign Ministry, 11 November 1852, Relaciones Exteriores, Legajo A 441, Expediente 1–16, 1846–1862: "Certain British subjects on their arrival from Turks Island at Puerto Plata were refused permission to land and otherwise treated in an unfriendly manner." See also Robert Schomburgk to Ministry of Foreign Affairs, 12 June 1854, Relaciones Exteriores, Legajo 7, Expediente 1–13: Complains here about the "harsh and unconstitutional treatment which Thomas Wilson, a British subject residing at Porto Plata, received. . . . [He was] placed in a vile prison where he was left under great sufferings for five days"; he had been accused of "taking up a bunch of plantains which he found on the public road." Robert Schomburgk to Ministry of Foreign Affairs, 5 August 1854, Legajo 7: "Dr. Jackson. . . .a more unjust sentence could scarcely have been given. . . .such a violent

act of interference with the liberty of a British subject. . . . injuries he has suffered since
an attack was made upon his life." Robert Schomburgk to Ministry of Foreign Affairs, 3
October 1854, Legajo 7: "arbitrary and unconstitutional treatment Thomas Wilson, a British
subject residing at Porto Plata received." Robert Schomburgk to Ministry of Foreign Affairs,
23 June 1854, Legajo 7: Thomas Wilson was "treated in such a harsh and unconstitutional
manner. . . . Wilson must either work for Alejandro Fanfan three months or remain in
prison six months and do public work. To condemn a British subject to work by force and
gratuitously for another person" was akin to "the curse of human society, 'slavery.'"

5.   Robert Schomburgk and Jonathan Elliot to Foreign Ministry, 29 February 1852, Relaciones
       Exteriores, 1851. See also Jonathan Elliot to Foreign Ministry, 19 August 1852, Relaciones
       Exteriores, Legajo A 441, Expediente 1–16, 1846–1852: "[Edward] Roth, United States
       Commercial Agent at Porto Plata," complains that "he is not respected in his office. . . . a
       woman called Frances Brown who has been residing some six months at Porto Plata and
       having an American protection [sic] from the United States agent in Cape Haytian, was
       ordered to leave the country immediately."

6.   Robert Schomburgk to Foreign Ministry, 20 July 1853, Relaciones Exteriores, Legajo 6.
       Expediente 1–7, 1853.

7.   Department of State to Foreign Ministry, 9 July 1857, Relaciones Exteriores, Legajo 10,
       1857, Expediente 1–23.

8.   Jonathan Elliot to Ministry of Foreign Affairs, 3 October 1857, Relaciones Exteriores,
       Legajo 10.

9.   Jonathan Elliot to Foreign Ministry, 25 October 1857, Relaciones Exteriores, Legajo 10.

10.   Robert Schomburgk to Foreign Ministry, 15 January 1857, Relaciones Exteriores, Legajo
       10, Expediente 1–33, 1857.

11.   Captain of British Schooner to President of D.R., 9 November 1857, Relaciones Exteriores,
       Legajo 10.

12.   Earl of Malmesbury to Felix Delmonte, 16 March 1858, Relaciones Exteriores, Legajo 11.

13.   Jonathan Elliot to Ministry of Foreign Affairs, 13 March 1857, Relaciones Exteriores,
       Legajo 10.

14.   Robert Schomburgk to Foreign Ministry, 13 March 1857, Relaciones Exteriores, Legajo 10.

15.   Martin Hood to Ministry of Foreign Affairs, 22 October 1857, Relaciones Exteriores,
       Legajo 10.

16.   Robert Schomburgk to Foreign Ministry, 4 January 1857, Relaciones Exteriores, Legajo 10,
       Expediente 1023.

17.   Robert Schomburgk to Foreign Ministry, 30 April 1852, Relaciones Exteriores, 1851,
       Correspondencia Official, Expediente 5: Bremen seeks to recognize the D.R., the latter
       having "only a population of 50,000. . . . its commerce is of very great consideration" and
       has "extensive connections with Puerto Plata." Dr. Emil Querner to "His Excellency Senor
       Santana, President of the Republic of San Domingo," 1 January 1859, Relaciones Exteriores,
       Legajo A 441, Expediente 1–16, 1846–1862: "I offer Your Excellency my services may it be
       in regard to colonization, of political, social, or military institutions. . . . being born and
       educated in Germany, I have studied the art of medicine. . . . took part in the revolution
       in 1848 as a captain. . . . [I] am engaged at present to design plans of colonization of the
       northern part of Canada for the Government. But this country is too poor, too triste, too
       cold as to earn a favourable effect."

18. Martin Hood to Foreign Ministry, 5 September 1857, Relaciones Exteriores, Legajo 10.

19. Robert Schomburgk to Ministry of Foreign Affairs, 29 January 1853, Relaciones Exteriores, Legajo 6, Expediente 1–7, 1853.

20. W.S. Courtney, *The Gold Fields of St. Domingo* (New York: Anson P. Norton, 1860). Emphasis original.

21. A.K. Shepard, *Papers on Spanish America* (Albany: Munsell, 1868), 22. See also Joseph Warren Fabens, *Facts about Santo Domingo Applicable to the Present Crisis: An Address Delivered before the American Geographical and Statistical Society at New York, April 3, 1862* (New York: Putnam, 1862).

22. Arthur Folsom to William Seward, 8 October 1866, Roll 9, M9, *Despatches from U.S. Consuls in Cap-Haïtien*, NARA-CP.

23. David C. Keehn, *Knights of the Golden Circle: Secret Empire, Southern Secession, Civil War* (Baton Rouge: Louisiana State University Press, 2013), 8.

24. Entry, 19 April 1858, in Scarborough, *The Diary of Edmund Ruffin*, 177–179.

25. Memorandum on Treaty between Spain and the Dominican Republic, 18 February 1854, Relaciones Exteriores, Legajo 7, Expediente 1–13. Translation from Spanish.

26. Robert Schomburgk to Ministry of Foreign Affairs, 18 October 1854, Relaciones Exteriores, Legajo 7.

27. Jonathan Elliot to Ministry of Foreign Affairs, 27 December 1854, Relaciones Exteriores, Legajo 7: "the American captain Beckley . . . now in prison . . . , awaiting his trial, is sick and requires medical attendance." See also James McIntosh to Felix Delmonte, Ministry of Foreign Affairs, 31 May 1858, Legajo 11: William Read of Boston was "imprisoned and otherwise maltreated," then forced to depart from Santo Domingo and "abandon his property and business."

28. James McIntosh to Buenaventura Báez, 26 May 1858, Legajo 11. Emphasis original.

29. James McIntosh to Buenaventura Báez, 1 June 1858, ibid.

30. Eustis Hubbard to William Seward, 15 April 1861, Roll 9, M9, *Despatches from U.S. Consuls in Cap-Haïtien.*

31. Arthur Folsom to William Seward, 16 August 1864, ibid.

32. Whiteman, *The British West Indies and African Immigration* (London: Richardson, 1860), New-York Historical Society. Cf. Pedro L. San Miguel, *The Imagined Island: History, Identity & Utopia in Hispaniola* (Chapel Hill: University of North Carolina Press, 2005).

33. Translation of remarks by Don Felipe Ribero y Le Moyne, 16 March 1863, FO23/47, NAUK.

34. Martin Hood to General Ribero, Captain General, 5 March 1863, FO23/47, ibid.

35. Memorandum by John Horne Darrell, 23 March 1863, FO23/47, ibid.

36. Martin Hood to Earl Russell, 20 March 1863, FO23/47, ibid.

37. G.L. Cheeseman to Martin Hood, 14 October 1863, FO23/48, ibid.

38. Martin Hood to Earl Russell, 15 July 1863, FO23/47, ibid.

39. Martin Hood to Earl Russell, 18 April 1862, FO23/46, ibid.

40. *Douglass Monthly*, March 1861.

41. Martin Hood to "My Dear Sir," 15 February 1862, FO23/44, NAUK.

42. Martin Hood to Earl Russell, 18 July 1862, FO23/46, ibid.

43. Proclamation of Don Carlos de Vargas y Cerveto, 23 October 1863, FO23/46, ibid.

44. Martin Hood to Earl Russell, 31 July 1862, FO23/46, ibid.
45. Martin Hood to Earl Russell, 19 April 1862. FO23/46, ibid.
46. Letter from Consul G.L. Cheeseman, 9 August 1862, FO23/46, ibid.
47. Martin Hood to Earl Russell, 20 September 1863, FO23/48, ibid.
48. Martin Hood to Earl Russell, 5 December 1863, FO23/48, ibid.
49. Martin Hood to Earl Russell, 6 December 1863, FO23/48, ibid.
50. Martin Hood to Earl Russell, 18 February 1864, FO23/48, ibid.
51. *New York Herald*, 10 March 1865, Etats-Unis, Affaires Diverses, 58–60, 1864–1865, MAE–Paris. See also the clippings on France in Mexico in this same file: *New York Times*, 4 July 1865; *New York Herald*, 18 December 1865; Clipping, 28 November 1865: "trouble on the Rio Grande. . . . two French war steamers in the Rio Grande."
52. Clipping, circa 1864–1865, and *New York Herald*, 15 December 1864, Etats-Unis, ibid. See also Cathryn J. Prince, *Burn the Town and Sack the Banks: Confederates Attack Vermont* (New York City: Carroll & Graf, 2006).
53. *New York Herald*, 17 November 1865: "Negro atrocities" and "Negro revolt" in Jamaica, Etats-Unis, Affaires Diverses.
54. Jane Cazneau to Moses Beach, 24 September 1862, *Cazneau Papers*.
55. Jane Cazneau to Moses Beach, 9 October 1862, ibid.
56. Jane Cazneau to Moses Beach, 25 August 1865, ibid.
57. De B. Randolph Keim, *San Domingo: Pen, Pictures, and Leaves of Travel, Romance and History. From the Portfolio of a Correspondent in the American Tropics* (Philadelphia: Claxton, Remsen, & Haffelfinger, 1870), 18.
58. Letter from Governor Henry Allen, 8 January 1865, Etats-Unis, Affaires Diverses, 30–32, 1861–1864, MAE-Paris.
59. *The National Era*, 17 March 1859, citing the *Savannah Republican*.
60. *The Provincial Freeman*, 13 October 1855.
61. Remarks by Senator Ulloa, 24 March 1865, in David G. Yuengling, ed., *Highlights in the Debates in the Spanish Chamber of Deputies Relative to the Abandonment of Santo Domingo* (Washington, D.C.: Murray & Heister, 1941), 9.
62. M.M. Gautier to Joseph Fabens, 10 March 1869, Roll 1, T801, *Notes from Dominican Legation in the United States to the Department of State*, NARA-CP. See also, "Convention Between the Dominican Government and Robert M. Funkhouser and Associates for the Establishment of a Mail Steamship Line Between the Ports of New York and New Orleans in the United States of America and those of the Dominican Republic," 8 October 1868, Huntington Library, San Marino, California.
63. For documentation of the case of Pelletier and the foregoing, see "The American and Haytien Claims Commission. The Untied States vs. the Republic of Hayti in the Matter of the Claim of Antonio Pelletier. Record. Washington, D.C., 1885," Harvard Law Library. See also Inventory of Archives in Haitian Legation in United States, 1863–1889, National Archives of Haiti, Port-au-Prince.
64. Ernest Roumain to William Seward, 28 July 1863, Roll 1, *Notes from the Haitian Legation in the United States to the Department of State, 1861–1906*, NARA-CP.
65. Joseph Lewis, U.S. Commercial Agent in Port-au-Prince, to Victorin Pleasance, Secretary of State for Foreign Affairs, 8 May 1861, Roll 1, *Notes from the Haitian Legation*.
66. Statement, 15 August 1861, ibid.

67. Eustis Hubbard to William Seward, 13 April 1861, Roll 9, M9, *Despatches from U.S. Consuls in Cap-Haïtien.*

68. Eustis Hubbard to Antonio Pelletier, 6 April 1861, ibid.

69. Letter from Henry Byron, 8 May 1861, CO301/31, NAUK.

70. Pelletier Record, Harvard Law Library. See also "Protocol . . . à Washington Pour Le Regelement de Reclamations Pelletier et Lazare," 28 August 1884, in *Recueil des Traites de la Republique d'Haiti. Tome Premier, 1804–1904, Publication de la Secretaire d'Etat des Relations Exterieures, Imprimerie de l'Etat,* 1945, 208, Ministry of Foreign Affairs, Port-au-Prince. In the same volume, see also "Protocole Additionnel . . . Signe dans Le But de Prolonger jusqu' au 28 Julliet 1885 le Terme Prevue par Le Protocole Haitiano-Americain de Washington pour La Soumission à un Arbitrage des Reclamations Lazare et Pelletier."

71. Logan, *Haiti and the Dominican Republic,* 44.

72. M.B. Bird, *The Victorious: A Small Poem* (Port-au-Prince: de Cordova, 1866).

73. *New Orleans Tribune,* 1 November 1866.

74. *The Elevator,* 5 February 1869.

75. *The Loyal Georgian,* 10 August 1867.

76. *The Elevator,* 31 July 1868.

77. *The Elevator,* 29 November 1867.

78. Arthur Folsom to William Seward, 10 May 1865, Roll 9, M9, *Despatches from U.S. Consuls in Cap-Haïtien.*

79. Matthew Casey, "Between Anti-Haitianism and Anti-Imperialism: Haitian and Cuban Political Collaboration in the Nineteenth and Twentieth Centuries," in Carla Calarge et al., eds., *Haiti and the Americas,* 54–73, 61.

80. Secretary of State for Foreign Affairs to "Mr. Consul," 4 January 1868, Roll 1, *Notes from Haitian Legation.*

81. P. Pujol to Secretary of State, 8 January 1868, Roll 1, *Notes from the Dominican Legation.* In the same collection and reel, see Report by M.M. Gautier, 29 November 1869: Santo Domingo sought to lease Samaná for 50 years which would "in no wise affect . . . national security."

82. Joseph Fabens to Hamilton Fish, 20 April 1869, ibid.

83. Selma F. Rubin, "The United States Commission of Inquiry to the Dominican Republic, 1871" (M.A. thesis, University of Miami, 1965), 46.

84. David Leon to Secretary of State for Foreign Affairs, 9 April 1869, FO23/59, NAUK.

85. A.S. Green to Foreign Office, 9 February 1865, FO881/1339, NAUK.

86. Documents on Samaná, 10 January 1868, 40B–B11, SEN40A–B9, National Archives and Records Administration, Washington, D.C.

87. General Pujol to William Seward, 18 January 1868, ibid.

88. Petition by "Undersigned Members of the Central Committee of the Government elected by the will of the people of the Cibao Provinces," circa 7 October 1867, Roll 1, *Notes from the Dominican Legation.*

89. Gregorio Luperon to "Sir," 5 August 1869, ibid.

90. M.M. Gautier to Joseph Fabens, 22 June 1869, ibid.

91. Joseph Fabens to Hamilton Fish, ibid.

92. Translation of Speech by J.B. Zafra at Session of the National Dominican Congress, 16 December 1867, Roll 1, *Notes from Haitian Legation.*

93. Louis Achille de Pitti Fernandie to U.S. Secretary of State, 5 February 1868, Roll 1, *Notes from Haitian Legation.*

94. George Raester to William Seward, 27 May 1868, Roll 1, *Notes from Haitian Legation.*

95. "A.T." to "President" of United States, circa 1868, Roll 1, ibid.

96. Jacmel "Committee of Public Safety" to William Seward, 30 September 1868, ibid.

97. Evariste La Roche to Secretary of State Hamilton Fish, 30 April 1869, ibid.

98. Evariste La Roche to "Sir," 6 May 1869, ibid.

99. Evariste la Roche to to Hamilton Fish, 21 May 1869, ibid.

100. J. Leon to Minister of Finance, 22 May 1869, ibid.

101. Stephen Preston to Secretary of State, 30 June 1870, Roll 2, *Notes from Haitian Legation.*

102. Stephen Preston to Hamilton Fish, 8 December 1870, ibid.

103. Stephen Preston to Hamilton Fish, 8 December 1870, in John Y. Simon, ed., *The Papers of Ulysses S. Grant, Volume 21: November 1, 1870–May 31, 1871* (Carbondale: Southern Illinois University Press, 1998), 46.

104. Hamilton Fish to Ebenezer Bassett, 9 February 1871, in ibid., 147.

105. Amandus Meyer to Hamilton Fish, 14 December 1869, Roll 1, *Notes from the Dominican Legation.*

106. Clipping, 3 February 1870, Roll 2, *Notes from the Haitian Legation.*

107. Arthur Folsom to General Salnave, 23 September 1865, Roll 9, M9, *Despatches from U.S. Consuls in Cap-Haïtien.*

108. J. Delmonte to William Seward, 10 August 1868, Roll 1, *Notes from the Dominican Legation.*

109. Buenaventura Báez to Joseph Fabens, 2 April 1869, ibid. See the proclamation by Báez on the vote to join the United States, circa March 1870, FO23/61, NAUK.

110. M.M. Gautier to Santo Domingo, Department for Foreign Relations, 9 March 1869, Roll 1, *Notes from the Dominican Legation.*

111. M.M. Gautier to "Your Excellency," 6 July 1869, ibid.

112. M.M. Gautier to William Seward, 9 July 1869, ibid.

113. E.K. Owen to George M. Robeson, 18 January 1870, ibid.

114. E.K. Owen to George M. Robeson, 18 January 1870, attached is Petition signed by Luperon and his comrades, 9 December 1869, ibid.

115. David Leon to My Lord, 9 December 1869, FO23/59, NAUK. At the same site, see also David Leon to My Lord, 9 April 1869, FO23/59.

116. M.M. Gautier to R. Perry, U.S. Commercial Agent in Santo Domingo, 1 January 1870, Roll 1, *Notes from the Dominican Legation.*

117. Hamilton Fish to Evariste Laroche, 7 October 1869, Roll 58, M99, *Notes to Foreign Legations in the United States from the Department of State, 1834–1906,* NARA-CP.

118. Memorandum, circa 1870, Roll 1, *Notes from the Dominican Legation.*

119. C.H. Poor, Rear Admiral of U.S. Fleet to George Robeson, Secretary of the Navy, 12 March 1870, Roll 6, T56, *Despatches from U.S. Consuls in Santo Domingo.*

120. M.M. Gautier to "Most Excellent Sir," 16 May 1870, Roll 1, *Notes from the Dominican Legation.*

121. Report by Buenaventura Báez and M.M. Gautier, 16 April 1870, Roll 1.

122. William Cazneau to Hamilton Fish, 17 May 1870, ibid.

123. Raymond Perry to William Cazneau, 4 May 1870, ibid.

124. William Cazneau to Raymond Perry, 4 May 1870, ibid.

125. M.M. Gautier to "Most Excellent Sir," 17 May 1870, ibid.
126. Raymond Perry to Hamilton Fish, 20 February 1870, Roll 6, T56, *Despatches from U.S. Consuls in Santo Domingo.*
127. Raymond Perry to William Cazneau, 13 May 1870, ibid.
128. William Cazneau to Raymond Perry, 6 May 1870, ibid.
129. Raymond Perry to Hamilton Fish, 10 December 1869, ibid.
130. C.H. Poor, Rear Admiral, to George Robeson, 12 March 1870, ibid. Adjacent to this correspondence, see "Boletin General" of 5 March 1870 from the D.R., claiming substantial support for annexation.
131. M.M. Gautier to "Most Excellent Sir," 12 December 1870, Roll 1, *Notes from the Dominican Legation.*
132. Report from Raymond Perry, 28 December 1869, Roll 6, T56, *Despatches from U.S. Consuls in Santo Domingo.*
133. Spencer St. John to Earl Granville, 5 September 1871, CO23/62, NAUK.
134. Letter to Earl Granville, 1 October 1872, FO23/63, ibid.
135. G.H. Harding to William Seward, 4 September 1867, Roll 1, T486, *Despatches from U.S. Consuls in St. Marc.*
136. Selma F. Rubin, "The United States Commission of Inquiry to the Dominican Republic, 1871" (M.A. thesis, University of Miami, 1965), 56.
137. G.H. Harding to Department of State, 18 September 1867, Roll 1, T486, *Despatches from U.S. Consuls in St. Marc.* Emphasis original.
138. Amy Wilentz, *Farewell, Fred Voodoo: A Letter from Haiti* (New York: Simon & Schuster, 2013).

11. ANNEX HISPANIOLA AND DEPORT U.S. NEGROES THERE? 1870–1871

1. Memorandum by President Grant, 1869–1870, in Simon, *The Papers of Ulysses S. Grant, Volume 20*, 74–76. See also Yves L. Auguste, *Haiti et Les Etats-Unis, 1804–1862* (Sherbrooke, Quebec: Editions Naaman, 1979).
2. Samuel G. Howe to President Grant in Samuel G. Howe, *Letters on the Proposed Annexation of Santo Domingo, in Answer to Certain Charges in the Newspapers* (Boston: Wright & Potter, 1871). See also Jean Price-Mars, *La République d'Haiti et La Républicaine Dominicaine: Les Aspets Divers d'Un Problème d'Histoire de Géographie et D'Ethnologie* (Lausanne: Imprimerie Held, 1953).
3. Speech of Hon. Oliver P. Morton of Indiana Delivered in the Senate of the United States, December 21, 1870, Huntington Library, San Marino, California.
4. Samuel Howe to President Grant, June 1871, in Simon, *The Papers of Ulysses S. Grant, Volume 22*, 23.
5. Stanislaus Goutier to State Department, 27 February 1871, Roll 10, M9, *Despatches from U.S. Consuls in Cap-Haïtien*, NARA-CP.
6. Stanislaus Goutier to General Nord Alexis, 3 February 1871, ibid.
7. General Nord Alexis to Stanislaus Goutier, 4 February 1871, ibid.
8. Comment, in Eric Paul Roorda et al., eds., *The Dominican Republic Reader: History, Culture, Politics* (Durham: Duke University Press, 2014), 141.
9. Tansill, *The United States and Santo Domingo*, 341.
10. *The Weekly Louisianan*, 20 July 1871.

11. Frederick Douglass, *Autobiographies* (New York: Library of America, 1994), 846.

12. Edward Jackson Holmes, "Observations Made While in the House of Charles Sumner, Dec. 25, 1870 to June 19, 1871," Massachusetts Historical Society, Boston.

13. Speech of Hon. Charles Sumner . . . on his St. Domingo Resolutions Delivered in the Senate of the United States, March 27, 1871, Violations of International Law and Usurpations of War Powers, University of Virginia. Cf. Speech of Hon. James Harlan of Iowa, Delivered in the Senate of the United States, March 29, 1871 (Washington: Rives & Bailey, 1871), New York Historical Society.

14. Speech of Fernando Wood of New York in the House of Representatives, January 9, 1871, University of Virginia.

15. Speech of Hon. Charles Sumner of Massachusetts on the Proposed Annexation of "The Island of San Domingo," Delivered in the Senate of the United States, December 21, 1870, University of Virginia.

16. Howe, *Letters on the Proposed Annexation*.

17. Daguillard, *A Jewel in the Crown*, 45, 49.

18. Speech by Hon. Carl Schurz of Missouri, Delivered in the Senate of the United States, 11 January 1871, Missouri Historical Society, St. Louis. The same speech can also be found at the Huntington Library in San Marino, California.

19. Howe, *Letters on the Proposed Annexation*.

20. Speech of Hon. Job Stevenson of Ohio in the House of Representatives, January 10, 1871, University of Virginia.

21. Speech of Hon. Oliver P. Morton of Indiana, Delivered in the Senate of the United States, December 21, 1870, Huntington Library, San Marino, California.

22. Speech by Hon. Zachariah Chandler of Michigan, Delivered in the Senate of the United States, May 28, 1870, Chicago History Museum.

23. Cornelius Cole, *Memoirs of Cornelius Cole* (New York: McLouglin, 1908), 220–222, 230, 233–234, 237.

24. Benjamin Wade to "President," 7 March 1871, Benjamin Wade Collection, Chicago History Museum.

25. President U.S. Grant to the Senate, 31 May 1870, in *A Compilation of the Messages and Papers of the Presidents: Prepared under the Direction of the Joint Committee on Printing of the House and Senate, Pursuant to an Act of the Fifty-Second Congress of the United States, Volume IX, 1897*, 4015, Missouri Historical Society, St. Louis.

26. Quoted in Andrew D. White, *Autobiography of Andrew D. White, Volume I* (New York: Century, 1905), 484.

27. Samuel Hazard, *Santo Domingo, Past and Present, with a Glance at Hayti* (New York: Harper & Bros., 1873), viii, 215, 485.

28. White, *Autobiography of Andrew D. White, Volume I*, 490.

29. Howe, *Letters on the Proposed Annexation*.

30. President U.S. Grant to President Buenaventura Báez, 7 July 1870, in Simon, *The Papers of Ulysses S. Grant, Volume 20*, 188.

31. Comment, June 1870, in ibid., 180.

32. Howe, *Letters on the Proposed Annexation*.

33. Memorandum from H.K. Storks of War Office, 1 March 1871, Departement des Affaires Etranger, 828, Legation d'Haiti à Londres, 1871–1874, ANH.

34. "Regulations for the Admission of Foreigners to Her Majesty's Dockyards," 16 January 1871, in ibid.

35. Invitation, 27 April 1871, in ibid.

36. Letter to Charles Villervaleix, 10 December 1874, in ibid.

37. Letter to Charles Villervaleix, 23 December 1874, in ibid.

38. Letter to Port-au-Prince, 16 July 1874, in ibid.

39. Secretary of State for Foreign Affairs to Stephen Preston, 9 May 1874, Random File (inadequately filed), ANH.

40. Copy of Convention between the Dominican Republic and United States, 3 February 1873, Haiti, Affaires Diverses, 1870–1874, MAE-Paris.

41. Report, 23 October 1873, ibid.

42. Benjamin Wade to "My Dear President," 6 March 1871, *Benjamin Wade Collection*, Chicago History Museum.

43. M.M. Gautier to "Most Excellent Sir," 27 March 1871, Roll 1, *Notes from the Legation of the Dominican Republic*.

44. Letter to President Grant, 22 August 1871, Roll 2, ibid.

45. Stanislaus Goutier to Commander of U.S. vessel, 9 February 1871, Roll 10, M9, *Despatches from U.S. Consuls in Cap-Haïtien*.

46. Translated Leaflet from Luperón, circa 1871, ibid.

47. Andrew White, *Autobiography of Andrew D. White* (New York: Century, 1905), 500–502, 504, 507.

48. Remarks of Congressman Samuel Cox, 10 January 1871, in Simon, *The Papers of Ulysses S. Grant, Volume 21*, 88.

49. Howe, *Letters on the Proposed Annexation*.

50. *The Weekly Louisianan*, 20 July 1871.

51. James de Long to O.H. Browning, 7 December 1867, Roll 3, T330, *Despatches from US Consuls in Aux Cayes*, NARA-CP.

52. Translation of Decree, 15 January 1869, ibid.

53. James de Long to Secretary of State, 6 March 1869, ibid.

54. James de Long to Secretary of State, 5 May 1869, ibid.

55. Letter to Secretary of State Hamilton Fish, 19 December 1869, Roll 9, M9, *Despatches from U.S. Consuls in Cap-Haïtien*.

56. U.S. Consul to U.S. Admiral, 3 March 1870, Roll 10, M9, ibid.

57. Rubin, "The United States Commission of Inquiry to the Dominican Republic," 87.

58. News Report, 29 March 1871, in Simon, *The Papers of Ulysses S. Grant, Volume 21*, 291.

59. Dana Minaya, *Freed U.S. Slave Emigrants of 1824 to Samaná* (College Research Ctr., 2012), 33.

60. William S. McFeely, *Frederick Douglass* (New York: Norton, 1991), 277.

61. Rubin, "The United States Commission of Inquiry to the Dominican Republic," 89.

62. Frederick Douglass, *Autobiographies* (New York: Library of America, 1994), 848.

63. Howe, *Letters on the Proposed Annexation*.

64. Rubin, "The United States Commission to the Dominican Republic, 1871," 96.

65. Letter from Gerrit Smith to Hon. Mr. Churchill, 22 December 1870, Massachusetts Historical Society, Boston.

66. John Bell Hepburn to President Grant, 8 November 1870, in Simon, *The Papers of Ulysses S. Grant, Volume 21*, 299–300. Emphasis original.

67.   John Bell Hepburn to President Grant, 25 July 1869, in Simon, *The Papers of Ulysses S. Grant, Volume 20*, 13.

68.   Ed Horton to President Grant, 2 November 1870, in ibid.

69.   Henry Allen to President Grant, 20 November 1870 in ibid.

70.   President Báez to Rear Admiral Poor, 29 March 1870, SEN41B–B7, National Archives and Records Administration-Washington, D.C. Hereafter denoted as NARA-Washington, D.C.

71.   John Irwin to Rear Admiral Lee, 1 January 1871, ibid.

72.   Statement by Gregorio Luperón, no date, ibid.

73.   Secretary of State Hamilton Fish to Ebenezer Bassett, 16 November 1870, in Simon, *The Papers of Ulysses S. Grant, Volume 21*, 146.

74.   Ebenezer Bassett to Hamilton Fish, 25 January 1871, in ibid., 146.

75.   Ebenezer Bassett to Hamilton Fish, 23 November 1872, in Simon, *Volume 23*, 195.

76.   Lt. Commander Selfridge to Secretary of Navy, 14 July 1869, SEN41B–B7, NARA-Washington, D.C.

77.   Report from Matanzas to Secretary of Navy, 27 May 1869, ibid.

78.   *New York World*, 25 March 1870.

79.   Christopher Teal, *Hero of Hispaniola: America's First Black Diplomat, Ebenezer Bassett* (Westport, Connecticut: Praeger, 2008), 88.

80.   James de Long to William Seward, 20 September 1868, Roll 3, T330, *Despatches from US Consuls in Aux Cayes*. Emphasis original.

81.   A. Hilchenbach, U.S. Consul to G.H. Hollister, 6 April 1869, SEN41B–B7, NARA-Washington, D.C.

82.   *The Elevator*, 20 September 1867.

83.   James de Long to William Seward, 20 September 1868, Roll 3, T330, *Despatches from US Consuls in Aux Cayes*.

84.   W.A. Gould to Secretary of State, 28 January 1871, Roll 4, T330, *Despatches from US Consuls in Aux Cayes*.

85.   W.A. Gould to General Dominique, 29 November 1870, ibid.

86.   Copy of Letter from the United States, 11 December 1869, Haiti, Affaires Diverses, 1870–1874, MAE-Paris.

87.   Report from Spencer St. John, 4 September 1871, in Haiti, Affaires Diverses.

88.   W.A. Gould to Hamilton Fish, 7 January 1870, Roll 3, T330, *Despatches from US Consuls in Aux Cayes*.

89.   W.A. Gould to Hamilton Fish, 31 January 1870, ibid.

90.   Hamilton Fish to Ebenezer Bassett, 31 May 1872, Roll 95, M77, *Diplomatic Instructions of the Department of State*, NARA-CP.

91.   W.A. Gould to Hamilton Fish, 4 May 1870, Roll 4, T330, *Despatches from US Consuls in Aux Cayes*.

92.   W.A. Gould to J.B. Davis, 23 June 1870, ibid.

93.   U.S. Consul to Hamilton Fish, 15 January 1870, Roll 10, M9, *Despatches from U.S. Consuls in Cap-Haïtien*.

94.   U.S. Consul to Hamilton Fish, January 1870, ibid.

95.   Stanislaus Goutier to General Nord Alexis, 22, ibid.

96.   General Nord Alexis to Stanislaus Goutier, 25 June 1871, ibid.

97. *The Weekly Louisianan,* 28 May 1871.
98. 3 May 1874, ibid.
99. *The Elevator,* 17 July 1868.
100. 16 August 1867, ibid.
101. Hazard, *Santo Domingo, Past and Present, with a Glance at Hayti,* 461.
102. Keim, *San Domingo: Pen, Pictures, and Leaves of Travel,* 110.
103. *The Weekly Louisianan,* 10 August 1872.
104. E.P. Smith to James de Long, 20 July 1868, Roll 3, T330, *Despatches from US Consuls in Aux Cayes.*
105. Superintendent of Contrabands to Chief Quartermaster, 2 April 1864, in Ira Berlin et al., eds., *Freedom: A Documentary History of Emancipation, 1861–1867* (New York: Cambridge University Press, 1993), 333–334.
106. Rebecca J. Scott and Jean M. Hebrand, *Freedom Papers: An Atlantic Odyssey in the Age of Emancipation* (Cambridge: Harvard University Press, 2012), 1–2.
107. R.J. Lackland to Judge David Irvin, 16 November 1868, *Lackland Papers,* Missouri Historical Society, St. Louis.
108. R.J. Lackland to Judge David Irvin, 30 July 1869, ibid.
109. Hamilton Fish to Stephen Preston, 10 June 1873, Roll 58, M99, *Notes to Foreign Legations in the United States from the Department of State,* NARA-CP.
110. Hamilton Fish to "Sir," 14 February 1870, Roll 95, M77, *Diplomatic Instructions of the Department of State,* NARA-CP.
111. Hamilton Fish to Ebenezer Bassett, 9 February 1871, ibid.
112. Stanislaus Goutier to State Department, 30 March 1872, Roll 10, M9, *Despatches from U.S. Consuls in Cap-Haïtien.*
113. Hamilton Fish to Ebenezer Bassett, 9 February 1871, in Simon, *The Papers of Ulysses S. Grant, Volume 21,* 147.
114. Daguillard, *A Jewel in the Crown,* 45.
115. U.S. Consul to Hamilton Fish, 18 July 1870, Roll 10, M9, *Despatches from U.S. Consuls in Cap-Haïtien.*
116. John Bell Hepburn to President Grant, 4 April 1875, in Simon, *The Papers of Ulysses S. Grant, Volume 26,* 450–451. Emphasis original.
117. Secretary of State Hamilton Fish to President Grant, August 1875, in ibid.
118. Thomas Webster to President Grant, 12 March 1869, in Simon, *The Papers of Ulysses S. Grant, Volume 20,* 10.
119. Ebenezer Bassett to President Grant, 17 March 1869, in ibid., 10–11.
120. George Vashon to President Grant, 18 March 1869, in ibid., 11. Emphasis original.
121. Stanislaus Goutier to State Department, 10 January 1871, Roll 10, M9, *Despatches from U.S. Consuls in Cap-Haïtien.*
122. Stanislaus Goutier to State Department, 25 January 1871, ibid.
123. Report, 23 March 1872, FO83/379, NAUK.
124. H.R., "The Insurrection in Jamaica," 1865, Chicago History Museum.
125. "Statement of A.E. Phillips, Late Acting United States Consul at the Port of St. Jago de Cuba, Showing the Circumstances and Events which Forced him to Abandon his Post and Seek Protection at Jamaica, West Indies, from the Violence of a Spanish Mob," 1870, Chicago History Museum.

126. Message from President Saget to Senate and House, 6 June 1872, Roll 10, M9, *Despatches from U.S. Consuls in Cap-Haïtien.*
127. Message from President Saget, 12 August 1873, ibid.
128. Memo from Vice Consul, 4 November 1873, Roll 1, T486, *Despatches from U.S. Consuls in St. Marc*, NARA-CP.
129. Colonial Bank of London to Charles Villervaleix, 29 August 1874, in Légation à Londres, ANH.
130. Letter to Charles Villervaleix, 23 April 1874, in ibid.
131. Letter to Charles Villervaleix, 9 June 1874, in ibid. At the same site with the same correspondents, see the 23 July 1874 letter.
132. Stanislaus Goutier to State Department, 5 August 1872, Roll 10, M9, *Despatches from U.S. Consuls in Cap-Haïtien.*
133. Joseph Fabens to President Grant, 18 October 1873, in Simon, *The Papers of Ulysses S. Grant, Volume 24*, 276–277.
134. Melvin Knight, *The Americans in Santo Domingo* (New York: Vanguard, 1928), 7.
135. M.M. Gautier to Hamilton Fish, 1 May 1873, Roll 2, *Notes from the Legation of the Dominican Republic.*
136. Letter to Charles Villervaleix, 9 January 1874, in Légation à Londres, ANH.
137. Letter from Port-au-Prince, 27 January 1874, in ibid.
138. Letter from London to Port-au-Prince, 1 June 1874, in ibid.
139. Letter to Charles Villervaleix, 23 August 1874, in ibid.
140. Secretary of State for Foreign Relations to Stephen Preston, 9 May 1874, Random File, ANH.
141. Secretary of State for Foreign Relations to Stephen Preston, 19 January 1874, Random File, ibid.
142. Hamilton Fish to Ebenezer Bassett, 21 September 1875, Roll 96, M77, *Diplomatic Instructions of the Department of State.*
143. Clinton Rice to Clement Haentjens, 25 February 1893, Légation à New York et a Washington.
144. Correspondence, 30 April 1874, and *Daily News*, 7 April 1874, in Légation à Londres, ANH.
145. Letter to Port-au-Prince, 15 June 1874, in ibid.
146. Charles Douglas to Assistant Secretary of State, 13 January 1876, Roll 1, T662, *Despatches from United States Consuls in Puerto Plata*, NARA-CP.
147. Charles Douglas to Hamilton Fish, 6 October 1876, ibid.
148. Mrs. William Cazneau, *Our Winter Eden: Pen Pictures of the Tropics* (New York: WC, 1878), 45–47, 59–60, 65, 108–110, appendix.
149. Will of Jane Cazneau, 27 January 1877, *Cazneau Papers.*
150. *New York Evening Telegram*, 27 December 1878, ibid.
151. Memorandum from Haiti's consul in Hamburg, 20 August 1862, Random File, ANH.
152. Report from L.R. Baker, Vice Consul of Haiti, in Wilmington, "Master's or Conductor's Oath on Clearing Outward, District and Port of Wilmington," 29 March 1882, Random File, ibid.
153. Secretary of State for Foreign Relations to Stephen Preston, 9 May 1874, Random File, ibid.

154. "Eighth and Annual Message to Congress," 5 December 1876, in Simon, *The Papers of Ulysses S. Grant, Volume 28*, 68–69.

155. Interview with U.S. Grant, 6 July 1878, in ibid.

156. T. Thomas Fortune to Clement Haentjens, 17 May 1894, Département des Relations Extérieures, 740, Légation d'Haiti à New York et à Washington, ANH.

157. Atlas Steamship Company to Clement Haentjens, 25 August 1893, in ibid.

158. Annette Wood to "The Haytian Consul," 8 June 1894, in ibid.: Her mother left "my native home Santo Domingo . . . during the insurrection of 1863 or 1864. . . . her children were then in the United States," but she now wants to return and reclaim property; "the farm is situated 7 miles from the city of Porto Plata and was well stocked with cattle. . . . it is on the road which has the American church. [My] mother[']s name was Mary Buck. . . . I am a Haytian by birth but the property is in Santo Domingo." She then lived in Baltimore.

159. Attorney Homer Morris, Cincinnati, to Clement Haentjens, 1 October 1895, in ibid.: " . . . whether Hayti or San Domingo ever paid to France the 150,000,000 francs agreed upon in 1825 as indemnity for losses suffered by French colonists."

160. "Protocol of an Agreement for Submission to an Arbitrator of the Claim of Charles Adrien van Bokkelen, Signed May 24, 1888," in *Recueil des Traites de la République d'Haiti Tome Premier, 1804–1904, Publication de la Secretaire d'Etat des Relations Exterieures. Imprimerie de L'Etat*, 1945. Ministry of Foreign Affairs, Port-au-Prince.

161. Glen Jamison to "the Haytian Consul," 19 November 1894, in Légation d'Haiti à New York et à Washington, ANH. This resident of Orange, Texas, wanted "information on coffee growing in Hayti," including the "price and quality of land and a general description of the country."

162. J.L. Campbell to "the Haytian Minister," 21 October 1895, in ibid.: "I hereby make application for position of the Haytian consul for this port."

163. G. Jarvis Bowens, M.D., to Clement Haentjens, 4 November 1895, in ibid.: "having come in contact with many subjects of color of your and other nations. . . . would be prudent, profitable & public to establish a consular service here wherein a man of color would have charge of affairs. . . . as Norfolk is a large & growing seaport I think quite a number of business enterprises might be established between this and other Haytian ports as a result of such a consular service."

164. Theophilius G. Steward, *The Haitian Revolution, 1791 to 1804* (New York: Crowell, 1914).

165. Frederick Douglass, "The Miracle of Haiti," in Mercer Cook and Dantes Bellesgardes, eds., *The Haitian American Anthology: Haitian Readings from American Authors* (Port-au-Prince: Imprimerie de L'Etat, 1944), 31–32.

166. Martha Ellen Davis, "Asentamiento y Vida Economica de Los Immigrantes Afroamericanos de Samaná: Testimonio de la Profesora Martha Willmore (Leticia)," *Boletin del Archivo General de la Nacion*, 32 (Num. 119, 9–12, 2007): 709–734, 710, 720, 724, 727.

167. Phil Pastras, *Dead Man's Blues: Jelly Roll Morton Way Out West* (Berkeley: University of California Press, 2001), 71.

168. *New York Amsterdam News*, 24–30 October 2013.

169. Gerald Horne, *W.E.B. Du Bois: A Biography* (Santa Barbara: ABC-Clio), 2010.

170. Wyclef Jean, *Purpose: An Immigrant's Story* (New York: HarperCollins, 2012), 36–37.

Index

402

Index

gens de coleur, 197; French nationals, indemnities for, 146, 177; Holstein, Ducoudray, 133; Inginac, Joseph Balthazar, 145; Jamaica, 193, 195; Lovell case, 192; MacKenzie, Charles, 146; Manumission Society, 162; Paul, Thomas, 150; racial equality, 23; refugee black artisans, call for, 149; South Carolina, trade with, 141–142; trade proclamation, 147; United States, refugee blacks from, encouragement of, 23, 149–150, 163; U.S. nationals in, indemnities for, 175; Vesey, Denmark, 131

Brazil: abolitionism, 29; Bahia, 14; foreign diplomats, color of, 243; "Revolt of the Tailors," 14; slave insurrections/revolts, 14; slave trading, 210; slavery, 117, 166, 207–208, 294; sugar production, 119

Bridgetown, Barbados, 70

"brigands" (the term), 21

Brisbane, Charles, 134–135

Britain: African refugees from Dixie fighting for (*see* Carolina Corps (a.k.a. Black Corps)); African troops, deployment of, 14, 49, 52, 87, 123, 134; Black Jacobins, 89, 159; Christophe, Henri, 107; colonial convicts, dumping of, 169; Confederate States of America, relations with, 26; Dixie, invasion of, 123; Dominican Republic, relations with, 216–217; Dominican Republic, trade with, 228; Dominican Republic, U.S. annexation of, 263; foreign diplomats, color of, 243; France, relations with, 13, 32, 62, 177; free people of color/*gens de coleur,* 87, 88, 109; Grenada, relations with, 13; Haiti, loan to, 295;

Haiti, relations with, 24, 129, 137, 144, 146–147, 173, 178, 181, 182, 206, 222, 258; Haiti, U.S. annexation of, 263, 309; Haitian Revolution (1791-1804), 58, 106, 327n2; Hispaniola, intervention in, 78, 87–88; Hispaniola, relations with, 78–79, 84; Illinois, 33; Mexico, relations with, 188; New Orleans, 108; St. Vincent, 63; slave trading, 118, 159; slave trading, abolition of, 52; Spain, relations with, 32; Texas, U.S. annexation of, 188; Toussaint L'Ouverture, 88, 94, 98; United States, relations with, 14, 41, 66, 82–83, 85–86, 88, 141, 142, 153, 159; U.S. Civil War, 241, 269; U.S. Negroes, 276; U.S. slavery, British-Haitian alliance against, 107–108

British abolitionism: abolition of slave trading, 52; French abolitionism, 39; Haitian Revolution (1791-1804), 109–110, 127; Haiti's existence, 152; Hispaniola, 1791 insurrection in, 39–40, 52; maintenance of British colonies, 73; strength, 118; United States, 9; U.S. Negroes, 276; U.S. recognition of Haiti, 242; Wilberforce, William, 40

British Empire, 14

Brody, Charles, 305

Brougham, Henry, 135–136, 319n46

Brown, John, 25–26, 174, 244–245, 246, 251

Brown, John, Jr., 244, 250–251

Brown, William Wells, 29, 220, 251

Buchanan, James, 204, 262

Buck, Mary, 399n158

Burr, Aaron, 16, 322n72

"Bush Negroes," 73, 76, 87

Butler, Pierce, 36–37, 41, 54–55, 81